POLAND 1939-1947

THE POLITICS OF LIBERATION SERIES

General Editors: Geoffrey Warner and David W. Ellwood

John Coutouvidis & Jaime Reynolds

POLAND 1939-1947

Leicester University Press
1986

First published in 1986 by Leicester University Press
First published in the United States of America 1986 by
Holmes & Meier Publishers, Inc.

Designed by Douglas Martin
Phototypeset by Alan Sutton Publishing Limited, Gloucester
Printed in Great Britain by The Bath Press, Avon

The publication of this book has been assisted by a grant from the
Twenty-Seven Foundation

British Library Cataloguing in Publication Data

Coutouvidis, John
Poland 1939–1947. – (the Politics of liberation series)
1. Poland – Politics and government – 1918–1945 2. Poland –
Politics and government – 1945–1980 3. World War,
1939–1945 – Poland
I. Title II. Reynolds, Jaime III. Series

ISBN 0–7185–1211–1
ISBN 0-7185-1273-1 Pbk

Contents

Part Two The Struggle for Power in Poland and the Establishment of Communist Rule

Illustrations

Maps *page*

Figures *page*

Plates *between pages 186 and 187*

Tables

Editors' foreword

EARLY IN 1945, Josef Stalin enunciated the following proposition to a visiting delegation of Yugoslav Communists: 'This war is not as in the past; whoever occupies a territory imposes on it his own social system. Everyone imposes his own system as far as his army has power to do so. It cannot be otherwise.' (Milovan Djilas, *Conversations with Stalin*.) The purpose of the volumes in the Politics of Liberation series is to examine the liberation of Europe at the end of the Second World War in the light of this statement, which involves taking a new look at the link between international and national politics in both western and eastern Europe from the moment when the defeat of the Axis became apparent to that when the boundaries of the post-war political, economic and social systems were definitively established. The act of liberation from German occupation is seen as the focal point of this period, and the series sets out to examine the way in which the perceived national interests of the liberating powers – Britain, America and Russia – were translated into policies in the liberated countries, and the extent to which these policies were modified to take account of local forces and situations. In particular, while it has long been recognized that a key factor in the communization of eastern Europe was its liberation by the Red Army, the role played by Anglo-American forces in influencing developments in western Europe has received much less attention, and the series will aim to redress this balance.

Of necessity, each country is the subject of a separate volume in the series, but a common framework of enquiry unites them all. A number of areas have been defined as being of particular importance in each investigation: the nature of the country's political, economic and social system prior to enemy occupation during the Second World War and the impact of the occupation on this system; the nature, strength and long-term objectives of the Resistance movements in the country, its relationship to political forces from the pre-war era and to outside influences during the conflict; and the composition, strength and objectives of a government in exile or a well-defined alternative leadership abroad, if any, and the relationship of such a leadership with the host government. Examination has also to be made of the plans of the liberating power or powers with regard to the country, their attitudes towards the interests and activities of each other in the country, and the contrasts, if any, between their short-term and long-term objectives. The form of the liberation process itself, its speed and duration, the machinery used to regulate relations inside the country and the degree of intervention by the liberating powers in the country's process of reconstruction at its earliest stage all must be considered. Finally, the duration or otherwise of the political, economic and social arrangements which emerged at the time of liberation and the traces of the conflicts of that time remaining to the present day are critically examined.

Within this common approach, individual authors have nevertheless been left considerable scope to draw out specific features of each national situation; practical comparison is left to the reader. It is hoped that in this way questions will emerge which will take the comparative politics of the Second World War in Europe beyond the venerable problems of the 'origins of the Cold War', the 'development of European unity', or the 'rebirth of European democracy' round which they have revolved for so long. Much of the writing on resistance and liberation in the Anglo-Saxon world has so far tended to concentrate on the military as opposed to the political and economic aspects of the subject and while no one would want to deny the value of this kind of history it is clearly incomplete.

The sources for a series as envisaged are now plentiful. The German archives for the Second World War, which go into considerable detail concerning the politics, economics, etc., of occupied Europe have been available for research for some years. More recently, extensive British and American archives have been opened to scholarship. Nearly every European country has an institute for the study of its wartime resistance movement in which are to be found collections of primary documents, clandestine newspapers, oral testimony and other sources. While Russian archives are not of course open to unauthorized researchers from the West, the amount of Russian literature dealing with the role of the U.S.S.R. in liberating eastern Europe and based upon these archives is now voluminous. Individual East European governments and communist parties have also published collections of documents and official histories of the subject. In addition, all the contributors to the series are familiar with the local historiography of the countries they treat and are thus able to take into consideration the influence of debates and analyses not normally accessible to the English-speaking reader.

G.W./D.W.E.

POLAKOM, W KRAJU I NA OBCZYŹNIE

Preface

POLAND'S EXPERIENCE occupies a special and tragic place in the history of the Second World War and the construction of post-war Europe. No occupied country fared worse at the hands of the Nazis between 1939 and 1945 or fought with such determination and heroism to regain its independence. Yet the defeat of the Germans in 1945 also marked the defeat of the Polish Government-in-Exile and the underground State in Poland, which together held the allegiance of the vast majority of the Polish people. Poland was liberated from the Germans, but fell under the domination of the Soviet Union which very many Poles regarded as a second hostile power. The Communist-led government installed in Poland was viewed from the start by a large part of the Polish nation as neither legitimate nor truly Polish. Many Poles would argue that within the Grand Alliance Poland was the only 'Ally' which lost the Second World War.

A good deal has been written in English on the Polish question as a problem of international relations between the Great Powers during and after the war. The future of Poland is well recognized as one of the key issues in the negotiations between the Big Three on the post-war settlement in Europe and as a significant factor in the onset of the Cold War. However, there has been very little exploration of the impact of these great external events from the point of view of Poland's internal politics. While we would not for a moment deny the huge importance of external pressures – arising from Soviet policy and East–West relations – in shaping the basic pattern and course of Poland's development, we would argue that her own political forces and culture have also had a far greater influence throughout Poland's recent history than is generally assumed in the West, or indeed by many in Poland. This volume focuses on this Polish perspective on the politics of war, liberation and reconstruction. We hope it will go some way to fill what has hitherto been a gap in the literature on modern Polish history.

One of the reasons for the comparative neglect of Poland's internal politics is of course the problem of obtaining primary source material from the Polish and Soviet archives. This material is not generally accessible to Western scholars for the relevant period. However, at least so far as the Polish documentary evidence is concerned, a great deal of important material has now been published in little-known Polish secondary sources and by Polish émigrés in the West. For example, most of the transcripts of meetings of the Central Committee of the Polish Workers' Party between 1944 and 1948 have now been published in major part or in full, together with many other useful internal Communist Party and government papers. We hope that the present study will bring this largely unexplored material to the attention of students of recent Polish and Eastern European history.

Naturally, many questions will remain unanswerable unless or until the Soviet and Polish archives are opened to independent scholars. Where this is so, we have tried at least to indicate what the outstanding questions are and to set out the current state of and gaps in our knowledge.

The Polish émigré archives in London have been of immense value to both of us in providing further material. We would like to record our indebtedness to the staff of the Polish Institute and Sikorski Museum, the Polish Underground Study Trust and the Polish Library.

The book is divided into two parts. Part One, written by John Coutouvidis, draws on primary source material first considered in his Ph.D. thesis 'The formation of the Polish Government-in-Exile and its relations with Great Britain, 1939–41' discussed at the University of Keele in 1975. It examines the Polish Government-in-Exile from its formation in France to its disintegration and isolation towards the end of the war, looking in particular at the relations of the 'London' Poles with the Allied Powers.

Part Two, written by Jaime Reynolds, is based on his Ph.D. thesis 'The Polish Workers' Party and the opposition to communist power in Poland 1944 to 1947' (London University: L.S.E., 1984). Some sections of chapters 6 and 7 were previously published in a different form in an article 'Lublin versus London: the Party and the Underground in Poland 1944–45' in *The Journal of Contemporary History*, 16 (1981). Part 2 deals with the internal struggle for power in Poland during the German occupation and the immediate post-war years against the background of Soviet power in Eastern Europe and traces the consolidation of Communist rule up to the elections of 1947.

We are indebted to many people and institutions who have made this book possible. We would like to thank Geoffrey Warner for his acute and invariably helpful editorial advice and also Peter Boulton and his colleagues at Leicester University Press for excellent professional assistance.

John Coutouvidis wishes to thank the North Staffordshire Polytechnic for its generous provision for research; Merrilyn Coutouvidis for essential help and even more for her constant and loving support; Professor Paul Rolo, until recently Head of the History Department at the University of Keele, for wisdom and friendship, advice and guidance so kindly given over many years; Mrs M.G. Kempton for unstinting efforts with the typescript and Mrs B. Wacewicz for personal qualities which served as a source of inspiration. To friends and family he owes a debt of gratitude for the hospitality that made his work a pleasure.

Jaime Reynolds would like to record his gratitude to George Schöpflin and the late Lucjan Blit for their advice and assistance as research super-visors and to the Social Science Research Council and the Polish gov-ernment (through the British Council) for the awards which enabled him to collect the material on which Part Two of the book is based. He owes a special debt of gratitude respectively to Dr Antony Polonsky for his interest and encouragement over a number of years, and to his friends in Poland, parents, mother-in-law and wife for their generosity, encouragement and support.

Following convention, the authors bear sole responsibility for the text that follows.

J.R./J.C.
October 1985

Abbreviations

AK	*Armia Krajowa*	Home Army
AL	*Armia Ludowa*	People's Army
BBWR	*Bezpartyjny Blok Współpracy z Rządem*	
tx2		Non-party Bloc for the Support of the Government
CBKP	*Centralne Biuro Komunistów Polskich*	
		Central Bureau of Polish Communists
CCS		Combined Chiefs of Staff
DSZ	*Delegatura Sił Zbrojnych*	Armed Forces Delegation
FAO		Food and Agriculture Organization
GL	*Gwardia Ludowa*	People's Guard
GOP	*Grupy Ochronno-Propagandowe*	Defence-Propaganda Groups
GRP	*Główna Rada Polityczna*	Chief Political Council
KBW	*Korpus Bezpieczeństwa Wewnętrznego*	
		Internal Security Corps
KC	*Komitet Centralny*	Central Committee
KNP	*Komitet Narodowy Polski*	Polish National Committee
KPP	*Komunistyczna Partia Polski*	Communist Party of Poland
KRN	*Krajowa Rada Narodowa*	Homeland National Council
MO	*Milicja Obywatelska*	Citizens' Militia
ND	*Narodowa Demokracja (Endecja)*	National Democratic Party
NKN	*Naczelny Komitet Narodowy*	Supreme National Council
NKVD	*Narodovy komisariat vnutrich dyel*	
		Soviet People's Commissariat for Internal Affairs
NOW	*Narodowa Organizacja Wojskowa*	National Military Organization
NPR	*Narodowa Partia Robotnicza*	National Worker's Party
NSZ	*Narodowe Siły Zbrojne*	National Armed Forces
NZW	*Narodowy Związek Wojskowy*	National Military Union
ORMO	*Ochotnicza Rezerwa Milicji Obywatelskiej*	
		Citizens' Militia Volunteer Reserve

OZON	*Obóz Zjednoczenia Narodowego*	Camp of National Unity
PKP	*Polityczny Komitet Porozumiewawczy*	
		Political Consultative Committee
PKWN	*Polski Komitet Wyzwolenia Narodowego*	
		Polish National Committee of Liberation
POW	*Polska Organizacja Wojskowa*	Polish Military Organization
PPR	*Polska Partia Robotnicza*	Polish Workers' Party
PPS	*Polska Partia Socjalistyczna*	Polish Socialist Party
PS	*(Organizacja) Polskich Socjalistów*	
		(Organization of) Polish Socialists
PSL	*Polskie Stronnictwo Ludowe*	Polish Peasant Party
PZPR	*Polska Zjednoczona Partia Robotnicza*	
		Polish United Workers' Party
RPPS	*Robotnicza Partia Polskich Socjalistów*	
		Workers' Party of the Polish Socialists
SD	*Stronnictwo Demokratyczne*	Democratic Party
SDKPiL	*Socjaldemokracja Królestwa Polskiego i Litwy*	
		Social Democracy of the Kingdom of Poland and Lithuania
SL	*Stronnictwo Ludowe*	Peasant Party
SL'ROCh'	*Stronnictwo Ludowe 'Ruch Oporu Chłopów'*	
		Peasant Party 'Resistance movement of the Peasants'
SN	*Stronnictwo Narodowe*	National Party
SP	*Stronnictwo Pracy*	Party of Labour
SZP	*Służba Zwycięstwu Polski*	'Service for the Victory of Poland'
UB	*Urząd Bezpieczeństwa*	Security Office
UNRRA		United Nations Relief and Rehabilitation Administration
UPA	*Ukraińska Powstańcza Armia*	Ukrainian Insurrectionary Army
WiN	*Wolność i Niezawisłość*	Freedom and Independence
WRN	*Wolność, Równość, Niepodległość*	
		Freedom, Equality, Independence
ZMK	*Związek Młodzieży Komunistycznej*	
		Union of Communist Youth

ZPP	*Związek Patriotów Polskich*	Union of Polish Patriots
ZSCh	*Związek Samopomocy Chłopskiej*	Peasant Self-help Union
ZSL	*Zjednoczone Stronnictwo Ludowe*	United Peasant Party
ZMW 'Wici'	*Związek Młodzieży Wrejskiej 'Wici'*	
		Union of Rural Youth
ZWM	*Związek Walki Młodych*	Youth Union of Struggle
ZWZ	*Związek Walki Zbrojnej*	Union for Armed Struggle

Translations of Polish terms used in the text, with hints on pronunciation

Note: The hints on pronunciation are given once only and relate solely to sounds foreign to an Anglophone.

aktyw (sound *y* as *i* in *ink* and terminal *w* as *vf*)   party activists
polituki (*u* as *oo*, *i* as *ee*)   political officers in the armed forces
Wola ludu (initial *w* as *v*)   'will of the people'
Trybuna Wolności (*ś* as *sh*, *ci* as *tshee*)   *Tribune of Freedom*
Sanacja (*j* as *y* in *you*)   clean up – the term used by the regime which ruled Poland from 1926 to 1939
Kresy   the eastern borderlands of pre-war Poland
akowcy (*c* as *ts*)   members of the Home Army
aparat   the State apparatus
Delegatura   the political leadership of the Polish underground state during the war
Sejm   the Polish parliament
Tygodnik Powszechny (sound *ch* as in Scottish *loch*)   *Universal Weekly*
Dziś i Jutro (sound *Dz* as *g* in *gem*)   *Today and Tomorrow*
Zryw Narodowy   *National effort*
Gazeta ludowa   *Peoples News*
Robotnik   *The Worker*
Nowe Wyzwolenie (*ie* as *ye* in *yes*)   *New Liberation*
Piast   PSL newspaper in Kraków (*ó* as *oo*) named after medieval Polish ruling dynasty; also the label of Witos's Peasant Party
Chłopi i Państwo (sound *ł* as *w*, *ń* as *ene* in *scene*)   *Peasants and the State*

PART ONE

THE DEFEAT OF THE 'LONDON' POLES: THE GOVERNMENT-IN-EXILE AND THE DIPLOMATIC BACKGROUND TO LIBERATION

1   From independence to exile

FOREIGN DOMINATION of Poland had left a lasting impression on political outlooks and the conduct of national policy since the mid-eighteenth century when Poland was little more than a client state of Russia; the termination of her statehood, which came with the partitioning of Poland between Russia, Prussia and Austria, followed by increased Russian control of an even greater portion of her territory in the settlements following the defeat of Napoleon in 1815, left many Polish people with a hatred of their oppressors. Their fear of occupation, together with a pride in the glories of historic Poland, were factors contributing to the extreme nationalism which characterized Polish political life, uniting Poles of widely differing political persuasions in a yearning for freedom, a dream set against the reality of Poland's geopolitical position.

Though there was an abundance of political parties, even before the First World War, the lack of experience in the processes of government meant that the distinction between intention and realization in politics was insufficiently appreciated and the equation of the two was rarely achieved. When this did occur, as in the rebirth of Polish independence, it was more the result of external circumstances than the product of Polish statesmanship. The power at the disposal of Polish policy-makers was rarely sufficient to achieve their aims. Awkward compromise rather than consensus characterized the political heritage, as did a related recourse to forceful and unconstitutional methods. Significant also is a legacy of conspiracy and of politics in exile.

In the decade before the First World War political activists in Galicia, prominent among whom were Józef Piłsudski, Kazimierz Sosnkowski and Władisław Sikorski, formed secret military organizations. The most important of these was the Riflemen's Association (*Związek Strzelecki*). Piłsudski believed that Polish independence could be achieved only by military means. The opportunity to prove this came in July 1914 when Poland's partitioning powers were at war. Piłsudski, who regarded Russia as Poland's worst enemy, led his Legions, recruited from the Riflemen's Associations, into Russian Poland. He called for an uprising. His expectations were shown to be premature and this did not occur.

Instead, Piłsudski became a leader of the Supreme National Council (*Naczelny Komitet Narodowy* – NKN) which was formed in Kraków. It was comprised of Polish members of the Imperial Diet together with politicians from Galicia and representatives from Russian Poland who worked with the Austrian government to form a Polish army. Sikorski, who headed the NKN's military department, was responsible for the task which was made difficult by clashes with Piłsudski over the incorporation of his free corps into the Polish Legions.

The NKN had an associated elite intelligence group, the Polish Military Organization (*Polska Organizacja Wojskowa* – POW), which survived after the disbandment of the Legions – three Polish military brigades, subordinate to Austrian orders. Representing mainly Left and Centre opinion, the NKN included Stanisław Kot as propaganda organizer, and the peasant leader Wincenty Witos, together with a large part of his Polish Peasant Party (*Polskie Stronnictwo Ludowe, Piast*). The NKN considered that the future of the Polish State depended on the army, taking the view that while there was an army there was a people. However, there was disagreement about the future of the Legions. In opposition to the other NKN leaders, Piłsudski urged caution in expanding them and came instead to rely increasingly on his underground military body, the POW. He was aware that neither Austria nor Germany would further the cause of Polish independence and decided to wait on events, feeling that the greatest opportunities would be offered by the revolution in Russia and the raising of an army there.

Sikorski saw the future differently. He wanted a Polish army to emerge in Poland free of the conflicts of loyalty which arise from dependence on other nations. Strongly held views and clashing policies by dominant personalities were to remain a feature of Polish politics; the internecine quarrels of this period continued in independent Poland and played a determining role in the politics of the Polish State after its defeat in September 1939.

The developments in Galicia were matched in Russian Poland by the formation, in November 1914, of the Polish National Committee (*Komitet Narodowy Polski* – KNP). This Right-wing, anti-German body, supported by a volunteer Legion, was composed largely of members of the National Democratic Party (*Narodowa Demokracja* – ND, popularly known as the *Endecja*). It was under the leadership of Roman Dmowski, who also clashed with Piłsudski.

For the advocates of Polish nationalism the 1916–21 period intensified their problems, particularly that of gaining support for their cause. At the same time it provided the possibility of independence. On 5 November 1916, Kaiser Wilhelm II of Germany and Emperor Franz-Joseph of Austria proclaimed a 'Kingdom of Poland' and a Polish army. This made a strong impression on Poles, and was met by great enthusiasm, particularly amongst Polish youth, though it was given little credence by many of their leaders, who believed that Poland's resurrection would have to come from the nation's own resources. It was followed, in March 1917, by a declaration of support for Polish independence by the Provisional Government in Russia.

By July 1917 German successes led them to press for a transfer of the Polish Legions from Austrian to German allegiance. Piłsudski refused and was arrested and imprisoned in Germany, though the work of his group continued.

In the meantime Dmowski and the KNP had left Russian Poland for Lausanne and in August 1917 declared themselves the Government-in-Exile of a restored Polish State. They soon moved to Paris, intent on obtaining Allied recognition. Despite Dmowski's efforts in Paris, and those of the NKN in Kraków, it was over a year before the creation of a Polish State became a condition of peace by the Western Allies. The intervention of the United States, the Treaty of Brest-Litovsk (1918) and the collapse of the Central Powers combined to bring this about, together with such energetic Polish efforts as Ignacy Paderewski's (on behalf of the KNP) in wooing President Wilson to the cause of Polish independence.[1]

On 10 November 1918, a day after the revolution in Germany, Piłsudski was in Warsaw. While in prison he had dreamed of a moment such as this, with Poland's neighbours rendered impotent by the chaos of revolution, and once released he was quick to exploit the possibilities. Within four days of his arrival, the Germans had completely abandoned Warsaw, assured by Piłsudski of a safe retreat across Poland and endowing him, before they left, with the title of Chief of State.

Two rival bodies now claimed to represent the Polish State. The Paris Committee enjoyed the very Allied support that Piłsudski lacked, whereas it did not control the administration and army on Polish soil, which the latter did. It fell to Paderewski to attempt a *modus vivendi* between the two groups. He went to Poland as a representative of the KNP and persuaded Piłsudski, who realized the need for Allied support on the frontier question, to come to an accommodation with the KNP. As a result, a compromise cabinet was formed and quickly recognized by the Allies.

In Paris the problem of Poland's frontiers was being considered by the peacemakers. The Supreme Council's agreement on a German/Polish frontier disappointed Dmowski and left until later a decision on the question of the eastern territories including Galicia and Teschen. (*Cieszyn*, Silesia, was disputed between Poles and Czechs. The eastern area of the former Austrian duchy was awarded to Poland in July 1920. The western area – Transolza, *Zaolzie* – was annexed by Poland from Czechoslovakia in October 1938: see below, p.17.)

In the meantime Piłsudski was making his own plans for the East. These involved the use of armed force, in his opinion the only measure of a nation's strength; he intended to bind together the fragile republics of Lithuania, Byelorussia and Ukraine to realize his federal dream, and indeed by the autumn of 1919 Polish forces had brought large areas in the north

—++ the Curzon Line of 11 July 1920
—·—· the Spa Line of 10 July 1920
— — — — the German-Soviet frontier arranged between
          Ribbentrop and Molotov, 28 September 1939,
          which lasted until the outbreak of war between
          Germany and Russia
········· the Armistice Line proposed by the Soviet Union
          on 29 January 1920
—··—·· the 1921-39 Polish-Soviet frontier established
          by the Treaty of Riga, 19 March 1921

Map 1   Poland and adjacent states between 1919 and 1939.

and east under their control. The extent of this territory corresponded roughly to that claimed by Dmowski in Paris in March 1919. Piłsudski's intentions, however, went further and since the Bolsheviks also had their programme of federation for these territories a clash between Poland and Soviet Russia was bound to come. The Russo-Polish War of 1919–20 was a war of movement in which Poland experienced dramatic changes of fortune.[2] After the capture of Kiev in May 1920, the Red Army's counter-attack followed swiftly and by August Warsaw was threatened. A governmental crisis resulted and the cabinet, headed by Władysław Grabski, called on the Allies for help. Consequently undertakings known as the Protocols of Spa were signed by the Polish government on 10 July 1920. These amounted to a major climb-down, particularly on the question of the eastern frontier, which it was agreed should follow the Curzon Line.[3] However, the situation changed once more with a Polish breakthrough by Sikorski's Fifth Army which pushed back the Russian forces to a line running from the river Dvina in the north to the Dniester in the south. These positions formed the basis of the subsequent frontier settlement embodied in the Peace Treaty of Riga signed on 18 March 1921.

The tortuous process of creating the Polish State was finally over though the frontiers were to remain provisional; in the west the Germans had been forced to concede too much and in the east the result was a stalemate. Revision was inevitable. At the time, though, having become allied to France in February 1921, Poland was established as a State in the European balance of power system.

Economic and social background

THE new Poland was a classic example of underdevelopment; her social and economic structure was predominantly rural.[4] Of 27.2 million inhabitants, three-quarters lived in the countryside and 63.8 per cent derived their livelihood from the soil. The creation of a surplus in agricultural products for the purpose of trade, income from which could pay for capital investment in the process of modernization, was hampered by several factors. Fecundity (15.3 births per 1,000 inhabitants), illiteracy (32.7 per cent) and inefficient farming practices created limitations which were compounded by runaway inflation. This was itself partly a consequence of the war; making good the physical devastation created enormous demands which the economy was inadequate to meet. The need for new markets and the legacy of three disparate imperial economies were further factors in an inflationary spiral which continued uncurbed until 1924. There was so much to be done and so little with which to do it.

Agricultural reform was a priority. Lack of mechanization, servitude and medieval-style strip farming persisted among the peasants. Their crop yields were low and the quality of their stock was poor. Of the 15.5 million peasants the majority worked holdings of 5 hectares or less on 15.3 per cent of the land. Such units were barely self-sufficient. At the other extreme 1 per cent of holdings were over 50 hectares and occupied 52.9 per cent of the land. Of this over 70 per cent was privately owned and over half was in estates over 1,000 hectares. A redistribution of land was seen as a social necessity and was put into effect by the Land Reform Bills of 1920 and 1925. However, implementation was slow and the annual parcellation of 200,000 hectares barely kept pace with the rapidly rising population, so that by 1939 the agriculture problem was further from solution than it had been in 1918.[5]

Between the wars the distorted vestiges of feudal values permeated Polish society as a whole. The noble owners of the largest estates had, until the eighteenth century, played a dominant role in Polish history. The parliament (*Sejm*) was formed from their nominees and their policies, which largely served their interests as grain-producers and landowners, included extreme exploitation of the peasants and little or no hope of agricultural reform. Interpersonal quarrelling amongst the nobility and a system of 'Liberum Veto' which meant that any member of parliament could veto a law favoured by all the rest, also made government extremely difficult.

During the nineteenth century the intelligentsia, and the officer corps which came into being during the Napoleonic Wars, emerged as influential social groups. They adopted certain of the landowners' prejudices against trade and industry, while variously supplanting the former aristocratic egotism with the democratic values of their century embodied in liberalism, nationalism and socialism.

The intelligentsia comprised a very broad membership drawn from the bureaucracy and the professions – it was the dominant urban class. Poland lacked both a strong bourgeoisie and a strong proletariat. This may be accounted for by a relative lack of industrialization, except in Upper Silesia and in and around Kielce, Warsaw and Lodz, and to a lesser extent in Poznań and Kraków. Poland's two major industries were metallurgy and textiles but both suffered from a lack of capital and enterprise. The former was linked to the backward tradition of Polish agriculture and to cultural attitudes, and may also be explained by Poland's failure to attract outside loans; the latter likewise had its roots in the cultural history of the country.

Poland's industry was not only concentrated geographically and organizationally (by cartels) but much of it was controlled by the State. In contrast most trade was characterized by its small scale of operation – most often at the level of the individual shopkeeper or businessman. Much of it was in Jewish hands as Jews did not share the dominant cultural prejudice against commerce. They were widely dispersed throughout Poland and in 1921 numbered 2,110,000 or 7.8 per cent of the population. They were largely urban and populated whole towns and large sectors of the cities. Such concentration, coupled with different values, provoked the fervent anti-semitism common throughout Eastern Europe.

The destruction of Jewish society by the Germans during the Second World War evoked this response in a letter from Poland: 'The Jews have lost their dominating position especially in the economic world . . . and Polish society will not admit that they should re-obtain the strongholds they have lost.'[6]

Polish xenophobia not only had a bearing on the Jews but was also directed at other conspicuous minorities living in Poland. A distinction in this regard needs to be made between territories west and east of the Curzon Line. To the west there lived a Polish majority, amongst whom lived Jews and Germans. The latter group numbered 1,770,000, mostly living along Poland's western frontier in the provinces of Poznania and Pomerania. Territories to the east of the Curzon Line did not have a Polish majority. According to the 1931 census, these border lands (*Kresy*) contained a population of 10,768,000 of whom 37 per cent were Ukrainians, 36 per cent Poles, 9 per cent Byelorussians, 8 per cent Jews and 7 per cent Polesians. Russians, Germans and Lithuanians each made up 1 per cent.[7]

Complex in its ethnography and history, the *Kresy* posed the most difficult of the many political problems for the new Poland. Its peoples had come under Polish hegemony in 1386 after the marriage of Queen Jadwiga to the Lithuanian Prince Jagiełło. This Jagellonian Commonwealth (the *Rzeczpospolita*) left an indelible mark on Polish consciousness. The new territories became the proving ground of Polish nationalism where to be Polish was to be Catholic and a defender of Western civilization against the barbarians from the East.

Polish dominance in the *Kresy* declined in the eighteenth and nineteenth centuries. Many of the estates, owned by the *Slachta* (country gentry), were confiscated by the Russians in retribution for the owners' role in the risings of 1830–1 and 1863–5. Another consequence of Russian rule was the attraction of millions of peasants to the Orthodox Church and thus towards a Russian orientation. The growth of nationalism amongst the non-Polish peoples also posed a political threat.

The eastern provinces were of critical importance to the newly independent Poland. To Piłsudski their importance was primarily strategic, a buffer zone in the east which made Russian intervention in Polish life more difficult. Sikorski, who like Piłsudski was born in the *Kresy*, held similar views.

The political and diplomatic prelude to the Second World War

THE constitution of the Second Polish Republic was finally adopted on 17 March 1921. Modelled closely on the French system, real power lay with the legislature made up of a *Sejm* (lower house) and a Senate. Of the two the *Sejm* was vastly more powerful. The president, as titular head of State, had the right to appoint the government but not to dissolve parliament. In this way Dmowski's National Democrats hoped to insure themselves against Piłudski if he became president.

The political system of the new Polish State was fragmented. No party or grouping was strong enough to provide a firm basis for stable government. In the period from 1918 to 1926, when Piłsudski overthrew the parliamentary regime, no fewer than fourteen governments held office. The National Democrats dominated the Right in the spectrum of Polish politics. Theirs was basically a middle-class party, supported by white-collar workers and much of the intelligentsia. It was strongly nationalistic and grew increasingly anti-semitic from the 1920s. The party had, in the elections of 1919 and 1922, formed joint lists with the Christian National Party of Labour. This Catholic party gradually freed itself from dependence on the *Endecja* and in 1925 changed its name to the Christian Democratic Party. In the Centre was the *Piast* Party, led by Wincenty Witos and supported, in the main, by well-to-do peasants. On the Left was the Liberation Peasant Party (*Wyzwolenie*) and the Polish Socialist Party (*Polska Partia Socjalistyczna*, PPS). The Communist Party of Poland, whose history is dealt with in some detail later, remained politically insignificant throughout the interwar years.

The principle universal suffrage, enshrined in the new constitution, brought a new set of factors into Polish politics. These were the parties of the minorities. They tended to ally themselves with parties of the Left and Centre. National minority parties frequently held the balance of power or had an influence out of proportion to their numbers. This was not a healthy situation as Polish groups began to lose faith in democracy and to look towards the army to maintain Polish hegemony.

The elections of 1922, themselves marked by violence, were held after an unsettled start to the new republic's history. A popular government led by Moraczewski and dominated by Piłsudski held office for three months at the turn of 1918/19. This was followed by a government headed by Ignacy Paderewski. However, Paderewski resigned as prime minister in December 1919, the year after his triumphant return from Versailles. He had had enough of political deviousness and returned to the piano. (He was to re-emerge as a political figure in the late 1930s.) Then came the war with Russia which prompted the establishment of a government of 'National Defence'.

Piłsudski, opposed by the Right and supported by the Left, declined to stand as president in the elections of 1922. Instead, his friend Gabriel Narutowicz was elected. Two days later, on 16 December, Narutowicz was assassinated. The resulting crisis was resolved when M. Rataj, speaker of the newly elected *Sejm* and acting president, appointed a non-party government under General Sikorski.[8] This ministry lasted only five months (December 1922–May 1923), but uncovered the major problems facing Poland after independence, as well as giving the premier a foretaste of the dissension in Polish political life.

It can be said that in foreign affairs Sikorski's government made considerable headway. Poland's eastern frontier gained formal recognition at the Ambassadors' Conference of 14 March 1923 and support for the same was forthcoming from the League of Nations. August Zaleski, Polish minister in Rome from 1922 to 1926, was particularly notable for his success in obtaining strong Italian backing for Polish claims. Relations with France were close but talks with the French general staff in September 1922 had led Sikorski to the conclusion that although Germany was clearly identified as the mutual threat, Western opinion tended to treat Russian territorial claims sympathetically.[9] Nevertheless, at a time when Germany and Russia were weak, Polish foreign policy was successful. In contrast there were setbacks in internal affairs, particularly finance and land reform. Sikorski's government fell victim to the struggle between the Right and the Left over these important questions. Because of disagreements with Piłsudski and his followers, Sikorski was denied any further position of authority (apart from command of the Lwów Corps from 1925 to 1928) until after the outbreak of the Second World War.

No succeeding government was able to mobilize sufficient support in the *Sejm* for a workable majority which could attempt a solution to the internal problems which beset Poland. Crisis followed crisis, culminating in Piłsudski's *coup d'état* in May 1926. This event coincided with a growing awareness that Poland's international position could be endangered by the revival of German influence, seen in such developments as the Locarno agreement, German membership of the League of Nations and the renewal of the Treaty of Rapallo.

It was likely that in time Germany and Russia would regain their power. In these circumstances Polish diplomacy between the wars was based on two principles: firstly preservation of the equilibrium between the two either by maintaining a strict impartiality towards them both, or by drawing closer to one or the other depending on the balance of power within the triangular relationship; secondly, the protection of Poland from her neighbours through alliance with other Great Powers or through multilateral security agreements. In pursuit of this policy of balance, post-1926, Piłsudski took personal charge of approaches to Russia, leaving Zaleski, who was foreign minister (1926–32) to deal with the rest of foreign affairs. With the signing of the Litvinov protocols in February 1929, a satisfactory relationship was achieved with the Soviet Union which made possible the conclusion of the Non-Aggression Pact of July 1932 between the two countries.[10] Piłsudski hoped to underwrite Poland's frontiers with the ambitious plan of creating a system of States under Polish leadership stretching from the Baltic to the Black Sea. Piłsudski also instructed his under-secretary of state at the foreign ministry, Colonel Józef Beck, to concentrate on the solution of the Transolza, Danzig, Lithuania and minorities questions (see below, pp.14–17). Beck had proved himself energetic in home affairs and in November 1932 replaced the more cautious and conservative Zaleski.

As the new foreign minister took over news broke of German-Soviet military conversations. This was a sharp reminder of Poland's exposed position and of the danger of a rapprochement between the two ex-partitioning powers. Beck's response was to tackle the problem of a resurgent Germany by seeking an agreement with her to balance the Polish-Soviet treaty. Since Poland was neither in a position to check the rate of growth in German or Russian power, nor strong enough to act independently against either or both, much depended on the skill of Polish diplomacy and the degree of realism of her policy. In retrospect Beck's assessment of Hitler's attitude to Poland was sadly awry.

> The main problem which I had to face at the initial stages as Minister of Foreign Affairs was the new character of German-Polish relations. In Germany, the Nationalist movement under the leadership of Adolf Hitler rose quickly to power, showing considerable dynamic strength . . . the whole world, almost without exception, identified by habit every dynamic movement in Germany with anti-Polish activity. All political leaders in the world warned our diplomatic representatives that Hitler meant a strong anti-Polish trend in German politics. I retained in my mind one contrary voice which reached us from outside. The grey-haired but wise and experienced Swedish King Gustav V summoned our envoy and told him: 'Everybody says that Hitler's first aim would be anti-Polish activity. I met him on my journey through Berlin and I am not convinced of it. This man is above all interested in internal reforms and he has no anti-Polish complex . . .' It struck me that Marshal Piłsudski had at a distance quite the same feeling. That was why at the moment when for the first time I had to take up a position with regard to this problem in a parliamentary discussion, the Marshal advised me to leave aside the excitement of the European press and in speaking of Germany use definitions which would be steadfast but also calm and moderate and would not anticipate the future as bearing exclusively negative possibilities.[11]

This underestimate of the dynamic and aggressive character of Nazism in relation to Poland, and the associated neglect of informed opinion to the contrary marked Polish foreign policy until the beginning of 1939 and were symptomatic of a deep malaise in the Polish government.

Since the May coup, the key positions in the State administration had been filled by military personnel such as Beck who had a disdain for the democratic process and a worshipful regard for Piłsudski's dictates. Therefore by 1930, when Piłsudski was losing his vigour, others were hesitant to take decisions where he failed to give a lead. The government styled itself *Sanacja*, which denoted the 'reform' it had in mind for parliament. It tried, at first, to exercise power constitutionally but by the elections of 1928 Piłsudski was losing the support he had had, from the parties in the Centre and on the Left, because of his outspoken criticism of the *Sejm*. He ignored opinion contrary to his own; democratic procedures were foreign to his nature. In this he had the support of the government, who muzzled any effective opposition.

In an attempt to organize a grouping to contest an election on behalf of the *Sanacja* a 'Non-party Bloc for the Support of the Government' (*Bezpartyjny Blok Współpracy z Rządem* – BBWR) was formed in January 1928. It was organized by Piłsudski-ites of long standing – former legionnaires such as Adam Koc and members of the POW. Directing their main attack against the *Endecja* they succeeded in drawing support away from the Right and Centre and did particularly well in the *Kresy*. Pressing home their advantage, the core of the BBWR, known as the 'colonels group', proposed the constitutional changes long advocated by Piłsudski, particularly the strengthening of the executive at the expense of the legislature. The proposals provoked violent reactions, culminating in a huge rally in Kraków on 29 June 1930. The crowds called for the resignation of the president, Ignacy Moscicki, who was a close friend of Piłsudski. The Marshal was himself pilloried as an enemy of democracy.

Once again, as in 1926, Piłsudski lost patience. He ordered the arrest of 79 people, variously members of the PPS, the *Wyzwolenie*, the National Workers' Party, the *Piast* (including its leader Wincenty Witos), the National Democrats and several Ukrainians. They were interned at the fortress at Brześć. This act caused a scandal which marked a parting of the ways between the nation and its leaders.

In 1935 a new constitution was adopted. It greatly extended the power of the president who could now appoint and dismiss the prime minister, appoint one-third of the members of the Senate, dissolve the *Sejm* and appoint his own successors in time of war. These provisions were tailor-made for Piłsudski. However, he died on 12 May 1935 and President Moscicki was re-elected.

After Piłsudski's death the 'colonels group' ruled until the outbreak of war, led by Moscicki, Edward Smigły-Rydz (inspector-general of Polish forces) and Beck. Attempts were made to revive popular support for the *Sanacja*, a noteworthy example being the formation of a new political organization in 1937 called the Camp of National Unity (*Obóz Zjednoczenia Narodowego* – OZON). This failed, however, and instead there was an increased tendency towards authoritarian rule by the oligarchy. A cycle of protest and repression came to characterize the regime. In this context the peasant strike called on 15 August 1937 was, in Polonsky's words, 'the most serious outbreak of social unrest in Poland in the whole inter-war period.'[12] The strike, organized by the new leader of the Peasant Party, Stanisław Mikołajczyk, who was later to succeed Sikorski as Poland's prime minister, was brutally put down.

A less radical opposition to the *Sanacja* also took shape in 1937. The 'Front Morges', formed in 1934 and named after the Swiss town where Paderewski was living at the time, was absorbed into Karol Popiel's Party of Labour. Sikorski was closely involved in promoting the merger and, with his close friend Marian Kukiel, joined the new party. At the time it had little impact as an alternative to the regime. Its real significance was felt after the outbreak of war.[13]

In the meantime the 'colonels group' had to contend with an international environment which had changed dramatically since Hitler's rise to power. Self-reliance became the keynote of their foreign policy particularly with regard to the four problems identified by Piłsudski: Danzig, the Minorities Treaty, Lithuania and Transolza.

The task of maintaining good relations with Germany while guarding Poland's rights in Danzig, as accorded to her under the Treaty of Versailles, proved too great for Polish diplomacy. Indeed it was more than the combined efforts of Poland, France and Great Britain could accomplish during the diplomatic prelude to the Second World War. Even before this, however, numerous attempts towards a solution of the Danzig question were made. In the early 1930s, while the Polish government was seeking accommodation with Germany through diplomatic channels, its attitude towards Polish rights in the free city hardened. In June 1932 the Polish destroyer *Wicher* entered Danzig harbour. In March 1933 the guard was ostentatiously strengthened at the Polish arms depot at the Westerplatte. Without entering into the controversy that surrounds Polish intentions at this time it is clear that Poland wished her presence to be felt and intended to be mistress of her own destiny. This was shown again in Beck's reaction to Mussolini's abortive plan of March 1933 for a four-power directory of European affairs. He declared that if any state wanted to take possession of a 'single square metre of our territory, the cannon will speak: they know that in Berlin . . . I am afraid that this is not well known enough in London and Rome, or even in Paris.'[14]

Neither real nor apparent coercion, however, played a role in Polish attempts to come to terms with Germany. The New Order in German politics was seen as an exceptional opportunity for strengthening 'our own position in the European balance of power'[15] and the Polish-German Pact of Non-Aggression signed in January 1934 was a result of this.

Between the signing and the ratification of the pact, Beck went to Moscow in order to allay Soviet fears over the Polish-German agreement. At the time relations between Poland and Russia were good and Beck was able to overcome Soviet suspicions by offering to extend the Polish-Russian agreement for another ten years. In this way the principle of 'balance' in Polish foreign policy was adhered to and Poland asserted her independence in European politics.

In September 1934 she denounced the Minorities Treaty unilaterally. Poland decided to withdraw the problem of her minorities from the jurisdiction of the League of Nations. The debate at Geneva seemed positively dangerous from the government's point of view; any encouragement of separatism went against its policy of Polonization. The League of Nations seemed no longer to be of use to Poland in other respects. Proposals for an Eastern Locarno, a collective pact of mutual assistance in Eastern Europe to be guaranteed by France, followed from discussions between the Soviet and French foreign ministers in May 1934. It was feared that France was trying to extricate herself from her responsibilities in Eastern Europe by allowing Soviet Russia, newly elected to the League, a major role in that region. An anti-German coalition, theoretically led by France, would in practice give the Russians freedom of action in the East. This was unacceptable to Beck who regarded the Soviet Union as Poland's main enemy. The plan was also rejected to preserve the Polish policy of balance.[16]

At Geneva, in the 1930s, Poland stood out as an *enfant terrible*. Her uncooperative attitude stemmed from a feeling that the League had developed into a club for the major powers, so from her point of view it was defunct, though the opportunity for contacts outside the confines of the assembly was useful.

In her quest for security, Poland seemed, since the May coup, to be looking towards Britain rather than France. A conversation in Geneva between Beck and Eden, under-secretary of state at the Foreign Office and Lord Privy Seal, in October 1935, confirms this and both Beck and the Foreign Office in London thought the discussion significant. During this conversation Beck referred to lingering memories of the early 1920s, particularly Lloyd George's critical views of Poland. He felt, however, that more recently there had been a marked improvement in understanding between the two nations. He reminded Eden of his warm welcome in Warsaw, in April 1935. Eden responded by assuring Beck that things had changed and that there was a real respect among informed opinion in England for the manner in which Poland had confronted her difficulties, both political and economic.

The two ministers went on to discuss the international situation. In the course of this exchange Beck told Eden of a conversation that he had had with Hitler in July of that year concerning the Baltic. The German chancellor had told him that he had considered closing Poland's outlet to the sea but had decided against it because he did not wish to contend with a disgruntled neighbour. He had assured Beck that Polish independence and rights would be recognized.[17]

Beck remained keen to make the British government aware of Poland's position and visited London in March 1936, May 1937 and April 1939, but it was not until August 1939 that a treaty was made between the two governments. In the meantime Europe was to experience, with increasing severity, the effects of Hitler's policies. His remilitarization of the Rhineland in March 1936 dramatically confirmed fears in Poland regarding the efficacy of the League and the nerve of the French. France's weak protests against Hitler's gamble indicated that she would act neither in the West nor in the East. For the French system of alliances to be effective against German aggression Soviet troops would have to cross Polish territory, a possibility quite unacceptable to the Polish government. Piłsudski and his followers equated any presence of Soviet troops on Polish soil with the loss of independence. This was one of the most important dogmas of Polish interwar policy. The crisis called for a review of Poland's foreign relations with a view to dealing with either possible threats from Germany or the consequences of a Soviet counter-move against these.

Paweł Starzenski, Beck's secretary, recorded Beck's views after a holiday they spent together in Venice in September 1937.[18] Beck considered relations with Great Britain to be improved though he thought it a little early to speak of a permanent agreement between the two at that stage, desirable as he considered this. He felt that the non-aggression pact was sufficient protection as regards Russia because she was too weak to start a war on her own initiative. As to Germany, Beck remembered the Marshal warning him that when he (Piłsudski) died all the odium of their joint policy would fall on Beck. He had continued the Marshal's policy of rapprochement with Germany. The non-aggression pact had prevented French attempts at friendship with Germany at Poland's expense and had given her added importance internationally. Nevertheless he refrained from collaboration beyond the terms of the pact. The same was true of the agreement with Russia.

Beck believed the best way of dealing with these two powers was to improve relations with Hungary, Romania, Yugoslavia and Italy and to create a 'Third Europe': a neutral zone, led by Poland, from the Baltic to the Black Sea. An East European federation was not a new idea in Polish thinking. In previous centuries Poland had been able to act as a major power by leading the group of small European States whose territories extended as far east as Kiev in the Ukraine. To Piłsudski and Beck, Jagellonian Poland provided the model for their concept of a 'Third Europe'. This was a dream in their desire for the revival of Poland as a great power. It would also create a barrier to German expansion eastward and become an alternative to the anti-Comintern Pact as a protection against Russia. However, at the time, Lithuania and Czechoslovakia were blocking this path.

These States became Beck's major preoccupation during the Anschluss crisis. His views on the fate of Austria were no secret; her collapse (as indeed was that of Czechoslovakia) was a foregone conclusion. Apparently blind to the relevance of the other States 'ceasing to exist', he concluded that the Austrian problem was 'remote from us and concerned us comparatively little, . . . but, our counter-move should be most careful'.[19] The counter-move depended to some extent on the reaction of the Western Powers. In the event, Hitler's move went unchecked but with attention focused on Austria, Beck took the opportunity to effect a forceful solution to the problem of relations with Lithuania. The former grand duchy had been the focus of Poland's expansionist aims in the period immediately after the First World War. For Piłsudski in particular Lithuania was more than an historical and cultural extension of Poland. The Vilna region, which contained a majority of Poles, was a piece of his homeland of which he was particularly fond and its incorporation into the new Poland gave him great personal satisfaction. He also had designs on the rest of Lithuania. An attempt at a *coup d'état* in Kovno by members of the POW in the summer of 1919 was discovered by the Lithuanian government. Since then its antagonism towards the Polish State had hardened, which created in annoying political and diplomatic impasse. Beck's chance to clear this came after an incident in which a Polish soldier was shot on the border of the two countries. This led to an ultimatum forcing the Lithuanian government to engage in diplomatic relations with Poland.

A similar heavy-handed display of 'independent action' was seen in Beck's conduct during the Munich crisis. He bore a grudge against the Czechs for their action in January 1919 when Prague ordered the invasion of Transolza (Zaolzie) despite an earlier agreement between the Czechoslovak and Polish National Councils to partition the disputed district. A plebiscite, carried out in July 1920 on Allied orders, confirmed Czech claims. Beck took the view that the Czechoslovak State was artificial and he disagreed with her foreign policy.[20] More specifically he was working for Polish control of Transolza and even threatened the use of force if Poland's interests there were not considered.[21] Synchronizing his demand with Hitler's pressure on Czechoslovakia Beck acted not only against advice from Britain and France but also against growing criticism at home. As it turned out, the Munich settlement was reached as Beck had dreaded, without Polish participation, and it was decided that Polish claims to the Transolza area should be settled in the future. Beck reacted by issuing an ultimatum to the Czechslovakian government on 30 September, demanding that they cede the area to Poland. On 2 October Polish troops marched into Transolza. The gain was hollow and rather pathetic. Its significance was summed up by Beck's secretary:

> The regaining of Transolza was without doubt in Piłsudski's political plans, one of the parts of an unwritten testament foreign policy charged to Beck. . . . He accepted entirely every order and objective of the Marshal, and applied them, even in the changing pattern of power in Europe. He often said in our small gathering: 'I never betrayed the Marshal while he lived, how could I do it now, when he is no longer with us? . . .'. Beck's relationship to Piłsudski could only be compared to that of a son to the memory of a beloved father.[22]

The Czechoslovak State had not fallen completely apart as Beck had hoped, but it had fallen under German influence. Hitler offered not an inch of her remaining territory to either Poland or Hungary. Thus the Polish desire for a common frontier with Hungary came to nothing.

His policy in a shambles after Munich, Beck himself was soon to feel the harsh realities of German pressure. Hitler wanted Danzig, that cornerstone of Polish-German relations, returned to Germany and a motorway link constructed from Germany, through the corridor, to East Prussia. As a consequence of this Beck hoped for closer links with Great Britain which Britain proposed in the form of a declaration by Britain, France, Poland and Russia to the effect that any action threatening any European state would occasion the four Powers to consult together as to 'what steps should be taken to offer joint resistance to any such action'.[23] The Poles and French were hesitant about the declaration though the Soviet government accepted it on 24 March.

The British were keen 'to manage affairs so as to secure the support of Poland'[24] and won Beck's approval for an announcement by Chamberlain to the House of Commons offering a guarantee against German aggression. The statement was made on 31 March 1939. British press emphasis on the 'free negotiations' mentioned by Chamberlain annoyed the Poles, who secured Foreign Office assurances that the British government had no intention of pressing Poland to make any concessions to Germany.

On 4 April the British and Polish foreign ministers met with Chamberlain. As a result of the meeting, relations between the two countries altered from a position of mutual interest in keeping the peace to mutual obligation in the case of a direct attack on either party. Beck claimed this as a great success at his press conference and one might agree that 'Poland was no longer an isolated potential victim of German aggression; an attack on her would, in all likelihood, launch a world war.'[25] Others saw flaws in the agreement; its terms had been of less interest than its value tactically as a deterrent to the Germans; there was no definite assurance that an attack on Danzig was tantamount to an attack on Poland; and there was no economic clause assuring Poland of British material aid.

The real value of the arrangement with Britain is doubtful since it did not deter Hitler. The only possibility of doing so lay in some arrangement with Russia, which Beck avoided, continuing merely to hope for a solution to the Danzig problem, while at the same time pressing for a stronger alliance with Britain. At that stage, Britain was also wary of a closer relationship with Russia, and the government rejected Russian proposals for an agreement between Britain, France and Russia because of possible effects on Poland.

At the same time, the British foreign minister saw the dangers of allowing Britain to 'get into a position in which the issues of war and peace depended solely on the judgement of the Polish Government'.[26] The British received little comfort on this score from Beck's 5 May speech to the *Sejm*, when he said that a self-respecting nation did not make unilateral concessions such as the Germans were demanding over Danzig and the corridor. An impasse over the issue had been reached.

Poland now sought to capitalize on the agreement with Britain and Count Edward Raczynski, the Polish ambassador in London, presented the British foreign minister with a request for aid of about £60 million which Chamberlain refused because of both internal and external pressures.

Meanwhile tension in Danzig mounted as Polish customs inspectors were sent a note by local authorities preventing them from carrying out their duties. This was interpreted by the Poles as a direct challenge to the Danzig statute and hence within the bounds of direct Polish interest as perceived by Beck. Britain and Poland had been discussing the terms of a treaty for some months and Raczynski now put the case for speedy completion of this agreement both for its deterrent value and as a 'counterpoise to the failure of the financial negotiations'.[27]

Britain, together with France, also sought an agreement with Russia and on 11 August British and French military missions arrived in the Soviet capital to be faced, a few days later, by Soviet demands for their (Soviet) troops to be granted right of passage through Poland. The Poles believed this request to have an ulterior motive. On 20 August, speaking for both the government and the military, Beck said that Marshal Voroshilov, who led the Soviet delegation as people's commissar for defence, was 'attempting today to reach in a peaceful manner what he had attempted to obtain by force of arms in 1920'.[28] Beck also thought it would lead to immediate declaration of war on the part of Germany. The talks were a failure. The next day the Soviet press announced the conclusion of a commercial credit agreement between Russia and Germany and the day after announced a Russo-German pact of non-aggression. In fact, neither Poland nor the Western Powers regarded the announcement of the Nazi-Soviet pact as necessarily entailing an end to Russian assistance should war break out. Beck's response to Western pressure to accept the Soviet terms was to agree to the possibility of military cooperation once hostilities broke out, but to reiterate the Polish case against the desired agreement with Russia in time of peace.

On 25 August the Anglo-Polish agreement was signed. It was an unholy alliance; Poland and Britain found themselves thrown together in the special circumstances of the diplomatic prelude to the war. Nothing but fear of Hitler brought the two together. Their alliance was an attempt to play for time in the hope that they would deter Hitler from further use of force in the conduct of German foreign policy. It is only with hindsight one can say that this reasoning was wrong. It would have been better to prepare to fight the war than attempt to delay it.

On 29 August the German chancellor delivered his ultimatum to Poland. He repeated the demands he had made after Munich. A familiar scene was being acted out but this time Hitler's victim did not capitulate under diplomatic pressure. Negotiations between the two governments broke down on 31 August 1939. In the early hours of the next day Germany invaded Poland.

The British and French governments reluctantly declared war on Germany on 3 September 1939. The discrepancy between the actuality of war on Polish territory and the response by Poland's Western allies was stunning. Yet, in reality, could Polish requests for the immediate fulfilment of Anglo-French obligations to Poland have been met by more than words? Could the British and French have helped the Poles? There were 25 German divisions in the west compared with 110 French but the latter needed three weeks to mobilize and apart from a token move towards the Saar the French army remained inactive. The calculation in London and Paris was that Poland would last out against Germany long enough for this mobilization to take place.

The collapse of Poland on 27 September, leaving just a few pockets of resistance, meant that German forces began their return to the west sooner than expected. France then froze in a defensive posture. As for the British, who had only two divisions in the field, they 'never expected to save Polish independence at the beginning of the war only to restore it after they had defeated Germany'.[29]

The Polish government was itself pessimistic about the military situation despite the Allied declaration of war. In view of the massive German assault, it felt a withdrawal should be made to the south-east corner of the country. It thought in terms of establishing a fortified camp in anticipation of the counter-offensive by the Western Allies and considered it wiser to make the move at that time rather than retreat later fighting every step of the way. The decision to evacuate the government from Warsaw was made on 5 September.

On 17 September, when the relentless onslaught of the German forces had swept the government to Kuty, Poland was invaded by the Soviet army, which occupied the area agreed to in the secret protocol to the Nazi-Soviet pact. This was defined by a line running through Przemyśl and Brest-Litovsk (Brześć) and reduced Poland to the 'narrowest ethnographical boundaries' of which G.V. Chicherin, the Soviet foreign commissar, and G. Stresseman, the German chancellor, had spoken in 1925.[30] Now, fourteen years later, Molotov was Soviet foreign commissar. He justified the Soviet action by saying that the Polish government had 'disintegrated' and had, in fact, 'ceased to exist', leaving Poland 'a suitable field for all manners of hazards and surprises, which may constitute a threat to the U.S.S.R.' Moreover he said that his government could not view with indifference the fate of Ukrainians and White Russians 'who live on Polish territory'. He concluded: 'At the same time the Soviet Government proposes to take all measures to extricate the Polish people from the unfortunate war into which they were dragged by their unwise leaders, and to enable them to live a peaceful life.'[31] Similar sentiments had been expressed by Chicherin during the Russo-Polish War of 1920. In August of that year a Polish Revolutionary Committee, the potential nucleus of a future Communist government, had been established to the rear of the advancing Red Army. Only time would tell how far history would repeat itself in the Second World War.

The immediate consequence of the Soviet invasion of 17 September 1939 was to oblige the Polish government and High Command to leave their country. The next day they crossed the Romanian frontier. The history of their fate then becomes confused before personalities and policies emerged from the melting pot and a new Polish government was formed in France.

2 In Angers and London, 1940

DURING THE EARLY hours of 18 September 1939, before crossing the Romanian frontier, the Polish foreign minister sent the following instructions to Poland's ambassador in London:

> The military situation in Poland in the current conflict is such as to necessitate the transfer abroad of the seat of the President of the Republic and of the Government. The Polish Government has the honour to inform the Government of His Britannic Majesty that it is today contacting the Government of the French Republic concerning the extra-territorial exercise of its powers on French soil.[1]

If the intention of the Polish government was therein made clear by Beck, its achievement proved more difficult than he could have anticipated. Hopes that the Romanian government would not hinder the passage of the Polish authorities *en route* for France were not to be fulfilled.

In London the War Cabinet discussed the fate of Poland. It is, however, clear from the record that Romania, even more than Poland, now became its concern. It was thought probable that the Germans had agreed at Moscow to the invasion of eastern Poland and it was a 'disturbing' thought that some 'similar secret agreement' might have been made in regard to Romania.[2] Already Germany had warned Romania that if the Polish government were allowed to establish itself on, and direct the war from, Romanian soil, this would be regarded as a breach of Romanian neutrality by Germany, who would be obliged to take sanctions against her.

As to the Russian invasion of Poland, this did not involve Britain in war with the U.S.S.R., since although the agreement with Poland provided for such action 'if Poland suffered aggression from a European Power' there was a 'further understanding' that 'the European power in question was Germany'. The War Cabinet was even against the British ambassador lodging a protest at the Kremlin as requested by the Polish ambassador in London. Instead, the minutes record that the cabinet supported Chamberlain's proposed statement that 'His Majesty's Government had learned with indignation and horror of the action taken by the Government of the U.S.S.R. in invading Polish territory'. They pledged their support for the Poles by saying that 'this action neither altered in any way the position in this country in relation to Poland nor weakened the obligations which we had solemnly undertaken to Poland'. But, quite clearly, the British government did not wish to offend the Soviet Union. They concluded

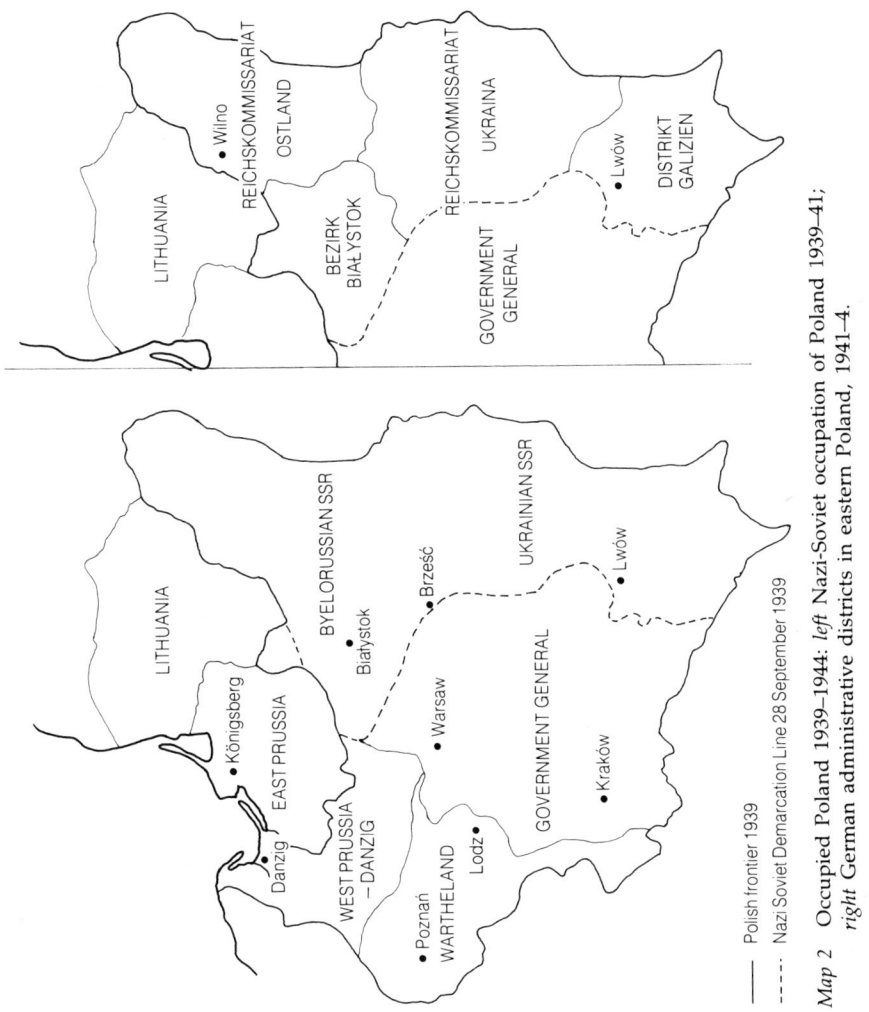

Map 2 Occupied Poland 1939–1944: *left* Nazi-Soviet occupation of Poland 1939–41; *right* German administrative districts in eastern Poland, 1941–4.

'although the Soviet aggression had added further tragedy to the history of Poland, His Majesty's Government still retained complete confidence that on the conclusion of the war, Poland would be restored'.[3]

The Romanian government was equally unwilling to offend the Soviets and a decision to intern the Polish government was taken on 18 September when the Russians were in occupation of that part of Poland which bordered on Romania.

The Poles depended heavily on the attitude of the British government and looked to Britain for any pressure she could bring to bear on Romania to secure the release of the Polish authorities. The British War Cabinet agreed that although there was no longer any free Polish territory it was important that a Polish government should remain in existence in order to organize the use of Polish resources against Germany. These resources were identified as a large sum in gold, certain naval units and considerable Polish manpower capable of being organized into divisions for use on the Western Front.[4] As to safe passage through Romania, it was decided to employ the most cautious approach; the chosen means of bringing pressure was the legal argument that 'under international law the Romanian Government was under no obligation whatsoever to intern civil members of the Polish Government'.[5] A message to this effect was sent.

Meanwhile, in Romania, most Poles felt that their government should resign. This was urgent since unless the president appointed a successor who was in France, or on his way there, thus ensuring the existence of the legal Polish government, the fear was that a puppet regime would be installed in Warsaw. This fear proved groundless because after some initial consideration of such a scheme both Hitler and Stalin rejected the idea. A rump state could have been a cause of friction between the two powers and so it was rejected in favour of the traditional Russo-German policy of settling their differences over Poland by partitioning her. Moreover, they agreed on 28 September 1939 that 'neither party would tolerate in its territory any Polish agitation which affected the territories of the other party';[6] liaison between Gestapo and NKVD was close.

The German half of Poland was itself subdivided according to Hitler's decree of 8 October 1939. Western Poland was incorporated into the Third Reich. The new provinces were Wartheland and West-Prussia-Danzig. The remaining portion of Poland, under German occupation, came to be known as the 'Government General'.

In contrast to Hitler's swift and decisive moves in Poland, Stalin's policy was hesitant. He had been over this ground before and was alive to the problems which had exercised his mind in 1920 when he was political commissar to A.I. Yegorov, the commander of the Soviet South-Western Front. As well as experiencing the strength of Polish nationalism, he had then developed three attitudes which were to colour his future policies. First was a reluctance to move Soviet forces too far ahead of their supplies.

Second was a fear of the potential nationalism of Ukrainians and White Russians living in Russia's western marches. Third was a wariness of the intentions of Finland and Romania towards Russia in time of war. It should also be noted that Stalin saw the capture of Lwòw as a priority in the Polish-Soviet War of 1920. He believed that its conquest would open the way for a Bolshevik march to Hungary, Romania and the Balkans.[7]

In the opening stages of the Second World War Stalin turned his attention to legitimizing his territorial gains. On 10 October 1939 Wilno (Vilna) was transferred to Lithuania in an attempt to secure the republic's loyalty to Russia.[8] Then, on 21 October, a plebiscite was held by the Soviet authorities in occupation of Polish territory. Its results were announced in Moscow on 1 November 1939. Western Ukraine was to be incorporated into the U.S.S.R. by union with the Ukrainian Soviet Socialist Republic. Similarly western White Ruthenia (Byelorussia or White Russia) was to unite with the White Ruthenian Soviet Socialist Republic.[9]

During much of this time Poland was technically without a government; the internment in Romania created a dangerous interregnum. In London, Halifax was impatient and disturbed at the delay in arranging for the constitution of a Polish government which could legally function in France. Kennard, the British ambassador to Warsaw, who escaped with Beck, had informed the Foreign Office of Polish opinion, particularly amongst opponents of the regime, such as Sikorski, who had also gone into exile:

> The Polish collapse and hasty retreat into Romania have caused great resentment amongst representative Poles. The Marshal (Smigły-Rydz) and Colonel Beck are especially criticized, and it is freely stated that Polish people will not entrust their future destiny to their former leaders.[10]

The French government, in sympathy with this opinion, made it clear that it would not support the formation of a government representative of the *Sanacja*.

After many difficulties, the position of the president, and therefore the legal existence of the Polish State, was secured by the appointment of Władisław Raczkiewicz.[11] Attention in Paris then concentrated on the formation of a government and the establishment and command of a Polish army in France. The basis of the Franco-Polish agreement concerning the creation of a Polish division there was signed on 21 September. It put a Polish general in charge of a Polish division under French High Command. Sikorski, who was considered by French officials as France's closest friend, was appointed commander of the Polish army in France. Concurrent with the appointment in the military field, the formation of the new government was also rapidly proceeding. Choice of a premier called for compromise between the demands of the Sikorski group and the wishes of the newly appointed president working within a constitutional framework which was under strain from the pressures of politics in exile. After much dispute President Rackiewicz agreed to appoint Sikorski prime minister. Thus on 30 September 1939, the transfer of the supreme offices of the state was completed, and their 'constitutional continuity and legality remained intact',[12] but the power of the president was altered in what is known as the 'Paris Compromise'.[13] This was a manifestation of the problems besetting the émigré Poles. While Sikorski and the democratic opposition were undoubtedly popular with the majority of Poles and with the Allies, the supporters of the *Sanacja* constituted a formidable political group in exile. Their interest lay in maintaining the powers of the president as defined by the 1935 constitution. To Sikorski and his group these were unacceptable. With French support they persuaded Rackiewicz to agree to consult with the prime minister over matters on which he could have acted independently in the past. From the manoeuvres of the two groups Sikorski emerged the winner; the prime minister's executive role overshadowed the president's, even though the president's influence on crucial matters was still evident at times in the future.

General Sikorski, as prime minister, also held the portfolios for justice, internal affairs and military affairs, although his experience in political office, before the May coup, had been but brief. In the ten years before the outbreak of war, Sikorski had divided his time between writing and political opposition. He had often visited France. Greatly to the chagrin of the Polish government he was made much of there, especially by the military authorities. Sikorski's government of 'National Unity' represented all the more important parties and currents of political thought.

Certain personalities were associated with different phases in the political history of independent Poland. General Sosnkowski, the president's heir apparent and minister without portfolio, was one of the few officers of high rank to come through the invasion of Poland with distinction. He had been close to Piłsudski from the period up to 1926 and remained a great favourite of the officer corps. Zaleski, minister of foreign affairs, was identified with the first phase of the *Sanacja*. Colonel Adam Koc, minister of finance, was closely associated with its later phase. Together they presented Sikorski with a formidable threat.

The *Endecja* were represented in the cabinet by Marian Seyda, minister without portfolio, and Stanisław Stronski, vice-premier and minister of propaganda. On the left of the political spectrum, the PPS was represented by Jan Stanczyk, minister of social welfare. Aleksander-Lados, minister without portfolio, represented Wito's Peasant Party. Karol Popiel, undersecretary for social welfare, General Kukiel, under-secretary for military affairs and General Haller, minister without portfolio, were closely associated with the Centre Catholic Party of Labour (*Stronnictwo Pracy* – SP).

The new government marked a radical change in Polish politics in that, while including some Piłsudski-ites, the old regime was replaced by a government comprised of representatives of the former opposition, from both the Left and the Right. They came to power in dramatic circumstances; the military disaster, flight to Romania and internment of the government offered the opportunity for change which had otherwise been impossible in Poland since Piłsudski's *coup d'état* of May 1926. The extent to which the Sikorski government differed in its policies from those of its predecessors remained to be seen.

Reaction to the new Polish government was favourable. A message had been sent to Raczkiewicz by members of the former government expressing their loyalty to the new administration and, at the same time, tendering their resignations. The prestige of the government increased proportionately with the growing and outspoken criticism of the former government, particularly from Poles in Romania. The High Command was being accused of negligence both because they had not provided better air defence and because, all through the summer of 1939, they had been selling their anti-aircraft guns abroad. Piłsudski's successor, Marshal Smigły-Rydz, was accused of leaving the country prematurely and abandoning the troops, and Beck of having left reconciliation with the Western Powers too late to be of assistance. The British government was criticized and the French even more so, for interference in Polish internal affairs, particularly over the composition of the new government. Much of this talk was of course the by-product of intrigue amongst Poles jockeying for position in whatever new administration might emerge.

Important institutional and political changes were soon to come following the government's move to Angers, from where a presidential order was issued on 2 November dissolving the *Sejm* and Senate.[14] This left a void which had to be filled and subsequently the Council of Ministers received for its consideration a presidential decree for the creation of a new National Council. Debate on this concerned the elections to the Council. Sosnkowski made the obvious point that at the time elections were impossible but the Council of Ministers accepted the declaration which stated that for the 'duration of the unusual circumstances caused by the war a National Council would be appointed to act as the President's and Government's consultative organ'.[15] This body would give an opinion on all matters brought to its attention by the government which concerned the State budget and the future political system of the State. Although it was to be left to the National Council to agree on its own rules of procedure, motions could only be put when at least two-thirds of its members were present. A simple majority would then be required to carry the motion. Membership was confined to a minimum of 12 and a maximum of 24 to be appointed by the president at the suggestion of the chairman of the Council of Ministers. Neither members of the government, civil servants nor military personnel on active service would be eligible for membership. However, members of the government were allowed to take part in its sittings without the right to vote. It was agreed that the president could dissolve the National Council at the request of the prime minister.

The distance between government and nation had somehow to be bridged and the National Council was seen as one way of achieving this. It could only be regarded as a poor substitute for the *Sejm* and Senate since its members could not be elected by the people and under these circumstances the powers granted to do it could not be as great as those bodies had enjoyed, and its subordination to the Council of Ministers was set down in its constitution. Its composition was dictated by the government, in particular by Sikorski who was dominant in all decisions made over this issue.

Kennard, the British ambassador to the Polish Government-in-Exile, reported that Sikorski had had pointed out to him that there was very little hope of 'any member of the present Polish Government in exile being acceptable to the Poles in Poland after the war'. Kennard believed that Sikorski could spare himself the fate of Marshal Smigły-Rydz only by avoiding 'the role of man of destiny and by insisting that he was only holding office provisionally and would be ready at any moment to lay his power in the hands of the Polish Nation'.[16]

Lewis Namier, a Polish expert and expatriate who was professor of modern history at the University of Manchester 1931–9, held a similar opinion. In comparing the fate of the émigré Poles with that of their compatriots under German occupation he wrote:

> however well the émigrés may work or fight those who have been left behind or who have stuck to their land or posts, will entertain a feeling of superiority over the émigrés, or even a grudge against them. This is a matter of human psychology. A marked radicalisation of the Polish masses may easily be the consequence of the defeat and emigration: they will not necessarily distinguish between those who had been responsible for the mismanagement of the Polish State and the defeat of the Polish Army, and those who had no share in the Government.

Namier also recognized that not every one of the governing class had left. Moreover he believed that it was from among those who had remained that the new leaders would be found and with whom it was important for the Polish government to keep in touch. Apart from difficult circumstances this presented a problem as it was a question of mental attitude: 'it is important that the émigrés in their minds should be subordinate themselves to those who have stayed behind'.[17]

Sikorski appeared not to be heeding such advice. Early impressions gained from reports reaching the Foreign Office in London were of a man determined to effect a number of changes which would sustain his own political existence through a series of crises where his critics were many and their protests loud. Without going too far in condemning the old regime and excluding everybody connected with it on the grounds that it was so loathed by the Poles in Poland, the changes Sikorski proposed attempted to introduce into the government elements which enjoyed the confidence of Poles in Poland, such as Professor Kot of the Peasant Party. As Kennard commented, however, in view of the 'undoubted hatred of the Poles in Poland for the regime that seems to them to have been responsible for Poland's misfortunes', Sikorski had a good excuse for 'getting his own back' on those who he believed had 'behaved unfairly to him after 1926.'[18]

The attitude of each of the parties represented in the National Council towards the government was displayed during the debate on 5 March 1940 which followed Sikorski's first speech to the National Council since its inauguration. Sikorski's theme was the Government-in-Exile and its attempts to lay new foundations for the future of a strong, united and democratic Poland. He spoke of the failures of the pre-war regime and the danger of repeating such mistakes through intrigues amongst sections of the Polish community in exile, and he appealed for support for his government.[19]

Bielecki, representative of the National Democrats, said that his party would cooperate with Sikorski's government in Poland and in exile to free the nation from its captors. His party would work towards this end and support the government since it was the only legal government of Poland; this was despite reservations as to its composition and political direction. He recognized their common cause of drawing people of opposing ideological and political views round the same table but warned that working together did not mean mindless acceptance of all the government's policies.[20]

Through its spokesman, M. Kwiatkowski, the Party of Labour pointed out that, in the face of government's call to everyone to work for Poland, a number of defenders of the old regime stood apart. It supported the prime minister's remarks that such attempts to undermine the government should not be tolerated and declared its own complete faith in Premier Sikorski's government.

The views of the Socialist Party were similar. 'As members of the National Council we should support the Government in exploiting every possibility of helping both the population at home and the evacuees.'[21] The Peasant Party was even more positive in its support of Sikorski. They said he had been known and respected over a long time for his democratic beliefs. His radical break from old *Sanacja*-dominated *Sejm* endeared him to the Peasant Party who supported his attempts to build a new Poland in which the 25 million peasants would play a more decisive political role.

The party representatives on the National Council thus offered overall support for the government, but within the Council itself division did exist, as indicated during the debate on procedure. The tendency of individual members to argue at length over relatively insignificant matters also emerged. Though a waste of time, it suited the government. The National Council was free to expend its energies in this harmless way, as long as the parties remained loyal. Sikorski's government had ensured that the National Council could not threaten the government but could serve as a useful source of moral support. It is in the light of his attitude towards the National Council that his policy towards the organizations developing in Poland against German and Russian occupation should be seen.

The first of these, called 'Service for the Victory of Poland' (*Stużba Zwycięstwu Polski*–SZP) was formed on the orders of Marshal Smigły-Rydz. These orders were transmitted by General Julius Rommel, commander of Warsaw's defences on 27 September 1939 (the day before the capital's surrender) to General Michał Karasiewicz-Tokarzewski. Alongside the SZP there developed a political organization, the Chief Political Council (*Główna Rada Polityczna* – GRP). Tokarzewski, himself a Piłsudski-ite, recognizing the importance of giving the SZP a wide political base, encouraged their cooperation. However, a situation in which both the military and political underground movements had created their own organizations was not to Sikorski's liking. In turning his attention to Poland after the formation of his government in France, Sikorski's first act was the creation, on 13 November 1939, of the Union for Armed Struggle (*Związek Walki Zbrojnej* – ZWZ). This organization came under the control of General Sosnkowski through the Committee of Ministers for Polish Affairs which he headed until August 1941.

In January 1940 the resistance movement in Poland was divided territorially: Tokarzewski, based in Lwów, was given the command of Polish forces in the Russian zone of occupation. Colonel Stefan Rowecki, based in Warsaw, was given the equivalent appointment in the zone under German occupation. This arrangement, disturbed by Tokarzewski's capture by the Russians in March 1940, lasted until the end of June when Rowecki was placed in charge of a unified ZWZ Command for the whole of Poland.

Sikorski also ordered the dissolution of the GRP, replacing it in February 1940 with the Political Consultative Committee (*Polityczny Komitet Porozumiewawczy* – PKP). Within this organization the chief representatives of the political parties of the underground movement were: the Socialist Kazimierz Puzak; Stefan Korboński who represented the Peasants; Aleksander Dębski the Nationalists; and Franciszek Kwiecinski the Party of Labour.

In practice this Committee was subordinate to the military organization, the ZWZ. As Jozef Garlinski explains, this state of affairs still did not suit Sikorski and the Polish Government-in-Exile.[22] With the prospect of power in post-war Poland in mind the government appointed a delegate, who was based within the PKP, to whom the military command was made subordinate. Sikorski thus hoped to ensure his control over the underground State. The delegate, Cyryl Ratajski, a member of the Party of Labour, who was appointed on 2 December 1940, was directly responsible to the Polish Government-in-Exile. This effectively curtailed the political power of General Rowecki who, though widely held in esteem in Poland, had previously supported the former regime and was therefore politically suspect in the eyes of the ex-opposition majority in the government who wished to keep the military out of politics. Sikorski's own situation belied that policy. He did not intend to heed advice to separate his military from his political function, believing that the war justified his stance.

The new Polish government and the Allies, 1939

AT the first full meeting of the Council of Ministers, held on 6 October 1939 in Paris, Sikorski proposed a declaration to Poland in which he referred to the concord between himself and the president and to his own position at the head of a government of national unity and of the military. 'From the reassurances of Poland's allies', he said, 'we know that they will continue the battle with us for the eventual triumph of freedom, law and justice. Poland will emerge from this battle strengthened – to endure for ages.' He concluded that the causes and responsibility for the disasters which had led to the occupation of the whole of Polish territory by Germany and Russia would be decided by 'history and the Nation', after 'the liberation of our land'. The Council of Ministers agreed to the declaration.

Regarding military affairs, the prime minister announced that the training of Polish soldiers in exile was getting under way. He felt sure that a call up in France would provide between 15,000 and 20,000 men. In addition, about the same number of troops was reported to be arriving in Salonika and Istanbul from Hungary and Romania. General Kleeburg was authorized to marshal Polish men and material arriving from these sources. As regards the air force, it was hoped that two or three units would concentrate in England and one, two or three in France, with a further three coming from the U.S.A. and Canada. General Haller was to go to North America, as the representative of the government, to facilitate the organization of such air force units.

Sikorski was anxious to ensure that the fact that both government and army were on French soil did not lead to too close an identification of Poland with French interests. He hoped that Zaleski's proposed visit to London would redress the balance between Franco-Polish and Anglo-Polish relations. The foreign minister stated his intention to contact Lord Halifax, members of the British government and of the opposition. It was agreed that his task would be to obtain an agreement whereby Germany would be held responsible for territorial and material losses in Poland; in addition he was to seek the support of the British government to prevent Germany giving further Polish territory to Soviet Russia. Zaleski pointed out that the French and British governments were afraid of pushing Russia further into Germany's grip, a fear which prevented a really forceful approach, but he said he would take the opportunity to enlighten the British government of the Soviet danger and to prepare an appropriate policy in the matter for the future. At this time the Polish government was most worried about the French attitude towards the Soviet Union. Sikorski commented that Russian action in Poland had created confusion in French minds, but he believed that the French government's policy of extreme caution towards the Soviet Union could be effectively influenced in Poland's favour by pressure from the British government. He concluded the discussion by saying that after the destruction of Germany, it was imperative to create a system in Central Europe, headed by Poland, to act as a counterweight to both Germany and Russia. A summary of these rather vague conclusions was sent out in the 'Government Instructions to the Directors of the Legations' which ended with the hope that 'all concerned would work towards the creation of a new Poland whose government was the expression of National Unity'.[23]

On 17 October Zaleski reported the outcome of his recent three-day visit to London. He told his colleagues that his meetings with the leading figures of all parties in Britain were conducted in a cordial atmosphere, in contrast to the bitterness evident in Franco-Polish relations at the time. Zaleski had suggested that Soviet action in Poland should, for the present, be played down and attention concentrated on Germany, blaming her for all Polish losses since he did not believe that the Soviets were wholeheartedly cooperating with Germany or that they would think it in their interest to see a victorious Germany neighbouring on Russia. He reported that the British foreign secretary accepted his views and offered this as an example of good Anglo-Polish relations suspecting, however, 'that as the war developed, Soviet policy might evolve in unexpected directions'.

Regarding his conversation with Chamberlain, Zaleski concluded that while the British policy-makers did not have a determined policy towards Soviet Russia at that time, they might, in the future, seek Soviet help against Germany which would be 'contrary to Polish interests', bearing in mind 'Soviet agitation on ethnic grounds'.[24]

Members of the government were generally happy with the outcome of Zaleski's visit but, in the discussion that followed, Sosnkowski urged the necessity of attaining parity in relations with the Allies. Stronski saw in Chamberlain's attitude no danger of being treated like Czechoslovakia or Austria before the outbreak of war, but he feared that unless Poland was treated on the same level as France by the British government, decisions concerning Polish affairs could be made without prior consultation by London.

This fear was soon confirmed over the matter of Polish frontiers. Soon after Zaleski's visit to London, Chamberlain was questioned in the Commons about how much territory had been added to Poland by the action of the Polish armies over and above the areas agreed on by the Treaty of Versailles, and what areas the British government intended to recognize as the boundary of Poland.

The reply given in the House on 19 October 1939 by R.A. Butler, parliamentary under-secretary of state for foreign affairs, was as follows:

> The Treaty of Versailles did not lay down the area of the Polish State, but dealt only with the frontier between Poland and Germany. Such parts of this frontier as the Treaty did not exactly define were left for determination, after the holding of a plebiscite, by the Conference of Ambassadors. The frontier so arranged has not been altered by the action of Poland. The other frontiers of Poland were subsequently settled by other international arrangements.[25]

The answer to the question about the areas His Majesty's Government intended to recognize as the boundary of Poland was not then given. However, speaking on 26 October, Halifax said that 'the Soviet frontier with Poland now coincided with the Curzon Line'.[26] The Polish government were taken aback by this. They expected consultation as an ally and this must have been foremost in Sikorski's mind as he and Zaleski left for London on 14 November.

In his talks with Chamberlain, Sikorski pointed out that beyond the demarcation line which the Soviets had established in Poland, there lived 'more than five million Poles, nearly as many Ukrainians, three-quarters of a million White Russians, as many Jews and not one Russian'. Since none of these people wished to be integrated into the Soviet Union, its latest territorial demands were, in his opinion, without foundation. He insisted that 'the problem of Eastern Europe should be decided on a plane other than the one demanded by the Soviet Union'. Sikorski wanted an assurance from the British government that it would condemn any territorial acquisition by the Soviet Union at Poland's expense. Instead he was told that it was too early to make any decisions about Poland's frontiers. Reassured that Halifax's speech of 26 October should not be treated as an official statement of the British government, it was nevertheless clear to him that the issue of the Russo-Polish frontier remained open. Later, he told his Council of Ministers that the matter would have to be taken up again. At the same time, he still upheld the principle that Poland should be a strong maritime nation, with a more substantial outlet to the Baltic than she had hitherto had, and claimed he had gained acceptance of this in Great Britain.

With regard to the military affairs, Sikorski conceded the difficulty of finding resources to equip 100,000 Poles when 4 million French and 250,000 British soldiers had to be prepared for action, but nevertheless he felt that given the 'goodwill' of the allies 'everybody can be mobilised'.[27] It was agreed in London the Polish armed forces should be organized into Polish units 'and employed on a footing of equality with the armed forces of the Allied Powers for common action under the orders of the Allied

High Command'.[28] Sikorski impressed the British with the need to form a Polish division in Canada. It was noted that such a force would, 'keep in being the entity of the Polish nation as one of the original allies, and it would be of importance from the point of view of opinion in U.S.'[29] This conclusion was sent to the cabinet's Military Coordination Committee which responded most favourably. 'We strongly favour the proposal that Polish units should be formed in this country, in Canada, and in France, and we recommend that this should be pushed on as fast as possible by the departments concerned.'[30]

Decision-making in the military sphere was also discussed while Sikorski was in London. He reported that he had made 'yet another positive step'. He had learnt that the British and French authorities had agreed to establish a permanent staff committee on the Supreme War Council. It had been reported that the head of the Polish Government and Commander in Chief 'ought to participate in *some* [emphasis added] sittings of this Committee'.

The situation with regard to Soviet Russia was less satisfactory. France and England did not wish to 'push the Soviets into the German grasp' as Sikorski well understood and yet, he told his cabinet, 'our allies in time will have to understand the danger which threatens the West from the East. The hour will come when they will have to resist politically and eventually militarily the further advance of the Red Army in the West.'[31]

These points were reiterated in a document sent both to the French and to Halifax in which the Polish government also pressed for full reports as an ally on the Supreme War Council. It was particularly concerned about the rebuilding of the Polish army and active Allied collaboration with a view to 'regularising the arrival in France of young recruits from Poland and of soldiers interned in certain countries'. It said that the two 'Occupying Powers have condemned the Poles to death by starvation' and that all reports from Poland led to the conviction that 'failing regular relief in the way of food, clothes and medicines, the next winter will cause the most fearful ravages among the population'. It urged that supplies be sent on a long-term basis.

A preface to the document included impassioned reference to the suffering of the Poles from 'misery, cold and hunger' and said that they had been 'massacred, shot, deported (and) herded into concentration camps'. It spoke with pride of Polish unwillingness to compromise with the enemy and the inability of the Germans to find even a minor candidate for a pro-Hitler government in Poland; of the willingness of what was left of the Polish police to face internment in concentration camps, if necessary, in support of the secret loyalty sworn to the Angers government; and of unanimity in the Allied cause of 'the peasant and the landowner, the workmen and the priest, the artisan and the intellectual'. It sought proper help in this 'resistance unparalleled in history'.[32]

The minute by Makins on the Polish document summed up the reaction of the Foreign Office to this plea for better treatment. He wrote that he had much sympathy for the Poles but believed that they would have to modify their expansionist ambitions and that it was likely to be 'difficult enough to give them back a country which is a going concern'. He interpreted the Polish document as a bid for full recognition of Poland's status 'as an Allied state which has fulfilled its obligations and which is called upon now and in the future to play a decisive role in the reconstitution of Central and Eastern Europe'. He thought that such recognition would strengthen 'the will to resist of the Polish nation, which would thus, at the appropriate moment, be in a position to render great and precious military service to the common cause'.[33] The official Foreign Office response along these lines emerged in due course.

The French reply on 12 May 1940 favoured Polish participation in the deliberations of the Supreme War Council whenever a question appearing to affect Polish interests was to be examined.[34] There was little joy in this reply for the Polish government; nothing in it suggested that the Allies were prepared to treat it as an equal or to support its goal of the restored Polish State playing a major role in European politics. That Poland should play the dominant role in a united east central Europe was central to the government's thinking. Thus a declaration issued to 'all people in the occupied Republic of Poland', which referred to the September campaign as the 'greatest defeat of Western Slavdom in the thousand-year battle with the German deluge' claimed that 'out of the tragedy a united association of Slav states would emerge within the framework of a new political configuration of east-central Europe'. Sikorski believed that such an association would form a bloc of nations between the Baltic, Black and Adriatic seas 'which would stem the German tide in the West and separate Germany from Russia'.[35] This was an old Polish dream to which the Government-in-Exile was to devote much of its energies.

As a subject for discussion within the Council of Ministers, the Soviet Union was noticeably absent, at this stage, and was not mentioned in official declarations. One reason for this was of course the marked lack of support for Polish interests against the Soviet Union by the Western Allies. Another explanation for the silence about Russia was uncertainty as to the relationship between the two powers occupying Poland. Reports of tension between Germany and Russia were reaching the Polish government. One such report, dated 28 October 1939, urged 'the acceptance by Poland of the present situation regarding the territories taken over by the Russians'. This would greatly ease the relationship with Poland's allies since it would remove the formal and moral obstacles to a gradual entry by the Soviets to the anti-German coalition. The recognition of Soviet gains by Poland and her allies would be:

the first condition enabling the USSR to embark on a road towards a closer relationship with Britain and France. If this were to happen the Soviets would support Poland as an independent state, without aiming to incorporate her into the Socialist republics, provided of course that Polish policies towards the Soviet Union were friendly. What emerges is that the political and military stance of Russia *vis à vis* Germany will change completely.[36]

While it was inconceivable that the Polish government would voluntarily make the sacrifices suggested, the possible change in Russo-German relations had to be considered seriously, though until the Russians also found themselves on the receiving end of German force, the Polish government felt it could do no more than acquaint the Western Allies with its position on the question of frontiers, leaving open the question of its relationship with Russia at this stage; the behaviour of the Soviet authorities towards Poles could not, in the government's view, be distinguished from that of the German authorities in occupied Poland.

Poland under Nazi-Soviet occupation

THE first year of war brought calamities upon Polish society such as to defy adequate description. Perhaps this haunting vignette, typifying the condition of millions on the move within Poland and out of Poland to the Soviet Union and Germany goes some way to convey the horror of it all:

> It was early in December 1939. The winter was extraordinarily severe, the temperature falling to 30 degrees of frost (C.). At Mielec I saw a train full of deportees from Bydgoszcz enter the station. It was composed entirely of cattle-trucks, sealed, without windows, without water, lavatories, or any heat. The journey had lasted three days and three nights. The people confined in it were mainly women and children. When the trucks were opened, there got down from them spectres who could scarcely stand upright, all dirty and emaciated, in a state of terror. They began to undo their baggage. I approached and saw that it was frozen children, frost bitten. One, two, ten, twenty, thirty or more. None of the mothers wept, they were as if petrified. Two half-dead children had great lumps of ice on their cheeks: it was their tears frozen on their pale faces.[37]

The lives of the majority who were spared the rigours of forced migration were blighted in other ways.

In the Government General, which Czesław Miłosz described as the experimental laboratory in which Nazi policy made 'excellent material for a study in human madness', the authorities acted in accordance with dictates from Berlin.[38] These ranged from the persecution of Jews for ideological reasons to the provision of Polish labour to fuel the needs of the German war economy. After a number of half-hearted attempts to establish a puppet government, Governor Hans Frank set about controlling his subjects by a variety of methods. In response to the growing strength of Polish refusal to collaborate, he applied the principle of divide and rule; certain national or ethnic minorities – Russians (until the summer of 1941),

White Russians and especially Ukrainians – were treated better than ethnic Poles. All were favoured in comparison to Jews. Arrests were numerous from September 1939. At first, with the exception of round-ups of labour, the victims were individuals rather than groups. However, from August 1940, starting in Warsaw, the authorities proceeded with mass arrests. The intelligentsia, sent away to concentration camps – principally to Auschwitz (Oswięcim) – suffered the most in these actions.[39] The city itself, as with other large centres of population, was divided up into three sectors: German, Polish and Jewish.

Living conditions deteriorated very rapidly in the non-German sectors. The price of food rose by massive proportions. The statistics for many were meaningless in a situation where some foods became unobtainable. Of those who managed to get rations, most, after the summer of 1941, were on a starvation diet. It suffices to say that the death rate in the Jewish ghetto prior to its liquidation in 1942 was in the region of 158 per 1,000 inhabitants compared to an average pre-war figure for Poland of 10 per 1,000.[40] Deaths through starvation and disease were added to deaths through military and police action and compounded by death in the death camps where millions met their end in the German gas chambers of Poland.

If, in their actions in Poland, the Germans 'blackened hell', Soviet policy in the first two years of the war did not make it any lighter. It is estimated that well over a million Poles were deported to the East in four vast convoys starting in February 1940 and ending in June 1941. The exact fate of many of these prisoners – civilians as well as soldiers – is still unknown. However, the testimony of those who survived suggests that after the German attack on the Soviet Union on 22 June 1941 the fate of Poles in Poland could only improve in the sense that there was only one devil to overcome.

God, too, had a role to play. In a memorandum to the British foreign secretary dated 17 February 1941, Kennard reported that churches throughout Poland were filled to overflowing. Priests and convents were involved in resistance. 'Sermons openly alluded to the Resurrection of Poland.'[41] Hope of victory over the Germans was never abandoned. Poles never lost confidence in their own ability to survive for the duration of the war. What sustained them in spirit was a love of their country. As so often in their history they took strength from dreams of freedom and the vision of a resurrected Poland. This belief in the indestructibility of the nation despite the vicissitudes of history gave them the will to survive that enraged their enemies and, at times, took forms which exasperated their friends.

This will expressed itself in a multitude of acts of resistance – ranging from non-cooperation to acts of sabotage. Yet for all this it was always understood that victory would really only be achieved by help from outside. In commenting upon the results of resistance activity in Poland in 1941, it was stated by General Sosnkowski, the head of the Polish underground under Sikorski: 'such actions are a proof of the spirit of resistance which dominates in Poland, (but) they cannot be regarded as likely to bring about a weakening of Germany's military power'.[42] Polish forces had to be organized and armed to meet the enemy on an equal footing. The opportunity for this presented itself best at the side of the Allies in theatres of war outside Poland. Until the summer of 1941 the Soviet Union was, in this context, regarded as fair game by the Polish Government-in-Exile.

The fighting Ally

ON 30 November 1939, the Russo-Finnish war erupted and was thrust into the public eye by the appeal from the Finnish government to the League of Nations on 2 December. The Finnish appeal against the Soviet invasion found a ready response from the Polish government. At its first meeting in the new year it decided to aid Finland despite the very considerable difficulties inherent in the task. In particular, Latvia and Estonia would not allow the passage of Polish *matériel* 'because of their dependence on the Soviet Union'; without this, the manpower the Poles had to offer was not very useful to the Finns. Zaleski told his colleagues that significant help could only be offered by obtaining French agreement to allow Poland some Swedish war *matériel* for this purpose. Even if the French were agreeable, though, Sikorski contended that the British government would prevent the use of Polish naval units to aid Finland, 'because a state of war between Russia and Britain does not exist'.[43]

What the government could do was clearly dependent on the willingness of the Allies to allow Polish aid to reach Finland. An opportunity came for Sikorski to discuss this, and the crisis as a whole, when he and the French premier met on 4 January 1940, to sign the Polish-French military agreement. Sikorski pointed out that the Finnish war opened out new possibilities for the Allies 'if only they would exploit them'. He described Bolshevism as 'a colossus of weak internal structure and with a worthless army' and urged that the offensive be taken against it in Finland, where he foresaw a role for Polish troops. Daladier agreed. He declared himself in complete agreement with open war against Bolshevism, though adding that the British were applying brakes on this. He said that both the French and the British were quite openly supplying aircraft, artillery, small arms and even tanks to Finland and suggested that if the British did not actually declare war, the kind of aid they offered might well amount to that, an eventuality which he stressed would suit France. He reiterated acceptance of General Sikorski's suggestions for an offensive on the Finnish sector, which Sikorski saw as 'a great step forward in tidying up the problem of creating a Polish Army'. Reporting to his ministers Sikorski observed that the French were easier to negotiate with than the British: 'The French behave fairly in agreements. The one just signed allowed the means of building up an army in exile in France to the advantage of the Government, but the same was not true in Britain.' He complained most of all about the lack of Polish representation on the Supreme War Council. Although it had been agreed to include a Polish general here when Polish matters were to be discussed, this was not enough for Sikorski. He argued that since 'The British betray an unwillingness to countenance our participation in the Council', there should be closer cooperation with the French who would not 'compromise with the Germans and also with those who were deciding in favour of a confrontation with Soviet Russia, most probably in Finland'.[44]

At the government's meeting of 24 January 1940, at which Sikorski informed his ministers that Daladier himself had formally proposed the formation and despatch of a Polish division to Finland, it was agreed that although this would mean a 'certain postponement' in the formation of a Polish army in France, this would be compensated for by joint activities with French and Canadian brigades fighting on the Finnish front. Sikorski commented that: 'The despatch of these three brigades draws Britain and France into war with Russia which, for a variety of reasons, is welcome to us.'[45] As it turned out, the Allied decision to send detachments to Finland came too late. The Finnish army faced a strong adversary and it was only a question of time before they had to accede to Soviet demands. Nevertheless the issue remained of major importance to the Polish government until the cease-fire on 13 March 1940. It felt that the presence of Polish forces on Finnish territory would be living proof of Poland's existence and involvement on the Allied side, and that in failing to take the initiative the Allies lost the political and military gains to be had from involvement in Finland, by which was meant a blockade of the 'iron route' from Sweden to Germany and the opportunity of diverting Hitler against the Soviet Union. Moreover it was thought that 'the practical means of determining the Eastern European and especially Polish frontiers had been lost'.[46]

The conclusion of the Russo-Finnish war was followed by the German attack on Norway on 6 April. This gave the Poles their opportunity. The 'Podhalanska Brigade' was sent to Norway. Sikorski told his government that Polish troops were going to Norway, 'to fight for Poland and, in the spirit of fine Polish tradition, for the freedom of other nations'. Moreover to Sikorski's surprise and delight, he was invited to attend a meeting of the Supreme Allied War Council. It was 'a turning point', he said, for Poland, which had now emerged as 'an old and sovereign ally of the Western Powers'. His presence at the Allied meeting was even more significant, he believed, than Polish participation in the war, since, 'in Poland this fact will strengthen faith in the Allies enormously'. He told his ministers that they must exploit this great success to the full, particularly as the communiqué to be issued after the meeting had to present to the world, a 'Poland completely equal with the Allies' and to end once and for all 'the myth so maliciously put out by the Germans, that Poland is merely the drudge of the other powers'. He concluded that great tact would be necessary to prolong this success.[47] For the government, and for Sikorski in particular, a high-water mark in Polish fortunes had been reached.

Sikorski's euphoria was tempered by fears of a recurrence of Russophile tendencies in Allied policy. He considered two developments particularly dangerous to Polish interests. The first concerned discussions in Moscow between Molotov, Commissar for Foreign Affairs, and Stafford Cripps, soon to be appointed British Ambassador, which led to talk of an Anglo-Russian trade agreement. The second was the attempts of French censorship to cut from his next broadcast the part referring to the return of 'all territory to the Motherland'.

The government's aim was to restore its pre-war frontiers, and this was put forward as government policy. It declined to enter into further discussions with France on the matter. But discussions went on within the Council of Ministers. Sosnkowski saw danger not so much in the Russophilism rooted in French opinion as in the toleration by the French government of propaganda 'which denied Poland the territories in question', and he urged the necessity of issuing a strong official declaration to the Allies concerning these frontiers.

Kot agreed with this proposal. He also emphasized the need to counter 'influences . . . working against us in the West', by which Kot meant the activities of the Czechoslovakian authorities in exile who were believed 'responsible for feeding French circles with doubts about the Government's ability to free itself from the influences of the *Sanacja*, and for propagating ideas on future boundaries in Eastern Poland in favour of Soviet interests'. In view of this, Sosnkowski counselled that they should sort out the limits of their policy towards Russia: 'We lack a definite conception. At the moment discussion on war aims starts, this must be to hand. Time is on our side, if the French and British are not already involved in defining these aims. It seems, however, that this is not so and that we are likely to be surprised.' Zaleski asserted the 'loyalty of the allied governments in the matter of Polish frontiers' and supported pursuit of the policy to restore the *status quo ante bellum*. On the strength of information that trade negotiations between Britain and the Soviet Union had broken down, he anticipated an Allied declaration of war on Russia and her consequent collapse.[48] Stronski proposed the convening of a committee of ministers to consider such questions of foreign policy at the end of May. However, time was against them. Momentous events of war intervened. On 10 May the Germans opened their attack in the West.

By the time the next government meeting opened in Paris on 20 May 1940 Holland had collapsed and Sikorski described Hitler's 'present concern with beating the French, British and Belgian armies which are located in the north'. There was no feeling yet amongst the ministers that the situation was desperate. On the contrary, as far as Sikorski was concerned, things were looking up – particularly on the political front. He reported that Roosevelt was most concerned with the fate of the Allies in the war and was making help readily available as well as preparing his government for greater involvement in the situation. He also had 'Mussolini's assurance that Italy would not come out actively on the side of Germany'.[49] On 28 May, the day the Belgians surrendered to the Germans, Sikorski reported that, although the failure of the Belgian army had not drastically affected the situation, the Allies were nevertheless having to leave Calais and Ostend, consolidating their position around Dunkirk. The most important thing, however, was 'to keep spirits up on the Allied side. . . . As Poles we must set an example in this situation.'[50]

Paris was taken on 14 June 1940 and now the main concern of the Polish government was its own evacuation and that of its armed forces. It was assured that despite British difficulty in evacuating their own forces, everything possible would be done for the Poles. This is confirmed by a telegram from the Foreign Office: 'Please inform the Polish Government, Commander-in-Chief, Western approaches, is being instructed to do what he can to evacuate such Polish troops as can make their way to Western Ports.'[51] Sikorski, already in London, spoke with Halifax on 19 June. The British foreign secretary told him that he would support the request he had made to the Admiralty with regard to the evacuation of as many of the Polish troops as possible as 'it was absolutely essential that they should not fall into the hands of the enemy'.[52] These assurances were also given to Sikorski by Churchill when the two premiers met on the morning of 19 June. Churchill's greeting made a deep impression on Sikorski. 'Tell your army that we are comrades in life and death. We shall conquer together.' The two shook hands. At a later date Sikorski confided to Ciechanowski 'that handshake meant more to me than any signed treaty of alliance or any pledged words'.[53]

On that morning of 19 June the two premiers discussed the Russian problem. The Polish leader stated that he was 'not advocating a policy which might provoke Russia', but warned against 'cherishing any illusions regarding the Soviets and their policy towards the Allies'. Churchill denied having such illusions and ventured that 'Hitler might be tempted to strike against Russia'.[54] According to Raczynski, Sikorski then 'touched on the idea of getting the Russians to agree to the formation of a Polish Army in the territory under their control' and enlarged upon this with Halifax in the afternoon.[55] Halifax asked for a note in writing. On Sikorski's instructions, Raczynski drew up the following memorandum:

> The Polish Government, considering the defeat of Germany as the principal object of the war, does not intend to create difficulties which might prejudice the discussions between the British and Soviet Governments, in connection with the appointment of Sir Stafford Cripps to Moscow. On the other hand, the Polish

Government is determined to spare no effort to improve the tragic situation of the Polish population in Soviet-occupied territory and in the Soviet Union itself (prisoners of war detained there) in order to create, with the agreement of the Soviet authorities, a Polish army of some 300,000 men for service against Germany.

In the present circumstances, the Polish Government ventures to suggest the attachment to the staff of the British Embassy in Moscow, on a confidential and unofficial basis, of a Polish official . . . to study the Soviet attitudes, and the possibilities of carrying out the plan suggested above. . . . It goes without saying that the suggestion in the present aide-memoire cannot in any way be interpreted as signifying any waiver of the indefeasible rights of the Polish State which have been violated by the aggression of the Soviet Union.[56]

This memorandum was to have serious repercussions within the Polish government.

Sikorski's thirty-day crisis, 19 June–19 July 1940[57]

ON the evening of 21 June, the Polish president and his party which included Zaleski and the finance minister Strassburger, were met at Paddington Station by the king. Ambassador Raczynski, who was also on the platform, noted that General Sikorski did not appear at the station and sent word that he was very tired by his journey and would call on the president later. In fact he did not call on him for many days and also refused to receive Zaleski because he and other ministers had left France for England so hastily. Raczynski commented: 'Sikorski's behaviour towards the President and Foreign Minister marked the beginning of a lengthy crisis within our Government after its transfer to London.' But Sikorski went to ground for reasons more important than the hasty retreat of his ministers from France, although this had annoyed him. His own position had been threatened by internal political strife. Now, on the threshold of a new exile, it was to become even more precarious. He knew, before the arrival of the presidential party in England, that Rackiewicz had decided to replace him as head of government. Zaleski was being championed by opponents of Sikorski, supporters of the former regime, who were taking this chance to remove him from power. They had been severely criticized for their alleged incompetence in allowing the Polish army to be overrun so quickly by the Germans and now they took courage from the fate of France. How much better had the French fared in the face of a German onslaught? Had Sikorski's command been more successful than that of Smigły-Rydz, his predecessor? This feeling, heightened by the chaotic evacuation, carried over to England the old political animosities between the *Sanajca* and the opposition, and was about to erupt in a governmental crisis in London. As Raczynski explains, a major cause of this crisis was Sikorski's conduct on the eventful 19 June.

Sikorski's attempt to enter into relations with the USSR without consulting his Government aroused criticism . . . Zaleski, who reached London on 21 June, took the matter up with Sikorski, as soon as he was able to see him, and as a result the memorandum of 19 June was withdrawn.[58]

The chaos in France had made it difficult for Sikorski to consult his ministers and he had taken a personal initiative on the Russian question without the knowledge of Zaleski.

The circumstances that surrounded the drafting of the memorandum and its original form also raised misgivings in Raczynski's mind. He states that a few days before Sikorski arrived in London, the TASS representative there, Andrew Rothstein, suggested to Stefan Litauer of the Polish news agency (PAT) that semi-official contacts be made between the Polish and Soviet governments. Litauer recorded the suggestions made in a memorandum he gave to Sikorski on his arrival in London. Prior to his meeting with Churchill of 19 June Sikorski asked Raczynski to examine, and to comment on, the points contained in Litauer's paper. This envisaged the creation of a Polish army in Russia, the appointment of an unofficial Polish observer to the staff of the British Embassy in Moscow and touched on 'the possibility of some concession in regard to our frontier with the Soviet Union, and on the question (of course purely theoretical) of our consent to the passage of Soviet troops through Poland'. On Raczynski's insistence this portion of the memorandum was crossed out and did not feature in its final form as submitted to Halifax. Raczynski concludes that the main reason for Sikorski's 'feverish interest' in Litauer's memorandum was his determination to create a sizeable Polish army, even if it required 'the help of the devil himself'.[59] Although this explains Sikorski's motive for his initiative of 19 June, it is worthwhile to show in greater detail than that contained in the ambassador's memoirs what the chances were of creating a Polish army and how far Sikorski was prepared to go to achieve this end. As before, Foreign Office records shed much light here. Kennard, who had also spoken with Sikorski on 19 June, reported:

> The Polish Prime Minister said that he wished to speak to me on a subject which had not hitherto been discussed between our two Governments, which was the relations between the Allies and the Soviet Union.
>
> General Sikorski said that the present Polish Government, and he himself in particular, had decided that they did not wish to place any obstacle in the way of an improvement of relations between the Western Powers and the Soviet Union by continuing their predecessor's policy of provocation towards the latter country. It seemed that the Soviet Union was beginning to realise that the Polish nation could not be annihilated, and recently the Soviet Government had wished to get into contact with the Polish Government. He himself was not opposed to such contacts, on condition that the question of the eastern frontier of Poland was freely discussed and that the persecution of Poles in Soviet-occupied Poland should cease. . . . (The) Soviet Union in Poland seemed to have adopted a more reasonable attitude during the last 10 days and in Lithuania they had even asked the Polish Officers, who had sought refuge in the country, to enlist in the Red Army. . . . He quite understood the allies desire to improve their relations with the Soviet Union,

> though he thought that we should be disappointed if we hoped for effective collaboration, since the Soviet Government were above all afraid of Germany.
>
> I told Sikorski that . . . His Majesty's Government were doing their best to find some basis for agreement which might contribute towards detaching the Soviet Union from Germany. If Polish Government for their part were able to take parallel action . . . all to the good.[60]

In this conversation with the British ambassador Sikorski reveals a positive desire to come to grips with the question of relations with the Soviet Union with less reserve than the memorandum submitted to Halifax suggests. The free discussion about Poland's eastern frontier, indicating that this was negotiable with the Russians, suggests that Sikorski's thoughts on the possibilities of rapprochement with the Soviet government were out of step with the rest of his government, in particular the president and Zaleski. This was very apparent as the Polish crisis in London developed.

The enlistment of Polish officers in the Red Army, which Sikorski saw as an indication of the ameliorating attitude of the Soviet government towards his government and therefore to be taken advantage of, was a development which the Foreign Office had been following closely.[61] On 7 June, Preston, the British minister at Kovno, sent the following information: 'I am credibly informed that the Russians are forming at Stanislava a Polish Red Legion with Polish troops interned in Russia. Treatment is said to be good and all former rank restored. Polish Officers in Lithuania would be grateful to learn whether Polish Government wishes them to join these legions.'[62] It was felt in London that this was 'a very awkward question for the P.G.', particularly as it was reported that the 'Russians wanted to have an officer corps in preparation for a "Polish People's Army", and a "Polish People's Republic".'[63] It was decided that Kennard should obtain the Polish viewpoint. He replied, 'Polish Minister for Foreign Affairs would be grateful if H.M. Minister at Kovno could be instructed to inform Polish officers in Lithuania that, in the opinion of the Polish Government, Russian proposal is very suspect and should certainly not be accepted.'[64] This reflected Kennard's own feelings on the question. He believed that if such legions were formed by Russia, the Germans would try to do likewise, and the result would be a similar situation to that in 'the last war when Polish legions were to be found in Russia, Germany and Austria and many of the subsequent internal difficulties in Poland arose out of the quarrelling of the members of those different legions'. Kennard felt furthermore that if the Poles had to make a choice between the two, they would be 'more likely to work with the Germans than with the Russians since collaboration with the Russians implied the acceptance of a lower culture . . . , the negation of their strong Catholic faith, and acceptance of Communism with all that implied'.[65] This was a fairly accurate representation of the Polish attitude to Russia but most Poles would surely have seen the assumption of their preference for Germany as showing extraordinary ignorance of their feelings.

While Kennard thought the Poles would turn towards the Germans, Lewis Namier believed they should be directed towards the Russians. He suggested that it was in Britain's interest to support Sikorski in creating a Polish legion. 'Poland could only exist in the long run if assured of either German or Russian support and . . . it was clearly much safer for us if she turned to Russia than to Germany. If such a move encouraged the Germans to start German legions then this could hardly be concealed from the Russians and would also react favourably on British interests.'[66]

The opinion of British Military Intelligence was that

> it certainly seems that as the Polish troops are interned in Russia they must be completely subject to any proposal . . . which the Soviet might make . . . if they are formed into Polish Red Legions the result would probably be no worse from the political aspect and might be better; that is to say, the Polish Officers might be able to restrain extremists, and the men would at least retain a certain amount of self-respect and discipline. We know that Col. Mitkiewicz, the head of the Polish Mission here, is inclined to agree in principle. Germany being the main enemy, he thought it would be an advantage to form a nucleus of Polish troops on the Soviet-German frontier. . . . Since dictating above I have seen Col. Mitkiewicz who quite definitely agrees. *Any* Polish formation is a future asset.[67]

There was a clear divergence of opinion on the question of a 'Red Polish Legion' between Zaleski's Foreign Ministry and Sikorski's War Ministry. That a brake on closer Polish-Soviet relations was being applied by the former is made abundantly clear in this record of a conversation between Balinski of the Polish Embassy in London and Maclean of the Foreign Office on 6 July 1940. Balinski began by questioning whether there was any real community of interests between Britain and the Soviet Union and whether 'we were likely to make any sacrifices in return for what might prove illusory political advantages'. Maclean replied that 'Anglo-Soviet interests coincided in preventing Germany from dominating Europe and that the problem was being approached in a realistic spirit.' Moreover there was no question of sacrificing the interests of any of 'our Allies for the *beaux yeux* of Mr. Stalin'. Reassured by this comment, Balinski next referred to the proposal which had originated with General Sikorski that 'we should endeavour to establish relations of some kind between the Polish and Soviet Governments and encourage the Russians to form a Polish Legion in Soviet-occupied Poland for use against Germany'.[68] Balinski was himself against the idea from the start, mainly on the grounds that the Russians were not concerned with the Polish government in London and would not invoke its help to employ Poles against Germans.

Balinski failed to see what Sikorski came to realize, namely, that the best way of ensuring that the Soviet government did not ignore the Polish government in London on such and other issues was by the resumption of diplomatic relations between the two. A year was to elapse before this was achieved; all else apart, Sikorski did not feel secure enough to force the pace at this stage when relations between him, the president and Zaleski continued to deteriorate.

The crisis was worsened by the proposals dealing with the government's reorganization made by Sikorski at the first meeting of the Council of Ministers in London. He began with a report on his talks with Churchill.

> The British Premier gives the impression of being totally decisive and is full of faith and energy. . . . An attack by Hitler on England could come at any moment. . . . English discipline and the spirit prevailing in the community make an excellent impression. According to the head of the British Government, the arrival of a Polish division in England would raise further the present high morale.[69]

He calculated the strength of the Polish forces on arrival in England at around 25,000 (British estimates give a figure of 16,000). These men would provide three infantry brigades, one armoured brigade and an air force.[70] In this context Sikorski said that Churchill had agreed to the adjustment of the military agreements 'to present circumstances', accepting, moreover, that 'the Sovereign rights of Poland will be strictly observed'. He then went on to say that armed forces apart: 'Civilians who were not part of the Government apparatus would be taken care of completely by the British Government. . . . It is therefore essential to undertake a segregation of Poles who are gathering at rallying points.' He stressed the necessity of considerable reductions in the government's apparatus. He announced that a Commission, headed by General Sosnkowski, was reviewing the matter, and anticipated that they would recommend a reduction in the number of ministries in the government. Only the Praesidium of the Council of Ministers, the ministries of Foreign Affairs, the Treasury and Information and Documentation would remain. In this connection, 'under-secretariats of State would be wound down and all current contracts withdrawn'. He concluded his report by emphasizing that the 'seriousness of the situation' demanded 'ruthless action against the atmosphere of intrigue and gossip, which has held sway lately'.[71]

Sikorski's intention to reorganize the Polish government in London by reducing its personnel was the factor which finally precipitated the crisis which had loomed, ever more threatening, since the evacuation from France. By 4 July two Foreign Office officials discussed the storm raging amongst the Poles. Savery, counsellor at the British Embassy to the Polish government, called on Strang, assistant under-secretary at the Foreign Office, to tell him of the problems in Polish government circles. Their cause, he said, was the attempt to get rid of Zaleski and 'the whole staff of the Polish Foreign Office of the *ancien régime*'. He thought it would be as well to 'take the bull by the horns at an early stage and put an end once and for all to all these intrigues'.[72] The suggestion for intervention by the Foreign Office was taken up on 6 July, when Kennard advised Sikorski to cool the crisis. He had little success; Sikorski was too preoccupied considering his cabinet meeting that day to pay much attention to such words of caution. The meeting was long and controversial, dealing as it did with the swift evacuation from France and possible government reorganization.

Accusation and counter-accusation were made of over-hasty departure for England. Zaleski and Stanczyk and their respective ministries, Foreign Affairs and Social Welfare, fared particularly badly in the argument and Kot, minister without portfolio, threatened his own resignation and the withdrawal of the Peasant Party from the National Council unless those who had not performed their duty were removed from office.[73] This unleashed an interparty struggle which destroyed any remaining vestige of unity amongst Polish political exiles.

At the cabinet meeting on 8 July, the controversial proposals concerning the restructuring were given in a report from Sosnkowski entitled 'The High Command and Departments of the Republic on British Territory' which had been produced by a committee of ministers under his chairmanship. Their recommendation envisaged the absorption of the Ministry for Military Affairs into the High Command and the elimination of the Ministry of Social Welfare. This led to bitter wrangling and the threat from Stanczyk that his party would withdraw from the government.[74]

On 9 July Sikorski held fruitful talks with the Socialist Lieberman and Mikołajczyk of the Peasant Party. He told his ministers, at the meeting of 11 July, that as a result of these discussions he could offer a compromise solution. He proposed the establishment of a committee of ministers to look after the interests of Polish evacuees abroad, to be chaired by Stancyzk.

The debate on reorganization which had monopolized the business of the Council of Ministers ever since its first meeting in London had obscured the precariousness of Sikorski's personal situation since the events of 19 June. Its extent came to light when he informed the Council of Ministers of intrigues against himself which 'were so audacious that he had been warned of an attempt on his person'. He warned all against challenging his authority on British territory, 'where without doubt, the standing of the head of the Government of the Republic is at its highest', and was adamant that he would not allow intrigues to dissipate the 'moral capital which had accrued to the Government through the bravery of the army'.[75]

Returning to his proposal for reorganization, the motion was carried with Stancyzk voting against and Kot abstaining. Stancyzk declared that he was forced to leave the government and threatened to approach the president and his party on the matter, suggesting that the PPS would no longer cooperate with the government. Zaleski, who had played little part in the discussion so far, warned against the deepening of divisions in this way. Although he did not believe that the British government would intervene in the internal affairs of the Polish Government he considered that they would be intolerant of internal wrangles which could prove harmful and warned that they were aware of what was going on.[76]

This was indeed the case; Foreign Office records give a full account of the crisis as it developed, and give penetrating insights into its causes. Frank Roberts of the Central Department recorded information he had had from Kennard about the situation. The *chef de cabinet* of the President's Office had informed Kennard that the president proposed to dismiss Sikorski from office within the next 24 hours because of his self-centredness and failure to work in with colleagues and his insistence on handling matters outside the military sphere, with which he was not competent to deal. There was also concern that Sikorski had not curbed the activities of Kot, who seemed set on pursuit of his own personal vendettas. The *chef de cabinet* also told Kennard that it was hoped to establish a government 'on much the same lines', under Zaleski, and, if possible, with the cooperation of General Sikorski as C. in C. and minister of war. Kennard and Savery both felt that the President had every justification for his action and that it was probably a pity that the trouble had not been allowed to come to a head when it first developed shortly after the arrival of the Polish government in this country. 'General Sikorski, with all his qualities, was not fit to be the P.M. as well as C. in C.' Roberts then asked Savery what the effect of this would be on the army. Savery's opinion was that personal devotion to General Sikorski was lacking and he recalled 'a good deal of criticism (perhaps unjustified) that more troops had not been saved in France and that their condition on their arrival in this country had not been satisfactory'. Savery also suggested that there was a general feeling 'that General Sikorski should spend more time with his troops and less over his political activities in London'. Roberts ended his minute: 'Kennard has warned the private secretaries of these developments, as the Secretary of State was lunching with General Sikorski tomorrow, by which time a decision should have been reached one way or another.'[77] A settlement was in fact reached in time for lunch and it was one in which Kennard played some part. He had been instructed by Halifax to make it clear to those concerned that it was regarded as essential that these differences should be amicably settled. He reported back on talks with Łepkowski, the chief of the president's chancellery and his principal adviser. Kennard had told him that while the British did not wish to express any views as to the nature of the differences between the president and General Sikorski, 'H.M.G. felt it essential that an early settlement should be reached, as any serious crisis of the Polish Government could only react unfavourably on Allied interests generally.' Apparently the president fully appreciated this aspect of the question and stated that General Sosnkowski and Seyda, the National Democrat minister without portfolio, had been acting as intermediaries between himself and Sikorski. The president had yielded on various points but insisted on the separation of the duties of commander-in-chief and president of the council. Kennard was asked to urge Sikorski to accept this demand. He did but Sikorski refused. He said that he could not agree to the separation of the duties of commander-in-chief and president of the council, as he had been 'unanimously accepted by all parties in Poland as such' and, were he to relinquish either of these functions, it would react unfavourably on the Polish forces. He protested that he had nothing to do with all the quarrels and intrigues which were going on, and said that his one desire was to carry on the onerous duty of reconstituting the Polish army. He anticipated a compromise solution in the near future.[78]

The minutes of the government meeting of 19 July reveal that 'the crisis initiated by the demand for the change in Government . . . and for the formation of a new Government headed by August Zaleski, was resolved, thanks to the mediation of Minister Sosnkowski.' Apparently it had been suggested to the president that the matter of the separation of military from political functions should be taken up in discussions between himself, the government and the parties. President Rackiewicz asked General Sikorski to form a new government, supported by 'harmonious co-operation between the parties', and adhering to the principle of National Unity. Sikorski assured him that the government would be reorganized in such a way that the administrative boundaries would be carefully delineated so as to prevent any imbalance of power between one minister and another. The meeting concluded with the revelation that Zaleski had been threatened with 'dire consequences' by a group of officers unless he refused President Raczkiewicz's commission for him to head the new government. Although Sikorski said that those responsible for the action were to be dealt with 'so severely as to deter anyone from taking similar action in the future', it was this action by a group of Sikorski's friends in the General Staff which finally deterred Zaleski from forming a new government.[79]

The outcome of the month-old crisis only gave cause for greater resentment between Zaleski, who was supported by the president, and Sikorski. Sikorski had emerged victorious in this particular contest. As Strang noted: 'Sir H. Kennard told me this morning that the Polish "crisis" had now been settled and that there would be no change in the Government. General Sikorski had won, as we thought he would. There is, in fact, no alternative to him, and we shall have to bear with his idiosyncrasies. As a man and a public figure, the Poles cannot easily do without him.'[80]

This conclusion had been reached independently by Namier. In a conversation with Strang, Namier emphasized that it was essential not to lose those Poles who 'were really doing the work of organising the Polish cause abroad and whose position is therefore strong with the people in Poland'. Namier referred in particular to General Sikorski and to Professor Kot, 'the latter of whom represented the great mass of the Polish peasantry'. He was afraid that M. Zaleski, 'being naturally lazy, although entirely honest', was allowing himself to be used by intriguers, many of whom had been connected with the old colonels' regime (i.e. the *Sanacja*) to down General Sikorski. In his view, M. Zaleski 'cut very little ice now in Poland and it would therefore be fatal if they [the intriguers] were to win the day'. Strang confessed to considerable sympathy with Namier's views.[81]

Regarding army opinion of Sikorski, Savery records the observation of the secretary general of the Polish Foreign Ministry, Tarnowski, that the soldiers looked on Sikorski as a symbol rather than as a human being, and willingly paid him 'the respect which they considered to be due to the commander in chief of that army', while also wondering why he did not abandon the 'civilians and semi-civilians in London who did not count at all' to come instead to share their lot.[82] Sikorski's political role strained his relationship with his forces. Much of the criticism of Sikorski was due to his failure to visit them at the Scottish camps to which they had been posted, ostensibly to guard the coast, though even when Sikorski did visit his troops in July 1940 he did not gain their whole-hearted loyalty.

The position of the Polish troops, inactive in a foreign country, was an unenviable one. It was felt at the Foreign Office that to give the troops something to do would prevent them quarrelling amongst themselves.

> If we can find some activity for the Polish troops in this country, this will help to maintain the morale of the Poles in Poland. The fact that the Poles have a Government at Claridges Hotel does not have any great psychological effect, but if we can send out news that may percolate through to Poland that the Poles still have an Army which is actively engaged, this encourages the inhabitants of Poland. No mention is necessary of the fact that the Polish Army only consists of 16,000 men in England and 6,000 in Egypt.[83]

From Sikorski's point of view this force was big enough to build upon, particularly as he hoped to supplement it by drawing from the large Polish manpower available in Canada. This hope was the main topic of discussion at a meeting held between Sikorski and the British Chief of Staff General Ismay to consider the organization of Polish forces after the fall of France.

A recruiting centre in Canada was very much to the fore in Sikorski's thinking. He realized that he would have to discuss the question independently with the Canadian government but told Ismay that he sought the prior support and assistance of Britain particularly with regard to financial arrangements. The response was not encouraging. It was pointed out to him that there was no shortage of manpower in Britain but there was a dearth of equipment. Sikorski did not see this as an immediate obstacle as the Canadian recruits would need an initial period of training during which little equipment would be required. Despite advice to concentrate his efforts on organization of his forces in England he pressed the 'moral value' of a force in Canada and pursued the matter energetically in the months to come. It became a stumbling block in the negotiations between the British and Polish governments.

Reporting on the state of the negotiations at the cabinet meeting of 12 July, Sikorski said that 'everything was going to the Government's advantage. The conditions laid down were better than those given by France, and the agreements would soon be signed.' He concluded: 'this is a great plan and a great success.'[84]

And so, with the matter of Canada outstanding, the Anglo-Polish military agreements were signed on 5 August 1940, 'with an unusual amount of ceremony for such an occasion'.[85] For Sikorski this was a major achievement and a significant advance in relations between the two countries. He underlined his historical meaning of the agreement which was

> a development of the ones before, and which granted all our requirements. It will be the basis for the closest co-operation between Great Britain and Poland which should be of decisive importance for the future. The advantages of this agreement should be understood even by our politically over-active émigrés, who instead of complaining and criticizing should get close to the British nation.

He intimated that relations with Britain should not be limited to army matters, but that 'wider contacts should be made in the field of British politics and social and intellectual life'.[86] A year after the signing of the Anglo-Polish Alliance, the following short declaration on Polish policy was agreed by the Council of Ministers: 'Poland is allied with Great Britain and in accordance with this the Polish Army will fight arm in arm with the British Army wherever the need arises.'

Sikorski's wish was to consolidate his and the government's position in Britain. He was determined that nothing should undermine 'the priceless capital of trust which the British accord us today'.[87] The military agreements enabled Poland to participate in the war in a manner more worthy of a great nation and state and were, from a personal point of view, seen by Sikorski as a recognition by the British government of his own position as leader of the Polish government. The success in the field of foreign policy matched his own personal triumph in retaining his position as Poland's political and military supremo. For him this was the light at the end of the tunnel through which he had journeyed since the evacuation from France. It marked the end of a chapter in the history of the Polish government. Much of what had been achieved after months of effort to establish the machinery of government was swept away. Yet much remained on which to build. Sikorski emerged in a particularly favourable light. His energy and clarity of mind at a time when others panicked was remarkable. That he never once considered any course of action other than to continue the fight against Germany was less so. No other possibility was conceivable. The logical conclusion of the policy which clearly emerged in

France, a consistent commitment by the Polish government to pursue the war against Hitler, was nevertheless sought with extraordinary vigour. The involvement of a Polish force in Norway demonstrates this policy in practice. It also suggests real efforts to realize the government's long-standing ambition to gain the confidence of, and parity with, the British and French governments. The reaction of these governments to Polish demands for participation on the Supreme War Council shows how difficult this had been to achieve. The reasons are clear. The Polish government was weak, totally dependent on the help of its allies and sympathizers, and able to exert little pressure. Yet the need for recognition as an ally of equal rank was very real to Sikorski. He insisted on involvement around the table and in the field, not only to establish his government's credibility in the eyes of the Allies but also for the sake of Polish support at home and abroad. Sikorski had come through a most trying period and survived serious attempts to oust him. He remained as head of government and chief of armed forces after his evacuation from France. Though temporarily abated, Sikorski's conflict with Zaleski and Raczkiewicz was soon to re-emerge. Nevertheless, with the appointment, in October 1940 of his close associate, Stanisław Kot as minister of internal affairs, the balance of power within the Council of Ministers had shifted unmistakably in Sikorski's favour. He was determined to exploit this advantage to the full in attempting to break the political mould which he had inherited from the Second Republic.

DURING THE FIRST half of 1941 the Anglo-Polish alliance, though still unequal, was based on greater mutual confidence and a closer identity of interests than at any other time of the war. Poland had replaced France as Britain's chief ally, while the Soviet Union continued its benevolent neutrality towards Germany.

Despite strains between the various factions in the Polish government and the wider emigration, Sikorski, firmly supported by the British, was able to override critics of his style and policies. It was not until the question of Soviet-Polish relations came to the fore with the entry of the U.S.S.R. into the war in June 1941 that a crisis, more serious than that of June 1940, arose in the Government-in-Exile. Sikorski, again under fire for his policy and style of leadership, was at least confident of his standing with Churchill. The warmth of the relationship between the two prime ministers is evident at the beginning of the new year. On 7 January 1941, Sikorski had written to seek Churchill's view of the suitability of that time for his proposed visit to Egypt and America. Seven days later he received the following reply:

> I have given much thought to your letter. . . . If I am to consult my personal feeling and wishes, I must frankly say I hope very much that on reflection you will decide to postpone your tour. It is a great help to me to know that you, as the leader of the largest Allied force in this country and as Prime Minister of our first Ally in the war, are available to give help and guidance at a time when we may at any moment be faced with a heavy attack from the enemy and the Polish Army may be called . . . to fight at our side. This, my dear General, is my personal view, but of course, I should not wish to stand in your way if you feel that your duty lies elsewhere.[1]

Churchill's words pleased Sikorski, as indicated by his response: 'My dear Prime Minister, thank you very much for your letter of January 24th. I appreciate what you say and I am very glad to know that you feel the Polish Forces have an important role to play in the defence of this country.' Flattered to think his presence was required in Britain he asked Churchill whether he would help him to send someone in his place if he did not go to Egypt. He explained that there were nearly 10,000 Polish troops in the Middle East and that a number of problems had arisen which needed to be sorted out by his ministry. He wished to send some staff officers and proposed to ask Major Cazalet, Conservative M.P. for Chippenham and liaison officer with Sikorski's government, if he could accompany them to facilitate contacts with the British authorities in Palestine. Sikorski was particularly interested in the possible use of Polish troops from there against the Germans in the Balkans and the decision whether or not to go to the Middle East was a difficult one. It was complicated by his desire to go to the United States because he saw 'so much amongst the 5 million Poles there both for the future of Poland and also for the benefit of the Allied cause'. He saw the Poles in America as a sort of reserve which could provide the drafts needed for the Polish air force, navy and army and felt that organization of these new Polish forces so important to the Poles in Poland was possible only on American soil. He told Churchill that Paderewski was then in the United States 'exercising on our behalf his unique moral authority', to secure the favourable attitude of the Americans for the drafting of recruits into the Polish forces, and also the consent of the administration to 'include Poland among the countries which they are prepared to assist with credits and military equipment needed for the new fighting units'. He asked Churchill to ensure the credits Poland needed 'within the frame of the Anglo-American financial arrangements', and ended 'I am convinced my dear Prime Minister, you will understand and sympathise with this point of view, and not refuse your help in all these vital matters for the future of my country'.[2]

Churchill exerted pressure on the Foreign Office to send a favourable reply: 'All possible consideration should be given to this very faithful and courageous statesman',[3] and Eden informed the British ambassador in Washington that: 'We should of course treat any Polish requests as sympathetically as possible and do our best to help. These Polish recruits in the New World are not only a necessary source of man-power for the Polish forces, but of great symbolic significance.'[4]

The telegram found Sikorski already in North America, on his first visit there which lasted from 24 March to 9 May 1941. He created a favourable impression, particularly in Washington where Roosevelt not only approved of recruiting for the Polish armed forces but also allowed Lease-Lend material to be used to equip them. Moreover, according to the Polish ambassador, 'we were assured that there was not the slightest doubt in the minds of any of the military or civilian U.S. officials as to Poland's status as a fully fledged partner in the struggle'.[5]

This was the kind of recognition for which Sikorski was working and from this point of view his American trip was a great success, though he was disturbed by rumours in the American media, some of which spoke of a rift between himself and Zaleski. The foreign minister was reported to have been incensed at the irregular manner in which Sikorski conducted business. In this instance it concerned the consignment of American aid to Poland and Zaleski was angry that the Foreign Ministry was not consulted in this matter. On his return to London Sikorski pointed out that, as head of government, he did have the power to make decisions which would only be ratified by the government retrospectively. The nature of the problem and the distances involved perhaps excused Sikorski on this occasion. Zaleski was more worried about the consequences of such action in the field of foreign policy as a whole. Zaleski's concern was shared by Raczynski who wrote: 'The Prime Minister . . . has been quietly building up his own apparatus for the conduct of Poland's foreign relations.'[6]

Sikorski and the Russian Question, 1940–1

THESE suspicions were well-founded. Zaleski was too conventional in his approach to foreign politics for Sikorski and was much the more cautious from the start and his voice carried less and less weight as Sikorski systematically by-passed him and the Foreign Ministry. This had happened during the flight from France on 19 June 1940 when Sikorski had taken an initiative primarily intended to strengthen Polish bargaining power by raising an army in Russia. Then a month later, unbeknown to Zaleski or the rest of the government, the British Foreign Office received information through Sikorski's close adviser Professor Lewis Namier and Colonel Kedzior, the chief of staff to General Sikorski, to the effect that Sikorski and Namier were anxious to work for a rapprochment with Russia with a view to reconstituting a new Polish State at the expense of Germany. The letter said that they were anxious that Britain should avoid any action which might tend to force Russia and Germany into greater collaboration and were against any proposition to revive Polish interests in the Ukraine, which was seen as a Soviet sphere of influence. The letter ended by saying that Namier wished his views to be well known in Foreign Office and service circles.[7]

The debate on reorganization had so monopolized the business of cabinet meetings in the latter half of 1940 that clarification of foreign policy had been neglected. At the meeting of 7 January 1941, Haller, minister without portfolio, stressed the urgent need for the government to define its foreign policy and in particular its attitude towards the Soviet Union: 'We are constantly being asked about it.'[8] Neither he nor Zaleski knew that Sikorski had, a week earlier, given his views of foreign policy in a wide-ranging discussion with a British official. H.M. Jebb of the Ministry of Economic Warfare had listened to Sikorski's criticisms of the old regime and of Smigły-Rydz and Beck in particular. He reported Sikorski's belief that ultimately the Russians and Germans were bound to clash.[9] Sikorski hoped for a large-scale attack by Germany on Russia with the object of obtaining oil from the Caucasus and expected that the Russians would be fairly easily defeated. The net result would, 'after a shorter or longer period, be anarchy both in Russia and in Germany, under the cover of which it would be possible for the Polish Government to return to Warsaw and set up a reformed Polish State'.[10] Sikorski's views were seen, at the Foreign Office, as indicative of his prejudices with regard to the past and a certain amount of wishful thinking regarding the future. They were nevertheless found interesting as an indication of the lines along which Sikorski's mind was moving.

The Polish prime minister did share some of these views with his ministers at the meeting of 15 February 1941, concentrating his remarks on military developments. He began by saying that the German High Command had ordered its forces to be ready by 2 March for a major offensive against Britain, though he said that from information received it could not as yet be ascertained where the Germans had decided to attack, though he felt that the German posture was offensive in the West and South and defensive in the East.[11] It is against this background of uncertainty with regard to German intentions that Polish views began to take on a worrying aspect for the Foreign Office. In February 1941 both the president and Sikorski made public speeches which implied that Poland should emerge from the war with her post-Versailles frontiers fully restored, if not extended. Savery reported that Sikorski had said at the opening of a Polish labour exchange:

> In the future Poland will not be able to shut herself up within the frontiers of 1939. She will be obliged to enter into close understanding with her neighbours in order to create a sufficiently strong bloc and be able to oppose any attempt which may be made to repeat the catastrophe which twenty years after the termination of a world war has once more shattered the world.[12]

A speech made on the radio by Raczkiewicz was more outspoken and gave rise to concern. The president said:

> When in September 1939 Poland opposed the German aggressor, her other neighbour, Soviet Russia, unmindful of the validity of mutual treaties which had settled the historical differences between Poland and Russia, at the height of the Polish German war treacherously invaded the Eastern areas of the Polish Republic. . . . Situated geographically between the East and the West, during all the thousand years of her history, Poland opposed the imperialism of Germandom in the West and of the Muscovite World in the East . . . Lithuania, Latvia and Estonia lost their independence owing to the temporary subjugation of the Polish Republic, which was a strong and just pillar of European equilibrium . . . Poland succumbed to violence after an extraordinarily sanguinary struggle, a struggle on two fronts. Hundreds of thousands of soldiers and defenceless citizens were buried beneath the ruins of heroic Warsaw, beneath the ruins of hundreds of towns and thousands of villages. The war trampled over every part of Poland and in Poland today there is not one family which does not mourn the loss of one beloved. . . . The Germans are systematically starving the population of Poland . . . Soviet Russia does not lag behind in the persecution of Polish citizens. The lot of Poles deported in masses to the forests of Siberia and Central Asia, without consideration for age and sex, is terrible beyond words. . . . The Polish nation is fighting to regain what she acquired twenty years ago by her own effort by international law and of which she has been deprived by violence and superior

force. . . . We are fighting on . . . (Poland) will not and cannot give up anything she justly owned.[13]

Questioned in Parliament about the broadcast, Butler replied that it was to the Polish people, and did not give the impression that Britain was at war with Russia, as alleged. Further, he said that the responsibility for Anglo-Soviet relations rested with those governments.[14]

If public utterances by Polish leaders raised such questions, what they said privately was even more worrying to the Foreign Office. Bruce Lockhart, the British representative with the Czechoslovakian Provisional Government, sent a report of a conversation between Sikorski and Beneš.

> From President Beneš's point of view the conversation was very satisfactory but contained one unpleasant surprise. It began with a discussion of first principles, and there was agreement on two resolutions, (1) that, however the war went, Poland and Czechoslovakia would support one another at the peace settlement and (2) that, if Russia advanced beyond her present frontiers in the event of a German collapse, Czechoslovakia would come to the aid of Poland in resisting this advance. There was also a large measure of agreement on other aspects of the Polish Czechoslovak problem.
>
> It was not until the exchange of views had covered a wide field that General Sikorski produced his surprise. In Britain, he said, political opinion had changed considerably during the past three months. All parties, including the Labour party, were now anti-Russian, and the general public shared this feeling. Now was the time for Poland to benefit from this change of sentiment. He proposed to issue immediately a statement declaring that Poland required the full restoration of her Eastern frontier. . . . He suggested that Czechoslovakian support of this Polish war aim would benefit the cause of Polish-Czechoslovak collaboration.
>
> Not wishing to create a deadlock, President Beneš tried to dissuade General Sikorski from raising this issue at this stage of the war. He suggested that the British Government might be embarrassed by premature declarations about frontiers which could be determined only by the course of military events. . . . General Sikorski replied that the British Government were already pledged to restore Poland's former frontiers.[15]

Reaction at the Foreign Office to this report was swift and concerned. In case Sikorski was bluffing Beneš or deceiving himself, Bruce Lockhart was instructed to tell Beneš that the British government were not committed to any frontiers and that there appeared to be some misapprehension on the part of General Sikorski. The same message was to be conveyed to the Polish government, whose views on the question of post-war frontiers were of vital interest to the British government, which had not yet given public expression to war aims.

The Foreign Office was confronted with a very awkward problem at a time when British policy towards the Soviet Union desperately needed to be free of any such embarrassments. British efforts at rapprochement with the Soviet Union had already come to the notice of the Polish government. Churchill had said in the House of Commons on 5 September 1940:

> We have not adopted at any time, since the war broke out, the line that nothing could be changed in the territorial structure of various countries. On the other

hand, we do not propose to recognise any territorial changes which take place
during the war, unless they take place with the free consent and good will of the
parties concerned.[16]

The British government's readiness to give its consent in November 1940
to Soviet proposals for the recognition of their annexation of the Baltic
States was seen by the Polish government as contradicting Churchill's
statement. Halifax's assurance to Zaleski in his letter of 27 November 1940
that any such recognition would be a temporary arrangement to await a
definite solution at the end of the war failed to convince the Polish
government. It saw the danger of winning the Soviet Union as an ally by
making sacrifices of which the Soviet Union could then avail itself in future
attempts to revise the Treaty of Riga.[17]

The hardening of the Polish attitude on the question of the eastern
frontier was seen as a major obstacle to Anglo-Soviet understanding. This
point was made in an article, 'Anglo-Russian Understanding – A Polish
Factor', by Sir Bernard Pares, former director of the School of Slavonic and
East European Studies at the University of London. He also wrote of how,
in the confusion after the First World War, millions of Russians were
placed under Polish rule only to be recovered by Russian forces who had
marched in 'when the Germans broke the back of the new Poland and the
Polish Government was in flight'.[18] Officially, too, the Polish government
was given to understand that the issue of Poland's frontier with Russia
was seen as an impediment to better Polish-Soviet relations.

Hitler's attack on Russia

ON 19 June, three days before Hitler's invasion of Russia began, Sikorski
informed the cabinet of his conversation the previous day with Sir Stafford
Cripps, British ambassador to the Soviet government, who was then in
London for consultations. Sikorski saw the hour as 'a decisive moment in
terms of war between Germany and Russia', and said he and Cripps were
united in the belief that Hitler's attack on Soviet Russia was imminent.
Cripps's view was that given the recent trends in Russo-German relations,
'it would be best for ourselves and for you if the Germans should advance
into Russia and occupy all Polish territories, and then be stopped by the
Russians beyond that line. That would remove from the agenda the Polish
question which has so far weighed heavily on Anglo-Soviet relations.'[19]

Sikorski then asked what the attitude of the Soviet leaders was towards
Poland. Cripps told him that in his talks with them Poland had not been
mentioned, but he believed that she would be in the very near future and
he urged Sikorski to prepare a list of names from which, at the appropriate
moment, a choice for 'unofficial ambassador' in Moscow could be made.[20]
In the meantime Cripps had urged that instructions should be issued to all
Polish legations stressing the need not to cause any difficulties at this

delicate juncture; then he went on to say that in the event of an understanding between Poland and Russia he was convinced that for geographical reasons Poland could be of greater help to the Soviet Union against the Germans than could Britain, since there was 'a great number of Polish officers and soldiers in Russia'.[21]

Sikorski told his ministers that as regards action against Germany on Soviet territory he had stressed to Cripps that there could be talk of forming Polish divisions only after an unreserved recognition by the Soviets of Polish sovereign rights and the ending of the wrong-doing towards the Polish people. He said that in law Poland was at war with Russia, and in the event of a Russo-German war she would remain neutral, though he concluded that 'without doubt the Germans will always remain enemy No. 1 for Poland'.[22]

When the German offensive in the East opened on 22 June 1941, the news was greeted with unconcealed relief by all Poles. As Stronski put it, 'to no other country in the world does it matter so much as to Poland whether Germany and Russia co-operate or whether they fight each other.' Sikorski issued his 'Instructions to the nation and diplomatic posts'. They are of interest because they did not distinguish between the German and Russian occupant, 'yesterday's allies'. Moreover, 'the Polish Government did not see under the present circumstances [i.e. as long as Russia did not recognize the pre-1939 borders of Poland] the way to engaging in co-operation with Russia', a position which he concluded was fully appreciated by 'our British ally'.[23]

Zaleski elaborated on this point by informing the cabinet of a talk with Eden during which he asked the British government not to use such terms as 'alliance', 'allies', in relation to Russia, and also not to engage in discussions with Russia on Polish affairs without close agreement with the Polish government. Zaleski suggested it was as a result of this conversation that the speech made on the day of Hitler's invasion of Russia, in which Churchill declared that any 'state which fights on against Nazidom will have our aid', contained nothing to worry the government.[24] Reserving his judgment momentarily on this, Sikorski asked the cabinet to agree to the text of his speech to Poland which he intended to broadcast the next day. This was agreed after he had emphasized that nothing as yet indicated the means to an understanding with Russia and that the initiative would have to come from the other side. He closed the discussion with a pessimistic assessment of Churchill's speech which he saw as devoid of a programme for the future and disappointingly silent about Poland, as well as having 'very warm, too warm an approach to bolshevik Russia', which might even be 'damaging'. Sikorski intended to use his speech to correct this fault and a copy was sent to Churchill for his information.[25] Sikorski hoped to promote a political commitment on the part of the British towards Polish relations with Soviet Russia. The speech, delivered on 23 June, caused a marked reaction from the British. One and a half hours before Sikorski spoke, Eden arrived after a meeting of the War Cabinet (attended also by Cripps) to ask for a 'toning down' of the speech. He warned of the adverse effect it would have on British and American public opinion, and urged that any difference with the Bolsheviks should be laid aside for a later time, as the British government had declared a positive desire, for the present, to cooperate with the Soviets against the Germans. Sikorski succumbed to this pressure and the speech as delivered differed from the text agreed by the president and Council of Ministers. It bore, as he put it, a more 'diplomatic' tone. Furthermore, he agreed with Cripps that for a period of seven to ten days the initiative for a clarification in Polish-Soviet relations would be taken by the British, in particular by Cripps in Moscow, bearing in mind the plight of Polish citizens in Russia. (Of an estimated 1,230,000, 180,000 were members of the Polish armed forces taken into captivity.)[26]

The British government now pressed the Polish government to come to an agreement with Russia for the sake of its own relations with its new ally. As Churchill elaborated:

> The attitude of Russia to Poland lay at the root of our early relations with the Soviets . . . the British Government were in a dilemma from the beginning. We had gone to war with Germany as the direct result of our guarantee to Poland. We had a strong obligation to support the interest of our first ally. At this stage in the struggle we could not admit the legality of the Russian occupation of Polish territory in 1939. In this summer of 1941, less than two weeks after the appearance of Russia on our side in the struggle against Germany, we could not force our new and severely threatened ally to abandon, even on paper, regions on the frontier which she regarded for generations as vital for her security. There was no way out. The issue of the territorial future of Poland must be postponed until easier times.[27]

As it turned out there were no 'easier times'. The shape of things to come was already discernible. July 1941 was a turning point in Anglo-Soviet relations as well as the beginning of a new chapter in the affairs of the Polish government. Its fate now depended increasingly on Soviet policy. The Polish question became one of the main subjects of a dispute which was to sour Great Power relations.

The Polish government was faced with a dilemma. All Poles in exile were united in their caution over the question of relations with the Soviet Union. They believed that Western governments had a tendency to treat the Soviet Union over-sympathetically. The West had to be reminded of the dangers of Communism, of which, because of their closer proximity, the Poles were very much aware. This view made agreement with the Soviet Union in August 1939 unthinkable, yet a pact with that country was signed two years later. The explanation lies much more in a change of circumstances and leadership than in any change of heart.

The Polish-Soviet treaty

THE German offensive against Russia set the stage for a period of intense diplomatic activity between the British, Soviet and Polish governments, resulting in a dramatic change in official relations between Poland and Russia. The new relationship with Russia had extensive repercussions within the Polish government and precipitated a significant shift in the Polish-British alliance. The drama started slowly. At the Council of Ministers' meeting of 28 June, Sikorski reported that, as yet, there had been no reaction to his speech from the Soviets but that it had been well received in British and American circles. He informed his ministers of rumours from German sources that a 'government' was being formed in Warsaw as well as 'legions' to oppose the Soviets. Stronski reported a conversation between Litauer of the Polish news agency (PAT) and a correspondent of Tass who confirmed the lack of any instruction from Moscow to the Soviet ambassador in London. He said that at the Soviet Embassy it was felt that Sikorski's demand for a return to Poland's interwar borders would be rejected and the Russians would insist on renegotiation of the Treaty of Riga. Apart from this Moscow would agree to a discussion of all the points raised by Sikorski with the proviso that frontiers would be settled at a later date. Not forgetting the Byelorussians and Ukrainians the Soviet government would fully recognize the present Polish government and wanted good relations with an 'ethnographical Poland'.[28]

In the meantime Eden saw Maisky, the Soviet ambassador, as soon as he could after Sikorski's broadcast. He reported, on 24 June, to the British Embassy in Moscow:

1. I had a conversation with the Soviet Ambassador this evening on the subject of Polish prisoners in Russia. I said that M. Maisky would no doubt have heard or read General Sikorski's broadcast last night and I hoped that he would share my view that, in the light of past history, General Sikorski's attitude was moderate and reasonable. We should, of course, like to see an improvement in Russian-Polish relations and it would greatly conduce to that end if the Soviet Government could adopt a generous attitude in respect of the Polish prisoners they held. . . . Could not the Soviet Government make a start with the release of some of these prisoners soon?

2. Maisky was not responsive to my appeal. He said that, if I insisted, he would, of course, transmit my suggestion to his Government, but he much hoped that I would not press him to do this just now. The Soviet Government regarded the Polish Government as a reactionary government which was fundamentally hostile to Russia. Since they had been in this country the Polish Government had made it plain that they were at war with Russia. How could the Soviet Government be expected to release the prisoners of a country with whom they were still at war? I did not accept M. Maisky's description of the Polish Government and pointed out that it was certainly less reactionary than the Polish Government of pre-war days, with whom, after all, Russia had relations. It was not surprising that the Polish Government felt that the Russian attack upon them last year when they were being invaded by Germany was a cruel deed. The essential, however, was to concentrate upon present considerations. These Polish soldiers were invaluable fighting material and, if they

could be released, they would form a valuable reinforcement in the war against Germany. It might be that the Polish Government were not friendly to Russia. It was certain, however, that their chief enemy was Germany. M. Maisky demurred to this and said that I underrated the hostility of a man like M. Zaleski, for instance, to Russia.

3. After some further discussion M. Maisky reiterated his appeal that I should allow events to develop for the next few days before pressing him to make representations. He himself would prefer that the matter should be allowed to drop. I said that I could not agree to that, but I would consider the matter further and speak to the Ambassador again in the course of the next few days.[29]

Within the Foreign Office it was thought that Maisky's reaction could hardly have been worse. Sikorski, meanwhile, unaware of the substance of the Eden-Maisky talks, elaborated his views on Polish-Soviet relations in a conversation he had on 3 July with Ernest Bevin, minister of labour in Churchill's Cabinet. The Polish premier said that he would like the Soviet government 'to declare null and void' the German-Soviet treaty of non-aggression of August 1939, and the German-Soviet friendship and frontier agreement of September 1939, which partitioned Poland between Germany and the Soviet Union. He was glad that the Soviet government now appeared to be adopting a more favourable attitude towards Poland as, for example, in recognizing the predominantly Polish character of the city of Lwów by setting up an administration containing a majority of Poles.

Bevin wanted to know what the Polish government would do in return for the Soviet government. Sikorski intimated that while the Polish government would not actually surrender their claim to the pre-war frontiers, both the Lithuanian-Polish and Polish-Soviet frontiers might be matters for discussion. This point is particularly noteworthy. It seems to imply that Sikorski was prepared to be flexible on the eastern frontier of Poland once the Russians accepted Polish sovereignty in the area. This was how the Foreign Office understood it.

Bevin and Sikorski agreed that there would be advantages in creating an economic bloc in Eastern Europe, stretching from the Baltic States to Greece and including Poland. Sikorski then listed the proposals which the Polish government wished to put to the Russians when the time was right:

1. that Polish prisoners of war and deportees should be released;
2. that these prisoners of war and deportees should be recognised by the Soviet Government as Polish citizens;
3. that the Soviet Government should recognise the right of the Polish Government to protect them (Poland was willing to spend her gold reserve for the benefit of these Polish citizens in the Soviet Union);
4. that the Soviet Government should receive, as a Polish representative, one of the persons on the list given by General Sikorski to Sir Stafford Cripps;
5. that the Polish Red Cross should be allowed to work in the Soviet Union;
6. that a Polish Army should be created in Russia;
7. that the Soviet Government would cease anti-Polish propaganda.
8. Poland, for her part, would be willing to come to some compromise arrangement about the Soviet-Polish frontier after the war. Poland would seek compensation at Germany's expense to the westward.[30]

As to other matters, Bevin announced that he proposed to make a broadcast to the Polish people shortly and asked Sikorski if it would be possible to say something reassuring on the subject of agrarian reform. He said that the existence of large landed estates in Poland, run on feudal lines, caused difficulty to left-wing opinion in England. Although large landowning was a significant feature of Polish agriculture and some archaic survivals persisted, Sikorski denied that conditions in Poland could be described as 'feudal' and contrasted them favourably with conditions in Britain. As regards agrarian reform, the Polish government ruled out the collective system as practised in the Soviet Union and the parcelization of the land into small holdings of 3 or 4 acres which were insufficient to support a family. More positively, they would readjust the holdings of land in Poland in such a way as to be of the greatest benefit to Polish agricultural economy. This Sikorski described as 'absolutely necessary', since Poland was 'predominantly a peasant state'. They intended, he said, to create small holdings of from 20 to 25 acres, and to reduce the large estates so as to be most advantageous to the economy of the country as a whole. These policies found favour with Bevin.

Strang recorded that the Foreign Office would await Sikorski's memorandum giving the points on which the Polish government wished an approach made to the Soviet government but meanwhile took note of 'two interesting points' from the general's exposition: firstly his statement that 'the Polish Government would be ready to reach a compromise with the Soviet Government about the Polish eastern frontier' and that it was 'in the west (at the expense of Germany) rather than in the east, that Polish aspirations lay' and secondly 'his statement of Polish agrarian policy after the war'.[31]

On the afternoon of 4 July, the Soviet ambassador in London called on Eden. He told the foreign secretary that the Soviet government had been considering their relations with Poland, Czechoslovakia and Yugoslavia and had decided to give facilities to all three States to form 'national committees' in the U.S.S.R. These committees would be allowed to form national military forces to which the Soviet Government would supply arms and equipment. All Polish prisoners of war in Russian hands would be handed over to the 'Polish National Committee', 20,000 altogether, not nearly so many as General Sikorski had suggested. The Russians assumed that these forces would fight with them 'against the German aggressor'.[32]

Turning to the matter of Polish frontiers, Maisky told Eden that the Russians favoured the establishment of an independent national Polish State, the boundaries of which would correspond with ethnographical Poland. He foresaw that certain districts and towns occupied by Russia in 1939 might be returned to Poland. As to the form of internal government to be set up, the Soviet government saw this as 'entirely a matter for the Poles themselves'. Maisky said that if Sikorski and his government found these statements of policy acceptable, the Soviet government was prepared to make a treaty to form 'a common front against German aggression'.[33]

The timing of the publication of this declaration and a more exact definition of 'ethnographical Poland' were left undecided in this discussion, the substance of which was communicated by Eden to Sikorski late that same afternoon. In an account of this meeting given to Dormer by Eden, Eden recorded Sikorski's recognition of the importance of the message while at the same time emphasizing 'the Pan-Slav character of this Russian move'. He pointed out that there were no Czechs and few Yugoslavs in Russia so that 'the only purpose' of forming national committees from these countries was 'to emphasise the Pan-Slav nature of Russian policy', though at a later stage in the conversation he even suggested the possibility that the Russian move was intended to prevent the development of a Polish Balkan bloc from north to south, such as he sought, by recreating Russian leadership in the Balkans instead. As to the creation of a Polish National Committee in Russia, Eden recorded Sikorski's view that this was unnecessary, that: 'Poland had a legal government and the correct procedure was for that government to be invited to appoint a representative at Moscow, which he would be glad to do.' Regarding frontiers, Eden noted Sikorski's wish that Russia should be made aware that the Poles 'required . . . that Russia should nullify the treaties she had made with Germany in 1939'. He also 'contended that the Soviet Government's figure for prisoners could not be accurate' and mentioned a recent Soviet press release which referred to 180,000 Polish prisoners-of-war. Following more discussion, however, we are told that Sikorski admitted 'that the Russians might not be willing to arm so large a number of Poles at once' which could 'explain the wide discrepancy in figures'. Eden noted the Polish desire for 'a number of their deportees to be freed', and undertook to arrange a meeting between the general and Maisky the following week after informing the latter of the gist of the Polish reply.[34]

Almost immediately after this meeting Eden saw Maisky and put Sikorski's points to him. Maisky took note of these and asked various questions, as reported by Eden to Cripps:

[He] asked me whether the Polish Prime Minister had intimated his willingness to make a treaty to resist aggression with Russia and also whether he had accepted the plan of an ethnographical Poland. I said that, as regards the former, my impression was that it would be wise to clear up first the question of national committees. General Sikorski had raised with me the attitude of the Soviet Government towards his Government, and I said it seemed to me clear that the Soviet Government must be willing to recognise his Government, for otherwise there would have been no advantage in speaking of a treaty between the Soviet Government and the Polish Government. M. Maisky agreed. As regards ethnographical Poland, I could only repeat General Sikorski's expression of opinion as to the advisability of not discussing frontiers at present.[35]

Sikorski consulted his ministers the next day before meeting Maisky for the first time. He reported his talk with Eden. He then told them that they were experiencing 'a rare moment of historical decision'. On it, he said, depended the nation's fate, 'actualities mattered rather than words'. He pointed out the importance of retaining the support of their British ally at such a crucial time and to this end advocated avoidance of the term 'Treaty of Riga' both because it was so unpopular in Britain, and because it would add to the difficulty of demanding an official cancellation by the Soviets of the Soviet-German agreements of 1939. 'We have', he said, 'to exploit to the full the sympathetic treatment by the British Government of our main postulates. The British Government, urging a Polish-Soviet agreement, and acting as a go-between in this matter, is taking upon itself no mean responsibility.' He then announced that, at Maisky's request, he had agreed to a talk with the Soviet ambassador at the Foreign Office. Each minister, in turn, urged caution but wished the premier well. Zaleski, a self-confessed 'connoisseur of Moscow's asiatic method of diplomacy', whom Sikorski had invited to the meeting, advised the adoption of an assertive manner in talking to Maisky, 'who would then quickly concede, especially if we stress our distrust of Soviet ideology'.[36]

At his meeting with Maisky, Sikorski made the following points: firstly, the discussion of frontiers was not material, provided the Soviet government denounced the 1939 treaties with Germany; secondly, there should be a return to normal relations between the two governments. This would be formalized by the appointment of a Polish ambassador in Moscow. Once relations were restored the Polish government would, thirdly, agree to collaborate with Russia against the Germans. In connection with this a Polish army was to be formed in the Soviet Union. Its status would be similar to that of the Polish forces in Britain. Finally, Polish prisoners in Russia were to be set free. 'On these conditions the Polish Government would agree to the signing of a treaty with Soviet Russia.'[37]

Events were moving too fast for Zaleski. The outcome of this first official encounter between the two sides prompted him to give Eden two stiffly worded notes. The first, of 7 July 1941, emphasized Polish lack of confidence in an agreement with the Soviet Union unless past wrongs were corrected, in particular the frontier question.[38] The second, of 8 July 1941, concerned Polish territories and the Baltic States annexed by the Soviet Union between 1939 and 1940.[39] At the Foreign Office the Polish foreign minister's interest in presenting, for the record, his unabridged perception of Soviet policy was recognized. Strang saw that the Polish Government-in-Exile could not afford to make concessions which would discredit them at home but he hoped Zaleski's notes could be kept private. Although they did not altogether exclude some eventual territorial adjustments on Poland's eastern frontier 'they were sufficiently rigid/severe to make our task of honest broker no easy one'.[40]

The next meeting between Sikorski and Maisky took place on 11 July when the Soviet ambassador stated that his government were: (i) willing to leave the question of frontiers; (ii) willing to denounce the Soviet-German treaties; (iii) agreeable to the resumption of diplomatic relations; and (iv) agreeable to the creation of a Polish army on Soviet soil.[41] Eden suggested that these points might be embodied in a political agreement, and 'heads of agreement' were circulated to both parties.

The British foreign secretary was indeed hard at work. He informed Cripps that he was negotiating with Sikorski and Maisky on the basis of 'drafts drawn up here and communicated to both sides'. He said that the drafts consisted of a four-part agreement, a protocol relating to the treatment of Polish citizens in Soviet Russia and a secret protocol relating to territorial claims. He commented:

> I am not hopeful of reconciling the two parties on the basis of these two texts. The main difficulty in regards to the agreement itself is to draft it as not to prejudice the divergent views held respectively (by) the two parties as to the Polish-Soviet frontier and as to the validity of the Treaty of Riga.[42]

On the Polish side this was indeed causing great difficulties, particularly for Sikorski. He had called a Council of Ministers' meeting on 12 July at Seyda's insistence. The latter wished to hear the prime minister's opinions on the latest phase of the Polish-Soviet negotiations, about which Sikorski had spoken at length to the National Council. Seyda stressed the necessity of reaching an understanding with the Soviet Union which would not question the validity of Poland's frontier before the Soviet invasion. He warned against the creation of a Polish army in Russia because it would be subject to Soviet propaganda and cautioned against the 'constant engagement of the personal authority of the head of government in talks with the Russians, which could be taken over by another government representative, eventually by the ambassador'.

Sikorski, recounting what he had said to the National Council, said that working from a situation that 'amounted to a fourth partitioning of Poland' was most difficult, 'particularly as going into details with the Bolsheviks endangered Polish State rights'. Moreover, he thought that such discussions might touch on the Treaty of Riga and thus make such talks unpopular from the British point of view. 'It could lead us into a situation without exit', he concluded.[43]

It was exactly this potential trap which worried Zaleski. On 12 July he sent a note to Eden giving his own response to the outlined Soviet proposals for a Russo-Polish agreement. Zaleski's draft incorporated under its first heading a requirement that the Soviet agreement should base any resumption of relations on the position agreed by the two governments before the outbreak of war. This meant the Soviet government accepting the validity of not only the Polish-Soviet Pact of Non-Aggression but also the Treaty of Riga.[44]

Zaleski's initiative made a difficult task worse for Sikorski as this Foreign Office minute suggests:

> Major Cazalet came round to see the Secretary of State this afternoon, and in his absence saw Mr. Strang and myself.
>
> He had been especially asked by General Sikorski to come up from the country. The General had explained to him that he had not wished M. Zaleski to put in his draft of the Polish Russian Agreement. . . . In order to keep the peace, he had, however, said that Zaleski could send it in if he wanted to.
>
> General Sikorski is apparently having rather a difficult time with some of his team, and in particular with M. Zaleski.
>
> Major Cazalet had the further suggestion to make that it might be useful if the Prime Minister could be moved to send a line to General Sikorski to the effect that he has heard from the Secretary of State of the efforts he is making to come to an agreement with the Russians, and how much his understanding of the necessity of such an agreement has been appreciated by Mr. Churchill. Major Cazalet thinks that a letter of encouragement in this sense will help to get the General over the next fence.[45]

Strang agreed with this suggestion. He minuted: 'We hope that it will be possible for the P.M. to send a message. General Sikorski is behaving extremely well under great difficulties.'[46]

Views were polarizing. Some Poles believed with Sikorski that the territorial question should be left for discussion at a later date, since insisting on a full recognition of territorial integrity at this stage would mean the end of a possible agreement with Russia; others believed with Zaleski that Polish territorial integrity was non-negotiable. A rift in the Polish government was again in the making. This one differed only in its proportions. And it was one which the Foreign Office wanted to prevent.

On 21 July, Dormer was sent to see the Polish president to speak to him on the following lines.

> Mr. Eden has now been working a long time for the conclusion of a Polish-Soviet agreement. H.M.G. attach the utmost importance to the early signature of such an agreement. Both the P.M. and S. of S. have done their utmost to secure a text which will meet the Polish point of view. Would the President impress upon his Government the urgent need for the conclusion of the negotiations and the signature of the agreement.[47]

The ambassador to the Polish government went to see Raczkiewicz that evening as directed. The president saw the difference between the Polish government and the Soviets now as 'very slight', and anticipated an early agreement. Dormer expressed satisfaction with this statement and requested that since the difference had been so narrowed down the Polish government would not insist too rigidly on the Polish point of view. The president mentioned the problem of satisfying opinion in Poland but Dormer replied that 'if the Polish Government were satisfied that the agreement safeguarded Polish interests', as the British government were, 'it ought not to be difficult to convince the Poles in Poland, and the

Russians in their own interests would be unlikely to undermine this in their propaganda'. The president concluded that 'the agreement was important for the Russians no less than for the Poles. He made no mention of the frontier question but spoke of the need to have the Polish prisoners set free. As regards this point he agreed with me that it was only through an agreement that this could be achieved.'[48] Dormer followed a report of this meeting with Raczkiewicz by a second one written a month after Germany's attack on Russia, which described the effect of this event. It said that there was 'unconcealed relief' amongst the Poles at the prospect of their two great enemies killing each other and in anticipation of the Russians being driven from Poland, 'thus leaving a single enemy to be dealt with'. It was assumed that 'the Allies would defeat Germany and Polish territory would be restored in its entirety'.[49]

Dormer found the attitude prevalent amongst Poles in London disappointing. Tarnowski (secretary-general of the Ministry for Foreign Affairs), for instance, was 'almost indignant' at the suggestion that a reply from the Russians could be of any interest. He anticipated that they would soon be driven out of Poland, and as far as he was concerned the question of Poland's frontiers would be no longer worth discussing with them.

Even after the Polish-Soviet conversations began in the Foreign Office, Dormer found a noticeable absence of confidence that the negotiations would produce results leading to any practical advantage. Most of the Poles he met seemed to regard the question of the frontiers as of greater importance than that of the Polish prisoners, largely because of the effect it would have on opinion in Poland. The Soviet government's reluctance to define its attitude over frontiers was interpreted as due to its intention one day to insist on the validity of the 'plebiscites' held at the time of the occupation.

Dormer noticed a doubt amongst the Poles whether English people understood 'the Russian mentality and Soviet duplicity'. Current press opinion in favour of the Russians following the German attack on them seemed to create the suspicion that the British support of the Polish case against Russia might now weaken. He remarked, 'I have not heard this said in so many words, and perhaps it would be nearer the mark to say that since the Russians became our Ally, the Polish nose feels a little out of joint.' Dormer concluded:

> It seems clear that the impelling motive with the Polish Government in concluding an agreement with the Soviet Government is their desire to stand well with his Majesty's Government, to whom they feel they owe a great debt of loyalty. At the same time, it is natural that they should be sensitive to the effects of any agreement they may conclude on public opinion in Poland, where the population is constantly exposed to German propaganda. To the Poles in Poland the Polish Government in London is a symbol of Free Poland, which they respect so long as it maintains an uncompromising defence of Polish rights, but the individual members of the Government have not that overwhelming prestige in Poland which Marshal

Piłsudski had in some periods of his career. For their own sake as a Government, and still more for the sake of the unity of the nation, they must convince their people that the agreement safeguards the national interests.[50]

The minutes on this reveal Foreign Office sentiment over Poland's predicament:

The Polish position is certainly a difficult one, but I cannot help feeling that over this issue, the Poles in this country, with the exception of General Sikorski, have shown the lack of political judgement which has handicapped Poland so much throughout her history. The agreement can hardly harm Poland's position and it may provide the means of improving it in many ways.

The Poles are certainly in a bad mood and dislike no longer being our No. 1 ally.

The best hope seems to be General Sikorski, who so far as I am able to judge, is a bigger man than most Poles, and able to rise above domestic squabbles.[51]

As the Foreign Office placed their hope in Sikorski, so he, for his part, looked towards the British government for support. On the day Dormer went to see the president, Sikorski met with his ministers. He could not hide his bitter disgust at the 'demagogic gossip . . . from our sick émigrés' and warned the ministers not to give in to these influences.

He equated realistic striving for the rebuilding of Poland with acceptance of the need for a Polish-Soviet agreement. He declared himself prepared to assume responsibility for the outcome of the negotiations. He criticized Zaleski and decried attempts to make major amendments to the draft treaty but told ministers that he hoped to gain British support to persuade the Soviets to denounce treaties concerning territorial change in Poland from September 1939 onwards. Recognizing the wider territorial aspirations of colleagues Sikorski warned against harbouring such illusions without the arguments to support them. He foresaw that Britain would have to 'leave us to our fate' if unrealistic demands were put 'which would affect Britain's position as a go-between'.

Sikorski described Britain as committed to such an extent that it had to see the negotiations through to a successful conclusion. He saw the British as loyal and told ministers that the 'support of Polish demands on the frontiers of 1939 was a British responsibility which had been accepted'.[52]

Zaleski's response was ferocious. He attacked Sikorski for taking upon himself the entire weight of the negotiations at a time when the government was about to 'take one of its most important decisions'. He said it was in British government interests for the Polish government to sign and concluded that 'never during the time of our stay here had the British Government pressed us so much as in the matter of signing the agreement with Russia'.[53]

The outcome of this long, bitter debate reached the Foreign Office in the form of a proposed press communiqué from the Polish Ministry of Information. It read: 'The Polish Cabinet discussed on Monday the basis of an agreement between Poland and the U.S.S.R. now being negotiated between the two countries with the active help of the Foreign Office. All Ministers of the Polish Cabinet took part in the discussion and after an exhaustive exchange of views the proposals put forward by the Prime Minister, General Sikorski, were carried unanimously.'[54]

In fact according to Strang's notes of 28 July Eden was unofficially informed that three Polish ministers – Zaleski, Sosnkowski and Seyda – had decided not to support the conclusion of the Polish-Soviet agreement. It was possible that the Polish president, 'under the influence of these three Ministers, would withhold his assent to the signature of the agreement'. Strang's notes continued to the effect that Sikorski feared that the president might decline to authorize him to sign the treaty, but was considering signing nevertheless. He wondered how this would be regarded by the British and the Russians. Strang noted that the draft agreement was not drawn up in the normal treaty form and did not, therefore, require ratification. It did not say in its terms that those who signed it were duly authorized by their governments, or had verified each others' full powers. 'This might perhaps indicate a way out', he concluded.[55]

Sikorski must have taken courage from this information. He was working under extreme pressure. Zaleski and the other two dissident ministers wanted to resign. Raczkiewicz refused to accept this and hoped to effect a compromise between Sikorski and the other three. He threatened to withdraw his consent to the signing of the Polish-Soviet agreement. There was no hope of a compromise between the two opposing factions in the government. Sikorski explained the crisis to a depleted Council of Ministers on 28 July 1941. It is interesting that in his hour of need Sikorski invited representatives of the three 'Parties of National Unity', Peasant, Labour and PPS, so that they could 'manifest their solidarity with the Government at such a decisive moment'. He told them that after the British had given 'significant assurances', Zaleski had intervened with demands which would only repeat the mistake made by Beck. In his view any further cooperation between himself and Zaleski was impossible. Were the Polish-Soviet agreement not to be signed then responsibility for this would have to fall jointly on the side of the Soviets and on to 'those gentlemen, who do not wish to allow its signature at any price'. He emphasized that 'Anglo-Saxon opinion' was behind him and not just that of the government. He concluded: 'We have to behave coolly, salvaging sovereignty, doing nothing which would promote the German or Soviet cause, or the creation of "government" in Moscow or Warsaw.' He asked for the meeting's full support to proceed with the agreement, informing his colleagues that the president requested a postponement of the treaty firstly because the three dissident ministers had tendered their resignations and secondly in the hope of improving the terms of the treaty. The entire Government approved the signature of the treaty; unanimity was made possible by the resignations of Zaleski, Seyda and Sosnkowski.[56]

Having reaffirmed this support again the next day Sikorski acted without the president's consent and he and Maisky signed the treaty in Eden's office at 4.15 p.m. on 30 July 1941.[57]

Sikorski's victory

THE Russo-Polish pact was a victory for General Sikorski and evidence of his firm control of the Polish Government-in-Exile. It brought to fruition a line of policy which he had initiated on 19 June 1940. As then, his attitude towards relations with the Soviet Union precipitated a crisis within the Polish government. Both crises were concerned essentially with a power struggle between the group led by Sikorski, representing political elements in opposition to the former regime, and those connected with that regime, headed by Zaleski. Zaleski's resignation on 25 July 1941 marked Sikorski's victory over the critics of his policy towards Russia. His ascendancy was confirmed by the statement of President Rackiewicz on 20 August 1941 that the treaty had ceased to be a source of difficulty between himself and Sikorski.[58]

The struggle had its links with the past; it has been traced to Piłsudski's coup d'état in 1926 after which government in Poland became increasingly dictatorial. Power lay with the *Sanacja* and any opposition proved ineffective. The outbreak of war and the consequent exile of the Polish government altered all this. The Polish government which emerged in France represented a radical change in Polish politics. Members of the former opposition grasped the opportunity provided by the internment of the government in Romania and the collapse of the colonels' authority with the military disaster in 1939. They also took advantage of the French attitude towards the government in general, and Beck in particular, to claim authority.

Morally, the position of the former opposition was strong. The governments formed after Piłsudski's death in 1935 were narrowly based, relying chiefly on control of the armed forces and bureaucracy to sustain power. Attempts to create a popular following through a party machine (OZON) were a complete fiasco. The September defeat discredited the colonels' regime and destroyed the pillars of its power, allowing the opposition parties to emerge as the true spokesmen of the Polish nation.

The process by which those who claimed the support of the majority became the government of Poland had complex legal and political ramifications, as we have seen. It also became fraught with intrigue. While this is, perhaps, a characteristic of all political systems it had been particularly pronounced in Poland's history and was, and had been, aggravated by the legacy of politics in exile which left the government without the control of the usual operation of constitutional checks and balances and also weak in terms of accountability to the nation.

Further special problems faced by Sikorski's government fall into two broad categories: those to do with foreign policy and those dealing with internal matters. Central to both was the major issue of Russia. The lack of internal consensus over war aims relating to Russia was pronounced. The political cleavage between ex-*Sanacja* and ex-opposition elements in the government deepened over the issue. The mediocrity of many government figures, and their inexperience, was highlighted by it. Alongside these problems there existed great uncertainty as to the geopolitical situation Poland would find herself in at the end of the war. There was no clear or 'realistic' view at this time to guide government policy.

Sikorski was well aware of some of these issues. It is to his credit, for example, that he insisted on making the government representative of the mass of Polish people. Unless that claim could be substantiated, he knew that acceptance of his government by allies and fellow-countrymen alike would have been all the harder to secure. However, he had experienced the grave difficulties of heading a coalition in the past and his dealings with the Council of Ministers since October 1939 did nothing to dispel his doubts about the efficacy of democratic methods. Democracy meant very little in practice in July 1941. Sikorski was not a politician. He was a soldier. Paderewski's advice to him on becoming prime minister, that he should take charge of Polish affairs in a military fashion by giving orders and punishing insubordination,[59] only reinforced Sikorski's own predilection. Moreover, he was determined to take sole charge of policy-making, particularly in the field of foreign policy. His reason for doing so was a compound of vanity and necessity. He felt he knew best and, in any case, could find few people whom he could trust with policy-making. There was a dearth of politicians and administrators of the right calibre and experience amongst the representatives of the former opposition in exile.

Although it may be said that the government as a whole suffered from mediocrity this would not necessarily have affected Sikorski's performance. He tended to operate within a narrow circle of trusted friends like Stanisław Kot whom he had known over a long period of time. He was suspicious of anyone who had cooperated with the former regime. Also, not prepared to listen to his critics, he isolated himself still further and perhaps justified accusations of arrogance.

With Kot zealously guarding Sikorski's position within the government, the latter felt able to expend his energies on issues he believed to be of paramount importance. First there was the army, and here Sikorski proved his mettle. His energy in effecting the organization of Polish forces in exile could only be admired. As commander-in-chief he lacked Piłsudski's charisma, but he was no less devoted to the troops than the late marshal. He could not see the harm of combining his posts as head of military and of government; the political post would best secure the interests of the Polish forces. His attitude towards the military coloured his outlook over the whole of Polish affairs. He believed that only through a military contribution could Poland demand the full rights of an ally which he so desperately sought and he therefore pursued the policy of exploiting every source of manpower possible to provide him with armed forces.

Sikorski's attitude towards France and Britain, respectively, was ambivalent. When in France he resented interference by the French government in Polish politics and he was keen to court the British in order to balance this influence. On the other hand, he found the British government striking tougher bargains in their agreements than the French. Both Allies disappointed him over the question of the status of the Poles in Allied decision-making. This disappointment ran deep in Sikorski. To him status and prestige were essential aspects of government.

The fall of France, despite the grave difficulties it caused the Polish government, was for Sikorski a blessing in disguise. The situation was sufficiently dramatic to forge strong links of comradeship-in-arms during the first meeting between himself and Churchill. In Churchill Sikorski thought he had found the acceptance he sought. Poland in June 1940 was Britain's only ally and the ally for whom she had gone to war. Despite defeat, Poland's spirit of resistance was, in Churchill's mind, something to be held up as an example. It lightened the gloom of the hour; furthermore, Sikorski and his government provided an alternative to Pétain's defeatism. Churchill realized that Polish national feeling merited respect and in Sikorski he recognized a great national leader. It is interesting to speculate how far the bearing of the Polish government, and in particular that of the Polish prime minister, influenced British policy towards the support of other governments-in-exile and in particular the Free French.

Relations between the Polish and British governments during the summer of 1940 remained warm and relatively uncomplicated. Though at first it did not share Churchill's opinion of Sikorski, the Foreign Office came round to accept this. Sikorski's vanity and the bickering amongst the exiled Poles were overlooked in the common cause of resistance to Germany. When Hitler attacked Russia, however, the relationship lost its outward simplicity. In Churchill's words, 'Hitler's invasion of Russia altered the values and relationships of the war'.[60] The event provided the test of the Anglo-Polish alliance formalized on 25 August 1939. Russia was again to pose an awkward dilemma for both governments, just as she had done during the diplomatic prelude to the war.

British policy towards the Soviet Union after the outbreak of war was not to antagonize her in any way. Several attempts were made to seek an agreement on trade. But on both sides more than trade was at stake. The British government wanted to limit Russian cooperation with Germany. The Soviet Union wanted Britain to recognize her territorial acquisition in east central Europe. There, Polish interests were directly involved. Any change in the British government's position towards Russia was bound to affect the interests of the Polish government.

Attempts by the British government at rapprochement with the Soviet Union were temporarily halted by the Russo-Finnish war, which the Polish government had hoped would lead to an Allied declaration of war on the Soviet Union. This hope was disappointed. When Hitler attacked in the West, Stafford Cripps was asked by the British cabinet to go to Moscow. Cripps, who was an advocate of close relations with the Soviet Union, was also critical of the policy of the former Polish regime towards Russia. Because of Polish hostility Cripps thought 'it naturally followed that when Germany overran Poland, and the Polish Government ran away . . . Russia entered Poland up to the Curzon Line.'[61]

Cripps's mission to Moscow failed to produce results. Stalin spurned all British efforts at rapprochement, fearing that any positive moves towards Britain would offend the Germans, whom he was desperately anxious to placate. Even the British resolve to recognize the *de facto* control by the Soviets over Polish territory and the Baltic States did nothing to change Stalin's attitude. This decision by the British government naturally distressed the Polish government. By insisting, however, that the British proposal in no way weakened the British government's commitment to the principle of non-recognition of territorial acquisitions during the war, Halifax was, for a time, able to pacify Polish fears. Indeed, the spring of 1941, which was before Hitler's military intentions became clear, Polish confidence had recovered so much as to embarrass the British government with public and private utterances which looked forward to a fully restored, if not enlarged, post-war Poland supported by her ally, Britain. These hopes ran counter to opinion in Britain. No sooner was Poland defeated by Germany than the British press showed signs of appeasement towards the Soviet Union combined with criticism of the Poles. *The Times* of 23 September 1939 said that with Poland defeated and overrun by the Germans: 'Russia could not let the White Russian and Ukrainian provinces fall into the hands of the Nazis, who would have formed them into separatist puppet states, a menace to Russia.' The next day, in the *Sunday Express* Lloyd George wrote an article under the heading 'What is Stalin up to?' in which he criticized the 'class-ridden Polish government' and praised the Soviet government for 'liberating their kinsmen from the Polish yoke'.[62]

Similar sentiments reappeared in the press in mid-1941. Now the Polish government was also being portrayed in an unfavourable light over the issue of anti-semitism. Persistent criticism over this question detracted from the favourable image created by Polish efforts during the Battle of Britain, in which the Polish kill ratio was twice that of the British.[63] Any illusions about Britain favouring Poland at Russia's expense were shattered by Churchill's unconditional invitation of the Soviet Union into the anti-Hitler camp after German forces attacked in the East on 22 June 1941. This hard lesson was soon followed by the understanding that British interests were involved in their pressure on Poland to sign the treaty with Russia at the end of July and Sikorski came to realize that signing this was the only way of keeping the British government's support. Exile had stripped the Polish government of the advantage held between the wars; in mid-1941 it was faced with the problem of coming to terms with the Soviet Union in a situation where independence was lost and, as Sikorski appreciated, without the option of rejecting cooperation with Russia.

This was not a view shared by Zaleski. To him any agreement with the Soviet Union ought to have a guarantee of Polish territorial integrity by Britain. When Britain would not give that, he felt that the Polish government should not sign, whatever pressure was put on it. The pressure was indeed great. The Foreign Office, and Eden in particular, on his first important assignment as Churchill's foreign secretary, worked hard to clear his path to a close Anglo-Russian understanding. Attention was focused on Sikorski, whose difficult position was recognized and on whom British hopes were pinned. He did not disappoint these hopes. On 5 July 1941, the very first day of contact between the Polish and Russian sides, Cadogan noted that Sikorski was 'very good. Firm but courteous'.[64] Cadogan himself pressed for an early agreement between the two nations. By the last day of the negotiations, his diary holds this rather jaundiced entry: 'Saw A [Anthony Eden] and Strang about P-R business. Both sides are crooks, but it looks as if we may get a signature this afternoon.'[65]

The importance to the British government of the agreement between Poland and Russia was revealed in a remark made by Eden to Sikorski on 8 June 1942. He told the Polish prime minister that the Anglo-Soviet Treaty of 26 May 1942 depended on the existence of a Polish-Soviet agreement.[66] While this may have been an exaggeration, the British government, and Churchill in particular, wanted a Polish-Soviet treaty as quickly as possible, in order to consolidate the new relationship with Russia. Admittedly, after the Anglo-Soviet pact of 12 July 1941, difficulties in the negotiations between the Polish and Soviet governments became a matter of secondary importance to the British. Nevertheless any Polish reluctance to come to terms with Britain's new ally was embarrassing and a problem which the British government could well do without.

The pressure on Sikorski to sign was such as to suggest that if it were a choice between the continued support of the Polish government as it then existed and harm to British interests in the form of new ties with Russia, then the Polish government would be the one to suffer. Sikorski saw the survival of the Polish government as being dependent on its alliance with Britain and he was not willing to endanger this by refusing to sign the agreement. The realities which were masked during the diplomatic prelude to the war were now recognized by him. He realized that the Anglo-Polish partnership, however Beck had tried to regard it, had never been an equal one. Its inequality was now confirmed. Sikorski also knew that Britain could not provide the assurances sought by Zaleski on Polish frontiers. Instead he believed that sufficient compensation for this lay in the alliance with Britain, that in return for signing the British government would continue to support his government and also, hopefully, take on the responsibility for Polish frontiers. Sikorski was willing to stake the whole of Poland's future on the Anglo-Polish relationship. This was certainly placing much more weight on the alliance than was originally intended.

Sikorski's policy reflected the predicament of the Polish Government-in-Exile. In a situation where its very existence depended on continued recognition by the British government its policy options were severely limited, particularly in the case where the interests of its host were at stake. In accepting this fact, remembering also that he actively pursued a policy of rapprochement with the Soviet Union, Sikorski displayed a sense of realism which was rare in Polish politics. His emergence as a Polish statesman of mark is significant in the history of the Polish government during the Second World War. The impression gained from the earlier part of this period is of a posturing figure whose sense of Poland's importance in the Allied cause was out of all proportion to her worth as an ally, though his demands to be treated as an equal partner in the struggle against Germany could be seen as justifiable attempts directed at maintaining Polish dignity. Throughout late 1939 and into 1941 Sikorski could have been seen as just another Pole with a grandiloquent turn of phrase, but this would not be a fair assessment. He was at his best when he talked in broad terms of major issues and in so doing served the same purpose as Churchill did for Britain and de Gaulle for France, emerging as Poland's Man of Destiny. This went against the advice of both critics and admirers. Yet it is difficult to see how this equation between Sikorski and his country could have been avoided. In a most dark and tragic hour of his nation's history, he held tenaciously to his belief in the strength and rightness of the Polish cause and in the eventual deliverance of his country from the defeat and humiliation it had suffered at the hands of its two historic enemies. Sikorski's indestructible patriotism was inspiring. He also had the good sense to see that concrete evidence of the will to contribute to the Allied cause needed to be provided, not only for prestige purposes *vis-à-vis* other partners in the alliance, but also for the sake of the morale of the Poles themselves. To this end he worked with persistent diligence and he was, above all, successful in his energetic pursuit of aid from his allies for the building-up of the Polish forces. In doing this he made a thorough nuisance of himself, particularly over the question of aid in recruiting an army in Canada. In short, in the period from the formation of the Polish government in France to Hitler's attack on Russia, one's general assessment of the Polish Government-in-Exile changes. The early scenes of comic opera change under Sikorski's direction to a serious representation of the Polish case. The true test of his statesmanship, however, came when the British government invited the Soviet Union on to the Allied side.

It would have hindered the Allied cause had the Polish government insisted on holding out over the agreement with Russia. Sikorski's importance lay in keeping clear the path that others sought to block. He offered his fullest cooperation over the signing of the pact with Russia, within the limits he gauged to be necessary for the maintenance of fundamental Polish interests.

By going against the strongest prejudices held by his countrymen, Sikorski showed he was not afraid of being unpopular. The agreement with Russia was more than a demonstration of Polish willingness to work for the Allied cause. It was a gesture necessary, in Sikorski's view, to obtain British commitment to support Polish interests in the new Europe that was to emerge after the war. Whatever illusions he may have had over the extent of Britain's influence over Polish fate he showed his statesmanship in appreciating his government's dependence upon Britain and in converting that dependence, which inevitably characterized the Anglo-Polish alliance as it had developed, into the basis of a working relationship. The value of this relationship, for the Poles, remained to be seen.

4   The growing isolation of the London Poles, 1942–1944

BRITAIN CONTINUED TO play a crucial role in Polish affairs after the summer of 1941. The Foreign Office hoped that if, in their negotiations with the Soviet Union, the Poles in London gave in on the frontier issue, they might preserve their government, whereas if they failed to do so they would lose out in both cases. Whatever influence the British government could exert on the Polish was, however, subject to a number of overriding factors, not the least of which was the ability of the London Poles to revise their attitudes fast enough to accommodate the enormous concessions demanded of them in response to Stalin's evolving policy towards Poland.

This chapter will discuss Russo-Polish relations in terms of the alliance which gained the epithet 'grand' with the entry of the United States into the war in December 1941. American influence with regard to the 'Polish Question' was, however, evident before the end of 1941 when the military situation on the eastern front was critical. Both Western powers came to the aid of Russia. The Americans were particularly forthcoming in this regard. Shortly after the commencement of Operation Barbarossa, Hitler's plan of campaign against the Soviet Union, Roosevelt announced the release of Soviet dollar resources to enable the Soviet government to purchase American arms. He then sent his aide, Harry Hopkins, to Moscow. There, Western aid was promised to Stalin and the knot binding the Americans, British and Russians was firmly tied.[1] Despite mutual fears of a separate peace there was to be no going back.

In August 1941 Roosevelt and Churchill reviewed the war situation. They proposed sending a joint mission to Moscow in order to ascertain Soviet needs and then produced a definition of war aims in the form of the Atlantic Charter. One of these aims was of great importance to the Polish government. It stated that the two powers 'desired to see no changes [in territory] that do not accord with the freely expressed wishes of the people concerned'.[2] For its part, the Soviet government gave qualified acceptance of the Charter. It considered that 'the practical application of these principles will necessarily adapt itself to the circumstances, needs and historical peculiarities of particular countries'.[3]

Between these points of view lay the seeds of problems for the future. In August 1941 the survival of Russia lay in the balance. The Ukraine was almost entirely in German hands. Leningrad was surrounded and Moscow threatened. Stalin was most concerned about a 'Second Front' for which he repeatedly asked the Western Powers. In the West his demands were received amid fears of a possible German-Soviet rapprochement.[4] The joint mission, which was preparing to go to Moscow to offer unconditional aid, wished to prevent such an eventuality. Before Lord Beaverbrook (minister of supply in the War Cabinet) and Averell Harriman (Roosevelt's personal representative) left London, they were approached, separately, by Sikorski. The Polish premier felt that he had an interest in material aid offered to the Soviet Union. Any arrangements under Lend-Lease could, he hoped, be extended to include the needs of the nascent Polish army in Russia. Sikorski's requests to secure for General Anders, its commander, the means to equip four to six infantry divisions were met by noncommittal answers.[5] In Moscow, however, Stalin got what he wanted: the assurance of an astonishing quantity of materials which made 'generous inroads into American and British supplies'.[6] This was entirely consistent with Beaverbrook's view of the war at that time: 'There is today only one military problem – how to help Russia.'[7] Though the implications of the Moscow meeting were, for Poland, profound her needs and interests were not given a high priority there. They had not even merited mention in Churchill's letter taken by Beaverbrook to Stalin.[8] Then, in Moscow, 'immediately on their arrival the guests were so fully occupied with an intensive programme of consultations and work that, despite all the promises given in London . . . they did not make contact' with the Poles there for several days. As it became clear that the Polish perspective (especially General Anders's military desiderata) was given no prominence at all at the talks, Kot, the newly appointed Polish ambassador to the Soviet Union, pressed for a British-Polish-American meeting which took place on 2 October. At this meeting Beaverbrook made it plain that Polish interests were being handed over to Russia and that the Polish question would mainly be dealt with by Stalin. He argued that even if it were possible to supply the Poles separately with material 'there wouldn't be any transport resources for it' as already these were insufficient to fulfil Allied obligations entered into with Russia. It was therefore Stalin's 'business to allocate something from this for the Polish Army'.[9]

Sikorski's disappointment with the outcome of the negotiations from the Polish point of view was expressed in a letter to Churchill written on 8 October: 'it was with profound regret that I learnt of the decision of the British representative to interpret his instructions as restricting the British contribution in material as destined exclusively for the USSR leaving it to the discretion of the Soviet Government to decide whether they can spare (any) for the use of the Polish Army.'[10]

Russo-Polish relations were soon to cool. Kot reported their steady deterioration since the signing of the Military Agreement in August 1941.[11] Sikorski responded by going to the Soviet Union, where he had important conversations with Stalin on 3 December 1941. During these talks the Polish leader presented himself as a man of goodwill who had never conducted or agreed with Polish policy directed against the Soviet Union over the past twenty years. Reinforcing these credentials, he also said he would back the Soviet leader in advocating a Second Front.

Sikorski then introduced a subject that plagued Polish-Soviet relations. He told Stalin: 'I have with me a list containing the names of approximately 4,000 officers who were deported by force and who presently still remain in the prisons and labour camps. . . . These people are here. Not one of them has returned.' Stalin replied: 'That is impossible, they have escaped . . . to Manchuria. . . . Surely they have been released, but as yet have not arrived.' They never did. The Poles kept asking the Russians about them and kept getting fobbed off, at first in private and then in public – after the Germans announced, in April 1943, the discovery of their bodies at Katyn.

Sikorski's interest in the missing officers was their use in the organization of a Polish army in the Soviet Union. He proposed to Stalin that it should be located in 'the Southern regions of the Semipalatinsk Province' and specified Tashkent, Alma – Ata and Southern Kazakhstan where a milder climate would benefit the health of Polish soldiers and of as many civilians as could be directed there. Sikorski also spoke to Stalin of a further move to Persia where the climate as well as 'the promised American and British help would allow these people to recover within a short time and form a strong army which would return here to the front and take over the section assigned to them . . . I am ready to declare that these forces will return to the Russian front.' Stalin replied, 'I am a person of experience and of age. I know that if you go to Persia you will never return here.'[12] Nevertheless, despite his evident displeasure at Sikorski's suggestion, he eventually agreed to the formation of seven Polish divisions in Russia and to the evacuation of 25,000 men as reinforcements for the 1st Army Corps serving in the Middle East.

The talks continued later over dinner. Stalin suggested discussion of frontiers which Sikorski declined. Sensing his unease with the topic, Stalin said that there was no need to quarrel over frontiers and offered the reassurance that no harm was intended in this respect. Why Sikorski refused such an opportunity to make a deal directly with Stalin was a question raised by his critics who believed that he should have done so at that juncture. Sikorski told Ciechanowski that he did not see any reason to discuss a frontier which had been settled in 1921 and that it was in any case unconstitutional for him to do so. More importantly, it was not a matter for discussion during war, 'in view of its imponderables'.[13] While he believed in the eventual victory of the Soviet Union against the German invasion, Sikorski expected further Soviet reverses in 1942. Thus talks about frontiers at this time would have been premature and Sikorski hoped for an eventual outcome which would allow Poland's eastern frontier to remain as defined by the Treaty of Riga. He expected to find Russia so exhausted by war as to render Stalin impotent in his designs on the frontier issue.

Stalin thought otherwise.[14] He had high hopes of victory in 1942 which explains why, during Russia's darkest hour, he should have been thinking at all about the territorial relationship between the Soviet Union and her Western neighbours. In the event Stalin conceded very little to Sikorski. The agreements reached in December 1941 add up to little more than a confirmation of the July treaty provisions.

Stalin's attention was fixed on an issue that was to impose a great strain upon the Anglo-American relationship. He demanded a Second Front. Churchill responded with a proposal to send a military mission to the Soviet Union to discuss the progress of the war. Stalin demanded more. He wanted both to discuss war aims and to 'plan for the post-war organization of peace'.[15] Without these topics on the agenda he was not prepared to receive a visiting party. The wider brief he had in mind led Churchill to offer Eden to accompany the mission and he accepted Stalin's provisos.[16] In doing so he laid open for negotiation matters of vital importance in the Polish government which now feared that concessions over the frontier question would be granted to the Soviet Union by Britain.

The American government also suspected a deal to be in the offing. Cordell Hull defined his government's position to Eden on 5 December 1941 by reiterating the principles of the Atlantic Charter.[17] This position must, however, be seen in the context of public opinion. In the U.S., as indeed in Great Britain, there was a swing in favour of the Soviet Union which was seen more and more as an heroic bulwark against Hitler.

On 16 December 1941 Eden arrived in Moscow. He was told bluntly what was expected of the visit by his hosts. To be considered a success it had to result in an Anglo-Soviet military alliance. Moreover, with regard to Poland, Stalin demanded Anglo-American consent for his idea that the 'Curzon Line with certain modifications' should become the frontier line between Russia and Poland. The Polish government had good cause to be concerned about the likelihood of an Anglo-Russian deal at Poland's expense. Stalin was undeterred by Eden's repetition of the principles of the Atlantic Charter and in any case British resolve to stand by these was fast eroding. On 26 January 1942 Stafford Cripps told Sikorski that Stalin's demands on the Curzon Line should be accepted.[18]

Churchill himself now thought the same, despite earlier assurances he had given Sikorski to the contrary. In a letter to Roosevelt, dated 7 March 1942, the contents of which were made known to Stalin, he stated:

> The increasing gravity of the war has led me to feel that the principles of the Atlantic Charter ought not to be construed so as to deny Russia the frontiers she occupied when Germany attacked her. I hope therefore that you will be able to give us a free hand to sign the treaty which Stalin desires as soon as possible.[19]

It is important to note two points. Firstly, in referring to Roosevelt like this, Churchill paid due regard to Washington's role before redefining the Anglo-Soviet relationship. Secondly, he wanted to keep Stalin in the war against Hitler at almost any price at a time when a Russo-German rapprochement through Japanese mediation was feared.

In their attack on Pearl Harbour on 7 December 1941 the Japanese had drawn the United States into the war. For the West the New Year brought in a series of shattering defeats in the Pacific (Philippines) and in South East Asia (Singapore). For Russia there was, in contrast, a glimmer of hope. Two days before the Japanese attack on Pearl Harbour, the Red Army launched a counter-offensive against the Germans. It succeeded in lifting the threat from Moscow.[20] Moreover, in forcing German retreats elsewhere along the Eastern Front the Red Army's successes highlighted the terrible price paid in German lives for Hitler's earlier advances; a quarter of the German complement of manpower there had been destroyed. Stalin's demands to Eden in December 1941 were based upon a new-found confidence.

The import of these developments was not lost on Sikorski. He decided to turn once more to Roosevelt for support in preventing 'a second Munich only shifted 180 degrees to the left'.[21] Roosevelt realized that concessions to Stalin would have consequences for American domestic policies. Polish Americans, for whom the frontier question was a test of presidential integrity, were in the main supporters of the Democratic Party. Roosevelt intended to maintain their loyalty. He assured Sikorski on 24 March 1942 that he would not back down on the principle that no territorial questions should be settled before the end of the war.[22]

Consistent with this assurance American pressure was in fact applied on the British government's negotiation of a treaty with the Soviet Union. The text of the Anglo-Soviet Treaty was sufficiently altered to satisfy the Polish government; Ciechanowski thanked Hull on 13 June 1942 for American help in removing the territorial clauses inimical to Polish interests.[23] This indicates some bargaining power on the part of the Polish government in its relations with the United States though this should not be exaggerated. When Molotov met with Roosevelt on 29 May 1942, the principles of the Atlantic Charter were but a spectre of past good intent. Roosevelt described a new world in which the main signatories of the United Nations declaration – Britain, the Soviet Union, China and the United States – would act as the world's policemen. The corollary of this was that the future would see the sovereignty of smaller nations considerably reduced; indeed, according to the American president, they would be disarmed and in this vision of post-war international relations Poland had no power. Molotov remarked that this might be a 'bitter blow to the prestige of Poland . . . (but) . . . observed warmly that the President's ideas for the preservation of mutual peace would be sympathetically viewed by the

Soviet Government and people'.[24] Molotov was also given to understand that there would be a Second Front in 1942. But in this regard the Russians were soon to be disappointed. The Germans' May offensive in Russia threatened Stalingrad by August 1942 and Stalin came to learn personally from Churchill (on 12 August) that there would be no Second Front that year.

Polish strategy and military developments in Russia and Poland, 1942

CHURCHILL'S visit to Stalin, which marked a moment of gloom in Anglo-Soviet relations, coincided with a sudden deterioration in Polish-Soviet relations. At the centre of this latter dispute lay the fate of the Polish army in Russia. The future of Sikorski's military strategy was based on the principle of unity of command for all Polish forces on all fronts and on the belief that Poland would be liberated in a coordinated action between the Polish government's forces in Poland and those abroad. Because of uncertainty over the directions from which Poland's forces in exile would re-enter Polish territory, Sikorski insisted on a sizeable Polish force in every theatre of war. His army in Russia, under the command of General Anders, was based at Yangi Yul near Tashkent. It consisted of six divisions, only one of which was equipped to fight. In February Anders was asked by Zhukov, then a major-general and liaison officer with the Poles, to prepare his division (the Fifteenth) for action on the Soviet front. Anders refused. His army was to fight in full complement or not at all.[25] Stalin responded by halving the Polish army's food allocation. Anders immediately flew to Moscow where he met Stalin and Molotov on 18 March 1942. It was then agreed that the soldiers for whom there was a shortage of rations should be evacuated to Iran. The evacuation of 40,000 Polish soldiers together with women and children was carried out almost immediately.[26] Anders, who feared for the future of the balance of his men, was determined to save the Polish army by withdrawing it completely from the Soviet Union to the Middle East. His intention undermined the policy pursued by Sikorski. A rift between the two developed and surfaced publicly when Anders appeared in London on 21 April 1942. Though the two parted on reasonable terms, relations between them worsened as Stalin pursued his policy against Polish interests in Russia. This culminated in the arrest in August of Polish delegates responsible to the Polish Embassy in Russia and in the evacuation of the remainder of Anders's army. By the beginning of September 1942, 70,939 Poles had left Russia for the Middle East.[27] The thousands who remained behind were cut off from all contact with the Polish government in London. Many Poles in Russia were, however, recruited into the Communist-controlled Polish army whose history is outlined in Part Two.

In strategic terms Sikorski had lost the military potential of the Polish prisoners-of-war left behind in Russia. He now had to focus his attention on his forces in Poland. The Home Army (*Armja Krajowa* – AK), came into existence on 14 February 1942. It had evolved from the SZP and ZWZ. They were joined by the Peasant Battalions (*Bataliony Chłopskie* – 'Be-Cha') and by Right-wing groups such as the National Armed Forces (*Narodowe Siły Zbrojne* – NSZ) and the National Military Organization (*Narodowa Organizacja Wojskowa* – NOW), 'and more loosely, by the diminutive, communist-led' People's Guard (*Gwardia Ludowa* – GL).[28]

In March 1943 the Polish estimate of the strength of the AK was 300,200. Though the exact figure was disputed the AK was the largest resistance movement in Europe. It is important to note, however, that resistance to the German invaders was, until the Warsaw Rising, kept to a minimum. The Polish government's aim was to preserve the AK until it could be used, at a decisive moment of the war, to secure Poland for the return of the London Poles.

Whatever the hopes for the future, the government's authority was being challenged in Poland from the spring of 1942 by what General Grot-Rowecki, commander of the AK, called the 'Soviet Communist action in Poland'. This was the title of a report, dated 17 July 1942, which he sent to London. The report brought to the government's attention the activity of the Polish Workers Party (*Polska Partia Robotnicza* – PPR) which had been formed in January 1942, and that of a propaganda campaign by the Kosciuszko Broadcasting Station in Moscow. Both tried to convince Polish opinion that the London-controlled AK was aiding the German de-struction of the Polish nation in its passivity. The claim was made that the PPR was the only centre of a 'general-national front' for active struggle and that the Soviet Union was 'the only saviour of the Polish nation'.

In this propaganda Grot-Rowecki recognized the development of an idea which might in time undermine the authority of the Polish gov-ernment throughout Poland. This was the impression that the 'Bolsheviks had taken over the protection of Polish territory' and planned a build-up of Communist forces which was to be backed by the 'whole might of the Red Army' in the coming liberation. Grot-Rowecki emphasized that while the 'political side of the Soviet propaganda was unpopular, except with the poorest in the countryside and small towns, the idea of actively fighting the German appeals to the populace'. He urged the government to tell the Soviet authorities to stop their action on Polish territory and to ask the Bolsheviks to say clearly what sort of action they wished to be taken in Poland by the Polish armed forces. He also suggested that the government should issue a wireless appeal to the Polish population to take orders only from the Polish authorities in Poland and to take part in the active struggle only when the proper authorities told them. The report added: 'If that is done, the writer is prepared to begin a reinforced guerrilla-sabotage action in Poland and something of the same sort in the east as from autumn of this year.'[29]

Grot-Rowecki's report, which was decoded in London in October 1942, was preceded in September by reports of the bombing of Warsaw by Soviet aircraft.[30] It gave substance to the fears expressed in communications reaching London from Poland from the beginning of 1941 that the main threat to Poland under German occupation was perceived as the threat of invasion 'from the Bolshevik side'. As far as 'Polish Society' was concerned, the government's most important task was 'to protect the country from an invasion of the Red Army'.[31]

The government agonized over its reply to Grot-Rowecki. Its thinking was conditioned by the fear, so cogently expressed by General Kukiel to Orme Sargent on 26 December 1942 in a discussion about Polish response to German military activity in Zamość that a premature rising would leave 'Poland dead as a spent bullet'.[32]

Grot-Rowecki was ordered in November 1942 to prevent any outburst of national insurrection. Furthermore he was told that 'the essential aim of the ultimate insurrection was the forestalling of the Russians in the liberation of Poland by the assumption of political power by the resistance'. In his orders to Grot-Rowecki, Sikorski also stressed that the AK should present 'a positive attitude towards the Soviet Union'.[33] This instruction was one which Sikorski himself found great difficulty with as Polish-Soviet relations took yet another turn for the worse.

Relations between Poland and the Western Allies now also came under considerable strain. In December 1942 Sikorski went to Washington for the last time. His discussions with Roosevelt are noteworthy only in their revelation of the limitations of Sikorski's understanding of the real situation. He believed conditions to be favourable to an assertion by the United States, Britain and Poland of their dominance in relations with the Soviet Union. He went to America to obtain Roosevelt's support for the Polish government's position on the frontier question. On this he drew a blank.

After his talk with Roosevelt Sikorski wrote a memorandum to Sumner Welles, the U.S. acting secretary of state, in which he recorded that Poland would repudiate any agreement conceding territorial claims to the Soviets. Sumner Welles asked Ciechanowski: 'Am I to understand that the Polish Government is determined not to sacrifice even an inch of its Eastern Territory?' The Polish ambassador replied that this was indeed his government's position and he went on to justify it by repeating some words Sikorski had used to him:

> I am sure he would agree that no Government, forced to function outside of its territory as a result of war, could hope to maintain its authority and keep the support of its nationals, if contrary to that nation's will, and without having the possibility of consulting its parliament . . . it were to agree to make any territorial concessions.[34]

This may be read as a summary of the problems faced by the Polish government at the end of 1942, as indeed it was from the moment it went into exile. The American government believed that Russia would emerge from the war greatly strengthened and the corollary of this view was that the granting of special Russian demands was to be expected. Yet the Polish government refused to accept this even when in January 1943 Ciechanowski was told by Sumner Welles that the United States was in basic agreement with the Soviet position over the Curzon Line.

Further evidence of a lack of British and American support for Polish interests came in the same month. On 16 January 1943 a note had come from Molotov to the Polish Embassy in Kuybyshev which stated that 'all persons who found themselves on Polish Territories occupied by Soviet forces on 1–2 November 1939 must forthwith consider themselves Soviet citizens.'[35] Polish appeals to the British and American governments in protest against this note drew no support.

The break with Russia

WITH the military balance on the Eastern Front swinging in favour of the Soviet Union in the spring of 1943, the future of Poland became increasingly open to Soviet initiatives. Each Soviet military victory further reduced the will of the Western Powers to intervene on Poland's behalf. On his return from the Casablanca Conference, 14–25 January 1943, Roosevelt told Ciechanowski that the moment was unfavourable for diplomatic intervention in Moscow because the Russians were 'in a phase of considerable success'. He advised the Polish government to 'keep their shirts on'.[36] Distressed at their isolation, the London Poles issued the following declaration: 'Polish territory within its frontier of 1st September 1939, and its sovereignty, are intangible and indivisible. No unilateral and illegal acts on anybody's part . . . are able to change this state of things.'[37] The subsequent events have endowed these words with a hollow ring.

During the night of 26–27 February 1943 the new Polish ambassador to the Soviet Union, Romer, met with Stalin and Molotov. The territorial problem was discussed in a manner best summarized by the following exchange: 'Romer: You won't find a single Pole who would deny Wilno and Lwów are Polish. I myself declare it in your presence. Stalin: I understand your viewpoint. We also have ours. We are quits. We shall make our statement.'[38] It was issued by Tass on 1 March and made public for the first time Stalin's claim to the Curzon Line:

> The leading Soviet circles are of the opinion that the denial of the right of the Ukrainian and Byelo-Russian people of reunion with their blood brethren bears witness to an imperialistic tendency. . . . Even the well-known British Minister Lord Curzon, in spite of his inimical attitude to the U.S.S.R., realised that Poland cannot put forward a claim to the Ukraine and Russian lands, but the Polish ruling circles still show no understanding in this matter.[39]

Such a vociferous debate about the fate of Poland ensued in the Western media that the British government decided to place curbs on the topic in the press in case it upset Allied unity. Moreover it decided the time had come to attempt, by direct negotiation, a solution to the problem that had poisoned Russo-Polish relations and that was threatening more besides.

In March 1943 Eden travelled to Washington. Before he left London he talked to the Soviet ambassador, Maisky, and was told that Russian demands at future peace talks included a Russo-Polish frontier along the Curzon Line with minor adjustments. Maisky also pointed out to Eden, as he had earlier, on 24 June 1941 that the Soviet Union would tolerate only a Polish government friendly towards itself and he specifically ruled out the London Poles in this context.

In Washington, Eden and Roosevelt agreed that 'whilst Poland will want her original boundaries . . . the big powers would have to decide what Poland should have'.[40] There was to be, as Ciechanowski understated, no 'strong intervention on behalf of Poland in Moscow'.[41]

At 9.15 p.m. on 13 April 1943, Berlin radio announced to the world the discovery of the bodies of about 10,000 Polish officers buried in mass graves in the Smolensk area. According to the broadcast, German troops were taken by locals to a place called Kosogory at the northern end of Katyn wood, an area occupied by the Germans since 14 July 1941. Here 'the Bolsheviks had perpetrated secretly mass executions'.[42]

Two days after this statement was broadcast the Soviet Information Bureau in London discussed it as 'fabrication by Goebbels' slanderers'.[43] On the same day that the Soviet release was issued, the Polish cabinet met to discuss the allegation of the Soviet mass-murder broadcast from Berlin. It decided to seek an explanation from the Soviet Embassy in London. The International Red Cross was also asked to investigate. At the time General Sikorski was in the Middle East visiting Polish troops and so on 16 April General Kukiel issued a detailed account of Polish-Soviet communications concerning the Polish officers missing since 17 September 1939. Kukiel's statement ended with the words:

> We have become accustomed to the lies of German propaganda and we understand the purpose behind its latest revelations. In view however of the abundant and detailed German information concerning the discovery . . . , and the categorical statement that they (the missing Polish Officers) were murdered by Soviet authorities in the Spring of 1940, the necessity has arisen that the mass graves discovered should be investigated and the facts alleged verified.[44]

This move angered Stalin into interrupting relations with Sikorski's government. On 21 April 1943, in a telegram to Churchill, he described the behaviour of the Polish government towards the U.S.S.R. as 'completely abnormal and contrary to the rules and standards governing relations between two allied States'. He was resentful that far from countering the 'infamous fascist slander against the U.S.S.R.', the Sikorski government had not found it necessary 'even to address questions to the Soviet Government or to request information on the matter'. He interpreted the simultaneous start of 'the anti-Soviet campaign' in the German and Polish press as 'indubitable evidence of contact and collusion between Hitler and the Sikorski Government' a view he saw further supported by the close correspondence of line taken by the respective press campaigns. He concluded that these circumstances led the Soviet government to believe that the London government had 'severed its relations of alliance with the U.S.S.R.' and 'for these reasons the Soviet Government has decided to interrupt relations with the Government'.[45] Three days later Churchill replied that far from Sikorski being pro-German or in league with them he was in danger of being overthrown by Poles who considered that he had not stood up sufficiently against the Soviet government. 'If he should go we should only get somebody worse. I hope therefore that your decision to "interrupt" relations is read in the sense of a final warning.'[46] Stalin refused to change his mind. Relations between the Polish Government-in-Exile and the Soviet Union were never resumed.

The government's isolation was intensified by the tragic death of General Sikorski on 4 July 1943. The aircraft bringing him back to London crashed on take-off in Gibraltar. Sikorski's death has been the subject of much debate and, in the absence of strong evidence to the contrary, foul play will continue to be a possibility which is given consideration. The matter is of sufficient notoriety to call for some comment here on the charge that the British were responsible for Sikorski's death. Stalin for one seemed to have believed it. Despite attempts to implicate Churchill in the affair the British prime minister's position is unassailable. On personal and political grounds he had a real interest in Sikorski's welfare. He admired Sikorski as much as he came to dislike his successors, none of whom perished by order of the prime minister. That is not to say that assassination as a possible solution to Polish problems was never considered in British policy-making circles. Kot, who was always regarded by the Foreign Office as much more troublesome than Sikorski, is referred to in a letter dated 30 July 1940 from Savery to Roberts in these terms: 'I think that all parties are now united in their desire to reduce K's [Kot's] powers. I hope they will succeed but I am afraid we shall never have any peace until we have him bumped off.'[47]

Though no such reference is found regarding Sikorski, threats to his life were discussed at the Foreign Office. He certainly had enemies amongst his compatriots who would have wished to see him dead. In October 1942 a Foreign Office minute records a conversation between Tytus Filipowicz and Savery in which the Polish ex-ambassador to Washington spoke of the growing unpopularity of Sikorski amongst Polish émigrés and warned of a possible threat to his life. This view was discussed as being over-emotional.[48]

Yet the man who had come to symbolize the spirit of the Polish nation during the war *was* suddenly lost. Sikorski's death was a disastrous blow to the London Poles. He had given substance to the Government-in-Exile, which some had regarded as an 'ephemeral fiction'. Within the international community he was an irreplaceable Polish asset. As regards his successor Stanisław Mikołajczyk, Churchill 'showed little sympathy for his feelings or understanding of his lack of international experience. . . . He felt he owed nothing to Mikołajczyk. The words he had uttered to General Sikorski in 1940 did not seem to apply to his relationship with the General's successor.'[49]

Be that as it may, the strengths of the new Polish leader lay outside the orbit of personal friendship with Churchill, or Roosevelt for that matter. It lay in the radicalism of his political beliefs, his leadership of the Peasant Party and in his relatively pragmatic approach to foreign policy. In exile he had built upon his interwar record as an opponent of the *Sanacja*. He was a keen supporter of Sikorski who returned this confidence in engineering the appointment of Mikołajczyk as minister of internal affairs and later as vice-premier after Kot went to Moscow in December 1941 as Polish ambassador.

The new prime minister pledged himself to continue with Sikorski's policy towards the Soviet Union. This simply was to normalize relations with that country while maintaining the support of Britain and America. It was to prove a most difficult task. The new Polish premier had also to reckon with the political opinions of a cabinet whose membership had altered after Sikorski's death. There was a new commander-in-chief of Polish forces and the separation of duties as between that post and premier had been effected.

President Rackiewicz's appointment of General Kazimierz Sosnkowski as commander-in-chief went against Mikołaczyk's wishes and indeed those of the majority of the cabinet; after all Sosnkowski had identified himself as anti-Sikorski when he resigned over the Polish-Soviet Treaty in July 1941. He was, however, extremely popular with the army. It was probably for this reason that the British government allowed the appointment to be made, despite views to the contrary from the Soviet ambassador. The Polish government's difficulty in maintaining the loyalty of its armed forces who were particularly critical of the London government for being too soft on the Soviet government was understood.

Polish forces and Allied strategy, 1943

THE foundation of Polish military strategy, particularly in regard to the AK, had been laid down by Sikorski in November 1942. It was in the spirit of his instruction to Grot-Rowecki that he directed Romer to offer Stalin a coordinated military effort between the Red Army and the AK. The Polish ambassador put the proposal to the Soviet leader at their meeting of 26–27 February 1943. Stalin politely turned the suggestion down. 'When the course of the War allows it, we shall certainly let you know Mr. Ambassador. For the time being, I cannot say anything more.'[50] The AK did not fit into Stalin's strategic plan as a force with which the Red Army would cooperate in pushing back the Germans. It was equally ignored in Western strategic plans.

Sikorski had tried, valiantly, to obtain Western aid for his forces in Poland, and Roosevelt had agreed to make the Lend-Lease arrangements available for this purpose, but strategic considerations went against the decision. In March 1943 the chiefs of staff drew up a priority list of aid to resistance movements. It read:

i   The Italian islands, Corsica and Crete;
ii   The Balkans;
iii France;
iv   Poland and Czechoslovakia;
v   Norway and the Low Countries;
vi   Far East.[51]

The Polish government was kept in the dark about these considerations. It was not until September 1943 that it was told that the AK had no role to play in the strategic plans of the Allied Powers in Europe. These were discussed at Quebec (12–24 August 1943) where the American plan for an invasion of Europe through Northern France was developed. It took some months, however, before operation 'Overlord' was finalized.

Another decision made at Quebec was that no aid be given to the AK. A memorandum by the joint staff planners, dated 18 August 1943, states in the language of the magician:

> It is assumed that Polish forces will continue to fight with the British and they need not be considered as sacrificed by non-support of the Polish 'Secret Army' as an organised unit. Moreover, the formation of Polish divisions and brigades can only be accomplished after the fall of Germany, at which time the existence of a formal Polish Army for the defeat of Germany would not be necessary.[52]

In this context the AK was not perceived by the Western Allies as a viable force against the Germans. Its strength was reckoned to be little more than a fifth of the number given in Polish estimates. It was calculated that to equip these 65,000 men for battle would require 500 sorties. And to what effect? It was estimated that this force so equipped could fight in isolation 'for about 20 days and its continued existence would depend on a break-through contact by other Allied forces within that time'. Moreover the Polish plan of transporting troops from Britain and the Middle East after the 'break-through contact' with the AK was turned down. It was agreed that its effect 'cannot be realised until such time as it is no longer needed'. No military justification could be found to establish a viable Polish army on Polish soil. The airlift could 'not be spared without seriously affecting other operations'. Irrespective of this, 'current intelligence digests indicate that Russia will violently oppose any army of the Poles in Poland due to the well-known Polish-Russian enmity'.[53]

The Polish plan referred to is contained in the report 'The Armed Forces and Secret Organization of Poland' made to the combined chiefs of staff (CCS) by Colonel Mitkiewicz on 17 July 1943. It based all Polish hopes on assistance to Polish forces from the Western Allies because the likelihood of Soviet assistance to the Polish Underground Army was judged by Polish political leaders as 'doubtful since the severance of diplomatic relations with Moscow and refusal on its part to enter into any political and military discussions'.[54]

The formal reply from the CCS reached London on 23 September 1943. It repeated the old arguments that: 'The Secret Army could not openly take an active part against the axis until direct land or sea contacts were immediately in prospect. There is also a lack of suitable aircraft for the delivery of large quantities of supplies to Poland.'[55]

In his conversation with Brigadier Redman of the secretariat to the CCS, to whom fell the unenviable task of breaking this news to the Poles, Colonel Mitkiewicz asked whether 'these arguments put forward were actually the main reason for the decision or whether the crux of the question lay elsewhere?' Redman agreed that 'the crux of the question was connected with the Soviet problem'.[56]

The Big Three and Poland's future frontiers, 1943

DURING 1943 the war had entered a phase of momentous victories for the Red Army. On the last day of January von Paulus surrendered at Stalingrad. By the end of July the German armies were pushed back to Kursk. The consequence of these achievements was to alter, dramatically, relations between the Big Three. Particularly important in this regard was Stalin's order of the day of 23 February 1943. He predicted that the Red Army alone would drive the Germans out of Russia, the Ukraine, Byelorussia and the Baltic States up to the western boundary of the Soviet Union. To the Polish government this suggested that the fate of Poland was increasingly open to Soviet initiatives, particularly as each Soviet military victory seemed to reduce further the will of the Western Powers to intervene on Poland's behalf.

In London it was feared that Stalin was thinking of stopping short of assisting the Allies in the final invasion of Germany. At the State Department in Washington concern was expressed at the exclusive wording of the order.[57] Stalin's apparent unilateralism required moderation; he had to be brought to the conference table. It seems that the Western Allies, no longer worried as they had been about Stalin lasting out against Hitler, were now concerned about his intentions in victory. His agreement to meet them at Teheran came as a great relief.

In preparation for this meeting, efforts were made to remove the irritations that were damaging relations within the Grand Alliance. We have referred to the strategic decisions taken at Quebec. Political issues were also examined there. The most important of these concerned the emergence of the eventual territorial settlement with regard to Poland's post-war frontiers. The idea that Poland would be compensated in the West for losses in the East was developed by Eden. Its origins can be traced back to the discussion between Bevin and Sikorski on 3 July 1941 when the relationship between a territorial settlement with Russia and Poland's western boundary was alluded to.

In Quebec Eden recorded that he and Hull had a 'brief but useful discussion about Soviet frontiers' on 23 August, and that he had given Hull a memorandum about 'probable Russian demands',[58] in which he referred to Stalin's information to the foreign secretary in December 1941, that the question of the U.S.S.R.'s western frontier was 'the main question for us in the war'.[59] Eden also told Hull that Stalin, Molotov and Maisky had all independently stated at some time between December 1941 and March 1943 that the Curzon Line with minor modifications would be a 'satisfactory basis for frontier settlement', and suggested it would be much easier to deal with the Soviets on 'Polish and other matters' if the two governments let them know that they were prepared to 'contemplate a substantial measure of satisfaction on what we understand Soviet territorial claims to be', without actually 'abandoning our principle of not recognising during the war any territorial changes'.

Eden also outlined the British government's view of what the Russians could expect, *viz.* Poland should receive Danzig, East Prussia and Upper Silesia in the west and be content in the east with the Curzon Line adjusted to include the city of Lwów in Poland. Further, there should be eventual recognition of Russia's 1941 frontiers with Finland and Romania, and of Soviet sovereignty over the Baltic States.

Eden further told Hull of exchanges of telegrams between the British prime minister and Stalin which showed that the latter sought closer consultation on future operations now that the Allies were embarked on operations which were likely to affect south-eastern Europe. He foresaw a suspicious and uncooperative Soviet attitude as likely unless the Russians received reassurances on this 'main question' of frontiers. Eden explained that the British did not wish to announce formally any understanding that might be reached with the Soviets, and suggested that they should also be asked to keep it to themselves until 'such time as it could be presented as part of a general territorial settlement'. This was because the type of publicity it could arouse from either the Soviet or the Polish side was uncertain. Eden saw this offer of satisfaction to the Soviet government on the point of frontiers as dependent on their willingness to play 'a useful part in post-war organisation as we conceive it'.

He continued his memorandum by saying that there could be no question of an actual agreement with the Soviet government on the frontier question at that stage. 'This would be contrary to the assurances we gave Poland in 1941 when the Soviet Polish Treaty was signed and again in 1942 at the time of the negotiations for an Anglo-Soviet treaty.' He proposed that the two governments should inform the Polish government that no final settlement of Polish-Soviet difficulties could be found without agreement on the frontier question. If agreement was delayed until the Soviet armies re-entered Polish territory 'it is our belief that a satisfactory solution would then be all the harder to obtain'.

Eden recognized the difficulty of Polish government acceptance of any surrender of former Polish territory but considered it might help them if the United States and United Kingdom governments were to recommend the outlined solution 'conditional on Poland receiving the compensation indicated'.[60] The Polish government was presented with this bargain on 9 September when Eden met Mikołajczyk. The British foreign secretary did not get very far with his suggestion at that time but pursued the matter again with Mikołajczyk on 5 October 1943. Eden very much wanted a positive response from the Poles. This would help him in his meeting in Moscow where the foreign ministers of the Big Three had agreed to meet prior to Teheran.

The Polish response disappointed Eden. Mikołajczyk was against the frontier issue being raised at all in the forthcoming discussion. What he wanted from the Western Allies was the fulfilment of the agreement to arm the AK and he suggested to Eden that the moment for an uprising in Poland had come. He went on to say: 'Such an action, carried out on a big scale, would require, however, a detailed understanding with the Russians and therefore the prompt re-establishment of diplomatic relations between Poland and the Soviet Union was imperative.'

Eden was greatly interested in this. Here was a suggestion which could bring a thaw to Russo-Polish relations, yet he was not hopeful that this would occur:

> I now know your point of view. You expect very much from me, but you have given me only one card up my sleeve which might be used as a trump in Moscow [the Polish diversion on a big scale]. I am not too optimistic about the prospects of my endeavours. Poland has been put on our agenda, but I do not know what can be expected from the other side. However, even in the event of failure one must keep in mind that the Moscow Conference is but a preparatory stage for the meeting of the responsible heads of government.[61]

Eden's visit to Moscow not only confirmed his pessimism as regards what could be achieved for Poland but also demonstrated his own isolation and the limitations placed upon British influence in the negotiations with his American and Russian counterparts.

A few hours before the sixth session of the tripartite conference, on 24

October 1943, Eden talked with Hull. The purpose of his call was to discuss the question of Soviet-Polish relations. The U.S. secretary of state made it clear that although his government took account of 'the large elements of Polish population in the United States' it saw Polish-Soviet relations more as 'a British problem in view of their treaty relationships'. He suggested that Eden ask Molotov 'whether he had any suggestions' on the issue.[62]

Similar lack of open American support for the British foreign secretary in his dealings with the Russians was demonstrated once again that same day at the conference table. Eden was determined to draw the Soviets into the open about their intentions in Europe. He introduced the item on the agenda dealing with agreements between major and minor allies by reminding the meeting that in June 1942 Molotov and he had agreed that, with respect to small states, it was undesirable to conclude during the war any agreements relating to the post-war period. It was their hope thus to avoid 'any scramble for special relationships with small powers'. Eden wished to forestall further agreements along the lines of the Soviet-Czech Treaty which was still in draft form, though he insisted that he was referring to a general principle.

In reply Molotov sought Hull's opinion. The U.S. secretary of state said that he had followed 'with interest and profit' the discussions on this subject but that he felt that Eden and Molotov were 'in a better position to discuss the matter'. Moreover, should they fail to reach agreement on this issue, 'there would be little value in his participating in those differences'.[63] Was the American government signalling its intention to stay clear of Anglo-Soviet disputes? Or was it perhaps saying that it would not automatically take sides with Britain against Russia? Without American support, Eden was obliged to withdraw his objection to the signature of the Soviet-Czech Treaty. Nevertheless, only two days after this rebuff, he made another attempt at checking Soviet initiatives in Europe.

Eden presented the meeting of 26 October with a proposed British draft of a Declaration on Joint Responsibility for Europe. The fourth point of this led to some discussion. It asked that the Allies would not seek to create any separate areas of responsibility in Europe and would not recognize 'such for others', but rather affirm their common interest in 'the well-being of Europe as a whole'. Eden asked Hull for his comments. The U.S. secretary of state again avoided openly supporting the British proposal. He gave as his reason that his government did not want to select any particular area or question for special consideration before the general principles were agreed on. In the absence of these he felt that he had 'little of a specific nature to add' and preferred to take his colleagues' advice on the matter.

Molotov, as over the discussion of the Soviet-Czech treaty, took the opportunity offered by Hull's reticence to press home a Soviet advantage.

He denied that his government would be interested in 'separate zones or spheres of influence' and guaranteed that there was 'no disposition on the part of the Soviet Government to divide Europe into small separate zones'. Then, in a thinly veiled reference to the federal policy of the Polish government he criticized the 'idea of planning schemes of federation at this time' and stated his government's belief that encouragement of such schemes was 'premature and even harmful'.[64] Federal plans were a major irritant to the Soviets by whom they were regarded as a *cordon sanitaire.*

This view coincided with a Foreign Office perception of Poland's federal policy that 'what the Poles really hanker for is a Scandinavian and East European *cordon sanitaire v.* Russia'.[65] Others in the Foreign Office saw in Polish claims on German territory the 'opening guns of Polish propaganda' intended to establish a negotiating position for the time when Polish frontiers were to be settled. In this light a most comprehensive statement of the Polish government's position on the matter was set out in a memorandum written by Raczynski to Eden as early as 17 December 1942. The minutes on this remark particularly on Raczynski's use of the phrase 'the Oder line' in sketching out Poland's western frontier and also on his suggested foundation of a Central European Federation as the whole basis of Polish territorial claims.[66]

Sikorski had developed both these points in speeches during his visit to the U.S. in December 1942. What alarmed Eden was that Lithuania was spoken of as a key member of Poland's proposed federation. Eden's minute on this speaks volumes: 'Sikorski is wiser than most Poles, but doesn't learn much all the same.'[67] In Moscow on 26 October 1943 Eden was careful not to link Britain with Poland's federal proposals. He was mindful of Soviet claims on Lithuania.

Towards the end of the Moscow Conference, Eden expressed his government's regrets that no diplomatic relations existed between Poland and the Soviet Union. He conveyed to Molotov the Polish government's desire to re-establish normal and friendly relations. Molotov said that this was the first the Soviet government had heard of such a desire and parried the message by referring to the Polish division on the Eastern Front which was 'fighting heroically' against the common enemy. He indicated the vital interest of Soviet Russia in the question of relations with her neighbour, Poland, and saw it as an issue that primarily concerned those two countries. He affirmed Soviet support for an independent Poland when there was a Polish government friendly towards Soviet Russia. Furthermore, when pressed for the Russian view of arming the 'Polish Secret Army' he replied that the questions of arms 'depended on the reliability of the people to whom you gave them'.[68] In the face of such opinions, Eden was hardly likely to play his 'trump card' (a Polish rising) in attempting a rapprochement between the Polish and Soviet governments.

Back in London, Eden met Mikołajczyk and other members of the Polish government on 12 November 1943. The Polish premier 'took note of the interest expressed by M. Molotov in an independent Poland', but wondered what sort of independent Poland Molotov had in mind and 'under whose domination'. The possibility of the Soviets setting up a puppet government was referred to by the two men but Eden said that this was not the impression he had gained at the Moscow talks.

What concerned Mikołajczk was that Soviet interests could perhaps be best furthered if there were no government in Poland. In this context he asked Eden 'what would become of the problem of security in the event of Soviet troops entering Polish territory? What does the British Government intend to do? What has it done in Moscow?'

'What could we do?', Eden asked in reply and went on to say that the question would be relatively simple but for the Soviet territorial claims. He pointed to the contrast with other members of the United Nations where native authorities were involved in negotiations to take over the administration and said, 'You have not allowed me to raise the territorial question according to the principle of compensation . . . I was therefore quite helpless.'[69] Asked whether the Russians had raised the frontier question, Eden replied in the negative. The Polish government was nonetheless sure that it would be raised at the impending conference at Teheran. In anticipation of this it issued, on 16 November, a formal rejection of the idea that it should renounce territory in the East for compensation in the West. Significantly, however, a different case was made informally. When Raczynski handed his memorandum to Eden he is reported as allowing that 'if, however, Poland's friends were to tell the Government that they must accept such and such a settlement in order to safeguard the future of Poland, this would create a new situation.' Moreover, four days previously in reply to Sir Orme Sargent's criticism that the Poles had prevented the Moscow Conference from dealing with the Polish Question, Raczynski said: 'We could not expect an exiled government like the Polish to take the initiative of proposing a surgical operation on the body of their country'.[70] Eden reported to the cabinet that 'it seemed that the Polish Government at last recognized that it was in their interest that a settlement should be reached on the question between Russia and Poland; but that the Polish Government might, in all the circumstances, *welcome the imposition of a settlement by the British and United States Governments*'[71] (emphasis added).

Less a surgeon than a soldier, Churchill suggested at Teheran that 'Poland might move westward, like soldiers taking two steps "left close".'[72] Stalin asked whether the changes would be made without Poland's participation and Churchill replied in the affirmative. Roosevelt said very little about Poland at Teheran. More concerned with cultivating Stalin's trust, he did nevertheless indicate his agreement though

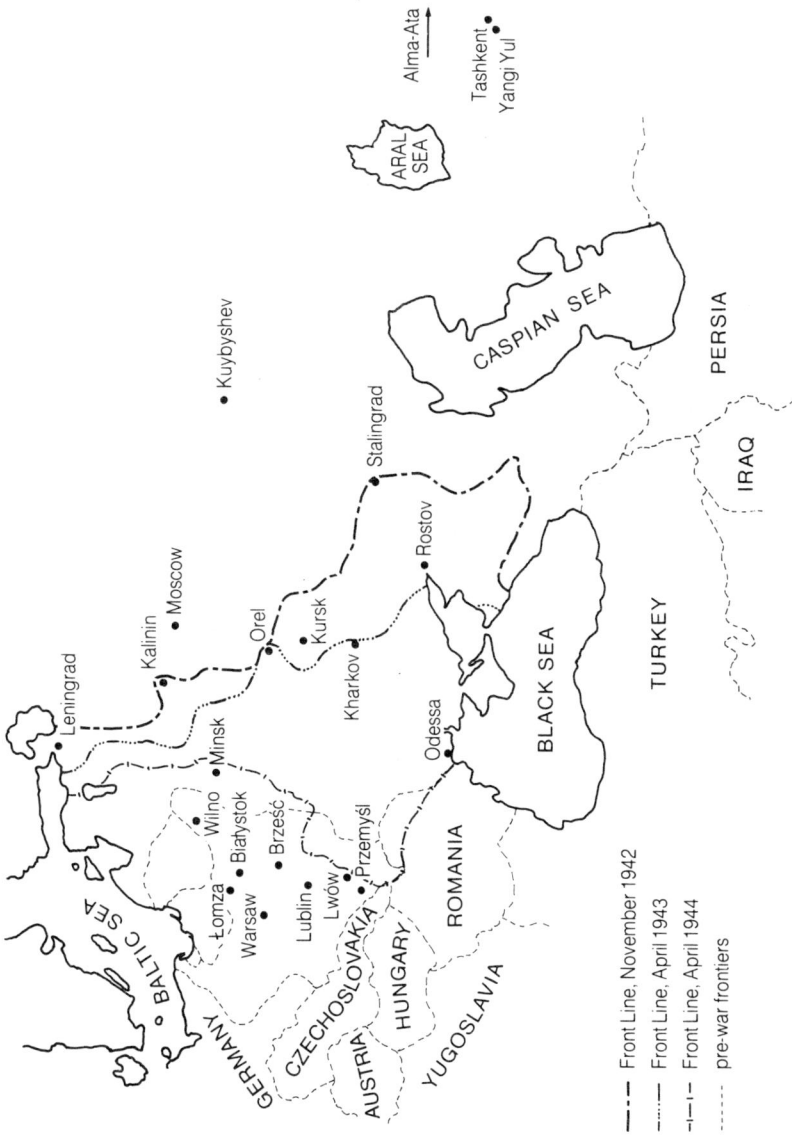

Map 3   The Eastern Fronts, 1942–4.

requesting that this be kept secret because of the presidential election to be held in 1944. The Polish vote was important to him as he freely admitted to Stalin. All three leaders recognized that a westward shift in Poland's territory was implied in the decision taken at Teheran that German territory was transferable.

The implications for Poland of the strategic and diplomatic decisions taken between August and November 1943 were of immense importance. The planned invasion of France put paid to the Polish hope that the Western Allies would 'start a Front in the Balkans' and made it clear that Poland would be liberated by the Red Army and not by the West. Moreover, by offering up Polish territory to the Soviet Union for the sake of Big Three cooperation the Western Allies conceded at Teheran that Poland's future was to be decisively influenced by Soviet interests and policies. This, at any rate, seems to have been the conclusion drawn by the Russians. As Mastny states:

> The Soviet Press and radio acclaimed the new spirit of Allied co-operation, emphasising pointedly the contrast between the emerging concern of the great powers and the 'falsely democratic attitude towards small states' which had failed to secure peace in the past. The apparent ease with which the Western Statesmen seemed ready to shed such an attitude may have astonished but otherwise only gratified Stalin. Molotov later recalled with irony and satisfaction the moment when they had unfolded their maps of Poland with the Curzon line already drawn as the future frontier. Indeed, as a Soviet diplomat privately put it, the Russians perceived the outcome of Teheran as giving them 'the right to establish friendly Governments in the neighbouring Countries'.[73]

Despite being kept in the dark about the full implications and conclusions reached at Teheran, the policy decisions of the London Poles were markedly coloured by the changed political environment. We have already shown that Sikorski had reckoned with the possibility of Poland's liberation by the Red Army. After his death on 4 July 1943 and the arrest of Grot-Rowecki by the Gestapo the development of strategy for the AK increasingly took account of this likelihood.

The 'Tempest' gamble

On 20 December 1943, the new commander of the AK in Poland, General Bor-Komorowski, issued the order for Operation Tempest. In it he accepted that the Red Army and not the Western forces would enter Poland in pursuit of the Germans. Furthermore, Tempest envisaged a situation in which the AK and the Red Army would cooperate in ejecting the Germans. An offer of working together was made by Romer in his discussions with Stalin. This willingness to cooperate was reiterated in an aide-mémoire from the Polish government to the Foreign Office, 30 December 1943:

> In view of the approaching time, when it will become necessary to issue the order for a general rising in Poland against the Germans we declare to the British Government our readiness, jointly with the participation of the Soviet Government . . . that Polish armed action should be included in the general strategic plans of the Allies.[74]

On 5 January 1944, the government issued a declaration in connection with the crossing of Poland's pre-war eastern frontier by Soviet troops. It reminded the world of the government's instructions to the underground authorities in Poland issued on 27 October 1943, *viz.*, 'to avoid all conflicts with the Soviet armies entering Poland . . . , and to enter into cooperation with the Soviet commander in the event of the resumption of Polish-Soviet relations.'[75]

In saying this they were reflecting the wishes of the British government which very much desired a resumption of relations between the Polish and Soviet governments; the headway made on the diplomatic front would otherwise lose its momentum and purpose. However, instead of agreement, Russo-Polish relations deteriorated further.

The Soviet government, noting that the London Poles had not accepted the Curzon Line, now demanded the reorganization of the Polish government itself. Churchill witnessed the fruit of his endeavours at Teheran perish in the frigid atmosphere of Russo-Polish relations and put pressure on Mikołajczyck to concede the points demanded by Stalin. He managed to get the London Poles to accept the Curzon Line as the *de facto* frontier line subject to adjustment at a peace conference and succeeded in getting them to issue new orders to the AK whereby local commanders would disclose their identity to and cooperate with the Red Army as it entered their respective districts in pursuit of German troops. He also pressed the Polish cabinet to agree to 'include among themselves none but persons fully determined to co-operate with the Soviet Union'.[76] These concessions were ignored by Stalin; on 22 January the formation of a Polish Committee of National Liberation (*Polski Komitet Wyzwolenia Narodu* – PKWN) was announced in Moscow.

Mikołajczyk responded to this impasse by travelling to Washington in search of American support for his government and its position. There he was treated with the attention due to a leading Pole in the year of the presidential election, but achieved nothing; Roosevelt was not prepared to offer the Polish government public support over its dispute with Stalin. He urged Mikołajczyk to talk matters over in person with Stalin.

Despite their diplomatic setbacks and the wide rift with the Soviet government, the London Poles pressed on with their existing policies. Their hopes were pinned on the success of Operation Tempest. If the AK were indeed to show the strength which the government believed it to possess then Poland would once more have stature sufficient to gain her a place at the negotiating table; only the AK could make up for the diplomatic disappointments of the previous months.

'Tempest' was intended to establish the London government in Poland ahead of any regime backed by the Kremlin. Despite the recent reluctance of the Western governments to back the London government, the operation gambled on their intervention on its behalf if the Red Army were to act against the AK; such Soviet behaviour in Poland would, it was hoped, re-establish the Polish government in favour with Churchill and Roosevelt and put them under moral and political pressure from their own electorate to intervene on the Poles' behalf.

'Tempest' was to present the Polish government in the best possible light. Yet, while there is evidence of some cooperation between an AK commander in Volhynia with detachments of the Red Army, 'Tempest' was never intended to herald the beginning of a new era in Russo-Polish relations. The operation's intention was to manifest through AK activity 'the existence of the Republic'. Moreover, the aim of the AK was not unreservedly to assist the Russians against the Germans. It was, as its commander Bor-Komorowski states, to give them 'minimal military help' thereby 'creating maximum political difficulties for them'.[77] As events were to show, the Russians were not deterred by the prospect of political embarrassment. In any case the Red Army had, since the spring of 1944, held such a dominant sway over the German military that the cooperation of the AK was of little consequence: Soviet territory was now clear of German troops. In May they had been ejected from the Crimea, in July from Minsk, Wilno, Lwów and Brześć. On the eighteenth day of the same month the Red Army crossed the Curzon Line. Before stopping at the Vistula it liberated Lublin and on 23 July the Polish Committee of National Liberation established itself there.

Bereft of any political or military support by the Western Allies in the face of these Communist initiatives on Polish territory Mikołajczyk had little option but to go to Moscow. There he saw Molotov on 31 July and Stalin on 3 August 1944. Both demanded of him an unambiguous acceptance of the Curzon Line as the Russo-Polish frontier. He was also advised to seek agreement with the Lublin Committee. Mikołajczyk did meet with leaders of the committee on 6 August and with Stalin again on 9 August 1944.

These negotiations were overshadowed by the Warsaw rising which broke out on 31 July.[78] Responsibility for the decision that the AK should occupy Warsaw lay with Bor-Komorowski; it had been accepted, with some reluctance, by the Polish government in London that the time and place of a general insurrection against the Germans would be at his discretion. Warsaw was chosen because an uprising in the capital city would arrest world attention whereas fighting in the countryside, as earlier phases of 'Tempest' had shown, could easily go unnoticed by Western political opinion. In General Okulicki's words:

> An effort was needed which would stir up the conscience of the world . . . and
> display our extreme goodwill to Russia, and which would even more strongly

accentuate her behaviour towards us. The battles which our units had fought . . .
could not accomplish this task.[79]

The AK hoped that a rising in Warsaw would achieve the aims set out in
Operation Tempest. The intention of the insurgents seems to have been to
capture Warsaw from the Germans and in so doing to test Soviet intentions
towards them in the full glare of the publicity that the setting of Poland's
capital would provide. This went sadly awry. As Polonsky explains:

> The plan was a gamble and it failed disastrously. The AK could only have been
> successful if the uprising had been followed quickly by the Soviet capture of
> Warsaw. Yet even as the plan was set in motion, it became clear that the Germans
> had repulsed the Soviet thrust and that the Red Army would not be able to take
> Warsaw for at least two weeks.[80]

On 9 August Stalin had told Mikołajczyk that he would drop arms to the
insurgents, but after the two weeks had elapsed he decided that Soviet
interests would best be served by doing nothing either through action by
the Red Army and other units fighting alongside or by aerial supply of the
AK by Western air forces. The latter stance raised protests in London and
Washington. But these were soon set aside for the sake of concord within
the Grand Alliance. In little more than a week after the surrender of the AK
at Warsaw (30 October 1944) Churchill, Eden and Harriman met with
Stalin in Moscow. The British foreign secretary informed Sir Orme Sargent
in a letter dated 11 October 1944 of what had been said:

> . . . Stalin was at great pains to assure the Prime Minister that failure to relieve
> Warsaw had not been due to any lack of effort by the Red Army. The failure was
> due entirely to the enemy's strength and difficulties of terrain. Marshal Stalin could
> not admit this failure before the world. . . . The Prime Minister said he accepted
> this view absolutely and he assured Marshal Stalin that no serious persons in the
> United Kingdom had credited reports that failure had been deliberate. . . . Mr.
> Harriman . . . said that the same was true of the people in America.
>
> 2.   The Prime Minister and I then sought to impress on Marshal Stalin how essential
> it was in the interests of Anglo-Soviet relations that the Polish question should now
> be settled on a basis which would seem reasonable to the British people. . . . The
> London Poles and Lublin Poles must now be told that they must agree together. If
> they refused or were unable to agree, then the British and Soviet Governments, the
> two great Allies, must themselves impose a reasonable settlement.[81]

Stalin was thus let off the hook by Churchill over the question of whether
he had deliberately withheld assistance from the rising. Erickson's view,
which backs up Polonsky's judgment with regard to the Polish gamble, is
that by 25 July Soviet forces moving forward towards the outskirts of
Warsaw had to go on the defensive. Field-Marshal Model's Panzer
divisions posed a real threat to Soviet lines of communication.[82] It would
have been consistent with Stalin's military strategy in both 1920 and in
1939 for this threat in summer 1944 to have been critical in preventing a
further Soviet landward thrust at this time.

Nevertheless more could have been done for the insurgents from the air.

Throughout August 1944 Stalin was reluctant to risk his aircraft in sorties over Warsaw. He also refused to provide facilities for British and American aircraft to drop supplies to the partisans. However, under Western pressure, well short of any threat to the 'grand' alliance, he agreed in September to Allied use of airfields in Soviet-held territory. But, as Norman Davies concludes, 'Stalin comes out of the episode with no credit. At the same time, there was little reason to expect that in the middle of the "Great Patriotic War" the Soviet Dictator should have made a generous gesture to people who were fundamentally opposed to everything he stood for.'[83]

The Moscow Conference, October 1944

TOWARDS the end of 1944, defeat of Hitler in the East by the Red Army seemed imminent. The ultimate fate of Central and Eastern Europe would then depend, above all, on Stalin's policies. Why then did the British try again to find a solution to the Polish Question? Churchill realized that Britain's influence over Stalin's policies arose, at least in part, from her relationship with Poland. In its widest context the Anglo-Polish alliance was 'symbolic of Britain's position in the struggle to defeat Hitler and conferred upon her the right to have a say in the making of the future of Europe'.[84]

The British foreign secretary had, however, witnessed new limits on British influence in the face of the positions taken respectively by America and Russia in Moscow a year earlier and these reverses had now to be rectified. At stake also was Churchill's prestige. He was determined not to allow the Polish problem to sour the moment of victory over Germany. Churchill therefore arranged for Mikołajczyk to join him in talks with Stalin in Moscow.

The Polish premier had agreed to this on condition that the proposed tripartite conference took into consideration the memorandum issued by his Council of Ministers on 29 August 1944. This described the Polish government's programme for the period following the liberation of Warsaw. It stated that representatives from the PPR would be included in the Polish government which was to 'take over the administration of the liberated lands' and to prepare for the imposition of its authority in areas to be surrendered by Germany. The PPR and the four parties represented in the Polish government in London would be given equal strength.

As to foreign affairs, the government had stated in the memorandum that its first priority was the resumption of diplomatic relations with the Soviet Union. This was to lay the foundation, after the war, of a 'durable Polish-Soviet friendship based on an alliance aiming at close political and economic collaboration between the two countries'. With regard to her eastern frontier, 'the main centres of Polish cultural life and sources of raw materials' were to be included within Polish frontiers. However, 'a final settlement of the Polish-Soviet frontier' would be decided by the new 'Constitutional Diet in accordance with Democratic principles'. Finally, the Polish armed forces would come under the authority of the Polish government acting in its capacity as a War Cabinet. It would be responsible for Polish-Soviet military collaboration. The memorandum added: 'The Polish armed forces in the Eastern Zone would come under Soviet Supreme Operational Command.'[85]

During talks with British and Soviet leaders in Moscow on 13 October 1944 Mikołajczyk made these proposals. His task of convincing the Soviet delegation of their feasibility was the more complicated because the Soviet government had, on the very day of his arrival in Moscow, recognized the PKWN as the new Polish government. Churchill suggested a way forward. A compromise between the London Poles and the PKWN was possible within the framework of Mikołajczyk's memorandum. The fact that the Polish Workers' Party was to be included among the five parties which were to form the future government did not in his view 'imply an intention to diminish the Committee's part in such a Government'.

In reply Mikołajczyk refused to accept the notion that the PKWN should, 'as one of the future principal parties' receive more than a fifth of the ministries within any new Polish government. Churchill thought otherwise. He believed it would be necessary to seek a more equal proportion between the government and the committee. Mikołajczyk disagreed with him once again, this time on the grounds that his government was recognized by Britain and America among others, whereas the committee had the backing only of the Soviet Union. He reiterated the principle in the memorandum that the new government would contain representatives of both groups in a four to one ratio in favour of the London Poles and expected on that basis to achieve recognition by 'all of the three Great Allies'. Minutes of the conversation continued: 'Churchill: So the memorandum is the best basis for discussion? Mikołajczyk: The memorandum is the best solution that we have been able to find.' Stalin did not accept this. In his opinion the Polish memorandum had two important defects which 'may make an understanding impossible'. The first was that it ignored the PKWN, who, Stalin reminded Mikołajczyk, were carrying out 'an important task in liberated Poland' and whose opinion had been influential at recent conferences of the Socialist and Peasant Parties. Stalin believed that an analysis of the situation showed that there was 'either no Government in Poland or else there are two, which amounts to the same thing'. He therefore recommended that a government should be formed on the basis of 'a compromise between the two authorities which claim to be the Government'.

Another defect of the memorandum, according to Stalin, was that it did not settle the problem of the eastern frontiers of Poland on the basis of the Curzon Line. 'If you want to have relations with the Soviet Government

you can only do it by recognizing the Curzon Line as the principle.'
Churchill followed immediately with the words: 'As regards the frontier
problems, I must declare on behalf of the British Government that the
sacrifices made by the Soviet Union in the course of the war against
Germany and its effort towards liberating Poland entitle it, in our opinion,
to a Western frontier along the Curzon Line.' He reminded Mikołajczyk
that this had been the declared British position throughout 1943 and
added: 'I also understand that the Allies will be continuing the struggle
against Germany in order to obtain, in return for the Polish concessions in
the East, an equal balance [he first said compensation and then corrected
himself] in the form of territories in the North and in the West.'[86]

Mikołajczyk was unobliging. He replied that over the question of
frontiers he was in disagreement with both Stalin and Churchill. Instead
he requested a 'generous conciliatory gesture on the part of the Soviet
Union'. In return for ceding 40 per cent of Polish territory he demanded a
'guarantee of our independence'. Stalin interrupted the Polish premier at
this point: 'Who is it that threatens the independence of Poland? Is it
perhaps the Soviet Union?' Mikołajczyk did not reply and perhaps lost an
important opportunity to expand on his fears.

Churchill now appealed to Mikołajczyk 'to make a great effort to help the
British Government in their endeavour'. The British prime minister pointed to
mutual obligations in the Anglo-Polish relationship: 'Though badly prepared,
Britain came into the war to save the Polish Nation from destruction. I think
our duty will have been fulfilled if as a result of this war a great, free,
sovereign and independent Poland arises and takes the whole nation under
her wing.' He then reiterated his position on Polish frontiers and added: 'I do
not think that in this state of affairs it would be in the interest of the Polish
Government to estrange themselves from the British Government.'[87]

A territorial settlement in line with Churchill's suggestion was entailed
in British support for the London Poles. Failure to oblige could have
resulted in a severance of relations. Mikołajczyk was faced with the stark
reality of the cost of his government's relationship with Britain. In case he
thought he could fall back on support from the United States Molotov
reminded him of the meeting at Teheran:

> I should like to add a few words about what was discussed in Teheran on the
> subject of Poland. All those who took part are here today with the exception of
> President Roosevelt . . . I can quite well remember that [he] said that he fully agreed
> to the Curzon Line and that he considered it to be a just frontier between Poland
> and the Soviet Union . . . we can therefore draw the conclusion that the Curzon
> Line does not only correspond with the attitude of the Soviet Government but it
> also has the concurrence of all of the three Great Powers.[88]

This was the first Mikołajczyk had heard of Roosevelt's acquiescence. He
simply asked: And may I learn what was decided in Teheran with regard
to the Western frontiers of Poland?

Molotov: The opinion was that the line of the Oder was just. I do not remember anyone objecting.

Churchill: I also agreed.

Eden: The formula in Teheran was that the new frontier of Poland in the West would go as far towards the Oder as the Poles would wish. (All concur).

Churchill: In East Prussia, the territories earmarked for Poland extend to the West and South of Konigsberg. Would *a new United Polish Government* [emphasis added] accept the Curzon Line, on these conditions, as the *de facto* Eastern frontier, with the reservation that the matter will be settled finally at the Peace Conference? I must add that I have not yet had the opportunity to discuss this suggestion with the Soviet Government.

Mikołajczyk: I have no authority to make such a declaration.

Churchill: I have not in mind a solemn declaration but 'a working formula'.[89]

But Stalin insisted upon something more definite. 'In order that the whole matter may be quite clear and that there may be no doubts I want to state categorically that the Soviet Union cannot accept Premier Churchill's formula concerning the Curzon Line.' (At this point the minutes record Churchill making a gesture of disappointment and helplessness.) 'I must add the following correction . . . to this formula: The Curzon Line must be accepted as the future Polish-Soviet frontier . . . I repeat once more: The Curzon Line as the basis of the frontier.'[90] Mikołajczyk asked Stalin whether the Curzon Line was identical with 'the demarcation line introduced in 1939?' Stalin ended the conference by replying: 'No, not by any means. The Curzon Line gives you Białystok, Łomza and Przemyśl.'[91]

Mikołajczyk's resignation

THE Polish prime minister spent a sleepless night, 13/14 October 1944. The conference had been a shocking affair for him. It undermined the credibility of his policies and thus the tenability of his position and that of the Polish government. He now realized that the Curzon Line would have to be accepted though he did not say so at the time. Knowledge of the decisions on this taken at Teheran negated assurances given in the past that territorial changes which took place during the war would not be recognized. Even more worrying to him was the demand for a fusion of 'the legitimate Polish Government' with that created by the Soviets. He saw in this a renunciation of the legal basis of the existence of the Polish government and hence of the continuity of constitutional authority in liberated Poland. He foresaw a future in which all 'ensuing acts would be imposed on the people of Poland in the presence of the Red Army and the NKVD'. Poland would thus lose her eastern lands and 'in the remainder of her territory, Poland's independence would be effaced by the rule of agents of the Comintern in Poland'. He concluded that the Polish government was expected to 'commit suicide of its own volition'.[92]

Mikołajczyk had talks with Churchill the next morning. The British prime minister urged his Polish counterpart to accept Stalin's demands. 'Everything hinges on one thing: the eastern frontier of Poland. If this is settled and announced, in one or two sentences, then agreement can be reached easily.' He foresaw irreparable damage to the fortunes of Poland if the chance of agreement were to be lost that day as it had been in January. This, he pointed out, had made matters worse. Now there was the PKWN who were going to be a 'frightful nuisance'. They would build up a rival government which would gradually take over authority in Poland. He warned that fighting would begin with the Russians siding with the rival government and that they would have a victorious army behind them. He urged Mikołajczyk to go to Poland to form a united government there and to separate himself from the hope of General Anders that after the defeat of Germany the Russians would then be beaten. To Churchill this seemed crazy.

> You cannot defeat the Russians. I beg you to settle upon the frontier question. You must take responsibilities. If you reach a formula with me I'll go to Stalin at 4 p.m. . . . If you agree on the frontier then the Russians will withdraw their support from the Committee. When I criticized the Lublin Poles last night Stalin on many occasions supported me. You are really dealing with Russia. . . . What does it matter supposing you lose the support of some of the Poles? Think what you will gain in return! Ambassadors will come. The British Ambassador will be with you. The Americans will have an Ambassador. The greatest Military Power in the world. You must do this. If you miss this moment everything will be lost.[93]

Mikołajczyk replied that to ratify the decision taken at Teheran was to sign a death sentence against himself. Angered, Churchill barked back that he was washing his hands of Mikołajczyk and was not going to 'wreck the peace of Europe because of quarrels between Poles'. He claimed that Britain was again preserving Poland from disappearance, 'but you will not play. You are absolutely crazy.' He repeated his warning that unless Mikołajczyk accept the frontier 'you are out of business for ever. The Russians will sweep through your country and your people will be liquidated. You are on the verge of annihilation.' Mikołajczyk then suggested that the three Great Powers should proclaim that they had decided on the frontiers of Poland without Polish assent. This is an interesting idea which suggests that Mikołajczyk, like Raczynski, wanted an imposed settlement. But Churchill did not oblige and became increasingly annoyed as the argument continued that afternoon and Mikołajczyk again insisted that he could not accept the Curzon Line as a frontier. Churchill exploded: 'You are no Government if you are incapable of taking any decision. You are a callous people who want to wreck Europe. I shall leave you to your own troubles. You have no sense of responsibility when you want to abandon your people at home, to whose sufferings you are indifferent. You do not care about the future of Europe, you have only your own miserable interest in mind. I will have to call on the other Poles and this Lublin Government may function very well. *It will be the Government'* (emphasis in the original). He refused to repeat to Stalin Mikołajczyk's suggestion that he should present his declaration as his own proposal in response to which the Polish government would confine itself to a purely formal protest and he cast doubt on whether the British government would continue to recognize the London Poles. He declared with passion that Great Britain was powerless in the face of Russia and repeatedly warned that Polish hatred of Russia was not the basis on which Mikołajczyk should decide Polish policy.[94]

Despite Churchill's suggestion to the contrary, Mikołajczyk returned to London to consult with his colleagues there. However, he found it impossible to persuade them to accept what was demanded of them. Only the Peasant Party was prepared even to consider this. On 2 November, Mikołajczyk told Churchill that he was facing strong objections as regards the solution proposed in Moscow. Barely able to contain his anger, Churchill responded 'let the Lublin Poles remain in control of Polish affairs. . . . So far as I am concerned I have done everything possible, I tried to persuade Stalin and I convinced him of the necessity of coming to terms with Poland. Today you might have been again in Moscow, with success at hand and, instead, you stay here, quite helpless.' It looked to Churchill as though Mikołajczyk had 'lost his bearings' and was 'stricken with paralysis', and he concluded, 'I have had enough of this and I withdraw my promises'.[95]

American support for Poland with respect to demands made at Moscow was, at a distance, more sympathetic. Yet, in a letter to Mikołajczyk, Roosevelt did not support the Polish case against the Curzon Line. However, he had instructed Harriman to intervene in Moscow on Mikołajczyk's behalf in the question of leaving 'Lwów and the oil district with Poland if Mikołajczyk confirmed that the Polish Government wished this at present'.[96]

On 24 November Mikołajczyk resigned. Nothing less than public Anglo-American guarantees of support of the Polish government's position against Stalin's demands would have prevented his doing so. As he explained to Winant, the U.S. ambassador to London, he could not take advantage of Roosevelt's offer to intervene with Stalin regarding the oil areas of Galicia and Lwów 'in as much as he was not able in any event to obtain the support of his own Government to the general boundary settlement which had been proposed by the Soviets'.[97]

The liberators who never were

DESPITE Mikołajczyk's ambition to take power in Poland he lacked the authority of his predecessor General Sikorski, which might have kept him in power in London, and felt he had no option but to resign. In doing so he was at least, as we shall see, free to play a role in Warsaw without the burden of premiership in exile round his shoulders. To Cadogan and others in London, Mikołajczyk's resignation meant 'the end of those silly Poles'.[98] Moreover, though recognition of the Government-in-Exile was not withdrawn by the Western Powers until July 1945, few in the West would have contradicted Stalin's view, expressed to Churchill on 8 December 1944, that 'Ministerial changes in the émigré Government no longer deserve serious attention.'[99]

The November 1944 crisis in effect eliminated everyone opposed to the settlement with Russia from further influence on events. This turning point in the affairs of the London Poles raises a number of questions. Why was the Government-in-Exile unable to salvage something from the difficult situation in which it found itself? And what was it that compelled it to intransigence so stubborn that it rendered itself politically impotent?

There is firstly the romantic view of Polish history to contend with. The belief in the value of heroic gestures rather than in a search for compromise did colour the policies of the London Poles. Moreover, it is difficult not to charge them with being unrealistic. Yet theirs was the generation which had witnessed the resurrection of Poland with little recourse to meaningful negotiations or political compromise. Appeals to the Polish government to face the facts of the situation in which it found itself at the end of 1943 could draw little response from men nurtured on nationalistic ideals founded on the concepts of courage and honour perhaps outside the experience of the western world in which Poland sought her place. Certainly the Polish perception of the justness of the Polish cause *vis-à-vis* Soviet Russia was not shared by the Western Allies during the Second World War.

They advised rapprochement with the Soviet Union to the heirs of an historical heritage in which this was anathema. The Russo-Polish treaty of non-aggression of 1932 and the Russo-Polish treaty of 1941 cut across deeply ingrained sentiment. The first must be seen in the context of the diplomatic language peculiar to the interwar years; non-aggression meant that each party to the treaty reserved the right to future aggression. For each the war of 1920 was a reality whose lessons would not be forgotten. The second was the fruit of Sikorski's political understanding and man-oeuvres and he took rapprochement with the Soviet Union to its very limits, in the belief that the military outcomes would once more favour Poland.

Mikołajczyk lacked faith in such calculations. His policy relied on thinking which went beyond the conceptual limits of the majority of his colleagues and he was unable to promote in them the changes in attitudes which he had undergone and which were required of his government by their allies. In his search for agreement with the Soviet Union he eventually came to accept Roosevelt's advice that this would require 'concessions on matters of prestige', a euphemistic reference to an erosion of sovereignty far beyond the pale in his colleagues' view.

The London Poles were victims of their status. As members of a Government-in-Exile they felt bound by the very constitutional and diplomatic obligations to which the government owed its existence. This left them in a dilemma portrayed by Raczynski in September 1941 as the impossible situation between 'the Scylla of the Atlantic declaration and the Charybdis of the Russo-Polish Treaty'.[100] It was recognized that the demographic changes wrought by Soviet policy in eastern Poland would affect local opinion in regard to the final configuration of the Russo-Polish frontier but, even assuming strict adherence to the second principle of the Atlantic declaration (no territorial adjustment without the consent of the inhabitants), the government felt it could not make concessions to the Soviets which in its view not only contrary to the interests of the Polish State but also contrary to the wishes of the overwhelming majority in Poland.

The Soviet threat to Poland's future was perceived by the London Poles as being even greater than that of the Nazis. Moreover, there was for them no comfort in a distinction that was drawn in the Foreign Office between the Russians and Germans in Poland in 1941: 'The Russians are concerned primarily to destroy not a national but a social order.'[101] All Polish émigrés in London would have qualified under Soviet policies then prevailing for deportation to 'the dark side of the Moon'.[102]

What worried Raczynski most about eastern Poland was the lack of a guarantee of Poland's frontier with Russia. Such a guarantee was ruled out by definition under the principles of the Atlantic Charter, and was an important omission from the Polish-Soviet Treaty of 1941. This Treaty was, as we have shown, significantly shaped by Anglo-Polish relations, in which context ambiguity existed in Polish minds over the meaning of British assurances as regards Polish frontiers. Churchill was, however, consistent in the view that 'we ourselves have never in the past guaranteed, on behalf of His Majesty's Government any particular frontier line to Poland'.[103]

The Polish government was in a trap, escape from which was possible only if the Western Allies, in good time, came to adopt the Polish perception of Soviet intentions in Europe. This hope was entertained by Kulski, legal counsellor at the Polish Embassy in London, in a conversation minuted by Gladwyn Jebb of the Foreign Office. He said that Kulski, 'like so many of his compatriots' thought that it 'may well be an aim of Soviet policy to occcupy the whole of Europe up to the Elbe and establish Soviet Republics in the existing States in Eastern and South Eastern Europe'. Kulski believed that the eastern frontier of Poland 'was not really the critical question, which was whether or not the Bolsheviks wanted to have a Sovietized Government in Warsaw'. He thought the 'best approach for Poland was a "wait and see" policy: Russia after all might be so weakened by the war that she would not represent a great force at the end of it as some people expected'.[104] This remained the false hope of the London Poles up to and after Mikołajczyk's resignation.

British policy with regard to Russia was also consistent, though more realistic. Indeed it is perhaps a worthy example of Morton's fork: Russian defeats had made it all the more necessary to placate Russia; Russian victories made it all the less possible to resist Russian demands. Moreover, as Jebb said to Kulski, there was 'no knowing what Soviet policy would turn out to be' and 'much would depend on where Soviet forces were at the end of the war'. He did not think that such a policy as envisaged by Kulski would necessarily be pursued by the Russians. He suggested that, on the contrary, if they should be convinced that 'both we and the Americans were firmly committed to hold Germany down in co-operation with them, they – [the Soviets] might come in time to see that their own interests would best be served by the maintenance of independent States in Eastern and South-Eastern Europe provided always that those States did not pursue an anti-Soviet line.' Kulski conceded that it should be possible to come to a reasonable arrangement with the Soviets. However, it all depended 'whether a Western drive by the Soviet Union would be likely to take place under the influence of fear or as a result of an imperialistic urge'. He suggested that 'the only force which counted today in Russia was patriotism and it might well be that patriotic elements in the Russian Army would insist on an imperialistic policy after the war'. Jebb told Kulski that he could only hope that his vision would not become a reality and that he genuinely believed that 'if Russia was treated as a sort of outcast it would then be more likely to happen than otherwise'.[105]

It is in this spirit that both the U.S. and the U.K. approached the Soviet Union in the conferences of the Big Three at Teheran, Yalta and Potsdam. Following Yalta Mikołajczyk accepted the decisions with regard to Poland. Territorially, Poland's eastern frontiers were to follow the Curzon Line 'with adjustments in some regions of 5–8 Kms. in favour of Poland'. Though Poland lost Lwów at Potsdam, she was compensated for these losses by being given a western frontier on the Oder and Western Neisse (see map 4). Stalin achieved the territorial settlement he desired. In Polonsky's words: 'The Polish Question which had been the subject of so much bitter controversy, was thus finally resolved by an agreed settlement.'[106]

Where did this leave the Poles? The answer to that question is offered in Part Two, though as far as the London Poles are concerned, 'it is almost an article of faith that one day Yalta will be undone'.[107]

PART TWO

THE STRUGGLE FOR POWER IN POLAND AND THE ESTABLISHMENT OF COMMUNIST RULE

5   From the KPP to Lublin

ABOUT 1 a.m. on 28 December 1941 six parachutists landed in fields in Wiazowna, near Warsaw. Despite the loss of a radio transmitter and the awkward fall of its leader, Marceli Nowotko, who broke his leg, the First Initiative Group of the Polish Workers' Party (*Polska Partia Robotnicza* – PPR) landed undetected. A week later in a sympathizer's flat in Żoliborz, a suburb of the capital, the party was formally established.[1] Some three years after Stalin's purge and disbandment of the Communist Party of Poland (*Komunistyczna Partia Polski* – KPP) in 1938, the Polish Communists once more had a political vehicle which enjoyed Soviet confidence.

In several respects circumstances seemed to favour the new party's growth. Uneasy though their alliance was, Poland and the Soviet Union were linked in the common struggle against Nazi Germany and, as we have seen, it became apparent that the Red Army and not the Western Powers would drive the Germans from Polish territory. For the first time in their history the Communists were able to combine their loyalty to the Soviets with Polish national interests and sentiments. This opportunity was enhanced by the ideological flexibility and lack of dogmatism which characterized the political line of the Soviet Union and the international Communist movement from 1941 until the late 1940s. Secondly, the interwar regime had been destroyed by Poland's crushing defeat in 1939. The Government-in-Exile had the support of all Poland's major political parties and the great majority of the population in Poland but, as Part One has shown, its distance from Poland and its dependence on the Western Powers, which placed higher priority on peaceful relations with the Soviet Union, were ultimately to prove fatal disadvantages in the struggle for power in post-war Poland.[2] Thirdly, as elsewhere in Europe, the experience of war and occupation weakened traditional allegiances and radicalized important sections of the population.[3] The Communists were optimistic that they could achieve a new and broad appeal based on the yearning of the Polish nation for liberation and the popular desire for radical reform and reconstruction. The Communists believed that the prestige and unity of Poland's wartime underground state, which had the support of almost all political groupings from far Left to far Right, would crumble as the end of the German occupation approached and conflicts of class interest heightened. In this situation the party would be able to win allies on the Left and

Centre and isolate its diehard opponents. The PPR would thereby avoid the political isolation and eventual fate of the KPP. Such was the thinking behind the strategy of the national front which, following long discussions in Comintern circles prior to its departure, the 'Initiative Group' placed at the core of the new party's outlook.

However, the two-and-a-half years from its formation until its assumption of power in Lublin in July 1944 were years of failure as far as the party's strategy was concerned. The premises on which the national front strategy was based were correct only in broad geopolitical terms, that is in relation to Poland's likely place in the post-war international order. Domestically, its assumptions proved false. The party was quite unable to escape the legacy of the KPP. It had very little success in harnessing radical forces or placing itself at the head of the struggle for national liberation. It was unable to expand much beyond the political base of the pre-war Communist movement, while the underground camp remained solidly united in its hostility to the PPR and had little difficulty in keeping it isolated. The prestige of the traditional political forces remained high, while anti-Soviet feeling, projected on to the PPR, did not abate but was fuelled by such factors as the revelation of the Katyn massacres in 1943[4] and the Soviet claim to much of pre-war eastern Poland. In sum, the fundamental weakness of the Communist movement within Polish society remained a constant between 1942 and 1944 while the military victory of the Soviet Union over Germany propelled it into government.

The movement was separated into two far-flung sections: the circle in Soviet emigration and the clandestine PPR in Poland itself. The failure of the PPR in Poland was not shared by the Polish Communists in the U.S.S.R., who had considerable success in enlisting the cooperation of the Polish emigration in the U.S.S.R. which had no other route to return to Poland and was able to participate in the Soviet victories of 1943–4. Strongly influenced by Soviet foreign policy requirements, the leading Communist group adhered closely to the national front strategy worked out in 1941. They attributed the difficulties encountered in its domestic application to what they saw as the ineptitude and sectarianism of the underground party rather than to any objective obstacles. In contrast the PPR was preoccupied with these obstacles and convinced of the need to modify the national front strategy to meet them. The original line of 1941: 'the national front without traitors and capitulators' had by 1943 reached a complete impasse. For many months during 1943 the underground leadership seemed directionless until at the end of the year, largely on its own initiative, it adopted a more radical 'democratic national front' and set up its own political centre, the Homeland National Council. This did not solve the problem. The Council won almost no support beyond the party itself and its formation generated a sharp, three-way debate amongst the Communists over strategy which persisted right up to the moment of liberation in July

1944. It would be no exaggeration to say that the path of the PPR from its foundation to power coincided with the steady erosion of its political strategy by internal realities.

The KPP legacy

THE KPP – the Communist Party of Poland – was formed in 1918 when the Social Democracy of the Kingdom of Poland and Lithuania (*Socjaldemokracja Królestwa Polskiego i Litwy* – SDKPiL) merged with elements from the left of the Polish Socialist Party. The KPP existed for two decades until 1938 when the Comintern, claiming that the KPP had been overrun by 'provocateurs', disbanded the party, and much of its leadership and *aktyw* fell victim to Stalin's Great Purge.[5] The PPR specifically disassociated itself from what were seen as the errors and false traditions of its predecessor. In 1947 Gomułka affirmed that 'it would be incorrect to define the PPR as a communist party. We are not a continuation of the former Communist Party of Poland. The first Congress of our Party confirmed that "the Polish Workers' Party is a new party. . .".'[6]

However, especially during the war, the legacy of the KPP weighed heavily on the PPR.[7] This inheritance had its root in long years of mutual rejection. On the one hand, for much of its existence the KPP had been at war not only with the Polish State, but with its entire body politic, including the legal opposition parties of the Left. On the other hand, in the eyes of the great majority of Poles, the KPP was a foreign, subversive agency of Moscow, bent on the destruction of Poland's hard-won independence and the incorporation of Poland into the Soviet Union. Labelled a 'Soviet agency' or the 'Jew-Commune', it was viewed as a dangerous and fundamentally un-Polish conspiracy dedicated to undermining national sovereignty and restoring, in a new guise, Russian domination.[8]

The KPP for most of its existence had little in common with those mass Communist Parties which operated in the open elsewhere in Europe. From its earliest days the KPP had been illegal. Party activists often spent more time in prison than at liberty. In 1932 when government repression was fierce, over 10,000 people were detained and nearly 7,000 were put under arrest for Communist activities.[9] Amongst the future leadership of the PPR, Bierut was imprisoned for six years, Gomułka for seven, Jóźwiak and Aleksander Zawadzki each for eleven.[10] The party operated underground. Much of its elite resided abroad permanently and congresses were normally held outside Poland. Party officials led an undercover existence with false identities and constant changes of address, ever-wary of informers and infiltration. Government repression prevented any true test of the party's electoral appeal. However even in its best year, 1928, when the KPP 'fronts' polled respectively in Lodz, Warsaw and the Silesian coalfield, its vote amounted to only 2.5 per cent of the total, very much less than its neighbouring German and Czech counterparts.[11]

Membership data bring out more vividly the narrow base of the KPP. Kowalski has estimated that the membership of the KPP in 1935 was between 7,400 and 8,200.[12] Membership in the 1920s had been less – about 3,500 in 1928–9.[13] Of the 1935 membership total, approximately a quarter were Jewish and no more than about 1,500 were factory workers.[14] Although the Ukrainian, White Russian and youth sections of the party supplemented its strength, these figures indicate clearly its failure to win mass support amongst the Polish population.

The other side of the party's isolation was the way in which the Communists distanced themselves from the political institutions and forces of the Polish Second Republic. This sprang to a large degree from the ideological stance of the party, its analysis of Poland's likely revolutionary development and its attitude to Polish statehood.

The KPP did not pursue the moderate and gradualist line adopted later by the PPR. Only in 1922–3 at the time of the Second Congress of the KPP, and again from 1934–5 when the anti-Fascist 'popular front' was adopted by the international movement did the KPP seek to construct alliances with parties from the mainstream of Polish politics. Even so, significant sections of the rank and file appear to have been unreceptive to calls by the leadership for moderation during these intervals.[15] For the most part, the KPP pursued a radical, ultra-Leftist line which Gomułka later described as its 'abstract revolutionism'.[16] This assumed that the Polish revolution would not be generated from within, but would follow a revolution spilling across the whole of Europe from the Soviet Union or Germany. In Poland it would take a classic Bolshevik course. Armed insurrection would be followed by the dictatorship of the proletariat, exercised by a tightly-disciplined, leninist cadre-party, the KPP, through councils of workers, peasants and soldiers. The revolutionary party would dismantle the bourgeois state and commence the construction of a Socialist state directly, without any transitional stages. The internal class-basis of the revolution would be the proletariat, poor peasants and oppressed national minorities. The KPP considered that collaboration with the bourgeois parties and particularly with the parliamentary Left (the Socialists and Peasant Party) was superfluous and would weaken the revolutionary commitment of the masses. In 1918–21, 1924–5 and 1929–34 the European revolution was judged imminent. Accordingly, party activity was not aimed at cultivating wide support inside Poland. Instead, it gave priority to preparations for the seizure of power. Attempts were made to arouse the working class through militant strike tactics and the national minorities through terrorist attacks on the Polish authorities and maximum support was given to the international movement.[17] The priority the KPP gave to furthering the international revolution and, in particular, to assisting the much larger

Communist Party of Germany, led the KPP to support the demands of the German minority in Poland. This may or may not have assisted the German Communists, but it was certainly highly damaging to the position of the KPP within Poland.[18]

In this scheme activity within the bourgeois state or in alliance with the mainstream parties could take place only on a temporary, tactical basis, when the prospect of the international revolution had for the moment receded and when it was felt that the bourgeois Right or Fascism constituted a real threat to the Soviet Union and the Communist movement. In such circumstances the use of defensive tactics, including support for non-Communist democratic opposition, was regarded as justified. It was such argumentation which led to the KPP lending Piłsudski its support in 1926 at the time of his coup against the Right-wing Peasant-Christian national government, a move which was rapidly condemned as the 'May Error'.[19] At no point, however, did the KPP abandon its detachment from the Polish political system to work within it for an internally-based revolution.

Closely related to the party's ultra-Leftism was its position on the 'national question', the matter of Polish statehood. Apart from its brief periods of moderation in 1922–3 and the later 1930s, the KPP, in Gomułka's words, adopted a position on Polish independence 'which did not even arouse any doubts, since it stood either for the organic integration of Poland as a soviet republic into the Union of Soviet Republics, or put forward the slogan of an independent Soviet Poland, stating at the same time that "for the KPP there can be no defence of the independence of bourgeois Poland".'[20] This open hostility to Polish statehood was a huge handicap in winning the support of a strongly nationalistic population which had only very recently recovered a precarious independence after more than a century of foreign domination. Nationalism was a force amongst the working class as much as any other stratum. In consequence, the influence of the Communists amongst organized labour trailed behind that of the Socialists, the National and Catholic workers' movements and even the *Sanacja*.[21]

During its early years, especially, the position of the KPP on the national question was strongly influenced by the revolutionary internationalism of the old SDKPiL. In 1920, during the Bolshevik advance on Warsaw, the Communists had formed a revolutionary government in Białystok and gave active support to the invading Red Army.[22] During this period the party's position was defined in the most uncompromising internationalist terms. One of its declarations stated that 'for the international camp of social revolution there can be no question of frontiers'.[23] In later years it was less the 'Luxemburgist heritage' of the SDKPiL than the party's subordination to the Comintern and Soviet foreign policy which accounted for its anti-national stance. This un-Polishness was self-reinforcing. Because of its unattractiveness to the Polish population and Polish parties, the KPP turned instead towards the national minorities. The disproportionate number of Jews amongst its membership and even more amongst its leadership was one reflection of this.[24] Another was the party's relative success in winning support within the Ukrainian and White Russian communities in the 1920s.

In practice the party's internationalism took the form of unquestioning loyalty to the Soviet Union. Though the leadership struggle in Moscow during the 1920s was reflected in the faction fights inside the KPP, this did not undermine the party's enthusiasm for the first Socialist state. However, Stalin's purge and disbandment of the KPP was a great trauma for the survivors. For some, like Gomułka, who had deep reservations about the character and line of the KPP, it confirmed the importance of a fresh start with a more nationally-based party which would be less dependent on the Soviet Union. Others, with deeper attachments to the KPP, did not revise their ideological outlook fundamentally and seem to have drawn the conclusion that Polish Communism must rehabilitate itself, avoid the disunity which had plagued it between the wars and regain Stalin's confidence.[25]

Some features of the KPP inheritance were more in evidence in later years when the PPR had already come to power, but three were felt deeply during the years of the occupation. The first was the persistence of the solid front of the entire political spectrum against the Communists. Even in 1942–3 when the Polish and Soviet governments maintained diplomatic relations with one another and the PPR platform was at its most moderate, the party was unable to gain the trust of any significant section of the underground camp, not least of its far Left. Efforts to form alliances with other groupings, whether with the leaders or the rank and file, produced almost no result right up to mid-1944. The PPR at no stage came near to emulating the success of the Czech Communists who were able to build on their pre-war role within the Czech political system to enter and play a major part in the wartime anti-German coalition. The second factor was the continuing narrowness of the Communists' base. Because of its lack of popular support the party was unable to command the attention of the underground state. Nor could it follow Tito's example by creating an alternative underground movement capable of supplanting that of the bourgeois parties. Despite its claims to be a new party and its national slogans, KPP veterans and sympathizers provided the bulk of PPR cadres.[26] In January 1943 its membership was said to be 8,000,[27] about the same as the KPP. Its estimated strength of 20,000 in mid-1944[28] was clearly of a very different order from that of the 'London' underground with its 350,000 Home Army troops,[29] although both claims should be treated cautiously. Partly because of its continuing isolation and weakness, the PPR displayed a third characteristic of the KPP – its sectarianism and disunity. This took the form of a persistent lack of consensus on the nature of the national front line. While some saw it as a radical departure from the strategic thinking of the KPP, others viewed it rather as a tactical variation on the old line, necessitated by international circumstances. Rank and file distaste for the liberalism of the new line and disputes in the leadership over how to implement it reflected this divergence.

'The national front without traitors and capitulators'

FOLLOWING the German invasion of the U.S.S.R. in June 1941, the Comintern rapidly abandoned its assessment of the war as a conflict between rival imperialisms and harmonized its line with the Soviet Union's new international alliances. The formula of the 'anti-Hitlerite national front' was adopted and, regardless of the PPR's formal independence of the Comintern, this line was adopted during the second half of 1941 as they prepared the party's launch.[30] The national front strategy in this, its broadest form, was maintained until 1943 in Poland and amongst the Soviet emigration in essence right up to liberation in 1944.

The strategy had two aspects. First it accepted the political structure and leadership of the underground state and the Government-in-Exile and attempted to gain entry to this coalition as an equal partner alongside the four other major parties. At this stage the Communists seem to have hoped to form a powerful and united working-class party including the Socialists,[31] which would play a prominent rather than a dominant role in the coalition. The formula employed was that 'a united and coherent working-class' would 'fight in the front ranks' of the underground movement.[32] Second, it aimed at constructing a coalition 'from below' around a platform of active armed struggle against the Germans. From the first weeks of its existence the PPR began to organize guerrilla units at a time when 'London' for tactical reasons avoided offensive measures of this kind. To capitalize on the grassroots support it was thought the guerrillas would generate, the party set up a network of 'National Committees of Struggle' (*Narodowe Komitety Walki*).

In both its aspects the 'national front without traitors and capitulators' failed abjectly and illustrated how far the Communists had exaggerated the factors working in their favour and wildly underestimated the problems they faced in winning support and overcoming the hostility of the mainstream parties. Although talks were held in February 1943 between the PPR and representatives of the leadership of the 'London' underground they only served to demonstrate how unbridgeable was the gap between the two sides and how widespread the opposition within the London camp to collaboration with the Communists, even of the most limited kind.[33] For 'London' the PPR was a political nuisance to be neutralized and isolated. Its patriotism was never taken seriously and it lacked the military or organizational strength to attract interest as a potential partner. Reporting in 1944 to the Moscow Poles, Spychalski admitted that 'the first attempts of the PPR to achieve a national front in struggle with the occupant produced almost no result. Quite simply, all the parties felt so strong in comparison with our movement that they did not consider opening negotiations with our party expedient.'[34]

Attempts to create a united working-class party fell on stony ground. The strongest political organization amongst the working class was 'Freedom, Equality, Independence' (*Wolność, Równość, Niepodległość*), known as WRN. The majority of active members of the pre-war Polish Socialist Party supported WRN which continued the adamant hostility to the Communists of its predecessor. Although modern Warsaw historians stress the significance of the Left-wing Socialists who remained outside WRN and formed the Organization of Polish Socialists (*Organizacja Polskich Socjalistów* – PS), one has admitted that the Left 'was at this time so weak that it could only dream of substantial influence amongst the working-class'.[35] Besides, even the Organization of Polish Socialists did not accept the PPR as a genuinely Polish party. At its 1942 Congress it defined its attitude thus: 'In relation to the PPR which is a new form of communist organisation in our country, the PS do not have confidence in the sincerity of its ideological platform, or in the autonomy of its political line and do not see the possibility of its participation in the democratic understanding.'[36] It was only after a succession of splits that the PPR succeeded in winning over a small splinter of sympathizers from the Socialist Left at the turn of 1943–4.

The campaign to build up popular support 'from below' around the guerrilla units was equally fruitless. The Communists' lack of local support, particularly in the more remote rural areas suited to guerrilla warfare, severely hindered the PPR's military plans.[37] As a modern party historian has observed, 'in spite of great efforts . . . the National Committees of Struggle failed to develop extensively in the terrain and in reality did not get beyond a conception of activity. A variety of reasons accounted for this . . . the weakness of the Party's own organisation, which was just in its initial period of activity, the effectiveness of the counter-action of the London underground as well as the unfavourable situation on the eastern front.'[38]

Instead of rapidly gaining influence within the underground movement as it had expected, the PPR leadership soon became embroiled in internal disputes. Party historians are divided over the extent of sectarianism amongst the KPP militants recruited into the PPR, but it is plain that the leadership did encounter resistance to the new line in some quarters.[39] Objections which had been raised already in the preliminary discussions on the new party programme among the Polish Communists in the Soviet Union recurred. For some the new line was too minimalist and retreated too far from that of the KPP.[40] Ideological considerations were behind disagreement over the party's name. Those who wished to stress its broad base preferred the label 'Polish Worker-Peasant Party'; those on the internationalist wing of the movement considered 'Workers Party *of Poland*' more appropriate than *Polish* Workers' Party.[41] Some ex-KPP activists would have nothing to do with the PPR, objecting to its 'non-class' character and the absence of public endorsement by the Comintern. Others demanded explicit commitment to Socialism.[42] Despite the attention the leadership gave to reassuring such doubters[43] the criticism continued. In July 1942, a full seven months after the party had been established, Nowotko reported to Dimitrov that 'the greatest difficulty is to break the sectarian frame of mind, especially among former members of the KPP, for whom everyone who is not a communist is an enemy', and went on to complain about the party's inability to broaden its base and national composition.[44] In late 1942 and into 1943 London intelligence reports pointed to continued internal divergences in the party where 'once again to a marked extent disputes between the leadership of the PPR and KPP *aktyw* have appeared'.[45] In January 1943 the Central Committee felt the need to warn its members: 'Every group/faction: this is the influence of alien class elements on the party; it is the disruption of the party . . . we must strengthen order and intra-party discipline.'[46]

This warning may have been a reference to events within the leadership itself which in late 1942 took a dramatic turn. Against the background of strains between the political (Nowotko) and military (B. Mołojec) chiefs of the party which had been evident as early as 1941,[47] and a wave of arrests by the Gestapo which extended to their respective families and intensified mutual suspicions, on 28 November Nowotko was murdered on the orders of Mołojec, who was himself subsequently executed on the decision of a party court of inquiry. The episode remains shrouded in mystery, but it was perhaps symptomatic of a certain demoralization at the top of the PPR as a result of its lack of success in the political sphere.[48]

Despite these setbacks, the new leadership of the party under Paweł Finder persevered with the formula of the 'national front without traitors and capitulators' for most of 1943. However, as the months passed its line became increasingly blurred. Externally, developments were encouraging. After Stalingrad in early 1943 the military balance on the Eastern Front began to shift in favour of the Russians and following the halting of the Germans' final great offensive at Kursk in July 1943, the Red Army began the westward advance which was to bring it to the frontiers of Poland in 1944. At the same time the position of the Polish Government-in-Exile in the Alliance was weakened in April when the Soviet government suspended diplomatic relations over the Katyn affair. Immediately the Soviet government began to form the Union of Polish Patriots (*Związek Patriotów Polskich* – ZPP) and a Polish Division amongst the émigrés in the U.S.S.R. In July the Government-in-Exile suffered a further blow when Sikorski was killed in an aircraft accident at Gibraltar. His successor as prime minister,

Stanisław Mikołajczyk, leader of the Peasant Party, lacked the prestige which Sikorski enjoyed in émigré political and military circles and amongst the leaders of the Allied governments.

However, the isolation of the Communists within Poland intensified. The rift between the Soviet and Polish governments buried for the time being any chance of further talks between the PPR and the London Delegation. In any case, by this stage the underground leadership had shifted to opponents of any compromise with the Communists.[49] In the aftermath of Katyn the party found it more difficult to win support and had to contend with an increase in anti-Communist propaganda as well as violence from the Right. In August the National Armed Forces (*Narodowe Siły Zbrojne* – NSZ) launched a campaign to 'cleanse the terrain of subversive and criminal bands', declaring that 'the PPR, People's Guard and various red partisans must vanish from the surface of Polish territory'.[50] At the same time 'London', which the Communists claimed tacitly supported NSZ violence, began preparations for its assumption of power in post-war Poland, plans from which the PPR was excluded. In August the 'Home Political Representation' (*Krajowa Representacja Polityczna*) was set up as a halfway house to a full underground parliament. This was formed in January 1944 in the shape of the Council of National Unity (*Rada Jedności Narodowej*). The four main political parties, the Peasants, Socialists, Party of Labour and National Democrats, issued a joint declaration defining an agreed programme of post-war reconstruction.[51] 'London' also stepped up the organization of the future infrastructure of power, establishing a secret network of local government and police and expanding the Home Army.

In January 1943 the Central Committee of the PPR met to review progress over the previous year. While reaffirming its pursuit of a 'broad national front of struggle without traitors and capitulators', it was clear that the leadership was looking for a way to escape the impasse it was in. Impressed by Tito's success and the armed resistance by the local peasants to German colonization in the Zamość region, the party turned for a while to the idea of a national insurrection.[52] However, it was aware of the difficulty it faced in breaking 'London's' monopoly of the patriotic platform. As an alternative, the PPR began to introduce new notes of social radicalism into its statements of policy and began to employ the slogan of a post-war 'democratic Poland'. These ideas were further developed in a programme issued in March.[53] Although internal pressures prompted such modifications of tactics, external considerations prevented the leadership from departing from its original strategy. The result was a blurred and somewhat incoherent line. Thus although the attempts to form the National Committees of Struggle were abandoned in mid-1943 and the party withdrew recognition of the Government-in-Exile, Gomułka later stated that 'for several more months [from the end of April] we did not change our basic political line towards the Delegation and the whole "London camp"; we were far from burning our bridges.'[54] As long as the possibility of a rapprochement between 'London' and Moscow existed, the PPR could not move over to radical opposition to the underground mainstream. It was not until after the October conference of foreign ministers in Moscow that the Central Committee decided that a resumption of Polish-Soviet relations was unlikely and began to clarify its line. All the same no bridges were burnt until the Teheran conference (28 November–1 December) had apparently confirmed the leadership's analysis of Soviet intentions.[55] By this time direct communications with the Russians had been broken.

The Polish Communist emigration in the U.S.S.R., much closer to Soviet thinking and free of the obstacles faced by the PPR in forming a broad national front, adhered much more consistently to the original version of the front. In its 'ideological declaration' of June 1943, the ZPP conformed closely to the 'anti-Fascist front' line. The aim of the ZPP, it stated, was to 'unite for the duration of the war all Poles residing on Soviet territory, regardless of differences in political, social or religious views, in one camp of struggle with Hitlerism'.[56] As Przygoński has noted, this was the line 'from which the PPR in Poland had already at this time begun to depart, putting forward the concept of a democratic front'.[57]

The democratic national front

THUS in late 1943 the line of the PPR underwent its first – but no means last – distinct modification. This shift from the 'anti-Fascist' to the 'democratic' national front was principally a response to the failure of the existing line to meet internal Polish realities. There is no evidence that Soviet prompting lay behind the shift. Indeed, the PPR seems to have strayed ahead of Soviet and émigré Communist thinking in 1943, with the result that in early 1944, when informed of the 'turn', the émigrés received it very critically.

The essence of the 'national front without traitors and capitulators' had been the Communists' acceptance of the political framework of the underground state and their attempt to gain entry to its leadership. The party made no overt claim to a leading role in this coalition and was prepared to work with any group, from Left to Right, committed to armed resistance to the Germans.

The 'democratic national front' was less broad and more radical. It rejected the legitimacy of the 'London' system and aimed at constructing a rival political camp, led by the PPR, by detaching 'democratic' elements, in particular the Socialists and Peasants, from what was viewed as the 'reactionary' leadership of the 'London' underground. The basis of this alliance would be a common programme combining national liberation with radical reform and its organizational expression would be a new political centre, the Homeland National Council (*Krajowa Rada Narodowa –*

KRN), a secret parliament of the parties which joined the front.

The idea of establishing some such organ was first mooted in PPR circles in early 1943, but Gomułka seems to have taken the decisive initiative while drafting a new version of the party's programme in September. After discussions between Gomułka and Finder, the secretary of the party, the proposal was put to the Central Committee and decided in principle on 7 November.[58]

The leadership did not decide what form the new centre should take at this meeting. There were in fact two differing conceptions of the purpose of the KRN, and by implication, of the character of the 'democratic national front'. Gomułka envisaged the KRN as a 'centre of political concentration', in other words as a point around which to gather a broad range of groupings which accepted its common programme, the manifesto.[59] The manifesto was to be the key element determining the area of cooperation with potential allies. The KRN would serve to dispute the monopoly of the London camp and loosen its hold on the 'democratic' parties which the PPR regarded as potential allies. Later he was to describe the KRN as a 'sort of coup d'état' in the underground,[60] in other words it would act as a catalyst to bring about a regrouping in Polish politics. From this standpoint the structural details of the KRN were of secondary importance, though Gomułka preferred to avoid a model which would fuel accusations that the PPR was intending to 'sovietize' Poland. As soon became clear, Gomułka saw no advantage in being specific on the form of the KRN and he was quite prepared to alter its character if this would assist the construction of a broad democratic front around the KRN manifesto.

Bolesław Bierut, on the other hand, led the group in the leadership which viewed the KRN rather as an 'organ of power', the cornerstone of a rival underground state firmly under the party's control which other groups would in time accept. For him the structure of the KRN was non-negotiable. If it proved an obstacle in the way of forming alliances, the party should wait until the other side gave way. In the meantime cosmetic alliances with splinters of the main groupings would suffice. The risk that the party would be suspected of aiming at the 'sovietization' of Poland did not worry Bierut, who insisted that the KRN should be underpinned by a network of local national councils.[61]

While Gomułka represented the current in the PPR which wished to rest power on a broad front of the Communists, Socialists and Peasants, Bierut was concerned above all with securing state power and was opposed to compromising on this point in order to widen the front. The two conceptions were fused untidily during the second half of November 1943. This was a disastrous time for the party; on 14 November Finder and another experienced member of the leadership, Małgorzata Fornalska, were arrested. Since they were responsible for communications, contact with Moscow was broken and not restored until early January. Within hours of the arrests Gomułka, Bierut and Franciszek Jóźwiak, who now constituted the top leadership of the party, went ahead with a pre-arranged meeting to decide the form of the KRN. Bierut's scheme of a local network was accepted without enthusiasm by Gomułka who, as he later recalled, did not wish to waste time and viewed the issue as secondary.[62] However, nine days later, unknown to the Soviets and émigrés, Gomułka was elected secretary in preference to Bierut and Jóźwiak.[63]

This outcome meant that the differences of view within the PPR leadership were not resolved in favour of either the Gomułka or Bierut–Jóźwiak conception before the KRN was inaugurated on New Year's Eve 1944. The timing of the inauguration was governed by tactical considerations: the imminent entry of the Red Army into pre-1939 Polish territory and the party's desire to pre-empt the transformation of the London Home Political Representation into a Council of National Unity. From the point of view of its political base, the establishment of the KRN was premature; at this stage very little progress had been made in winning over Socialists and Peasants.

The Socialist Left had undergone considerable regrouping during 1943, but remained aloof from the PPR. The Organization of Polish Socialists had split in April 1943. Some of its members had joined WRN, but the Left-wing, anti-London faction had formed a new body, the Workers' Party of the Polish Socialists (*Robotnicza Partia Polskich Socjalistów* – RPPS). With at most 1,500 members, the bulk of them in the Warsaw area,[64] the RPPS was, as Gomułka admitted, 'minute', though it was thought by the Communists to have a potential for growth.[65] Despite its very radical social programme and opposition to 'London', at its Congress in September 1943 the RPPS had characterized the PPR as 'representing Soviet influence' and by a large majority voted against collaboration.[66] In December, however, the RPPS agreed to talks, but rejected the Communists' concept of a 'democratic national front' around the KRN, proposing instead the idea of a 'popular front' of the Peasants, Communists and itself based on the new political centre which it had begun to form a few weeks before.[67] In the end, only a small faction of the RPPS, active in the Warsaw cooperative movement with whom Bierut had old contacts, entered the KRN. This tiny group of marxists led by Edward Osóbka-Morawski and Stanisław Szwalbe represented the total outcome of two years of Communist effort to win Socialist support.[68]

The party's failure to secure backing for the KRN from the Peasant Party (*Stronnictwo Ludowe* – SL) was even more striking. A formal invitation to the SL leadership did not even receive a reply. The Communists' hopes of recruiting at least a few SL activists 'from below' also came to nothing. In the end the party had to make do with Władysław Kowalski, a veteran KPP peasant activist, again brought in by Bierut.[69]

It has been suggested that Gomułka deliberately stayed away from the inaugural sitting of the KRN to express his dissatisfaction with the extremely narrow range of its membership. However, he later denied this emphatically.[70] Nonetheless he was very critical of the way in which the KRN fell so far short of his original conception. In a message to Dimitrov in March 1944 he wrote 'we did not want to form this representation on our own, but at the very least with the CK [Central Committee, i.e. the majority] of the RPPS'.[71] In his memoirs (1975) he stated plainly, 'I did not want the KRN to be a synonym for the PPR at all. The KRN was intended to be quite different.'[72]

For those like Gomułka who had envisaged the KRN as a centre of political consolidation for a broad democratic front, its failure to attract support beyond the PPR was a major disappointment. Others who viewed it rather as an embryonic organ of power were much less disturbed by this fact. As we shall shortly see, this divergence of outlook grew sharper in early 1944 as the failure of the KRN to escape its isolation became apparent.

The Communist emigration in the Soviet Union

THE size of the wartime Polish emigration in the Soviet Union is uncertain. Estimates by the ZPP put it at between 500,000 and 700,000 in 1940–1. 'London' sources suggested a million or more.[73] Only a relatively small part of this total was evacuated to the West in 1942 in the army commanded by General Anders. The Communist emigration was tiny – at most a few hundred people[74] – and until 1943 it was disorganized and dispersed. Some Communists were active in journalism, some in the Red Army or Comintern apparatus, but many others found themselves in labour brigades or camps. When the ZPP was formed some of these Communists were given positions in its leadership but most were assigned to the new Polish Division, chiefly to work in its political apparatus. They included a considerable number of the top figures in the post-war party – Berman, Minc, Radkiewicz, Zambrowski, Ochab, Zawadzki, Jaroszewicz and many other second-rank figures.

The Polish Communist group in the Soviet Union inevitably had a different perspective on political strategy from the party at home. Until 1944 their contact with the PPR was indirect, sporadic and provided only a very incomplete picture of the situation in Poland. Their thinking was much more closely geared to Soviet policy. Without any local rival for the patriotic cause it was relatively easy for them to recruit the non-Communist émigré masses into a broad front of struggle with the Germans. The principal problem which they faced was that of moulding these masses into a military and political force to place at the disposal of a future Communist government. These differing vantage-points influenced the character of the debate on strategy; in Poland the PPR leadership had to defend a broad, liberal line, which was not producing results, against criticism from its own Left. Within the emigration the Communists were almost oversuccessful in widening their base and feared that the nation-alistic and militaristic forces they had harnessed might overwhelm their influence in the army.

The strategic discussions amongst the émigrés were above all concerned with which element would play the key role in liberated Poland, the Communist Party or the Communist-led army. There was much greater agreement on the kind of issues which divided the PPR. The debate over the role of the political and military factors in post-war Poland was bound up with a struggle for dominance within the emigration, between civilian Communists in the Presidium of the ZPP and the military men in the command of the Polish Division. The Communists in the army political apparatus were inclined to occupy a middle position. In late 1943 this rivalry shaped discussions which were held to define more precisely the political aims of the emigration. Each of the three factions put forward its own 'theses' [*sic*]. Those of the army command, dubbed 'theses number one', were drafted by Major Jakub Prawin, but identified with the divisional commander, General Zygmunt Berling and his deputy, Włodzimierz Sokorski; Minc and Zambrowski wrote 'theses number two', reflecting the outlook of the *politruki*, while the view of the ZPP Presidium was embodied in 'theses number three', largely written by Alfred Lampe.[75] The debate has been described elsewhere in some detail,[76] so here we shall confine ourselves to saying that its outcome was a clear victory for the ZPP Presidium and its conception of party control of the army, rather than an independent political role for the military. This victory was consolidated with a series of personnel changes to strengthen the army political apparatus,[77] and the establishment in January 1944 of the Central Bureau of Polish Communists (*Centralne Biuro Komunistów Polskich* – CBKP). This organ for the first time provided the Communist émigrés with a unified leadership and a channel through which PPR communications with Moscow were increasingly directed.

During the debates on the 'theses' certain common assumptions amongst the Polish Communist emigration had emerged quite clearly. First, the émigrés took a very sanguine view of the feasibility of forming a broad coalition on the platform of national liberation. While the party at home had already limited its goal to a front extending only so far as the 'democratic' wing of the London camp, and had had in practice to make do with the very narrow base of the KRN, the émigrés remained convinced that a much wider 'patriotic front' was within their grasp. Prawin's 'theses' had declared that 'all, without regard to their political past who loyally and honestly stand on the ground of the political programme presented will be admitted to [the government] camp'.[78] 'Theses number two' insisted that 'the creation of a movement linking in a harmonious whole the homeland and the emigration is entirely realistic',[79] while Lampe viewed 'national solidarity' as a prerequisite of his conception of Poland's development towards socialism.[80] As became apparent in early 1944, the émigrés could not understand why the Communists at home had failed to win wider support, or why they had felt the need to radicalize their platform. They tended to ascribe this failure to what was seen as 'sectarianism' in the PPR.

Secondly, while the 'political' Communists insisted that the party should have a leading role, they did not mean by this that the underground PPR should exercise that function. Lip-service was paid to the formal subordination of the émigrés to the party at home and the CBKP was thus conceived as 'an organisation of the PPR abroad on Soviet territory'.[81] However, in practice the émigrés viewed the PPR as too weak and too out of touch with Soviet thinking to take the lead. 'Theses number one' had been criticized for undervaluing the part to be played by domestic forces, but Minc and Zambrowski too wrote of the need to create a 'unified leadership', arguing that 'the responsibility for achieving the task of consolidating Polish democracy falls on the ZPP and the Polish Armed Forces in the USSR, to which the course of events has granted immeasurably opportune and favourable scope for activity.'[82] As for Lampe's 'theses', they were intended as the basis for the programme of a Polish National Committee which the Presidium of the ZPP was preparing to launch in early 1944. This initiative, on which there was no consultation with the PPR because of the break in contact, was halted when news of the establishment of the KRN arrived. Otherwise the political hub of the Communist camp would have shifted decisively abroad. It is worth noting that although special attention was devoted to ensuring that representation on the committee would be given to right-wing opinion,[83] only a quarter of its seats were reserved for the homeland, compared to half for the Soviet emigration.[84] For the émigrés it was self-evident, formalities apart, that they rather than the PPR held the key to Poland's future. They took the view that their success in bringing the broad 'patriotic national front' strategy to fruition and in building an army 30,000 strong by the end of 1943 and 100,000 strong by mid-1944,[85] entitled them to the deference of the PPR rather than *vice versa*.

The 1944 strategy debate

THE proximity of power in early 1944 did not lead to any final crystallization of strategy by the Communists. Three different variations of the national front vied with one another right up to the moment of liberation and it was the unexpected rapidity of that liberation rather than any coming together of minds which shaped the party's course during its first weeks of power.

The lack of consensus within the leadership of the PPR over the intended character of the KRN and more generally over the nature of the 'democratic national front' became increasingly evident in the first months of 1944. At the same time the divergence between the 'patriotic national front' of the émigrés and the 'democratic national front' of the underground Communists became apparent.

The gap in thinking between Warsaw and Moscow was revealed once radio contact was re-established in early January, but the subsequent correspondence did little to diminish it. Gomułka's first message (12 January) provided a survey of political forces and the internal situation which Moscow had requested. The tone was optimistic. He claimed that a favourable transformation in public attitudes to the Soviet Union had occurred and that the possibility already existed of gathering 'considerable democratic forces' around the KRN.[86] The reply sent by the CBKP in February has not been published but it is clear that it contained extensive criticism of the changes which the line of the PPR had undergone since autumn. This emerges from the response of the PPR Central Committee in a letter of 7 March. This time the tone was decidedly defensive. Its assurances that 'the idea of the KRN has found general support amongst the broad masses' and that 'a strong foundation of support for the KRN is growing from below', were, as we shall see shortly, highly exaggerated and were contradicted by the party's reply to CBKP charges that it had failed to mount a broad coalition where other Communist parties had succeeded. The Central Bureau had seen PPR ultra-radicalism as the obstacle, but the Central Committee blamed factors beyond its control:

> The fact that up to now the PPR has not succeeded in achieving the creation of a national front in Poland on the pattern of Yugoslavia, Czechoslovakia or France results neither from sectarian political positions of the Party nor from our weakness, but from the attitude of our Party to Poland's eastern frontier question.

The émigré implication that a more tactful approach might improve things was scorned: 'If Saint Anthony's brotherhood stood for revising the eastern frontiers of Poland, it too would be branded by the reaction as a Moscow agency.'[87]

This defence did not satisfy the Central Bureau which in a note written, it seems, in May, repeated its criticisms and in effect told the PPR to abandon the 'democratic national front' and return to the broad 'patriotic national front' it had strayed away from in late 1943. The note gave a somewhat delayed welcome to the initiative of forming the KRN, but raised the same criticism that Gomułka had made of the structure which Bierut and Jóźwiak had insisted on. The CBKP considered that conceived as an 'organ of power' rather than a 'centre of political concentration', the KRN 'hindered winning over wavering elements'. But the Bureau's critique extended to the KRN programme which Gomułka had framed and to the very concept of a 'democratic national front'. According to Moscow, the programme paid insufficient attention to establishing 'a *broad political concentration* [original emphasis] which would be capable of drawing behind it or neutralising part of the bourgeoisie'; it was not 'the programme of a front but amounts to a narrowed national front'. The underground leadership had got out of step. It 'had not taken enough account of the complexity of the international situation. From this point of view [its radical] slogan of People's Poland is unacceptable as it is in conflict with the general political line.' But the CBKP implied that the PPR had also misjudged the internal situation and advised the party to take advantage of what the Central Bureau saw as a 'ferment' amongst the London parties. The watchword should still be 'a Provisional Government with a wide democratic base which will embrace alongside the KRN all groups standing sincerely for struggle with the Germans in alliance with the Soviet Union'.[88]

This advice did little to resolve the differences inside the PPR. On the one hand, however critically and reservedly, the Moscow Communists had endorsed the KRN. On the other, they had demanded a new drive to win over a broad coalition of allies. The émigrés did not see any contradiction between these two aims, and did not therefore address themselves to the issue which divided the underground leadership, namely how far it should be prepared to compromise on the structure of the KRN in order to win allies and broaden the national front.

As the correspondence between the PPR and CBKP reveals, the PPR leadership was reluctant to reveal its differences to the émigrés and appeared united in its defence of the KRN. Internally, however, strains increased. The party's efforts to broaden the base of the KRN were fruitless despite the growing certainty that the German occupation of Poland would be ended by the Red Army and not by the West. Although it proved easier to construct a network of provincial and local national councils beneath the KRN than had been the case with the National Committees of Struggle in 1942–3, this reflected improved party organization rather than any marked widening of support for the national front. The national councils were based on the PPR itself and the small groups linked with it and there was relatively little progress in detaching activists of the Peasant and Socialist movements 'from below'. The party leadership blamed this on the 'sectarianism' of local organizers, but the continuing solidity of the London camp was perhaps the chief obstacle.[89]

Little advance was made in expanding the tiny RPPS and Peasant groups which had joined the KRN. In January Osóbka-Morawski set up a pro-KRN central committee and began to campaign among the RPPS cells. However, only a few cells seem to have disowned the existing anti-KRN central committee. Indeed, as we shall see, the results were so limited that by May the Communists were divided over whether it was worth maintaining Osóbka's RPPS at all. Gomułka and his group in the leadership thought it might be wiser to liquidate it and concentrate their efforts on the 'old' RPPS, with which they conducted negotiations through February–March.[90] Overtures were also made to the leadership of the Peasant Party without result.[91] Meanwhile an attempt to generate an internal opposition in the SL was mounted in February around Władysław Kowalski and a few other Leftist peasants who had thrown in their lot with the PPR. This group took the name of the newspaper, *Wola ludu (Will of the People)*, which they began to publish. However, this was a very cosmetic venture and it was left to the Communists to print, distribute and even, to a large extent, write the paper.[92]

By spring 1944 it was clear that the KRN, though operative as an embryonic state apparatus, which would be used if the PPR found itself installed in power by the Red Army without having gained entry to the existing underground state, was quite useless as a means of rallying support and indeed actually alienated potential allies such as the 'old' RPPS.[93]

For Gomułka and others in the PPR leadership, notably Aleksander Kowalski, Ignacy Loga-Sowiński, Władysław Bieńkowski and Zenon Kliszko, the priority was to achieve the broadest possible front which would embrace in particular the Socialists and the Peasants and not only cosmetic splinter groups from the marxist fringe of these movements. Such a front would provide a genuine political base for a Communist-led government after liberation. Otherwise any new government would have only the meagre resources of the PPR and the KRN at its disposal and would be forced to rely very heavily on Soviet support to keep the London camp, still united, at bay. In the eyes of Gomułka and his supporters this was the rationale of the national front strategy and accorded clearly with the guidelines sent by the Central Bureau from Moscow in their recent messages.[94] Apart from general strategic considerations, Gomułka and the others interpreted recent diplomatic moves as indicating the possibility of a resumption of relations between the Soviet Union and Polish Government-in-Exile and were anxious to pursue tactics at home in line with this scenario.[95]

Bierut, Jóźwiak and Hilary Chełchowski, a more junior Central Committee member, saw in this a threat to the character or even existence of the KRN, which they feared would be sacrificed – along with Osóbka's RPPS and *Wola ludu* – in order to achieve a deal with the London groupings. They considered that the question of power in liberated Poland could be solved by the PPR itself with the active political support of the Soviet forces and that to make premature concessions to win Socialist and Peasant backing was undesirable. Writing three decades later, Gomułka made it clear that he regarded this stance as sectarian and as a fundamental retreat from the conception of a broad national front as the basis for mounting a broadly-based government on liberation. According to Gomułka the Bierut group:

> did not claim by any means that they excluded the possibility of a resumption of diplomatic relations. . . . They treated the matter as irrelevant. Their position

amounted to this: that I underrated the possibilities which the liberation of Poland by the Red Army opened for us; that with its help we would settle the problem of government in Poland as we liked; that at the same time I was underestimating the strength of our party, which in the new circumstances created by the Red Army's liberation of Poland would become the object of attention from the other parties.[96]

Bierut, describing Gomułka's attitude in 1948, said much the same:

During the creation of the KRN some comrades in our Party did not appreciate the true configuration of class forces and the special importance of the co-operation of these forces in the struggle for political power *with the armed might of the USSR, as a revolutionary, liberating force, as a class force, and not simply as the military force of an ally.* [emphasis added][97]

For Gomułka's group the imminence of the Soviet liberation of Poland dictated an intensification of efforts to create a broad front; for Bierut and Jóźwiak it provided an opportunity to escape the constraints imposed by this strategy and establish a more radical and Communist-centred government.

The dispute came to a head in May when the 'old' RPPS put forward the proposal that the KRN link-up with the Central People's Committee (*Centralny Komitet Ludowy*) or *Centralizacja* as it was called, a body comprising little more than the RPPS and the left of the Democratic Party (*Stronnictwo Demokratyczne* – SD). The two would then attempt to enter the 'London' Council of National Unity as a joint opposition. On May 19 the PPR telegraphed the Moscow Communists asking their opinion of this scheme. The reply, which arrived a few days later and may well have been influenced by Osóbka-Morawski, who had recently arrived in Moscow, expressed the view that the plan was a manoeuvre designed to subordinate the KRN to 'London'.[98]

Presumably this message had not been received when the Central Committee met (23 May) to discuss the plan. Wide differences were revealed in a sharp exchange of views. Bierut argued that the PPR should not collaborate politically with the *Centralizacja* because of what he claimed was its 'favourable' attitude to the London government and the difference between its ideas and those of the PPR on which forces would take power in liberated Poland. Jóźwiak saw the *Centralizacja* as a rival to the KRN which ought to be eliminated and he accused the Gomułka faction of overrating its importance and underestimating the strength of the party. Gomułka overruled these views and came down in favour of serious talks with the *Centralizacja* as the first step towards approaching the London 'democrats': 'We should do everything in order to link up and approach the SL (and) WRN together.'[99]

The next sitting of the Central Committee (29 May) was still more heated and brought out clearly the gulf in strategic thinking between the two sides. By this time news of Moscow's attitude to the merger plan and the reception by Stalin of Osóbka-Morawski and the other KRN representatives (22 May) had reached Warsaw.[100] This perhaps encouraged Bierut and Jóźwiak to stick to their guns. However, Gomułka and his colleagues were determined to persevere with the *Centralizacja* plan. They took the view that Stalin's public welcome for the KRN delegation was intended to reinforce British pressure on the Government-in-Exile to come to terms. Both sides claimed that they adhered to the national front philosophy and recognized the need for 'national consolidation', but the course of the argument revealed how differently they conceived this strategy. Bierut saw alliances with other parties and groups not as desirable in themselves, but as tactical devices to isolate and destroy the 'reaction'. As he put it, consolidation was required 'not because "we love each other", but in order to intensify the struggle'. Aleksander Kowalski, for the other side, expressed an altogether more conciliatory spirit and was ready to pay a considerable cost to achieve national unity: 'we should be ready to give up certain prerogatives, among others: exclusive representation which alone will form the government.' For Gomułka, the party's objective was to merge the KRN, *Centralizacja* and the 'London' Council of National Unity, purged of 'fascist elements' in 'one domestic, national representative body'. In other words he aimed to achieve the kind of broad coalition between the PPR, the Left Socialists and the London 'democrats' which was finally formed in June 1945. Jóźwiak, by contrast, not only rejected a deal with 'London', but regarded the *Centralizacja* as an unsuitable ally, arguing that it should be broken up and that only its 'democratic' wing could be trusted. In his opinion the KRN alone could exercise power and the national front should be extended only marginally beyond its present limits. The meeting concluded messily with Gomułka insisting on proceeding with talks with the *Centralizacja* over Bierut's protestation that there had been a change of party line.[101]

On 10 June it seems that Bierut sent a secret message to Dimitrov accusing Gomułka of political vacillation 'from sectarianism to opportunism', departing from 'collective work' and forming a faction in the leadership. He asked Moscow to step in to rectify matters.[102] In other circumstances such a conflict of outlook would very likely have led to the expulsion of the minority – in this case Bierut, Jóźwiak and Chełchowski[103] from the leadership. But in conditions of conspiracy, with power almost in their grasp and the attitude of the Soviets still very ambiguous, the conflict was left unresolved to await the further developments of events.

At the next Central Committee meeting for which we have a record (18 June) the rift was still apparent. Bierut played for time, arguing that 'at the moment it is not possible to assume that an understanding will not be made on the basis of the KRN . . . we ought to be cautious and not make commitments.' He and Jóźwiak agreed however to Gomułka's formula by which any talks would deal first with a joint political programme and only move on to the role of the KRN in the future power structure when agreement had been reached on the programme. Such an agenda would defer the question of the exclusivity of the KRN and would give wide scope for delay. However, Gomułka tried to put the issue beyond doubt in his summing-up, concluding that 'we shall not reach unification from above around the KRN and ought if the KRN proved an obstacle in the way of a political understanding, to give up the name KRN.'[104]

Some days later, on 1 July, a leader article written by Władysław Bieńkowski appeared in the PPR organ *Trybuna Wolności*, presenting the majority view as the official position of the party. It is most improbable that such an article could have appeared without Gomułka's prior approval. The statement brought the line of the PPR substantially into harmony with the 'patriotic national front' stance of the emigration and in fact the Central Bureau had called for just such a declaration in its April message. It spoke of the urgent need for 'a consolidation of all the forces of the democratic camp' and 'a broad national front embracing everything which stands for the struggle to liberate Poland'.[105] The party was back to the broad front formulae of 1942–3 and its objective, so the article implied, was once again the reconstruction of the Government-in-Exile rather than its replacement by the KRN. Indeed the statement made no mention of the KRN as a possible base for a new government bloc, an omission which, at least formally, fitted in with the Central Committee's decision to place the question of agreement on policy in the foreground. However, it also suggested a flexibility on the future role of the KRN which ran counter to the intentions of Bierut and Jóźwiak. In the leadership crisis of 1948 they were to cite this 'document of shame' as crowning evidence of Gomułka's abandonment of the KRN,[106] and as the first signal of his 'right-nationalism'.

Meanwhile the Moscow line continued to cut across the divisions at home. On 1 July, the same day that Bieńkowski's article appeared, the émigrés finally announced their formal recognition of the primacy of the KRN. This decision had been taken by the ZPP a week earlier presumably in response to Stalin's statement at a conference with the KRN delegates on 22 June that 'the core of the new government should be the homeland and the KRN'.[107] However, as a letter sent by the Central Bureau to the PPR on 18 July makes clear, the CBKP insisted that this should be accompanied by mounting of the broadest possible front. The Bureau bluntly stated that Soviet backing for the KRN would depend on an early broadening of its base and that this was an immediate priority. It also expressed dissatisfaction at what it saw as the continuing narrowness and 'inconsistencies' of the PPR line. It was worried by examples of the PPR's excessive radicalism, which it feared would alienate the peasantry and prevent the new government gathering the support of 'the majority of the nation'. The émigrés regarded this ambitious goal as not only possible, but imperative if the 'formation of a powerful reactionary underground, possessing a significant social base' was to be avoided. In what might be taken as a definitive statement of the philosophy of the broad national front – and no doubt of Soviet policy in mid-1944 – the Bureau formulated its strategic objective as being 'the creation of such an internal balance within which we shall be able to smash the reaction with our own internal forces'.[108]

The Polish Committee of National Liberation

IN the end geography and the speed of events at the front decided the relative influence of the different strategic conceptions on the party's line during its initial assumption of power. In mid-June when Bierut had argued for a waiting game and Gomułka was preparing the ground for a deal with the London 'democrats', the Soviet-German front was for the most part stabilized well to the east of the river Bug; five weeks later Red Army troops reached the Vistula. The unexpected extent and rapidity of this advance altered the whole context of the debate within the PPR and in effect decided the issue in Bierut's favour. The party would take power not in alliance with a broad national front of Peasants, Socialists and other groupings, but instead on the back of the Soviet army and within the framework of the KRN.

It was the émigré line nevertheless which had the most profound influence on the party's strategy in the first weeks of power. While the PPR leadership awaited the Soviet advance in Warsaw, in Moscow the émigrés put the final touches to the arrangements for assuming power. Messages from Moscow to Warsaw in July hinted that these preparations were getting under way but it appears that the PPR was only informed of the details by radio *post factum*.[109] Formally, in line with Stalin's instructions, the homeland was to form the core of the new government.[110] However, only seven representatives of the domestic wing of the national front were present in Moscow to participate in the discussions. Of these, three (Osóbka-Morawski, Rola-Żymierski and Spychalski) were second-rank figures in the KRN leadership, while the others were of no importance whatsoever. Not one of the top party leadership was available and Spychalski, the senior PPR spokesman, had left Warsaw in March and therefore knew nothing of the more recent debates in the party.[111] The Poles were inclined to await the expected arrival of further representatives of the KRN. However, these did not materialize and the Russians were anxious to finalize agreements. In meetings with Stalin and Molotov on 17–18 July the Poles were urged to go ahead with the immediate formation of a Committee of National Liberation to administer the liberated territories.[112] However, the Poles decided on 18 July to propose instead the creation of a 'KRN Delegation' to fulfil this role and the next day Stalin accepted this solution which at least formally embodied the supremacy of the KRN. On 20 July the new body held its first and only session at the end of which it was announced that Stalin had changed his mind and now insisted on his original conception of a Committee of National Liberation. The Poles had little choice but to accept this *volte-face* and, adding the word 'Polish', voted the Committee of National Liberation (*Polski Komitet Wyzwolenia Narodowego* – PKWN) into existence. Presumably Stalin had decided on reflection that to give such prominence to the KRN might provoke the Allies and hinder a deal with 'London' which was still in the offing. In terms of structure the change made virtually no difference.[113]

The political platform of the PKWN, its manifesto, was produced in Moscow on 21 July and was very much a Moscow product. Based on the draft declaration which Lampe had prepared the previous December for the abandoned Polish National Committee, it closely followed the émigré concept of the 'patriotic national front'. The manifesto called for 'national unity' and promised the restoration of all democratic freedoms, excluding only 'fascist organizations' from the legal political spectrum. It confined its criticisms of 'London' to its military strategy and the alleged illegality of the Government-in-Exile but refrained from broadening this into a general attack on the political profile of the underground. The KRN was recognized as 'the only legal source of authority in Poland', but the manifesto toned down several of the more radical statements of the PPR. For instance the pledge in the KRN programme to nationalize heavy industry, transport and banks was dropped. Instead the PKWN undertook to restore ownership to Poles expropriated by the Nazis.[114] The Central Bureau had explained the thinking behind such moderation in its letter of 18 July, where it had argued that the use of such radical slogans as 'People's Poland' and the nationalization of industry were 'not calculated to bring about fragmentation in our opponent's camp or to draw wavering bourgeois elements away from reactionary influence or to neutralise parts of the bourgeoisie'.[115]

The PKWN manifesto which served to define the party's strategic aims in its first weeks in power was thus largely framed by émigrés who had been out of Poland for five years and who regarded the assessment of the balance of forces at home by their underground comrades as mistaken. In line with Soviet thinking, the Moscow Poles believed that a mild social programme and a platform of national liberation would bring about the broad coalition of forces which had eluded the PPR since 1942. The summer months of 1944 would show that this faith was not well-founded. By October the Communists had no choice but to fall back on the Bierut–Jóźwiak conception of a cosmetic national front, based on the party itself and sustained by Soviet armed might.

6 'Lublin' and 'London', July to December 1944

THE POLISH COMMUNISTS took power in summer 1944 isolated and numerically weak. Speaking to the first gathering of party activists in liberated Lublin on 5 August, Gomułka admitted that the wartime efforts of the PPR to form a national front had failed to produce a result.[1] Twenty years later he returned to the subject of the internal balance of forces in 1944: 'the London crew had a great preponderance over us, a vast apparatus of cadres and material resources at its disposal. We had to rely on our own modest resources.'[2]

This of course left Soviet resources out of the calculation. In order to avoid total dependence on Soviet might, party strategy looked to the long-awaited regrouping of political forces which it assumed would now take place as Poland passed indisputably into the Soviet sphere of power and the burden of the war against the Germans moved from the 'London' underground to the Polish army fighting alongside the Russians. The expected disintegration of the London camp and the gravitation of its more pragmatic and radical components towards the Lublin regime would provide the PKWN with the internal base it lacked and enable the Communists to isolate and eliminate their die-hard opponents. The plan was set out authoritatively in the letter which the CBKP sent to the Central Committee of the PPR on 18 July.[3] The letter argued that the objective of establishing 'a genuinely national government gathering around itself the majority of the nation' could 'be fulfilled only by the determined and consistent realisation of the national front policy: the working-class under the leadership of our party will capture the leading position in the struggle for national liberation, achieving at the same time the maximum fragmentation of reactionary forces.' It continued:

> translating into class terminology, this means the struggle to destroy monopoly capital and great land-ownership, a struggle led by workers, peasants, intelligentsia, the petit-bourgeoisie, who will lead after them part of the middle bourgeoisie, neutralising its majority. At the same time a national front conceived in this way must guarantee the popular masses the maximum possibility of achieving their demands, while creating a favourable point of departure for the march towards changes in the political system.[4]

Reality failed to conform to this scheme. No significant regrouping of parties took place until mid-1945. The dividing line between London 'reactionaries' and 'democrats' proved less easy to draw than the Communists had expected and was in any case less in evidence than the divide separating 'London' from 'Lublin'. Moreover, faced with the problem of translating strategy into practice, the Communists came up against the fundamental dilemma which was to dog them for years to come. The kind of broad coalition bloc required to achieve the defeat of their opponents by political means demanded far-reaching compromises on policy and a relaxation of the party's hold on positions of power. In view of the party's acute lack of reliable manpower the danger existed that it would be swamped in such a block and thus lose the hegemonic role which it considered essential. On the other hand, a narrowly based front which embraced little more than the Communists and their client parties on the radical Left would preserve the party's leading role but at the cost of depriving it of the internal resources needed to defeat the opposition politically. Such a solution would leave the party with little alternative but to resort to police and bureaucratic methods and the direct application of Soviet power to deal with its opponents. Throughout its history the PPR was caught within this dilemma, never more so than during its first year of rule in 1944–5.

The unreality of the assumptions on which the July version of the national front rested was revealed within a couple of months. In October the party line hardened distinctly and by spring 1945 the momentum of this turn had swept it far adrift from the precepts of the national front. In May the leadership, facing a worsening political crisis and the loss of its authority within the governing apparatus, executed an abrupt *volte-face*, restoring in its essentials the general line from which it had departed the previous autumn.

The Lublin coalition

DESPITE its narrow base the administration installed in Lublin displayed, particularly in its first weeks of existence, many of the characteristics of a coalition. At its core lay the Communists, rarely occupying the more public positions, but dominating the key posts in the army, security forces, mass media and central government departments. The party itself was a coalition, between the émigrés and underground activists, between the old generation of KPP stalwarts and the younger ex-partisans, between idealists and pragmatists. Such differences in background and outlook were compounded by the differences which stemmed from the variety of vantage-points from which the political situation was viewed. The top leadership, keenly sensitive to shifts of mood in Moscow, the international picture and the broad balance of internal forces, saw things very differently from the activists sent out into the countryside to establish the rudiments of party organization and local government from nothing. A

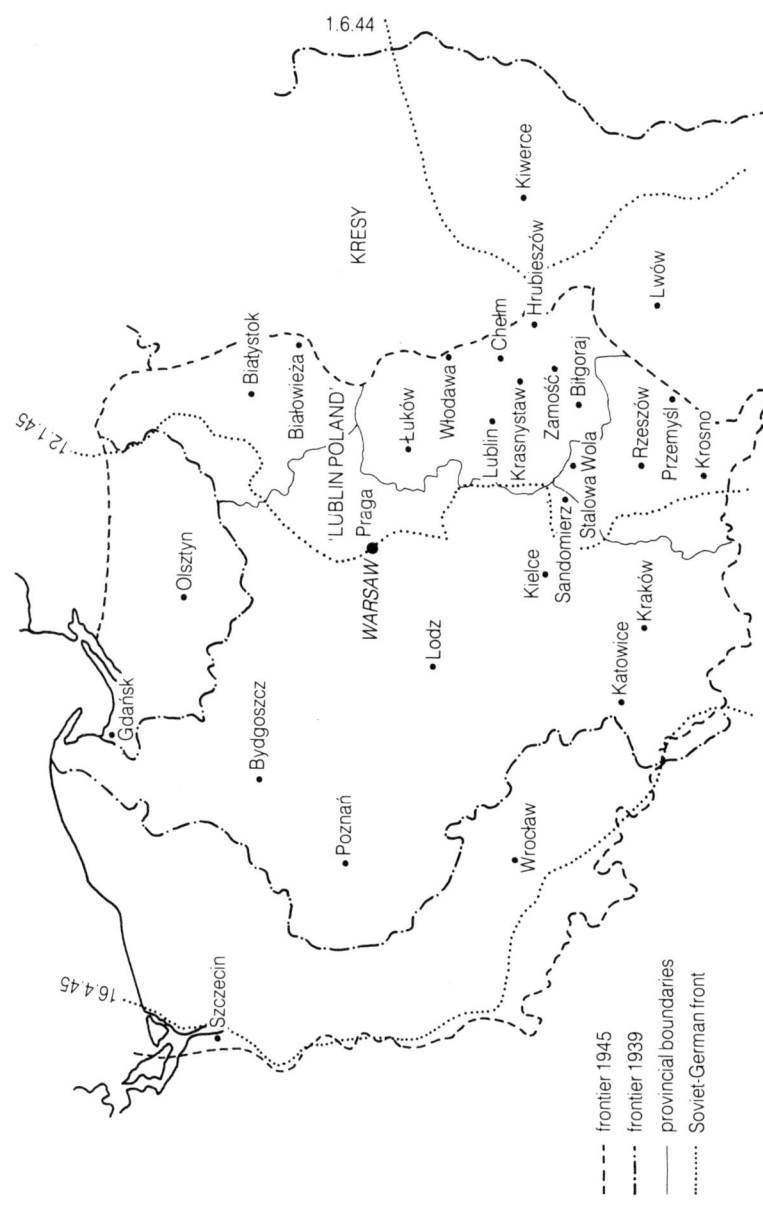

Map 4 'Lublin Poland', 1944.

security man with orders to prevent hostile infiltration and uncover 'reactionaries' differed in perspective from a political officer in the army given the task of winning the allegiance of fresh conscripts with five years of loyalty to 'London' behind them.

This heterogeneity was at its most evident in 1944 as the party made the transition from conspiracy to government. In one of its first circulars the leadership warned cadres of the problems that this process would involve: 'we have become a legal party, co-governing and therefore jointly responsible for all deficiencies, shortcomings etc. . . . On our work and activity, on our organisational skill in overcoming post-occupation chaos, on our correct party line at this crucial historical moment depends our success in winning over the majority of the nation. . . . Our party must learn how to govern.'[5]

The first organizational task was to form a unified leadership. This did not take place immediately. Although Gomułka addressed the first party meeting in Lublin on 5 August as secretary, it was Bierut who the same day arrived in Moscow for talks with Stalin and Mikołajczyk on the creation of a coalition government.[6] The Politburo seems to have been formally constituted on 29 August. Its membership comprised Gomułka and Bierut, but not Jóźwiak, from the underground secretariat of the PPR and Berman, Minc, Zawadzki and Radkiewicz who were coopted from the Central Bureau.[7] This apparent imbalance illustrates both the seniority of the Moscow group and Gomułka's weak hold on the leadership: none of the other members were his adherents. However, Gomułka may have found it easier to work with the new Politburo than the old underground secretariat, where he was outnumbered by Bierut and Jóźwiak.

During August and September the work of establishing a centralized organizational network for the party to replace the decentralized underground structure was completed. Provincial and district committees were formed everywhere except in the remoter parts of Białystok province where the PPR had had no wartime organization whatsoever. At this stage, with the local cells still few in number and the Central Committee apparatus at an embryonic stage (in September it had only 24 political workers), the district committees remained the focus of party activity.[8]

The membership of the party east of the Vistula in the final phase of the occupation has been estimated at about 5,000. It is claimed in addition that some 20,000 troops of the People's Army (*Armia Ludowa* – AL) were deployed in the Lublin region, though this figure may well be exaggerated.[9] In August and September it was primarily from this source that expansion of party membership took place, from 4,633 (1 September) to 8,960 (1 October). Distribution was uneven: over 70 per cent of members were concentrated in Lublin province, compared with about 12 per cent in Rzeszów and only 2 per cent in Białystok.[10] Even allowing for the exclusion from these statistics of some Communists in the army, the shortage of party cadres with which to govern a population of approaching 6 million was apparent. The scope for increasing membership was limited by the social structure of the liberated territories: apart from a few pockets of industrialization (Praga, Białystok, Lublin, Stalowa Wola), the region was overwhelmingly agricultural. At the end of 1944 as the factories began to resume regular production, the total industrial workforce was only about 85,000.[11] Moreover, especially in the towns, some party officials doubted the wisdom of expanding too fast, fearing a loss of political cohesion.[12] These doubts ran contrary to leadership policy which favoured a rapid growth. On 15 September the Politburo approved organizational instructions which relaxed recruitment requirements, 'opening wide the gates of our party for all who acknowledge the principles of the PPR programme'.[13] By the end of the year membership had risen to 21,649, thanks in part to the campaign staged around the parcellization of the great estates. However, there remained an acute lack of cadres. The influx of poor peasants and agricultural workers, who with other rural strata constituted at least 65–70 per cent of PPR members by December,[14] could not compensate in the short term for the absence of educated, politically sound activists. The other elements in the Lublin coalition – the Peasants, Socialists and the army and security forces – could only marginally alleviate the party's shortage of manpower.

The Peasant Party was by far the largest political movement in Lublin Poland, where nearly 85 per cent of the population lived in rural areas.[15] Although the SL was very weak in Białystok province, Lublin, Rzeszów and the liberated parts of Kielce and Warsaw were amongst its strongholds; the strength of the Peasant Battalions, the armed wing of the SL, stood at about 50,000 men in Lublin province alone.[16] The Communists saw the Peasants as an obvious and indispensable ally. As Gomułka told delegates at the first party meeting in August, 'the Peasants are our natural ally, and though in many cases their ideology and structure is different, we shall try to collaborate with them. The Peasants represent a serious force and without them nothing can take place.'[17]

The SL Resistance movement (ROCh) was a continuation of the pre-war peasant movement, and embraced the overwhelming bulk of politically active peasants within its rather loose ranks. It constituted the largest element within the London camp, providing about half of the strength of the Home Army,[18] and occupied many posts within the apparatus of the underground state. The choice of Mikołajczyk as premier of the Government-in-Exile reflected the importance of 'ROCh' within the resistance movement. During August and September 'Lublin' had high hopes of winning over 'ROCh' in its entirety or at any rate detaching a substantial section. While negotiations with Mikołajczyk were held in Moscow in early August and again in October, the authorities operated a relatively mild policy towards members of 'ROCh' and the Peasant Battalions. On 5 September 'ROCh' leaders held an illegal conference in Lublin itself. Several participants were arrested, but on indicating their readiness to cooperate with the PKWN were released and made their escape.[19] In fact the conference had reaffirmed its support for the London government and a boycott of the PKWN was declared in circulars issued at the beginning of August. Members working with the Lublin authorities were threatened with expulsion as 'traitors to the peasant cause'.[20] Although initially some 'ROCh' activists did find their way on to local national councils or into the militia, the boycott became more effective later and only a small proportion of the movement left the underground to throw in its lot with the PKWN.[21]

This group, which formed a rival 'Lublin SL' in August and September, was led by Peasant members of the PKWN: Andrzej Witos and Stanisław Kotek-Agroszewski. The 'Lublin SL' was not a serious rival for 'ROCh'. Its membership in December, by which time a local network had been established, is estimated at no more than 5,000–6,000.[22] The peasant movement did, however, provide the PKWN with a significant source of manpower in local government, although in many areas Peasant members of the national councils were closer to 'ROCh' than the 'Lublin' Peasant Party. In early November incomplete data show that the SL and Peasant Battalions constituted some 36 per cent of the membership of commune and district national councils as against 11 per cent for the PPR and 4 per cent for the Socialists and Democrats.[23] These figures probably underestimate the role played by the Peasants and in some districts such as Biłgoraj and Kraśnik they constituted as many as 80 per cent of councillors at the lowest tier.[24] The SL wielded considerable influence at higher administrative levels too. For example, Witold Jedliński, an SL member, was placed in charge of establishing administration in Rzeszów province. In this position he pursued an independent line, attempting to restore the pre-war elective local government system until he was removed on 29 September.[25] But it was Witos as vice-chairman of the PKWN and head of its Department of Agriculture and Land Reform, who could most affect policy. Until he was sacked in early October, one of the central planks of the PKWN programme, agrarian reform, was his responsibility.

In spite of its small size and separation from 'ROCh', the 'Lublin SL' proved an unsteady partner for the Communists. There were divisions over the leadership – no less than five candidates stood for chairman of the central committee at its September Congress[26] – as well as policy. An important section of the party opposed land reform in the shape forced through by the PPR, and inclined towards a compromise with 'ROCh' and Mikołajczyk. Many members of the party, reflecting the strong agrarian current in the Polish peasant movement, openly rejected Communist claims to hegemony and demanded a decisive say for their party.[27]

The Socialists, outside a few pockets of strength such as Lublin, Zamość and Krosno, had never been a significant force east of the Vistula. During the war the WRN had organizations in Lublin and amongst the oil-well workers of Krosno. Apart from groups in Biała Podlaska there appear to have been few traces of RPPS or Left Socialist activity in the region.[28] Osóbka-Morawski and Bolesław Drobner began talks with the other Socialists in Moscow on re-establishing the PPS even before the PKWN was set up.[29] However, within the PPR there were doubts about the wisdom of encouraging the emergence of a 'Lublin' Socialist Party, which might fall under the influence of the WRN. It was also feared that such a Socialist Party might develop into a competitor for the PPR in working-class areas. However, the PPR leadership decided that the balance of advantage lay in reviving the PPS. Gomułka stated its position in his 5 August speech: 'If we were to absorb certain elements from the PPS that party would be destroyed while we are after co-operation and it is in our interest that the partner organisation is strong so that it attracts those masses which we are not able to win over by ourselves.'[30] Locally, however, the situation was often confused. In Sandomierz, for instance, a 'Lublin PPS' branch began activity on 20 August with the approval of the Soviet military authorities. A few days later its entire membership joined the PPR, which took over the branch headquarters. The Socialists were coopted on to the district PPR committee, where they constituted a majority of the members. It was not until October that the Socialists split away from the PPR and reformed their own organization, on instructions from the PPS executive in Lublin.[31]

Within the leadership elected at the PPS Congress held in Lublin on 10–11 September there were three distinct currents of thought about the party's future. The group led by Stefan Matuszewski, the secretary-general, like many of the Communist leaders, envisaged a very limited role for the PPS. According to one modern Warsaw historian, Matuszewski saw the PPS

> not as an independent political factor, but as a useful 'label', which was supposed to neutralise the influence of the PPS-WRN as well as isolate the right-wing of the Foreign Committee of the PPS [i.e. the Socialists in London], both in its relations with Poland and with the Socialist parties in the West. At the same time the political authority of the PPS and its traditions, known to wide circles of Polish society, would make possible the widening of the narrow social base of the PKWN. . . . For these aims the existence of the PPS was necessary, but its organisational growth seemed superfluous, especially as it might become – as indeed it did in the following years – serious competition for the fast expanding PPR organisation.[32]

Matuszewski was amongst those who favoured the early merger of the two parties. In an article published on 9 November, he wrote: 'If today the PPS is consolidating its ranks, if today it is uniting all those who are scattered and those who were led astray or were disorientated, tomorrow work will begin on achieving unity of the worker's movement.'[33] Such an attitude on the part of the man who was in charge of the organizing of the party was one of the reasons for the shortcomings evident in this area. As Bardach has observed: 'the conditions were not created for the growth of the party in the localities, limiting it to traditional PPS areas. . . . [Because of] the conviction that the organisational unification of the workers' movement was imminent . . . the growth of the PPS, by activating former cadres linked in part during the occupation with the WRN, was deemed undesirable.'[34]

Bolesław Drobner, chairman of the party's Supreme Council, emerged as the spokesman for those who wished the PPS to play a much more positive role by recruiting actively among the party's traditional supporters including the rank and file of the WRN. This stance was popular with the activists, a large proportion of whom were formerly linked with WRN. Drobner's statement at the September Congress that 'the party offers a fraternal hand to the WRN-ites, let them return and join our ranks', was greeted with loud applause.[35] Drobner was also ready to praise the traditions of the pre-war PPS and assert the party's independence of the PPR.[36] At the September 1944 Congress he made the startling claim that the PPS throughout its history had 'stood steadfastly on the position of Poland's independence, in accordance with the theories of Marx and the views of Lenin and Stalin'.[37]

Osóbka-Morawski, as chairman of the PKWN and of the Central Executive of the PPS, was the most influential figure in the party. He shared Drobner's ambitions for the PPS, but was more circumspect in expressing them than his voluble comrade, who it seems often tried his patience. According to Drobner's deputy at the Department of Labour, Social Services and Health of the PKWN, Feliks Mantel, 'it was difficult to endure being with Drobner and more difficult still to work with him . . . he continually provoked Osóbka, preventing him from dealing with important problems. He denigrated the communists and the Soviet Union constantly.'[38] Osóbka, again according to Mantel's account, 'was not a puppet of the PPR, he did not give way to them. . . . Without personal ambition, he had nevertheless party ambitions. He was determined not to allow the PPR to push him to one side.'[39] This is borne out by other sources. In November Osóbka complained to Bierut that he was being treated like an 'accessory' (*doczepka*) and a month later the two clashed again, Osóbka exploding at Bierut: 'You have bandits and *Sanacja* men in your ranks, so purge yourselves and not our party.'[40]

Osóbka's advantage in the infighting within the leadership of the PPS and in his dealings with the Communists lay in his access to Stalin and the favour he found in the Kremlin. For example, in December after a visit to Moscow, Bierut informed the Politburo that Stalin's attitude to Osóbka-Morawski was favourable and that he had suggested that the PPR should rely on the Morawski group.[41] However, Osóbka seems to have been reluctant to use this Soviet support openly as a weapon against his rivals in the PPS. Thus he did not take advantage of Stalin's proposal that Drobner might be appointed PKWN representative in Moscow or Kiev, which would have effectively removed him from influence within the PPS. Osóbka also spoke up in defence of Drobner when he was criticized by Bulganin at a meeting in the Kremlin.[42]

While the PPS was not in a position to dispute PPR hegemony in the way that it did after mid-1945, neither at central nor local level did it tamely subordinate itself to the Communists. For example, Hillebrandt and Jakubowski, writing about the Praga suburb of Warsaw, state that:

> full confidence between the Praga PPR branch and the PPS group was lacking for a long time . . . Socialist activists frequently organised events – as a rule the same as those of the PPR – but separately, on their own initiative. In general PPS members showed more energy and discipline [in their own events] than in those staged jointly with the PPR. . . . Unhealthy rivalry also occurred. For a long time the PPS did not want to admit the PPR to some milieux, including working-class communities (e.g. the railway workers).

The situation in Praga improved only after widescale changes in the PPS leadership there in late November.[43] A report by the Warsaw provincial committee of the PPR for the period of 15 November 1944 to 1 January 1945 complained that:

> according to the information available 70% of the PPS *aktyw* is waiting for 'London' to return, or as they put it 'suitable cadres must be ready for when London arrives'. Like the SL, they direct their work to this end. They are trying to build up their organisation, fill responsible positions and take as little part as possible in joint activities. When we call them out they send representatives or greetings, but do not take an active part in campaigns and show little interest in political matters, at any rate on the outside.[44]

There is also evidence of tension between the Communist and Socialist elites. We have mentioned Osóbka's clashes with Bierut and Drobner's continual 'readiness for sharp debate'. More than once the PPS simply ignored PPR attempts to curb its influence. For example, it went ahead to form its own youth movement despite pressure from the PPR to submit to an all-party youth organization.[45] In November, Osóbka and the PPS arranged a Cooperative Congress in secret, with the result that the Socialists were able to re-establish their dominant position in the leadership of the Cooperative movement.[46] According to Edward Puacz, an émigré historian who obtained access to normally classified documents, there were some thirty meetings between Lublin representatives and Stalin during the second half of 1944. Their purpose was either to present joint PPR-PPS proposals to Stalin or to ask him to arbitrate between the two parties when they were in disagreement. This suggests that the Socialists were in a position to exert considerable influence and Puacz even argues that it was PPS pressure, culminating in an appeal to Stalin, which forced the subject of aid to the Warsaw uprising on to the PKWN agenda in mid-September.[47] Osóbka also implied, in an article published in later years, that Stalin overruled objections from Bierut and others to the immediate return to Warsaw as capital in early 1945, supporting the stand of the Socialists, Osóbka and Trojanowski.[48]

Such influence that the Socialists exerted sprang from their prominence in the top echelons of the PKWN rather than any organizational weight. The boycott operated by the underground WRN against the 'false PPS' was generally effective, particularly as far as experienced activists were concerned.[49] The hostility of such local Socialist leaders, Matuszewski's inactivity in the central secretariat and the absence of a strong PPS tradition in the region seriously restricted the growth of the party. At the end of 1944 it had perhaps 7,000–8,000 members.[50]

When the Soviet advance crossed the Bug, the First Polish Army numbered just over 100,000 men.[51] Initial plans for expansion envisaged, quite unrealistically, that the army would be quadrupled to some 430,000 men, organized as three armies of five divisions apiece.[52] Mobilization began at the end of August and during the next two months 66,000 recruits were conscripted, chiefly into the Second Army. It has been estimated that this draft fell short of the total liable for the first stage of conscription by between 20–40 per cent. To fill this gap it was decided to call up a further 46,000 men from the next classes.[53] The role of the London boycott of the mobilization will be considered presently, here we are concerned with the army as a political asset of the Lublin administration.

Though results fell short of the ambitious targets originally set, the creation of an army which by the end of the year numbered about 172,000 trained men[54] (plus 100,000 more undergoing training[55]) represented a major success for the PKWN and seriously weakened both the organization and authority of 'London'. This is not to say that the new recruits necessarily switched their allegiance. In very many cases the decision to submit to conscription indicated only a readiness to fight the Germans, rather than an endorsement of the Lublin regime. In a report written at the end of June Mieczysław Mietkowski, the head of the political apparatus of the First Army, described the political mood amongst recruits. These were conscripts from the eastern *kresy*, the main source of expansion of the army during the summer. However, it is unlikely that the mood of those called up in Lublin Poland differed greatly.

> A number of problems crop up amongst the new (recruits) in a form significantly sharper than among the old soldiers. The Ukrainian question . . . the frontier issue ('Lwów is a Polish city from long ago. . .') . . .
>
> It is worse in the formations stationed in the Przebraz-Kiwerce region. The local Polish population there is almost entirely under the influence of London propaganda. . . . The London government has immense authority amongst them. They imagine the future Poland basically as before. Attitude to the Soviet Union cool, with some hostile. . . . At first they looked on our army with great suspicion after coming into contact with officers who spoke Polish poorly or not at all. . .

. . . newly arrived units completely lack any political training apparatus . . . the human element is totally raw, remaining under the influence of London propaganda. Our propaganda does not get through to them. (Their) attitude to our army is full of distrust. Statements are made that it is 'a Polish mass run by the Jew-Commune' or that it is 'the Red Army in Polish uniforms'. Hatred of the Ukrainians is very great, generalised to the whole nation. Anti-Semitic feeling is fairly common.[56]

The value of placing this mass under military discipline and political influence was indisputable. However, in the short term the army demanded reliable cadres rather than providing them. This was apparent during the scare in October and November 1944 when the party feared it might lose control of its troops and the flow of political officers into administration and security had to be reversed.

The use of the army for civil purposes was necessarily circumscribed by the uncertainty over its allegiance. This was illustrated by the problems which arose in the use of troops to collect contingents from the peasantry. During September–October crack soldiers from the Special Storm Brigade were used for this purpose, but this unit – the forerunner of the Internal Security Corps (*Korpus Bezpieczeństwa Wewnętrznego* – KBW) – was only 1,053 strong in August and had grown to a mere 2,195 by November, when it was switched mainly to operations against the remnants of the London underground.[57] In its place ill-equipped and poorly-trained supply regiments consisting largely of Ukrainian and White Russian peasants were employed (presumably Poles were not regarded as suitable). These units proved both inefficient and insensitive.[58] About 600 officers and men were used to more positive effect during the parcellization of the great estates, when they participated in the distribution of about one-quarter of the total land involved and provided much needed support for the party's civilian land reform apparatus.[59] Even this limited contribution was invaluable in view of Lublin's shortage of manpower, but the army was able to alleviate the problem only marginally.

The security forces, the Citizens' Militia (*Milicja Obywatelska* – MO) and Security Office (*Urząd Bezpieczeństwa* – UB), were throughout 1944 still in the process of formation and like the army their political dependability was often suspect. In the first months the security apparatus was given priority over the army in the allocation of ex-AL partisans and specially trained army officers. However, the speed of its expansion inevitably involved relaxing recruitment standards. The UB had 2,500 officers by December 1944[60] and the MO had about 13,000 by early October.[61] The poor quality, lack of equipment and training, and low morale of these forces were discussed repeatedly in the Politburo and PKWN. In October the Communists decided on a drastic purge of the militia, transferring 50 per cent of its members into the army and filling the gap with soldiers.[62] Nevertheless two months later Jóźwiak, who had been appointed to command the MO, reported that 'the MO numbers about 14,000. The purge has shown that 7,000 needed to be dismissed.' He added that the 50 per cent transfer had not yet taken place.[63] But even these measures were unavailing and in May 1945 the MO and UB were once more subject to heavy criticism and further large-scale purges continued into 1945–6.

To sum up, by October 1944 the party east of the Vistula numbered perhaps 10,000 members. Its allies the 'Lublin' Socialists and Peasants, according to official figures, had together about 10,000 members. However, as Gomułka admitted, neither was very active, while 'the Democratic Party in general is not worth considering'. He added, 'our party is the real force'.[64] Apart from one or two thousand special troops, the army could not be trusted with assignments of a political nature. Work on organizing the militia and UB had only just begun. In many areas, the manpower of the security forces overlapped to a considerable extent with the membership of the party.[65] Nevertheless, these forces were regarded as being in need of a drastic purge. 'Lublin' could not rest its rule on these narrow resources. The failure of its efforts to broaden the national front into the London camp would leave no choice but to fall back on the Soviet factor and use more deliberately and extensively some of the 2.5 million Red Army troops massed on Polish territory.[66]

The party and the underground

THE party's line towards the AK in the summer and early autumn of 1944 was shaped by its broader commitment to the achievement of a national front. A discriminating policy was to be adopted towards the underground. As Radkiewicz, in charge of Public Security, later put it, 'we tried to differentiate between elements in the AK – fighting above all the NSZ, the most fascist, then the Piłsudski-ite, *Sanacja* core of the AK, while towards the Peasant Battalions we were very moderate.'[67] By stressing the need for national unity and the defeat of Germany, the Communists hoped to detach a large part of the rank and file of the AK, which would be used as the basis for a big expansion of the Polish army under Soviet command, leaving the reactionary sections of the AK officer corps and the Right of the London camp isolated.

The total strength of the AK in the territory of Lublin Poland in mid-1944 is impossible to estimate with any precision. The strength of AK units regularly based in the region a few months before was claimed to be between 100,000 to 150,000 troops.[68] However, the movement of units from the eastern *kresy* as the Red Army advanced, recruitment into the Polish army and Soviet round-ups had greatly complicated the position by July 1944.

As we have seen, during 1944 the underground state increasingly turned its attention to the problem of power in post-war Poland. As the likelihood grew that the Soviet army rather than the Western Allies would liberate Poland the question of how 'London' should respond to the advance on to Polish soil of the troops of a power with which it now had no diplomatic relations became extremely urgent. The Right-wing nationalists of the NSZ argued that the underground should prepare to continue its war with the occupant, whether Nazi or Soviet, by destroying pro-Soviet and Communist forces operating in conspiracy. However, this strategy was not one which the Government-in-Exile and the AK could adopt if it was to maintain any standing with the British and Americans or keep open the possibility of an accommodation with the Soviet government.

The tactics of the AK and the civilian organs of the underground towards the advancing Soviet armies as set out definitively in General Bor-Komorowski's order of 20 November 1943 were therefore to mobilize and offer assistance to the Red Army, in this way presenting the Soviets with the dilemma of either *de facto* recognizing 'London' as an ally, or repressing 'friendly' AK units, thereby risking friction with the Western Powers. The basic objective of operation 'Tempest', as the plan was code-named, was encapsulated in the following passage of Bor's order: 'I have ordered commanders and units, which will participate in fighting the retreating Germans, to reveal their presence to the Russians. Their task . . . will be to manifest through their action the existence of the Republic.'[69] These tactics were not intended to assist the Russians, whose aim, Bor wrote, 'is the destruction of the independence of Poland, or at least its political subordination to the Soviets',[70] but as a means to bolster the Polish cause amongst the Western Allies. As he put it, 'by giving the Soviets minimal military help we are creating political difficulties for them'.[71]

'Tempest' began in January 1944 when the Red Army crossed the pre-war frontier, but reached its peak during the huge Soviet offensive which began in late June and swept rapidly across the eastern *kresy* and during the second half of July into the territory to the west of the Curzon Line which Moscow recognized as Polish. AK units were mobilized in German-occupied areas with instructions to capture towns shortly before they fell to the Russians and establish Polish administrations there; they were then to welcome the advancing Red Army as hosts and reveal their forces to the local Soviet command. The tragic culmination of this plan was the Warsaw uprising, launched on 1 August in the expectation of the imminent Soviet entry into the capital.

In fact the commitment to revealing AK detachments to the Russians, though extensive, was not total. Bor, in the report he sent to Sosnkowski, the supreme commander in London, enclosing his order of 20 November, had added that 'in case of a second Russian occupation, I am preparing in the utmost secrecy the skeleton command network of a new clandestine organisation . . . it will be a separate network unconnected with the AK organisation, which has to a large degree been uncovered to elements in Soviet service.'[72] The new clandestine organization received the cryptonym *Nie*, and according to party historians was responsible for a number of the attacks on supporters of the Lublin Committee which occurred the following autumn.[73] Not only *Nie* remained underground; large sections of the AK were critical of the policy of leaving the conspiracy and reporting to the Russians. This was especially true of units linked with the National Party, on the anti-Soviet Right of the 'London' spectrum, belonging either to the National Military Organization (*Narodowa Organizacja Wojskowa* – NOW) or that part of the NSZ which had been merged into the AK. These formations retained a good deal of autonomy inside the AK and widely opted out of 'Tempest'.[74] Finally, the extreme-Right, National Radical wing of the NSZ, which had remained outside the AK, was, as we have seen, pursuing its own private war with the Communists.

Under the 'Tempest' plan, the Polish underground forces were to offer cooperation with the Red Army, but insist on retaining their identity as an integral part of the Polish armed forces loyal to the London government. The AK and its civilian network were, moreover, to negotiate solely with the Russian military authorities and hold aloof from any direct dealings with Lublin representatives. It was on these points that 'Tempest' came into collision with the national front strategy of the Communists.

Already in the eastern *kresy* 'Tempest' had set into a pattern of failure.[75] The Russians, unwilling to accept the political conditions implicitly tied to the cooperation proffered by the AK, had presented the Poles with the ultimatum of either joining General Berling's largely Soviet-officered Polish army or disarming and dissolving their units. The advance across the Bug into territory recognized by Moscow as Polish and the priority given to broadening the base of the PKWN, which now for the first time became directly involved in the confrontation, nevertheless made what happened in the Lublin region something of a test-case.

Lublin city itself was captured from the Germans in fighting between 23 and 25 July. Once shooting had died down, the AK and the government delegate for the city, Władysław Cholewa, began, in accordance with the 'Tempest', to take over the local administration. Proclamations were pasted up, the town hall occupied, State Security Corps (the underground's police force) patrols stationed in the streets and recruitment offices for the 'Lublin Battalion' of the AK opened. On 25 July the first PKWN representatives arrived, led by Edward Ochab, and the next day General Berling and Aleksander Zawadzki arrived at the head of regular Polish units. On the same day attempts were made, by Radkiewicz it seems, to open talks between the PKWN and the 'Londoners', who in line with 'Tempest', refused to enter negotiations with anyone except the

Soviet military authorities. On 27 July a meeting took place between General Kolpaczka, commander of the Soviet Sixth Army, Cholewa and Colonel Tumidajski, the area AK commander. Kolpaczka issued the usual ultimatum: the AK forces had either to join the Polish army fighting with the Red Army, or lay down their arms. The 'London' representatives followed their instructions and chose the latter alternative, adamantly refusing to recognize the PKWN.

It is worth noting that this meeting lasted until 29 July, whereupon Cholewa and Tumidajski were allowed to leave, though under surveillance. Apparently Radkiewicz and the Russians had not yet excluded the possibility that the underground leaders might revise their position. If this was the case, these hopes were entertained for only four or five days as the process of disarming AK units in the region got under way. On the one hand the 'Londoners' were alarmed by reports of arrests and deportations of AK officers and the internment of units, while on the other, PKWN security officials became convinced that the AK was handing over only a proportion of its arms and disbanding only a part of its network. In both cases these fears were probably well-founded.

The *Nie* organization has been mentioned, and in February instructions were issued which spoke of a 'second subsidiary network of civil and military leaders . . . which will remain underground, trying to establish contact with the Polish authorities and informing them of the fate of revealed representatives'.[76] There were besides numerous AK units, particularly those linked with the nationalist front, which disagreed with the 'Tempest' strategy and did not come into the open. On the other side, the Communists were not averse to using limited force in order to loosen what they saw as the hold of reactionary officers over the democratic mass of the AK. In practice this task was frequently left to NKVD (Soviet People's Commissariat for Internal Affairs) detachments charged with providing security behind the front. These units were hardly suited to drawing the fine distinctions such a policy assumed and from the start bloody clashes occurred between AK forces and those of the NKVD attempting to disarm them.[77]

The mutual suspicions were greatly intensified by the outbreak of the uprising in Warsaw on 1 August, which was interpreted in Lublin as a dire threat to its position, demanding a new aggressive stance to replace the flexibility and optimism of the first week of power. On 3 August Radkiewicz put the Security Department's view of priorities to the PKWN: '1/Mobilisation into the army of the broad mass of the AK. 2/The arrest of the AK commanders. Our tactics – offensive . . . the AK is attempting to seize Warsaw, to install its army and administration.'[78] The repercussions of this tougher line were felt in Lublin immediately. On 2 August Radkiewicz had told the PKWN that 'the AK command in Lublin formally agreed to lay down its arms, but did this only partially. . . . We must commence determined activity, with the probable use of repression. The AK has begun illegal work.'[79] The next day Tumidajski and Cholewa were brought in for further talks with the Russians with PKWN spokesmen in attendance. The 'Londoners' attempted to clarify the uncertainty over the treatment of their men, refusing once more demands that they subordinate their troops to the PKWN until such time as an agreement was reached between the Committee and Mikołajczyk, then in Moscow. The two men were thereupon arrested and despatched into imprisonment somewhere in the Soviet Union.[80]

The episode was duplicated in many other places: Zamość, Przemyśl, Rzeszów, Białystok and dozens of other towns and villages. In general, the confrontation lasted a few days before the Soviets intervened decisively and cleared out the AK authorities. The course of events in Lublin demonstrated the inevitability of conflict between the two sides as they carried out their instructions, for although both strategies aimed at avoiding an open clash, they were more concerned with extracting *de facto* recognition from the other of their claim to rule Poland. The outcome of the manoeuvring in July and August 1944 was hardly satisfactory for either side: the PPR captured the administrative machine, but thanks to Soviet military power, not the support of a broad national front; 'London' demonstrated its military and administrative presence, but also its total powerlessness in the face of Soviet backing for the PKWN.

Despite these setbacks to their respective strategies, neither side openly abandoned its tactics. 'Tempest' continued until October, fizzling out as the Soviet-German front stabilized. Amongst the Communists, the initial jolt of the Warsaw uprising gave way within a few days to a calmer appraisal of the situation. The arrival in Lublin of Gomułka and other leaders of the underground party was followed by reassertions of the broad national front line. In his first speech to the party *aktyw* on 5 August, Gomułka warned 'do not alienate other groupings . . . invite (them) to co-operate . . . by pursuing such a policy we deprive the conservative element of its weapons, we can isolate the reaction from the masses still under its influence.'[81] Over the following weeks the leadership persevered with this line, sustained by the Russians' apparent preference for a deal between Lublin and Mikołajczyk's following as well as the distinct possibility of the Red Army relieving the 'London' insurgents fighting in Warsaw. But on the ground, the strategies of both sides soon began to modify in the face of realities.

Having witnessed what had happened in Lublin and elsewhere, AK officers on the ground were most unhappy about carrying on with the policy of revealing their forces to the Russians. At least one commander wired Warsaw to confirm whether this order remained in force, adding that 'there is strong opposition amongst my officers and men'.[82] Białystok AK, under the command of Colonel Liniarski, disobeyed the order *en masse.*[83] By September, Bor himself had apparently dropped this aspect of 'Tempest' and began ordering AK concentrations to disperse and partisan units to dissolve. On 26 September he transmitted this message to Rzeszów command: 'Do not organise any conspiratorial AK units. Dissolve partisan detachments under Soviet *occupation* [emphasis added]. Disperse the troops.'[84]

Although Bor was by this time referring to the Soviet presence as an occupation, there is no satisfactory evidence that the *Nie* network was activated. Its command was pinned down in Warsaw and communications with the outside were severely disrupted. Bor, who was gambling on the Red Army relieving the insurrection in the capital, repeatedly and categorically forbade provincial commands to fight the Russians.[85] Clashes occurred all the same; orders to avoid conscription were misinterpreted by some units, which resisted with force or occasionally assassinated recruitment officers.[86] Shoot-outs also took place between NKVD detachments and AK units in the process of dispersal or remaining in conspiracy.[87] In some instances, AK officers disobeyed Bor's orders to dissolve and stayed underground to defend the population against marauding Soviet troops.[88] By the end of the year the Russians were claiming that some 300 Red Army officers had been killed.[89]

Such bloodshed, by no means all the work of the AK, was minimal in comparison with the level it was to reach in early 1945. But together with the growing feeling amongst party activists that they were being over-whelmed by the sheer inertia of the administrative machine, as well as fears for the allegiance of the armed forces, this violence reinforced the arguments of the hardliners in the PPR who were demanding a more radical solution to the problem of the underground.

The 'October turn'

THE party's moderation towards the Home Army and the 'democratic' wing of the London camp was maintained until early October. Its line was then abruptly transformed. By November a concerted effort to crush the AK was under way, an aggressive land parcellization campaign spearheaded a general radicalization of policy, while any deal with London had been indefinitely postponed. Although lip-service was still paid to the construction of the national front, in practice from October 1944 to May 1945 this strategy was submerged. Instead, the party pursued a narrowly-based, radical course which relied heavily on the repression applied by its own meagre security forces, greatly reinforced by Soviet units and advisers.

The 'October turn' was sudden and drastic. As late as 26 September the party leadership had affirmed that its objective was 'not only the main-tenance, but also the broadening of the national front . . . (and) unification of the nation, conceived as the active solidarity of all the main strata of the nation, of all the democratic parties.'[90] To the distaste of party militants, repressive measures were kept to a minimum. Edwarda Orłowska, secretary for Białystok province, complained that local activists came 'to us from the districts and say "What sort of power is this?" *Volksdeutsche* [Poles of German origin who declared their German nationality during the War] and traitors walk about the town. *Endeks* [National Democrats] openly make trouble and nothing happens to them. . . . Why so far has there been no death sentence? Ruthless repression should be applied against the leading (AK) commanders.'[91] From what other speakers at the same meeting said, it is clear that generally the party *aktyw* was not even armed at this stage.[92]

The level of arrests was restrained too. At the end of September Radkiewicz reported that only 3,000 (including 1,500 Home Army) people had been detained, most of whom had been pressed into the army. He admitted though that 'so far as arrests by the Soviet authorities are concerned, we do not have full data or information'.[93] In the army itself the stress was on integrating not only AK troops, but officers too. An instruction to *politruki* of the First Army dated 25 September ordered them to engender 'an atmosphere of friendly concern and fraternity' around AK officers, 'strongly emphasising the factor of national unity'. While noting the danger of hostile infiltration, it warned against the use of 'police surveillance methods'.[94]

Land reform, which the Communists saw as the key to capturing the allegiance of the peasants, was handled with the same restraint and was entrusted throughout the summer and early autumn to Andrzej Witos, head of the PKWN Department of Agriculture. Witos was a member of the Peasant Party, not noted for his radicalism. He planned gradual land reform 'in the majesty of the law' and was sceptical whether this would be administratively possible before the end of the war. Nonetheless, the Communists gave him a free hand and as late as 26 September stressed in a Central Committee circular that estate workers' committees (organized and often manned by the party) should cooperate with Witos's Land Offices.[95]

During the following week the party shifted its stance fundamentally. On 28 September amended instructions were issued to activists in the countryside claiming that 'even amongst some district officials of Land Offices and estate administrators, just those to whom the state has entrusted the implementation of land reform, there is a desire to delay and deflect it'. Estate committees were now advised to keep a close eye on Witos's administrators and special Land Reform Commissions were to be created in order, amongst other things, 'to nip in the bud every attempt to obstruct the reform by lackies of the reactionary landowners'.[96] This was a portent. On 4 October Radkiewicz, addressing the PKWN on security matters, digressed to announce the party's altered strategic perspective.

Claiming that 'a new situation, a new distribution of forces has arisen', he argued that there was now 'a distinct dividing line [between] the two centres: the PKWN and London, without any dividing line between Mikołajczyk and Sosnkowski' (leader of the London diehards). The attempt to differentiate between the various elements in the Home Army had not, he said, 'been confirmed by reality' and the divide between 'the PKWN and on the other side *all* the opponents of the PKWN', demanded that 'hitherto haphazard repression' give way to 'a period of planned, intensive work'.[97] A few days later, the land reform campaign was set in motion; Witos was dismissed and an improvised apparatus, led by special commissars with sweeping powers, forged ahead with the parcellization of the estates. Party militants were allowed off the leash against the underground also. On 9 October Gomułka declared that 'the state must reply to the terror; the time has come to begin the counter-attack.'[98] A Decree for the Defence of the State was issued at the end of the month, introducing draconian penalties for 'subversion'. By mid-November a local commissar could report that 'peoples courts have been set up; 30 AK have been shot, 500 arrested'.[99] In the army the *volte-face* was particularly dramatic. The 'open-doors' recruitment policy of the summer was abandoned, Gomułka stating bluntly that 'the AK on which not so long ago we were determined to construct the Polish Army, have in the overwhelming majority of cases turned out to be hostile elements'.[100] In November *politruki* received instructions contrasting sharply with those issued a few weeks before. 'Friendly concern and fraternity' towards the AK were now grounds for suspicion: 'Every political worker', the order demanded, 'must understand that today there is no room for any compromise with the AK in the army . . . treat advocates of a "neutral" or conciliatory attitude to the AK as AK members unless they immediately engage in active struggle with the AK.'[101]

The party's change of direction in October 1944 meant that in Poland the foundations of Communist power were laid in conditions of virtual civil war and overt reliance on Soviet force of arms. This outcome was at odds with the strategy pursued by the Communists (both inside Poland and in Soviet emigration) during the war, or indeed later in 1945–8 in Eastern Europe generally. What prompted this apparent aberration?

With the abandonment on 22 September of attempts by the Russians and Berling's troops to establish a bridgehead on the west bank of the Vistula, it became apparent that the Red Army would not be used to relieve the uprising in Warsaw.[102] Until then, this possibility had governed the political situation. As we have seen, the Home Army command restrained its forces outside the capital in order not to antagonize the Soviets, while Lublin was half-prepared for early entry into a coalition with part at least of the London camp and the incorporation into its army of thousands of armed, battle-hardened insurrectionaries. With the stabilization of the

Soviet front on the far bank of the Vistula and the collapse of the last pockets of resistance on the other side a few days later, the political situation was transformed. Whereas during the summer the PKWN had been able to some extent to capitalize on the patriotic elation which greeted the German retreat, the Soviet failure to save the uprising aroused a wave of popular hostility and bitterness towards the new authorities which undermined their appeal to national unity. Moreover, it would be several months before the advance could resume, until which time the PKWN would have to maintain its grip on power and establish a political base by means other than patriotic slogans and calls to battle against the Germans.

The implications of the Warsaw fiasco were sensed immediately in Lublin and doubtless discussed by the PKWN at a secret session held on 23 September.[103] But the party seems to have been perplexed by Soviet policy and uncertain how to tailor its own course to the new circumstances. The leadership's resolution of 26 September was perhaps intended to head-off questioning of the party's general line until Soviet intentions were known, but the questioning continued anyway. The next day, for instance, Rola-Żymierski showed the way the wind was blowing in a speech to the PKWN:

> the operation which the AK is undertaking in the terrain is becoming increasingly strong and determined. I have instructed that all materials be examined and am determined to take a clear position on this matter. So far we have sought a conciliatory way of dealing with the problem. As a result of the hostile activity of the AK and other organisations we were unable to achieve this. The state of affairs which has arisen in this country cannot be tolerated. The Polish population is living under terror and we do nothing about it. I feel we can no longer be passive observers.

Radkiewicz, who spoke next, supported this call for a more aggressive approach.[104] The next day, as we have mentioned, the Central Committee issued its amended and toughened instruction on land reform.

These moves preceded formal consultations to clarify Stalin's attitude. On 28 September a PKWN delegation flew to Moscow, staying until 3 October. The visit, as its leader, Bierut, reported on his return, 'was the result of our doubts over the general situation arising from the checking of activity on the Polish front and the failure of the Warsaw operation.'[105] Stalin, in his remarks to the full delegation, attributed the halting of the Soviet advance solely to military logistics and denied any political motives.[106] However, in conversations with its Communist members, he bluntly expressed his dissatisfaction with their political performance, particularly over land reform, and signalled a change of course. According to Bierut's subsequent report to the Politburo, 'Stalin cannot see revolutionary method in our approach. . . . He sharply criticised our softness, that up to now not one landowner has been imprisoned. . . . As he put it "get better or get out".'[107]

Hitherto, Soviet pressure had consistently tended to restrain the radicalism of the Polish Communists and stress the overriding importance of avoiding contention with the West over Poland. Now suddenly Stalin was reprimanding the Poles for their cautiousness. However, while it is clear that Stalin's intervention was a critical factor prompting the 'October turn', it would also seem that a significant and growing section of the Polish party had reached the same conclusion before the delegation's departure. Stalin's injunctions obviously demanded an urgent display of aggression from the PPR leadership, which complied without delay, but for much of the *aktyw* and at least part of the upper echelons of the party, Stalin was at last allowing them to go in the direction they favoured and which they believed the political situation demanded.

Many of the party activists, especially those charged with establishing the authority of the PKWN outside Lublin, had for some time been calling for a more aggressive line. These cadres were keenly aware of just how narrow was the support for the Lublin regime and felt increasingly exposed and powerless as the underground dispersed back into conspiracy. Sporadic assassinations, passive resistance and the continued domination by London sympathizers of large parts of the militia, local government and even the security apparatus set up by the Communists, aroused the fears and suspicions of such beleaguered cadres. These doubts were heightened by a growing feeling of *immobilisme* and wasted opportunity, especially over land reform,[108] as well as the ambiguous and unreliable attitude of the Communists' supposed allies amongst the Peasants and Socialists. The outlook of these militants was shaped both by their awareness that time was short in which to install an adequate state machine before the Red Army continued its advance and by deeply-rooted ideological traits. Veterans of the KPP who constituted the backbone of the *aktyw* of the PPR in many cases found the new national front strategy altogether too liberal and gradualist. Internal party reports frequently made reference to the distaste of older Communists for the tactics they were expected to apply. Ex-KPP cadres who had joined the PPR after liberation had, according to one report from Praga, 'a whole range of sectarian prejudices from the period of KPP work and it is difficult for them to adapt themselves to our Party's system of work in the current situation.'[109] At party meetings, hardliners found a receptive audience for their criticisms of the mildness of the official line. One of them, Witold Konopka, drew applause at a conference of the *aktyw* held on 10–11 October when he demanded that 'alongside campaigning against the AK, we must of course shoot at them and gaol them. By not shooting we are encouraging the enemy's impudence.'[110] Another KPP stalwart and prominent figure in the PPR leadership, Leon Kasman, encapsulated the mood of the militants: 'Our Party has succumbed to the parliamentary disease. With power in our hands, we have not applied terror towards the reaction. . . . We showed our enemies softness – not a single head has fallen.'[111]

Some modern Warsaw historians have argued that this sectarian strain in the party extended into the top leadership where it was represented above all by Jakub Berman, Hilary Minc, Roman Zambrowski and Stanisław Radkiewicz, all of whom had spent the war years in Moscow and were judged to be particularly subservient to the Soviets. The national front strategy, on the other hand, so it is claimed, was identified with that section of the party which had fought underground in Poland during the war and amongst whom Gomułka was the leading figure. The 'October turn' is presented as a victory for the hardline 'Muscovite' faction over the 'native' supporters of the national front.[112]

In fact, the differences within the party leadership over strategy tended to cut across the wartime divide. Thus the leading 'hawk' in the Politburo seems to have been Bierut, who had been in Warsaw from 1943. His views correspond to those of a vocal hardline element amongst the rank and file of the underground PPR. On the other hand, as we have seen, the broad national front strategy in the form crystallized in July 1944 had been largely the product of the Moscow emigration, closely reflecting Soviet requirements. The underground PPR inclined to a more radical 'democratic' national front and had been criticized for sectarianism by the Moscow group because of this. The 'October turn' in many ways vindicated the position of the 'natives' against the émigrés, and for all the differences in outlook between them, it was Bierut and Gomułka who took the lead in orchestrating the 'turn'. Moreover, the 'democratic' character of the national front was once again accented.

Ideological undercurrents and differing political backgrounds apart, by mid-September all sections of the party were increasingly disturbed by accumulating evidence of what was taken to be a wide-ranging conspiracy by London to overthrow the PKWN. Reports from local branches were alarming; rumours were put about that the PKWN would resign on 15 September; that the Germans were about to return; that the Western Allies were on their way or that a coup d'état was imminent.[113] The PKWN, deliberating on the situation in Warsaw, gave serious consideration to the possibility that Mikołajczyk was about to parachute into the city and establish his government there.[114] Disquieting reports were received from the army too. On 16 September the deputy-commander (political) of the 5th Infantry Division described the progress of political work amongst the civilian population:

> The AK, infuriated by this campaign, has gone onto the counter-offensive . . . a peasant PPR member of the organisational committee was badly wounded. The AK distributes masses of leaflets threatening those answering the call-up with death and makes armed attacks on conscripts. . . . The civilian authorities are timid and lack imagination. In Łuków there is no garrison commander . . . the Militia is

completely helpless. It must be stressed that the reserve of the population towards us is dictated to a large extent by fear of AK terror. . . . The troops still look on the PKWN with reserve, unconvinced of its permanence, and the majority still hope for an agreement with the London 'government'. AK activity has a depressing effect on the troops. . . . Almost 100 per cent of the soldiers are fanatically religious.[115]

A particularly worrying aspect of what was seen as a concerted campaign by the AK to undermine the PKWN was its apparent success in dissuading trained officers from joining the army. Rola-Żymierski informed the PKWN on 18 September that while the general mobilization was going according to plan, only 960 of the 2,400 officers required had been recruited.[116]

These fears did not abate. On 29 September the governor of Białystok province filed a particularly disturbing report: 'the AK is beginning to activate very intensively here . . . setting up armed detachments. In the Białowieża forests these are thought to number 17,000. Other large forests have their units too. . . . Unconfirmed rumours are circulating that a large-scale armed demonstration is being prepared, with 14 November or another later date being mentioned.'[117] The party leadership seems to have expected an insurrection against the PKWN timed to coincide with Mikołajczyk's arrival in Moscow for talks in mid-October.[118] His previous arrival in Moscow in August had been immediately followed by the outbreak of the Warsaw uprising, which the Communists were almost certainly right in regarding as no mere coincidence.[119] The desertion of whole units from the army – some 3,000 troops in all from the Second Army during October[120] – culminated on the night of 12–13 October with the desertion of much of the 31st Infantry Regiment, apparently at the instigation of the ex-AK officers,[121] and was seen as confirmation of such fears.

The picture which emerges is that by late September 1944 the leadership of the PPR was encountering increasing difficulties in convincing the rank and file of the correctness of its moderate course. The apparent reactivization of the AK and the hardening of the Soviet attitude to the prospect of a deal with London seemed to remove both the internal and external props of the broad 'patriotic' national front. Once Stalin had given the signal, the party with alacrity jettisoned the line it had been tied to for almost three years.

The underground and the aftermath of 'Tempest'

THE widespread belief within the PPR that the underground was not only still a military threat, but was also sufficiently belligerent to contemplate a rising against the Lublin Committee was quite mistaken. In fact, as we have seen, by September and October the AK Command was ordering its units to disperse and cease conspiratorial activity. With the capitulation of

Warsaw on 3 October, Bor went into German captivity along with many of his staff, while his successor, General Leopold Okulicki, escaped to begin organizing a new command in the Częstochowa region. This command was cut off from a large part of the AK network and was also viewed very suspiciously by government circles in London. Okulicki was regarded by many as a reckless officer too closely identified with Sosnkowski, the effective leader of the opposition within the emigration to the kind of concessions which might allow a deal with the Soviet Union. Okulicki's appointment was not officially endorsed until shortly before Christmas, by which time Mikołajczyk's government had been replaced by one composed of critics of his policy of seeking an agreement at the cost of concessions on the eastern frontier. In the meantime, General Tatar exercised temporary command of the AK by radio from England.[122]

Apart from these command problems, after the failure of the uprising and 'Tempest', the underground was in no state to undertake offensive operations. In the liberated zone of Poland, where several million Soviet troops were stationed, this would have amounted to suicide. In his 'Guideline for activity during the winter period 44/45', issued on 26 October, Okulicki admitted 'the great confusion and chaos' in the AK ranks and the need to 'overcome fatigue and a certain kind of stupor'. He laid stress on the importance of grouping together all military organizations under the AK, and preparing for the worst by adapting the conspiracy so that it could 'last out a possible Soviet occupation'. There was to be no armed resistance to the Russians, although the policy of revealing AK units was now specifically abandoned.[123]

These instructions no doubt failed to reach many *akowcy* in the field, but with very few exceptions, underground detachments were disinclined to take on Soviet and Communist forces; their objective was rather to elude NKVD round-ups or conscription by dispersing to their homes or into the forests and sitting out the winter until the Red Army resumed its offensive in the spring. Equally, the military formations linked with the Right-wing National Democrats, the National Military Organization and the NSZ had in general opted-out of 'Tempest', scattering their troops and burying their organization in deep conspiracy. In spite of Okulicki's calls for unity, the *endeks* were gradually detaching themselves from the AK and in November the National Military Union (*Narodowy Związek Wojskowy* – NZW) was created, envisaged by its founders as a rival framework for the nationalist forces. Even the extreme National Radical NSZ were relatively quiet in 'Lublin Poland', though in German-occupied territory they continued their war with Communist and Soviet partisans.[124]

The ascription of the overwhelming difficulties of the PKWN in late 1944 to underground activity had then very limited validity; such difficulties had their origin in the objective weakness of the PPR and the narrowness of its influence, rather than subversion or sabotage.[125] Nevertheless, the case for striking at the AK while it was weakened and the Russians were at hand was persuasive and this consideration may have lain behind much of the militancy drummed up in October.

The counter-attack

THE Lublin counter-attack, as Gomułka had defined it, lasted until May 1945. While continuing to employ the rhetoric of the national front, the Communists in fact unleashed a campaign of terror designed to destroy the same underground forces which a few weeks before they had been courting. By early 1945 party propaganda was equating the AK with the Gestapo.

The 'October turn' was viewed in various ways by the different sections of the party. For the militants it represented the final abandonment of a tactical stance dictated by international considerations but which seemed to them to have little relevance to the situation on the ground or basis in revolutionary marxism-leninism. The indications are, though, that for the leadership the turn was intended as a short-term tactical detour within rather than a departure from the national front strategy. It was assumed that a further attempt to reach argeement with 'London' would take place when this suited Soviet foreign policy and when 'Lublin' had strengthened its internal position and weakened that of its rivals. Meanwhile, the emphasis would be on 'capturing the majority of the working masses', especially the peasants through land reform, 'from below'. 'Combinations from above' with the bourgeois parties could await more favourable circumstances.[126] This was the intention, but the 'October turn' had a momentum of its own which was to sweep the party rapidly into positions quite incompatible with the national front.

The attempts to reach agreement with the leaderships of the underground parties and in particular Mikołajczyk's SL'ROCh' gave way to a policy of prising the rank and file of these parties away from those leaderships, a tactic which hitherto had been applied chiefly in order to exert pressure on party chiefs to compromise, but was now aimed rather at breaking up the 'London' organizations. On the surface the Communists' stance towards a deal with Mikołajczyk did not change immediately. On 17 October Bierut held unofficial talks with him in Moscow and as late as 3 December the Politburo reaffirmed its public position of favouring Mikołajczyk's entry into the PKWN.[127] But the true feeling of the party leadership was revealed in Bierut's remark to Stalin on 12 October that 'we want to reach an understanding [with Mikołajczyk], but would prefer that it takes place later'.[128] By mid-December, after Stalin had remarked that Mikołajczyk would not be allowed to return as long as the Red Army remained in Poland, the PPR line had hardened and a deal seems to have been ruled out for the foreseeable future.[129]

By this stage Stalin was ready to show his support for the PKWN more openly. At the end of the year he sanctioned the transformation of the PKWN into a Provisional Government and granted it official diplomatic recognition. This seal of approval was all the more significant since it was accompanied by a sharp weakening of the position of the Government-in-Exile at the international level. On 24 November, Mikołajczyk resigned, unable to carry the majority of his cabinet with his policy (which had the strong support of the British) of compromise with the Soviets and Lublin. A new government under the Socialist, Tomasz Arciszewski, was sworn in, but it had only the formal backing of the British and Americans. The former, in particular, continued to pin their hopes of a deal on Mikołajczyk and his supporters who now moved into opposition.[130] Within the underground political leadership in Poland, in which Mikołajczyk's Peasant Party followers continued to exert a considerable influence, the change of government was received unfavourably. The return of the Peasants to the government was regarded unanimously by the underground parties as 'very urgent and important'.[131] The SL pressed strongly for a vote of no confidence in Arciszewski and the resumption by Mikołajczyk of his premiership with a determined policy of seeking agreement with the Soviets even at the cost 'of very heavy concessions in the east'.[132]

The Communists diagnosed these developments as symptoms of 'a deep and lethal crisis amongst the London émigrés',[133] but they were not ready to renew their efforts to win over Mikołajczyk. In place of a political alliance with the peasant movement the Communists now concentrated on mobilizing the peasantry as a social class around the PKWN. Land reform was seen as the means to win over the allegiance of the rural population and undermine the base of the SL'ROCh'. 'The quicker the land is divided, the weaker will be the position of Mikołajczyk', as Gomułka put it.[134] This political consideration was given priority over both the economic argument that the new plots should not be inefficiently small and the claims of the landless estate workers to preferential treatment in the apportionment of the land. The party leadership repeatedly and categorically insisted that the benefits of the reform should be spread as extensively as possible and in particular that small and middle peasants should benefit. Local party activists who showed a tendency to exclude these groups threatened, in the opinion of the Central Committee 'to sow conflict . . . between small-peasants and agricultural labourers, between middle-peasants and poor peasants. . . . [This] will assist the work of the reaction amongst the middle-peasant masses.'[135] In some cases where the reform had deviated from central instructions the party demanded that the land be redivided and in a few instances those responsible were arrested.[136] This uncompromising response stemmed from the leadership's awareness that it was the middle peasants who carried the most political weight in the villages and who had to be won over if 'London's' rural base was to be broken.

The policy of by-passing the traditional peasant movement was also reflected in the Communists' new attitude to the 'Lublin SL'. Until October this party, small though it was, had embraced certain genuine sections of the traditional movement. Witos, Kotek-Agroszewski and others in its leadership, while prepared to work with the PPR did not tamely accept its hegemony. In the new atmosphere such independence was no longer tolerated. According to Bierut 'reactionary-kulak elements' had been allowed into the SL leadership.[137] As we have seen, the removal of Witos from the PKWN, followed shortly by that of Kotek-Agroszewski, heralded the hardening of the PPR line. On 22–23 November along with other independently-minded activists they were expelled from the SL leadership. The new leadership, which had been cleared with the Politburo in advance[138] comprised less troublesome figures: Maślanka, Janusz, Czechowski, Grubecki and so on, who it was thought could be relied upon to follow the Communists' lead. However, within a month the Politburo was concerned at the inactivity of this group and decided to delegate some of its own cadres to strengthen it. The Communists also envisaged a much more limited role for the SL. Gomułka warned that if the SL expanded as a mass organization it would be exposed to penetration by Mikołajczyk's followers. Berman went further and questioned whether the SL would be needed at all much longer. By this time the Communists were pinning their hopes of capturing mass support in the countryside not on the Peasant Party, however tame, but on a new organization, the Peasant Self-help Union (*Związek Samopomocy Chłopskiej* – ZSCh), formed in December to link together those peasants who had been drawn under party influence during the land reform.[139]

However, the political gains of the land reform could only compensate in small part for the party's failure to achieve an alliance with the peasant movement. The reform had only got under way in earnest in mid-October. By mid-November it was one-third complete and by 15 December, when peasant delegate congresses were held in each of the provinces, it was completed. In total some 212,084 hectares had been distributed between 110,000 households, creating 33,000 new holdings and expanding 77,000 existing ones.[140] About 14 per cent of the rural population had benefited. It was on this base that the party was able to rest much of its expansion in late 1944, from just under 9,000 members at the beginning of October to 21,649 by the end of December (which together with members still under German occupation brought the estimated strength of the PPR up to 34,000).[141] Zambrowski claimed that more than 100,000 peasants had taken part in the election of delegates to the first Congress of the ZSCh in December 1944.[142] This was an undoubted achievement and Stalin was reported to have been pleased with the progress of the reform.[143] On the other hand, the party remained extremely weak in most rural districts; over 80 per cent of peasants had not received land and despite recruitment of new members they were still spread very thinly. In Białystok province, PPR members had more than quadrupled between 1 October and 1 January, but still stood at only 781.[144] The Communists had gained a small foothold in the countryside, which nevertheless remained the domain of SL'ROCh' and the underground.

The role ascribed by the Communists to the 'Lublin PPS' also diminished after October. The emphasis moved from recruiting former members of the WRN to excluding them from political life. At the Socialists' Supreme Council on 17 November Drobner warned against these attempts to divide the party into its RPPS and WRN wings.[145] However, as we have seen, Drobner himself soon came under Communist suspicion and attempts were made to remove him from the PPS leadership and force Osóbka to purge the WRN.[146] There is also evidence to suggest that discussions were held within the PPR at this time on the possibility of a merger of the two parties.[147]

The radicalization of the party's line on land reform was paralleled by a change of tactics in relation to ownership and management of industry. The PKWN manifesto and party statements up to October had avoided using such terms as 'nationalization' and said little about the role of workers in directing the factories. Instead they stressed the commitment to early restoration of industrial concerns to their private owners.[148] Instructions governing the return of ownership of factories to their original proprietors were drawn up by Kotek-Agroszewski's Department of Public Administration, dated 18 and 23 September. However, when these were discussed by the PKWN on 7 October it was decided that the Department had acted beyond its competence and the instructions were shelved.[149] At the same time, the powers of the workers' own representatives on the factory councils which had sprung up in many branches of industry were broadened. An instruction of the PKWN Department of National Economy and Finances from September 1944 had entrusted factory management to three-man provisional committees comprising the director as chairman, a representative of the local authority and a delegate elected by the factory council.[150] Central Committee instructions put out on 2 October proclaimed the 'great role' to be played by the factory councils in managing their concerns. Although the powers of the factory councils were not defined in law until February 1945, the instruction opened the way to what amounted in effect to workers' control of the management of many factories. This became all the more evident when the more industrialized regions were liberated a few months later.[151] Within a week of the issue of the 2 October instructions party spokesmen were telling local factory activists that official policy was that 'the workers take upon themselves the entire responsibility for the factories'.[152]

The new line was also applied in the army, as we have noted, and in the administration of local and central government. The party's initial policy was to open wide 'the gates of the Polish Army to all soldiers and officers of the AK' and to employ civil servants regardless of their political background provided only that they had not collaborated with the Nazis and were not overtly hostile to the PKWN. This policy did not long survive the 'turn'. On 29 October Gomułka told the Politburo that

> the AK, on which not long ago we were determined to base the expansion of the Polish Army, have in the overwhelming majority of cases turned out to be a hostile element. In view of a possible agreement with Mikołajczyk, this danger is all the greater. The Army which we built may become an instrument in the hands of the reaction.

As for the administration: 'We have power at the top, but by no means do we have the whole apparatus in our hands. Revolutionary changes will not be brought about with the old apparatus.'[153] A fortnight later the leadership assembled the PPR *aktyw* in Lublin to announce the second stage of the new course: the 'democratization' of the army, particularly of the officer-corps, and of the state apparatus. 'Above all', Gomułka argued in his speech, 'the struggle for a democratic Poland is today a struggle for the state apparatus', which he defined as '1) the government, 2) the state administration, 3) the armed forces, 4) the courts and penal system'. Of these 'only one in its entirety is in the hands of democracy, i.e. the government in the shape of the PKWN. Elements hostile to democracy, elements on which the old *Sanacja* regime rested, have penetrated the others to a greater or lesser degree.' According to Gomułka the problem lay both in the shortage of politically reliable and experienced manpower and the lack of firm direction from the Communists who had been placed in charge of trained specialists:

> Polish democracy . . . was unable to train its own cadres as managers and organisers of state power in sufficient numbers. The reaction has such managers and organisers. . . . This fact enables the reaction to push its people into various organs of state, especially where on some vital section set by the camp of Polish democracy, the manager loses vigilance and falls into the political cretinism of specialism (*fachowość*).

Henceforth political commitment rather than qualification and experience was to take precedence:

> Experts of all kinds are needed, badly needed, by democratic Poland. But if a specialist makes use of his skills for the purpose of expert destruction, then Poland does not need such experts; such experts belong behind bars. In the place of such specialists it is better rather to put a good democrat, a good worker, peasant or *inteligent*, even if non-specialist and without experience.[154]

The first priority was the 'democratization' of the army officer-corps, where previously the party had hoped to employ widely ex-AK recruits. This policy was now reversed as the suspicion that the underground had gone on to the offensive, infiltrating the army with the intention of capturing control, had been confirmed in the eyes of the leadership and

Stalin by the desertions in October.[155] To avert this threat urgent steps were taken to strengthen the Communists' hold on the army and 500 party members were seconded to the officer corps. Also cadres from the wartime People's Army that had hitherto largely been sent into the militia were directed into the army political apparatus. Finally, it was decided to find 10,000 volunteers from amongst the working class and peasantry to 'pour a healthy, democratic stream into the ranks of the army'.[156] It is worth noting that these moves represented a strengthening of the influence of the former underground section of the party over the army, eclipsing somewhat the position of the émigrés who had hitherto dominated the political direction of the armed forces. Gomułka himself took charge of the campaign and a Military Department began functioning in the Central Committee.[157]

The obverse of this influx of dependable manpower was a purge of the ex-AK element in the forces. Although publicly distinctions were still drawn between the 'democratic' mass of the AK and their 'reactionary' commanders, in practice former AK members came under more or less indiscriminate suspicion. We have already seen how instructions to political commanders in the army on the treatment of AK officer recruits had hardened. The general attitude of the Communists to the AK after October, both in the army and outside, was summed up by Gomułka a few months later as follows: 'in practice, the attitude of our Party organisations was such that honest *akowcy* were not distinguished from the reactionary parts of the AK. They were put under arrest, because they were *akowcy*.'[158] Although the leadership later blamed sectarian elements amongst the rank and file for this extremism, there is clear evidence in the discussions held in the Politburo that by October–November 1944 the leadership was united in equating the bulk of the AK with the reaction[159] which it now aimed not simply to isolate and neutralize through political means, but to 'destroy' by repressive measures. Gomułka gave the lead in a speech on 10 October which introduced a new tone into official party pronouncements. 'Not only does the new democracy', he said, 'not assist the activity and development of the reaction . . . but on the contrary, it makes the destruction of fascism and all dark, backward and reactionary forces a condition of its existence.' He continued: 'the democratic camp and the PKWN will not hesitate to apply those measures which will once and for all liquidate the armed resistance. Efforts to win over the majority of the nation would be accompanied by the use of 'the severest repression towards the reaction . . . which is hiding under the cloak of Mikołajczyk'.[160] By February 1945 official party documents, without qualification, referred to the AK as the 'armed agency of the land owners'.[161] With this kind of language emanating from the centre, it was hardly surprising when local activists 'oversimplified their attitude to the AK by generalising hostility to all those who had at some time belonged to the AK'.[162]

The contradiction between the party leadership's calls for national unity and the intensified struggle against the London camp was most keenly felt at local level by the PPR *aktyw*. Not surprisingly, significant sections of the *aktyw* seem to have considered that the leadership was unrealistic in expecting the party to broaden its base substantially and deal with its opponents at the same time. This view was evident when Gomułka descended on the Praga PPR organization on 25–26 November. Praga, a working-class suburb of Warsaw, was one of the few areas in Lublin Poland where the PPR might have expected to establish a base amongst the industrial workers. This had not happened however. Gomułka, speaking to the local leaders of the party,

> assessed the activity of the Warsaw organisation of the PPR critically, using extremely severe terms in his speech. He said that the provincial committee lacked any idea how to work, had failed to break with conspiratorial habits, had made little contact with people, especially the workers, had a poor growth of membership, had not begun to organise cells in work-places as the Central Committee had directed, and that it lacked contact with the urban intelligentsia.

But for some at least of the *aktyw*, this was asking for the impossible: 'the criticism aroused the dissatisfaction of some of the members of the committee. They felt that the Central Committee Secretary was not sufficiently aware of the specific circumstances in Praga and that his assessment was not objective.'[163]

As noted at the beginning of this chapter, the abandonment of the broad national front left the party with little alternative but to resort to police methods and the direct application of Soviet power to deal with its opponents. Inevitably, the work of hunting down AK suspects was largely left to the NKVD. As we have seen, the Polish security forces were not yet strong enough to play more than a supporting role. Gomułka hinted at the party's acceptance of greater Soviet help in his 10 October speech when he said that 'it would not by any means be an interference in the affairs of a given country if the Red Army is one of those factors destroying fascism everywhere where it is to be found'.[164] On 18 October Stalin told Bierut and Osóbka in Moscow that the Polish forces were unable to cope with the security problem and the Soviet army would have to play a greater role than hitherto.[165] Party historians are largely silent on what this 'greater role' involved, but there can be little doubt that claims of mass arrests and deportations are true. In a letter written in 1956, General Zygmunt Berling, who had been removed from his command of the First Army but remained a member of the PKWN until December, dramatically described the situation in the last months of 1944 as follows:

> Beria's lackies from the NKVD wreaked devastation over the whole country. Criminal elements from Radkiewicz's apparatus assisted them in this without hindrance. During legal and illegal searches the population had its property stolen

and entirely innocent people were deported or thrown into gaol. People were shot at like dogs. Literally no one felt secure or knew the day or the hour. The chief military procurator told me on returning from an inspection which I had sent him on to prisons in Przemyśl, Zamość and Lublin, that over twelve thousand people were being held there. Nobody knew what they were accused of, by whom they had been arrested or what was intended to be done with them.[166]

Modern party historians mention that from mid-November to mid-January the Soviet and Polish forces were deployed for what was described as 'offensive operations' or 'disarming the terrain'. This involved mass identity checks on males aged between 16 and 50 and the arrest of suspects. It is not possible to gauge accurately the extent of the arrests: fragmentary official figures covering three districts in the southern part of Lublin province put the number of detainees at 664 but, especially where Soviet troops were used, it is probable that the round-ups were much greater.[167] At the same time, as we have seen, executions of AK officers began.

Although within a few months the PPR leadership was to become seriously concerned over the activities of the Soviet and Polish security forces, this was not the mood at the end of 1944. On the contrary, the party leaders were satisfied with the results of the measures against the AK and favoured stepping up the campaign against the underground. On 17 December the Politburo discussed security matters at some length, Radkiewicz claiming that 'the AK is experiencing an internal crisis . . . initially the AK fought to win the masses and lost'. His deputy, Roman Romkowski, reported that 'we have struck blows in the leadership (of the AK) in all the provinces and in Białystok against the NSZ too'. Gomułka argued that 'the London base is contracting; the AK leadership has recently been decimated'. However, there was agreement that the underground still posed a serious threat and was concentrating on 'diversionary work of a closed, sectarian character', and as Berman put it 'up to now in the fight with the reaction we have been cutting off the tendrils; we must get at the roots'.[168]

This assessment accorded with a general view in the leadership that the 'October turn' had paid off. Despite the continued elusiveness of the national front, the mood of crisis in the party, so much in evidence a couple of months before, had given way to an altogether more confident outlook. The agreed view in the leadership seems to have been that initial errors had been corrected and that the modified line had yielded rapid results. It was Berman who was the most enthusiastic: 'The process of change is going quicker than we had expected . . . in a short time we have constructed the *aparat*; there are successes'.[169] But Gomułka too gave an interview published on 7 December expressing considerable satisfaction with the progress which had been made, without any of the critical notes which he was normally not averse to sounding.[170]

By early January 1945, when the Soviet offensive was renewed, the PPR leadership was then in buoyant mood, having recovered much of the confidence which had deserted it in October. This mood did not last long; by April the party had again reached an impasse.

7 The spring crisis and the 'May turn', January to June 1945

THE RED ARMY resumed its advance on 12 January. Warsaw, systematically devastated by the Germans in the weeks after the collapse of the uprising, was liberated on 17 January, followed by Kraków and Lodz on the 19th, Katowice on the 27th and Poznań a month later. Pockets of resistance – Gdańsk, Szczecin and Wrocław – were mopped up in the last weeks of the war.

The rapidity of the advance transformed the political situation facing the PPR. Suddenly, the Communists found themselves with huge expanses of territory to organize and govern in central Poland and, after a short period of Soviet administration, in the former German western territories also. Simultaneously, the Lublin regime's protective Soviet shield moved away westwards. By no means all the Russian units pursued the German retreat, but the military and administrative resources at the disposal of the PPR shrank dramatically just at the moment when the demands made upon them multiplied. Compounding this shortage of manpower, the party's radical line left the Communists isolated within a considerably narrower front of allies than the previous summer. Moreover, the defeat of Hitler, although initially greeted by a wave of popular rejoicing and gratitude towards the Russians, deprived the Communists of their strongest patriotic asset. Post-liberation euphoria soon gave way to hostility towards the new authorities as Soviet marauding, the use of terror to crush the underground, and the dire economic conditions became apparent.

During the spring it became increasingly clear to most, though not all, of the party leadership that the narrower and more aggressive 'democratic national front' strategy which had it seemed suited the circumstances of Lublin Poland, did not meet the requirements of the new political situation. The crisis was evident in four main areas: the campaign against the AK and the underground, the economy, the national front itself, and in Soviet-Polish relations, both at international level and on the ground in Poland. By May 1945 the party leadership had concluded that the direction it had pursued in these areas since October 1944 was no longer correct. Rather than eliminating the opposition and widening the base of the national front, the party's policies appeared to be generating opposition, leaving the PPR in deeper isolation and dependence on Soviet assistance. In May and June the party line reverted in essentials to the broad national front line which the party had abandoned eight months before.

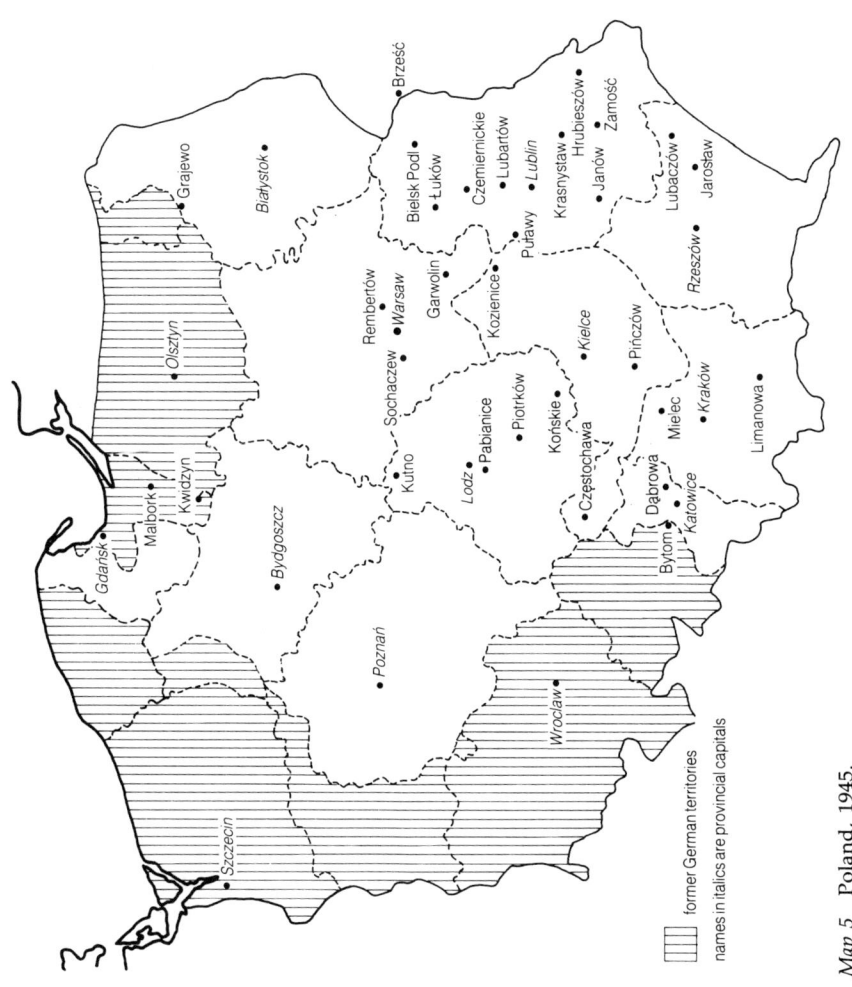

Map 5 Poland, 1945.

The revival of underground activity

THE counter-attack against the AK did not abate as the front advanced. However, after January the PPR was engaged in an attempt to terrorize the underground forces from a position of weakness. Party membership and the strength of militia and security organs mushroomed during the first months of 1945, but their political reliability remained extremely uncertain. The security apparatus and militia were still riddled with members of the underground,[1] while the Internal Army, soon to be renamed the Internal Security Corps, was only partly formed and trained by May 1945, when Moczar, one of its organizers, stated bluntly that it was not yet ready to take on the underground. What could happen when ill-prepared troops were deployed was mentioned by Gomułka: 'three Battalions of the Internal Army went out into the terrain and 2,000 people deserted'.[2]

This vulnerability left the party very heavily reliant on the remaining Soviet cover and those Polish security forces it had at its disposal. The employment of Soviet troops against the AK was an embarrassing necessity which came under heavy criticism at the May 1945 Plenum. Even Radkiewicz agreed that it was 'unfortunate that two Red Army regiments were sent to Białystok; Poles should be used against the AK. The attitude that the Red Army will establish order for us here is bad.' The Central Committee was also alarmed by the tendency of some local party chiefs to ignore the Politburo and pursue their own line using the security organs and the Russians. The UB apparatus, conscious of its key role in protecting the party's hold on power, began to slip from beneath party control. Gomułka went so far as to warn 'that a second state is beginning to grow up over our heads. The security organs are making their own policy, with which no-one is supposed to interfere.'[3]

The round-ups which began in November continued into spring 1945 on a big scale. Emigré sources claim that as many as 50,000 members of the AK were arrested and transported to Siberia at this time,[4] but of course there is no way of verifying this figure. Claims that some 8,000 people were incarcerated in Lublin castle at this time are plausible enough in view of official data revealing 1,646 arrests by the UB and MO alone in Lublin province between January and April. In the same operations, over 300 members of the underground were killed.[5] Internment camps were set up for the AK at Strobów, Rembertów, Piotrków and elsewhere. But as figure 1 clearly demonstrates, the repression, far from breaking the underground, contributed to the massive irruption of armed resistance in the spring.

To a limited degree this followed from the territorial extension of Communist rule to regions where the underground network had not been disrupted by 'Tempest' and Soviet policing, but about two-thirds of political murders were concentrated in the areas liberated in 1944[6] and the upsurge in guerrilla activity peaked in April–June, not in January–February when the AK and the Communists first came into contact in central Poland.

In spite of the repression, the stance of the underground remained generally defensive; resistance was offered on a sporadic and unplanned basis. Official historiography lays great emphasis on the *Nie* organization which it credits with an influence and degree of coherence it did not possess. In fact, the first three months of 1945 witnessed the virtual disintegration of the underground, with its leadership endeavouring to pick up the pieces, while rapidly coming to the conclusion that some kind of compromise had to be reached with the Russians. Non-recognition of the Lublin authorities and the conviction that the PPR was merely a Soviet puppet ruled out any direct approaches to the Polish Communists.

Okulicki at this time gives the impression of a man swept along on an irresistible tide of events. On 19 January he ordered – to the surprise and puzzlement, it seems, of London, of most of the AK as well as the Communists – the disbandment of the AK. Emigré historians claim the decision was unpremeditated and conditioned by the mood of defeatism within the movement and the urgent need to sanction its members' flight from NKVD round-ups.[7] Party historians argue rather that it had been planned in advance and was designed to prune down the AK, leaving only the dependable cadres of the *Nie* organization: the skeleton of the new anti-Soviet resistance.[8] Okulicki's order had indeed been ambiguous about the next step: 'We do not want to fight the Soviets, but we will never agree to live except in an entirely sovereign, independent, justly governed Polish state. The present Soviet victory has not ended the war.' President Raczkiewicz, endorsing Okulicki's order on 8 February, attempted to dispel the uncertainty, stating specifically that armed activity had ceased.[9]

The order added to the confusion and fragmentation reigning in the underground in the aftermath of the Soviet advance. Many of the conspirators, like the Russians, did not believe the order and simply ignored it, and began to repair and regroup the organization. In Białystok, for instance, Colonel Liniarski disobeyed the order and set up an independent 'Citizens' AK',[10] while the nationalists, who radically disagreed with the decision to disband, took further steps to revive their own military networks. And of course Okulicki himself did not cease activity, forming a central command for *Nie*, which apart from this never really got off the drawing-board.[11]

The centrifugal processes at work in the military arm of the underground were matched by fission within its political leadership. As we have seen, in November Mikołajczyk, ready to settle with the Lubliners on terms favoured by the British and Americans, was dumped as premier of the Government-in-Exile and replaced by the intransigent Arciszewski. Mikołajczyk's Peasant Party went into opposition and following the commitment of the Big Three at Yalta in February 1945 to the creation of a

Polish coalition government, it succeeded in winning over Delegate Jankowski and most of the underground political leaders to Mikołajczyk's line. By March 1945 the London camp was dividing in two, just as the Communists had intended nine months earlier, with the peasant movement and the Centre groupings searching for a way out of conspiracy and entry into coalition with the PPR, while the intransigents were left isolated. Significantly the former AK, as represented by Okulicki, with some reservations, fell in with Jankowski.

The talks held between the Russian military command in Poland and the fifteen underground leaders headed by Jankowski and Okulicki at the end of March, which terminated with the arrest of the fifteen and their disappearance to the Soviet Union where they were put on trial in June, demonstrated the risks which the AK and the *Delegatura* were prepared to take to promote a deal. Okulicki had at first refused to participate, but finally caved in to Jankowski's persuasion and Russian insistence on his presence.[12]

The arrests certainly increased the difficulties facing the Communists and must have significantly contributed to the irruption of underground violence in April, May and June which brought Poland to the brink of civil war.[13] Other factors too prompted the upsurge of guerrilla activity: the season – spring was suited to partisan warfare; the mass arrests, which propelled thousands of young men into the forests; and the realization that militia and security posts, or even prisons and internment camps often represented easy targets. The use of Red Army units and 'workers' brigades' to collect food quotas from the peasants also aroused a great deal of conflict. These factors accounted equally for the activization of Ukrainian nationalist insurgents in south-east Poland. But besides, Yalta seemed to promise a new phase and the end of the Communist monopoly in the administration. The defeatist, defensive mood which had weighed on the underground for months began to give way to a more offensive and hopeful one.

Soviet attempts to stamp out the resistance continued unabated. On 26 April London heard that:

> The pacification has begun of Garwolin, Łuków, Lubartów and Zamość districts. The Soviet Army surrounds villages and transports all the men, other than youngsters and the elderly, eastwards. The arrests numbering between ten and twenty thousand have provoked a mass exodus to the forests and the formation of irregular armed units, which nevertheless adopt a passive attitude, only defending themselves when attacked. The Soviet Air Force bombed the Czemiernickie forests.[14]

The report, even if exaggerated, indicates accurately enough the degree of fear and terror sweeping the countryside. By no means all the armed units remained passive either. On 24 April, guerrillas overran the town of Puławy, massacring the local security policeman. A couple of days later the same happened in Janów, then Kozienice, then Grajewo. These were sizeable towns. Militia posts in the countryside faced an unenviable task – on the night of 27–28 March formidably armed and trained UPA (Ukrainian nationalist) units simultaneously wiped out the entire system of militia stations in Lubaczów and Jarosław districts, while in Białystok province, acccording to official data, some forty militia offices had been demolished by March.[15] In May pitched battles took place between security forces and ex-AK units led by 'Orlik' (Marian Bernaciak) and 'Łupaszko' (Zygmunt Szendzielarz).[16]

The party's hard line had weakened and scattered the underground without seriously undermining its support and prestige amongst the bulk of the population. Mass arrests and internment created an atmosphere of tension and hostility to the Communists in which clandestine activity proliferated and the underground, like a hydra, sprouted new members as fast as the security forces picked off the old. When the Central Committee Plenum met in May, the leadership attempted to reassert its control over a security apparatus which had itself lost its grip on the underground. Gomułka concluded the Plenum by saying that the existence of 'certain elements of crisis' was undeniable. 'In the reactionary camp there is a crisis, but we have been unable to narrow its base. We are unable to fight the reaction without the Red Army. That says something about (our) base.'[17]

Industry and the working class

THE upsurge in underground activity was primarily a protest by the traditional rural communities of central and eastern Poland against the new order and indicated how shallow were the party's roots in the villages. In the towns and cities the political hold of the authorities was more secure and violent opposition limited. Nevertheless by the spring the Communists had to contend with a wave of discontent and industrial disruption amongst the urban working class, where they had hoped to find their strongest support.

The Polish economy was in ruins at the end of the war. National income, which had stood at 17.7 billion zloties in 1938, had fallen by 1945 to 6.8 billion. Industry had suffered particularly badly: some 65 per cent of industrial plants had been destroyed. The population had declined from 35 to 24 million – a loss which disproportionately severely affected the skilled labour force, management and technicians.[18] Cities like Warsaw, Wrocław and Gdańsk had been devastated. The occupation had also left deep psychological scars on those who had survived. The urban population had experienced Nazi rule at its most oppressive and had suffered the harshest material hardships. The legacy of the underground struggle continued to exercise a strong hold on large sections of the population for many years to come. This was to be seen in the conditioning of a whole generation to violence and fear, conspiracy and civil disobedience and in the intense loyalty to the memory of the AK and the secret state. In the economic sphere wartime habits such as the permanent 'go-slow' in production, the sanctioning of pilfering both on patriotic grounds and for the sake of survival, and the black market, died hard. There were besides specific post-war social problems: an influx of untrained and often illiterate labour from the countryside to the towns; the existence of pockets of extreme poverty, exceeding even the general level of hardship, amongst widows, the unemployed, the Warsaw lumpenproletariat, for instance.[19] Reactivation of industry and distribution was hampered by a virtual collapse of the currency in early 1945, as the wartime currencies were replaced by Polish zloty. For a time in many areas, vodka, spirit or sugar were used as a means of exchange to pay industrial workers and even state employees. By May 1945 the shortages of currency and credit had given way to fears of inflation.[20] With many of the urban population living at or below subsistence level, and workers receiving pay in kind rather than cash, the slightest disruption in the flow of food supplies was critical to the maintenance of production, which in any case stood in April at only 19 per cent of its 1937 level.[21] Absenteeism was a great problem, averaging 10–20 per cent daily and in some industries over 20 per cent.[22] In March and April when the material conditions of the workers sank to a new low – real earnings in the first half of 1945 were less than 10 per cent of their value in 1938[23] – short strikes became rife.

For days at a time food was unavailable. The authorities had estimated that forced collection of food quotas would provide about 1 million tons of grain and 1.9 million tons of potatoes in the economic year 1944–5. In fact only 681,000 tons of grain and 845,000 tons of potatoes were collected. As the army and Red Army had priority for such supplies, no more than 20 per cent of these stocks could be made available to the civilian population in spring 1945.[24] Minc told the May Plenum that there had been some 'progress' – 'a month ago there was no bread in Lodz, now they're calling for dripping'.[25] Where such shortages were combined with resentment at the favourable treatment reportedly received by others as well as political agitation by opponents of the government, the party was unable to restrain the workers. It is worth quoting at some length a report sent from Lodz to the Central Committee by Loga-Sowiński, the PPR secretary there; it covers the period 15 April–15 May.

> Against the background of food-supply difficulties strong tension of feelings in the factories. In the period of this report, especially in the past few days, a dozen or so brief strikes in Lodz, Pabianice, Końskie. . . . The strikes last as long as the shop-floor meetings which the works councils call immediately the stoppage begins. . . . Factory cells display complete impotence towards the strikes. As a rule the meetings are very stormy; the workers, and especially the women workers,

heckle the speakers; they should: 'Fine democracy, when there's nothing to eat'; 'The parasites stuff themselves as always, and the worker starves', etc. . . . We receive letters from workers asking why office-workers have good dinners with meat, why speculators go unpunished, why the shops are full of manufactures, only the government cannot find a way to feed the workers. . . . It is clear that the strikes are initiated by people sent in by the Reaction. The resentment of the workers over low pay and poor provisioning creates pretty fertile ground for strike-mongers.[26]

Loga-Sowiński added that such 'outbursts of dissatisfaction among the workers inspired by the Reaction cannot in any way be regarded as a general index of their mood'. However, as his report shows, the authorities were keenly aware of the political dimension to these protests and attempted to dissociate economic grievances from broader political discontent. Sometimes this seems to have been successful. 'On 24 March', the party committee in Warsaw reported, 'a public meeting of over a thousand people from the operational groups [organized to clear the ruins of the city] gathered at 24, Żurawa street with the intention of demanding bread. The direct intervention of the Party committee prevented a further demonstration and resulted in the meeting ending with pro-government slogans.'[27] Emergency measures were taken to overcome the shortages. The party press announced that:

In mid-July, just before the harvest the Warsaw PPR Committee was warned that once again there was no flour in the city stores and that stock-piles were sufficient for only 2–3 days. The City Hall proved helpless. Not having time to organise workers' brigades, the Warsaw committee immediately sent a team of its own staff to Sochaczew district. They brought back 80 tons of flour. The next PPR group was sent to Kutno bringing further tons of grain and famine was again averted.[28]

In line with the party's tactics of mobilizing the population in mass campaigns and to compensate for its own lack of manpower, the Communists preferred, whenever possible, to despatch workers' brigades into the countryside to collect food quotas. Altogether about 100,000 workers were said to have taken part in these brigades.[29]

But improvised measures and propaganda could not conceal the political threat posed by the economic difficulties. Minc, speaking to the Central Committee Plenum in February, drew a direct link between the regime's authority and the success of its management of the economy:

If the Provisional Government today comes to the newly-liberated regions with authority as the real administration of the country, this has happened because, amongst other things, this Provisional Government was able in general to overcome the economic difficulties in the territory liberated earlier . . . it was able . . . to feed the population and to reactivate industry more or less efficiently . . . it succeeded in introducing a rationing system. . . . The future of democracy and our triumph depends on whether we are able to solve all our economic problems.[30]

However, progress up to May fell short of the Communists' hopes. The Politburo was especially concerned over the continuing low level of productivity in industry which Gomułka described as 'catastrophic'.[31] Moreover, the wave of strikes, which one speaker at the May Plenum described as 'the most important element of the crisis'[32] continued with stoppages in Silesia, the Dąbrowa basin, Warsaw, Olsztyn, Częstochowa and elsewhere.[33]

The experiment in 'workers' control' through the factory councils also failed to produce the expected political dividends, but rather heightened the decentralization of management which was in any case unavoidable during the first stages of industrial recovery. Factories tended to operate as autonomous units, sometimes even refusing to distribute their products to other factories in the production chain,[34] and works' councils, representing shopfloor opinion, encroached on the already reduced powers of management.

The decree on works councils was passed after four months of discussion on 6 February and remained in force effectively until the end of May. Works councils were to be formed in all concerns employing more than 20 people and were to represent the interests of employees in relation to the employer, as well as 'watch over the increase and improvement of production of the concern in accordance with the general guidelines of state economic policy'. In factories under state or local government control – the vast majority – the works council was entitled to direct representation in the management board, more or less on a par with the director. The director was required to consult the council on a continuous basis and such matters as taking on or discharging workers and their pay and provisions were for joint decision.[35]

The party leadership seems to have looked to the works councils to provide a powerful check on the activities of management, which in many cases was suspected of political unreliability. At the February 1945 Plenum Minc stressed the wide role to be played by the councils which were to be given 'influence over who will be the director of a given factory and will be able to say "no, this one's bad and this one is good"'.[36]

The problems posed by this arrangement soon became evident. Frequent conflicts arose between directors, together with specialist technical staff, on the one hand, and the factory councils, on the other. The workers' representatives considered that the managements had failed to adjust their thinking to the new order in industry and were refusing to allow the councils an adequate say in decision-making.[37] The specialists in return argued that the councils undervalued their role. A particular bone of contention was the councils' tendency to reduce differentials and productivity bonuses, and to exclude non-manual staff from a share of the profits.[38] In some cases the party's radical line unleashed an ultra-radical response from the workers which some commentators have defined as 'anarcho-syndicalist' in character.[39] The party was critical of these tendencies. Loga-Sowiński reported from Lodz that the workers' councils had 'an incorrect attitude to the directors, [there is] a tendency to fight them, remove them and put in their place workers. We are not yet ready for this.'[40] The Communists were also against egalitarianism in pay. In April the PPR-controlled Central Commission of the Trade Unions declared that the operative principle on wages should be 'equal pay for equal work', elaborating that

> in setting rates for particular categories of workers and staff one should be guided by their qualifications and professional skills. . . . Where technical conditions allow, a system of piecework should be applied which will have a positive effect on the increase in production. . . . Also, where technical conditions allow, a bonus system should be put into operation.[41]

Frequently such conflicts had a strong party political flavour. In many factories, despite calls by the PPR leadership to share power, the Communists monopolized the works councils. This led to conflict with both the legal and the underground wings of the Socialist movement. The PPR monopolism also extended from the top to the bottom of the trade union apparatus. 'In the Central Commission of the Trade Unions out of 23 members, 19 were members of the PPR and 4 of the PPS. The composition of the union executives in the largest industrial centres such as Lodz and Katowice was similar. In Lodz only one member of the PPS sat on the Regional Union Committee, while in Katowice it consisted exclusively of members of the PPR.'[42] In Lodz, again according to Loga-Sowiński, 'monopolist tendencies are universal. Comrades resist changes to the benefit of the PPS in factory councils or national councils, although their composition is in this respect blatantly unjust.' It proved very difficult for the party leadership to overcome this obduracy. 'Everywhere we hear the same argument: we did not work in order to hand them seats now. [There is] suspicion and antipathy towards PPS members. Where Party directives are carried out it is formally, without conviction.'[43] As one modern historian has noted, 'despite the suggestions of the Central Committee of the PPR . . . changes in union leaderships took place very slowly. PPS representation in the Central Commission of the Trade Unions itself was not extended until the 1st Congress [November 1945].'[44] Central instructions were ignored, it seems, by local party organizations, and the leadership's campaign from May onwards to stamp out monopolism was only partially successful. At the December 1945 Congress Zambrowski listed a whole series of unions where the situation was still unsatisfactory: 'without doubt the balance of forces on the executives of these unions, so far as the PPR and PPS is concerned, does not correspond to the balance of influence at the grassroots, in the factories.'[45]

Such distortions not only created tension between the Communists and their Socialist allies, but in some cases strengthened the appeal of anti-government Socialists who continued to play the role of spokesmen for the workers outside the PPR-dominated unions and factory councils.

According to a report from Warsaw, 'the WRN holds sway in a great many PPS factory circles and engages in openly reactionary activity . . . our comrades' ultra-leftism exacerbates these conflicts'.[46] During February and March the leadership of the WRN under Kazimierz Pużak and Zygmunt Zaremba attempted to reactivate their network, issuing instructions ordering a boycott of the Provisional Government's political apparatus, but involvement in trade unions, factory councils and other social and economic organizations. The WRN was also to agitate for a fairer and more efficient system of food supply and higher wages.[47] In mid-March Pużak made a tour of industrial Upper Silesia and held one meeting inside a Bytom coal mine.[48]

In May the party leadership shifted the emphasis from the workers' prerogatives to the need to improve discipline and raise productivity. The experiment in workers' control had blurred managerial responsibility, reinforced ultra-radical deviations from the central party line and, in many cases, fear of losing control of the councils had resulted in the alienation and exclusion of potential allies rather than the broadening of the party's appeal.

The national front

THE third area where by May 1945 the party's strategy had reached an impasse was within the national front itself. The Communists' monopolist tendencies and conflicts with the Socialists in the trades unions and factories were symptomatic of more general strains within the governing coalition. After October the party's attitude to its allies had reflected the underlying ambiguities in its strategy. On the one hand its continuing commitment to constructing a national front required the existence and growth of the 'Lublin' Socialist and Peasant Parties to rally support for the Provisional Government and draw off the rank and file from the 'London' parties. On the other hand the narrowing of the front and offensive against the underground meant in practice that the party was more assertive in enforcing its 'leading role'. This meant keeping tight control of its allies' organizations and strict filtering of recruits to prevent pro-London elements taking over.

The trade-off between safeguarding PPR hegemony and broadening the base of the regime reappeared sharply in early 1945 as the legal parties expanded rapidly in the newly-liberated territories. As table 1 demonstrates, the very rapid growth of the PPR up to April was followed by an equally dramatic shedding of members during the following months, so that by June the marked imbalance in the size of the three main government parties, evident in Lublin, had given way to near equality. Such global figures give only a rough indication, of course, of the relative organizational strength of the parties, but they do show that, alongside the

PPR, two mass parties had emerged which in some areas at least presented the Communists with real competition. In Kraków, Katowice and Gdańsk, for instance, the PPS was able to outpace the Communists.[49]

Table 1. Membership of the PPR, PPS and SL in the first half of 1945

	PPR	PPS	SL
1944 December	21,649*	7,663*	5,000*
1945 January	69,239	–	–
February	176,337	–	–
March	262,652	–	–
April	301,695	124,428	–
May	255,904	–	–
June	206,510	156,832	200,000
July	188,904	–	–

* Figure for liberated territories only.
Sources:
N. Kołomejczyk, *PPR 1944–1945: (Studia nad rozwojem organizacyjnym partii)* (Warsaw, 1965), 275, 277; A. Reiss, *Z problemów odbudowy i rozwoju organizacyjnego PPS 1944–1946* (Warsaw, 1971), 69, 119, 189; A. Przygoński, *Z zagadnień strategii frontu narodowego PPR 1942–1945* (Warsaw, 1976), 315; R. Halaba *Stronnictwo Ludowe 1944–1946. Niektóre problemy rozwoju organizacyjnego i działalności politycznej* (Warsaw, 1966), 83.

Moreover, the manner of the expansion of the PPR was assessed very critically by the Politburo which at the end of April put the process into reverse.[50] In circulars issued on 7 May, the Central Committee stated that expansion had led to 'a series of negative phenomena', singling out the absence of any selectivity in signing-on recruits which had allowed corrupt, careerist and 'ideologically foreign elements' to join the party, thereby discrediting it and assisting its opponents.[51] The 'open doors' recruitment policy operated during the first weeks after the end of the German occupation placed virtually no restrictions on new members who were 'registered', often before cells had been organized, without any investigation of their views or background. The Central Committee was particularly disquieted by the massive expansion in Poznań province, a region with very little Communist tradition[52] and an old stronghold of the National and Christian Democrats. Between the end of February and the beginning of May membership there rose from under 2,000 to over 60,000. During May this figure was pruned back to 27,000.[53] Such wild fluctuations suggest that the real level of recruitment to the party was much less than the official figures indicated and that in very many cases recruits lacked any deep political commitment to the PPR. Material and career considerations undoubtedly motivated a large part of the new membership, as Zambrowski admitted some months later:

admittance to the Party took place in contravention of all the principles obligatory in our Party . . . [members] were not admitted, but signed-up, or as it was called at the time – registered. Anybody who applied was registered and amongst them tens of thousands of people were registered who joined the Party to get a job, to get some work, to get into the Militia.[54]

In the countryside the second stage of the land reform which began in February and benefited altogether 262,000 families was accompanied by mass recruitment. In the towns too the party had considerable patronage at its disposal. In Lodz, for instance, in March and April the party distributed nearly 9,000 housing units.[55]

In such circumstances it was not difficult to enlarge the formal membership without significantly alleviating the party's basic weaknesses and even intensifying some of them. The shortage of reliable cadres remained. Aleksander Zawadzki complained to the May Plenum that 'we are trying to fill every position with a PPR member, but we do not have enough people who will follow the Party line'.[56] The influx of members without any previous association with the Communist movement did not in many cases dilute the sectarian tendencies of party veterans; rather the opposite. 'Careerist elements' were accused of ultra-Leftism and an incorrect attitude to allied parties.[57] The rapidity of the expansion had also resulted in a loss of organizational coherence by increasing the remoteness of the central party apparatus from local cells.[58] Above all, the majority of the leadership does not seem to have considered that the party's growth indicated any real advance in broadening the base of the Provisional Government, the continuing narrowness of which lay behind the lack of political stabilization and symptoms of crisis.[59]

As we have remarked, the 'Lublin PPS' was in no position to challenge PPR hegemony effectively in 1944 and in spite of disputes within the government coalition, the Communists found it easier to impose a subordinate status on the PPS than on the Peasants. However, from early 1945, the PPS gained strength despite the boycott declared by the WRN and succeeded in capturing a foothold in traditional Socialist strongholds. Although only a handful of the more prominent pre-war figures in the party, most notably Adam Kuryłowicz, Henryk Świątkowski, Henryk Wachowicz and a little later Józef Cyrankiewicz and Kazimierz Rusinek, threw in their lot with the new organization, at local level it proved easier to win over activists and members.

The Communists viewed this process with some apprehension. In February, even before it was properly under way, the sharpest dispute to date between the two parties developed as the Communists attempted to prevent what they argued was an influx of WRN supporters into the PPS which the Communists feared would return to its old ideological stance.[60] In the Central Committee Aleksander Kowalski warned against exaggerated suspicion and confusing 'real PPS-ites' with 'enemy agents',[61] but the

Politburo was inclined to stress the danger. Gomułka's report displayed the ambiguity in the party's strategy: its commitment to the national front combined with hints to the *aktyw* to keep tight checks on potential recruits linked with 'London':

> Our Party sees and realises the benefits that the existence of the national front and co-operation with the PPS, the Peasants and the Democrats bring to the cause of rebuilding Poland and laying the foundations of democracy. Our Party draws a distinction between those Socialists standing for the unity of the democratic camp and those WRN elements, alien to socialism, which squeeze into the PPS with the aim of pushing it onto the wrong course. We consider that decidedly hostile WRN elements ought to be excluded from political life.[62]

Within the PPS leadership only Matuszewski and his group accepted the Communists' analysis wholeheartedly. Matuszewski went so far as to insist that: 'People from the WRN have no place in the reborn party and their ideology must be ruthlessly combated.'[63] But other speakers at the PPS Supreme Council on 25–26 February favoured a more liberal attitude to the WRN rank and file as well as towards the pre-war traditions of the party, taking the view that the threat of a WRN take-over was exaggerated and that the Right could be contained.[64] But behind the discussion of the WRN and party traditions lay the question of the role of the PPS in the government coalition and the general political situation. As usual Drobner did not mince his words, complaining that 'in grassroots circles of the PPR there is a conviction that only the PPR has the right to govern'. It was necessary, he went on, 'to dispel fear amongst our members, to make them aware that we are not a department of another party, but that we are an equal, sovereign party'.[65] Such sentiments were supported by Kuryłowicz, Obrączka, Motyka and others, in many cases linked with the Kraków PPS organization.[66] Between the Kraków and Matuszewski wings of the party, Osóbka-Morawski's group still dominated the leadership. Of the twelve Central Executive members elected in February, eight had belonged to the pro-KRN RPPS. Kuryłowicz and Matuszewski were included too, but not Drobner, who was replaced as chairman of the Supreme Council by Świątkowski from the pro-Communist Left.[67] The resolutions passed also represented a rejection of Drobner's stance.[68] Nevertheless, Osóbka-Morawski, with greater circumspection than the Kraków activists, was working towards the expansion and increased independence of the PPS, calling, for instance, on ex-Socialists to leave the PPR and join his party.[69] Talks were also started in February between the PPS leadership and WRN leaders from Kraków associated with Zygmunt Żuławski.[70]

The strains in Communist–Socialist relations at the top were paralleled by much sharper conflicts at local level. In Kraków, according to Aleksander Kowalski, 'an atmosphere of intrigue and suspicion reigned between the PPR and PPS. [Włodzimierz] Zawadzki [the local PPR secretary] told the PPS leadership to their faces that he had his people amongst them and knew what resolutions they passed.'[71] In Upper Silesia Socialist meetings were broken up by the Communists,[72] while in May the Ministry of Public Security had to issue instructions not to arrest members of the PPS and Peasant Party without clearance from above.[73]

Similar processes were at work in the legal SL. More than the PPS, its expansion rested on members of the underground party who now left the conspiracy without revising their outlook or abandoning their allegiance to Wincenty Witos and Mikołajczyk, the pre-war and wartime leaders of the movement.[74] The resumption of legal activity by former 'ROCh' members, and indeed whole organizations, was made easier by the rift between Mikołajczyk and the London government after his resignation as premier. The party in Poland supported his position and attempted to force London to retreat from its intransigent stance with threats to withdraw from the underground apparatus.[75]

However, the leadership of the SL remained in the hands of the pro-Communists. After the liberation the *Wola ludu* group took over from the executive installed in Lublin and this change was endorsed, with some dissent from Maślanka and others, at the Supreme Council held in Lodz on 25–26 March.[76] But a more significant conflict emerged between Bańczyk, the party president, who inclined towards a compromise with 'ROCh' and Kowalski, his deputy, who represented the Communists' line. On this occasion the Kowalski faction was able to shape the resolutions passed and Bańczyk's followers were heavily outnumbered on the new executive.[77] But although the PPR could still ensure that the SL leadership was controlled by its nominees, the movement at local and even provincial level was to a considerable degree under 'ROCh' influence. By May, the political tension in the country generally was reflected in the growth of open opposition in the SL to the Communists and the government which the leadership found increasingly difficult to restrain. At a congress of the peasant youth organization, *Wici*, and again at a meeting of SL deputies to the KRN, fierce attacks were made on the Communists and their management of the government, while anti-Communist feeling in the provincial organizations prompted the leadership to issue a special circular which called for party discipline and underlined the need for cooperation with the PPR.[78]

By May 1945 the PPR tactic of constructing the national front 'from below' had met only very limited success. Although it had been possible to embrace memberships of many thousands within the framework of the allied parties and place at their head executives dominated by pro-Communists, it had proved far more difficult to break old allegiances and win the loyalty of the new members for the government coalition. The difficulty was heightened by the resistance of many local party activists to working with organizations which they considered were riddled with underground and reactionary connections.

By May the Communists judged the situation in the PPS to have improved since February, when they had feared that it might slip from under the control of the pro-Communist group. However, the PPR concluded that it was because the Socialist leadership was not automatically subservient to the PPR that this improvement had taken place.[79] The situation in the SL was, on the other hand, extremely unstable, the Communists concluded, because it was led by 'our people' who had very little contact with the rank and file members. The domination by pro-Communists at the top had turned out to be an obstacle which stood in the way of winning over the mainstream of the movement. The treatment of the SL as 'an annex of the PPR' and as 'an appendix which had to be tolerated' had been mistaken. As Gomułka put it, a new course was required, 'so that the SL can become an independent party, with equal rights in the coalition . . . there are many peasant activists within our grasp who we have yet to win over.'[80]

The question of sovereignty

'OUR central problem is state sovereignty', declared Edward Ochab at the May Plenum, 'the war is over, the Red Army should leave Polish territory.'[81] The Soviet presence was indeed a crucial ingredient of the political crisis, casting doubt not only on Poland's sovereignty, but also on the sovereignty of the party leadership within Poland and even within the party itself.

The lesser problem was the relationship between the Politburo and the Kremlin. Berman and Finkielsztajn, who were both closely involved with Soviet-Polish liaison, agreed at the Plenum that Stalin respected the right of the Poles to direct their own affairs. According to Berman, 'Stalin stands for Poland's sovereignty and knows what the PPR understands by sovereignty.' The problem arose at a lower level of the Soviet apparatus, as Finkielsztajn pointed out: 'There is a difference between the position of Stalin on sovereignty and how the Soviets in the terrain conceive this matter.' He added that the fault also lay with the over-cautiousness of the party itself: 'Poland's foreign policy must coincide with the principles of the Soviet Union's policy, but within the framework of that policy we are able to defend our own interests; there is a lot of room for independence. We have not exploited these possibilities, we have not been active.'[82]

Uncertainty over Soviet policy towards Germany caused disquiet in the party leadership and was considered to be one area where Poland would need to assert her claims more energetically. It was feared that if Moscow decided to court German opinion it could be at the expense of Poland's claim to the territory up to the Oder-Neisse.[83] Such fears were heightened by delays in the handover of administration of these territories to the Poles. The sudden resumption in mid-May by the Russians of administration in Szczecin, which had earlier been transferred to the Provisional Government, was especially worrying. Ochab demanded a strong protest, 'it is a political defeat, an alarm signal. And now there are rumours about Wrocław.'[84]

But the need to press Polish interests more vigorously than hitherto during the peace settlement was a less immediate problem than putting a stop to the political interference and marauding of Russian officers and troops stationed in Poland. The lawlessness of some Red Army units was having very damaging effects on public opinion. According to Aleksander Zawadzki, 'the population in Silesia was enthusiastic towards the Soviet Union. Today its attitude is decidedly unfavourable . . . the debauchery of Red Army troops returning from Germany, marauding and outrages . . . alienate the nation from the Soviet Union.'[85] Plundering took place both in the form of individual 'trophy-hunting' as well as on an organized basis. In May, despite decisions taken during Bulganin's latest visit, many factories and much of the transport system remained under Soviet administration and its dismantling and removal eastwards continued.[86] As we have seen, the Red Army was also widely used to liquidate the AK. According to a report from Białystok province, 'up to now the partial destruction of the bands has been carried out mainly by the Red Army (not enough Polish Army); this has had a negative effect on the mood of the population'.[87] Soviet 'advisers' also played a major role in the UB, where Radkiewicz agreed that their impact had recently been damaging.[88] But it was the Soviet commanders stationed in the localities who were considered by the party leaders to have created the most trouble with their interference in affairs outside their competence which often cut right across the PPR line. According to Zambrowski, 'not only the Central Committee makes Party policy. The military commanders do as well. In Lodz, for example, they summon precinct committees without the provincial committee knowing and send them to rallies; Red Army troops campaign for *kolkhozy* [collective farms].'[89] In Malbork and Kwidzyn the Soviet authorities prohibited the formation of PPS, Peasant and Democratic Party branches.[90]

The tendency of some local party organizations to follow the lead of the Soviet and security organs rather than central directives was particularly disturbing to the Central Committee. The inexperience of local cadres, the danger and often isolation in which they worked, the ultra-radical euphoria which gripped much of the *aktyw* and especially the KPP veterans during the first months of power, not to mention the calls from above for greater vigilance and tough measures against the reaction, lay behind this tendency. Local cells looked to the real sources of their strength: the Soviet presence and the security forces and the party's hold on the state apparatus rather than the uncertain and frequently ineffective assistance of the allied parties, or even of the central party network itself. This was one of the main counts against Włodzimierz Zawadzki who was removed as party secretary

The 50th Infantry Regiment of the Home Army (AK) on the march in Volhynia, February 1944, filing past a roadside shrine often found in this part of Poland.

Contact made in Volhynia between officers of the AK and Red Army, photographed in the spring of 1944.

A close-up of the meeting: Colonel Fiedorov of the Red Army (third from the left) in the company of Polish officers (left to right, Captain Klimowski, Captain Jaworski, Major Sztumberg-Rychter) of the 27th Home Army (AK) Volhynia Infantry Division.

Soldiers of three armies liberating Wilno in July 1944. In the centre of the group is a member of the AK flanked on the right by an infantryman of the Red Army and on the left by a soldier of General Berling's Polish Army raised in Russia. (The original photograph is creased along a fold.)

A soldier in the Polish Army reading a call to arms in defence of political unity posted up in Wilno in the summer of 1944.

Detachment of the AK going into German captivity after the capitulation
of Warsaw in October 1944. A standard bearer holds aloft the Polish flag.

Civilians leaving the ruined capital.

Life returns to Warsaw: street scenes photographed in the period spring – summer 1945.

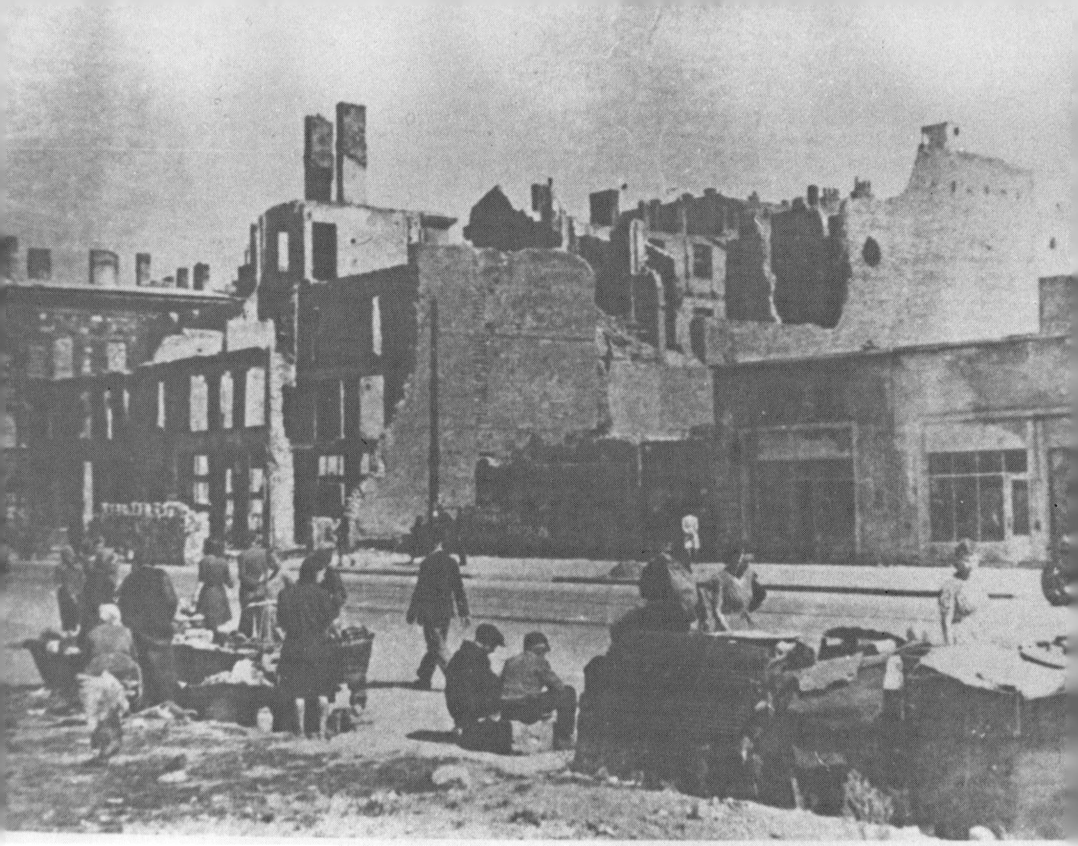

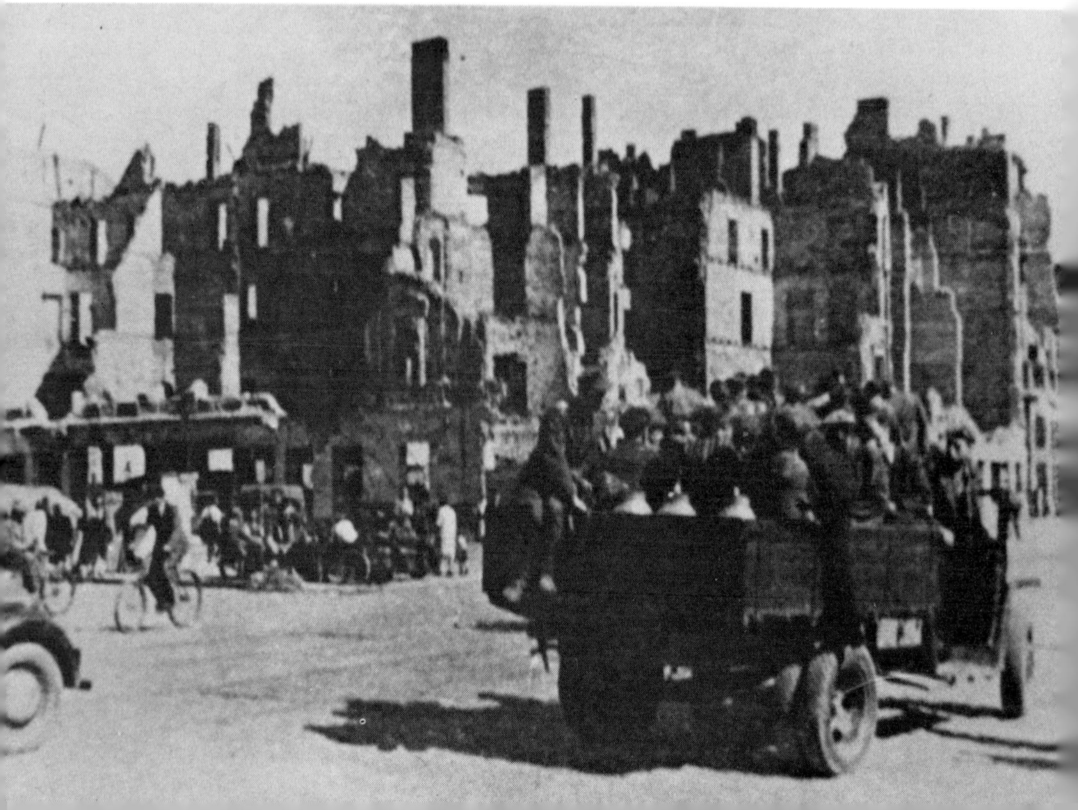

for Kraków on 16 April. Gomułka accused him of following his own line 'which substituted Security for the Party's policy', while Berman categorized his deviation more precisely: 'Jasny [Zawadzki] formulated the theory that every problem in Poland may be solved by the aid of the Red Army. This is a Trotskyist theory of revolution carried on bayonets.'[91] Zawadzki seems to have been made a scapegoat for what was a more general phenomenon. His running of the Kraków organization accorded with the feelings of much of the *aktyw* there and there was some dissatisfaction at his sacking.[92] Indeed such was his popularity with the Communist veterans at grassroots level in the city that in November they rebelled against the Central Committee and elected him as a delegate to the Party Congress. The leadership responded by expelling him from the party.[93]

The degree to which the party leadership had lost control of internal events was highlighted by the opening of negotiations between the Soviet military authorities and the leadership of the underground at the end of March, which as we have seen, concluded with the arrest of the fifteen London delegates and their subsequent trial in Moscow. While much has been published in the West about this episode,[94] we know nothing about the motives of the Russians in seizing the Poles or how and at what level the decision to do so was taken. However, it seems clear that the Polish Communists did not participate in any of the preliminaries leading up to the 'talks', nor in the charade on 27–28 March which seems to have been executed by the NKVD without any outside assistance. It is difficult to reconcile the coup with the party's wider efforts to establish its national credentials and stabilize the political situation and it seems unlikely that the Politburo would have allowed what was an embarrassing affront to its authority to have occurred if it had had any influence on the decision. Probably the Communists were presented with a *fait accompli*. This was the view of the underground leadership which replaced the arrested delegation. The new delegate, Stefan Korboński, informed London that: 'Lublin government circles consider the arrest of the fifteen by the Soviets a great mistake. They themselves are washing their hands of it.'[95] It is worth noting that Wincenty Witos was also arrested on 31 March by the NKVD, driven to Brześć on the Polish-Soviet border and then, mysteriously, driven back and released. Although Witos apparently thought it was his poor health which cut short this strange journey, it seems more probable that it was political intervention, perhaps with the Soviet government, or perhaps from the Polish leadership.[96]

By May all sections of the leadership of the PPR seem to have been agreed on the urgency of sharply reducing the role of the Soviet forces and asserting the party's primacy in directing affairs in Poland. Gomułka summed up this feeling with the remark that 'the masses ought to see us as a Polish party. Let them attack us as Polish communists and not as an agency.'[97] The strategy of using the Red Army to crush 'London' while the party established a political base and consolidated its hold on the state apparatus had failed. The repressive measures of the Soviet forces had proved an obstacle to stabilization, had reinforced the Communists' isolation and fuelled the opposition.

The 'May turn'

BETWEEN mid-April when Zawadzki was ousted (Gomułka called his dismissal 'the first warning step'[98]) and early June, the party line was put into reverse. Although he claimed that there was no '180 degree turn; only a "recognition of deviations"', Gomułka at the same time demanded that 'a real, fundamental turn in the policy of grassroots organisations' should take place. His claim that 'the line from the occupation, the line of the July manifesto, remains in force', was disingenuous since in practice a very different line had been pursued since October 1944.[99] The London camp was in no doubt that the party was following a new course; on 12 June Korboński informed London that: 'During the past few days a sudden and fundamental change has been executed in the Lublin press and tactics.'[100]

The essentials of the new line were unveiled at the Central Committee Plenum held on 20–21 May and announced to the top party *aktyw* at a special conference a week later. As usual the turn was accompanied by a redefinition of the party's strategic formula. In October the twin tests of support for the national front were active commitment to the destruction of the opponents of the PKWN and the establishment of a 'democratic' Poland. In May all that was required was recognition of the authority of the Provisional Government and compliance with its decrees. Thus the 'democratic national front' of 'struggle with the domestic reaction for a strong, democratic Poland'[101] of October, gave way to the more inclusive broad or united (*wspólny*) 'democratic national front' embracing 'all those groups and political activists who recognise the Provisional Government of the Polish Republic . . . (and) express a readiness to assist the implementation of all state instructions.'[102] Gomułka elaborated for the *aktyw* what this meant:

> We are not opening the doors for everybody. We have one basic criterion. We say: we will co-operate with those groups and political elements which above all recognise the Provisional Government as the only authority operating in Poland on the basis of the national will and . . . undertake to co-operate with the government in rebuilding the country. Provided these conditions are fulfilled, we consider both discussion and criticism as possible if it does not conflict with the fundamental principles of the democratic front.[103]

In the terminology of one Warsaw historian, the formula applying from late 1944 to spring 1945 of 'he who is not with us is against us' or even 'not everyone who is with us *is* with us', was now replaced with the same criterion in force the previous summer: 'he who is not against us is for us'.[104]

The turn-around was most evident in a revision in the party's attitude to the AK. The blanket condemnation of the AK 'from beginning to end, without distinction between leaders and led',[105] was now replaced with a policy of distinguishing the 'honest AK' from 'the reactionary part of the AK'. It was admitted that unjust arrests of AK members had driven others back into conspiracy.[106] According to underground reports to London, posters with the slogan 'Down with the AK and NSZ cut-throats' disappeared and in their place it was confirmed 'in all the press and official statements that the AK are heroes'.[107] On 30 May a partial amnesty was ordered, covering those arrested for connections with the AK who had not actually participated in armed resistance to the new authorities and had not held command positions in the AK. The same order instructed the use of propaganda to persuade 'as many people as possible to leave the forests'.[108]

Methods of combating the partisans changed too. Priority was given to deploying Polish units rather than Russians against the underground. On 24 May the Internal Security Corps (KBW) was formed from the existing Interior Armies and some regular units, and the 1st, 3rd and 9th Infantry Divisions were ordered to eastern Poland for duties against the guerrillas.[109] A new emphasis was placed on the political aspect of operations as well. An all-party 'Supreme Political Commission to Combat Banditry' was created under Gomułka's chairmanship,[110] and special 'agitprop groups' were attached to anti-insurgency units. The instructions issued to these groups stressed the need to deprive the guerrillas of their popular base and prestige. They were depicted as 'bandits' who 'murder peasants, soldiers and militiamen, steal from the population and state property, want to prevent the country's reconstruction . . . and Poland benefiting from the blessings of peace.' Group members were to avoid parading their party allegiances, but appear as 'representatives of the population, of the democratic camp'. The key to military success was 'the complete isolation of the bands from the population, and the resistance of the population to the bands.' Assurances were also given that partisans and deserters who gave themselves up to the authorities would not be punished.[111] The change of tactics resulted almost immediately in talks opening between the authorities and guerrilla units in some areas.[112]

Industrial policy also underwent a marked transformation. Its keynote now was the improvement of productivity and labour-discipline and an end to the radical experimentation and improvisation which had reigned in the factories over the previous months.

The problem of raising productivity was considered by the Politburo to be of foremost significance in achieving economic recovery and political stabilization.

> The situation which exists today in this area is not just unsatisfactory, but one must say, outright alarming, outright catastrophic. If we do not solve the problem of increasing labour productivity then we will not solve any of the problems which stand before us in this both economically and politically difficult situation, we will not maintain democratic power in Poland.[113]

This was a victory for the view of Minc's Ministry of Industry, so it seems, over trade union representations. As early as 2 April Minc had issued instructions on measures to raise productivity which ignored the role of the trade unions and works councils.[114] The trade unions had, on the other hand, still argued, in a resolution of 21–22 April, that the subsistence of the workers was 'the deciding question' determining their productive capacity.[115]

The first step taken to bring about this improvement in productivity was a marked curbing of the powers of the works councils in favour of the management. In May the wide role which the councils had played in practice in the factories for some months received legal regulation as the February decree came into force. At the same time instructions were issued on holding formal elections.[116] At the May Plenum, however, the leadership came down strongly in favour of 'the increased and strengthened authority of the director, engineer and foreman', which was spelt out as meaning that while the management and works council ought jointly to decide questions concerning the employment and laying off of workers as well as housing, rationing and other material and social needs of the workforce, 'the director alone decides all matters relating to the economic and technical management of the concern as well as matters related to bonuses.'[117] On 1 June Minc's ministry issued instructions limiting the role and powers of the councils 'in the name of efficient economic management'.[118] This move was discussed at a National Industrial Conference held on 2–3 June.[119] As Gołębiowski has commented, 'in consequence of the decisions taken the works councils and labour-force were deprived of direct influence on the economic management of concerns.'[120] Thus, just as elections got under way and the membership of the councils was broadened, they lost their hold on the factory purse strings.

Complementing these changes there was a further centralization in the overall management of the economy. Individual concerns were brought more closely under central direction,[121] and 'the emergency measures reminiscent of Soviet war communism [in 1918–21]' by which the economy had been run since mid-1944[122] began to be tempered by the first moves towards systematic planning. On 8 June ministries received instructions to draw up plans.[123]

On pay, the Central Committee reaffirmed its rejection of egalitarianism in favour of linking wages to productivity and skills, with non-manual employees receiving a share of profits. Wage-rates were to be reformed throughout industry during June. Simultaneously prices were to be revised so as to increase the profitability of industry while avoiding large price rises in basic consumer goods, manufactures for agriculture and industrial raw materials. Transport and service charges were to cover costs, with reduced fares for certain groups, especially for workers.[124]

Even before the Plenum steps had been taken to speed up the reprivatization of small and middle industry under temporary state management. An Act of 6 May embodied fairly liberal terms governing the restoration of factories to their original owners and an Industry Ministry circular of 15 May was designed to accelerate this process.[125] At the Plenum itself Gomułka complained that the party had not been able to revitalize the private sector, and he called for a far bolder policy[126] while the economic resolution demanded a greater role for 'private initiative' and trade. With some reservations the Central Committee gave its backing for a large-scale expansion of *Spolem*, the main established cooperative organization in Poland, grafting the ZSCh coops on to this network.[127] This represented a retreat, for the time being, by the Communists who had hoped to set up the ZSCh as a separate cooperative movement under their influence. It was also a concession to the Socialists who had strong links with *Spolem*. In early May Minc had severely criticized the 'old cooperative movement', arguing that its structure did not suit the new political and economic regime. This had aroused a stout defence of existing arrangements from the Socialist cooperators led by Jan Żerkowski, president of *Spolem*. By the time of the coop. 'parliament' in Lodz on 10 June these differences had been resolved, largely to the satisfaction of the PPS. Minc abandoned his critical stance and fell in with the decision not to create a separate new movement.[128]

Within the party leadership the question of the role of the cooperatives was bound up with deeper programmatic problems. Its economic standpoint remained ill-defined and although Minc took the lead in attempting to systematize the party's improvisations into a model his analyses still lacked precision and were not enshrined as official positions. At the February 1945 Plenum he had devoted some attention to theoretical matters, concluding that the present stage was characterized by the struggle between 'private capitalism', which was 'unrestrained, uncontrolled, unregulated, without a bridle, collar or muzzle' and 'state capitalism', which involved the handing-over by capitalism of a 'part of its profits to society', and the removal 'of its most venomous speculatory fangs'.[129] In May he commented on the view that Poland was experiencing an NEP-style coexistence of private and state sectors, a view he described as 'thoroughly wrong and dangerous'. He argued that Poland was in fact 'a capitalist system undergoing a democratic revolution', and that this was different.[130] Some members of the leadership were prepared to consider very unorthodox solutions to the problem of defining Poland's unorthodox economic arrangements. Ochab suggested the concept of a 'Cooperative Republic', but Zambrowski spoke against this.[131]

In practice May 1945 saw the introduction of the 'three-sector model' in which state, cooperative and private sectors existed side by side. For the Socialists this model was looked upon as a satisfactory long-term arrangement. The Communists, on the other hand, viewed it as a transitional stage suited to the initial years of economic recovery and consolidation of power, but from 1947 pressed for its transformation towards Socialism, by which they meant the clear supremacy of the state sector over reduced and dependent cooperative and private elements.

THE EMERGENCE OF the tripartite economic model was paralleled by the institutionalization in May and June 1945 of the multi-party system based on the PPR, Socialists and Peasants. In addition, two smaller organizations, the Democratic Party, representing the urban intelligentsia and trade, and the Party of Labour (*Stronnictwo Pracy* – SP) representing Catholics, were allowed to organize. The National Party, the anti-Communist wing of the PPS and former AK circles were prevented from organizing their own legal parties and either joined the legal 'opposition', ceased political activity or operated in conspiracy. The Communists were not of course prepared to allow the other parties to threaten their hegemony within the government coalition or their control over the key instruments of state power: the army, security, police and penal system, upper levels of the administrative apparatus and the media. Nevertheless it is fair to say that from mid-1945 until early 1947 a genuinely pluralistic party system functioned in Poland in which the Communists could not automatically rely on their allies to follow their lead as was to be the case by 1948–9.

The development of this system followed from the Communists' decision in May to broaden the national front and, in particular, to relax their hold on the leadership of the Peasant Party and allow the recruitment of members of 'ROCh' on a large scale. At the Plenum the use of 'plants' to direct the policy of the SL leadership was heavily criticized and it was decided that particularly discredited figures such as Janusz (the deputy-premier) and Bertold (minister of agriculture), should be removed. However, the use of plants 'for information purposes' was continued.[132] The Communists seem to have hoped that even without their direct intervention the bulk of 'ROCh' could be contained within the existing legal SL and that the minority of the party committed to cooperating with the PPR would be able to keep Mikołajczyk, on his return, in check.[133] Zambrowski, speaking confidentially in August, said that the party's initial tactics had been to force Mikołajczyk to join 'a single, united party, on the platform of the existing SL, in which the SL would have a majority'.[134] Confident that the pro-Communist factions would continue to guide the direction of the SL and PPS, the Politburo was prepared to envisage a wide range of free debate among the coalition parties, pledging itself to the 'principle of equality, of discussion and agreement of the more important resolutions and steps . . . the encouragement of debate and admission of criticism, and also opposition, as long as it does not clash with the basis itself of the coalition.'[135]

The party's attitude to the PPS also changed from May 1945. The campaign of February to prevent an uncontrolled expansion of the PPS by playing on the alleged WRN menace was discontinued and the question of merging the two parties was placed on ice in favour of an indefinite period of partnership.[136] This special partnership of the workers' parties, the 'united front', was given a new emphasis. With the way open for Mikołajczyk's return and the emergence of an independent Peasant Party, the Socialists assumed a pivotal role in the government coalition. Even before the Plenum the PPR leadership had been applying pressures on its local organizations to allow the Socialists a larger share of posts in industry and the administration and this was accompanied by policy concessions to the PPS – especially in the economic field. An example of this was the Communists' *volte-face* on coops. And while the party declared its 'aspiration' to the leading role in the national front, the Politburo made it clear to the *aktyw* that this role would have to be earned through political work and could not be claimed as of right.[137] The PPR had been forced to recognize that the Socialists could no longer be treated as a 'department' of the party, but would have to be handled as a coalition ally which was aware of its value to the Communists; a value which steadily rose as Mikołajczyk moved into open opposition and the elections drew closer.

The May Plenum also introduced fundamental changes in the party's attitude to its relationship with the Soviet government. The Politburo accepted the criticisms by Central Committee members of infringements of Polish sovereignty, and the unassertiveness of foreign policy hitherto. New emphasis was placed on Poland's sovereignty and independence and party propaganda disclaimed any intention of 'sovietizing' the country. In the foreign policy sphere, Gomułka, concluding the Plenum's deliberations, went so far as to state that 'the Soviet Union's change of course towards Germany should not bind us', adding that 'the problem of sovereignty was correctly put in the discussion'.[138]

This determination to follow a more independent foreign policy was expressed in the occupation on 19 June by Żymierski's troops of Zaolzie, a border area over which the Polish and Czech governments were in dispute. The use of military force to press the Polish claim against the Soviet Union's close ally can hardly have pleased Moscow. Without resorting to such dramatic gestures, the Russians were persuaded at the beginning of July to hand over the administration of Szczecin.[139] Also in August, the Poles rejected Stalin's proposal for joint companies to exploit the Lower Silesian coalfield.[140]

The problem of reducing the Soviet presence in Poland had been considered at length during the Plenum and it had been decided to pursue with greater vigour efforts to persuade the Russians to adopt a less provocative profile. Soviet military administration was largely withdrawn in July and August.[141] Polish calls for tougher measures against Red Army marauders also brought a response. By the end of the year court martials and in some cases the public execution of offenders had resulted in a significant reduction in outrages against the local population.[142] But as Gomułka candidly admitted, there was no point in demanding a departure of all the Soviet forces; 'we would not have enough of our own forces to put in their place.'[143] The handover of policing operations to the Polish army seems to have continued into 1946. As late as the first half of 1946 Soviet fatalities in clashes with the underground were still running at around 10 per cent of those suffered by Polish pro-government forces and civilians, a proportion much the same as it had been during the first half of 1945.[144] Nonetheless, from June 1945 the army was Polonized as Russian officers seconded during the war returned home. According to Żymierski, speaking in September 1946, some 14,000 Soviet officers, including 40 generals, had departed.[145] The British Embassy in Warsaw detected a major reduction in the presence of Soviet troops in Poland at the turn of 1945–6 and the ambassador, Cavendish-Bentinck was inclined to accept as true a statement by the Polish government on 30 January 1946 that the number of Soviet troops had been reduced to 250–300,000.[146]

Finally, the May Plenum heralded the transformation of the Provisional Government into the Provisional Government of National Unity following agreement at talks held in Moscow between the Warsaw Poles and Mikołajczyk on 21 June. The three Allied Powers had agreed on a formula for the reconstruction of the Provisional Government months before at Yalta. The communiqué issued on 11 February at the close of the conference had stated that:

> A new situation has been created in Poland as a result of her complete liberation by the Red Army. This calls for the establishment of a Polish Provisional Government which can be more broadly based than was possible before the recent liberation of western Poland. The Provisional Government which is now functioning in Poland should therefore be reorganised on a broader democratic basis with the inclusion of democratic leaders from Poland itself and from Poles abroad. . . . This Polish Provisional Government of National Unity shall be pledged to the holding of free and unfettered elections as soon as possible on the basis of universal suffrage and secret ballot. In these elections all democratic and anti-Nazi parties shall have the right to take part and to put forward candidates.

Molotov, Harriman and Clark Kerr were authorized as a commission to consult members of the Provisional Government and 'other Polish democratic leaders from within Poland and abroad'.[147]

The work of the commission proceeded slowly. The stumbling block was Mikołajczyk. The British and Americans regarded his inclusion in the reconstructed government as essential. However, at Yalta Stalin and Molotov had stated that Mikołajczyk was unacceptable to the Warsaw

Poles.[148] Molotov again took this line at a meeting of the commission on 27 February.[149] Polonsky suggests that pressure from the Polish Communists may indeed have prompted the Soviet veto on Mikołajczyk.[150] If so, it seems likely that as in October 1944 (cf. chapter 6, p.161) the advice from Warsaw was that the time was not yet ripe to deal with Mikołajczyk, rather than that such a deal was unacceptable in principle.

Sometime in April or May the Soviet and Polish authorities seem to have decided that it would be safe to run the risk of Mikołajczyk's return. In a letter of 7 April to Churchill, Stalin had offered to use his influence with the Warsaw Poles to make them withdraw their objections to Mikołajczyk, provided he declared his acceptance of the Yalta decisions on Poland.[151] Mikołajczyk did this on 15 April.[152] However, it seems unlikely that the Poles shifted their ground before the May Plenum. None of the speakers at the Plenum referred to the possible implications of Mikołajczyk returning; indeed there was no discussion at all on the reconstruction of the government.[153] It was left to Gomułka in his summing up to state that the party aimed to form a democratic coalition and that it was in its interest to solve the problem of the Provisional Government along the lines of the Yalta decisions as soon as possible.[154] Ten days later, during Harry Hopkins' placatory trip to Moscow, Stalin finally agreed to the resumption of talks with Mikołajczyk.

In executing the May 'turn' it seems, therefore, unlikely that the party was simply falling in with decisions already taken in Moscow to allow Mikołajczyk's return. The absence of discussion on reconstructing the government indicates that this was not the Central Committee's principal concern. Moreover, all the indications are that, in contrast to October 1944, Stalin had not given a firm lead to the Politburo. The discussion at the Plenum was remarkably frank and members of the leadership openly disagreed in their interpretation of the political situation. When Stalin was mentioned, it was to make it clear that he understood and supported the party's wish to assert its sovereignty and independence.

The Communists recognized that Mikołajczyk's return was the price they would have to pay to achieve early Western recognition of the Provisional Government. Western recognition was important both in order to secure aid for Poland's economic recovery and to ensure maximum Polish influence at the forthcoming peace conference which was to determine the extent of Poland's territorial gains in the north and west.[155] The discussion at the May Plenum focused on the problem from this specifically Polish perspective and these Polish interests appear to have been paramount in the leadership's decision to seek an early deal on reconstructing the government.

Although international considerations clearly played a part in the May 'turn', the speeches made at the Plenum were dominated by internal concerns: the economy, the underground, relations with the allied parties and the Soviet role in Poland. The Communists regarded international recognition of the Provisional Government as important but a lower priority than the question of power in Poland. Gomułka made this clear a few weeks later in Moscow when he told Mikołajczyk:

> if we do not reach agreement we shall return home without you. You may be certain that in two or three months time our government will be recognised by the Western Allies. . . . But even if it happens that we have to wait longer – then we shall wait, but we shall never hand over power.[156]

It was then, above all, the progress of the party's efforts to consolidate its position and broaden its mass base which determined the extent and timing of its change of course in May. The hard-line democratic national front adopted in the previous October had, in the view of the majority of the party leadership, served its purpose of securing the party's hold on power and was now propelling the country towards a political crisis which would find the PPR isolated and totally dependent on the Russians. It was this spectre which most concerned the May Plenum and convinced the Central Committee that a major change of tactics was required. The reorientation was not confined to a revision of policy towards the Mikołajczyk Peasants, but extended widely to take in other political groupings, security policy, industrial ownership and management, the economic model, Poland's national sovereignty and intra-party matters. One section of the party argued that the modification of the line should not go so far. This included KPP veterans like Włodzimierz Zawadzki who wanted to step up the use of the Red Army and security forces against the underground, or Konopka who warned of a Rightist deviation in the party threatening its leading role.[157] This group was easily isolated as 'sectarian', but within the leadership Berman too expressed a minority view. Though he rejected Zawadzki's 'Trotskyism' and recognized that the party must 'first complete the bourgeois revolution', Berman argued from Soviet experience that the party's narrow base signified great difficulties, but not a crisis. He viewed the increase in underground activity as the result not of a revival in popular support for London, but of the work of reactionary elements and claimed that 'what we see as a danger is [in fact] the excessively slow tempo of our own activity in relation to changes taking place. We have failed to follow up our own successes.' According to Berman, sectarianism was not a reaction to the crisis, but rather an 'illness' arising from the Luxemburgist tradition of the old KPP.[158] The implication of this was that the existing line was basically correct and major adjustments unnecessary. But Gomułka's group and most of the ex-émigrés for whom Zambrowski emerged as the main spokesman, but including Aleksander Zawadzki, Ochab, Wierbłowski, Finkielsztajn and Radkiewicz, came down decisively for a change of direction, justifying it by stressing the severity of the crisis. The position of Bierut, Minc and Spychalski is difficult, on the evidence available, to assess. Gomułka had the majority behind him in concluding that it was:

undeniable that there are certain elements of crisis. It is a crisis when the base narrows. . . . If our base was growing sectarianism would not occur. If the SL executive could build a real SL, the SL problem would not arise. . . . In the reactionary camp there is a crisis, but we have not been able to narrow its base. There is a lack of confidence in the Provisional Government. We cannot fight the reaction without the Red Army. That says something about [our] base.[159]

He added, in an undoubted reference to Berman's speech, that 'some people say that it took a long time for Soviet authority to be established. The comparison is incorrect. We are not establishing a Soviet system. We want to establish a democratic coalition.'[160] In May 1945 the majority of the PPR leadership believed that the political crisis demanded the formation of such a broad-based democratic coalition and that the party's hold on the key areas of power was sufficiently secure to allow it to run the risks involved. The next nine months were to convince the PPR that those risks were still too great.

8   National unity? June 1945 to February 1946

ON 23 JUNE ROMAN ZAMBROWSKI reported to the Central Committee Secretariat on the outcome of the Moscow talks with Mikołajczyk:

> The formation of the National Unity Government is a success. Its core is the Provisional Government. Five ministers out of 21 are from the London Government, which means that the (existing) government has been extended, not replaced. We have not made political concessions to London. The trial of the Sixteen [the 15 underground leaders arrested in March and Aleksander Kwierzyński of the National Party who had been arrested earlier] cuts off the retreat of Mikołajczyk and Stańczyk [one of the leaders of the émigré PPS] to the London reaction.[1]

The deal with Mikołajczyk indeed appeared to be a major success for the Communists. The terms of the agreement left the framework of the Provisional Government, and within it the dominant position of the PPR, intact. Moreover, the regrouping of the London camp which the Communists had sought fruitlessly in 1943–4 had come about at last. They had driven a wedge between the London 'democrats' led by Mikołajczyk, and the diehards, who regarded any deal with the Lublin camp as capitulation. The results of the regrouping were evident in a general stabilization of the political situation and a marked fall-off in underground activity after June (see figure 1). The consequences of Western recognition of the Provisional Government were soon evident also. The flow of economic aid from UNRRA (primarily, that is, from the U.S.A.) began in September.[2] And at Potsdam in July the Polish delegation which included Bierut, Mikołajczyk, Gomułka and Osóbka-Morawski secured *de facto* recognition by the Great Powers of a Polish frontier on the Oder-Western Neisse Line.[3]

However, the Communists were aware that, despite this success, the return of the London 'democrats' and the lower Soviet profile in Polish affairs would place the party's hegemony within the government coalition at risk. Zambrowski pointed to the danger in his report to the Central Committee Secretariat:

> the entry of Stańczyk, Żuławski, Witos, Mikołajczyk and Kiernik into the Government and KRN represents a strengthening of anti-PPR elements, sowing distrust towards the Soviet Union. There is a danger of the London elements blocking together as well as of attempts to form a PPS-SL bloc against the PPR. The question of a fifth party arises with the invitation to Popiel [leader of the Catholic Party of Labour]. . . . It is essential to strengthen cooperation with the PPS and SL. The

leadership group in the SL is weak and fissile, lacks wide support and will find it difficult to prevent Mikołajczyk, Kiernik and Witos returning in triumph.[4]

The period from June 1945 to February 1946 was a testing time when the Communists sought to consolidate and make permanent the advantages they had won at the conference table in Moscow and at the same time avert the inherent dangers to them in the new political situation. The legalization of the mainstream peasant movement and the elections, expected for the first half of 1946,[5] cast a shadow of uncertainty over the Communists' hold on power. As Gomułka put it, 'the elections are the last resort which the reaction wants to win and around which it concentrates all its hopes and forces.'[6] The party was under no illusions about the likely outcome of a contest: 'it must be expected that if the PSL [Mikołajczyk's *Polskie Stronnictwo Ludowe*] fought the elections independently . . . as well as if the democratic parties split over the elections – the PSL would have a serious chance. . . . We as a party must . . . pursue those tactics which will ensure us electoral victory.'[7]

Until February 1946 those tactics were to secure the integration of the London 'democrats', and in particular Mikołajczyk's followers in the peasant movement, into the national front, or more specifically, a single electoral bloc of the six coalition parties. Although the Communists were at no stage prepared to concede their leading role in such a bloc, they continued to regard the mainstream peasant movement, in more or less its existing form, as the foremost potential partner for themselves and the PPS in the 'worker–peasant alliance' and the principal means to extend the base of the national front into the countryside. In essence, they aimed to put into practice the conception of the broad democratic national front which they had sought without success to achieve in 1943–4 and had returned to in May 1945.

However, Mikołajczyk and the overwhelming majority of his party were not prepared to accept the bloc on the terms that the PPR demanded. Mikołajczyk recognized the necessity of working closely with the PPR,[8] but he was not prepared to accept an electoral bloc which would preserve the Communists' leading role in the coalition. Nor did he believe that the PPR was sufficiently strong to force him to do so. Although he had little confidence that the elections would be free and unfettered, he considered that the size and organizational strength of the peasant movement and the configuration of international forces were such that he could capture the leadership of the government coalition from the Communists and himself dictate the terms on which his party would cogovern with the PPR.

On his return to Poland following the Moscow talks, Mikołajczyk proceeded to put this strategy into effect with immediate and conspicuous success. In August his Polish Peasant Party (PSL) was legalized and within a few months had a mass membership considerably larger than that of the Communists and their allies taken together. The pro-Communist SL almost ceased functioning as its members went over *en masse* to the PSL. By spring 1946 the PPR leadership, though significantly not its PPS allies, had all but abandoned hope of bringing the PSL into the national front and were convinced that urgent and aggressive measures were needed to recover the political initiative and fend off Mikołajczyk's challenge. As in October 1944, the Communists decided that the question of power had to take priority over the quest for a more broadly-based national front.

The worker–peasant alliance

THE Communists considered that there were only two courses open to Mikołajczyk and his followers in the new political situation which had arisen as a result of the Moscow agreement. The first was for the 'London' Peasants to assume the role of a subordinate partner to the 'Lublin' parties in the national front, taking their place as one arm of the worker–peasant alliance under the hegemony of the workers' parties and, in particular, the PPR. On condition that they accepted the leadership of the PPR in the coalition once and for all, the Communists were prepared to concede to the Peasants a greater share of influence in the government apparatus and even allow them some freedom to express loyal opposition from within the national front. In the longer term the PPR believed that, cast in such a role, the peasant movement would evolve into an important prop for the future social and economic transformation of Poland.

The only alternative for the 'London' Peasants, in the Communists' view, was that of outright opposition to the 'democratic camp' in tacit alliance with the anti-Communist underground. This the PPR would not tolerate. If the Peasants took up such a stance, the Communists made it clear that they would use force to dismantle the movement's organization and make it impossible for Peasant activists to operate in the open. The Communists would look elsewhere for a partner in the worker–peasant alliance.

In the period from mid-1945 to February 1946 the PPR sought to force Mikołajczyk to make a clear choice between these alternative courses. The Communists seem to have decided from the start[9] that the acid test of Mikołajczyk's true intentions would be the PSL's 'attitude to the question of the worker–peasant alliance and to the problem of uniting in a joint electoral bloc'.[10] However, their allies in the leadership of the PPS did not accept this approach until November, when, at least formally, it was the Socialists who took the initiative of inviting the PSL to join an electoral bloc. Under strong pressure from the two workers' parties, the PSL leaders finally entered negotiations in February 1946.

Despite increasing tension between the Communists and the Peasants as 1945 wore on and pessimism as to the possibility of winning the consent of Mikołajczyk and his supporters[11] to an electoral bloc, until February the preference of the PPR leadership was to keep the PSL within the national front. Gomułka made this clear at the commencement of the negotiations in a speech delivered to the Central Committee on 10 February which provides the fullest statement of the party's view on the choice which lay before the PSL:

> the creation of an electoral bloc is the main objective of our Party. . . . We are endeavouring to form a bloc of the six political parties [i.e. including the PSL]. Why do we want this and what shall we gain by it? . . .
> Above all we shall guarantee the hegemony of the political line which commenced with the policy of the KRN and later the PKWN. By forming this bloc of six we shall disappoint all the hopes of our domestic reaction for a change of government in Poland. . . . All those reactionary elements which are today pinning their hopes on the PSL would be, quite clearly, profoundly disappointed and would of necessity be forced to alter their attitude to the PSL. By achieving the bloc of six we could establish political stabilisation in the country. . . . The creation of a bloc of six is beneficial not only from the point of view of our party, but from the national point of view. . . . The bloc is a state imperative.[12]

The Politburo considered that it would be worth making limited, but not insignificant political concessions to win PSL compliance:

> We must realise and say clearly that we would have to make certain concessions to the PSL in the state apparatus without however handing them hegemony. . . . However strengthening the PSL in the state apparatus within the bloc of six would not in fact be dangerous since the bloc of six must strengthen the leftist tendency and forces in the PSL. If the PSL joined us in the bloc it would be combated by the entire reaction. . . . A strengthening of the PSL in local government would also have to follow. The question of local government elections on different principles would then arise.[13]

The party leadership continued to see within the PSL considerable social potential as a partner in the worker–peasant alliance. Although he considered that the ideology of the PSL leadership was basically 'bourgeois-liberal' in character and that 'as the party furthest to the right' it had inevitably attracted support from 'reactionary, fascist elements', and had become 'the defender of the social interests of various capitalist strata, above all kulak, business and speculating layers', Gomułka warned the Central Committee that:

> We must not close our eyes to the fact that a substantial number of people who are gathered within the PSL ought not to be there considering its character – above all poor peasant elements. . . . However this should be seen as a temporary phenomenon and the poor amongst the PSL rank and file should be looked at as a factor which should cause centrifugal tendencies to grow inside the PSL. The interests of this poorer layer are diametrically opposed to the interests of the kulaks and speculators and we must recognise that there exist real possibilities of these centrifugal tendencies increasing.[14]

However, if the PSL refused to enter the bloc, thus disputing the hegemony of the PPR by contesting the elections as an independent force, 'or more precisely', as the Communists saw it, 'in a bloc with the reaction and the illegal organisations',[15] it would no longer be combated tolerantly as a loyal opposition, but would be treated on a par with the outlawed reaction:

> If the PSL does not go along with the bloc of six, it places itself not just in opposition to the government, but makes its party a factor splitting the unity of the democratic front. Therefore we would conduct our struggle with the PSL primarily from the angle not of a struggle against an opposition, but with those who smash and disrupt democratic unity.[16]

Gomułka had spelt out rather more explicitly what this meant in a speech he had made a few months before, when he had said that for those determined to provoke an electoral confrontation 'the Polish Workers' Party has only one reply: with opponents and enemies of democratic Poland we speak only in the language of struggle.'[17]

If such aggressive tactics became necessary, the bloc parties would continue to look for the support of the peasant masses which had hitherto followed Mikołajczyk. But instead of the evolutionary approach of integrating the bulk of the PSL into the government front and prodding it steadily Leftwards, the PSL would be broken up. Its 'reactionary' elements would be suppressed and the rank and file gathered into a new mass party based on the rump of the 'Lublin SL'. As Gomułka put it:

> our main task would have to be to work for a clear differentiation inside the PSL so that it will be possible to detach from it the democratic elements which are indisputably to be found within the ranks of that organisation. These democratic elements must be linked and mobilised with an electoral bloc of the four democratic parties. . . . The [Lublin] Peasant Party . . . has great potential influence on the poor peasantry amongst the PSL rank and file.[18]

Thus the Communists were uncompromising in defending the two crucial advantages which in their view they had gained in Moscow: their hegemony in the State apparatus and the separation of Mikołajczyk and his followers from the London diehards. As late as February 1946 the party was endeavouring to transform the Moscow deal into a deeper alliance, on its own terms naturally, with the PSL as a whole, or at any rate its major part. Simultaneously, it indicated that any attempt by the PSL to challenge these two essential points, by forcing an electoral contest, would not be tolerated.

Mikołajczyk and the tactics of the PSL

UNTIL 1947, to a very large degree Mikołajczyk dominated the tactical direction of his party. Witos, the ailing elder statesman of the movement, died in October 1945 having played little more than a symbolic role in the party during the last months of his life.[19] The third major figure of the interwar years active from 1945 was Władysław Kiernik, a cautious and flexible politician with none of Mikołajczyk's wartime prestige. Despite some earlier doubts, it was not until after the 1947 elections that Kiernik and the leaders of the wartime underground 'ROCh' organization, Józef Niećko and Czesław Wycech, began openly to dispute Mikołajczyk's leadership.

Stanisław Mikołajczyk was born in 1901, the son of a peasant who had emigrated to work in the Westphalian coalfield. Later the family returned to Poznania, where Mikołajczyk's father bought a small (6 hectares) farm near Krotoszyn. Mikołajczyk took part in the Wielkopolska uprising in 1918–19 and the Russo-Polish War in 1920. After elementary school, he completed his education with short courses at agricultural college. He was a fairly successful farmer and in 1930 he was able to buy a 20-hectare farm near Wągrowiec.

Mikołajczyk began his political activity in 1922 when he joined Witos' *Piast* Peasant Party. In 1927 he helped to found the youth section of *Piast* in Wielkopolska and was its chairman from 1928 to 1930. After 1930 he was effectively leader of the Poznanian peasant movement and won prominence in the national leadership of the unified Peasant Party. He sat as deputy to the *Sejm* between 1930 and 1935 and was secretary of the *Sejm* club and the Supreme Council of the SL. By the mid-1930s he had emerged as a leading domestic spokesman of the section of the movement which favoured active opposition to the *Sanacja* regime (many of the older leaders of the party, e.g. Witos, Kiernik and Bagiński were in exile). Mikołajczyk was in effective charge of the SL during the violent confrontations which took place with the authorities between 1936 and 1938, when mass demonstrations, a boycott of government directives, the organization of 'self-defence' groups in the villages and, above all, peasant strikes were used to press for the restoration of representative government.

In the September campaign, Mikołajczyk fought as a private soldier and then escaped via Hungary to France where he became chairman of the Foreign Committee of the SL and vice-chairman of the National Council (i.e. the Polish Parliament in exile). He was one of Sikorski's main allies in Paris and London and from September 1941 to July 1943 was deputy-premier and minister of internal affairs in the Government-in-Exile. On Sikorski's death he became prime minister.[20]

The considerable political reputation which Mikołajczyk enjoyed when he returned to Poland in 1945 was entirely destroyed by his defeat and subsequent flight from the country in 1947. Many Western accounts of the post-war struggle for power in Poland, including his own which was published in exile in 1948, depict him as a simple, straightforward – not to say naïve – liberal democrat who made the mistake of believing that the PSL would be allowed to win the elections, or if not, that the West would intervene on his behalf at the crucial juncture.[21]

In reality, Mikołajczyk was by 1945 a seasoned politician with a wide range of experience in both government and opposition. His background was, in many ways, particularly appropriate for the political circumstances of post-war Poland. In the 1930s he had led the SL at a time when its scope for activity within the parliamentary arena was severely limited and the movement had been forced increasingly to resort to extra-parliamentary and economic opposition to the authoritarian military regimes of Piłsudski and Śmigły-Rydz. Although he had no direct experience of the underground struggle against the Nazi occupation, he had played an important role in its organization from abroad as minister for internal affairs between 1941 and 1943 and prime minister in 1943–4. His premiership had also given him a considerable insight into the workings of Great Power diplomacy.

This experience had taught him to be a realist. Perhaps more than any other Polish politician, he had understood that Poland's future depended not on solemn treaties and undertakings, but on the real interests of the Big Three. He also recognized that the success of his party's bid for power would not depend on its popularity alone, but crucially on its organizational strength and capacity to withstand the repressive measures which the Communists would undoubtedly use against it. He understood that the elections would not in themselves decide the struggle for power and that the Soviet Union, not the Western Powers, would settle the issue. In his view, therefore, the key to the situation lay in demonstrating that Poland was ungovernable without the peasants and thereby convincing the Soviet government that its interests would be best served by a Poland in which his party was allowed to play a full role.

In the longer term, Mikołajczyk did not regard the prospects as unhopeful. Two days after the Moscow agreement, Averell Harriman reported that:

> Mikołajczyk does not expect the full freedoms which he would like for Poland and the Polish people. On the other hand he is hopeful that through the strength of the Peasant Party a reasonable degree of freedom and independence can be preserved now and that in time after conditions in Europe become more stable and Russia turns her attention to her internal development controls will be relaxed and Poland will be able to gain for herself her independence of life as a nation even though he freely accepts that Poland's security and foreign policy must follow the lead of Moscow.[22]

In the international sphere Mikołajczyk had nothing but contempt for the London diehards who while 'apparently giving up nothing, had lost everything'.[23] In his view reality demanded that Poland accommodate herself to her passage into the sphere of Soviet military power. He excluded the possibility of an armed clash between East and West which might, as the diehards hoped, reverse this development.[24] Rather he expected the alliance against Hitler to continue in the post-war world, with both Poland and the Soviet Union relying heavily on Western aid for years to come in order to reconstruct their ruined economies. This economic

constraint on Stalin and the Polish Communists would allow a compromise solution to the Polish question: Poland would ally herself closely
to the Soviet Union in foreign policy and internally anti-Soviet groups
would be excluded from political power, but the constitutional and
economic order would be modelled on the Western pattern. The Peasants,
as the largest party, would lead a representative coalition government
which would include the Communists. The aim of the PSL leaders was to
achieve the kind of relationship with the U.S.S.R. which was taking shape
in Finland.[25]

His acceptance by the Russians was crucial to Mikołajczyk's strategy. He
aimed at nothing less than supplanting the Communists in their role as the
main beneficiary of Soviet confidence and as protector of Soviet interests in
Poland. In a speech delivered shortly after his return, he explained the
kind of alliance he was seeking:

> The need for a Polish-Soviet alliance is understood by the peasants. . . . What in
> essence does the Polish-Soviet alliance rest upon? On mutual respect for the
> sovereignty and socio-economic systems existing in these states and on mutual
> non-interference in internal affairs. . . . At the highest levels we have never met
> with the denial of one of these basic points . . . on the contrary, we have always met
> with complete good will. . . . We consider that neither for Russia, nor for Poland
> would it be good if the question of confidence, collaboration, of sincere co-operation
> and friendship were to rest on only one or two parties. We feel that the more we can
> convince our eastern neighbour that co-operation and the alliance is supported by
> the widest possible groups in society, the more long-lasting will be its ties. The great
> extent of PSL influence amongst the peasant masses will play an important and
> positive role in shaping the co-existence of these two states.[26]

This policy may have appeared naïve in the light of later events, but
until mid-1946 the portents for its success seemed favourable. Official
Soviet pronouncements were very moderate in tone in accordance with the
stance of respect for Polish sovereignty and of disengagement from
internal affairs on which the Communists had since May 1945 also based
their strategy. In February 1946 Stalin in a speech made in Moscow
indicated that this Soviet moderation would continue,[27] while in Warsaw
Lebiediev, the Soviet ambassador, expressed his 'complete confidence in
Mikołajczyk himself'.[28] The British advice to Mikołajczyk was to take
Stalin's assurances at face value and proceed on that premise. Rumours
that the Russians would not accept Mikołajczyk as premier were ascribed
to PPR sources and were thought to have little foundation.[29] While only
limited significance could be attached to speeches and rumours, the
landslide victory of the Hungarian Smallholders' Party in Soviet-
supervised elections in November 1945, as well as the continued reduction
in the size of the Soviet military presence in Poland, seemed to bear out
Mikołajczyk's assessment of Russian intentions. He thought that the
Russians would not provide the Polish Communists with the kind of
support they would require to prevent the PSL winning the elections. In

conversation with the British ambassador, Cavendish-Bentinck, in January 1946 he said he 'was certain that the Communist leaders would think out other plans to remain in power when the elections go against them' but that it would be difficult for them 'to remain in office without the active support of the Russian Army for which purpose it will be necessary for the Soviet High Command to increase their forces in Poland; he added that these had been further reduced during the past few weeks.' In reply to Cavendish-Bentinck's enquiry whether the Communists would be able to use the Polish army to retain power, Mikołajczyk said 'that if it came to a clash between the Army and the people the Polish soldiers would refuse to act.'[30]

The role of the Western powers in Mikołajczyk's thinking was less prominent than most accounts suggest. His experience as premier of the Government-in-Exile had taught him better than anyone that Britain and the United States were determined not to become embroiled in a confrontation with the Soviet Union over Poland. His private contacts with Western diplomatic circles confirmed the limited scope of their support but this did not deter him.[31] The value of his connections with the West was twofold. First, he hoped that Anglo-American diplomatic, and more important, economic, pressure on the Communists and the Soviets would act as a constraint and check the use of overt repressive measures against his party. Secondly, his popular image as a statesman with the solid backing of the Western powers added greatly to his credibility and the credibility of the peasant opposition. The widespread popular assumption that the Western Powers were ready to intervene on Mikołajczyk's behalf gave him a major psychological advantage over the Communists and his rivals in the PSL. He actively cultivated his image as a man of the West, for example making a visit to the United States in November 1945, where he saw Truman. Even the Communists did not sense how shaky was the reality behind the reputation: in February Gomułka told a party audience that 'the Anglo-Saxon states are very widely committed . . . in recent times we are witnessing severer forms of pressure on us . . . abroad great significance is attached to the elections'.[32]

In the domestic sphere the lynchpin of Mikołajczyk's strategy was, as we have mentioned, the mobilization of the peasant movement in order to demonstrate that political stabilization and effective government depended on the peasants' continued support for and participation in the coalition. In Mikołajczyk's eyes the Moscow agreement had proved the indispensability of his party to the Communists. His objective was to return to Poland and capitalize on this indispensability. In a revealing remark made in a speech delivered in Poznań in October 1945, he tried to make it clear that the hard bargain which the Communists had forced on him in the Moscow negotiations on the shareout of ministries in the Provisional Government resulted not from his naîvety or the Communists' negotiating skill, but rather from his belief that the detailed terms of the agreement were of little importance in comparison with the underlying strength of the forces which had made the agreement:

> I know how to accommodate myself to reality without running to the law. I shall not cry if undertakings are not kept. I could recite the Moscow agreement. But if the SL which came out into the open in Lublin [i.e. the pro-Communist Peasant Party] had sufficed alone there would have been no need to extend the (regime's) political base by forming the Government of National Unity.[33]

He was confident that regardless of the Communists' control of the levers of government in Warsaw, his party would be able to capture control of local government in the countryside, thereby frustrating at the grassroots any attempt at widescale falsification of the election results. He accepted that such attempts would take place, but believed that in the rural areas at any rate the Communists would lack the resources to make these effective unless they resorted to extreme measures which would create international difficulties and destabilize the situation at home, neither of which would suit Stalin. Apart from the elections, Mikołajczyk thought that the needs of economic reconstruction and the supply of food for the towns would force the Communists to make political concessions to the peasants. This economic leverage was already brought into play by autumn 1945 when the Communists had to face not only strikes over food shortages in the towns but also problems in obtaining quotas from the peasants. The attitude of the PSL leadership in this crisis was ambivalent.[34] Mikołajczyk's belief in the indispensability of the peasant movement and in its capacity to counter the attacks of its opponents conditioned his reaction to the Communists' and Socialists' electoral proposals.

His aim was not to achieve a *modus vivendi* with the Lublin parties, but to outflank them and win Stalin's confidence. Until this were done, in his view, no deal made with the Communists would have any substance.[35] His attitude to the Socialists was almost as sceptical, combining long-standing mistrust of the reliability of the PPS from pre-war and wartime days with disbelief in the authenticity and independence of the 'Lublin' Socialists.[36] The key consideration was the question of 'hegemony'. Mikołajczyk certainly did not share the Communists' view that their hegemony in the coalition had been agreed in Moscow and he was totally opposed to an electoral deal which would institutionalize their advantage. Wójcik, the PSL secretary-general, expressed the party's position in a speech to the KRN in January 1946: 'We have always endeavoured to maintain the very best possible worker–peasant co-operation . . . on one condition, that the political representation of our working class brothers gives up its desire for supremacy over the peasant movement.'[37] The strong agrarian tendency in the PSL, with which Mikołajczyk sympathized, aimed at establishing the hegemony of the peasant movement itself, with the workers' parties playing second fiddle in the coalition.[38] However, even the more cautious wing of the party rejected PPR hegemony and hoped for a sizeable PSL contingent in any future government and in the *Sejm* to act as a brake on the Communists. Kiernik inclined to this view. After a conversation with him in January the British ambassador reported to London that Kiernik and a few older members of the PSL:

> would be prepared to advocate consenting (to the bloc) if they could obtain terms which would break the present hegemony of the Communist Party . . . as they fear that despite all precautions the elections may not be free and unfettered, and that even if they are free and the PSL win, the Communist Party will not quietly abandon power. . . . Kiernik frankly admitted as a further reason that if the PSL were victorious at the elections and formed a Government, such a Government would soon lose popularity as the Polish people are at present expecting that the change of Government will work wonders.[39]

But for this group too the question of hegemony was crucial as Kiernik made plain in a speech in his constituency some months later: 'we cannot allow the PPR which is in a minority to obtain hegemony over us'.[40]

Mikołajczyk's conviction that his party was indispensable and that the Communists lacked the strength to sustain themselves in power by force, meant that he did not take the threatening undercurrent of their propaganda very seriously. He was anxious to delay as long as possible and minimize the attack on his party organization which he expected would take place during the immediate run-up to the elections. However, he hoped to turn any increase in political tension to his own advantage by demonstrating the strength of popular backing for the PSL and the Communists' inability to counter it. He correctly reasoned that a rise in the political temperature would intensify the pressure not only on the PSL but on the Communists and their allies too. In fact, as the Communists alleged, Mikołajczyk's agreement to participation in the talks on the electoral bloc was purely tactical. In mid-January he confided to Cavendish-Bentinck that 'his object in not refusing outright the request of the Communist and Socialist parties for a single list is to reduce the period between open refusal by his party to agree to a single list of candidates and the elections and thus to avoid as long as possible open hostilities with violent repressions on local leaders of his party.'[41]

The rise of the PSL

BOTH the Communists and Mikołajczyk were thus pursuing strategies which assumed that worker–peasant cooperation should continue but collided on the issue of which side was to be the dominant partner. Mikołajczyk was determined to break the hegemony of the Communists and aspired to establish his own. Until early 1946 it was the PSL which held the initiative and the Communists who were on the defensive and, naturally, Mikołajczyk had no intention of abandoning tactics which seemed to be working. It was rather the strategy of the PPR which was undermined by internal developments during the latter half of 1945.

We have seen how at the international level Mikołajczyk was able to maintain his reputation as a statesman enjoying full Western confidence and support, while Stalin's intentions remained inscrutable but not discouraging for the PSL. Domestically the PSL was advancing on all fronts. By early 1946 it had captured large sections of the Communists' hard-won rural base, penetrated deeply into the local administrative apparatus and generated a series of strains within the parties of the former Lublin coalition. At the same time the Communists' hopes that Milołaj-czyk's return would bring about an evaporation of the popular dis-content which had disrupted industrial production and fuelled armed violence in the countryside during the spring were disappointed. The political climate remained unstable despite the relaxation, a combination of circumstances which caused increasing alarm within the PPR.

Mikołajczyk's first major success was within the peasant movement itself. It was tacitly assumed during the Moscow talks that 'ROCh' and the 'Lublin SL' would merge to form a single united party once the coalition government was formed and seats in the new cabinet were allocated on this premise. The Communists initially hoped to force the 'London' Peasants into a united party dominated by Lublin elements, according to the same plan which was executed more or less successfully in the case of the Socialists and the Catholic Party of Labour.[42] Mikołajczyk's followers, who clearly had a much sounder appreciation of the situation in the movement, proceeded from the start to activate their own organization based on the wartime and pre-war leadership which held a conference in Warsaw on 8 July and constituted itself as a provisional party executive. At this meeting the question of tactics towards the existing SL was discussed. A couple of days previously the strength of support for Mikołajczyk within the 'Lublin SL' had been clearly demonstrated when its Poznań organization (with the approval of the national executive) had elected Mikołajczyk as its president. This confirmed the confidence of the 'ROCh' leaders that in Kiernik's words, 'the liquidation of the hitherto fictional SL is inevitable'.[43]

The pro-Communist element in the leadership of the SL which was led by Władysław Kowalski had been thrown off balance by the strength of pro-Mikołajczyk feeling amongst the rank and file as well as many of the provincial activists. The so-called Centrists in the party led by Stanisław Bańczyk and Bolesław Ścibiorek seized the opportunity to force Kowalski's resignation as party vice-president, reinstate several suspended critics of the leadership and open talks with Mikołajczyk.[44] Mikołajczyk responded by offering the 'Lublin SL' a one-third share of seats on the national executive. The Centrists at first held out for more, but a month later put forward a compromise on Mikołajczyk's terms.[45] By this time, however, the Communists had changed tactics. At the end of July they and Kowalski decided that in any merger the 'Lublin' element would be submerged beneath the Mikołajczyk majority and that it would therefore be preferable to keep a separate 'Left' SL in existence. On 5 August attacks on Mikołajczyk began in the SL press,[46] and on 8 August Zambrowski informed the PPR Secretariat that:

> since up to now the situation has developed towards the outnumbering of the present SL by the Mikołajczyk group . . . [which has] revealed itself to be alien to the political line of the democratic camp and . . . which basically aims at restoring the pre-1926 [the year the parliamentary system was overthrown] system, we have recognised that there is no possibility of uniting these two parties; the existing poor and middle-peasant one, with democratic bloc, worker-peasant alliance and Soviet alliance traditions – and the middle-peasant and kulak pre-war Piast-type one. Our task is to give our peasants support . . . to instil them with a sense of the grandeur of their political heritage, to accentuate clearly the line of division between the Mikołajczyk group and the existing SL.[47]

The Bańczyk–Ścibiorek compromise was thrown out by the Leftists on the executive and on 22 August Mikołajczyk grasped the opportunity to legalize his own independent Polish Peasant Party.[48]

The troubles of the pro-Communists in the SL now began in earnest. One after the other the local and provincial organizations of the party declared for Mikołajczyk while within the rump of the party Bańczyk and Ścibiorek won wide support for their concept of a united, Centrist Peasant Party.[49] The Socialists were particularly well disposed to the prospect of the emergence of such a party which would be a potential partner for the PPS in a Socialist–Peasant alliance of the sort which had been common in the 1920s. On the other hand, the Kowalski faction, with a narrow and shaky majority on the executive, took an uncompromising pro-Communist line and its relations with the Socialists were marked by strong mutual antipathy.[50] The final split between the Centrists and the Left took place on 23 September at a meeting of the party Council. Bańczyk attempted to use his wide support on the Council to reorganize the executive, while Kowalski and his supporters attempted to oust Bańczyk and coopt their sympathizers to the Council. Amid stormy scenes Bańczyk, who claimed the support of 32 of the 76 Council members, led his followers in a walk-out from the meeting.[51] Attempts by the PPR to heal the split failed and on 25 September 20 members of the Centrist group were expelled by the Left faction.[52]

The pro-Communists' victory had been a Pyrrhic one. They had kept control of the central organization in Warsaw but without difficulty Mikołajczyk had captured the bulk of the grassroots network. Małopolska (Kraków, Rzeszów, Katowice) and Wielkopolska (Poznań, Bydgoszcz), traditional bastions of the movement, went over to the PSL more or less *en masse*, while in Warsaw, Lublin, Lodz, Kielce, Gdańsk and Wrocław provinces the PSL captured a large part of the organization. By November it claimed 200,000 members.[53] The position in Warsaw province, described in a PPR report, was typical:

> All except two members of the Provincial Executive have declared for the SL. However in the districts things are much worse. . . . The PSL are extraordinarily active . . . the SL behaves completely passively. Not only do they not care about their position, but one gets the impression that they want 'to be taken over'. . . . At present they are waiting . . . 'at ease' while the PSL meanwhile cleans up the organisation from under their noses.[54]

No reliable figures are available which would allow us to estimate the extent of the collapse of the 'Lublin SL' with precision. The party claimed 300,000 members in August 1945 but no further figures are available before 1947. Nevertheless, there is no reason to dispute Słabek's statement that 'at the turn of 1945/46 the SL organisation went over to the PSL virtually in its entirety'.[55] So weak was the SL in early 1946 that it was not included in the talks on the electoral bloc – to the intense chagrin of its leaders who feared that the Communists had, like the Socialists, decided that in the future it would have little role to play.[56]

The loss of the Bańczyk Centrists had been a severe setback. Amongst them were men such as Bronisław Drzewiecki and Franciszek Litwin who like Bańczyk had added some authenticity to the pro-Communist SL and had been linked with it since the *Wola ludu* group was formed in early 1944. Apart from a few veterans of the pre-war KPP peasant 'fronts' (Kowalski, A. Korzycki, M. Gwiazdowicz) the main prop of the leadership were the so-called *Kadzichłopi*, a group of somewhat discredited former *Sejm* deputies who had been active in the 1920s on the Left of the peasant movement and had later opposed Witos' leadership of the SL to the extent of lending support to the *Sanacja* regime in the late 1930s (J. Putek, S. Fidelus, A. Langer, S. Wrona, A. Waleron, H. Wyrzykowski). This group was naturally anathema to the mainstream movement and did little to widen the base of the party.

The Bańczyk group, following its secession, attempted during September–October to legalize itself as a third Centrist Peasant Party. This added to the Communists' discomfiture since the PPS lent vocal support to the proposal. The differences of view between the PPR and PPS over the future of the peasant movement were revealed at a joint meeting of their leaderships on 27–28 September.

Osóbka-Morawski, speaking for the majority of the Socialist leadership, set out the case for a Centrist solution:

> the PPS differs from the PPR in its assessment of the problem of the SL. The PPS stands for greater tolerance towards the Peasants than does the PPR. The Peasants do not understand the situation. With a tolerant course it would be possible to win them over, For various reasons the influence of the SL hitherto has been minimal. If

Bańczyk, Drzewiecki and the others were to drop out of the SL, that influence will decrease to a minimum, damaging our camp and strengthening Mikołajczyk. An agreement between the SL and Bańczyk and Drzewiecki would be the best way out, but if that turns out not to be possible – the formation of a third party would be a lesser evil than if Bańczyk and Drzewiecki joined Mikołajczyk.[57]

Gomułka replied for the Politburo of the PPR:

the PPS accuses us of pursuing the wrong policy towards the Peasants since Lublin times. Already we have explained that it was then not possible to apply a different policy from the one we adopted. . . . We shall agree with comrade Osóbka-Morawski and there will be no divergence between us in relation to the Peasants if as a basis for the worker–peasant alliance we choose a real and simultaneously democratic force in the countryside. . . . Today perhaps the PSL constitutes the greater real force, nevertheless it is not sincerely democratic. The SL is a lesser real force, but it is genuinely democratic. If we choose the real force and support it despite its anti-democratic potential that would be the wrong course and could lead to unfortunate consequences. . . . A third party based on Bańczyk, which the PPS would back with enthusiasm, is objectively speaking unnecessary and harmful. Logic teaches that factions struggle against one another. If that minority which left set up a party, it would conflict with the radical majority which was left. And ideologically, after all, this group inclines towards the PSL.[58]

Although the Socialists subsequently abandoned their support for Bańczyk's group, which in November joined the PSL, the PPS leaders had little confidence in the ability of the pro-Communist SL to rally support to the national front from the mainstream of the peasant movement. The communiqué at the end of the September meeting indicated clearly that the Socialists looked beyond the SL for allies: 'the PPS whole-heartedly supports the left SL and all Peasants who unreservedly and loyally work towards the political aims of the Government of National Unity.'[59] For the present, as we have seen, the Communists had not ruled out an alliance with the PSL and favoured an electoral agreement with Mikołajczyk. However, while the Communists regarded such an alliance as desirable, provided that their leading role was preserved, the Socialists regarded an agreement with the Peasants as essential and they were prepared to go further than the PPR in making concessions to achieve it. In particular, the Socialists themselves now questioned the hegemony of the PPR and saw an alliance with the Peasants as a way to strengthen their own position in the national front. Osóbka stated at the September meeting that until a short time before 'there existed the conviction that the PPR leads and has to lead in Poland. Now we must . . . emphasise that the working class leads.'[60] As Gomułka told the Central Committee, 'the PPS would like to be as it were in the middle of the configuration of forces in Poland, with the PPR on one side and the PSL on the other.'[61]

Mikołajczyk's success in rallying the peasant movement was a major setback for the Communists. Not only had the PSL drawn off a very large part of the organization and rank and file membership of the SL, it had even won back the Bańczyk group which had broken with 'ROCh' in 1944.

In the process it had brought to the surface strains between the PPR and the Socialists.

As the Peasants went over *en masse* to Mikołajczyk, much of the infrastructure of government in the countryside also fell under PSL control. In the villages the Communists relied heavily on the SL to man local government, the administration of agriculture and mass organizations such as ZSCh and *Wici*, the rural youth movement. In local government in November 1945, the SL held 25 per cent of seats on Provincial National Councils, 31 per cent at district level and 50 per cent at commune level.[62] Switches of allegiance amongst these councillors allowed the PSL to make rapid inroads into local administration. In Kraków province, for example, by the end of the year the PSL had 25 per cent of seats at both district and commune level.[63] This was just the start of a process which continued for most of 1946 and enabled the PSL to establish a dominant position in the lower tiers of local government across much of rural central Poland. In the villages the Communists lacked the strength to halt this trend. In the Peasant strongholds of Kraków and Rzeszów, Kiernik as minister of public administration was even able to install PSL members as provincial governors.[64]

Wherever possible, the PPR used its influence at central government level to halt the PSL advance.[65] In local government the 'Lublin' parties continued to dominate the Provincial National Councils which nominated members to the KRN. The PSL was therefore prevented from securing more than a small minority of seats in parliament (see table 2). Nevertheless, the Communists were in a minority in the KRN also and were heavily dependent on the PPS and their other allies to keep the PSL in check.[66]

Table 2.   Party representation on the KRN 1945–6

	August 1945[a]	December 1946[b]
PPR	100	139
PPS	77	112
SL	56	60
PSL	3	55
PSL *Nowe Wyzwolenie*	–	2
SD	16	38
SP	–	8
Non-party/others	31	30
TOTAL	283	444

Sources:
a B. Syzdek, Polska Partia Socjalistyczna w latach 1944–1948 (Warsaw, 1974), 249–5.
b PPR. Rezolucje, odezwy, instrukcje i okólniki komitetu centralnego i.1946–1947 (Warsaw, 1961), 214.

The Communists' loss of influence in the rural bureaucracy was accompanied by a general contraction of their base of support in the countryside. Apart from the defection to Mikołajczyk of most of the peasant movement the party itself lost members during the summer. In August 1945 it had 61,000 peasant members but by September this figure had fallen to 53,800. Although it had climbed back to 66,000 by December,[67] recruitment in rural areas was markedly slower than in the towns. The proportion of peasant members in the PPR in the spring had been 37 per cent; by December 1945 it had fallen to 28 per cent.[68] The continuing activity of the armed anti-Communist underground was blamed for this.[69] It seems more likely that the real reason was that in many country areas the party's organization was too weak to withstand the emergence of the PSL as the dominant force in the villages. Zambrowski indicated the party's concern over this problem and in particular the party's lack of good peasant cadres at the First Congress of the PPR in December 1945:

> provincial and district committees treat our Party's 60,000 members in the countryside as second-class members of the Party. The needs of rural cells are worst served, they meet least often, they are least looked after. The abundant, committed and authoritative *aktyw* which came forward in the ranks of the PPR during the implementation of land reform has for the most part been squandered and incorrectly spread around the state administration, behind desks and so on. . . . We must achieve . . . a shift back to work on a mass scale in the countryside.[70]

The position in the Peasant Self-help Union, which with over half a million members was an important channel of party influence in the countryside, was said by September to have reached a crisis. An internal party report commented that the 'Union's members have stopped paying their subscriptions. In those districts where SL executives have been taken over by the PSL, the Peasant Self-help offices have been as well. Self-help cooperatives are vegetating without any possibility of growth' – kept down it was said by the (PPS-dominated) *Społem* coops and the (PSL-dominated) Land Offices.[71] Mikołajczyk's followers succeeded in capturing many local branches of the Union and even the provincial sections in Poznań and Gdańsk. Only concerted efforts by the PPR, including the arrest of PSL delegates, prevented the PSL securing the majority at the national Congress of the ZSCh in March 1946.[72]

The PPR was powerless to prevent *Wici*, the 400,000-strong peasant youth movement, from falling into PSL hands. Its congress in December 1945 has been described as 'a huge pro-PSL demonstration' and the president and his deputy (J. Dusza and M. Jagła) were both members of the PSL Supreme Council.[73] A few days before the PSL had captured control of the Polish Teachers' Union at its first post-war congress. Of 1,500 delegates it seems that only about 30 were Communists.[74] The paucity of PPR influence within the teaching profession had been a cause of leadership concern for some time. In September 1945 the party launched a campaign to expand its following in the schools,[75] but a few months later Zambrowski lamented over the 'pathological opposition towards our democratic system of a large part of the teaching profession'.[76] A number of factors limited the appeal of the PPR amongst teachers, including the general anti-Communism of the intelligentsia and their depressed material conditions. Moreover the Peasants had great influence within the profession. The SL 'ROCh' had largely organized the underground schools system during the war and one of the leading wartime educational activists, Czesław Wycech, a prominent member of the PSL, was from 1945 to 1947 minister of education.

To sum up, the legalization of the mainstream peasant movement in mid-1945 did not so much extend the government's base in the country-side, but rather allowed the traditional political structure of the villages to resurface. In the spring, despite their numerical weakness, the Com-munists had held the levers of power in their hands by monopolizing local government and the ZSCh, excluding their opponents from the 'Lublin SL' and *Wici* and employing the UB to overcome political obstacles. However, by the end of 1945 the PSL was running the villages.

The illegal opposition

DESPITE the concessions in the political apparatus the Communists had made to the other coalition parties, the stabilization of the political and economic situation, which had been one of the main objectives of the 'May turn', was only very partial. Underground activity, lawlessness, strikes and protests persisted. For the Communists this continuing climate of uncertainty and their failure to generate any marked shift in popular feeling towards themselves was unexpected and troubling. For Mikołaj-czyk, on the other hand, the absence of stabilization bore out his claim that only the PSL could provide Stalin with a secure and friendly Polish government.

Despite the regrouping of political forces in 1945, the underground remained one of the main obstacles to stabilization. The formation of the Provisional Government of National Unity in effect marked the end of the underground state formed in 1939–40, which had survived, battered, until mid-1945. At a meeting in Kraków on 27 June the political leadership of the movement formally disbanded and announced this publicly on 1 July.[77]

The military underground, commanded since Okulicki's arrest by Colo-nel Jan Rzepecki, had been reorganized in April as the Armed Forces Delegation (*Delegatura Sił Zbrojnych* – DSZ), in part because the *Nie* organization was known to the Russians, but also it seems as a more strictly military formation than its predecessor, firmly subordinated to the political leadership of the underground.[78] While setting itself the task of 'liquidating particularly harmful persons' and 'armed resistance to the nation's destruction as well as the depopulation and devastation of the country',[79] the DSZ sought to curb uncoordinated resistance and two appeals were issued in May to this effect.[80] The DSZ succeeded in gathering together rather more of the old AK network than had *Nie*, but a considerable part, including the National Democrats, remained outside, and its organization was still far from complete in August 1945 when, following the dissolution of the underground state, it followed suit.[81]

However, only about 44,000 people took advantage of the amnesty of August–September 1945. For the most part these were members of the Peasant Battalions. Old loyalties and mistrust of the authorities dissuaded most of the AK/DSZ and nationalists from revealing themselves.[82] According to estimates of the Ministry of the Interior, which must be very approximate, some 80,000 people remained active in the underground in 1945 and about 60,000 in 1946.[83]

As figure 1 below shows, although the peak of anti-government violence in spring 1945 fell off sharply in June–July, it thereafter remained almost constant at a level of about 200 assassinations of officials and government supporters every month – a considerable number. In some areas, in particular most of western Poland and the urbanized regions, armed resistance was slight. But across much of central Poland it persisted on a wide scale, while in the remoter parts of the east and south of the

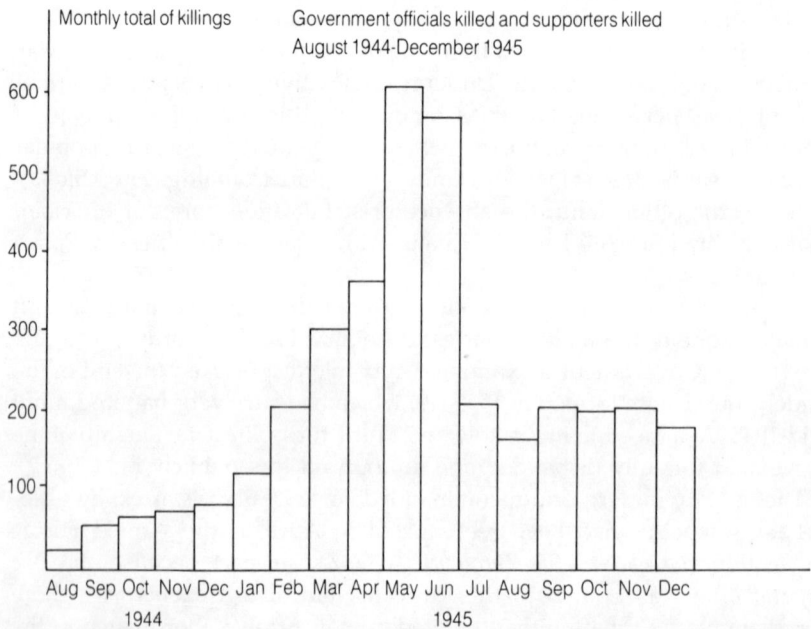

Fig. 1   Government officials and supporters killed, August 1944–December 1945 (computed on the basis of data in *Polegli w walce o władzę ludową*, Warsaw, 1970).

country government forces were confined to the towns, under virtual siege.

Two main underground networks were active in 1945–6. Freedom and Independence (*Wolność i Niezawisłość* – WiN), established in September 1945, was based on the former membership of the AK/DSZ. The National Military Union (NZW), the armed wing of the underground National Party, was formed in November 1944, and by mid-1945 had absorbed much of what remained of the NSZ. There were also regional organizations such as the Conspiratorial Polish Army 'Lasy' (Lodz province), or that of 'Ogień' (Podhale) and 'Łupaszko' (Pomorze). These networks sustained a considerable degree of organizational coherence until late 1946.[84] In addition, the Ukrainian nationalist movement, active along the south-eastern border, was particularly well-organized and effective.[85]

Apart from the full-scale insurgency by the Ukrainian nationalists, the Polish guerrillas too were capable of inflicting considerable damage to the authority of the government. On 4–5 August 1945, for instance, some 250 men, equipped with seven lorries, occupied Kielce, captured its key points and stormed the prison to release 376 prisoners.[86] A month later a smaller group, again transported in lorries, attacked Radom prison, allowing the escape of 292 prisoners.[87] Early in 1946 NZW 'Special Action' units carried out a 'pacification' of pro-government White Russian villages in Bielsk Podlaski District which had delivered quotas on time. Forty-six inhabitants were killed.[88]

Such incidents, accompanied as they were by a host of less dramatic shootings and attacks, had a disastrous effect on party morale and support in the countryside. It is clear from reports to the Central Committee that the security problem remained serious during the second half of 1945:[89]

'security in Kalisz district is beneath criticism. Chocz commune and in part Kościelec are almost continuously under the terror of the bands' (*Poznań*, July– August). 'The activity of the terrorist bands has decreased significantly. There are nevertheless districts such as Ostrów Mazowiecki, Ostrołęka, Garwolin, where up to now it has not been possible to venture outside the towns. Militia posts have been withdrawn; in the communes our authority does not in reality exist' (*Warsaw*, August–September). 'The wrecking on two occasions of the prisons in such strategically vital places as the towns of Kielce and Radom and their virtual occupation has undoubtedly strengthened the reaction'. . . . 'Party work in some districts, such as Kozienice, Sandomierz and Pińczów, encounters immense difficulties . . . due to the marauding bands . . . (in Pińczów) Party activity literally exists only in conspiracy. It is impossible because of the intense terror of the bands . . . to conduct activity in the terrain' (*Kielce*, September–October). 'In Zawiercie district our Party has been unable to expand since as a result of the activity of the bands, five of our commune committees were forced to suspend activity' (*Katowice*, December).

The Communists' lack of resources to combat the underground and the pervasiveness of the mood of uncertainty is shown by a report from Rzeszów for October–November:

> Since the unfortunate close of the London conference of Foreign Ministers
> [11.9.–2.10.45] we have observed a steady growth in the impact of reactionary
> rumours that a third world war will break out. This has caused a steady increase in
> anti-Soviet, anti-PPR, anti-democratic feeling as well as of the reactionary terror. In
> a number of districts the appearance of new terrorist bands or the expansion of old
> ones and their increased activity has been evident. . . . In some of the districts it is
> difficult to master the situation in view of the inadequate strength of the Militia and
> Security forces and the limited possibility of employing local army garrisons [lack of
> political training]. . . . [There are] frequent refusals by whole units to take part in
> operations. Many of the officers [display] decidedly unfavourable, not to say hostile
> feeling. . . . The Party has in some districts to a large extent been forced
> underground.

In many rural areas the underground was clearly capable of countering the
Communists' police resources. The PSL was allowed a free run, while the
party was forced into hiding.

Clandestine organizations were active in the towns too, where they
mounted protests and circulated anti-government literature. Although
armed resistance was much less common than in the countryside there was
much unrest. Working-class protests were frequent and often it seems took
an anti-semitic turn. In August *Endek* elements, so it was claimed, provoked
a pogrom in Kraków and attempted to do the same in nearby Rąbka,
Chrzanów and Miechów.[90] Strikes in the Lodz textile mills and following
month were blamed by the Communists on 'reactionary elements' and
anti-semitic overtones were once more evident.[91] 'Very strong anti-semitic
feeling' was reported amongst the employees of the Rzeszów aircraft factory
in November.[92] Students for the most part were vociferously anti-
Communist and the *Endeks* retained some of their pre-war influence in the
universities, especially in Kraków and Poznań.[93] But student rebelliousness
was evident in Lodz too where in December, following demonstrations,
some 100 students were arrested and the university closed early.[94]

As we have said, the Communists were determined to keep in place the
wedge they had driven between Mikołajczyk and the reaction. They feared
that a situation might develop in which underground activity would
complement Mikołajczyk's legal opposition. Following the October 1945
Plenum the Communists renewed the 'class struggle' against the reaction.
This they hoped would complete the destruction of the underground.[95] At
the same time they launched a propaganda campaign to warn Mikołajczyk
against taking advantage of the situation. They did not at this stage accuse
him of allying his party with the reaction, but rather of ambivalence:

> the reaction would like to assign to Mikołajczyk the role of a trojan horse. . . . This
> raises a basic question: what attitude does the other side take to these plans? . . .
> Today it is still too early to give a definitive reply to this question. All the same it is
> striking that Mikołajczyk and his group do not repudiate the reaction in a conclusive
> way, but maintain a discrete silence . . . and what is worse there are even those in
> the PSL who do not hide that they would willingly take the help offered to them by
> the other side.[96]

Mikołajczyk had in fact commented just a week before that 'peasants know how to count . . . there are so many of us . . . that we do not need to look to any help from the reaction'.[97] But he did not accept the Communists' all-embracing definition of the reaction. He applied the term only to former *Sanacja* circles and Right-wing Nationalists, traditional enemies of his party who regarded him as the betrayer of the Government-in-Exile and now looked to the armed overthrow of the coalition government or a third world war.[98] The fact that moderate sections of the AK and the National Party remained underground and that popular outbursts took place was, in the view of the PSL, the consequence of Communist repression and excesses rather than mass support for the diehards.[99]

Nevertheless, leaving aside the *Sanacja* and NSZ extremists there was indeed a great deal of affinity in terms of short-term political objectives as well as social base between the legal and illegal oppositions. Apart from Białystok province where the Peasants were weak and the underground numerous and particularly uncompromising, the two movements both drew the bulk of their support from the same social groups in rural central and eastern Poland. Most of the rank and file of the underground were peasants, as were many of its officers, while others were often drawn from the rural intelligentsia, especially from among teachers.[100] Despite their political differences, in most areas the PSL supporters had far more in common with their former AK colleagues than with their official allies from the PPR.

There was also much in common between the political outlook of the PSL and much of the underground. The Right wing of the underground based its strategy on the assumption that armed conflict would sooner or later break out between the West and the Soviet Union and directed its energies to preparing for a rebellion inside Poland when this happened. The PSL was, especially at first, viewed with hostility by this element. However, as Mikołajczyk moved into opposition its general attitude shifted to one of non-aggression if not active support.[101] However, the stronger current in the underground geared its tactics closely to those of the legal opposition. WiN in particular seems to have been conceived by its founders as a kind of underground party which would provide a moderate rallying point for former members of the AK who might otherwise be drawn to the *Endek* extremists.[102] Its 'ideological guidelines' of September 1945 closely paralleled PSL thinking, apart from the demand by WiN for a renegotiation of the eastern frontier settlement. The guidelines called for the restoration of civil rights, drastic curbs on the powers of the security forces and full Polish sovereignty. WiN viewed free elections as 'the only correct way' to achieve this, and although it did not intend to contest such elections, it declared that it would 'exert every effort so that [the seats] would be found in the hands of genuine Polish democracy', and to ensure that the results were not falsified. The guidelines welcomed the programme of the Government of National Unity 'in many of its fundamental features', but criticized the distortion of the programme to serve 'the political objectives of one party'. The decision of the previous underground leadership to cooperate with the coalition government in 'open struggle for its aims' was greeted as 'sensible and courageous', and WiN considered that the legitimacy of the Government-in-Exile had ceased and called on the emigration to return home. Although the movement aimed at 'freedom and independence as conceived by Anglo-Saxon society' it recognized that 'the maintenance of good political relations and economic cooperation with the Soviet Union' was 'necessary and positive'. Armed activity was not ruled out, but WiN disassociated itself from 'the anti-democratic activity of extreme groups' and admitted that 'self-defence' had often taken 'too severe a form'.[103] There is evidence that the rank and file members of the underground regarded the emphasis on the political character of WiN sceptically and tended to see it as a straightforward anti-Communist military organization[104] and changes in its command during 1946 reinforced this tendency.[105] Nevertheless, the elections remained at the centre of WiN activity and the movement's *raison d'être* was largely removed by the defeat and collapse of the PSL in early 1947.

The fact that in Poland, alone amongst the East European satellites, the underground anti-Communists continued to play a significant role through 1945–6 had obvious implications for the viability of the party's strategy. First, it hindered the Communists' efforts to escape their political isolation and gather a mass following. This was particularly so in the remoter country areas where armed attacks made it difficult for the Communists to establish even the rudiments of an effective organization. But even in the towns it was not easy for the party to break the remnants of wartime solidarity, the prestige of the AK and the widespread popular view that party membership was tantamount to collaboration with an occupying power. Secondly, the Communists' insecurity and suspicion towards potential allies was greatly intensified by the continued activity of political conspiracies and guerrilla groups. They were acutely aware that their hegemony in the government was shaky and saw clearly the danger of a complete loss of control if it was relaxed. Thirdly, the activity of the underground gave teeth to the whole opposition movement and reduced the effectiveness of the Communists' censorship and the media. Mikołajczyk could point to the long-standing conflicts between his party and the forces which composed the underground, but by fuelling the atmosphere of instability and paralysing the political machine of the PPR, the underground enhanced the viability of the Peasant opposition. Unlike the legal bourgeois parties elsewhere in Eastern Europe, the PSL did not feel compelled to avoid confronting the Communists. Its leadership felt that it could emerge victorious from such a showdown because the alternative would be to slide to civil war, which the Russians would not allow.

The mood in the PPR

ALTHOUGH Gomułka and the leadership continued to condemn 'sectarianism' within the party and to argue for the line adopted in May 1945, the growth of the Peasant opposition and the persistence of clandestine activity prompted calls for a harder line from the *aktyw*. The formation of the Government of National Unity had not been popular with many activists. A report from Warsaw province for August described the mood at a series of meetings of the *aktyw*:

> A characteristic feature noticeable at all these meetings was the serious disquiet and disorientation aroused in the Party's ranks by the formation of the Government of National Unity, the audacious stunts of the reaction and at the same time the contraction [in the role of the PPR]. Such cries as: 'We need a Dzierżyński'; 'Put an end to Kerensky-ism'; 'Enough talk: when do we begin to fight the reaction?', were to be heard at the meetings. The report on the political situation, the call to organise struggle with sabotage and the reaction and to turn a blind eye to (PSL) ministerial and procuratorial decisions – brought a sigh of relief.[106]

In November the same tendencies were revealed at the conferences preceding the Party Congress. Kasman reported to the Secretariat of the Central Committee that:

> In general the conferences took the form of serious debates. . . . Comrades raised the subject of the struggle against the reaction and the call for strong government. It was apparent that there was concern amongst the Party rank and file that the system of power of People's democracy should be safeguarded. The tendency to overcome difficulties by administrative pressure was fairly widely in evidence. At several conferences a number of speakers put forward the slogan of the dictatorship of the proletariat in various forms, which met with applause. . . . The sectarian tendencies . . . result in general from an inability to overcome the difficulties which we encounter in the struggle for influence amongst the masses, as well as from KPP traditions mechanically carried over to present circumstances. The sectarian mood results not from an oppositionist attitude to the Party line but rather from a failure to understand and digest it. . . . At numerous conferences in small-town working-class centres, which ought to be strongly linked with the countryside, the issue of the worker–peasant alliance was dealt with weakly or not at all.[107]

Kasman mentioned rebellions which had taken place against the Party line at conferences in Kraków and Lodz. In the former, where Włodzimierz Zawadzki still enjoyed considerable popularity, the conference had demanded a change of policy, rejecting the national front and calling for the dictatorship of the proletariat.[108] Although Ochab doubted whether 'the general ultra-leftist tendency' would give rise to an organized Left faction at the congress, he did think that it was necessary for the leadership to speak out against this trend.[109]

In fact, several members of the leadership including Ochab were given a rough ride by the Left at the congress. As one of the delegates from Lodz later reminisced, Gomułka had to answer hardline critics of the party's moderation towards the academic profession. The hardliners had interrupted Bieńkowski's speech with such cries as 'Down with the reactionary professors!'. Gomułka also had to reply to Daniszewski and others who argued that the PPR lacked a clear conception of where it was heading and had departed too far from the traditions of its Marxist predecessors. But the sharpest attack on the leadership was led by Maria Kamińska, second secretary of the Poznań committee and a prominent figure in the KPP in the 1930s:

> In her speech she delivered a crushing condemnation of the work of the Land Offices as hotbeds of the landlords and their supporters, of the land commissioners of the Ministry of Agriculture for indolence; she criticised the State Repatriation Office for sluggishness and poor organisation of repatriation, lack of energy in combating the PSL and the reaction etc. However it was not only the content, but the form which was decisive. She spoke with such fluency, so suggestively and convincingly . . . that she carried the entire congress with her. Time and time again the audience responded with bursts of applause or made shouts of approval. . . . Later in Edward Ochab's summing-up it turned out that on a number of matters Kamińska had been wrong. Ochab, replying to Kamińska, argued that according to her everybody, especially those at the top, was at fault, except the Poznań committee. He pointed out that a great many of the weaknesses of the Poznań party organisation resulted from the poor work of the provincial committee: that it was necessary to go to the peasant, to the countryside, combat the reactionary elements, but not to look to Warsaw, to the security forces, to think that decrees solved everything. But he spoke less convincingly, perhaps even too monotonously, so that the conference-hall received his speech rather reservedly.[110]

Unfortunately the proceedings of the February 1946 Central Committee Plenum, with the exception of parts of Gomułka's opening speech from which we have already quoted, have never been published. The resolution adopted suggests that the Plenum backed the leadership's preference for a bloc of six and a deal with the PSL but without really expecting that this would transpire.[111] The conflict between the tactics of the PPR and Mikołajczyk was increasingly apparent. He had captured the peasant movement and won control of much of the rural political infrastructure. The Lublin coalition had been seriously weakened: the SL had virtually collapsed, recruitment to the PPR had slowed down and divergences in outlook between the PPR and the PPS had come to the surface. Underground activity continued on a wide scale and there was growing discontent amongst the Party *aktyw*. No doubt all these factors weighed on the discussion. Aleksander Zawadzki was doubtless not alone in admitting that the party's line had yet to yield dividends:

> At present we find ourselves in a more difficult situation than at the beginning when we crossed with our army and the Red Army [into Poland]. The liberation of the country pushed everything else into the background. . . . A year has passed.

People have looked us over, have got down to work. And at the same time the reaction has regenerated and begun to activate.[112]

With such thoughts in mind, the Plenum placed the party in readiness for a probable change of course: a move away from the version of the national front which had prevailed since May 1945 and the adoption of a more aggressive policy towards the PSL.

The Church and the Catholic camp (I)

IN many ways the Polish Catholic Church, always one of the strongest in Europe, emerged from the Second World War with its prestige and position as the defender of Polish nationhood enhanced. The patriotic stance and suffering of the vast bulk of the clergy during the German occupation and the transformation of Poland from a state populated not only by Roman Catholics, but also by Greek Catholic, Orthodox, Jewish and Protestant communities into a homogenous Catholic one, led in the later 1940s to a certain renaissance of the Church in Poland.[113]

For the Communists the Church represented a spiritual and social force with which it was difficult to find a common language, but which nevertheless they recognized as being too deeply-rooted and resilient an institution to attack directly. Until 1949–50 when relations degenerated into open confrontation, the party's policy towards the Church was generally correct and respectful. While in the long term, the Communists assumed, the influence of the Church would gradually wither, for the present the political neutralization of the Church was their main goal. At the Central Committee Plenum of June 1946, the party defined its attitude as follows:

> The Central Committee of the PPR . . . steadfastly stands for full religious toleration, respect for religious feelings and traditions as well as Church institutions, demanding at the same time complete respect for the laws and regulations of the authorities of the Republic as well as that religious feelings must not be made use of in political disputes.[114]

The government's repudiation of the Concordat in September 1945 seems to have been motivated by this same outlook that Church and State should operate in different spheres, rather than by any hardening of policy towards the Church.

At the same time Catholicism had for many years been a political as well as a social and religious force. In interwar Poland the two main Catholic political groupings, the Christian Democrats and the National Workers' Party, had merged in 1937 to form the Party of Labour (SP) led by Karol Popiel. This party remained small and assumed a position of liberal opposition in the *Sanacja* regime. In the wartime underground its influence grew somewhat since Sikorski was closer to the SP than to any other of the four main conspiratorial parties. Other Catholics were drawn to the Right, to the National Democrats and the *Sanacja*, while on the Left the Peasants and Socialists drew much of their support from the Catholic masses despite certain anti-clerical currents amongst their activists and leaders. After the war the PPR displayed a good deal of hesitancy towards the idea of allowing the re-emergence of a Catholic political movement. Though such a movement would clearly be a gain for the national front, it would be difficult to prevent it moving to the Right and forming a potentially very dangerous opposition centre.

The attempt by the Communists to cultivate the neutrality of the Church and to generate support amongst Catholics for the government continued throughout the period. But by mid-1946 the relative success hitherto of this strategy began to reverse and two processes became observable: one was the narrowing of government influence amongst politically active Catholics; the other was the increasing engagement of the Church hierarchy on behalf of the opposition. Thereafter a slow but steady deterioration in relations between Church and State took place until by 1948 the Church itself had again assumed its traditional mantle as the protector of the nation against its rulers.

From 1944 to 1946 the Communists achieved some success in their efforts to win the constructive neutrality of the Church. Considerable attention was paid to reassuring the faithful that the party posed no threat to religious freedom. Chaplains were attached to Polish army units, Church lands were excluded from the land reform, the Catholic University in Lublin was reactivated, the Communist mayor of Kraków made a courtesy visit to the archbishop, Bierut attended church and through Jerzy Borejsza, the Communist publishing overlord, in particular, the party sought contact with Catholic circles. One outcome of these soundings was permission for the Kraków Catholics, in April 1945, to begin publication of a weekly paper, *Tygodnik Powszechny*. Later the same year a group of Warsaw Catholics started another weekly, *Dziś i Jutro*. Even London circles admitted that this campaign had yielded results. In June 1945 in a report to the Government-in-Exile, Korboński, the acting-delegate, wrote:

> As for the situation of the clergy in Poland, we observe a flirtation by the Lublin Committee with them, including Sapieha [archbishop of Kraków]. Priests and their property are not touched and the Committee endeavours to win the support of the clergy, which in part they have succeeded in doing.[115]

The authorities do indeed seem to have established a *modus vivendi* with the Kraków Curia quite early. This was of particular value since during the wartime exile of the primate, Cardinal Hlond – an absence which aroused some criticism – Archbishop Sapieha of Kraków effectively led the Polish Church and was its most respected figure. Sapieha and the circle of Catholic journalists and academics around him, though undoubtedly conservative in their general outlook, took a typically Galician pragmatic attitude, rejecting either a boycott of or confrontation with the new authorities, and advocated instead a policy of involving themselves in public life and attempting to influence as much as possible the changes taking place. As one Catholic writer has put it, they 'inclined to stabilisation and some sort of engagement in what had arisen'.[116] It was this philosophy which *Tygodnik Powszechny* put forward.

Following the formation of the Government of National Unity and the return of Hlond in mid-1945, the episcopate began to take a more assertive stand against materialism and for the reconstruction of Poland on Christian principles. At their conference in Jasna Góra in October 1945 the bishops expressed their regret at the government's repudiation of the Concordat, stressed the incompatibility of Christianity and materialism and called on Catholics to vote in the coming elections

> according to their Catholic conscience, in other words to elect the candidates of those parties which undertake to realise a social and political programme in agreement with Christ's teaching . . . under our modern democratic constitution . . . the overwhelming Catholic majority in the country has the right to be represented in the *Sejm* by parties suited to its religious convictions and ethical principles.[117]

The bishops seem to have concurred on the whole with the viewpoint of Hlond, which was more uncompromising than that of the 'Sapieha bloc'. Hlond, who became primate in 1926, had a reputation as being on the political Right. Before the war he had attracted criticism for his amenable attitude to the *Sanacja* regime[118] and his alleged anti-semitism.[119] After 1945 he took the view – at least in conversation with the émigré circles with whom he maintained contact – that Poland was experiencing a temporary phase which would soon be transformed by intervention from the West or the collapse of Soviet power. After discussions with Hlond in Rome late in 1946, the 'London' ambassador to the Vatican reported back to the Government-in-Exile that 'his [Hlond's] conviction as to the temporary and provisional character of the Warsaw "government" revealed itself very clearly.'[120] Hlond was inclined to emphasize the gulf between Christian teaching and Communist materialism. In his first major address in Poznań in October 1945, he bluntly stated that despite certain points of agreement 'in fundamental matters there is such a vast difference between Christianity and materialism that it is not possible to reconcile them theoretically.'[121] A year later, en route to the Vatican, he spoke with a representative of the Government-in-Exile who reported Hlond's views as follows:

> at present, just as last year, he takes the position that a temporary cease-fire is possible between the communist world and the world of western culture and Christianity but there is no possibility of compromise. Such a deep ideological conflict must sooner or later lead also to a clash in the realm of material forces.[122]

Working from these assumptions Hlond was much less inclined than the Kraków Catholics to seek a long-term *modus vivendi* with the new order.

Not only did he studiously avoid any official contact with government dignitaries,[123] but he was lukewarm towards the idea of a Catholic Party operating under the current political arrangements.[124]

At the Moscow talks of June 1945 it had been agreed that Karol Popiel would return to Poland and, tacitly, that his Party of Labour would resume legal activity. Mikołajczyk, whose relations with Popiel were not good, broadly favoured the reactivization of the SP but did not regard this as a priority and, in Popiel's view, had not done enough for his party in Moscow.[125] The Socialists, Osóbka and Szwalbe, hoped to see the SP emerge as a conservative centre party which would tend to keep the Peasants on the Centre-Left.[126] The PPR though was quite determined to prevent the emergence of a conservative oppositionist SP.[127] In this they were relatively successful until spring 1946, executing the same manoeuvre which failed so dismally in the case of the PSL. This involved grafting on to the leadership of the underground (Popiel) SP a group of individuals committed to close collaboration with the PPR.

In early 1945 Gomułka had made contact with Zygmunt Felczak and Feliks Widy-Wirski, the leaders of a small, Leftist splinter of the Party of Labour called the *Zryw Narodowy*. After talks Widy-Wirski was appointed governor of Poznań and Felczak deputy-governor of Pomorze provinces.[128] Felczak, who led the *Zryw* group until his death in July 1946, was a genuine catch for the Communists. He had been a prominent figure on the Left of the National Workers' Party and then the SP in Pomorze during the 1930s and had vociferously opposed the *Sanacja*. During the war he had been one of the chief organizers of the underground Party of Labour and for a spell was its leader and representative in the political leadership of the wider underground movement. But in late 1942 the Left lost control of the SP and Felczak split away to form *Zryw*.[129] Widy-Wirski, who before the war had been active both in pro-*Sanacja* student circles and then in Popular Front organizations, was a little-known figure who was prepared to comply closely with PPR wishes.[130] *Zryw* viewed Catholicism as only a very loose framework for its political ideas and seems to have had almost no contact with the Church hierarchy. Its influence was largely confined to the Left-wing of the former National Workers' Party in western Poland and was in any case very limited. Felczak hoped to see the emergence of an independent SP, working in alliance with the communists and based chiefly on the Catholic workers.[131]

Although *Zryw* represented only a small minority of the Party of Labour's membership, the Communists succeeded in forcing the Popiel-ites to accept a fifty-fifty split on the party's national executive. Popiel's supporters had begun organizing a legal party immediately following his return, but the authorities refused legalization until a compromise had been reached with the *Zryw*-ites. An attempt was made to form a separate Christian Party of Labour, just as Mikołajczyk had set up the PSL independent of the 'Lublin SL', but this too was denied legalization. In November 1945 the Popiel-ites gave way and accepted merger with *Zryw*. Only Popiel's casting vote as chairman gave them control of the evenly divided executive.

This was a favourable outcome for the Communists. They had secured the establishment of a party which through the Popiel-ites had good contacts with influential sections of the Church, especially in the Kraków Curia, and the support of these quarters, but in which the pro-Communist faction would check any opposition tendency and influence the development of the party. The Popiel majority had accepted these terms confident that they could rapidly erode the position of the *Zryw* group by activating the party locally and then calling a national congress to elect a new leadership which would reflect more accurately their overwhelming support amongst the rank and file. The Communists were equally determined to prevent any disturbance of the *status quo*.

Quite apart from the *Zryw* group, the Communists had some success in cultivating the active support of elements of the Catholic intelligentsia in close contact with the Church with a political background very far removed from Communism. In Warsaw a group of 'radical Catholics' led by Bolesław Piasecki and dominated by his followers from the pre-war Fascistic *Falanga* movement offered their assistance to the Communists. It seems certain that Piasecki had won the support of the Soviet security forces for the initiative.[132] In a memorial presented in July 1945 this group argued for close collaboration between Catholics and marxists around a programme of radical reform and national reconstruction.[133] In November the group was allowed to begin publication of its own journal, *Dziś i Jutro*, and became perhaps the most committed ally of the Communists and the pro-Soviet orientation in Poland.[134] The *Dziś i Jutro* circle had at this stage reasonably good relations with the episcopate. Hlond even gave a donation to assist in the costs of launching the paper,[135] while one of the circle described Sapieha's attitude as 'fair to the end'.[136] In 1945–6 the Church seems not to have taken the hostile attitude to the 'radical Catholics' it was to assume subsequently.

A separate, even smaller, current of pro-government Catholic opinion was represented by Aleksander Bocheński, who in 1947 was elected for Kraków as one of the three 'Progressive Catholic' deputies in the *Sejm*, and Ksawery Pruszyński, a well-known journalist and writer. Their ideas were an elaboration of the Kraków school of positivist conservatism, which rejected the romantic tradition in Polish history and proclaimed the need for realism and the acceptance of the new political order.[137]

The Communists attached considerable significance to courting sympathetic Catholics; Gomułka and Bierut appear to have been directly or indirectly involved in contacting such circles and Jerzy Borejsza, the party's publishing overlord, was particularly active in this field.[138]

Although it would be wrong to exaggerate the extent of the Catholic elements they won over, it was true nonetheless that these groups exercised an influence beyond their numbers and at the turn of 1945–6 provided the Communists with a bridge to the wider Catholic political movement and to the Church itself.

THE PERIOD FROM spring to autumn 1946 was marked by increasing political polarization and tension as the parties prepared for the coming elections. The long-awaited negotiations between the Communists, Socialists and PSL on the proposal to form an electoral bloc broke down on 22 February 1946. In reply to the workers' parties' offer of 20 per cent of the seats in the next *Sejm* for the PSL (as against 70 per cent for the 'Lublin' parties), Mikołajczyk had demanded that in any bloc representatives of the countryside (i.e. the PSL and SL) should have 75 per cent of the seats.[1] The failure of the talks was followed by the postponement of the elections, expected in the first half of the year, until the autumn and then the winter of 1946–7.[2] In their place, a referendum held at the end of June provided an inconclusive opening round to the coming battle.

As we have seen, in the months after the formation of the Government of National Unity, the PPR had sought to force Mikołajczyk to make a clear choice between full alignment of the PSL with the national front (and hence tacit acceptance of Communist hegemony), and outright opposition 'in a bloc with the reaction and the illegal organisations'. The outcome of the talks was seen by the PPR as final proof that Mikołajczyk had chosen the latter path. The party concluded from this that an accommodation with the PSL in its existing form and under its existing leadership was no longer realistic and that the time had come to commence open struggle with the opposition. Preparations for the elections should ensure that the PSL was prevented from mounting an effective challenge for power.

In terms of the national front strategy, this represented a decisive turn away from the conception of a broad national front embracing the mainstream of the peasant movement which the PPR had with more or less consistency sought to achieve since 1943 and which in mid-1945 had appeared briefly to have come to fruition. The emphasis which the party had hitherto placed on drawing the peasant movement as a whole away from the reaction now gave way to propaganda which aimed to establish 'links between the PSL and the reaction'. The Communists no longer looked to the PSL for partners in the worker–peasant alliance, but to the rump of the 'Lublin' SL and any 'democratic' elements which could be persuaded to break with the PSL 'from below'.

The crucial strategic question was how and with what resources the PPR would neutralize the PSL and manage the elections: Mikołajczyk believed that the Communists would be unable to crush the PSL unless the Russians intervened directly on their behalf. However, as we have seen, such a course would have been contrary to the conception of Poland's development held by Gomułka and a significant section of the party leadership. This aimed to establish a balance of forces within Poland which would enable the national front to defeat its opponents with its own internal resources. Those elements in the leadership which in 1944–5 had inclined to an external solution to the question of power had been silenced by the damage done to the party by its close dependence on the Soviet forces in the period between October 1944 and May 1945. In any case, the indications were that Stalin was equally anxious to avoid direct intervention and the costs this would entail in terms of Soviet relations with the West. Also, as we shall see, there is evidence that at this stage Stalin may not yet have been convinced that a satisfactory deal with the PSL was unattainable.

However, the internal resources at the disposal of the Communists in 1946 were still very limited. In spite of the expansion of the party and the security forces over the previous year, in many parts of the country the Communists lacked sufficient reliable manpower to hold the opposition and the underground in check and administer the elections. The army was an important additional source of manpower, but in early 1946 the political allegiance of many of the troops was an unknown factor. The 'Lublin SL' and the splinter-groups detached from the PSL during 1946 were far too weak to reinforce significantly the narrow base of the national front in the countryside.

These circumstances underlined the vital importance of the Socialists within the national front. The PPS was by 1946 a mass party with considerable popular appeal among Polish society. It played a major part in the apparatus of central and local government and the administration of the economy where the Communists were heavily dependent on the Socialists to ensure that key positions of power were kept in the hands of their allies. The PPR was acutely aware that the support of the PPS was essential to defeat Mikołajczyk's challenge. For its part, the Left-wing leadership of the PPS was convinced that the workers' parties must remain united to prevent Mikołajczyk gaining power and to secure the continuation of the political programme of the Lublin coalition: however, it did not share the view of the PPR that a deal with the PSL was no longer realistic. Indeed, it regarded further concerted efforts to achieve an electoral agreement as essential, both in terms of the national and its own party interest. It considered that an open confrontation with the PSL after the February talks was premature and that it might be possible to avoid a clash altogether if the Left parties pursued a more flexible course.

As the PPR went on to the offensive, these differences came into the open. During the summer, the Socialists launched a widescale campaign to reverse the increasing polarization in the country and restore national unity. Particular emphasis was laid on the special role which the PPS might play in any future coalition government. The Communists were deeply alarmed by what they feared was an attempt by the Socialists to supplant them at the head of the national front. However, constrained by the need to preserve the united front with the PPS and possibly unsure of Soviet wishes, they did not openly oppose the campaign.

For Mikołajczyk the developments of spring and summer 1946 appeared to bear out his conviction that the Communists would be unable to prevent the PSL from winning a substantial number – if not a majority – of seats at the coming elections. Despite the increase in tension and the repressive measures applied against the PSL after February, the Communists' attacks did not develop into the decisive showdown which he had expected. His party was not expelled from the government and in many areas was able to continue to operate and expand its influence without serious hindrance until late 1946. Within the PSL Mikołajczyk's leadership and policy remained virtually unquestioned while the divisions in the national front were evident for all to see. The referendum, held in the midst of the dispute between the PPR and the PPS, demonstrated the capacity of the opposition to frustrate the Communists' efforts to fabricate the results and the continuing narrowness of popular support for the PPR camp. At international level, there was no sign despite increasing East–West tension of a major hardening of Soviet policy or any slackening of Western support for his cause. The Catholic Church ruled out a compromise with the Communists and indicated its tacit commitment on behalf of the opposition more and more clearly.

Mikołajczyk therefore saw no reason to respond positively to the Socialists' overtures. He did not regard the PPS as a genuinely independent force and was not attracted by a compromise in which the Socialists would in effect occupy the pivotal position. In the end it was the PPS which was forced to give way. Its efforts to revive the broad national front of mid-1945 collapsed in September–October when it became apparent that neither the PPR nor the PSL was prepared to concede on the fundamental question of leadership in the future government. In September, the PPS leadership accepted the inevitability of a bloc of four parties and concentrated its energies on maximizing Socialist influence on the government to be formed after the elections. The failure of the Socialists' bid to reconstruct the broad national front opened the way for the Communists to begin in earnest the offensive against the PSL. Within a matter of weeks, this offensive destroyed the opposition as an effective force and secured once and for all that the Communists would determine Poland's future development.

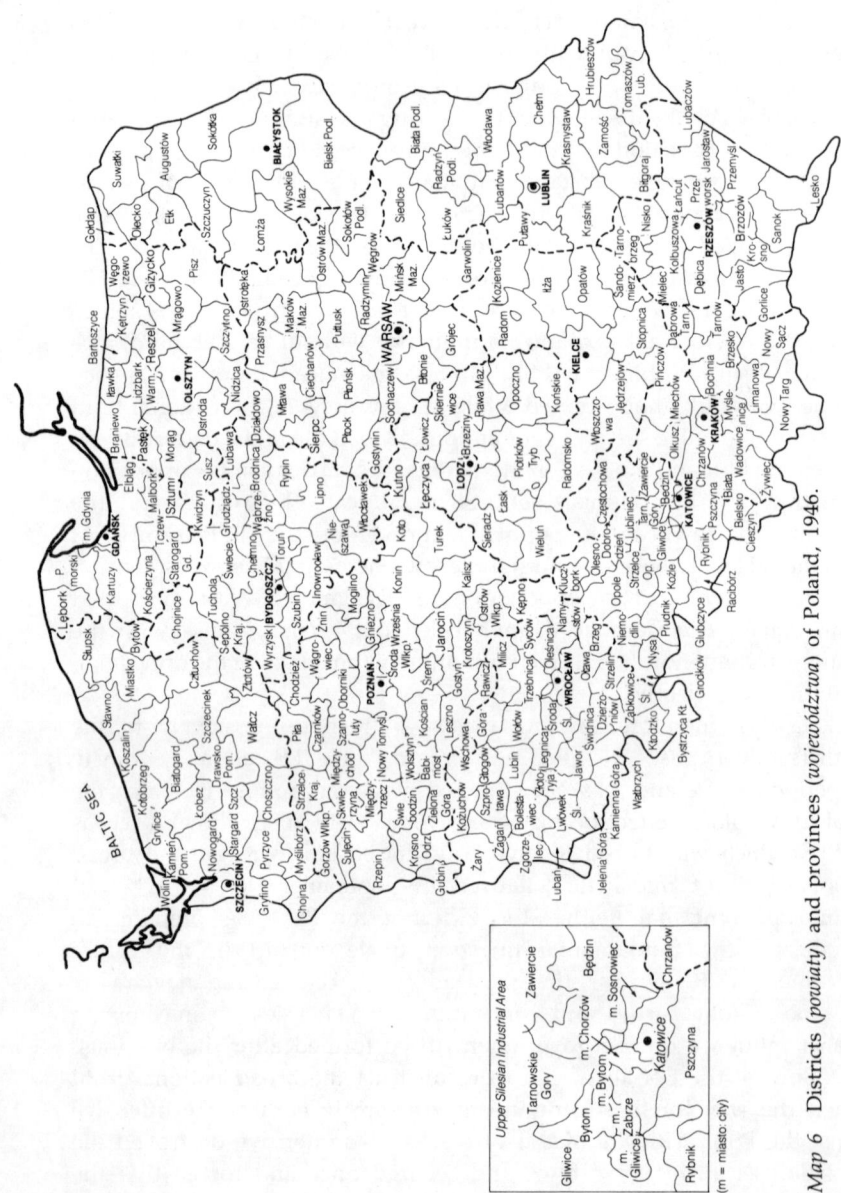

Map 6   Districts (powiaty) and provinces (wojewódstwa) of Poland, 1946.

'General storm'

As we have seen, the ground for the PPR's change of course in February had been prepared at the Central Committee Plenum on the 10th. The party leadership began to organize the offensive against the PSL immediately after the collapse of the negotiations on the bloc on 22 February.[3] The campaign was launched at a mass meeting of the PPR and PPS *aktyw* in Warsaw on 27 February. By the beginning of March headlines in *Gazeta Ludowa*, the organ of the PSL, told of a 'general storm' on the party.[4]

Gomułka's speech to the Warsaw meeting on 27 February signalled the main lines of attack on the PSL which were to be developed in the following weeks. The first was to identify the PSL with the reaction. According to Gomułka, by rejecting the bloc, the PSL leadership had 'chosen co-operation with the reaction'.[5] This cooperation was to be seen both in the political support given by the underground to the PSL and cases of alleged participation by PSL members in illegal organizations.[6] The second line of attack was to encourage internal opposition to Mikołajczyk within the PSL. Gomułka drew a clear distinction between the policy of the leadership group in the PSL and the wishes of the mass of the peasantry, including many of the rank and file members of the PSL. At this stage, the Communists hoped that it would be possible to mount a significant anti-Mikołajczyk faction within the peasant movement.[7] Thirdly, Gomułka stressed the importance of unifying the democratic bloc, and in particular strengthening the alliance of the PPR and the PPS, in preparation for the elections.

In terms of the party's strategy, the new course marked a clear shift away from the 'broad national front'. Although the Communists still aimed to split the peasant movement, after February they saw no real possibility of averting an open clash with the PSL if they were to keep power. They regarded Socialist hopes that a more moderate course might still win the PSL away from the reaction as a dangerous illusion. In a speech delivered on May Day in Katowice, Gomułka claimed that:

> Two forces, two political blocs are at work in the nation. . . . The first is the democratic bloc with the working class parties at its head, the second . . . is the reactionary bloc, which the PSL has in reality joined. . . . Let nobody think that there is some third road. There is no third road.[8]

As political tension increased and the hoped-for split in the PSL failed to materialize, the identification of the PSL as a whole with the reaction became steadily more pronounced in PPR propaganda. In a speech made in Warsaw on 30 April, Gomułka accused the PSL leaders of corrupting their organization and of 'inculcating their supporters with a fratricidal spirit' as well as being 'linked by a great many ties with the reaction'. He claimed that:

> The difference between the PSL and the illegal fascist organisations is beginning to disappear in some areas . . . many local PSL organisations have become the cover for hotbeds of diversionaries and bandits. Many of these organisations are deeply

corroded and controlled by these elements. The organizers and executors of fratricidal murders and criminal diversionary acts stood (and doubtless stand) at the head of certain PSL organizations.[9]

The same speech contained a clear warning that the PPR was contemplating outlawing the PSL – i.e. a reversion to the situation that had applied before mid-1945:

> The time has come to say to the PSL leadership that . . . in accordance with the Yalta and Potsdam conference resolutions, only democratic, anti-fascist organizations may conduct legal activity. Our system, our rule of law in reconstructed Poland is democratic. But there is no democracy in the world which would allow the forces of conservatism to indulge in acts of bloody violence, terror and anarchy. Therefore our democracy will also respond to such acts with repression and will regard this reply as proof of the rule of law. The leaders of the PSL should pay attention to all this.[10]

Although the PPR no longer regarded the broad national front as viable, Gomułka made it clear that the party would deal with the opposition with its own internal resources. He alluded to this in his speech on 27 February with the remark that 'we are a sovereign state and we do not want foreign help with the elections, since we do not need it'.[11] And on 30 April he reiterated that the national front was capable of defeating its opponents: 'Polish democracy with the parties of the working class at its head will find sufficient strength to thwart the plans of the reaction.'[12]

Despite the differences between the two on policy and tactics, the party regarded the united front of the PPR and the PPS as the cornerstone of its strategy in the period up to the elections. Gomułka, in particular, laid special stress on the importance of the united front, claiming that 'all the social reforms and gains by the working people achieved so far are above all the result of the united collaboration of the working class. The united front is a great achievement.' He admitted, however, that many within the PPR and PPS did not yet share this view.[13] According to Gomułka, the alliance with the Socialists would be the key to victory over the PSL:

> We need fear no opposition as long as the working class is united, as long as our decisions, all our moves against our opponents and also all our steps in the direction of the reconstruction and development of Poland are agreed and executed jointly. That is the basis, the foundation of our victory.[14]

The practical consequences of the party's new offensive course were felt straight away. The ZSCh Congress, held in Warsaw on 10–12 March, provided the occasion for the first major confrontation. As we have seen, the PSL had captured control of much of the local network of the ZSCh in the second half of 1945. To prevent the PSL taking control of the national organization – thereby eliminating the most important remaining source of Communist influence over the peasants – the PPR used every means in its power to exclude PSL delegates and pack the Congress with its own supporters. During the opening session Mikołajczyk staged a walk-out at the head of some 700 of the delegates in protest at the irregularities. Later the same day the security forces made their first raid on the headquarters of the PSL in Warsaw, making six arrests and confiscating various documents.[15]

Violence against PSL members increased markedly from February. Such attacks were not of course a new development and there had been a number of notorious killings of PSL activists in 1945.[16] However, the attacks became more common during spring 1946. At least 21 PSL members were murdered between February and April and at least 25 were killed in May alone.[17] The PSL ascribed the attacks to the security forces, and produced many eye-witness accounts in support of these allegations.[18] It seems certain that in many cases members of the UB were indeed implicated, although the evidence that there was an organized campaign of terror is thin.[19] Nevertheless the PPR leadership bluntly rejected the claims of the PSL and gave strong public support to the activity of the security forces.[20]

Arrests amongst the opposition also became commonplace. One source – referring to Silesia – notes the continual arrests of members of the PSL accused of cooperation with the underground from April onwards.[21] In the same region, the activity of the Party of Labour, which had considerable local support, was virtually paralysed by sweeping arrests in March and April.[22] Censorship of the PSL press was also tightened at this time and in May the Ministry of Public Security for the first time banned PSL branches in two districts.[23] A further seven were banned within the next month.[24]

At the same time, there was a general activization of the security forces, aimed primarily at stamping out the underground. In February the KBW was deployed in Białystok, Warsaw and Lublin provinces for its first major operation against the underground. Some 10,000 troops took part, detaining 6,000 suspects, over 300 of whom were shot after summary court martial.[25] On 29 March Żymierski announced a nationwide offensive against the underground and a State Security Commission, paralleled by provincial committees, was set up to co-ordinate the campaign. In all between 150,000 and 180,000 soldiers and militiamen were put at the disposal of the security committees, chiefly in eastern Poland.[26] Soon round-ups of suspects resumed on a considerable scale. In Kielce province, for example, 1,600 'suspects' were arrested in a UB-army operation between 12 and 15 April.[27]

However, despite the increasing belligerence of the Communists, in spring 1946 the PPR was not yet strong enough to launch an all-out effort to crush the opposition. Its hold over the apparatus of central and local government remained weak in many areas and the organization of the security forces as a reliable arm of the party was far from complete.

On paper, at least, the PPR was no bigger than it had been in spring 1945. On 1 January 1946 its membership was 235,300; by June 1946 this had increased to 347,105 (the membership in April 1945 was 302,000).[28] Although the party's organization had been improved and the number of cadres had grown, these gains had been very uneven and in many rural areas where support for the PSL and the underground was greatest, there had been little or no progress. Table 3 shows that the expansion of party membership was concentrated in the western and northern territories and in the major cities where the PPR was able to exercise firmer control over economic administration and local government.[29]

Table 3.   Rate of expansion of the membership of the PPR by region, January to June 1946

	PPR membership		Index of increase
Province/city	*January 1946*	*June 1946*	*(January 1946 = 100)*
(i) Old territories			
Kraków province	21,196	22,571	106
Lublin province	12,155	14,379	118
Kielce province	24,295	29,194	120
Lodz province	16,515	19,969	121
Rzeszów province	5,646	6,856	121
Warsaw province	25,896	33,356	129
TOTAL	105,703	126,325	120
(ii) Mixed territories			
Białystok province	2,581	3,579	139
Śląsk-Dąbrowa province	35,589	50,278	141
Poznań province	26,779	39,847	149
Bydgoszcz province	24,207	35,978	149
Gdańsk province	5,244	11,647	222
TOTAL	94,400	141,329	150
(iii) New territories			
Olsztyn province	2,560	6,169	241
Wrocław province	9,965	26,363	265
Szczecin province	4,109	12,533	305
TOTAL	16,634	45,065	271
(iv) Cities	8,984	15,048	167
Lodz city			
Warsaw city	9,729	19,348	199
TOTAL	18,713	34,396	184
OVERALL TOTAL	235,450	347,115	147

Source: PPR. Rezolucje, odezwy, instrukcje i okólniki komitetu centralnego i 1946–i 1947 (Warsaw, 1961), 212.

Table 4.   Membership of the PPR, PPS, and PSL by province, first half of 1946

Province	PPS December[a] 1945	PPR December[b] 1945 Total	Peasants	PSL	Date
Białystok	860	2,581	813	6,000[c]	ii/iii.46
Bydogszcz	20,362	24,207	7,753	?	
Gdańsk	8,735	5,244	1,367	6,069[d]	i.46
Katowice	22,486	35,589	3,684	35,000[e]	i.46
Kielce	12,344	24,295	6,920	50,000[f]	iii.46
Kraków	35,500	21,196	5,625	100,000[g]	i.46
Lodz	10,529	16,515	5,134	?	
Lodz city	12,873	8,834	–	?	
Lublin	3,464	12,155	7,774	24,000[h]	i.46
Olsztyn	1,766	2,560	988	8,000[i]	iii.46
Poznań	13,042	26,779	8,468	70,000[j]	mid.-46
Rzeszów	8,152	5,646	2,159	70,000[g]	i.46
Szczecin	4,000	4,109	1,600	18,000[i]	ii.46
Warsaw	14,543	25,896	9,905	65,000[g]	xi.45
Warsaw city	11,014	9,729	–	?	
Wrocław	14,700	9,965	3,664	50,000[i]	vi.46
TOTAL	194,107	235,300	65,854	502,069+	

Sources:
a   A. Reiss, Z problemów odbudowy i rozwoju organizacyjnego PPS 1944–1946 (Warsaw, 1971), 301, 313, 317.
b   N. Kołomejczyk, PPR 1944–1945 (Studia nad rozwojem organizacyjnym partii (Warsaw, 1965), 289–90.
c   H. Majecki, Białostocczyzna w pierwszych latach władzy ludowej 1944–48 (2nd edn, Warsaw 1977), 144.
d   R. Wapiński, Pierwsze lata władzy ludowej na wybrzeżu gdańskim (Gdańsk, 1970), 100.
e   J. Gołębiowski, Pierwsze lata 1945–1947 (2nd edn, Katowice, 1974), 332.
f   J. Naumiuk, Polska Partia Robotnicza na Kielecczyźnie (Warsaw, 1976), 348–9.
g   J. Borkowski, 'Rola i działalność Mikołajczykowskiego PSL 1945–47' (unpublished doctoral thesis, Warsaw, 1958) gives a figure of 170,000 members of the PSL in Małopolska (i.e. Kraków, Rzeszów and part of Katowice provinces) for Jan. 1946. E. Olszewski, Początki władzy ludowej na rzeszowszczyźnie 1944–1947 (Lublin, 1974), 173, gives an estimate of 70,000 for Rzeszów province alone for May 1946.
h   I. Caban and E. Machocki, Za władzę ludu (Lublin, 1975), 109.
i   B. Pasierb, Ruch Ludowy na Dolnym Śląsku w latach 1945–49 (Wrocław, 1972), 143.
j   A. Dobieszewski and Z. Hemmerling, Ruch ludowy w Wielkopolsce 1945–1949 (Warsaw, 1971), 106, say that the figure of 70,000 members is mentioned in PSL and PPS sources. Paid-up membership was 20,362 in 1945 and 39,725 in 1946.

In terms of mass membership, the PPR fell short of the PSL and was only slightly ahead of the PPS. In January 1946 the PSL claimed 540,000 members and the PPS 194,000.[30] Of course, these figures give only a general idea of the relative strengths of the parties; new members were often simply registered *en masse* and the number of active, paid-up members was considerably less than the total. However, this was true for all the parties and as we shall see in many rural areas at least, the PSL was a match for the Communists in terms of its organization as well as the size of its membership. As table 4 shows, the PSL was by far the largest political force in the provinces of central and eastern Poland – Kraków, Rzeszów, Poznań, Kielce, Warsaw, Lublin – and even in Szczecin and Olsztyn amongst the new western and northern territories. This ascendancy was overwhelming in comparison with the peasant membership of the PPR. Elsewhere,

Table 5.   PPR and PPS membership in urban areas at the turn of 1945–6

Province/city	*PPR membership in urban areas* (December 1945)[a]*	*PPS membership in urban areas+ (December 1945/January 1946)[b]*
Białystok	508	c. 400
Bydgoszcz	6,060	5,727
Gdańsk	1,794	3,978
Kielce	6,054	c. 4,000
Kraków	5,813	18,260
Lublin	1,277	c. 1,500
Lodz (province)	1,595	c. 1,127
Lodz (city)	8,834	12,873
Olsztyn	267	250
Poznań	3,745	4,425
Rzeszów	638	c. 3,000
Szczecin	337	c. 500
Śląsk-Dąbrowa	15,566	c. 7,742
Warsaw (province)	1,352	–
Warsaw (city)	9,729	11,014
Wrocław	1,702	3,035
TOTAL	65,271	c. 77,831

*   That is members of town committees (*komitety miejskie*) of the PPR.
+   That is members of the PPS in provincial towns (*miasta wydzielone*).
Sources:
a   Kołomejczyk, *PPR* . . ., *op. cit.*, 309–16.
b   Reiss, *op. cit.*, 316–17.

particularly in the urban areas of Warsaw, Lodz, Gdańsk, Kraków, Rzeszów and Wrocław provinces, the membership of the PPS outstripped that of the PPR (see table 5).

Only a relatively small proportion of the total party membership was suitable for responsible political work. The shortage of reliable, experienced and capable cadres remained acute. In December 1945, Zambrowski stated that the Central Committee's records of members holding responsible posts in the party and State apparatus and those with higher education, contained only 6,358 names.[31] Although these records were not complete, it was clear that the *aktyw* available to the Central Committee was far from sufficient to satisfy the party's needs. Even in critical areas, such as the training of organizers for the elections (which incidentally began only at the beginning of 1946), provincial committees of the PPR found it difficult to find appropriate people. A Central Committee circular dated February 1946 complained that despite instructions, some of the provincial committees had sent 'people entirely at random, without suitable qualifications' to the first course organized by the party's Central School.[32]

The PPR leadership was particularly concerned about the weakness of the party organization in the countryside. Exhortations to the local *aktyw* to extend their activity outside the country towns seem to have had little effect. A Central Committee circular 'on mass Party work in the countryside' issued on 1 April admitted that:

> the majority of Party organisations have yet to make a start on enacting the Party Congress resolution on the expansion of mass activity in the countryside. In particular the Central Committee considers that communes and villages are not adequately served by the Party *aktyw* and have up to now remained outside the scope of our Party's mass activity. The run-up to the elections demands from us the extension of mass activity to the countryside. Party organisations cannot therefore confine themselves to gathering peasants in country-towns, but ought to focus on a systematic campaign of mass-meetings in the communes and villages.

This campaign was to begin immediately and be given special priority, with the 'best *aktyw* . . . regardless of position held' being mobilized to organize it.[33] The party also paid special attention to the organization of protests against Mikołajczyk and the PSL during celebrations of *Zielone Święta*, the traditional peasant holiday in May.[34]

Efforts were also made to revive the pro-Communist Peasant Party. This had been virtually moribund at local level in most areas since the formation of the PSL. In provinces where the peasant movement was traditionally strong, its membership was insignificant in comparison with that of the PSL. In Kielce in March 1946 it claimed 3,700 members (compared with 50,000 in the PSL); in Rzeszów in June 1946: 3,680 (PSL: 70,000).[35] Many of these members were only loosely attached to the party. In Poznań, for instance, out of 5,000 SL members in March 1946, only 656 actually held party cards.[36] The leadership group in the SL remained weak and divided – some elements, it seems, inclined towards an alliance with the PSL.[37] The Communists apparently concluded that the relative independence they had allowed the SL leadership in running the party after May 1945 had failed. Gomułka told the June 1946 Plenum that 'in practice our approach . . . was to let the SL grow by itself. It has not grown. The conditions are right for it to become established as a powerful force, but we must help it.'[38]

The PPR's control over the upper levels of the army and security forces was secure, but the allegiance of the lower ranks in a clash with the opposition was uncertain. As we have seen, Mikołajczyk was convinced that the army would refuse to act on behalf of the Communists in a confrontation with the 'people'. And indeed army units did refuse outright to take part in operations against the underground in Rzeszów province.[39] The militia was often unreliable too. Gomułka claimed that the anti-Communist underground had succeeded in penetrating the militia and that for a time they had agents in the Supreme Command of the MO.[40] In Warsaw province the Communists reckoned that a large part of the MO was on the side of the opposition.[41] WiN was allegedly active within the MO command in Olsztyn province.[42] A major purge of the militia which had led to the dismissal of 20,000 officers in 1945 continued throughout 1946.[43] The party's hold on the UB was more secure, although even here the leadership considered that it was inadequate.[44] Also, by no means all UB functionaries were PPR members. Figures for Warsaw UB in 1946 show that 63 per cent belonged to the PPR, 4 per cent to the ZWM, 3 per cent to other parties and 29 per cent were non-party.[45] Nationally, it has been estimated that at the turn of 1945/46 87.6 per cent of UB officers and 73.3 per cent of militia officers belonged to the PPR.[46]

As the likelihood of a showdown with the PSL grew, the PPR took urgent steps to reinforce the security forces at its disposal. In February, just as the talks on the block reached breaking-point, the government took the decision to form ORMO – the Militia Voluntary Reserve (*Ochotnicza Rezerwa Milicji Obywatelskiej*). Its function was to provide 'a fighting force, capable of combating banditry in the defence of order and democracy'. Recruits were drawn from the PPR and the PPS and 'the better elements amongst the SL and the SD'. The party was told to accept recruits from the PSL only if they were 'democratic in outlook'.[47] In practice, the PSL played no part in ORMO which in many areas was a paramilitary extension of the PPR, and to a much lesser degree of the PPS.[48] By mid-March the new organization had 40,000 members[49] and by the end of 1946 over 100,000. Two-thirds of these were members of the PPR or its youth movement.[50]

However, it was to be some months before ORMO was ready for action against the underground. In the meantime, the security operations in the countryside and the increase in political tension led to a marked upsurge of violence which showed that the armed underground remained a real threat to the Communists in many rural areas of the country. In some provinces the breakdown in security reached crisis proportions. Kozik, writing about Kraków, comments that 'that state of security deteriorated with each successive month, despite counter-measures and the season of the year which created unfavourable conditions . . . the situation in the province, as other authors agree, can be defined as approximating to a state of civil war.'[51] Figure 2 illustrates how the level of violence against government supporters increased in spring 1946.

As in spring 1945, the tougher line against the opposition and the underground provoked a backlash which in many areas the PPR and security forces were hard-pressed to cope with. One of the Communists' main lines of attack after February was the campaign to reduce the influence of the PSL in central and local government.[52] As tables 6, 7 and 8 show, by 1946 the PSL had secured a substantial presence in both the representative and executive arms of local government, especially at the lower levels. At the upper levels of the bureaucracy and in the towns and regions, such as Silesia, where the PPR was relatively numerous, the PSL was either given only token representation or excluded altogether. Its gains elsewhere reflected its own organizational strength and popular support and the inability of the PPR to man the administrative apparatus at grassroots level.

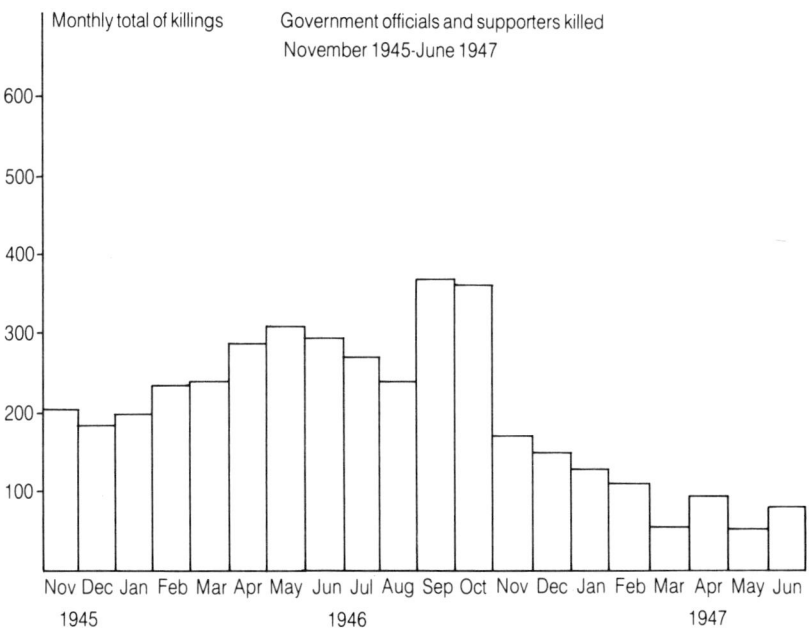

Fig. 2 Government officials and supporters killed, November 1945–June 1947 (computed on the basis of data in *Polegli w walce o władzę ludową*, Warsaw, 1970).

The weakness of the PPR and its allies was also reflected in the extensive dependence on non-party representatives on national councils. In Białystok province 90 per cent of commune national council members at the end of 1945 were non-party.[53] The scale of the PSL presence in the local bureaucracy was clearly a threat to the Communists' capacity to administer the elections in their favour. It also underlined the importance of the alliance between the PPR and the PPS, which was the third significant force in local government.

Table 6.   PPR, PPS and PSL membership of national councils, August 1946

National council	PPR	PPS	PSL
Provincial	314	226	121
District	1,623	1,035	1,213
Commune	5,209	2,322	7,600

Source: J.W. Gołębiowski and W. Góra (eds), *Ruch robotniczy w Polsce Ludowej* (Warsaw, 1975), 84.

Table 7.   PPR and PSL strength on various district and commune national councils, 1946

Province (date)	District N.C. seats		Commune N.C. seats	
	PPR (%)	PSL (%)	PPR (%)	PSL (%)
Kraków[a] (i.46)	27.2	20.9	24.4	20.5
(x.46)	20.8	37.2	11.8	51.9
Poznań[b] (v.46)	27.6	30.1	21.8	33.2
Rzeszów[c] (vi.46)	15.4	37.1	5.8	54.3
Kielce[d] (vi.46)	28.6	30.6	20.8	38.8
Wrocław[e] (ii.46)	30.2	0.5	?	?
Katowice[f] (xii.45)	21.6	0	28.0	2.6

Sources:
a   K. Ćwik, *Problemy współdziałania PPR i PPS w województwie krakowskim* (Krakow, 1974), 310–13.
b   A. Dobieszewski and Z. Hemmerling, *Ruch ludowy w Wielkopolsce 1945–1949* (Warsaw, 1971), 110.
c   E. Olszewski, *Początki władzy ludowej na rzeszowszczyźnie 1944–1947* (Lublin, 1974), 182–3.
d   J. Naumiuk, *Początki władzy ludowej na Kielecczyźnie 1944–1947* (Lublin, 1969), 191.
e   A. Kowalik, *Z dziejów Polskiej Partii Robotniczej na Dolnym Śląsku w latach 1945–1948* (Wrocław, 1979), 97.
f   J. Kantyka, *Na drodze do jedności* (Katowice, 1973), 183.

Table 8. Role of the PSL in local government administration, 1946–7 (percentage of posts held by PSL)

Province (date)	Starostowie (prefect)	Burmistrzowie (mayor)	Wójtowie (commune adminis-trator)	Sołtysi (village adminis-trator)
Poznań (vi.46)[a]	17.5	3.4	38.5	25.0
Katowice (vii.46)[b]	0	0	5.1	12.6
Kraków (iii.46)[c]	20.0	7.9	38.1	52.6
Olsztyn (iv.46)[d]	11.7	35.3	38.1	?
Rzeszów (iii.47)[e]	?	?	42.1	44.9
Gdańsk (vi.46)[f]	0	.... 12.3		?

Sources:
a   Dobieszewski and Hemmerling, *op. cit.*, 111.
b   R. Halaba, *Stronnictwo Ludowe 1944–1946. Niektóre problemy rozwoju organizacyjnego i działalności politycznej* (Warsaw, 1966), 203.
c   W. Góra (ed.), *PPR w walce o niepodległość i władzę ludu* (Warsaw, 1963), 116.
d   E. Wojnowski, *Warmia i Mazury w latach 1945–1947. Życie polityczne* (2nd edn, Olsztyn, 1970), 109.
e   Olszewski, *op. cit.*, 181.
f   R. Wapiński, *Pierwsze lata władzy ludowej na wybrzeżu gdańskim* (Gdańsk, 1970), 118.

Urgent steps were taken to improve the organization of the PPR in local government. The party leadership had been critical of provincial and district committees for poor organization in this area for some time. Zambrowski complained to the party's First Congress that PPR members of national councils:

> are not always sufficiently active . . . in most [national councils], especially at the district and commune level, they do not form groups or meet as groups, they do not prepare themselves for meetings of the council, they show insufficient initiative. . . . Comrades in provincial, district and town committees tolerate a state of affairs where inter-party consultative committees discuss and decide matters which belong to the national councils.[54]

In March the Central Committee set up departments in each provincial committee to deal with administrative and local government affairs and to activate PPR councillors and local officials.[55] At the same time a purge of PSL supporters in the local administration began. A Central Committee circular issued in March stated that:

> the apparatus of state and local government ought to be an effective instrument in the hands of democracy in the struggle with the reaction. National Councils . . .

should play a decisive role in that struggle and in the purging of the state and local apparatus of hostile and destructive elements.[56]

Wójcik, the secretary-general, informed the executive of the PSL at its sitting on 10–11 April of the effects of the purge. He reported that, for example, in Lower Silesia 17 out of 18 PSL prefects (*starostowie*) had been sacked within a period of two weeks, along with a considerable number of lesser officials.[57]

Overall, however, the policy of squeezing the PSL out of state apparatus fell well short of its objectives. As tables 6, 7 and 8 show, the PSL maintained a strong position in local government in many areas after spring 1946. Table 9, based on data for Kraków and Kielce provinces, suggests that the PSL continued to make inroads until the end of the year.

Table 9.   Party representation on commune and district national councils in Kraków and Kielce provinces, 1946*

Province (date)	District national councils			Commune national councils		
	PPR (%)	SL (%)	PSL (%)	PPR (%)	SL (%)	PSL (%)
Kraków[a] (i.46)	35.1	15.3	27.0	29.9	28.4	25.1
(vi.46)	28.9	6.0	44.3	–	–	–
(x.46)	25.5	8.8	45.5	15.0	5.9	66.1
Kielce[b] (i.47)	–	–	–	19.2	13.6	52.2
(vi.46)	30.4	20.1	32.6	24.8	20.6	46.5
(xi.46)	29.8	19.1	31.5	22.5	10.6	58.2

* *figures include only PPR, PSL, PPS and SL members*
Sources:
a   F. Ryszka (ed.), *Polska Ludowa 1944–50. Przemiany społeczne* (Wrocław, 1974), 263; Ćwik, *op. cit.*, 310.
b   Naumiuk, *Początki . . .* , *op. cit.*, 191, 231.

There seem to have been a number of reasons for this. The PPR was not yet ready organizationally to undertake a thorough-going purge of local government. A year after they had been formed, the Central Committee admitted that the local government departments of the provincial committees of the party were still not in a position to extend their activity to rural communes.[58] Also, three PSL ministers continued to sit in the government and although their powers were gradually whittled away, they were still able to achieve local victories in the State apparatus.[59] Perhaps the key factor preventing an all-out purge was the attitude of the Socialists who until the autumn still sought a compromise with the PSL. It was only after the PPS leadership accepted the inevitability of a confrontation with the PSL that the elimination of the influence of the opposition in the State apparatus began in earnest. The signal for this was expulsion of the PSL from the network of all-party consultative committees that in effect decided the distribution of political appointments and the 'party key' in the administration. This did not take place until late September.

The PSL: weathering the storm

MIKOŁAJCZYK seemed to the British and U.S. ambassadors 'highly worried and very nervy' about the Communists' offensive against his party.[60] He feared the expulsion of the PSL from the government and 'the formentation of disorders throughout the country' as a pretext for requesting Soviet intervention, followed by rigged elections in which the PSL would be suppressed by the security forces.[61] Nevertheless, he was not deflected from his strategy. He was determined not to compromise on the question of the bloc. In reply to Cavendish-Bentinck's observation that he had perhaps 'been opening his mouth a bit wide' in demanding 75 per cent of seats on a joint list, Mikołajczyk admitted:

> that he had done so on purpose as he was determined that there should not be a joint list of candidates . . . he feared however that the other parties would insist on a resumption of inter-party negotiations as they were bent on achieving a single list.[62]

Critics within the PSL of his conduct of the negotiations were silenced by a unanimous vote of approval for his stand at a specially called national conference of provincial leaders of the party on 2 March.[63]

In fact Mikołajczyk decided to meet the 'general storm' head-on. He believed that the confrontation with the Communists could be turned to his advantage and that in any case his party would lose more by entering the bloc than by continuing the struggle outside it. He assumed that the PPR would use intimidation and falsification of the results in the elections to achieve a majority in their favour.[64] However, he expected that despite the repression the PSL would still be able to use the elections as a demonstration of its strength and capture enough seats to obstruct changes to the constitution.[65] His main objective was to force the PPR to the limit to ensure that in order to obtain a majority 'the efforts which the Communist leaders will have to adopt to secure this result will show the strength of the opposition.'[66]

Mikołajczyk hoped that as the struggle between the Communists and his party intensified, external pressure on the PPR would increase. At a sitting of the executive of the PSL on 25 May he argued that 'if Polish society holds out, counting on its own strength, it may also receive foreign help.'[67] No doubt most of his colleagues took this to be a reference to diplomatic and economic pressure by the Western Powers and indeed Mikołajczyk endeavoured to extract the maximum political leverage from this source.[68] However, he also continued to work for an accommodation with the Russians and this may have been the real significance of his remark. He hoped that the Russians would ultimately be persuaded by the extent of popular support for his party to throw their weight behind a compromise. On 12 May Mikołajczyk told Cavendish-Bentinck of his hitherto abortive attempts to arrange 'a confidential and unofficial talk' with Lebiediev, the Soviet ambassador, adding that 'sooner or later the Soviet Government are likely to find themselves faced with the alternative either of having to occupy this country militarily or acquiescing in a Government headed by himself. He believed they would choose the latter.'[69] A few days later (probably 15 May) he at last obtained an interview with Lebiediev and tried to convince him that a PSL-led government would bolster the Polish-Soviet alliance. He warned that the Soviet Union would be blamed if bloodshed broke out.[70] Although Lebiediev was 'not particularly responsive', Mikołajczyk does not seem to have been discouraged and it appears that a further meeting took place on 31 May.[71] These approaches were doubtless linked with the talks which Stalin held in Moscow on 23–26 May with Lebiediev and the leaders of the PPR and PPS. The outcome of these talks, as we shall see, suggested that Stalin had not finally ruled out a deal with the PSL.

Internally too, Mikołajczyk sought to outflank the Communists and Socialists rather than to find a compromise solution. His response to the Communists' offensive was to launch a protest campaign of mass meetings, starting early in April with a tour of Silesia where he addressed large crowds in Katowice and Opole.[72] These meetings – the last to be granted official permits – were met by counter-demonstrations from the PPR and were followed by attacks on PSL activists. Nevertheless, the campaign continued with demonstrations of PSL strength at gatherings held to celebrate public holidays, at funerals of murdered PSL activists, at dedications of PSL banners and even at an international football match and a scout rally.[73]

The campaign was characterized by an overt appeal to urban working-class support, as the choice of the industrialized cities of Silesia for Mikołajczyk's first tour indicated. He is reported to have declared in Katowice that 'the workers' parties have no monopoly on the workers' and to have urged the PSL *aktyw* to 'go amongst the ranks of the workers'.[74] Despite the doubts of the agrarian wing of the party who feared that PSL recruitment in the towns would lead to an influx of *Endek* elements,[75] from late 1945 the party seems to have undertaken the formation of urban circles on a wide scale. In December 1945 the PSL had 800 members in Ursus, an industrialized suburb of Warsaw; a few months later it had 1,353 members in Poznań city – about half of them organized ini factory circles.[76] Mikołajczyk believed that the PSL would be able to mobilize working-class support against the Communists if they attempted to crush his party. Following a conversation with Mikołajczyk on 12 May, the British ambassador reported to London that he 'gathered . . . that if he [Mikołajczyk] is ejected from the Government he will try to cause any resultant disturbances to take the form of strikes nominally for higher wages rather than a political outburst.'[77]

The political and economic situation in the towns favoured the PSL campaign. Discontent, generated by the harsh economic conditions and the general increase in political tension, was widespread. As in early 1945, the government faced severe difficulties in maintaining basic food supplies and preventing sharp price rises in the winter months of 1946. Against this background, a wave of strikes took place in the spring, notably in the Lodz textile industry, the Gdańsk-Gdynia docks, the Silesian coalfield and in Warsaw, Radom, Kielce and Częstochowa.[78] Generally, the strikes were brief protests arising out of food shortages or suspicions that the available food was being distributed unfairly. Usually the workers resumed production once extra rations were issued. But often the strikes also had anti-government overtones and were attributed by the Communists to the continuing influence of reactionary elements amongst the working class.[79] In some cases the PSL may have been involved. The Communists blamed the PSL for organizing strikes in Warsaw on the eve of May Day and short stoppages which took place on the railways, in the Schicht factory and among the telephone employees.[80] The situation was regarded with alarm by the PPR and PPS which issued a joint declaration warning that they would oppose 'any attempt by PSL wreckers to split the working class with every means at their command'.[81] Urban unrest was also expressed in demonstrations against the government. The most serious took place on Constitution Day, 3 May, when despite a last-minute ban on processions, large-scale protest marches occurred in Kraków, Katowice, Gliwice, Sosnowiec, Bytom, Lodz and numerous other towns. In Kraków and Gliwice rioting broke out after clashes between demonstrators and police units.[82]

Mikołajczyk's readiness to rise to the Communists' challenge and his determination not to enter the bloc conditioned his attitude to the attempts of the PPS leadership to find a compromise. He and the great majority of the PSL leaders regarded the PPS as little more than a stalking horse for the PPR and believed that its following in the country and many of its activists would swing behind the opposition rather than accept a joint list with the Communists. The PSL gave open encouragement to the anti-bloc faction of the PPS led by Zygmunt Żuławski,[83] which was fiercely opposed to the Centrist leadership of the party around Osóbka, Cyrankiewicz and Szwalbe.

By May, the tension and doubts which had been evident in the PSL leadership when the Communists began their offensive had given way to a mood of greater confidence and unity. Cavendish-Bentinck found Mikoł-ajczyk 'in better spirits than I have seen him for some time past'.[84] The PSL had weathered the 'general storm'. The party had not been ejected from the government and, as we have seen, had generally maintained its position in the State apparatus. Kiernik and a few others who had questioned Mikołajczyk's uncompromising line on the bloc had rallied behind his leadership,[85] which clearly had the overwhelming support of the rank and file. Despite the increase in repressive measures against the PSL its popularity was undiminished. Finally, it was clear that the PPR and PPS were sharply divided on strategy and tactics.

The PPS: 'The third road'

ALTHOUGH the leadership of the PPS fell in with the PPR offensive against the PSL, it did not share the Communists' view that Poland had split finally into two camps and that a clash with the PSL was now unavoidable. The dominant Centrist faction in the PPS, led by Osóbka, Cyrankiewicz, Szwalbe, Rusinek and Hochfeld, did not accept that the failure of the February talks should deflect the workers' parties from the broad national front strategy and their efforts to forge an alliance with the mainstream peasant movement. It considered that the 'obstacle to forming an electoral bloc, to achieving full worker-peasant unity, is above all that relatively narrow group of activists which was connected with the London Government Delegation.'[86] The Socialists argued that 'We ought not to describe the whole of the PSL as reactionary and by doing this estrange its healthy elements from positive cooperation . . . a wise policy will assist the process of their coming closer to us.'[87] The PPS favoured a tougher line towards the PSL – and the rhetoric of the Socialists was often more menacing than that of the PPR[88] – but such language was intended to force the PSL, or at any rate its more pragmatic leaders, back to the negotiating table. Even as the February talks collapsed, Osóbka asked the PSL spokesman to reconsider and offered them a week to withdraw from their position.[89]

These accents were muted at first; by May and June, as tension in the country grew and the PPS became seriously alarmed at the Communists' increasing belligerence, they grew louder. Initially, however, the PPS leaders were more concerned to preserve the united front with the PPR and defeat the anti-bloc faction in the party led by Zygmunt Żuławski, which had considerable influence amongst the rank and file.[90] Despite their differences with the PPR, the Centrists were determined at all costs to maintain the hegemony of the workers' parties within the government. They accepted that if a bloc of six parties with the PSL was not achieved, the PPS would collaborate with the Communists to defeat the PSL in a bloc of the four 'Lublin' parties. For the Centrists this was the overriding priority, as Osóbka made clear: 'the most important problem is to maintain political power in the hands of the world of labour. . . . Therefore the four democratic parties . . . must win a majority even without the PSL.'[91] They feared that the alternative would be a regeneration of Right-wing forces which the Communists and the Russians would crush by force:

> We are certain that having once handed over power, we would have to wrench it back from the hands not of conservatives, but fascists, not through the ballot box, but by force. . . . We are genuinely afraid of unleashing elements which will either have to be crushed with Cromwellian fanaticism, or will rule out the possibility of a peaceful development towards socialist democracy in Poland. . . . We are afraid of the spread of attitudes which might justify the Soviet Union's lack of confidence towards Poland.[92]

The Centrists believed that only through the united front could they exercise a moderating influence on the Communists and avoid a narrowly-based, forced construction of Socialism in Poland on the Soviet model.[93]

Despite the strength of opposition to the alliance with the PPR in the provincial organizations of the PPS in Kraków, Warsaw, Katowice and elsewhere,[94] the Centrists, supported by the Left, had no difficulty in outvoting the Żuławski group at the party's Supreme Council on 31 March–1 April.[95] The Council reaffirmed the party's commitment to the united front and the bloc and agreed that the PPS should put forward a proposal to hold a referendum before the elections.[96] Having removed the threat from the Right, the Centrists turned their attention, with growing urgency, to their efforts to reverse the polarization between the Communists and the PSL. At a sitting of the party executive on 14 May, the Left (Świątkowski, Matuszewski and, in particular, Stanisław Skowroński) accused the Centrists of wavering and demanded closer cooperation with the PPR against the PSL. However, the majority decided in favour of a concerted attempt to reach a compromise with the Peasants. Stańczyk, on the Right of the party, went as far as to argue that 'if we do not achieve a bloc of six, we could have a revolution on our hands'.[97] The Centrist position was set out in an article by Szwalbe, the party president, entitled 'For a correct evaluation of the attitude of the PPS to the PSL and the Party of Labour', which appeared in *Robotnik* on 24 May. Szwalbe – no doubt with Gomułka's recent Warsaw speech (see p.233) in mind – bluntly contradicted PPR claims that the situation had polarized to the point where the legality of the PSL was in doubt:

> 'private' farmers and businessmen have their own economic interests and must have their own political representation to express these economic interests. All those comrades who, oversimplifying the situation, consider that there is no place for politically moderate parties in contemporary democratic Poland are mistaken. There is such a place and in the interest of the normal development of Poland's political situation, this place must remain. All thought then of delegalising such parties would be fanciful.[98]

The article concluded with a clear offer to resume negotiations to reach a compromise around an all-party bloc:

> We shall fight the PSL more and more sharply. . . . But at any time if the PSL agrees to the maintenance of government by democracy . . . in the way that we conceive it (which does not exclude struggle over socialism) . . . then the PPS, doubtless in full agreement with the PPR, will propose substituting conflict with an internal pact of the six parties which would be so beneficial for Poland, an agreement based on the principle of recognition of the true role of the PKWN parties in general, and the workers' parties in particular, in sustaining, deepening and continuing genuine democracy, not the formal democracy of *Chjeno-Piast* times [i.e. the right-centre coalitions between Witos's followers and the Christian Democrats in the 1920s] or from before September 1939, but the new democracy founded on the social reforms decreed by the PKWN and the KRN and the new style of government in Poland.[99]

The timing of the Socialists' offer was probably governed by the hope that it would influence the PSL executive which met on 25 May to decide its tactics in the referendum. The PSL leaders, though fully aware of the PPS attempts to promote a compromise,[100] voted for a contest.

However, such tactical considerations were not paramount. In fact, by this stage the disagreements between the PPR and the PPS over strategy were such that Stalin had become involved. Between 23 and 26 May a Polish delegation including Gomułka, Bierut, Szwalbe and Osóbka made a publicized visit to Moscow to discuss Soviet credits and the general political situation. No details of the discussions are available, but it is apparent that Stalin did not veto the PPS campaign to reopen talks, which continued with renewed vigour on the delegation's return. Rather, it seems that Stalin's attitude prompted the Communists to soften their line and accept – at least formally – that a further attempt to draw the PSL into the bloc should be made before the elections. On his return, Gomułka warned the Central Committee at its Plenum held on 2 June of the likelihood of new talks with the PSL:

> The PPS is convinced that a six-party electoral bloc is possible, real, immediate. Our view is different. We consider that the six-party bloc will not come about. All the same, it cannot be excluded that because of the position of the PPS, we shall, as it were, be forced tactically to take certain steps which will help to convince the PPS of its illusions. This means being able, on the basis of some sort of experience with the PSL, to convince the PPS that its calculations are mistaken.[101]

In its resolution the Plenum stated that decided opponents of Mikołajczyk within the PSL could expect to find 'a common tongue with the Polish democratic parties, despite ideological and programmatic differences' and 'forms of loyal, constructive co-operation'.[102] This was a distinct moderation of the party's public stance.

The Socialists put their own gloss on the Communists' very limited retreat and pressed on with their efforts to achieve an agreement. On 8 June Szwalbe published a further article in *Robotnik* entitled 'More on the attitude of the PPS to the PSL'. This reiterated the Socialists' commitment to the broadest possible alliance 'of the entire working countryside with the entire labouring population of the towns . . . an understanding not only with the "red" countryside, but also with the "green" as well as the "red and white" [colours of the peasant movement and the Polish national flag] and not only with the SL.' While the political battle with the PSL would continue, the PPS was determined to seek:

> a way through to those masses organised in the PSL movement which in reality agree with the new order in Poland and genuinely wish to improve or influence its future development, even if in the spirit of their own 'moderate' ideology. The resolutions on the PSL of the Plenum of the Central Committee of the PPR on 2 June deal with this issue in the same way. Despite rumours, the PPR, sharply attacking the reactionary and negative attitude of the PSL to the Polish system, also explicitly spoke of the possibility of finding a common tongue with Peasant-democrats.[103]

The PPS leadership was much encouraged by the formation of the *Nowe Wyzwolenie* group which opposed Mikołajczyk's tactics in the referendum and was expelled from the PSL in June. The PPS saw this as a potential third peasant party of the sort which they had hoped the Bańczyk group would form the previous September; such a party would be a natural ally for the Socialists.[104] However, as Osóbka made clear in a speech on 9 June, the PPS aimed to win over not only the dissidents, but also those remaining inside the PSL who had doubts about Mikołajczyk's tactics.[105] On 19 June he appeared to go even further in a speech which proclaimed the need for national unity and flatly denied the identification by the Communists of the PSL with the opponents of the national front:

> if someone asked me the question what we most need, I would reply – national unity. . . . Today not only the four political parties which founded the KRN, but also the SP and the PSL, accept in principle all the political and programmatic assumptions of our camp.[106]

Convinced as they were that the Socialists' hopes of a deal with the PSL were illusory, with the referendum only a matter of days away, the Communists had no choice but to fall in with the PPS, whose collaboration would be crucial to producing a favourable result when the votes were counted.

The referendum

THE failure of the talks on the electoral bloc placed a question mark over the timing of the election. In early April the PPS, supported by the PPR, put forward the proposal, which had been in the air for some months,[107] that a referendum should be held before the elections. The proposal was accepted by the KRN at the end of April and the date of the referendum was fixed for 30 June. The electorate were asked to vote on three issues: abolition of the Senate (the upper chamber of the Polish parliament); approval of the economic reforms provided for in the Land Reform and the 1946 Nationalization Law; and approval of the new frontiers of Poland. For the PPR the referendum was a convenient way to delay the elections, which were now expected to take place in the autumn.[108] It would also place the PSL in a political dilemma. If the vote was unopposed, the Communists could claim the result as a vote of confidence in the government. On the other hand, the Peasants were long-standing critics of the Senate and would have to reverse their policy to oppose the Communists on this issue. A contest on the economic reforms or the new frontiers would compromise Mikołajczyk's progressive and pro-Soviet stance. For the Socialists, the referendum had the additional advantages of providing further time to seek a compromise with the PSL and reassuring the PPS rank and file over the postponement of the elections.

At first, it seemed that the PSL would not contest the referendum. Its executive met on 10–11 April and decided to accept the referendum as the price for fixing the date of the elections. When it was suggested that the PSL might force a contest, both Mikołajczyk and Kiernik were opposed.[109] Mikołajczyk's view was that 'if, prior to the referendum, he and his party could feel sure that the elections will be held and these will be reasonably free . . . his party would not advise members as to how to vote . . . as, if the elections are in fact held, it will later on have no importance.'[110] However, during May opinion in the PSL leadership hardened in favour of a contest. The majority favoured recommending members to vote 'no' to question I (abolition of the Senate) and 'yes' to questions II and III. Some favoured an even tougher line (a boycott or 'no' votes on questions I and II). The party Council on 26–27 May gave overwhelming support for the first formula. Only 10 out of 128 Council members voted for the 'three times yes' formula which would have avoided a contest, and 3 voted for a boycott.[111] Mikołajczyk explained to the British ambassador after the Council that:

> at first he had thought the C[entral] C[ommittee] of the P[olish] P[easant] P[arty] should not give any advice to its members as to how to vote in the referendum but should regard this as unimportant and should concentrate on preparatory work for the elections. However, he subsequently changed his mind . . . for the following reasons. If the referendum produced a majority in favour of the abolition of the Senate, this would result in the election only being for one chamber instead of two. Should this one chamber have, as a result of the elections being rigged, a two-thirds majority prepared to obey the orders of the Communist leaders, it would be possible for the latter to change the constitution forthwith and turn this country into a totalitarian Communist state. On the other hand with 2 chambers the operation would be more difficult. Moreover, a large negative vote on the proposed abolition of the Senate would help to show the strength of the opposition.[112]

Despite the Communists' efforts to generate internal opposition to Mikołajczyk within the PSL, only a small minority dissented from the decision to force a contest. The most prominent critics of a 'no' vote, Zygmunt Załęski, Kiernik and Kazimierz Bagiński, were opposed largely for tactical reasons and fell in with the majority once the decision was taken.[113] A handful of lesser figures, led by Tadeusz Rek, deputy-secretary of the party, came out publicly against the decision and were immediately expelled. Although this group began publishing its own newspaper (with the help of the bloc parties) and formed a new party, the PSL *Nowe Wyzwolenie*, it was unable to win over any significant support from the grassroots of the PSL. It was widely viewed as a Communist 'front', though its orientation was closer to the PPS.

The official results of the referendum were not issued until 12 July. According to these figures, the results of the voting were as shown in table 10. The turnout was 85 per cent. Mikołajczyk, who produced evidence of widespread irregularities in the voting arrangements and the count, issued separate figures covering just under 30 per cent of the polling districts where PSL sympathizers had succeeeded in witnessing the count. According to these returns, 2,770,351 (83.5 per cent) voted 'no' to question I in these areas.[114]

Table 10.   Official results of the referendum, 30 June 1946

Question	'Yes' %	'No' %
I (For abolition of the Senate)	68.2	31.8
II (For the land reform and nationalization law)	77.3	22.7
III (For the new frontiers)	91.4	8.6

Source: Głos Ludu, 12 July 1946.

Generally the voting seems to have been conducted correctly.[115] However, even at this stage some blatant irregularities took place. One PPR electoral official from the Chełm region recounted in his memoirs (published in 1974) making off across the meadows with the ballot box in one hand and a pistol in the other, several hours before voting in a pro-PSL village was due to close.[116] It was during the count that the Communists intervened to falsify the results. Instead of the votes being counted locally, as provided for in the regulations, the count took place at district level, in most cases without PSL scrutineers present.[117]

Although the Communists claimed victory, it was clear that the referendum was a major setback for the party, in both political and organizational terms. According to the British ambassador, the Communists were 'appalled at the small vote they secured'.[118] Even the official results betrayed the continuing failure of the PPR and its allies to capture public support. A heavy vote for the opposition had been expected in the countryside, where political brigades often required protection by the army and ORMO units when they ventured into the villages.[119] However, in the towns they had expected that a combination of economic and administrative pressures on government employees and support for the

Left amongst the urban working class, would produce a respectable vote. In fact, the outcome in many of the towns appears to have been disastrous for the bloc. In Kraków city, according to the official figures, the vote on question I was 'yes': 23,162; 'no': 120,840 (84%).[120] In Kielce, Częstochowa and Radom the official returns did not conceal 'yes' votes and turnouts well below average.[121] Apart from Kraków, Poznań (53%), Rzeszów (79%) and Stalowa Wola (80%) voted 'no' to question I on the official figures. The last two, both industrial towns, also voted against nationalization and the land reform on question II by majorities of 73 and 68 per cent respectively.[122] There were rumours of a landslide vote against the government in Katowice and there was open talk in Communist circles about the fiasco in Lodz, which had been regarded as a PPR stronghold.[123]

Apart from the voting itself, the strength of hostility to the Communists revealed in the campaign preceding the referendum came as a sharp jolt to the PPR. According to Hillebrandt and Jakubowski, writing of Warsaw, the party had little experience of campaigning amongst the public. Canvassers 'sometimes met open hostility to the Party . . . there were cases of assaults on canvassers, they were whistled at and pelted with rotten fruit'. This reception was unexpected:

> contact during the pre-referendum campaign with the broad mass of the population in Warsaw enabled the party to ascertain more accurately the mood of groups with which it had hitherto not been in touch: the unemployed, small craftsmen, the petit-bourgeoisie, housewives. Their mood was, according to reports of the PPR Provincial Committee, worse than expected. It had not been realised that there was so much unemployment, especially amongst women and the young. The universal fear of losing homes, shops, sheds or small workshops with which owners were, it was supposed, threatened and which made them hostile or suspicious towards the new authorities came as a surprise. Canvassers also confirmed that strong prejudice against the new government as well as hopes of a change in the political system, pinned chiefly on the PSL and the person of Stanisław Mikołajczyk, still existed in many neighbourhoods.[124]

The referendum had made abundantly clear how far the PPR was from achieving a broad base of popular support for the national front, or even from winning the allegiance of a significant section of the urban working class.

The referendum had also demonstrated the ineffectiveness of the party's organization in many areas. Despite the measures taken to produce a positive result, in Kraków and elsewhere the bloc had been unable to prevent the opposition scoring embarrassing local victories. These upsets seemed to confirm Mikołajczyk's conviction that the Communists lacked the organizational resources and manpower to prevent his party winning a substantial number of seats at the elections.

The machinery for counting the votes had been set up in mid-May. Central Committee instructions issued at the time made no bones about the fact that local party committees were to ensure that these electoral commissions were manned by 'people who have demonstrated actively their allegiance to the democratic camp and who desire the maintenance of People's Poland'.[125] This meant the wholesale exclusion of the PSL from the electoral apparatus. At provincial level, the PSL forced its representatives on to only three commissions (Poznań, Lodz, Kraków) out of seventeen and in the polling districts its representatives were present on only about 3,000 of the 14,000 commissions.[126] But where the PSL was strong, it was able to breach the monopoly of the Communist bloc. In Poznań city five of its members were commission chairmen, in Jarosław five commissions were composed entirely of PSL members and in Lubaczów nearly all were.[127] In Kraków province, all 30 commission chairmen in Dąbrowa District, 23 out of 28 in Limanowa District, 46 out of 75 in Biała District and 20 out of 62 in Nowy Targ District, belonged to the PSL. Out of 560 commission members in Nowy Targ, just 12 were in the PPR; in Limanowa only 2 out of 280.[128]

The Communists' grip on the electoral machinery was shaky not only in the Peasant strongholds, but also in the towns where the PPR was heavily dependent on the Socialists.[129] The attitude of the Socialists seems to have been the decisive factor governing the efficiency of the management of the results. In Kielce province where the Leftist leadership of the local PPS cooperated closely with the PPR, the Socialists played a big role on the electoral commissions. Despite the local strength of the PSL the Left parties succeeded in producing voting figures that were better than average.[130] In Rzeszów and Stalowa Wola the PPS vote was thought to have gone against the government, while in Kraków not only did Żuławski tacitly support the opposition, but the ever-present friction between the local PPS and PPR had been sharply exacerbated by the summary replacement of the Socialist chairman of the provincial electoral commission by a Communist.[131] The referendum underlined the fact that the Communists would have both to intensify measures against the PSL network in the villages and to secure greater cooperation from the Socialists if they were to arrange a satisfactory outcome to the elections. On their own they were still not ready organizationally to take on the opposition.

After the referendum

THE summer months of 1946, between the referendum and the unleashing by the PPR in the autumn of the offensive which dispersed the PSL and the underground and enabled the bloc parties to manage the elections successfully when they were finally held in January 1947, offered the last opportunity to return to the compromise of June 1945. By this stage, the chances of agreement were slight. The two main protagonists, the majority of the PSL led by Mikołajczyk, and the PPR, were determined to join battle. It was the Socialists and a minority within the PSL led by Kiernik and Wycech which endeavoured to avoid the clash.

The Communists, shaken by their failure to win wider support in the referendum, took their retreat from the broad national front line of mid-1945 one step further. The 'general storm' in the spring had failed to fragment the PSL or curb its influence, largely because the Socialists had been unwilling to cooperate in applying more than limited pressure on the opposition. After the referendum, the PPR leadership gave priority to strengthening the alliance with the Socialists as the springboard for a much more intense and effective offensive against the PSL. The purpose of the offensive would be to eliminate the bulk of the PSL from further political activity. In the Communists' view the referendum had shown that only a small part of the PSL could be drawn into the democratic camp, the majority led by Mikołajczyk being irredeemably linked with the reaction.

Gomułka set out the party's position in his first post-referendum speech, delivered at a meeting of the PPR and PPS *aktyw* in Warsaw on 6 July. While claiming that the bloc had won a great victory, his conclusions betrayed the failure of the party's earlier strategy. He argued that the referendum had confirmed the PPR view that the PSL was incapable of playing a Centrist role between the Communists and their allies, on the one hand, and the anti-Communist underground on the other. It had also shown the continuing strength of the reaction, which was 'even stronger than we had thought'. Gomułka based this interpretation on the following analysis of the results. The referendum had provided a 'straightforward and clear-cut line of division between democrat and reactionary'. Among those who had cast negative votes, a small number, about 10–12 per cent, had followed PSL instructions (i.e. 'no' only to question I). This section of the electorate could be considered as 'the right wing of the democratic camp' which had 'demonstrated its distaste for the present government while accepting the basis on which democratic Poland rests. This group is in opposition to the government, however that opposition is within the framework of democratic Poland.' The PPR was not friendly to this element, but was not hostile either and had no intention of persecuting it or hindering its activity. On the other hand, the remainder of the opposition, the 'reactionary, fascist Mikołajczyk PSL', embracing all those who had cast more than one negative vote (i.e. a large majority of the voters in some areas) were to be eliminated from political life. Gomułka ended his speech with a call for 'a mighty, lightning offensive . . . against the reaction, against the Polish fascists, against the bandits and diversionaries', the success of which, he stressed, would depend on the cohesiveness of the united front.[132]

The implication was that the referendum had confirmed the conviction of the PPR leadership that there was no possibility of achieving an electoral bloc with the PSL or even a substantial part of its following. Indeed, the PPR and PPS could only hope to retain power at the elections by means of a 'mighty offensive' against the PSL and the underground. In effect this would require the suspension of the broad national front which the

Communists had sought to construct with varying degrees of conviction since May 1945 and its substitution by what amounted to a temporary proletarian dictatorship of the united front of the PPR and the PPS.

Mikołajczyk and the majority of the PSL leadership and activists were not deflected from their course by the outcome of the referendum, rather the opposite. The official results had come as no surprise. It had been apparent to Mikołajczyk for weeks before the vote and indeed before the PSL decided on a contest, that the Communists planned to manage the results very carefully.[133] However, according to the British ambassador, Mikołajczyk was 'so encouraged by the real results of the referendum which far exceeded his expectations'.[134] Opinion on the PSL executive and Council was strongly in favour of his opposition line and there is little doubt that grassroots party members would have resisted any compromise with the Communists, even if the leadership had agreed to join a single list.[135] Mikołajczyk was ready to discuss limited local electoral pacts providing they formed part of a broader political understanding and did not leave the PPR hegemony intact. However, he was opposed to any discussion of a nationwide bloc. As in February, his real objective in any negotiations was to extract a firm date for the elections, which he was determined would be basically competitive.[136]

Mikołajczyk's general strategy was unaltered. He was still optimistic that the PSL could capture leadership of the government coalition by winning the confidence of the Russians, enlisting Western diplomatic and economic pressure, holding together the PSL electoral organization and sustaining a mood of resistance and uncertainty in the country. His aim as reported to the British ambassador remained:

> victory for his party secured by international supervision, followed by the formation of a coalition Government: 50% of the Ministries being reserved for his people. His policy then would be to go slow, avoid antagonising the Russians, prevent as far as possible any reprisals, avoid a purge and concentrate on keeping agriculture and industry going. He was convinced he could get on with the Russians and that the immediate result would be an all-round relaxation of tension.

The only alternative, he told the British, would come about if Poland were abandoned by the West and would involve:

> the continued suppression of his party, rigged elections . . . and the affirmation of a totalitarian Communist regime. This would throw the people into despair, violence would increase, more and more people would take to the woods, public security would be reduced to nothing, the Government, unable to control the country with its own resources (he does not think the Government can rely on the militia) would call in more Soviet police and troops, and a state of smouldering civil war would ensue.[137]

He seems to have put much the same arguments to Lebiediev during a long conversation in early July during which he again asserted that the Russians needed the PSL.[138]

Internationally circumstances still seemed to favour his approach. The British were, it was true, averse to his idea of international supervision of the elections, chiefly on practical grounds, and the Americans, to the annoyance of the British and the U.S. ambassador, Bliss Lane, were prone to lapses in their support for Mikołajczyk, as for example in their decision on the eve of the referendum to unfreeze credits to the Polish government.[139] However, their basic attitude was underlined by the delivery to the Poles on 19 August of strong notes demanding a decision on the date of the elections.[140] In September Mikołajczyk sent his emissary, Kulerski ('Mr Carter'), to London to sound out the Foreign Office. The outcome was satisfactory. When Kulerski informed the British that Miłoł-ajczyk 'earnestly hoped that we would pursue our policy of linking economic help to political questions and get the Americans to do the same.[141] The attitude of the Russians was at this time more puzzling than at almost any other time. Not only were there clear signs that Stalin's confidence in the PPR was at a low ebb and that he was ready to look elsewhere to achieve stabilization in Poland, but Molotov's overt appeal to German opinion in a speech on July[142] highlighted the shakiness of the Communists' claim that they were the best guarantors of Polish interests and showed the risks involved if the pro-Western wing of the government, represented by Mikołajczyk, was forced out of office.

Internally PSL tactics altered little either. Despite growing repression, mass demonstrations continued. On 28 July Mikołajczyk addressed 10,000 peasants at Krotoszyn and delivered a strong attack on the government's economic and political policies. On 4 August he spoke at a rowdy meeting in Gdańsk.[143] However, after the referendum emphasis was placed on developing a more disciplined, semi-conspiratorial cadre-organization. In effect, the party stepped back towards the underground it had left in 1945 in an effort to counter infiltration, avoid the repressive measures taken against its activists by the authorities, and ensure that an organizational network remained intact for activization during the elections.[144] In sum, the PSL during the summer of 1946, far from modifying its oppositionist stance, was digging in for the coming battle.

In the aftermath of the referendum the minority in the leadership, led by Kiernik and Wycech and supported by Załęski and Niećko, which had reservations about Mikołajczyk's tactics pressed hard to keep open the possibility of a compromise. But although alarmed by the obvious determination of the PPR to go to any lengths to retain power and the general increase in tension which had found bizarre expression a few days after the referendum in a pogrom of Jews in Kielce and the surrounding district,[145] this group was prepared to consider only an electoral bloc in which the PSL had 40–50 per cent of the seats and the hegemony of the PPR camp was broken.[146]

The Centrist leaders of the Socialist Party, Osóbka-Morawski, Cyrankiewicz, Szwalbe and Rusinek, also felt that the referendum had demonstrated the correctness of their calculations. On the one hand, it had shown that the hold of the Left on power was tenuous and would not long survive a split in the 'united front' of the kind advocated by Żuławski and others on the Right of the party. And on the other, it had underlined the acute danger of drift away from the national unity platform of the PKWN and the coalition government towards a virtual dictatorship of the proletariat in which there would be little place for the PPS. They pointed to the need to avoid a recurrence of the mistakes of early 1945, fearing that the same indiscriminate condemnation of the London camp which had occurred then might now be applied to the PSL.[147] The Socialists were, despite the intransigence of the Communists and much of the PSL, not to mention the PPS hardliners led by Matuszewski, determined to make one further, serious, concerted attempt to bring the Peasants into a bloc.

The strains within the united front apparent before the referendum were heightened in its aftermath by sharply divergent interpretations of its significance. The Socialists emerged as defenders of the national front conception, while the PPR adopted a line which a year before its own leadership had denounced as sectarian. The divergence arose from the difference in the parties' assessment both of the viability of the broad governing coalition and the extent and character of the opposition. While Gomułka argued that the referendum had provided a clear-cut dividing line between democracy and reaction, the PPS view was altogether more liberal. Rusinek, speaking for the Socialists at a sitting of the trade union executive in early July, argued that 'those who regard all the "no" votes as the votes of fascism and black reaction over-simplify the situation' and suggested that apart from Right-wing and conservative elements, the 'no' voters included also,

> those objectively dissatisfied, the homeless, the poorly-paid, the hungry and ill-clothed. It was not calculated opposition or class-hostility to the new political system which they expressed, but only despair at their material condition, the social inequality which they see, at injustices, sorrow and disappointment experienced every day.[148]

In Socialist eyes the reaction was much less threatening and all-pervasive than the Communists claimed in proposing drastic counter-measures. Rather the united front should remain on the course it had adopted a year before. As Osóbka-Morawski put it to the Council of the PPS on 25 August:

> the referendum confirmed our political position regarding the policy of the six-party bloc. . . . At the present historical stage only the policy of close agreement of the six parties is beneficial for Poland. . . . Whoever causes the break-up of the six-party bloc will carry a great responsibility before history and the nation. Of course, if a six-party bloc does not come about, there will be a five-party or four-party one and I am convinced that it will be victorious. . . . Only it is a shame that this same victory

would have to be bought at the cost of serious conflict and undue sacrifice which with luck might be spared.[149]

Renewed talking on forming a six-party bloc began almost immediately after the referendum and continued on and off until early October when the PSL Council declared finally for a separate list. The discussions went through three distinct phases. During July the negotiations were held chiefly between Wycech and Kiernik, from the PSL, and representatives of the PPR. In August it was the PPS leadership which took the initiative with a rather more serious and determined attempt to achieve an understanding. During September it became apparent that this effort had failed and the PPS reluctantly moved back into line with the PPR, while Mikołajczyk's critics within the PSL fell in with the uncompromising stance of the majority of the party.

The first round of talks in July revealed the wide gap between the two sides. Mikołajczyk had agreed to Kiernik and Wycech holding discussions only with the proviso that 'there could be no question of a bloc'.[150] The Communists for their part were not prepared to consider any other electoral arrangement or to go beyond giving the PSL (with *Nowe Wyzwolenie*) 25 per cent of the seats in such a bloc. In addition, the exclusion of Mikołajczyk was to be a condition.[151] When the PSL executive met on 27 July to decide its attitude to these proposals, Wycech and Kiernik were unable to attract any support for a motion rejecting the bloc while leaving open the door for talks on a more limited electoral agreement. Mikołajczyk's motion insisting on a separate PSL list was passed almost unanimously,[152] and on 2 August the party activists from the provinces gave his line their backing.[153] The same week he renewed hostilities with speeches in Krotoszyn and Gdańsk. The PPR, which had agreed to participate in the talks chiefly to convince the Socialists that a deal was impossible, also resumed physical and propaganda attacks on the PSL at the end of July.[154] In their view the time for talking was over, the time to launch an offensive to disperse the opposition had arrived.

'The banner of national unity'

FOR the Socialists, however, this point had not yet been reached.[155] Adamant on the need for a bloc with the PSL, the PPS Centrists considered that greater determination was required to bring this about and that the Communists would have to offer concessions to attract the PSL: these should include dropping the demand for Mikołajczyk's exclusion.[156] On 29 July *Robotnik* carried the first of a series of articles by Osóbka-Morawski under the title 'Who will raise the banner of National Unity?'. This marked the beginning of a concerted drive by the PPS leaders to achieve a compromise in which their party would play a key role.[157] In the view of the Socialists, what was required was internal peace and not the further polarization advocated by the Communists and their own Left wing:

> today, when we need unity so much and when that unity is so lacking, the PPS ought to make every effort to construct it as broadly and quickly as possible. I consider that the PPS is suited to this role. In order to achieve success in the area of national unity two basic things are necessary: to genuinely *want* it and *to know how* to achieve it. That the PPS wants it ought not to arouse any discussion or doubts.[158]

The PPS was inclined to concede considerable ground to the PSL to win its accession to the bloc. They were ready to open talks with an offer of 33 per cent of *Sejm* and cabinet seats and some, such as Szwalbe and Wachowicz, were willing to go as far as 40 per cent – a figure which would have satisfied Kiernik. Osóbka stated publicly that his party envisaged 'such a balance and procedure in parliament, that without the agreement of PSL and SP members, [the Constitution] could not be passed.'[159]

The PPS moves provoked a profound crisis in relations between the two workers' parties. The Communists were deeply alarmed by the Socialists' open advocacy of a reconstruction of the government coalition so as to deprive them of their leading role. In their determination to prevent this, the PPR leaders seem to have contemplated abandoning the basis of the alliance with the PPS which had been central to their strategy since May 1945. This would have marked the end not only of the worker–peasant alliance, but also in effect of the united front as well.

First, the Communists attempted to oust Osóbka-Morawski from the premiership. In April, in order to reassure the PPS as repression against the opposition was stepped-up, Henryk Wachowicz, leader of the Lodz PPS, was appointed deputy-minister of public security. On 1 August, just three days after the publication of Osóbka's call for national unity, *Robotnik*, though not the PPR press, announced that Wachowicz had resigned. The reason for this was that Wachowicz, probably with Osóbka's approval,[160] had ordered the release from arrest of a veteran Socialist, Antoni Wąsik; Radkiewicz, the Communist minister of public security, on hearing of this had ordered Wąsik's rearrest.[161] Wąsik was not an important figure and doubtless the Communists' main purpose was to reassert absolute control over security matters and indirectly to undermine Osóbka's position as prime minister.[162] On 5 August the Socialists replied to this pressure for Osóbka's removal with what amounted to a show of force in Warsaw. Large crowds of PPS supporters marched through the city and loudly demonstrated in favour of Osóbka outside the prime minister's office.[163] Cyrankiewicz stoutly defended the PPS line in his speech to the marchers:

> we are an independent party and we are an equal party and we have every political and moral right to fight for that equality. A great campaign to consolidate society has been undertaken by Comrade Osóbka-Morawski in the name of the PPS. We need internal peace. A broad coalition of democratic parties, guaranteeing each

other mutual co-participation in government and excluding all aspirations to mono-party rule, is required. *The attempt has once more been undertaken to assure Poland peace through an understanding of the parties.*

He added the observation that 'amongst the perpetual suspicions that someone else has mono-party tendencies . . . lie frustrated hopes for one's own monopoly of power. This must end.'[164]

Without, it seems, informing the Socialists, Gomułka, Bierut and Minc had in the meantime flown to Moscow for further talks with Stalin (2–7 August).[165] Stalin's advice did not, however, settle matters; Osóbka remained as premier, but the PPR remained firmly opposed to further talks with the PSL. On 13 August the Secretariat of the PPR Central Committee assessed the differences between the Mikołajczyk and Wycech-Kiernik groups in the PSL and concluded that these were 'insignificant . . . on the critical issues they are entirely at one. They [Kiernik and Wycech] have set their demand in the election at 40%, which shows there is no possibility of negotiating with this group.'[166] At the same time the Central Committee seems to have given its approval and assistance to an attempt by the Left faction in the PPS to capture the leadership of the party and put an end to the Centrists' overtures to the PSL.[167]

This episode was the subject of fierce debate at the time and again more recently amongst historians of the PPS in Poland.[168] According to the Centrists the Matuszewski group attempted a putsch which was intended to remove the leadership by force. The Left claimed that its activities aimed only at organizing internal opposition to the Centrist line of the party. Strains between the two factions had been apparent before the referendum and during July the Centrists did not prevent changes in the leadership of local party organizations which strengthened the Right at the expense of the Left.[169] On 29 July, the same day that Osóbka launched his campaign, Stanisław Skowroński, the most outspoken Leftist in the leadership and secretary of the Kielce organization, was expelled from the party over protests from the PPR.[170] On 9 August the Left responded by circulating amongst the *aktyw* a petition, signed by 28 leading figures in the party, which warned that as the result of 'an offensive by hostile WRN elements' the danger had arisen of 'a distortion in the political-ideological face' of the PPS which cast it in the role of a 'champion of compromise with the PSL and Mikołajczyk'. The petitioners denied the need for 'serious and unjustified concessions' to the PSL and declared their support for the Communist conception of an offensive against the opposition. They also demanded the cooption of more Leftists to the inner leadership of the party (i.e. Secretariat and Political Committee).[171] The Centrists were not deflected, however. In the provincial Socialist press Drobner and Wachowicz published articles supporting the leadership[172] which drew a polemical reply from Gomułka,[173] while Cyrankiewicz made a direct approach to Mikołajczyk, proposing talks.[174]

At this stage, some of the Leftists, including Skowroński and perhaps Matuszewski, planned and possibly attempted the putsch. Hochfeld, one of the leading Centrists gave his version of events to Denis Healey of the International Section of the Labour Party in a conversation a few weeks later, which Healey reported as follows:

> the Communist Party told the PPS that Moscow had forbidden them to approach Mikołajczyk again. The PPS refused to accept the instructions, so one of its own national executive members, Matuszewski, the Minister of Information, began to organise the control of the executive by crypto-communists, the expulsion of Cyrankiewicz and the others, and the fusion of the PPS with the Communist Party, all this to take place at the next meeting of the executive.[175]

Osóbka-Morawski, speaking to the PPS Council on 25 August, made the same claim: 'We have proof that a putsch was attempted, the take-over by force of the editorial offices of *Robotnik* and the Central Executive Committee.'[176] According to Hochfeld's version, the Socialists outflanked this coup by appealing direct to Moscow:

> Cyrankiewicz heard of the plot and demanded to see Stalin. Stalin agreed, so Cyrankiewicz Szwalbe and Osóbka-Morawski flew to Moscow to ask Stalin two questions:
> 1) Does Stalin want a single-party state in Poland? If not, the PPS must be left independent within the limits of Soviet Foreign Policy, and given greater representation in the Polish Government in proportion to its greater mass support than the CP.
> 2) Does Stalin want civil war after fake elections, or will he agree to an attempt to persuade Mikołajczyk to enter common lists with a fairer proportion than suggested before? Stalin gave way on both points. The PPS is to have a larger representation in the government after the the elections, and Mikołajczyk is to be approached again with a genuine offer of collaboration.[177]

The circumstantial evidence supports this description of events. The PPS leaders seem to have made a trip to Moscow on 18/19–21 August.[178] It was Berman, the Politburo member chiefly responsible for Kremlin-PPR liaison, who according to Osóbka ordered the Leftists to call off their plans to seize the leadership.[179] Certainly, the PPS behaved after their supposed visit to Moscow with renewed confidence. The same day Osóbka had a lengthy conversation with the U.S. ambassador[180] and on 25 August he held a ninety-minute talk with Cavendish-Bentinck in which he 'made a strong plea that HMG should support the P[olish] S[ocialist] P[arty] on the ground that his party constituted a moderate element, and that if supported by HMG and [the] U.S. Government [it] would have less reason to look to [the] Soviet Union.' Osóbka added that 'the elections would make no difference, and that it was necessary that Poland should be governed by a coalition of Communists, Socialists and a Peasant group, all of whom would have equal power but that the Socialist party, which would gain in strength, would together with the Peasant group, be able to control the C(ommunist) P(arty).'[181] On 23 August the PPS reopened talks with the PSL, offering 25 per cent each for the PSL and the PPR, with 20 per cent of the seats in the bloc for themselves and 30 per cent for the other three parties. This formula came very close to breaking Communist hegemony.[182] Next, at a meeting of the party Council on 25–26 August the leadership moved against Matuszewski and his group, which had been left at its mercy by the turn of events. A purge of the Leftists was instituted, Matuszewski was suspended from the party and the leadership's efforts to achieve a bloc were given a vote of approval.[183]

The PSL followed the dispute between the workers' parties closely and at its height on 18 August decided to hold a special congress on 15 September to decide election tactics, a move which may have encouraged the Socialists to press on with their campaign. However, Mikołajczyk did not waver in his refusal to consider a bloc. He informed the PPS on 28 August that his party might agree to limited local pacts, but insisted on competitive elections in most areas.[184] Two days later he told his executive that since the Socialists' offer was confined to a general bloc, it was 'unacceptable' and that he was opposed to any further discussion of such a bloc, although some looser agreement giving a 'decisive majority' to the PSL, PPS and Popiel SP might be considered.[185] The same sitting decided that because of the postponement of the KRN due for 31 August at which the election ordinance and date were to have been settled, the PSL special Congress would also be put off.[186] The same evening Mikołajczyk, in what appeared to the Socialists to be a calculated affront, left the country for three weeks (30 August to 19 September) to attend a conference of the FAO in Copenhagen.[187] From there he sent his secret emissary, Witold Kulerski ('Mr Carter'), who told the British that 'there was as yet . . . no strongly led movement among leading Socialists which could be relied on'.[188]

The final round of the campaign to draw the PSL or part of it into the bloc took place in early September. After further consultations with the Russians, the PPS, this time jointly with the PPR, repeated the offer of 25 per cent of the seats in the next *Sejm* for the PSL and *Nowe Wyzwolenie*. The PSL was given until 11 September to respond.[189] Kiernik again indicated a readiness to compromise if the PSL were given 40 per cent,[190] but Mikołajczyk ignored the offer entirely.[191]

The Communists considered that with the passage of the 11 September deadline, the time had come to begin the offensive against the PSL.[192] However, the Centrist leaders of the PPS, despite their growing conviction that a deal with the PSL was unattainable,[193] managed to keep the offer of a compromise on the table a little longer. On 13 September the workers' parties published a joint open letter to the PSL which in the redraft demanded by the Socialists once again called on the Peasants to respond to the proposals for a six-party bloc.[194]

The Socialists did not wait for the PSL's formal reply which was decided at the party's Supreme Council meeting on 6–7 October. On 26 September, at a conference of the four bloc parties, Cyrankiewicz for the PPS agreed to abandon attempts to form a six-party bloc and accepted the exclusion of the PSL from the system of interparty consultative committees.[195] This amounted to the expulsion of the PSL from the national front and signified that the PSL would be prevented from exerting influence on the administration of the elections. The Socialists' change of course was announced in the press the next day.

External factors undoubtedly played a part in the decision of the PPS leadership. Stalin's personal views were no doubt an important influence. There is strong evidence that a joint delegation of the PPR and PPS leaders visited Moscow on 28–30 August for talks with the Russians on strategy.[196] According to Mikołajczyk's account, published in 1948, it was at this meeting that Stalin dictated how the elections and the repression of the opposition were to be conducted.[197] It is indeed true that the talks came at a time when the Soviet government's policies at home were hardening distinctly.[198] However, it is unlikely that Stalin ruled out further efforts to reach an agreement with Mikołajczyk. The immediate outcome of the visit was a renewed offer by the PPS and PPR of a deal which the Communists had hitherto opposed. At the time the PSL leadership was far from discouraged by the visit. Kulerski, Mikołajczyk's emissary, told the British that the Russian attitude had shown the same flexibility which the Socialists had found during their separate visit a few days before. 'In general', Kulerski reported, 'Stalin had conveyed the impression that he must have peace in Poland and that the present regime had not conducted its affairs in a manner which ensured this. He had intimated that they must really try and do a deal with the PSL on less unfair lines.'[199] The talks, as a perceptive Socialist commentator later wrote, were probably inconclusive.[200]

Apart from direct Soviet advice on the internal situation, it seems that the evolution of East–West relations with regard to Germany and the implications of this for the permanence of Poland's western frontiers had a major influence on the attitude of the PPS leaders. As we have said, Molotov's pro-German speech in July doubtless contributed to the determination of the PPS to achieve national unity at home. On 6 September the U.S. secretary of state, Byrnes, made his reply in a speech in Stuttgart which placed a question mark over American backing for the Oder-Neisse Line. Despite Mikołajczyk's public criticism of the speech,[201] the PPR seized the opportunity to tar the whole pro-Western orientation and the PSL in particular with accusations of unreliability on the issue of the frontiers. Byrnes' speech cast doubt on the value which the Socialists had placed on the continued participation of the PSL in the government coalition. It also underlined the need to secure Stalin's firm support for the Oder-Neisse frontier and to restore his confidence in the ability of the PPR–PPS alliance to stabilize the political situation in

Poland. Stalin may have given the Socialists assurances on the frontier question during the talks held in August. Molotov's statement of 17 September confirming the integrity of Poland's frontiers made the Soviet position clear.[202]

The PPS leaders were also under various forms of pressure from the Communists. As will be shown in the next chapter, the PPR reviewed its line towards the PPS at the Central Committee Plenum held on 18 September. The Plenum revived the prospect of a merger of the two workers' parties, an issue which had largely been dropped since the period of the Lublin Committee. It also began a campaign to influence PPS policy 'from below' through joint meetings of local activists of the two parties. More personal forms of pressure may also have been brought to bear on the PPS leaders; Rusinek, for instance, was from May to September 1946 under investigation by a special prosecutor after allegations had been made about his conduct in Stutthof concentration camp during the war.[203] It is doubtful though if these factors played much part in the Socialists' acceptance of the four-party bloc. The pressures on the PPS had been much greater in July–August when the Centrists had out-manoeuvred their Left-wing critics and the PPR. Moreover, the party leadership's abandonment of the six-party bloc was accompanied by re-emphasis of the special role for an independent PPS in Poland's future and the consolidation of the Centrists' control over the party organization.

However, the fundamental reason for the PPS leadership's decision to abandon its fight for a six-party bloc was its acceptance that in view of the entrenched positions of both the PSL and the PPR this objective was simply unattainable. Consistent with the strategy they had pursued since 1944, the PPS Centrists believed that in these circumstances they had no choice but to ally their party with the PPR in the coming confrontation with the opposition. Only in this way could they ensure that power would remain in the hands of the Left without resort to direct Soviet intervention, and preserve the possibility that the PPS would be able to broaden the base and moderate the policies of the government formed after the elections. Hochfeld, the leading Centrist theoretician, explained the leadership's reasoning in a confidential speech delivered to a conference of the PPS youth organization in September. He frankly told the delegates that in the absence of agreement on the bloc, the alternative to fabrication of the elections would be national disaster:

> We will not give up power . . . we are a party which took power in exceptional circumstances at a time when there was the threat of a political void. To hand over power in such a moment . . . would lead to catastrophe, not to some different government. If only it were a matter of handing power to Mikołajczyk. But no, it would be handing power to anarchy. We would find ourselves between the bands of the NSZ and intervention by the Soviet Union. . . . Under no condition whatsoever can we allow such a situation to arise. So it is an open secret that if it comes to an electoral showdown, those elections will be fabricated.[204]

He had no doubts that the Communists possessed the means to manage the elections, nor any illusions about what this might mean for Poland's future development:

the PPR has the sources of power in its hands – the army, the security forces, a large part of the state apparatus, industry. . . . They can do as they please. They do not want to use this power against society but they are able to do so. And then there would be nobody to help; Uncle Sam will not come to our aid; at the most he will suspend a loan. But that will only damage Polish society, not help. Soviet mistrust would increase enormously and the possibility of rebuilding Poland with our own hands would sharply diminish. Our ideas of socialist humanitarianism and our hopes of rebuilding the Polish economy by raising the living standards of Polish citizens, and not at the human cost and personal sacrifice that was necessary in the Soviet Union, will be gravely at risk.[205]

Hochfeld saw little possibility of avoiding this outcome, but nevertheless considered that the PPS should persevere with its efforts to extend its influence and salvage what could be saved from the break-up of the coalition government:

Will the bloc come about? This is rather doubtful. The opposition is so great, that in view of the hostile attitude of the PPR, our efforts to bring these two madmen to an agreement will be impossible. What should we do? Maybe throw the towel in and tell the PPR to govern on its own. Or we could say something different. We will not be the ones to fabricate the elections, but we hope to enter the new situation as strong a factor as possible, with the greatest amount of power in our hands. . . . The PSL has already lost its opportunity; it's finished. The PPS remains on the battlefield. . . . It remains in order in a difficult situation to win that 5% chance of saving Poland's links with the West. . . . We must do the dirty work in order that a cleansing of the atmosphere for clean work may follow from this 5 or 10% chance. This might or might not succeed, we do not know, but we must not give up.[206]

As will be shown in the next chapter, the PPS leadership attempted to put this strategy into action in the following months. But many party members rated its chance of success even lower than Hochfeld and sensed that Poland had reached a crossroads rather than a temporary detour. As one of the speakers who replied to Hochfeld's speech put it:

We will see that after the liquidation of the PSL, the turn of the PPS will come. The conception of dependence on the Soviet Union is an opportunity for the PPR. There is no place for us within that conception. . . . Fabricated elections will weaken us, we are selling out. The consequence of fabricated elections is sovietisation of Poland.[207]

The Church and the Catholic camp II

THE development of a generally cool but correct relationship between Church and State authorities during 1945 has been described above.[208] In spring 1946, as the Communists commenced hostilities against the PSL in earnest and Mikołajczyk took up the challenge, relations between the government and the Church began to show some strain. This was to be seen in a gradual shift in the Church's position, from neutrality towards tacit support for the opposition, and increasing pressure from the Communists in an effort to stop this trend.

This political tension in the country was discussed by the bishops in conference at Jasna Góra on 22–24 May. In the communiqué issued afterwards, the bishops roundly condemned the lawlessness and violence, the responsibility for which they placed implicitly, though unmistakably, on the Communists.[209] Shortly afterwards Borejsza sent a representative to Hlond to warn him that the party viewed the communiqué as a 'declaration of war' and that reprisals would be taken. But this threat seems to have been designed chiefly to lever Hlond into making a statement favourable to the government or at least publicly visiting Bierut as president before the referendum. Hlond refused to do either.[210] Instead, on the very eve of the referendum, a letter from the Pope containing a veiled attack on Communism was read out in the Polish churches.[211]

Once more the Kraków Catholics showed a rather more conciliatory attitude than Hlond and the Church as a whole. Their reluctance to assume a position of fundamental oppositon or negation towards the new political order was expressed in an article by Jerzy Turowicz published in *Tygodnik Powszechny* on 7 April.[212] Popiel and his followers in the leadership of the Party of Labour took much the same view. In February the SP executive had called for a compromise between Mikołajczyk and the Democratic Bloc and in May at the congress of the Kielce organization of the SP he delivered a sharp attack on Mikołajczyk for not facing up to political realities and accepting the logical consequence of his return to Poland by joining the bloc.[213] Popiel seems indeed to have seen his role in the party, and of the party in the country, as essentially that of a mediating force.[214] However, the tough line of the episcopate, the increasingly violent trend of Communist policy and the strong sympathy for the opposition amongst the SP grassroots made this line very difficult to maintain. In March Popiel told the British he was on the verge of dissolving the party, lamenting that 'it was quite impossible to carry on. It really was a delusion to think otherwise.'[215] In May the leaders closest to the Church raised once more the question of disbanding the party.[216]

Instead, according to Bujak under pressure from the episcopate,[217] the SP – or more accurately the Popiel faction – moved over to Mikołajczyk's oppositionist position. On May 21–22 the party executive adopted a formula advising its supporters to vote the same way as the PSL in the coming referendum, while stating that a pro-government vote (three times 'yes') was also admissible. The *Zryw*-ites concurred for fear that otherwise the party would be dissolved.[218] This formula failed to prevent an open split between Left and Right during the campaign. While Popiel and his supporters campaigned for a 'no' vote to question I, the Communists,

Socialists and *Zryw* faction endeavoured to swing the party back to its former neutralist line. At a meeting of the national executive on 25 June only Popiel's casting-vote defeated a motion censuring the activities of the Right, after Józef Gawrych, hitherto a supporter of Popiel,[219] had gone over to *Zryw*.[220] The *Zryw* faction refused to accept this result and on the eve of polling issued public calls for a pro-government vote.

Complicating the dispute within the SP over referendum tactics was the forthcoming party congress, for although the *Zryw* faction had momentarily captured control of the national executive, no more than 5–10 per cent of congress delegates were on their side.[221] The expansion of the SP in early 1946 had been less selective than the *Zryw*-ites had hoped and been based chiefly on the old Christian Democratic strongholds, Silesia and Kraków, rather than the Christian labour tradition of western Poland where the Left was rather stronger.[222] The Communists tried to correct this trend by arresting activists from the Right of the party,[223] but at one provincial conference after another the rank and file demonstrated their support for opposition to the government and weakened the *Zryw* group.

The conflict came to a head immediately after the referendum. The Communists were reeling from the unexpected size of their defeat and their united front with the Socialists was strained to breaking-point. Simultaneously they were faced with the prospect of a takeover of the Party of Labour by the Right at its Congress due to be held on 19–20 July. It is worth noting that *Zryw* was prepared to accept a compromise which would have given Popiel a clear majority on the executive while leaving them with 40 per cent of the seats. They would not accept Popiel's offer of 25 per cent and demanded instead a postponement of the Congress and purge of the membership.[224] Szwalbe's attempt to mediate resulted in a meeting of the two factions with himself and Zambrowski on 13 July at which Szwalbe appealed to Popiel to accept the terms offered by *Zryw*, promising at the same time a relaxation of the authorities' measures against the SP. Zambrowski, speaking 'brutally, but for the first time sincerely', took a tougher line. According to Popiel,

> he defended the methods used against the SP. They were in present Polish realities proper and necessary. After the experience with the PSL – Zambrowski said, we cannot allow the unhindered growth of a second political party, all the more dangerous than the PSL in that it rested on a unified ideological position. These words clearly showed and I understood them to mean that the other side had also had enough of this bizarre 'co-operation'.[225]

No agreement was reached and the following day the takeover of the party by the *Zryw*-ites took place, the Congress was declared postponed and several of Popiel's supporters, though not Popiel himself, were suspended from the executive. After the protests of the Right had been rejected by the prime minister and the KRN, it announced on 18 July that the party had suspended its activity. Within a month the local organization of the party had been largely disbanded, while the minority set about salvaging what they could.

Mikołajczyk claimed that the elimination of the SP was a rehearsal by the Communists for their coming attack on the PSL.[226] This is unlikely. The Communists had a clear interest in maintaining the existence of a broadly neutral Catholic party in which sympathetic elements had a strong influence. The dissolution of the SP followed its marked shift towards the opposition and many weeks of pressure to force it to resume its initial unaligned stance. The Communists were even ready to concede Popiel a majority on the executive to achieve this. As it was, the bridge which the government bloc had established with the Catholic camp was now closed. In September the bishops bluntly rejected the claims of the *Zryw*-ite SP to represent Catholic opinion[227] and although it survived as a separate organization until 1950 it remained isolated and fissile with nothing like the popular base of the party in 1945–6.[228] The Socialists certainly felt a mistake had been made and in September 1946 and again in spring 1947 encouraged Popiel's attempts to form a new Christian Party of Labour.[229] The root cause of the decision of the SP Right seems to have been their clear preference by mid-1946 for withdrawing from politics rather than compromising on the oppositionist character of their party.

This seems to have suited the Church which, as polarization took place in the country, found it increasingly embarrassing to be identified with a particular party so closely. If the SP resumed a middle position the Church would be seen as distancing itself from the opposition. If, on the other hand, the SP allied itself with the PSL, the Church would be drawn into open confrontation with the Communists.[230] In fact, the rift between the Church and the government grew wider in any case as the elections approached. Church statements criticized the government and gave tacit support to the PSL. At the third post-war conference of the episcopate at Jasna Góra on 8–10 September, the bishops repudiated the pro-government rump of the SP and issued a proclamation on the elections which reasserted the right of the episcopate to involve itself in public affairs, forbade Catholics to join parties whose principles or activities were in conflict with Christian teaching, and told the faithful not to vote for 'those lists whose programmes or methods of government are inimical to common sense, the well-being of the Nation and the state, Christian morality or the Christian view of the world.'[231] The Left-wing parties saw the declaration as a victory for Hlond's tough policy towards the government.[232] This did not deflect the Communists from their cautious line towards the Church. Despite personal attacks on Hlond,[233] the party carefully avoided being drawn into open conflict with the Church and continued to cultivate its remaining links with Catholic circles throughout the election period – to little effect, as we shall see.

10 'A mighty lightning offensive', September 1946 to spring 1947

Mobilizing the party–State apparatus

DESPITE THE SOCIALISTS' last-ditch efforts to keep open the possibility of a deal with Mikołajczyk, in September the Communists pressed ahead with preparations for the 'mighty, lightning offensive' which Gomułka had called for two months before. Demonstrations held on 8 September to protest against Byrnes' Stuttgart speech served as a symbolic opening shot, and in Warsaw ended with a mob sacking the offices of *Gazeta Ludowa*, the PSL's daily newspaper.[1]

On 18 September the Central Committee of the PPR met in plenary session for the last time before the elections to consider the general political situation. Only fragmentary extracts from the speeches made at the Plenum have been published. However, it is clear from these and the resolution which was carried that the discussion centred on two main issues: relations with the PPS, which will be discussed in the next section; and the campaign to crush the PSL and the underground in the run-up to the elections.

The Central Committee presented the divide between the Democratic Bloc and the PSL in stark terms:

> the elections must settle the great historical confrontation between progress and backwardness; between democracy and fascism; between the road leading to a great and prosperous Poland with its frontiers resting on the Oder Neisse and the Baltic, and the road of political recklessness and national catastrophe; between the sacred rights of working men, the peasant and the white-collar worker, and the base interests of parasites, profiteers, speculators, ex-landowners and dispossessed monopolists.[2]

The resolution reaffirmed the party's commitment to a limited form of pluralism, offering:

> complete freedom for the opposition parties if in defending their principles and distinctive programmes they separate themselves from and combat actively all forms of fascist ideology and methods, as well as every kind of illegal struggle or terror.[3]

There would be no place for the PSL, which the Plenum claimed had 'placed itself outside the democratic camp' and was 'tightening its alliance with the fascist underground and the fascist emigration'. In a clear reference to the coming offensive, the Central Committee warned that:

> Polish democracy has proved that it has sufficient strength to thwart the reaction's every move. PSL calculations on obtaining dominance in Poland by allying themselves with the underground and getting help from their foreign protectors will meet with the determined resistance of the masses and will be completely crushed.[4]

The election campaign would require 'the mobilization of all the constructive forces in the nation' to 'crush and shatter the centres of the reaction in Poland'.[5]

In the view of the party leadership there was a clear cleavage between the 'democratic camp' on the one side, and the 'reactionary camp', including the PSL, on the other. Great stress was placed on the linkage between the PSL and the underground and the association of the PSL with espionage and subversion. One of the main tasks of the *aktyw* in the period leading up to the elections would be 'to reveal the true face of the PSL: in reality the ally of Anders and the bands of the fascist underground'.[6] PSL branches were described as often being no more than a legal cover for the activity of the WiN and NSZ.[7] The Plenum discussed ways of giving publicity to the alleged connections between the PSL and the illegal opposition, including the use of political trials, and the identification of the two was a constant theme of trials in the following months.[8] Much less emphasis than in the past was placed on the presence of democratic elements in the PSL which might be won over.[9] The leadership's clear message to the party rank and file was to deal with the PSL in the same indiscriminate and repressive way as it was dealing with the armed underground. In effect, the party was acknowledging that it had been unable to isolate the reaction and that its offensive would embrace not only the diehard anti-Communist Right, but also wide sections of Centre and Left-of-Centre opinion grouped within and around the PSL.

In this situation, the crucial strategic question was whether the internal resources at the disposal of the PPR would be adequate to the task of neutralizing the opposition and managing the elections without provoking serious international repercussions or a political destabilization at home in which the Russians might decide that they had to intervene directly. As Bierut put it:

> We are living through critical times when old political structures die away and new ones come into being . . . the task of politicians and leaders is to steer the state in a way which will spare the nation from unnecessary loss and reduce the unavoidable conflict to a minimum.[10]

In late 1946 it was still an open question whether the Communists would be able to achieve this. The fact that they did was due principally to the successful mobilization of the party organization and the organs of the State under Communist control, particularly the central and local bureaucracy, the army, the militia and the security forces.

The PPR expanded rapidly in the latter part of 1946 and early 1947, and at the same time there was a mass activization of its members to carry out tasks associated with the election campaign. Membership grew from 347,000 in June, to 420,000 in September, to 556,000 in December 1946 and by June 1947 had reached 849,000.[11] As before, organizations in the western and northern territories increased in size faster than those in central and eastern Poland and the proportion of urban workers increased as the party continued to shed its predominantly peasant character of 1944–5.[12]

Motives for joining the PPR were various. It is important not to discount the genuine appeal of the party's programme in radical and Left-wing quarters. The party displayed a vitality and offered a vision in the 1940s which was eroded in later years. Others were drawn to the PPR because it seemed the most effective route to participation in the political, cultural and economic regeneration of Poland.[13] For many others party membership provided an opportunity for social advancement. But these were constant factors that can have played little part in the sudden expansion of the party in the election period. Nor is there any convincing evidence of any spontaneous movement of opinion which could explain the growth. In fact, most new members appear to have joined the PPR not through spontaneous choice, but because material pressures or incentives of one kind or another were brought to bear. In the countryside, for example, party membership was not correlated with differences in size of landownership, but was heavily concentrated amongst peasants and former agricultural labourers who had benefited from the land reform.[14] In the towns strong pressure seems to have been placed on white-collar and manual workers to join the PPR. The personnel supervisors who were attached to most offices and factories to ensure that the more important posts were occupied by government supporters appear to have stepped up their activity before the elections.[15] The British consul in Lodz reported that workers in government-run undertakings had been issued with discharge notices, with the offer of re-employment on condition that they joined the PPR.[16] The rationing system and housing allocations provided other means to persuade people to join the party.

These methods of recruitment were effective, particularly in the towns, and especially amongst office-workers, managers, government employees and the like, as a means of extending the influence of the party and in weakening the sense of solidarity which was essential to sustain the opposition. However, the level of commitment and political education of the recruits was often very low. In 1946 systematic political training of PPR members had hardly begun.[17] The situation was particularly bad in the countryside, where the party remained very weak. Rural cells tended to be little interested in affairs outside their locality and not infrequently members were said to be under the influence of the Church.[18] The expansion of the party was primarily a consequence of its tightening grip on the State and economic apparatus: it did not represent a real broadening of the popular base of the PPR which remained narrower than that of any other Communist party in Eastern Europe.[19]

The election involved an unprecedented mobilization of these members at all levels. A special network of *trójki* (triumvirates) was established within the party at provincial, district and local level to organize the campaign, and all members were required to follow their instructions in the period until the elections. As a rule, one member of the *trójka* was simultaneously the chairman or deputy-chairman of the electoral commission responsible for administering the elections and counting the votes in each area. Another was in charge of the citizens' electoral committees which were established throughout the country, typically to serve a village, a block of flats, a factory or an office.[20] Although the party was unable to establish a full network of *trójki*[21] and often had to rely on cadres from outside to man them (in Kraków province, 1,000 activists were brought in from Silesia to reinforce district committees[22]), the apparatus seems to have been generally effective in securing the party's control over the electoral machinery and ensuring a high level of participation by PPR members in the campaign. The most reliable cadres were appointed to the electoral commissions, of which there were some 5,000 in the country as a whole. These were manned largely, or in some areas, exclusively, by the PPR. Although there were only about a third as many commissions as there had been in the referendum, the numbers of cadres required to staff them was still considerable: over 1,500 in Lublin province and more than 2,000 in Kraków province, for example.[23] The role of PPR members in the citizens' committees was important also. The purpose of the committees was to mobilize the other bloc parties and non-party sympathizers, to organize canvassing and, above all, to make arrangements for open, collective voting.[24] Some 5,000 PPR members in Kraków province, 11,000 in Warsaw city and 19,000 in Upper Silesia sat on the committees.[25] In all, about 200,000 party members took part in door-to-door canvassing.[26]

The party also paid special attention to expanding ORMO in the immediate pre-election period. A Central Committee circular issued in October instructed party committees to assign quotas of members to ORMO in order to increase its overall strength from 70,000 to 150,000 by 1 December. The PPS and SL were also to be asked to provide recruits. Units were to be formed in each town, rural commune and place of work.[27] Although the target strength does not appear to have been reached, 106,000 ORMO reservists were deployed on election day.[28] In other words, some 60,000 party members were placed under arms for the campaign.[29]

The party apparatus in the State bureaucracy was also mobilized to ensure that the organs of central and local government were pitched against

the opposition. Thus, publicity on behalf of the bloc parties was coordinated and distributed by the Ministry of Information and Propaganda.[30]
More fundamentally, the Communists, with the support of the other bloc
parties, made maximum use of their majorities on the KRN and in the
provincial national councils to make certain that the administration of the
elections would be firmly under their control. The electoral law was carried
by the KRN on 22 September by a majority of 306 to 42. Apart from
providing for a distribution of seats which discriminated in favour of the
bloc by over-representing the western and northern territories and
industrial centres where the PSL was less well organized, the law allowed
wide scope for manipulation and malpractice. The main criticisms made by
the PSL were as follows. First and foremost, the administration of the
elections was entrusted to the electoral commissions whose members were
to be appointed by the provincial national councils (and not, as in the
referendum, the district national councils on which the PSL was often
strongly represented).[31] As a consequence, the PSL was almost entirely
excluded from influence on the conduct of the elections.[32] Moreover, the
law did not define the rights of tellers. In practice, commissions insisted
that PSL tellers obtained certificates of good character from the UB before
they were admitted to the count, with the result that in contrast to the
referendum, only a handful of PSL and independent witnesses succeeded
in attending.[33] The reduced number of polling districts facilitated central
control over the count and in rural areas often meant that peasants had to
travel long distances in order to cast their votes. The commissions were
empowered to strike from the register people alleged to have collaborated
with the Germans during the war or to be involved with the underground.
Large numbers of PSL sympathizers seem to have been struck off on these
grounds.[34] These measures and the invalidation of lists of PSL candidates
in ten constituencies (i.e. one-fifth of the total, and all areas where the
peasant movement was particularly active), and the widespread application of open, collective voting on 19 January, ruled out any real possibility
of the PSL winning a substantial number of seats and ensured that the
Communists would have free rein to produce a favourable result.

However, the purpose of the election offensive was not only to frustrate
the electoral challenge of the PSL, but also to undermine the Peasants as an
effective political force. The administrative apparatus played an important
part in this process. From September onwards there was a marked increase
in the use against the opposition of what party historians term
'administrative methods'.[35] These included the arrest or repeated detention
of PSL activists. According to Wójcik, from mid-November PSL
sympathizers were summoned to UB and MO offices on a mass scale for
so-called 'interviews'. Over 100,000 people were estimated to have received
such summonses.[36] The wave of arrests which took place from September
onwards extended, for the first time since early 1945, to the top leadership

of the party. The first major figures to be arrested were Stanisław Mierzwa, vice-president of the Kraków provincial committee, and Karol Buczek, editor of *Piast* and president of Kraków city PSL, on 23 September.[37] By 1 December, according to Mikołajczyk, 22 members of the Supreme Council of the PSL, 7 members of provincial executives, 147 members of district executives and 670 members of commune executives had been taken into custody, along with many thousands of ordinary party members.[38] The PSL press was hit particularly hard. The police operation against it began in autumn 1946.[39] On 25 September the UB raided the press department at PSL HQ, sealing off its offices and confiscating various documents. This action was aimed against the PSL's uncensored internal news sheet.[40] In the following weeks a series of arrests among PSL journalists and a clamp-down by the censor crippled the PSL press.[41]

In addition, bureaucratic means were used to apply pressure on voters to support the bloc, while a purge of the local administration weakened PSL influence and ensured that local government staff worked actively on behalf of the bloc. In Kielce province, for example:

> a series of changes were made at prefectorial and vice-prefectorial level. Prefects were replaced in Stopnica, Włoszczowa, Kielce and Sandomierz districts; a whole range of vice-prefects were also replaced. A school was organised at provincial level to train commune secretaries, with the students drawn from people holding sincerely democratic views and above all from the PPR. They were used to strengthen local government, replacing many of the existing PSL officials who had until then acted as chairmen of the national councils in many communes. These changes, made on the eve of the elections, had a positive influence on the attitude to the Democratic Bloc of the lower levels of the administration. To a large degree, they accounted for the active involvement of the majority of state and local government staff in work related to the elections.[42]

The Communists also tried to reduce or isolate the PSL groups on the national councils,[43] and in at least one district where this proved impossible the entire national council was dissolved.[44] In many areas the local and security authorities simply prevented the PSL from operating in the open as a political party. Internal party meetings were frequently prohibited (PSL public meetings had been banned since spring 1946). District executives were suspended or dissolved in more than a dozen areas after September, most of them in the weeks immediately before the election.[45]

A crucial part in the offensive was played by the army and security forces, especially in the rural areas where the party was weak and the influence of the PSL and the underground most marked. Security operations against the underground were stepped up during the election period and at the turn of 1946–7 the regular army was used as the basis for defence-propaganda groups (*grupy ochronno-propagandowe* – GOP) which were sent into the countryside, ostensibly to campaign on behalf of the bloc and to prevent the armed underground from disrupting the elections.

Between 5 and 21 December 2,300 GOP were deployed and 2,600 between 28 December and 20 January. In all, 62,438 regular Polish army troops took part, supported by activists of the bloc parties, 9,800 KBW troops, 4,600 UB officers, 16,700 militia and 16,200 ORMO reservists.[46]

In reality the role of the GOP was far from purely defensive. They carried out some 850 operations against the underground, during which 341 alleged members of the underground were killed and over 5,000 arrested.[47] Their activities were also directed against the PSL. The GOP were instructed actively to oppose PSL propaganda.[48] The example of Rzeszów province shows what this meant in practice. There the GOP dissolved 75 PSL circles and obtained the resignation from the PSL of 2,555 members, while 129 SL, 6 PPR and 3 ZWM circles were established. In addition, 27 commune and 61 village administrators, as well as 9 other officials, were replaced.[49]

The employment of the regular army on such a scale against the opposition was of considerable political significance. It demonstrated that the PPR's control over a large section of the army (the troops seconded to the GOP represented about 40 per cent of the army's total strength[50]) was much more secure than Mikołajczyk had thought. The army occupied a special place in the hearts of many Poles and its wide involvement in the campaign on behalf of the bloc was of major psychological importance. But above all, the army provided the Communists with the resources to make up for the deficiencies in the party's organization and popular base in the countryside. On their own, the UB and KBW were not strong enough to do this, while the political reliability of the militia was often uncertain. The successful use of the army and the extensive paramilitarization of party members in ORMO enabled the Communists to neutralize the opposition without resorting to extensive direct assistance from the Soviet forces. The Russians were able to keep a low profile throughout the elections. There was no recurrence of the situation of 1944–5 when Red Army and NKVD units were used against the underground on a wide scale. Asked by the British ambassador what part the Russians were playing in the elections, Mikołajczyk spoke only of their role *behind the scenes*, in the security apparatus, where he believed that the number of Soviet 'advisers' had increased and that they were directing the campaign against his party, and in the top echelons of the PPR, which in the shape of Berman was, he claimed, in daily contact with the Soviet ambassador.[51] In his account of the elections published in 1948 he referred to Russians in the security apparatus and the officer corps of the Polish armed forces, but also described the effective and disciplined way the Polish army was used against the PSL.[52] While it is impossible on the present base of evidence to identify clearly the extent of Soviet activity in Poland at the turn of 1946–7, it is apparent that this activity was well concealed. What was evident was the onslaught by the PPR and its Polish resources against the opposition.

The democratic bloc

ALONGSIDE the party-State apparatus, the chief prop of the Communists was the national front, now reduced to the alliance of the four 'Lublin' parties: the PPR, PPS, SL and SD. The September Plenum reaffirmed that the PPR looked to this alliance as the popular base on which to achieve the programme defined in the 1944 PKWN Manifesto and as a major weapon in the coming offensive against the opposition. The resolution declared that:

> the Central Committee will endeavour as before to strengthen the close and friendly co-operation of the 4 parties of the PKWN which have formed a powerful centre for the consolidation of all the democratic forces of the nation. That co-operation is and will be the guarantee of the full realisation of the principles of the July Manifesto, the guarantee of a lasting worker–peasant alliance . . . the Electoral Bloc of the 4 Parties will play a decisive role in the struggle to smash the reaction and in the political stabilisation of the country.[53]

The cornerstone of the bloc was the alliance between the PPR and the PPS. Following the crisis in the united front during the summer, the September Plenum examined relations with the PPS in unprecedented depth. The central importance of the partnership was reaffirmed and 'sectarian and domineering attitudes' towards the PPS (perhaps a reference to the putsch episode) were criticized by Kowalski and others.[54] But although Gomułka stressed the continuity of the party's line on the united front and in particular on the question of the eventual merger of the two parties,[55] the September Plenum presaged the shift in the party's position on the PPS which became clear after the elections. Since May 1945 the Communists had followed a policy of allowing the PPS considerable freedom to develop as a broadly independent mass party exercising – at least formally – joint hegemony with the PPR within the national front. The PPS was seen as a key factor broadening the base of the front and as a vital ally for the PPR in fending off the challenge of the PSL. However, from spring 1946 as rivalry and political differences between the two workers' parties became more pronounced and the Centrist leadership under Osóbka and Cyrankiewicz steered an increasingly independent line as the Matuszewski Left lost ground, the Communists became seriously alarmed at the trend of events in the PPS. The September Plenum noted these developments and concluded that the Socialists' efforts to reach a compromise with the PSL and their demands for parity in the allocation of offices in the state and economic administration constituted an attempt to capture hegemony for the PPS in the democratic camp.[56] The Central Committee appears to have questioned the wisdom of allowing the PPS to develop as a second workers' party in 1944–5. Now the time had come to curb its independence and re-emphasize its junior role in the united front. According to Sierocki, the main points of the Central Committee's assessment were as follows:

Exceptionally favourable conditions for closer co-operation had existed during the period fo the PKWN and the Provisional Government. Later the PPS had grown stronger in part because of the absorption of WRN-ite and right-wing elements. In attempting to obtain support in non-proletarian quarters of society, a partial return to the old pre-war traditions of the Socialist movement had occurred within the PPS. History had shown . . . that the PPS was a nationalist, Piłsudski-ite and anti-Soviet party. It had also been a reformist party, and it still was. Thus for it to gain hegemony . . . would be a 'backward step'. Despite the changes that had taken place in the Polish Socialist movement, it had remained an integral part of European social democracy. As in social democracy everywhere, the Western orientation played a great part in its conception of Poland's foreign policy. In domestic policy, the PPS was inclined to make the greatest possible concessions to the PSL in order to achieve the social reconstruction of the country at the least social cost. In the Plenum's view all of this demanded that the future development of the Polish socialist movement would have to be watched very closely, all the more so in view of the recent confrontation with the united front [i.e. the Matuszewski faction] elements. The Plenum . . . confirmed that the PPS 'was developing into a regressive political force'.[57]

Gomułka seems to have led the attack on the PPS's supposed hegemonistic ambitions, while emphasizing the importance of continuing the alliance, with the Socialists playing second fiddle. Again according to Sierocki, 'particularly severe statements about the PPS were to be found in the speech of the Party's general secretary, Władysław Gomułka. He said that the PPS, not being a Marxist party, was unable to bring about socialism. . . . Therefore the PPS could not exercise hegemony in the workers' movement and would have to be satisfied with the position it had occupied hitherto.'[58]

The objective of a single workers' party was for the first time to be made explicit. The resolution passed at the Plenum declared that:

The strengthening of the united front through joint activity and gradual convergence of the positions of both workers' parties in matters of key importance is a basic objective of the policy of the PPR in aspiring towards the complete political unity of the working class.[59]

The party would in future concentrate its attention primarily on fostering cooperation with the grassroots organization of the PPS 'from below'.[60] A campaign of joint meetings was to be organized with the purpose of weakening opposition amongst the PPS rank and file to the united front. Meanwhile contacts with the leadership would continue and talks would proceed with the aim of reaching a formal agreement on future policy and joint activity. Gomułka warned the Plenum that difficulties could be expected on both fronts. In relation to the campaign of joint local meetings:

we must expect obstruction [from] the [PPS] leadership, but not give up. It will be difficult to agree everything with the PPS. We are now raising the question of making an agreement between the leaderships so that certain matters will be formalised. We will pursue this even though it will require concessions from both sides.[61]

At this stage the shift in PPR policy was felt more in terms of the organizational relationship between the parties than on policy or programme. The Communists continued to proclaim their commitment to the three-sector economic model, the three-year economic reconstruction plan and the multi-party system – all basic tenets of the PPS Centrists' philosophy.[62] In addition the Communists, and in particular Gomułka, publicly associated the PPR with 'the best tradition of struggle for Poland's independence' of the PPS, while sharply criticizing the KPP's record on the same issue.[63] The PPR still hoped to harness the two traditions of the working-class movement but after the September 1946 Plenum the Communists were clear that this process would involve the fusion of the two traditions within a single united party, not an indefinite continuation of the partnership of the two separate parties which had developed over the previous two years.

The Communists' plans to redefine the character and direction of the united front were at odds with the political strategy of the PPS leadership and anathema to many activists. As we have seen, the Centrists had accepted the four-party bloc against the PSL with great reluctance. Though convinced that the united front must continue and anxious to improve cooperation with the Communists, the Centrists aimed, as Hochfeld had put it, to ensure that the PPS would 'enter the new situation as strong a factor as possible, with the greatest amount of power' in its hands. They had no intention of acknowledging the hegemony of the PPR, or of abandoning the claim of the PPS to play an independent and equal role in the government that was formed after the elections. Even as the party was resigning itself to the inevitability of joining the Communists' offensive against the PSL, these objectives were forcibly restated. On 15 September Cyrankiewicz told a meeting of the PPS *aktyw* in Wrocław that: 'The united front . . . the alliance of equal parties, the PPS and the PPR, is the basis of everything that we are building in Poland. Equal means no mutual suspicions, no hegemony, no disloyalty, no dogma of infallibility in either of the parties.'[64] The same day at a huge public meeting in Lodz, Osóbka declared that 'the role of the Polish Socialist Party at the present time is immense, we have taken on our shoulders the burden of raising the banner of national unity . . . the role that the party should play is in the first rank.' Drobner, who also spoke, argued that history had given the PPS 'the right to lead the workers' movement and the camp of Polish democracy'.[65]

The differences of outlook were reflected in the 'pact of unity of activity and co-operation' which was signed by Gomułka and Cyrankiewicz on 28 November. The negotiations which had preceded the pact had been long and difficult.[66] The main problem was the question of hegemony. According to one member of the PPS Supreme Council, the talks had indicated 'that the leadership of the PPR is of the opinion that the PPR is the principal, the leading, the governing party, and the PPS only has to help.'

The draft of the pact proposed by the Communists had covered the joint offensive against the opposition, merger of the PPR and PPS youth movements, and eventual fusion of the two parties. The PPS counter-proposal had presented its position 'strongly, clearly and independently. If the PPS makes its contribution to the economic reconstruction of the country and the consolidation of democracy, then to the same extent the right to govern should extend to the PPS.'[67]

The pact in its final form fell short of the objectives which the PPR leadership had set out at the September Plenum, but extracted important concessions from the PPS in many areas. The PPS reaffirmed its commitment to assist in the offensive against the opposition, undertaking to exert all its strength 'to liquidate the bands of the fascist underground', and to give full support to the security organs in restoring 'calm and the rule of law'. Above all, the PPS accepted the formula that it should 'fight the PSL which has slipped into the role of a legal extension of the reactionary underground'. The PPS also agreed to the principle of 'closer co-operation and joint activity in all spheres of state and social life' and accepted joint party meetings and ideological training. The Socialists were to undertake 'uncompromising struggle against the influence of anti-Soviet and reactionary WRN-ite ideology' within the party. Last, but not least, the Communists secured a reference to eventual amalgamation of the two parties, although no urgency was expressed, and it was implied that a merger would be preceded by a gradual process of deepening cooperation and ideological convergence.

However, the Socialists seem to have got their way on a number of points. Most important, there was no suggestion that the PPR occupied a leading role in the united front and indeed, the principle that 'both parties, as separate, independent and equal political organisms, will respect each others' organisational structure' was given particular prominence. The PPS right to be consulted was embodied in the provision that 'both parties will agree a line on important political and economic issues before any public statements' were made. The Communists reaffirmed their support for the government's moderate economic policy and to the principles of the programme which had been set out in the PKWN manifesto in 1944. Lastly, the two parties pledged themselves to work for the achievement of the worker–peasant alliance. While no mention was made of the SL, the pact specifically stated that the two parties should 'assist the process of secession of real democrats from the PSL' – a reflection of the Socialists' strongly held view.[68]

As well as the declaration of principles in the pact, which was published, the two parties reached agreement on various detailed matters set out in an annex to the pact which was kept secret from the wider party *aktyw*.[69] Under this annex, both parties undertook to agree their electoral tactics, observe parity in appointments to the electoral commissions and apply severe sanctions (including expulsion) against members who did not comply with the terms of the agreement. Disagreements were not to be revealed in public, though in exceptional cases and as a last resort, differences could be indicated by abstention. The parties agreed on the need to ensure that the four-party bloc obtained a decisive majority in the next *Sejm* and decided on a preliminary percentage allocation of seats. In the next government the PPR would nominate the president and the PPS the prime minister.[70] The allocation of certain other portfolios was agreed and the PPS was to have deputy ministers of public security and foreign affairs. The PPR was to receive a vice-presidency of *Społem*, the Socialist-dominated cooperative union. Both sides accepted that the principle of equality should not be interpreted as parity in appointments to posts in the state administration. State officials (including vice-ministers) were to take instructions from their superiors and not from their party. Disputes were to be referred to joint committees of the two parties. The prime minister's right to allocate funds was made conditional on the agreement of the PPR. It was decided to establish joint mediation committees at central, provincial and district levels to sort out disputes between the parties. Finally, they were to cooperate in combating non-union industrial action and apply sanctions against the organizers if they were party members.[71]

Party historians claim that the signing of the pact – and by implication the decision to accept the Communists' electoral strategy – was greeted with approval by the decided majority of the *aktyw* and members of the PPS.[72] But this seems highly improbable. It is most unlikely that the differences of view and the deep mistrust which had existed between the two parties in many parts of the country just a few weeks before could have been dispelled so quickly. Although the pact affirmed the independence and equality of the two parties, the PPS had been forced to give ground to the PPR in a number of important areas, notably on the question of eventual merger. If the degree of active participation by PPS members in the election campaign is anything to go by (an estimated 30 per cent took part),[73] it seems clear that the attitude of the majority of the rank and file to the pact was hostile, or at best apathetic. However, there seems to have been little open effective opposition to the leadership's line. In part this was because the anti-bloc Right of the party had already been outmanoeuvred by the Centrists. The joint meetings organized by the Communists in September and October no doubt helped to isolate the Right,[74] but the main factor seems to have been the activity of the general secretariat under Cyrankiewicz. The powers of this apparatus had been increased in August 1946 when the secretaries of the PPS provincial committees had been subordinated to the general secretariat. Since the provincial secretariats had charge over the party organization at local level, this meant that the entire *aktyw* was brought under central control.[75] The general secretariat used these powers to root out local leaders, both on the Left and the Right, who were critical of the national leadership. In November special delegates from the centre orchestrated the replacement of former-WRN Rightists in the leaderships of Kraków and Rzeszów provincial committees.[76] The biggest purge took place in Upper Silesia where the Right which had captured the leadership at the end of September had maintained contacts with the PSL and resisted joint meetings with the Communists. In mid-November the general secretariat reorganized the provincial committee and installed Tadeusz Ćwik, one of Cyrankiewicz's main lieutenants, to supervise the election campaign.[77] The impotence of the anti-bloc faction in the face of the Centrists' party machine was symbolized by Żuławski's resignation from the PPS in November.[78]

Other critics of the pact agreed to abide by it, while playing down its significance. Drobner, who led the criticism at the Supreme Council of the party on 4 December, argued that 'people are losing faith in the PPS and are saying – you have betrayed us, you have sold yourselves for a ministerial portfolio.'[79] But despite his reservations about joint training and warnings against unification of the parties, except as a long-term goal, he was satisfied that the pact contained little that was new and voted with the majority for ratification.[80] No doubt any activists were persuaded that the pact was the best compromise that could have been obtained in the circumstances and that it was essential to maintain party unity around the Centrist leadership if its strategy of preserving the PPS as an independent, equal partner of the PPR was to have any chance of success.

The Socialists' agreement to the offensive against the PSL and the pact certainly did not imply any retreat from this strategy. Indeed the Centrists' efforts to establish a strong and separate organizational and ideological identity for the PPS were at their most intense in the later months of 1946 and the first half of 1947. Particular attention was paid to associating the party with the historical and patriotic traditions of the pre-war PPS. In November, for instance, mass meetings were held throughout the country to celebrate the 54th anniversary of the foundation of the PPS.[81] The leadership did not miss a chance to point out the contrast between the record of the PPS on the national question and that of the KPP. Thus Osóbka publicly contradicted the view that the PPS had been responsible for the failure of the Left-wing government formed in Poland at the end of the First World War, arguing that much of the blame lay with the Communists 'who had an incorrect attitude to the problem of Poland's independence'.[82] Attempts were also made to define the party's position within the broader context of Socialist theory. The Centrists were anxious to show that their rejection of Western social democracy did not imply acceptance of the sovietization of Poland. In December Rusinek told an International Socialist Conference in Prague that:

> Until a short time ago there were disagreements in the Marxist camp on the question of the route to power. . . . We are familiar with two models and both turned out to be wrong. The first, advocated by orthodox Marxists . . . declared that

the 'dictatorship of the proletariat' is the only correct and the only possible road to socialism. This 'infantile leftist' conception divided the socialist camp. The reformists whose error lay in an excessively mechanistic view of the development of economic relations, gained the upper hand. . . . The reformists were deprived of dialectical thought by fear of the dictatorship of the proletariat and led astray by a falsely conceived legalism. . . . The orthodox communists applied their one formula to every country without regard to the objective conditions of the given country . . . both conceptions . . . were false in the sense of there being only two roads to socialism. For history has shown us a third road, and that third road means for Poland – the Polish road.[83]

For the Socialists the essential feature of the Polish road was the preservation of a substantial degree of individual liberty and political and economic pluralism. The election offensive was viewed as a necessary, but temporary evil. Once the elections were out of the way and the PSL no longer posed a threat to the Left's hold on power, constitutional safeguards would be introduced and the machinery of repression would be wound down. As Hochfeld put it, the task of the new system of government was to 'build up the sphere of freedom and civic liberty, to liquidate . . . the transitional limitation of those freedoms and liberties'.[84]

Table 11. PPS and PPR membership by province at the turn of 1946–7

Province/city	PPR membership (Jan. 1947)[a]	PPS membership (date as shown)
Białystok	6,040	1,600 (Jan. or Feb.)[b]
Gdańsk	17,601	20,237 (1 Jan.)[c]
Kielce	37,558	28,610 (end Feb.)[d]
Kraków	28,563	44,500 (end Jan.)[e]
Lublin	16,071	7,143 (Jan. or Feb.)[b]
Lodz – province	25,762	16,319 (Jan.)[f]
Lodz – city	25,032	23,908 (Jan.)[f]
Olsztyn	11,305	6,027 (end Dec.)[g]
Pomorze	61,061	42,471 (Jan. or Feb.)[b]
Poznań	66,604	43,000 (Jan.)[h]
Rzeszów	9,213	11,417 (end Dec.)[i]
Szczecin	30,971	25,199 (Jan. or Feb.)[b]
Śląsk-Dąbrowa	88,352	67,462 (1 Jan.)[j]
Warsaw – province	42,697	26,563 (Jan. or Feb.)[b]
Warsaw – city	29,034	29,160 (end Dec.)[k]
Wrocław	60,016	45,255 (end Dec.)[l]
TOTALS	555,880	438,871

Sources:

a   PPR. *Rezolucje, odezwy i okólniki komitetu centralnego, i 1946– i 1947* (Warsaw, 1961), 212.
b   PRO, FO 371, 66093/N/6349.
c   S. Przywuski, 'PPS w województwie Gdańskim 1945–48. Powstanie, organizacja i formy działania' *Z pola walki* (1978), no. 1 (81), 166–8.
d   J. Naumiuk, *Początki władzy ludowej na Kielecczyźnie 1944–1947* (Lublin, 1969), 273.
e   K. Ćwik, *Problemy współdziałania PPR i PPS w województwie Krakowskim, 1945–1948* (Kraków, 1974), 192–3, 208.
f   W. Stefaniuk, 'Lodzka organizacja PPS 1945–1948' (Lodz, 1980), 281–2.
g   E. Wojnowski, *Warmia i Mazury w latach 1945–1947 Życie polityczne* (2nd edn, Olsztyn, 1970), 176.
h   K. Robakowski, *Rola i działalność PPS w Wielkopolsce i na Ziemi Lubuskiej w latach 1944–48* (Poznań, 1973), 49–50, 59.
i   E. Olszewski, *Początki władzy ludowej na rzeszowszczyźnie 1944–1947* (Lublin, 1974), 250.
j   H. Rechowicz, *Pierwsze wybory 1947* (Katowice, 1963), 80.
k   B. Hillebrandt and J. Jakubowski, *Warszawska organizacja PPR 1942–1948* (Warsaw, 1978), 80.
l   K.B. Janowski, 'Kształtowanie się jedności ruchu robotniczego na Dolnym Śląsku (1945–48)', *Z pola walki* (1971) no.3 (55), 60.

The main outward sign of the Socialists' campaign to widen their influence and counter-balance the Communists within the national front was the recruitment drive launched in August with the goal of increasing membership of the PPS from 250,000 to 500,000 by the end of 1946 and to 1 million during 1947.[85] In fact, the recruitment effort only began in earnest in October; nevertheless by early 1947 membership had reached almost half a million and by the end of the year was approaching three-quarters of a million. Details of the relative strength of the two parties by province at the time of the elections are given in table 11. The growth of the PPS caused disquiet amongst the Communists who found themselves in competition with the Socialists for members in many industrial areas and suspected that a substantial proportion of the PPS recruits were former supporters of the PSL who now saw the PPS as the best means to oppose the Communists.[86] The drive was to be a major factor in the renewed crisis in relations between the parties after the elections, but it was not until mid-1947 that the PPS called a halt to recruitment on such a mass scale. The PPS leaders believed that their party's role in the election offensive would have major significance both for its own future and for the viability of 'the Polish road to socialism'. They feared that if the national front – and in practice this basically meant the PPR–PPS alliance – proved inadequate as a means of overcoming the opposition, the Communists would resort to repression on a much wider scale and the forced construction of Socialism. If this happened, there would be little place for an independent PPS; the Communists would rest their rule on the security apparatus and a far greater degree of direct Soviet support. This linkage between the maintenance of the Socialist–Communist bloc and Polish self-government lay behind Cyrankiewicz's warning just before the elections that 'the simple truth is that the question of the united front . . . lies at the root of the problem of Poland's independence.'[87] The PPS therefore made concerted efforts to demonstrate its cohesiveness and effectiveness as a political force in the elections, and hence its continuing value to the Communists as a partner. A month before polling day special conferences were organized to instruct PPS local government officials on their duties. The activists were told to cooperate closely with the PPR in accordance with the November pact and to play a full part in ensuring a favourable outcome, by for instance helping to organize open voting.[88] On 6 January the entire party membership was ordered to report to local branches to be allocated tasks for the election period.[89] Non-participants were threatened with severe party sanctions.[90]

However, the mobilization of the PPS was only partly successful. The *aktyw* undoubtedly played a key role in the management of the elections. The PPS representatives on the KRN and the provincial national councils collaborated with the PPR to make sure that the electoral commissions were monopolized by loyal adherents of the bloc. Some disputes occurred where the Communists feared that nominees put forward by the PPS could not be relied upon absolutely,[91] but none of these led to a break-down in cooperation. Despite the provisions of the November pact, the PPS did not generally achieve parity with the PPR on the commissions but whether this was due to the PPR rejecting PPS nominees, or to the PPS being unable to find enough suitable candidates, is unclear. Nevertheless, the PPS role was considerable, and a good deal greater than that of the Communists' other allies. It is claimed that a total of 15,000 Socialists were appointed to the commissions.[92] In areas where the PPS was strong, its share almost matched that of the PPR: in Upper Silesia it had 703 full members (PPR – 848); in Lodz city 308 (PPR – 316).[93] A few local commissions consisted entirely of PPS members: 19 out of 291 in Wrocław province, for instance.[94] Elsewhere the PPS was well represented: in Kielce province it had 26 per cent of commission chairmanships (PPR 54%, SL 20%, SD 1%);[95] in Kraków province 16 per cent of commission members belonged to the PPS (PPR 58%);[96] in Lublin province 20 per cent of members were in the PPS (PPR 68%, SL 10%, SD and non-party 2%);[97] in Olsztyn 22% (PPR 62%, SL 13%, SD 3%).[98] The Communists' control over the electoral apparatus depended on the PPS.

However, the PPS was unable to mobilize the bulk of its rank and file members. Although PPS members appear to have been more active than the SL or SD, and there was a better turnout than there had been in the referendum, in total only about 30 per cent of PPS members seem to have participated in the campaign.[99] In most provinces the PPR achieved a mobilization of between 60–80 per cent of its members.[100] Party historians attribute the difference to the tighter organization and discipline of the PPR,[101] but it is likely that dissatisfaction with the bloc in PPS quarters was also a major factor.

To sum up, the agreement forged between the PPR and the PPS to manage the elections and crush the opposition was unstable. Both parties accepted that harsh measures must be adopted to ensure that power remained in the hands of the Left, but beyond this immediate objective, their views diverged on the role the PPS would play in the 'Polish road to socialism'. The PPS hoped to assure its future influence by making itself the indispensable link between the Communists and the nation. But its contribution in the election offensive, though important to the Communists, was primarily in the bureaucratic sphere, in the electoral commissions, the national councils and the central and local administration. The PPS was far less successful in giving real substance to the national front by rallying mass popular support to the democratic bloc. Indeed, only a minority of its own members responded to the leadership's call to active participation in the campaign.

The SL and the SD were certainly much less important to the Communists as partners than was the PPS. Both were widely regarded, even within the bloc, as appendages of the PPR,[102] with little genuine popular following. Kowalski, the SL leader most trusted by the Communists, complained that in PPS circles the SL was viewed as a 'non-existent party' without support amongst the peasant masses.[103] However, especially from mid-1946, the Communists looked to the SL to provide the rural base of the national front. The PPR did its utmost to foster its expansion. The high degree of PPR intervention in the affairs of the SL and the forced character of the SL's growth is well illustrated by the 'plan of activity' of the PPR committee for Kolo district for September 1946. The committee was to:

> continue to lend assistance in organising SL circles. . . . Call a conference of SL members on 20 September for the purpose of electing a District Committee of the SL. Man this meeting with our members . . . sort out the matter of the local headquarters between the SL and the PSL. . . . Arrange for PSL members at the local level to go over to the SL.[104]

The campaign to expand the SL seems – on paper at least – to have had a significant effect in the period preceding the elections. By late 1946 it is estimated to have had 200,000 members, about the same number as in 1945 before the PSL was formed.[105] Much of the growth appears to have taken place amongst the settlers in the western territories. Membership of the SL in Lower Silesia was said to have jumped from 20,000 in August to 52,000 in January,[106] and in Upper Silesia from 4,800 in October to 25,800 in December 1946.[107] However, the allegiance of many of these recruits seems to have been only formal. In Upper Silesia, the increase in the number of members with party cards was just 144, the others simply 'declared' that they would join,[108] and the SL was able to provide only 71 activists for the 6,600 places on the electoral commissions. The pressure to make such declarations became particularly intense as the election campaign got fully under way. Meetings were organized at which the audience was called on to proclaim publicly that they were leaving the PSL to join the SL.[109] But such growth, generated by the arrival in the villages of army and police units or by pressure on settlers in the western territories who were economically dependent on the government, did little to broaden the base of the democratic bloc. The role of the SL in the election campaign was limited[110] and its membership remained notoriously inactive unless prodded by the PPR.[111] The Communists subsequently recognized that the SL was incapable of winning over many of the peasants they regarded as 'democratic' and after Mikołajczyk's flight they allowed the reconstructed PSL to operate as an alternative rallying point until 1949.[112] Moreover, even where the SL succeeded in recruiting ex-PSL supporters it was sometimes not strong enough to prevent them shifting the party to the Right, leading to tension with the Communists.[113]

The SD was even less of a factor in broadening the national front. It was not a mass party. In 1947 its national membership was only 27,783.[114] Its recruits were largely drawn from office-workers, shopkeepers, craftsmen, with a smattering of teachers and professionals.[115] The party was over-represented in the KRN and the provincial and town national councils, partly because of the relative abundance of well-educated people with administrative skills in its ranks. By the second half of 1946 the liberal-conservative wing of the SD led by Jerzy Langrod and Professor Adam Krzyżanowski, which was strongest in Kraków, had lost out to the staunchly pro-Communist faction.[116] There seems to have been no major opposition to the four-party bloc and Krzyżanowski was amongst those re-elected on the bloc list. Even so, the SD seems to have been able to provide only a few score activists in most provinces during the election campaign[117] and in at least one area some of its members refused to take part.[118]

In addition to the four bloc parties, the PSL *Nowe Wyzwolenie* and the reconstructed Party of Labour were tolerated as legal opposition parties within the national front and indeed in some areas they put forward candidates on the bloc list and were admitted to the national councils, interparty consultative committees and electoral commissions.[119] The attitude of the PPR leadership to these parties was lukewarm. Gomułka, speaking to a party audience, characterized them as 'free marksmen' (*wolni strzelcy*) and stated that the PPR would not campaign against them or 'scare the game away from their field of fire'.[120] But the Communist rank and file were often hostile. The Wrocław provincial committee described *Nowe Wyzwolenie* as a partner for the PPS against themselves and the SL and claimed it would become 'a second PSL, a shelter for reactionaries fleeing before our pressure from the PSL'.[121] In Białystok province SP activists were arrested or beaten up.[122] Nevertheless, *Nowe Wyzwolenie* established provincial and local branches during the autumn in preparation for the elections. Party historians in Poland are agreed that the new grouping made no real impression in the villages.[123] The party won 397,754 votes (3.5%) and 12 seats in the elections. After the elections the PPR lost all interest in *Nowe Wyzwolenie*. The pro-PPR faction led by Tadeusz Rek seceded to the SL in February 1947. In May the Communists admitted that the party 'had no real influence or significance at the grassroots'.[124] Nevertheless, the pro-PPS rump soldiered on until October, when it also joined the SL.

The *Zryw*-ite SP had continued activity after the departure of Popiel and his followers in July despite the open disapproval of the Church. The Communists and Socialists also courted independent Catholic opinion. In November the party press began carrying a number of articles restating the Communists' position of absolute freedom of religion as a *quid pro quo* for the political neutrality of the Church.[125] On 23 November an interview which Bierut had given Ksawery Pruszyński in which he made a clear bid for a *modus vivendi* between Church and State was published, attracting wide interest. Bierut denied any fundamental conflict between the aspirations of Church and State and argued that the Church had failed to respond to the genuine shift in the attitude of the Left in regard to religion and its attempts to reach a 'serious and long-term understanding'. The chief obstacles to such an understanding, he claimed, were the Germanophile tendencies of the Vatican and the use of the pulpit by certain elements of the clergy to make attacks on the government. But he added that the ruling camp was open to discussion on making a new Concordat and was willing to allow a separate Catholic grouping in the next *Sejm*.[126] The pro-government fringe of the Catholic camp led by *Dziś i Jutro* enthusiastically took up Bierut's call for a *modus vivendi*[127] and talks involving Cyrankiewicz, Władysław Wolski, the Communist deputy minister of public administration, Julia Brystygierowa of the ministry of public security and a number of Catholic activists including Stefan Kisielewski, were held on the proposed *Sejm* grouping.[128] At one stage it was suggested that up to 48 Catholic deputies might be elected.[129] However, this initiative seems to have been scotched by Hlond[130] and in the event only 3 independent 'progressive Catholics' were elected on the bloc list. The SP won 17 seats and 530,000 votes (4.7%). But apart from a mild success in Lodz city where it won 29 per cent of the votes and 3 out of the 10 seats, it failed to capture more than a small part of the Catholic vote. This was true even in its strongholds like Silesia and Kraków and despite the fact that in many areas it was the only tolerated alternative to the bloc parties. The results were viewed by the *Zryw*-ite leadership as a setback and sparked off a spate of infighting and ideological clashes within the party which lasted until its disbandment in 1950.[131] The attempts of the majority, led by Stefan Brzeziński, to revive a genuine Catholic labour party on the lines of the former National Workers' Party [132] were frustrated by Widy-Wirski and his followers who saw the role of the SP as no more than a 'transmission-belt' to Catholic tradesmen and artisans. [133] A telling indication of the inability of the SP to find any real grassroots following is the fact that by 1948 three-quarters of its income was provided by the government. [134]

In sum, the political base of the national front at the turn of 1946–7 was little wider than it had been in May 1945. There had been some gains: the PPR had doubled its membership and the PPS had established a genuine mass following. But the growth of the PPR had been concentrated in the cities and the western and northern territories; much less progress had been made in the rural areas of eastern and central Poland. The expansion of the PPS had been accompanied by a weakening of the united front which, though patched up for the elections, was fundamentally unstable. The national front had lost ground too, notably within the peasant movement. The mainstream of the movement which the SL had to some degree represented until the formation of the PSL remained solidly behind Mikołajczyk. Also, links with the Catholic camp had weakened markedly during 1946. The true difference between May 1945 and January 1947 lay not so much in any real broadening of the base of the national front, but in the strengthening of the bureaucratic and coercive resources at the disposal of the Communists: the party apparatus, the security forces and the army, the network of cadres in the central and local administration and in the management of industry and the trade unions, the leaderships of the allied parties and other social and economic institutions. The Communists owed their victory over the opposition neither, as party historiography suggests, to a massive spontaneous shift of popular support to the national front, nor to direct Soviet intervention as many had feared, but above all to the mobilization of the State-party apparatus and to a more limited extent the apparatuses of the allied parties, particularly the PPS.

'The reactionary bloc'

THE Supreme Council of the PSL met on 6 October to discuss the offer of a compromise that was no longer on the table. In his keynote speech Mikołajczyk made light of the expulsion of the PSL from the interparty consultative committee the week before, but made plain his view that a deal was out of the question as long as the Communists insisted on hegemony. He regarded the issue as one of confidence in his leadership:

> I should like to emphasise that at least as long as I am responsible for carrying out the policy of this party, I personally will never sign an understanding which on our part would allow the PPR and its satellites an entirely unjustified majority. You must decide in this matter. If you decide differently, I as a loyal member of the party will submit to that decision, without however taking any further responsibility for the policy of the party. [135]

An attempt by Wycech to keep the question open was overwhelmingly defeated, attracting only 5 votes against 115 with two abstentions (including that of Kiernik).[136] The minority bowed to this decision.

The general tone of Mikołajczyk's speech had been sombre. He warned the council that 'without doubt we have difficult days ahead of us' and admitted that 'in the hearts of some faith in the future had already been shaken'.[137] However, he argued that on balance the results of the PSL's activity had been positive and that it was right to carry on with the policy of opposition:

> The question arises – what next? . . . Do we really tell ourselves that there is no chance? And then what? We know the political results we have obtained; but in the conviction that our activity and contribution remained essential to the interests of the Polish state, we know also that we cannot and must not cease our fight.[138]

The cornerstone of his strategy remained the same. He continued to place faith in the resilience and political indispensability of the peasant movement:

> Is there really no balance on the credit side? There is. There is the most important achievement, namely that we exist, we have survived, we remain active and will endure. There is a second: we are the main object of interest; they hate us and rage at us but they take account of our existence and our position in a great many issues, because it is not possible to jump over or pass by the presence of the peasantry and its representation – the PSL.[139]

The resolution passed by the Council declared that if the party remained united 'the unyielding attitude of the peasant ranks will convince our political opponents of the futility of applying violence and coercion'.[140] Just a month before polling day Mikołajczyk was still hoping that despite the repression the PSL would manage to secure 20–30 per cent of the seats.[141]

He also continued to believe that international pressure and the danger of internal destabilization would constrain the Communists and prevent them from taking effective measures against his party. At the Council he reaffirmed his support for close links with the U.S.S.R.[142] On 10 October he sent a lengthy memorandum to Stalin in a bid to short-circuit the pressure the Communists were placing on the PSL.[143] At the same time he called on the British and Americans to step up economic pressure – pointing out that with economic prospects for the coming year verging on the 'catastrophic' and Soviet aid disappointing, the government would soon be forced to turn to the West for assistance.[144] But these overtures produced little result. Not only did Stalin ignore the memorandum, but the Soviet 'advisers' in the security apparatus were reinforced and Mikoł-ajczyk was forced to recognize that the Russians were not disposed to intervene on his behalf.[145] Moreover, when on 18 December Mikołajczyk delivered a protest against the election malpractices to the three Yalta powers, he was dismayed to discover that at first the Americans would not accept it.[146] The British and Bliss Lane managed to reverse this refusal and a series of exchanges between the Three Powers began, culminating in the Soviet statement of 13 January which bluntly rejected the protest and accused the PSL of involvement with the underground.[147]

Morale in the party fell as the extent of the repressive measures became apparent and as doubts grew if the falsification of the elections could in fact be frustrated. Mikołajczyk himself had warned the party to expect an 'exodus of the intelligentsia from our ranks'[148] and in November toyed with the idea of a change of tactics: a boycott of the poll combined with a peasant strike, in other words a return to the methods employed to oppose the *Sanacja* in the 1930s.[149] In the end, the party executive decided on 8 January to go ahead and contest the elections, boycotting them only in those constituencies where its lists had been invalidated.[150] The party seems to have been sustained in its resolve by a determination to go down fighting and by the fact that it continued to enjoy massive support in the country. For although the PSL had suffered heavy organization losses, political forces which had hitherto occupied a middle position rallied to them as the country polarized between the bloc and the opposition. This process was most apparent within the peasant movement itself where no significant open opposition to Mikołajczyk developed until after the elections. Even party historians admit that the PSL remained strong in the countryside. In Kielce province for instance 'the PSL still had a considerable membership . . . in Ostrowiec constituency its strength in autumn 1946 was estimated at about 15,000 . . . in Radom constituency at about 10,000 . . . the PSL-ites controlled the majority of commune and village administrator appointments in all the constituencies . . . the PSL was a relatively numerous organisation during the election period . . . it still possessed a great many sympathisers in society.'[151] In Lublin province 'despite a weakened organisation the influence of the peasant right on the countryside . . . was still quite large.'[152] In Rzeszów province in January 1947 8 prefects (out of 17), 120 commune administrators (out of 120), 900 village administrators (out of 1,244) belonged to the PSL.[153] The PPR committee in Gdańsk province reported on 19 October that it 'could not yet speak of a crisis in the local PSL at grassroots level'.[154] Although the party's activists were prevented from operating in the open, it seems to have continued activity on a semi-conspiratorial basis in many areas.[155] This concealed network was sufficiently effective to ensure that PSL lists were presented in all 52 constituencies.[156]

The most important ally of the PSL was the Catholic church. The bishops' September declaration calling on the faithful not to vote for parties whose outlook was 'inimical to . . . Christian morality or the Christian view of the world' was followed by a pastoral letter from Hlond on 20 October which, as he told the British, was intended 'to make it quite clear that the voters should vote for the Polish Peasant Party although the

Episcopate do not feel that this party is 100% satisfactory from their point of view.'[157] Hlond's hostility to the formation of an independent Catholic grouping in the *Sejm* seems to have been connected with the desire not to split the opposition vote.[158] In January the bishops issued a sharp rebuke to the *Dziś i Jutro* group for weakening the unity of the 'Catholic front' and trespassing on the prerogative of the hierarchy by publicly supporting the bloc. This was intended as a final warning.[159] Also, despite his personal support for the Oder-Neisse Line, Hlond was unresponsive to government suggestions that he should use the opportunity of a lengthy visit to Rome at the end of 1946 to mediate between the Vatican and Warsaw on the question of recognition of Poland's western frontier.[160] According to émigré sources, Hlond's main preoccupation during his talks in Rome was to make preparations for a new wave of pressure on the Church and possibly persecution which he expected after the elections.[161] The bishops' endorsement of the PSL was accompanied at local level by overt and often active support from the overwhelming majority of the clergy.[162]

The PSL also received support from the Socialist followers of Zygmunt Żuławski who stood as an independent on the PSL list in Krakó city. It was hoped to run independent Socialist candidates in Lodz and Częstochowa too, but the PSL lists in both cities were invalidated.

The PSL's other ally was the underground opposition. For although the party condemned the armed underground and vigorously denied the Communists' allegations that the two movements were linked, in social and political terms there was much common ground between the PSL and the illegal opposition and to an important degree the strategies of each of the movements depended on the existence and activity of the other. The Communists undoubtedly exploited the presence of the underground to justify repression of the PSL, but it is clear that the armed resistance was a major obstacle to the Communists in the small towns and villages, where it gave teeth to the wider opposition movement. Beyond this, the PSL argued that its existence as a legal opposition kept the underground in check and that the suppression of the party would be followed by a violent destabilization of the sort that had occurred in spring 1945. Mikołajczyk told the October party Council that he wished to

> emphasise what even our opponents must recognise, that the existence and sacrifices of the Polish Peasant Party protect Poland from chaos, and maybe from fratricidal struggle, because they sustain the belief of millions of citizens that it is still possible and necessary to resolve political problems through legal means. . . . I fear that the aim of those who call for the banning of the PSL is not the normalisation of relations in this country, but the outbreak of internal disorder so that by bloodshed they can achieve totalitarian power.[163]

There is ample evidence that the underground remained a force to be reckoned with in many parts of the country in the second half of 1946.

More supporters of the government, troops and officials were killed by the armed underground in the summer and autumn of 1946 than at any time since early 1945. One estimate puts the total membership of the underground, including small groups and loosely linked organizations, at approaching 100,000 at the end of 1946.[164] Although full-scale offensive operations by the guerrillas became rather less common as the year wore on, they did not cease.[165] Indeed the presence of the underground remained a major problem for the Communists in the eastern and central provinces. In Kielce province for instance:

> the armed underground sharply increased its activity after the referendum. . . . In July in Pińczów district, it destroyed the offices of 18 commune committees, murdered several Party activists and beat up about 60 others. Even the district committee offices in Pińczów were closed temporarily for fear of terrorist attacks. In Częstochowa district too almost the entire Party organization was terrorized. Commune committees and village circles of the Party did not meet and their secretaries and members . . . went into hiding or sought help from the district committee. The terror of the reaction was particularly evident in Kozienice, Radom and Iłża districts. . . . The head of the agricultural section of the Kielce provincial committee of the PPR wrote that 'in these districts Party members live in fear of their lives and property; they very rarely visit their homes and keep on the move. If the reaction continues to terrorise our members it will be difficult to get them to carry out the duties they will be assigned in connection with the forthcoming elections'.[166]

In Lublin province:

> the organization went through a period of stagnation between April and autumn 1946 in terms of the growth of its membership. In the villages of Łuków district, PPR members continued to conceal their membership of the Party. As a result of underground terror and the inability of the district authorities to organise members who had signed up, there was a complete break-down of contact between the PPR district committee and the rural areas. Many of the most active PPR members fled to the western and northern territories . . . some went into hiding in other provinces; the district committee was in touch with 60 members (out of 230), losing contact with the others for more than a year. A similar situation existed in several other areas controlled by the underground. In response to pressure from Party organizations the provincial committee of the PPR agreed not to send instructors to them in case this would reveal them to the neighbourhood.[167]

Finally, the Warsaw province, the PPR provincial committee reported late in 1946 that:

> From September the activity of the bands has increased, reaching unprecedented intensity. Innumerable attacks, with robberies and assaults are directed against Party members and the public security organs. The attacks have taken on a mass character. For instance in Sokołów and Gostynin districts where they are more and more audacious, e.g. a 30-strong band attacked the town of Wyszków and roamed around it for 24 hours.[168]

Table 12.   Activity of the armed underground, 1946–7

Month	'Terrorist' attacks	Robberies	Total	Government casualties (killed)
Jul 1946	355	569	924	356
Oct 1946	324	890	1214	234
Nov 1946	369	971	1340	271
Dec 1946	316	550	866	117
Jan 1947	213	287	500	179
Feb 1947	195	369	564	125
Mar 1947	–	–	463	104

In the event, the underground did not prove to be a major disruptive factor in the elections.[169] By January 1947 guerrilla activity had declined very significantly (see figure 2 and table 12). Party historians argue that the social base of the movement collapsed as the elections approached. According to this view popular revulsion with 'mass atrocities' committed by the underground, growing support for the bloc and the increased effectiveness of security operations against the guerrillas combined to undermine its hold on the villages and small towns.[170] In fact there seem to have been three main reasons why it was unable to respond to the Communists' election offensive. First, there was in practice little that the underground could do to affect the outcome of the elections, which depended above all on the effectiveness of the Communists' control over the electoral apparatus. Given the presence of the army, security forces and ORMO, it was a relatively straightforward task for the PPR to ensure the polling stations were defended from attack and to control the conduct of the voting and the count. Secondly, the underground seems to have been seriously weakened by the security forces' operations in the period before the elections. Although party historians attribute the upsurge of underground activity in September–November to an 'offensive' by the underground,[171] it seems more probable that many of the incidents occurred as the security forces stepped up their activities. During October and November incomplete figures show that over 2,500 'members of the armed underground' and suspects were arrested, and 344 killed in clashes with security units.[172] The GOPs arrested some 5,000 more and killed 214 in December and January.[173] The losses were particularly heavy in the political and military leadership of the movement. The president of WiN, Niepokólczycki, and 17 other members of the supreme command were arrested on 18 October. A new supreme command under Wincenty Kwieciński was rounded up in early January. WiN networks in the provinces were also devastated by arrests. In Lublin province, 879 WiN members were uncovered in September and October. Amongst those arrested were the deputy-commander and propaganda chief of the province, 2 area, 7 district, 4 subdistrict and 13 local commanders, the commanders of 3 armed units and 19 liaison officers.[174] WiN provincial commands in Bydgoszcz, Katowice, Olsztyn and Białystok were rounded up between September and December.[175] The National Party networks in Kraków, Rzeszów, Gdańsk and Bydgoszcz were broken by arrests in the second half of 1946 and the national leadership was detained in December, bringing to an end the activity of the party in Poland.[176]

These factors and the sheer practical difficulty of conducting guerrilla activity in harsh winter conditions no doubt account for much of the fall-off of violence in December and January. But, thirdly, political considerations were also important. Much of the former AK underground, notably WiN, had seen its struggle as complementary to the legal opposition and had pinned its hopes on the election. Armed resistance was primarily small-scale and defensive in purpose. The *raison d'être* of the movement was not to mount a guerrilla insurrection against the Communists which had no chance of succeeding against such unfavourable military odds, but to sustain the spirit of opposition to the PPR and ensure that the elections were conducted fairly.[177] Even the more Right-wing underground groups which looked to the National Party or the Government-in-Exile were sceptical about the value of widescale armed activity. The command of the military arm of the National Party, the NZW, had unanimously recommended the suspension of guerrilla activity as early as March 1946.[178] The Government-in-Exile was flatly opposed to armed struggle, fearing that the Communists would take advantage of this to provoke an insurrectionary outburst before the elections. In a declaration to the homeland issued in October 1946 it called on guerrilla units to leave the forests. While urging passive resistance, it warned against 'armed action, which in present circumstances can bring nothing except defeat', adding that 'the Polish question . . . is organically linked with the overall political situation of the post-war world. That situation contains within it the seeds of inevitable changes . . . preserve those forces essential for survival.'[179] With the defeat of Mikołajczyk and the consolidation of the Communists' hold on power a large part of the ex-AK left the underground during the amnesty in February–April 1947. But few of them were permanently reconciled to the new order and between 1948–56 many suffered persecution. Those diehards who did not take advantage of the amnesty in some cases continued guerrilla activity into the 1950s; others who believed that conflict between East and West was inevitable thought in terms of conserving their strength for more favourable times.[180]

The decline of the armed underground was not due to any sudden collapse of its social base as the elections approached. The underground remained a major force until early 1947. It was the crushing of the PSL which destroyed the political environment in which its activity had made sense in 1945–6.

The lines on which the country polarized at the end of 1946 were essentially the same as the divide which had existed in early 1945 before the formation of the Government of National Unity. Ranged against the 'Lublin' parties was a broad opposition movement which despite its internal differences was united by its refusal to accept Communist leadership of the government. This movement embraced the mainstream peasant movement, almost in its entirety, the Church and the overwhelming majority of the Catholic camp, the underground remnants of the AK and the National Party and a significant part of the Socialist Party. There is no doubt that in 'free and unfettered' elections the PSL would have secured a landslide majority. As it was, Mikołajczyk lost the struggle for power but ensured that the PPR was unable to rest that power on the broadly-based national front which the Party had endeavoured to create since 1942.

The elections

BY January 1947 the local organization of the PSL had been 'broken, dispersed and paralysed' in many areas. Nonetheless, the party still made its presence felt not only in its rural redoubts, but also in urban centres. In Warsaw, the PSL:

> campaigned vigorously . . . mainly by means of whispered propaganda and gatherings in private apartments and in front of churches. PSL members also distributed a great deal of literature, put up posters and organised public meetings. . . . Clashes between PPR and PSL canvassers were frequent.[181]

In Lublin students of the Catholic University organized a three-day strike which also spread to secondary schools and the secular university.[182] In Silesia where the PSL was unable to distribute leaflets legally it found other means: in Będzin literature was given out in a cinema while a film was showing.[183] In Wrocław province:

> slogans calling [on the electors] to vote for the PSL appeared on the walls of Kłodzko on 17 January . . . leaflets also appeared in Jelenia Góra and Dzierżoniów. The next day more PSL leaflets showed up in Milicz, Lwówek, Trzebnica, Jelenia Góra, Strzelin, Zgorzelec, Żagań and other districts . . . the culprits were not found.[184]

In Katowice in the last week before the election the PSL:

> obtained a couple of lorry-loads of propaganda material and sent out their people to post it up in the centre. The material was put up around the clock. The PPR organised a day and night rota in reply: as soon as a PSL poster appeared it was torn down.[185]

In the countryside the PSL was prevented from campaigning in many districts, but in some it had greater success. In Rzeszów province, for example, it only managed to conduct its campaign on a mass scale in

Krosno, Łańcut and part of Gorlice districts.[186] In Lublin province:

> the PSL was not able to organise mass propaganda in constituencies 16 (Zamość) and 17 (Chełm) at all and essentially conducted individual campaigning only . . . the party achieved wider activity in constituency 18 (Siedlce) where it organised public meetings. A considerable part of the local government administration was drawn into the campaign on behalf of the PSL in this area.[187]

The difficulties which faced the PSL may be illustrated by the experience of the Białystok provincial committee of the Party of Labour, which was regarded as part of the loyal opposition and therefore presumably treated more tolerantly than the PSL itself. Its report to Warsaw on the progress of the election campaign dated 16 January is worth quoting at length:

> Despite immense difficulties, the campaign has developed extremely well and augurs the very best results. The local inhabitants scramble for SP voting cards. On account of the success of our campaign at the local level, hindrance from representatives of the Bloc parties and the security organs has increased. SP posters are torn down or covered up by the ZWM as soon as they are put up and the only possibility that remains is direct leafleting at the doorstep, at markets and in front of churches. In addition, a number of people have been persecuted or given the sack for stating that they are going to vote for the SP list. Among others, engineer Budryk, who although not a party member, said he was going to vote for list number 2, was sacked from the Białystok power station.
>
> Because small businessmen are joining the SP, several craftsmen have been arrested in the past few days, amongst others the President of the chamber of commerce, Krukowski and Wojtasz. It is said that Krukowski has been released.
>
> In addition, on 16 January 1947 while he was giving out the party's eve of poll leaflets in the market place of Wysokie Mazowieckie, several individuals claiming to belong to the UB came up to Włodzimierz Gustyn, inspected his identity card, took him outside the town, took all the party's propaganda and burnt it, after which they beat up Gustyn severely and told him not to show himself in the district again. Besides beating him, they took all his documents. The Provincial Committee has reported this incident to the Military Procurator.
>
> Despite our great success, the Provincial Committee cannot guarantee how the elections will turn out since up to now not one of our tellers has been authorised [to attend the count], so that the Party has no possibility of checking the results of the election.[188]

On polling day, 19 January, the authorities did their utmost to ensure that voting was open. The conduct of the poll in Zory in Upper Silesia as reported by the local circle of the SP was probably fairly typical:

> There were no screens at all in the polling stations. The voting itself took place in full view. Nobody could avoid voting openly. Every voter was spied on by PPR members of the Electoral Commission, Militiamen, army officers etc. . . . the chairman of the Local Commission did not give the envelopes to the voters, but every voter had to place their ballot paper in the envelope which the chairman held in his hand with him looking at the ballot paper they had cast. No one but members of the PPR sat on the Electoral Commissions. If someone handed over a folded ballot paper it was immediately taken out of the envelope and unfolded to see if the voter had voted for a list other than number 3 [the bloc list]. No-one was allowed to fold their ballot paper which had to be placed in the envelope with the number visible.

Tellers were not admitted because the prefect had refused to sign their certificates of good character, despite the fact that the MO had given some of them a positive recommendation. Prefect Suchań did this deliberately so as not to allow any of the other parties' tellers into the polling stations where they could interfere with open voting and witness the count.[189]

The Communists considered that open, collective voting had been one of the most important factors in producing a favourable result.[190] In Kielce province about 90 per cent of the voters were said to have voted this way.[191] In Lublin province the proportion seems to have been between 30–45 per cent[192] and in Rzeszów province an average of 30 per cent chiefly employees of offices, factories and institutions and many villages.[193] According to PSL sources the arrangements made by the bloc for open voting broke down in many parts of the country.[194] There is some confirmation of this in PPR sources. Open voting failed in Kraków, Tarnów and other major towns in Kraków province, for instance.[195] In Rzeszów and Wrocław provinces there were cases of organized open voting for the PSL.[196] In Kielce province, where the PSL boycotted the poll after its lists had been invalidated, the UB estimated that about 10 per cent of the electorate refused to vote. In some areas of the province, however, the entire population stayed at home.[197] But even where the PSL was able to upset the bloc's voting arrangements it was unable to loosen its hold on the count. This ensured that the PSL was unable to repeat the local successes it had achieved in the referendum: in Kraków, for example, the official results gave the PSL-Żuławski list only 27 per cent of the votes.[198] The official returns for the whole country are set out in table 13.

Table 13. Official results of the election, 19 January 1947

	Votes	(%)	Seats
Democratic bloc	9,003,682	(80.1)	394*
PSL	1,154,847	(10.3)	28†
Party of Labour	530,979	(4.7)	12
PSL *Nowe Wyzwolenie*	397,754	(3.5)	7
Others	157,611	(1.4)	3‡

TURNOUT 89.9%

* PPS 116; PPR 114; SL 109; SD 41; SP 5; PSL *NW* 5; others 4.
† Including Z. Żuławski, elected as an independent socialist.
‡ Progressive Catholics

Sources: W. Góra, *Polska Rzeczpospolita Ludowa 1944–1974* (Warsaw, 1974), 219; S. Kuśmierski, *Propaganda polityczna PPR w latach 1944–1948* (Warsaw, 1976), 252.

How far the real results of the election, let alone the votes that would have been cast in 'free and unfettered' elections, differed from the official returns is impossible to say. PSL tellers witnessed the count through to the end in only about 100 polling districts. In some 1,100 more information was obtained from other witnesses. According to these data, 68 per cent of the votes were cast for the PSL and 22 per cent for the bloc.[199] At all events, the official returns could not change the fact that the popular base of the Communist camp remained much narrower than the party had hoped when it embarked on the national front strategy.[200] But neither could the PSL figures alter the reality that the elections marked the consolidation of Communist rule for decades to come.

'The new stage'

THE aftermath of the election confirmed that the struggle for power in Poland had been settled, albeit at the cost of alienating the great majority of PSL supporters from the national front. Mikołajczyk at first refused to accept defeat, rejecting suggestions from the PPR and PPS that he should leave the country[201] and persevering with his policy of uncompromising opposition to the new government. The majority of the party stood with him. The PSL supreme council endorsed this line when it met on 1–2 February, declaring that the new order was illegal and temporary.[202] Mikołajczyk and his followers in the *Sejm* assumed a position of outright opposition to the government, warning that the country was ungovernable without the PSL and that the political tensions and economic difficulties which had been fuelled by the elections would soon propel Poland into 'indescribable chaos' and 'anarchy'.[203]

But Mikołajczyk's strategy was in ruins. The PSL's protests over the conduct of the elections were ignored by the authorities. The reaction of the West to the results was confined to some mild economic reprisals and formal protests over the non-fulfilment of the Yalta agreement. The widespread belief – encouraged by Mikołajczyk – that the Great Powers would intervene decisively on his behalf was rudely disappointed. In fact, the West abandoned Mikołajczyk without ceremony. The British broke off all contact for several months. When Gainer, the new British ambassador, met Mikołajczyk in May, he admitted his discomfort:

> whichever way you cut it, we have in effect inevitably dropped Mikołajczyk since the elections. This of course we did deliberately first because we wished to avoid embarrassing Mikołajczyk, and secondly because it seemed more politic from our own point of view.[204]

The PSL had reaffirmed its commitment to close relations between Poland and the Soviet Union,[205] but the elections had made it perfectly clear that the Russians had no further interest in coming to terms with Mikołajczyk.

The party continued to operate legally, despite the fact that much of its local organization had been dissolved or driven into semi-conspiracy. The leadership seems to have hoped that it would be possible to preserve the basic core of the party organization until circumstances improved or a crisis developed which would force the Communists to recognize that they needed the PSL. However, despite serious economic difficulties in early 1947,[206] the political situation was characterized by stabilization, not crisis. In June the British Embassy reported that Poland had 'seemed calmer in the last three months than at any time since 1945'.[207] The upsurge of political violence which the PSL had warned would be the inevitable consequence of its suppression did not take place. As we have seen, underground activity tailed off after the elections; where it continued the security forces were well able to keep it in check. The PSL itself was allowed little opportunity to regroup the opposition. Attacks by the Communists on the party made its continued functioning as an independent centre of opposition virtually impossible. The party press was tightly censored, in the countryside branches were disbanded, premises closed and records destroyed, while many leading activists were under arrest.[208]

Moreover, the party was seriously split over strategy. At the February supreme council Niećko, Wycech and Banach, supported by a quarter of the delegates, demanded that the PSL should come to terms with the new regime to salvage what it could of the influence of the peasant movement. The move was defeated but the minority, refusing to bow to the decision, organized themselvs into a faction known as the *PSL-Lewica* (PSL-Left) which began to publish its own newspaper, *Chłopi i Państwo*. The rebels represented a genuine current within the peasant movement, drawing their supporters mainly from its economic, social and educational wing which was suffering as the political wing moved further and further into opposition. In March the leading rebels were expelled and in following months more expulsions took place. The Leftists carried their campaign to the rank and file of the party, but despite the credentials and record of their leaders, seem to have encountered great difficulty in breaking down the loyalty of the grassroots activists to Mikołajczyk's hard line.[209]

The flight of Mikołajczyk from Poland with American and British help on 20 October 1947 brought an end to the opposition activity of the PSL. The party remained in existence until 1949 under the leadership of the Leftist group which assumed control of the party organization and press immediately after Mikołajczyk's departure. The Communists hoped that the 'reborn PSL' would help to make up for the deficiences of the SL as a vehicle for winning peasant support and extending the government's influence in the countryside, but little was achieved. Some leading figures in the PSL who had not hitherto openly opposed Mikołajczyk, such as Czesław Poniecki, president of the Kielce provincial organization, Andrzej Witos and Kiernik (who returned from a visit to the USA to resume the party chairmanship) threw in their lot with the new executive. But evidence on how far the rank and file followed their lead, though very thin, suggests that most members stood aloof from the new organization. In Kielce province, for instance, PSL membership in spring 1948 was just 2,300 – compared with 47,000 two years earlier.[210] In Olsztyn membership in late 1948 was one-tenth of that in late 1946.[211] In Poznań, where at its peak the PSL had had between 40,000 to 70,000 members, by early 1949 it had just 5,000.[212] In the latter case, as Z. Hemmerling admits, 'despite the generally favourable attitude of the administrative authorities to the reborn PSL, organizational work did not produce the results expected. The reason for the lack of confidence was the fact that a dozen or so activists of the former PSL were still in prison.'[213] Another factor was the suspicious attitude of local Communist and SL activists, who despite central policy obstructed the revival of the PSL.[214] After two years of existence when the 'reborn PSL' was merged with the SL to form the United Peasant Party (*Zjednoczone Stronnictwo Ludowe* – ZSL) in November 1949 its verified membership was only 25,600.[215]

In the countryside the influence of the PSL opposition remained strong despite the election defeat and the suppression of party activity. A telling indication of the failure of the national front to generate any fundamental shift in allegiances at grassroots level was the way that PSL supporters continued to dominate the rural local government apparatus long after the party organization had ceased to function. In PSL strongholds it took two years for the Communists to establish a grip on the lower-level national councils. In April 1947 special commissions were attached to district national councils to carry out a purge.[216] In November, Warsaw issued a new circular complaining that commune councils were still overloaded with Mikołajczyk supporters, rich peasants and Right-wing 'independents'. The circular gave detailed instructions on how to expel such elements and ordered the formation of special party 'triumvirates' to reorganize the councils, adding that in communes where 'there are no Party members at all', a triumvirate from a neighbouring commune should carry out the purge.[217] H. Słabek concludes from a study of the representation of the various parties in village local government that despite its losses during 1947, the PSL remained a significant force until at least early 1948. In Kraków, even then it had 51 per cent of village administrators; in Lublin, 29 per cent, in Warsaw, 21 per cent, and, as Słabek points out, this index to some degree underestimates the influence of the PSL. It was in spring 1948 that the PSL was finally dislodged from the village councils.[218]

The liquidation of the peasant opposition left a political vacuum in the countryside which the Communists, SL and 'reborn PSL' were unable to fill. The PPR lacked any grassroots organization in much of rural central and eastern Poland. As late as the end of 1948 PPR cells had been established in only 45 per cent of villages; in Białystok province 85 per cent of villages had no party branch.[219] The SL remained weak and inactive. In September 1947, by which time the PSL was no longer a competitor, the paid-up membership claimed by the SL was about 180,000 and two years later the SL contributed just 230,000 members to the ZSL.[220] Considering the inducements offered to join, this was a far cry from the 500,000 to 800,000 members belonging to the PSL at its peak. The great majority of PSL supporters refused to compromise, replacing the active opposition of 1945–6 with passive disengagement from politics. A few weeks after the elections Zambrowski admitted the problem in terms which laid bare the deep gulf between the party and rural opinion:

> despite the defeat of the reaction and the PSL in the elections, the seeds of their ideology still weigh on the consciousness of the peasant masses. Distrust of the working class, political separation from the town, unwillingness to contribute through contingents to the reconstruction of the democratic state, a selfish and vegetative attitude to economic problems, apathy and hostility towards the momentum for reform of the progressive forces of the nation, suspicion towards the political ideas of peace and democracy – all these and similar failings disseminated by the PSL in the countryside will exert their influence on the outlook of the peasant masses for a long time to come.[221]

The brittle character of the agreement made between the PPR and PPS in November 1946 became obvious after the elections. As we have seen, the PPS viewed the election offensive as a historical necessity, justified in order to avoid what it regarded as the potentially disastrous consequences of a PSL victory. With the elections out of the way and the struggle for power resolved, the Socialists believed that the government camp should resume its efforts to win over a broad base of popular support for Socialism by offering a moderate and pluralistic economic and political programme and relaxing the exceptional repressive measures that they had deemed necessary during the elections. In essence, the PPS favoured taking up again the broad national front strategy where it had been left off in late 1946.

In the post-election discussions of the Polish road to Socialism the PPS argued that it should proceed in broadly evolutionary fashion on the basis of popular consent. Though rejecting classical parliamentary democracy, the Socialists proclaimed the strengthening of social control over political and economic institutions and the safeguarding of the rights of the individual *vis-à-vis* the state as fundamental features distinguishing the 'Polish road' from the dictatorship of the proletariat.[222] In the economic sphere the PPS stood by the three-sector model in which the private and co-operative sectors would play a major part alongside state enterprise. The road to Socialism would be determined, but gradual. Work should begin on laying the foundations 'at the quickest possible tempo, but that tempo should not be achieved at the cost of *excessive* [original emphasis] social effort, of some kind of new revolutionary upheaval, of demands beyond the capacity of the present generation.'[223] The fundamental condition for the construction of Socialism was that

> the majority of the population wanted it and that it was achieved in a way that suited its wishes, traditions, way of thinking, cultural relations and so on. In other words, we do not aim to repeat the course of the Russian revolution, which for Poland would be incorrect, for Poles would be unsuitable, and – what is more important – in the historical circumstances of today would be inapplicable.[224]

In Socialist eyes, the role of the national front and of the PPS in particular was, as before, to secure the active support of the widest possible section of society. The government camp should welcome openly all those who were prepared to work for the reconstruction of Poland on 'democratic' lines, with party affiliation and ideological allegiance very much a secondary consideration. Hochfeld expressed this attitude when he wrote that:

> the role of non-party citizens, who work and think honestly – even if sometimes critically – must increase . . . we need the active participation of all citizens.[225]

As for its own role, the PPS stood for strict observance of the November 1946 'unity of activity' pact, emphasizing that co-operation should be on an equal basis and that each party should respect the independence and organizational integrity of the other. The Socialists reaffirmed their commitment to eventual unification with the Communists, but insisted that this had to be preceded by a gradual – and bilateral – process of deepening collaboration and ideological convergence. It would be 'a long-term process' which 'could not be by-passed artificially' or 'accelerated by any kind of pressure'.[226] In sum, the PPS leaders saw no reason to modify in any major way the general strategy which they had pursued consistently since the end of the war and which for much of that time the Communists had also proclaimed.

However, the Communists did not contemplate a return to the broad national front of mid-1944 or mid-1945. The party's evolution away from this approach towards the use of force had been a response to its inability to undermine the opposition by non-coercive means. The Communists were acutely aware that the election offensive had not solved this dilemma. They rejected the Socialists' view that, as Gomułka put it

> the electoral victory of the democratic bloc has automatically solved all the problems of the further construction of People's Poland; that the working class and democratic government are no longer threatened by any danger; that the reaction in Poland has disappeared, or at least has been so weakened that its existence is hardly to be seen; that in short the elections have solved the problem of class struggle in Poland.[227]

Force – 'the class struggle' – was essential, for the opposition in spite of its setbacks was still a real threat to the new order:

despite its electoral defeat, the reaction continues to represent a serious danger to the people's power and with favourable circumstances could rapidly recover its strength . . . any underestimation of the strength of the reaction and its potential by party organizations and the state apparatus should be regarded as harmful.[228]

This sense of the insecurity of the foundations of the new government in terms of popular support, shaped the strategy of the PPR as it crystallized in 1947. The strategy was in essence a continuation and development of the aggressive, hardline stance of 1946, applied to the tasks of eliminating the influence of the reaction in society and preparing the ground for the 'Polish road to Socialism'. The party's principal task was to press on with the campaign it had launched in September 1946:

to mobilize all the parties of the democratic bloc for the further march forward on the road to People's Democracy, to the consolidation and development of our social system. . . . After the victory, after the destruction of the enemy, our party must not rest on its laurels since this would give the enemy the opportunity to regenerate its strength.[229]

The Communists still claimed that the new order rested on a broad front of workers, peasants, working intelligentsia and, to a limited extent, craftsmen.[230] In practice, however, they looked to the State apparatus and the party to drive Poland towards Socialism. Less and less emphasis was placed on the national front. This is not to say that the Communists abandoned the national platform. The Polishness of the PPR was strongly underlined in 1947. But the stress was on the party itself as an active, disciplined, ideologically-committed movement which would be able to carry the Polish revolution forward despite its limited support amongst the nation as a whole. The priority was no longer to draw forces outside the democratic bloc into the government camp, but to ensure that the zeal of the bloc parties was not diluted by ideologically alien elements and to break the influence of such forces in society.

The central role which the Communists expected the State apparatus to play in the building of Socialism was made very clear in the exchanges between the two workers' parties over the character of the 'Polish road' in the months following the elections. In referring to the State apparatus both sides had in mind, principally, the 'apparatus of state coercion', in other words the security forces.[231] Replying to Hochfeld's call for 'institutional checks' on the power of the state bureaucracy, Roman Werfel stated the party's view that, for all the differences between the 'Polish road' and the classical marxist-leninist path to Socialism:

the fundamental question for the victory of the working class remains the problem of breaking up the old bourgeois apparatus and putting in its place the workers' own apparatus – or in countries such as Poland – a State apparatus of all the common people (ogólno-ludowy) which will defend the people's power against every attempt to overthrow it.[232]

Far from limiting the state, Werfel declared that:

we must strengthen, expand, improve and make more efficient the State apparatus
. . . we must not do anything which might weaken or undermine it, or reduce its
significance.[233]

As for the danger of the bureaucracy losing contact with the people, Werfel
argued that this was not inherent in the nature of the State, but arose from
the human and ideological vestiges of the old bourgeois order. It would
cease to be a problem as the old ideology was rooted out and cadres drawn
from the working classes were drafted in.[234] In the meantime it could be
combated 'only on the basis of strengthening the apparatus of the people's
state';[235] 'institutional checks' would be positively harmful.[236] On grounds
both of theory and of practical politics, the Communists saw a security
apparatus, powerful and unfettered (except by party control), as
indispensable.

The other pillar of 'People's Poland' would be the party. This would not
be the PPR of 1946, but the new united party formed from the merger of
the PPR and the PPS. The April 1947 Plenum identified the relationship of
the two parties as the key factor in Poland's development and initiated
campaigns to prepare the PPR to accommodate the PPS and to break down
resistance within the PPS to 'organic unification'. After the Plenum,
recruitment to the PPR was reined back and a verification and vetting of
the existing membership was carried out.[237] The declared aim was to
transform its following 'from a party of PPR sympathisers into a party of
PPR members; moving the focus from indices of numerical growth to
qualitative criteria'.[238] At the same time the Central Committee launched a
major programme of political education designed to 'strengthen the
ideological backbone' of PPR members, and in particular to find and train
potential cadres to reinforce the party *aktyw*.[239]

Initially, the Communists' pressure on the PPS to make a serious start
on the process leading to merger met with fierce opposition from the
Socialists. The PPS stand led to a serious crisis in relations with the PPR
during May and June 1947, many of the details of which remain unclear.
As Holzer has written, it is difficult to say what happened behind the
scenes during these weeks. Confidential discussions took place between
the two party leaderships and within the PPS, while the pro-Communist
Left of the PPS, led by Matuszewski, was reactivated and began
publishing its own journal. As in 1946, it seems that the PPR was
threatening the PPS Centrists with replacement by a more compliant
leadership team. In this situation, at the end of June 1947, the Centrists
retreated. Though retaining control of the party and reiterating their
commitment to civil rights and the rule of law, they passed a resolution
affirming that 'the path of the PPS runs only on the left' and ruling out
any alternatives to the united front with the Communists. They also
agreed to a purge of the PPS membership and joint meetings with the
PPR at all levels.

After June 1947, resistance within the PPS to merger with the Communists was greatly weakened. The party leaders saw only two possible courses: a doomed confrontation with the Communists or gradual capitulation to their demands. The party virtually entrusted its fate to Cyrankiewicz, who was regarded as the man likely to play the PPS's few remaining cards with the greatest skill. Cyrankiewicz manoeuvred to defer the merger as long as possible. In his keynote speech to the 27th Congress of the PPS in December 1947 he declared that 'the PPS was, is and will be necessary to the Polish nation' and the delegates continued to assume that no early merger was likely.

However, against the background of deteriorating East–West relations in late 1947 and early 1948, PPR pressure on the Socialists was stepped up, starting at grassroots level and extending into the upper levels of the central government apparatus itself. A carefully orchestrated attack by the Communists on the influence of the PPS Centrists within the Central Planning office in mid-February 1948 seems to have particularly shaken the Socialist leaders.[240]

In March 1948, Cyrankiewicz abruptly changed course and agreed on behalf of the PPS that the merger should commence. Opponents of unification, including Osóbka-Morawski, were ousted from their posts. Once again, the full reasons for this *volte-face* remain obscure. Clearly, the sense of hopelessness in the PPS leadership, the various psychological and other pressures brought to bear by the Communists on the PPS activists, and the general trend of events within Poland and elsewhere in Eastern Europe (where the Socialist parties had undergone or were undergoing the same process of merger with their Communist counterparts) were the major factors.

The leadership crisis in the PPR which broke during the summer delayed unification until December 1948 when the Polish United Workers' Party (*Polska Zjednoczona Partia Robotnicza* – PZPR) was formed. By this time, the Communists had rejected Gomułka and in effect the national front strategy and the Socialists were able to exert little influence on the programme of the new party.[241]

As the leading role of the party was underlined and the independence of the PPS curbed, the significance of the national front decreased. The stress laid on ideological criteria in recruitment to the PPR was echoed in the other parties of the democratic bloc. Recruitment had continued on a mass scale in the first months after the election, but the Communists suspected the motives or at least the political commitment, of many of those who jumped on the bandwagon.[242] The April Plenum reversed the 'open doors' policy of the previous two years. Great emphasis was placed on the danger of infiltration of the democratic bloc by 'reactionary' elements, which it was claimed were attempting to subvert the national front from within.[243] Forces in society which the party had sought to coexist with since 1944, notably the Church, now came under attack. At the April Plenum Gomułka called for a rooting-out of

> the old, harmful and up to now only partially combated historical traditions, the daily impregnation of the nation's spirit with reactionary ideology by the Church; the education of youth, especially university youth, according to old idealist and reactionary academic conceptions.[244]

By the second half of 1947 campaigns were under way in the schools and higher education. The aim was to evolve 'Marxist teaching methods to destroy the ruinous influence of the reaction on children and working class youth [and] to develop in them a socialist view of the world'.[245] By September the episcopate was expressing its disquiet at what it considered was a 'deliberately directed hidden struggle with God and the Church' and called the Faithful to its defence.[246] The same radical and aggressive stance on the part of the PPR was seen in many other areas as the Communists abandoned the policy of building alliances with the existing political and social movements and sought instead to sweep them aside by transforming the nature of Polish society.

In many ways the campaigns initiated in 1947 were the precursors of the Stalinist offensives of the period after 1948. However, in 1947 they were placed firmly within a national context. They were undertaken not in conformity with the Soviet model of Socialist construction, but because in the party's view they were essential to the 'Polish road to Socialism'. It was in this national perspective that the essential continuity of the party's line with the objectives it had pursued since 1942 was apparent. Gomułka was in the fore in proclaiming the national platform, but in 1947 he spoke with the authority of the leadership as a whole. The general assumption was that having so recently found a 'national' solution to the struggle for power, there was every advantage in maintaining the national course as Poland moved towards Socialism. It was also assumed that Stalin held the same view – not only Gomułka, but the wider leadership too were puzzled by the implications of the establishment of the Cominform in September 1947[247] and carried on much as before. Gomułka told the inaugural meeting that in contrast to the old KPP, which had 'committed a great many errors . . . particularly on the national question', the PPR was a party of national independence (*partia niepodległościowa*). This had helped it immensely to broaden its political base in the working class and the nation as a whole.[248] As for the Polish-Soviet alliance, the key was to show that it was justified 'from the point of view of Polish *raison d'état*'.[249] After the Cominform session, the PPR insisted that its policies would remain unchanged:

> In the future as in the past, we will fight resolutely and without compromise to defend peace and to safeguard the interests of Poland. . . . The Communist and Marxist parties of all countries stand guard over peace, freedom and the independence of nations. . . . There is no question of the Soviet Union and the other People's Democracies intending to force their political systems on other

nations. . . . The Polish Workers' Party has shown that . . . it is building a strong and independent Poland; that it places the preservation of her independence and sovereignty above everything else. As far as the interests of the People's Poland are concerned . . . our Party knows no compromise.[250]

In this conception, the united party of the working class was to be the vanguard of the Polish revolution and the internal mass base on which it would rest. The alliance with the PPS – 'the foundation of People's Poland . . . the principal motor of all [its] victories and successes'[251] had been by far the most important fruit of the national front strategy and would provide the driving force on the 'Polish road to Socialism'. The Gomułka leadership aimed not simply to liquidate the PPS as a rival party and potential source of opposition, but to harness its constituency and national traditions for the new party. Unification would be based on an ideological platform of marxism-leninism and nationalism; it would not be 'mechanical'.[252] It would require a revision of attitudes on both sides.[253]

The *volte-face* by the PPS leadership in March 1948 may well have been prompted by the fear that the relatively favourable conditions for merger offered by Gomułka might not long remain on the table.[254] If so, the fears were well founded.

The crisis in the PPR leadership broke on 3 June 1948 when Gomułka addressed the Central Committee on the question of the ideological platform of the new united party.[255] While there is not space here to give a detailed account of the crisis, some of its main features should be noted. Gomułka's 3 June report argued that the party should reject the insensitivity of the old KPP attitude to Polish independence and incorporate the positive tradition of the PPS on the national question. Following some criticism of this position at the Plenum, the rest of the Politbureau adopted a statement rejecting Gomułka's report point by point and warning of the danger of a Rightist deviation if the 'nationalist and opportunist' traditions of the PPS were allowed to influence the programme of the new party. Gomułka responded on 15 June with a paper which bluntly rejected these criticisms and warned, in turn, of the danger of 'sectarianism' and a 'return to bad KPP traditions'.

At the same time as the dispute over ideological traditions, the issue of the relationship of the PPR to the Soviet Communist Party, which had already caused strains in the leadership at the time of the formation of the Cominform, became acute as the crisis in relations between Stalin and Tito worsened and Soviet pressure on the other East European states to accept overtly Soviet leadership and conform to Soviet ideological and economic practice sharply increased. While Gomułka resisted this process, most of the rest of the leadership rapidly fell in with the new orthodoxy during the summer of 1948.

Intermeshed with these developments, were divergences between Gomułka and some other party leaders over the nature of the national front strategy and the theoretical character of the state that was being constructed in Poland. These differences began to come increasingly to the fore as the party devoted more attention to theoretical matters from early 1947 onwards, although as we have seen, these political differences within the PPR over the meaning of the national front had existed since its foundation. Much attention was focused during the 1948 leadership crisis on the disputes in the underground leadership of the PPR in mid-1944 which it was alleged had first betrayed Gomułka's 'right-nationalist' tendencies.

Following his reply of 15 June to the Politbureau's criticisms, Gomułka appeared to be ready to compromise. He indicated that he would resign from the leadership and bow to the majority. Then claiming he was unwell he left for a two-month convalescent holiday. In July, another Central Committee Plenum was held (without Gomułka) to discuss the economic and agricultural programme of the new party. In accordance with a Cominform resolution of 29 June which had condemned Yugoslavia and announced the start of a general drive to collectivize agriculture, the Polish Communists accepted the principle of collectivization. This was a further issue of dispute with Gomułka.

The crisis came to a climax in mid-August when Gomułka returned to Warsaw and tried to resume work as secretary-general, though still in dispute with the Politbureau over collectivization, his interpretation of the record of the KPP on the national question and his refusal to accept a Politbureau resolution criticising his 'right-nationalism'. At a further Plenum at the end of August, Gomułka was replaced as secretary-general by Bierut, and persuaded to deliver a grudging self-criticism which nevertheless tacitly maintained his position on most of the key issues. The Plenum passed a resolution denouncing the 'right-nationalist deviation' in the leadership and launched the party on the Stalinist course it was to follow until Gomułka's return to power in 1956. The national front strategy had been finally eclipsed.

Conclusions

> This war is not as in the past; whoever occupies a territory also imposes on it his own social system. Everyone imposes his own system as far as his army has the power to do so. It cannot be otherwise.
>
> (Joseph Stalin to a group of Yugoslav Communists, 1945)

STALIN'S COMMENT TO the Yugoslav Communists quoted above is of course of particular relevance to Poland. Of the four countries initially covered in the Politics of Liberation series, Poland is the only one to have experienced the presence of the Red Army at the end of the war and to have emerged as a Communist state in the years that followed. Applied to Poland, Stalin's comment may be read as a statement of intent and not just as a generalized observation on the behaviour of occupying powers.

It was obvious to all concerned that once they had secured territorial possession of the country the Russians would not allow Poland to re-emerge in its interwar form. From 1941, when the U.S.S.R. was forced into the war on the side of the Allies, this truth governed Polish politics. There was no doubt that Stalin would impose a new social and political order on Polish territory if he was in a position to do so. The question was rather what concessions Stalin might make to Polish national identity as the new order was constructed. What territory would Poland be left with? How far and how fast, and with what degree of force, would the social transformation of Poland be undertaken? What extent of political, economic, religious and cultural pluralism would be tolerated? What links with the West could be preserved?

Part One of this volume has examined how the Government-in-Exile was undermined by these issues so that by 1944 it had lost all real influence over the course of events in Poland. The 'London' government was always a weak and fissile coalition, held together by common commitment to the patriotic cause, but riven by political differences from the interwar years, recriminations about the conduct of various of its members during the fall of Poland in 1939 and of France in 1940, and above all the question of Polish-Soviet relations. Apart perhaps from the brief period when Poland was Great Britain's major ally, from the defeat of France in mid-1940 until the German invasion of the Soviet Union in mid-1941, the London Poles' influence with the Allied Powers was not based on a true communality of interests. Beyond the immediate overriding objective of defeating Hitler, the perceived interest of the Allied powers lay in achieving a stable and peaceful post-war relationship with the U.S.S.R. rather than in meeting Poland's national aspirations. Poland's influence therefore depended critically on limiting her own claims to those that were consonant with the interests of the Western Powers, and exploiting to the full the debt of honour that Churchill in particular felt towards the Poles. Sikorski realized this and from 1941 his policy towards the Russians was closely aligned with that of the British. Because of this, his own personal authority within the Government-in-Exile and the continuing German advances into the Soviet Union until late 1942, Sikorski was able to maintain an illusion of considerable Polish influence on the Allies until his death in 1943. Under his successor, Mikołajczyk, this illusion rapidly dissolved. The Government-in-Exile was left high and dry by the transformation in the military situation in the East and the Big Three's moves to settle the Polish question in 1943–4. Mikołajczyk's efforts to achieve the basis for a deal with the Russians went too far for his cabinet colleagues but did not go far enough to satisfy Churchill, let alone Stalin. As a result, the Government-in-Exile both split apart and forfeited British and American support.

For part of the emigration, this outcome was preferable to reaching a compromise on Soviet terms. For these Poles it was unrealistic to imagine that, once in occupation, the Russians would be satisfied with anything less than the complete Sovietization of Poland. Poland's liberation was, for them, merely the replacement of occupation by one totalitarian power with that of another. The correct course of Government-in-Exile was to work to preserve Polish nationhood in a physical and spiritual sense, hoping that international circumstances would sooner or later create an opportunity for Poland to recover her independent statehood. Any concessions to the Russians, particularly from a position of weakness, would only serve to assist Stalin.

With the defeat of the London Poles, the focus of Polish politics returned to Poland itself and above all to the strategy and tactics of the PPR. Part Two of this study has analysed the attempts by the Communists and the other political movements inside Poland to shape her destiny within the parameters imposed by Soviet power.

The Communists' offensive against the PSL and the underground in the period leading up to the elections, and the rapid decline of organized opposition in their aftermath, marked the close of the struggle for power which had begun during the Nazi occupation and continued during the liberation. After 1946 the leading role of the PPR in the state was assured. The Socialists' attempt to preserve an element of pluralism from within the government camp had collapsed by 1948. Despite leadership crises and outbreaks of popular discontent in 1956, 1968 and 1970–1, it was not until the advent of *Solidarność* more than three decades later that the Communists again faced a major challenge to their monopoly of power.

The events of the turn of 1946–7 thus represented the culmination of the national front strategy which the party had tried to pursue with varying degrees of consistency since its formation in 1942. The essence of the strategy, as stated by the Central Bureau of Polish Communists in July 1944, was twofold. Its first purpose was to establish a 'truly national government supported by the majority of the people'. The national front was to 'embrace the workers, peasants, intelligentsia and petit-bourgeoisie'. In other words, the Communists aimed to win over much of the existing 'London' camp, leaving the diehard 'reactionaries' isolated and without a significant social base. Such a national front would provide a real bond between Polish Communism and the nation and form the 'point of departure on the road to changes in the system'. Through this regrouping the party would be able to achieve the second purpose of the strategy: to create a balance within Poland that would allow it to 'smash the reaction' with its own internal forces, that is principally by political means and without being forced to turn to the Soviet Union for direct military assistance.

As we have seen, the Communists encountered immense difficulties in putting this strategy into action and were repeatedly forced to modify their course. Virtually nothing was achieved in underground Poland. The attempt to establish a broad coalition around the PKWN in 1944 went off course within weeks. A combination of factors – its own insecurity, its numerical and organizational weakness and Stalin's doubts about its capacity to keep control of events, or even of its partners in the PKWN – caused the party to rely directly on the Soviet presence to crush the underground. By spring 1945 the PPR leadership found itself facing incipient civil war. In the provinces the security forces and party hardliners followed the lead of Soviet advisers rather than the Central Committee. The May Plenum reasserted the leadership's authority and steered the PPR back to the broad national front strategy that had in effect been suspended since October 1944.

Between June 1945 and February 1946 the national front strategy appeared to come close to fruition. There seemed to the Communists to be a real, albeit a steadily diminishing, possibility that the London wing of the Government of National Unity led by Mikołajczyk, or at least a substantial part of it, could be drawn into the national front under PPR hegemony. The attitude of the PSL to a joint electoral bloc was the test. However, Mikoł-ajczyk had different plans. He aimed at the reconstruction of the coalition government under PSL leadership with the Communists and their allies as the junior partner. He believed that the PPR would be too weak to prevent this unless the Soviet Union intervened directly on its behalf, and that in the final analysis Stalin would prefer to accept the new government rather than run the risk of internal destabilization in Poland and economic reprisals from the Western Powers.

Following the breakdown of talks on an electoral bloc in February 1946, the PPR concluded that it was unrealistic to hope for a deal with Mikołajczyk. It began to prepare for the confrontation with the opposition which it now believed to be unavoidable. The party tacitly accepted that its strategy had failed to detach the peasant movement and other sections of the London camp from the reaction. According to PPR propaganda, the PSL intended to fight the elections in an alliance with the reaction; it would therefore be allowed no further part to play in political life. However, the Centrist leadership of the party's only significant ally, the PPS, continued to believe that a broad national front, including the PSL, was attainable. This led to severe strains between the two parties. But the Communists were unwilling to sever their partnership with the PPS leaders, although in mid-1946 they appear to have come close to doing so. Such a rift would have spelt a return to the isolation in which the party had found itself in the spring of 1945. For this reason, and perhaps because the Russians were not yet ready to run the risk of a showdown between the PPR and the PSL, the Communists held their fire while the Socialists vainly attempted to resurrect the broad national front. In September 1946, it became clear that neither the PPR nor the Peasants were interested in a compromise. The PPS, appeased by the undertakings on future policy and the distribution of power in the government to be formed after the elections, took the only course which it considered was open to it, and fell in with the Communists' offensive against the PSL. It saw this as the only way to preserve some influence over the PPR after the elections and avoid the danger of Soviet intervention.

The results of the offensive demonstrated that the party had succeeded – probably beyond its expectations – in achieving what was intended as the second purpose of the national front strategy. The Communists had built up sufficient resources to be able to mobilize the State-party apparatus, the PPR rank and file, the bureaucracy, the army and the security forces, to overcome the opposition without having to call in the Red Army to help. Undoubtedly Soviet advisers played an important part behind the scenes, but their role was well concealed and the Red Army was able to maintain its low profile. The Polish Communists had consolidated their hold on the state with their own resources without provoking a major internal crisis, economic collapse or a breakdown in relations with the West. Mikołajczyk's confidence that they would be unable to do so had proved unfounded.

However, the national front *per se* had contributed little to this victory. The PPS leadership and *aktyw* played an important part in managing the elections, but neither the Socialists nor the Communists' other allies were able to draw the masses with them. The first purpose of the national front strategy – to rally the support of the majority of the nation and to isolate the reaction – remained unfulfilled. Contrary to the view put forward by party historians, the PPR had won the struggle for power despite the continuing narrowness of its popular base, not because it had succeeded in enlisting the support of the majority of the Polish nation. The party's recurrent resort to force to deal with its opponents, the unity of the peasant movement even in defeat and the dominant position of the PSL in rural local government in many areas, the strength of the underground opposition, the disastrous results of the referendum in those urban areas where the count was conducted fairly, the absence of party organization across many rural parts of eastern and central Poland into the late 1940s and the critical attitude of the Church, all belie the official interpretation that a widescale movement of opinion took place in the months before the election to produce a landslide in favour of the bloc. Whatever shift in opinion there was seems to have come after the election offensive when active opposition gave way to resigned acquiescence and disengagement from politics. Indeed, the polarization of forces in Poland at the turn of 1946–7 seems to have put yet another barrier between the party and large sections of the nation.

The reasons for this failure were then largely internal. The national front strategy assumed that it would be possible to achieve a national consensus for the party's vision of the future and that this would provide the climate in which it would be possible to neutralize the reaction by political rather than coercive means. However, the Communists were unable to achieve that internal consensus and were therefore obliged to use much greater repression than they had intended to consolidate their power. This is not to say that external factors, notably Soviet influence, did not play an important part in shaping the Communists' *tactics* – and not only their *strategy* – during 1945–7. We do not have the evidence to gauge accurately the extent of that influence, but it is safe to assume that it is considerable. However, one need look no further than the obvious inadequacy of the national front as an instrument to secure state power for the Communists to explain the strategy's lack of success. Stalin's diktats were in this sense secondary.

Party historians imply that if only the PPR had been allowed to persevere with the strategy after 1948, free of outside interference, it would have been possible, with time, to achieve an 'historical compromise' in Poland in which a genuine mechanism of consent between the nation and Polish Communism might have been established. But there is little substance to this. The essential features of the post-1948 phase were shaping up by 1946–7. The party had been propelled away from the national front and a harder, more aggressive and totalitarian course was in the ascendant by the time of the elections. As Zambrowski wrote many years later, while 1948 marked the 'great turn' to Stalinism in Poland, the road leading to the turn runs directly back to the crushing of the opposition at the time of the elections and the radicalization of the party's line in their aftermath (R. Zambrowski, 'Dziennik', *Krytyka, 6* [1980], 71).

In a longer term perspective, the failure of the national front meant that the new political order was thus fundamentally flawed from the start. The Communists held the State, but outside the party-State bureaucracy and the apparatus of coercion they lacked any firm internal basis on which to realize their social and economic objectives. The historic achievement of the Polish Workers' Party and the national front strategy was the creation of a political system which was, and has remained, one of the more effective in Eastern Europe in neutralizing opposition and managing crises with its own internal resources. But that system has been one of the least successful in establishing a mechanism of consent between rulers and ruled or in creating the conditions for economic and political stability. The roots of this failure lie firmly in the formative years of 'People's Poland' between 1944 and 1947.

In a sense, Poland's experience bears out the statement made by Stalin which was quoted at the beginning of this chapter. The fact of over-whelming Soviet military power has decided the basic characteristics of Poland's political structure since 1945. But the Russians have always avoided putting that military power to the test, preferring in practice to exert their influence by indirect means. With the partial exception of the period from 1948 to 1956 this has allowed Polish society and politics a degree of autonomy unparalleled in Eastern Europe. In that sense, the Soviet Union has never succeeded fully in imposing its social system on the Polish nation.

Abbreviations used in the notes

NOTE: Places of publication are given only for works published outside the United Kingdom. Commonly recognized abbreviations such as *J.* for *Journal*, *Rev.* for *Review*, have been used; other abbreviations are listed below.

APUST	Archives of Polish Underground Study Trust
CAB	Cabinet
CAHSD	Centralne Archiwum Historyczny Stronnictwa Democratycznego, Warsaw
DBFP	*Documents on British Foreign Policy 1919–1939*, ed. R. Butler and E.L. Woodward (1950)
DPSR	Documents on Polish-Soviet Relations
FRUS	Foreign Relations of the U.S.
PISM	Archive of the Polish Institute and Sikorski Museum, London
PRO, FO 371	Public Record Office, Foreign Office General Correspondence
PSZ	*Polskie Siły Zbrojne w Drugiej Wojnie Światowej (Polish Armed Forces during the Second World War)*, 1959
PWB	Polish White Book. *Official Documents Concerning Polish-German and Polish-Soviet Relations, 1933–1939* (n.d.)

Notes

1 From independence to exile

1. The question of Allied commitment, particularly that of the United States, to Polish independence at the end of the First World War is discussed in detail by T. Komarnicki, *Rebirth of the Polish Republic. A Study in the Diplomatic History of Europe, 1914–1920* (1957), 141–222.

2. See N. Davies, *White Eagle, Red Star, The Polish-Soviet War, 1919–20* (1972). Another, unpublished, study of the war which is worth consulting is Z.M. Musialik, 'The Soviet defeat on the Vistula, 1920, and the Weygand myth' (manuscript lodged with the Piłsudski Institute, London, 1973).

3. Poland's eastern frontier was not settled by the Treaty of Versailles. Rather, by article 87 of that treaty, Poland agreed that this boundary 'shall be subsequently determined by the Principal Allied and Associated Powers'. Cited by S. Konovalov (ed.), *Russo-Polish Relations: An Historical Survey* (1945), 33. On 8 Dec. 1919, the Supreme Council in its 'Declaration Relating to the Provisional Eastern Frontiers of Poland' defined a boundary for the northern section of Poland's eastern frontier.

   This ran down from the east Prussian frontier to the Galician boundary, upstream on the River Bug near Krilov. The line was not drawn farther south in this declaration because the Council was thinking of constituting the area or areas south and east [the eastern part of Galicia, one of the fragments of the Austro-Hungarian Empire which was being broken up], into a separate state. Consistently with this general idea, on November 21, 1919, it had adopted a 'Statute of Eastern Galicia' which provided for a twenty-five-year Polish mandate under the League of Nations, at the end of which the future status of the area was to be determined by the Council of the League. This specified the western boundary of the proposed mandate – which was to be the southern section of the eastern boundary of Poland proper. That designated line ran from Belzec on the former frontier between Austria-Hungary and Russia southwestward, passing west of Rawa Ruska and east of Przemysl [leaving the city and province of Lwow within the mandate], and thence to the Czecho-Slavok border. (H. Feis, *Churchill Roosevelt Stalin* (1959), Appendix, 'Note about origins and nature of the so-called Curzon Line', 657.)

   The line adopted by the Supreme Council was to be a 'provisional minimum frontier', see Harold W.V. Temperley (ed.), *A History of the Peace Conference of Paris* (1920–4), VI, 274. Any early opportunity to make it a permanent line was lost with the outbreak of the Russo-Polish war. However, at Spa in July 1920 this same line was proposed with Polish consent to Russia by the British foreign secretary, Lord Curzon (and thus became associated with his name), as an armistice line. The Soviet government turned down this proposal and subsequently agreed by the Treaty of Riga of 18 March 1921 to a frontier much more in Poland's favour. The 'Curzon Line' re-emerged as a 'catchword for a suggested Polish-Soviet frontier' during the war and eventually formed the basis of that frontier: see L. Kirkien, *Russia, Poland and the Curzon Line*, 2nd edn, (1945), 5.

4. See A. Polonsky, *Politics in Independent Poland 1921–1939: The Crisis of Constitutional Government* (1972). This excellent study, now a standard work, contains a particularly useful section, pp. 1–44, on interwar Poland's economic and social structure. However, his description of Lodz as the 'Polish Manchester' may perhaps require revision in the light of comments by N. Davies, *God's Playground. A History of Poland*, II *1795 to the present* (reprinted, with corrections, 1982), 163–77.
5. Polonsky, *op. cit.*, 458.
6. 'A letter from Poland', PRO, FO 371, 26723/C/278. See also letter, Savery to Roberts, 2 Jan. 1941, *ibid.*, C/181.
7. L. Kirkien, *op. cit.*, 47.
8. Polonsky, *op. cit.*, 109–13.
9. M. Kukieł, *General Sikorski, Żołnierz i Mąż Stanu Polski Walczącej (General Sikorski, Soldier and Statesman of Fighting Poland)* (1970), 60–1.
10. For text see *Documents on Polish-Soviet Relations* (DPSR) *1939–1945*, I, *1939–43* (1961), 12–15.
11. J. Beck, *Final Report* (New York, 1957), 20–1.
12. Polonsky, *op. cit.*, 428.
13. Formed in Feb. 1936, it represented most of the opposition to the regime established in Poland since Piłsudski's coup of May 1926. Most notably absent were Dmowski and his supporters who did not joint the front because they felt it was too pro-French and hence pro-Jewish: see A. Micewski, 'Sikorski a oppozyczja – czyli główny spór w Paryzu i Londynie', *Wiez*, no. 7–8 (1961), 202. A useful study entirely devoted to the Front Morges is by Henryk Przybylski, *Front Morges W Okresie II Rzeczypospolitej (Front Morges during the Second Republic)* (Warsaw, 1972). Przybylski endorses Polonsky's view that the opposition was badly organized and its efforts against the *Sanacja* ill coordinated, thus leaving that regime threatened less by external opposition than by dissension within itself: see Polonsky, *op. cit.*, 326. The divisions within the governing group were described to me by the late Aleksander Bobkowski, under-secretary of state for transport 1933–9. (See reference to him in the Preface to Beck's *Final Report*, 1957.) Bobkowski was also married to President Moscicki's daughter and his revelations about political activity in Poland in the interwar years were most interesting. I met him in Geneva in Aug. 1967. He admitted involvement in secret trade union activity over a number of years and exclaimed at one point, 'I was always a Communist.' His dramatic emphasis of the remark was, perhaps, for my consumption but reflected a belief in social justice common to all opponents of the policy of the ruling group within the *Sanacja*. A more equitable social and political system in Poland was also the concern of members of the Front Morges. However, Przybylski (*op. cit.*, 28–31, 43–5) is careful to point out the difference in approach to the attainment of these ends between constitutionalists like Sikorski and those like Witos who stood for radical changes verging on revolution. The Centre-Right response to the course of action proposed by the left was the concept of 'National Consolidation' (*ibid*, 70). This was, however, no more than a slogan before the outbreak of war after which it was translated into the 'National Unity' label with which Sikorski's government styled itself.
14. Quoted in Z.J. Gasiorowski, 'Did Piłsudski attempt to initiate a preventive war in 1933?', *J. Modern History*, 27 (June 1955), 145.

15. Beck, *op. cit.*, 24–5.
16. See B.B. Budorowycz, *Polish-Soviet Relations, 1932–39* (New York and London, 1963), 55–6.
17. See record of conversation between Beck and Eden in Geneva, 10 Oct. 1935, PRO, FO 371, 18899/C/7030.
18. See P. Starzenski, *3 Lata z Beckiem (3 Years with Beck)* (1972), 16–18.
19. Beck, *op. cit.*, 145.
20. *Ibid.*, 150–1.
21. According to Sikorski the Czechoslovakian authorities had managed to decipher one of Beck's telegrams to Lipski. It said that if Britain and France allowed Germany to occupy the Sudetan districts, Poland would at once march into the Teschen area. Minute, H.M. Jebb, 1 Jan. 1941 PRO, FO 371, 26722/C/188.
22. Starzenski, *op. cit.*, 166.
23. Minutes, Cab. 14 (39) 22 Mar. 1939 PRO, CAB 23/98.
24. Minutes, Cab. 15 (39) 29 Mar. 1939 PRO, CAB 23/98.
25. A. Cienciala, *Poland and the Western Powers 1938–1939* (London and Toronto, 1968), 236.
26. Minutes, Cab. 26 (39) 3 May 1939 PRO, CAB 23/98.
27. Raczynski to Beck, 10 Aug. 1939, no. 157. A. 1149/WB/2 PISM. Count Joseph Potocki, deputy director of the political department of the Polish Foreign Ministry during 1939, had misgivings about the value of the outcome of Beck's visit to London in April of that year. In a letter to Raczynski, 15 Apr. 1957, cited in Count E. Raczynski, *In Allied London* (1962), App. II, 342–3, he expressed his concern that Beck had failed to obtain an economic clause assuring Poland of British material aid. This was sought by Raczynski in Aug. 1939. In his letter to me of 18 Jan. 1972 Raczynski agreed that Potocki's opinion is valid. 'He and other of Beck's collaborators (*sic*) would have liked to press immediately for material proofs of British support. These, as we know, were not very generously offered, at a later stage in the summer of 1939.'
28. *Documents on British Foreign Policy, 1919–1939* (DBFP), ed. R. Butler and E.L. Woodward, third series (1950), VII, no. 88, 85–6.
29. C. Woodward (ed.), *British Foreign Policy During the Second World War* (1970–1), I, 10.
30. H. Roos (trans. J.R. Foster), *A History of Modern Poland* (1966), 174.
31. *Official Documents Concerning Polish-German and Polish-Soviet Relations, 1933–1939* (The Polish White Book) (PWB) (n.d.), no. 175, 181–90. The Soviet invasion of Poland and the Soviet government's justification of its decision to invade are discussed in a thesis which concentrates very largely on the legal aspects concerning the Polish Government-in-Exile, see George V. Lipski-Kaciewicz, 'The Polish Government-in-Exile and Great Britain 1939–45' (Indiana University, 1969, partial fulfilment for Ph.D.), 38–41. The main points he makes about the Soviet statement of 17 Sept. 1939 are firstly that it 'swept from its path its [the Soviet Government's] contractual network with Poland starting with the Treaty of Riga . . . and ending with the reaffirmation of the Non-aggression Treaty of July 25th, 1932, on November 26th, 1938.' It should also be added that the Russian invasion of Poland was a violation of the Pact of Paris, 1928, and the agreements reached in the Convention for the Definition of Aggression of 3 July 1933: see F.A. Voigt, *Pax Britannica* (1949), 118–19. And secondly, that the Soviet decision raised the legal question: 'Can a state disappear as the result of the occupation of its territory? International law leaves room for different interpretations, and certainly there is no consensus among authorities on international law on the conditions under which a state ceases to exist.' (Lipski-Kaciewicz, *op. cit.*, 40).

2 In Angers and London, 1940

1. Beck to Raczynski (copy to Paris), 18 Sept. 1939. Cyphers, no. 440, A.12.53/52. Quoted in J. Coutouvidis, 'Government-in-Exile: the transfer of Polish authority abroad in September 1939', *Rev. Int. Studies, 10*, no. 4 (Oct. 1984), 285–96.
2. Minutes, Cab. 19 (39) 18 Sept. 1939, PRO, CAB 65/1.
3. *Ibid.*
4. Polish resources abroad in 1939: there were three main sources of income available to the Polish government. The first and most important source consisted of loans. All the military expenditure was met in this way. Loans negotiated with its allies during the summer of 1939 were used to cover nearly all the costs incurred by the Polish government in the period 1939–41. The credit granted to it by the British government on 7 Sept. 1939 amounted to £8 million: see *Parliamentary Debates* (Commons), 17 Oct. 1939, CCCLII, cols 681–2. The French government's credit granted on 18 Aug. 1939 was for 500 million francs. What was not consumed before the war was used to pay for the Polish government's stay in France.

    The second source of income came from assets abroad. These included 38 vessels of the Polish merchant marine and the Polish gold. The latter had rather an interesting history. The decision to evacuate Warsaw, 5 Sept. 1939, prompted Col. Adam Koc, director of the *Bank Handlowy* (Commercial Bank), and under-secretary at the Treasury, to arrange for the transportation of the 75 tons of gold out of the capital: see R. Westerby and R.M. Low, *The Polish Gold* (1940), 1. This bullion was worth 463 million złoty. At 5.30 złotys to the dollar in 1939 it was the equivalent of $87 million: see Zygmunt Karpinski, *O Wielkopolsee i dalekich podrózach. Wspomnienia 1860–1960* (. . . *Memoirs, 1860–1960*) (Warsaw, 1971), 201. Karpinski, director of the Bank of Poland, arranged for the gold's safe keeping by the Bank of Paris into whose vaults it was placed on 28 Sept. 1939: *ibid.*, 212. For its subsequent history, see Low, *op. cit.*, 222–3, 225–32, 234–7. Having failed to get the gold back through diplomatic channels, the Polish Bank took the matter to the courts in the U.S. It sought, as compensation for its gold, part of the $728 million held by the French government in New York. Approximately $64 million were recovered by this legal suit in May 1941: see W.N. Hadsel, 'Allied governments in London – war efforts and peace aims', *Foreign Policy Reports*, xviii (1942), note no. 38, 254. No more of the value of its gold was ever recovered by the Polish Government-in-Exile. The third source of income was through contributions from Polish émigré organizations and individuals throughout the world and particularly in North America.

    The non-military expenditure of the government, its administrative budget, was calculated at about 10 million złoty a year: PRM-K. 102 (2) 6 Oct. 1939, PISM.

    The manpower for the reconstruction of Polish forces abroad, after the outbreak of the Second World War, came from various sources and their organization depended on a number of agreements between the Polish government and its Western Allies. Even before September 1939 provisions had been made between the French and Polish authorities for the formation of Polish forces in France. The Military Convention of 16 May 1939, signed by Generals Gamelin and Kasprzycki, allowed for a Polish force of 25,000 to be recruited from Polish citizens resident in France: see *Polskie Siły Zbrojne w Drugiej Wojnie Swiatowej* (PSZ) (*Polish Armed Forces During the Second World War*) (1959), II, Pt.I, 13. In 1939 there were 60,–70,000 Poles eligible for military service in France, 30,000 in Belgium, 3,000 in Great Britain, giving a total of about 100,000 men: *ibid.*, 21. In addition to these men there were the members of the Polish armed forces who left Poland after the September campaign. Those who reached France included 49,000 escapees from internment in Romania. (Thousands also joined Allied forces in the Middle East.) Taking into account Polish civilians who escaped to France and who were eligible for military service, and that the Franco-Polish Military Agreement of 9 Sept. 1939 (which superseded the Convention of 16 May 1939) allowed all eligible Poles living in France to serve with the Polish armed forces, some 150,000 men were available for recruitment by the Polish authorities in France: *ibid.*, 29. Following call-up notices which appeared in the official paper *Monitor Polski* (*Polish Monitor*) of 24 and 25 Sept. 1939 Sikorski was able to organize a Polish army in France made up of 7,661 officers and 74,600 men. This was integrated with the French army: see *ibid.*, 58.

Arrangements regarding the Polish navy were formalized by the Agreement concerning the Formation of the Detachment of the Polish Navy in Great Britain of 18 Nov. 1939. About three-quarters of the Polish navy had escaped the Germans and consisted of submarines, destroyers and auxiliary vessels: see L.M. Sayre, *Freedom in Exile, A Handbook of the Government-in-Exile*, 1972, 24. These naval units became attached to the British navy for the duration of the war. Although manned by Poles and commanded by Polish officers under the Polish flag, the Protocol to the Agreement specified that 'the Polish Naval Detachment, which shall form part of the British fleet, shall be under the operational control of the British Admiralty and shall co-operate with the British Navy in the manner found most suitable, under the orders of the British Commanders of the units to which the vessels may be attached' (PSZ, II, Pt.i, 153–6).

The Polish air force was at first split between France and Britain under the operational command of the air forces of those two countries. (Under the Franco-Polish military agreement of 4 Jan. 1940, which superseded the Agreement of 9 Sept. 1939, the Polish government was allowed to form a Polish air force on French soil: *ibid.*, 183–4.)

5.   Minutes, Cab. 22(39) 21 Sept. 1939 PRO, CAB 65/1.
6.   DPSR I, no. 55, 54.
7.   See Z.M. Musialik, 'The Soviet defeat on the Vistula, 1920, and the Weygand myth' (unpublished manuscript completed in 1973, Piłsudski Institute, London) 26, 218, and N. Davies, *White Eagle, Red Star, The Polish-Soviet War, 1919–20* (1972), 140, 210–11.
8.   See extracts from the Soviet-Lithuanian Agreement, 10 Oct. 1939. DPSR, I, no. 62, 62.
9.   See DPSR, I, nos 64–8, 64–70. Also W.J. Couch, 'General Sikorski, Poland and the Soviet Union, 1939–43', Ph.D. thesis, University of Chicago, 1970, 70–5.
10. Kennard, in Hoare to Halifax, 22 Sept. 1939, PRO, FO 371, 23151/no. 456, C/14615.
11. See J. Coutouvidis, *op. cit.* (note 1 above).
12. See W. Jedrzejewicz (ed.), *Diplomat in Paris 1936–1939, Memoirs of Julius Łukasiewicz, Ambassador of Poland* (New York and London, 1970), 372. Also J. Coutouvidis, 'The formation of the Polish Government-in-Exile and its relations with Great Britain, 1939–1941' (Ph.D. thesis, University of Keele, 1975), 88–94.
13. *Ibid.*, 9 and Appendix I, 331–2.
14. Text as approved by the Council of Ministers, in Appendix III, PRM-K, 102(5), 27 Oct. 1939, PISM. See George V. Lipski-Kacewicz, 'The Polish Government-in-Exile and Great Britain 1939–45' (Indiana University, 1969, partial fulfilment for Ph.D.), 46–54, in which the point is made that the

dissolution of the *Sejm* and Senate did not affect the president's right to legislate in time of war, as laid down by the Constitution of 1935.

15. Minutes, PRM-K 102(7), 23 Nov. 1939, PISM.
16. Kennard to Halifax, 13 Dec. 1939, PRO, FO 371, 23153/no.26/C/2059.
17. Namier to Butler, 28 Nov. 1939, PRO, FO 371, C/19304. See J. Coutouvidis, 'Lewis Namier and the Polish Government-in-Exile, 1939–40', *Slavonic and East European Rev., 62*, no. 3 (July 1984), 421–8.
18. Kennard to Halifax, 13 Dec. 1939, PRO, FO 371, 23153/no.26/C/20359.
19. Stenogram of the Inaugural Meeting of the National Council, 23 Jan. 1940, A 5/1a, PISM.
20. *Ibid.* True to his word, Bielecki, 'Dmowski's favourite disciple' withdrew the support of the nationalists by declaring them as an opposition to the government in 1942. See Reports on the Second National Council appointed on 3 Feb. 1942, PRO, FO 371, 31094/C/1755 and C/2097. The latter includes a detailed and interesting report, 'The Poles in the United Kingdom' by Prof. W.J. Rose of 5 Jan. 1942.
21. Minutes, A5/1a (4) 5 Mar. 1940 PISM.
22. See J. Garlinski, 'The Polish underground state (1939–45)', *J. Contemporary History, 10*, II (Apr. 1973), 219–60.
23. Minutes, PRM-K 102 (2) 6 Oct. 1939 and Appendix II, PISM.
24. Minutes, PRM-K 102 (4) 17 Oct. 1939, PISM.
25. *Parliamentary Debates* 5 (Commons), CCCLII, col. 1683.
26. *Parliamentary Debates* 5 (Lords), CXIV (1939), col. 1570.
27. Minutes, PRM-K 102 (7) 23 Nov. 1939, PISM.
28. Minutes Cab. 84 (39) 15 Nov. 1939, PRO, CAB 65/1.
29. *Ibid.*
30. Annexe to Minutes, Cab. 90(39) 21 Nov. 1939, PRO CAB 65/1.
31. Minutes, PRM-K 102(7) 23 Nov. 1939, PISM.
32. Copy of memo., Polish government to French government, enclosed in Kennard to Halifax, 13 Apr. 1940 PRO, FO 371, 24466/no.40/C/60077.
33. Minute by Makins, head of the Central Department of the Foreign Office, 26 Apr. 1940, PRO, FO 371, 2466/C/60077.
34. Transmitted in a report from Campbell to Halifax, 12 May 1940, PRO, FO 371, 24466/no.161/C/60077.
35. Minutes, PRM-K 102(10) 15 Dec. 1939, Appendix I, PISM. The creation of a federation of Slav States could only follow close cooperation between the Polish and Czechoslovak governments. See P.S. Wandycz, *Czechoslovak-Polish Confederations* (Indiana, 1956) and W.T. Kowalski 'Koncepcja konfederacji Polsko-Czechosłowackej w swietle dokumentów z lat 1939–43', *Zaranie Śląskie* (The concept of a Polish-Czechoslovakian confederation in the light of the diplomatic documents of the year 1939–43', *Silesian Dawn* [Katowice] No. 4 (Oct.–Dec. 1964).
36. Letter, J. Kowalewski to Sikorski, 28 Oct. 1939, PRM 1/7, PISM.
37. Cardinal Hlond, *The Persecution of the Catholic Church in German Occupied Poland* (1941), 66–7.
38. See C. Miłosz, *Native Realm. A Search for Self Definition* (transl. from Polish by C.S. Leach) (1981), 229–52, which constitute the chapter entitled 'The G.G.' in which the author describes his experience of life in the Government General. Elsewhere Miłosz equates German with Russian policy in Poland. See his *The Captive Mind* (transl. from Polish by J. Zielonko) (1953), viii. I was privileged to meet Miłosz at the Polish Library in London on 28 Mar. 1985. In discussion he reaffirmed his opinion that although their systems differed, no distinction could be made between the Germans and Russians as occupiers of Poland. This view

is rather different from our interpretation of the Polish experience, 1939–47.

39. See letter, Prince Radziwill, Warsaw, Dec. 1940, PRO, FO 371, 26723/C/278. With regard to recent historiography on German policy in Poland with particular reference to the destruction of the Polish intelligentsia in the context of the Holocaust, see the review article by R. Besell in *The Times Higher Education Supplement*, 19 Mar. 1982.

40. Statistic taken from the report on the 'Economic position in occupied Poland' forwarded by Raczynski to Eden, 26 June 1942, in PRO, FO 371, 31098/C/957 and the 'Statement on German crimes committed against the Jewish population in Poland' by J. Schwarzbart, member of the (Polish) National Council, 29 June 1942, PRO, FO 371, 31097/C/7107.

41. Kennard to Eden, 14 Feb. 1941, PRO, FO 371, 26723/C/1488/189/55. See also Dormer to Eden, 1 June 1942, PRO, FO 371, 31097/C/5951.

42. Letter from Sosnkowski, 10 Feb. 1941, PRO, FO 371, 26723/C/1766.

43. Minutes, PRM-K 102(11) 2 Jan. 1940, PISM. Under the terms of the Anglo-Polish military agreement Polish naval units came under the command of the Admiralty. See note 4 above.

44. Minutes, PRM-K 102(12) 9 Jan. 1940, PISM.

45. Minutes, PRM-K 102(15) 24 Jan. 1940, PISM.

46. Memo. by Kedzior, Apr. 1940, 1 PRMI/30 PISM. See B.D.P. Conduit, 'Britain's Arctic gamble: the Russo-Finnish war 1939–1940', *History Today*, 32 (Mar. 1982), 26–32.

47. Minutes, PRM-K 102(22) 26 Apr. 1940, PISM.

48. Minutes, PRM-K 102(23) 8 May 1940, PISM.

49. Minutes, PRM-K 102(24) 20 May 1940, PISM.

50. Minutes, PRM-K 102(25) 28 May 1940, PISM.

51. Halifax to Campbell, for Kennard, 17 June 1940, PRO, FO 371, 24468/C/7306.

52. Halifax to Campbell, for Kennard, 19 June 1940, PRO, FO 371, 24468/no. 192/C/7306.

53. J. Ciechanowski, *Defeat in Victory* (1948), 25.

54. DPSR, I, no. 75, 94.

55. E. Raczynski, *In Allied London* (1963), 58.

56. DPSR, I, no. 76, 95.

57. This section was first published as a paper circulated at the Sikorski Symposium, London University, SSEES, 26–27 Sept. 1983.

58. See Raczynski, *op. cit.*, 55–7.

59. *Ibid.*, 55–97.

60. Kennard to Halifax, 19 June 1940, PRO, FO 371, 24482/no. 93/C/7880/7177/55.

61. See Coutouvidis, 'Lewis Namier and the Polish Government-in-Exile', 427.

62. Minute by Makins, 9 June 1940, PRO, FO 371, 24482/C/7880.

63. *Ibid.*

64. *Ibid.*

65. Minute by Roberts on a conversation with Kennard, 6 July 1940, PRO, FO 371, 24482/C/7880.

66. Minute of a discussion between Roberts and Namier, 19 July 1940, PRO, FO 371, 24474/C/7639/252/55.

67. Letter, Beaumont-Nesbitt to Makins, 17 June 1940, PRO, FO 371, 24482/C/7177.

68. Minute by Maclean, 6 July 1940, PRO, FO 371, 24482/C/7880. Donald Maclean was promoted to second secretary at the FO, 15 Oct. 1940. He defected to Russia with Guy Burgess on 23 June 1951.

69. Minutes, PRM-K. 103(29), 26 June 1940, PISM.

70. *Ibid.* See note 4 above. Under the terms of the general agreement of 11 June 1940, Polish air force units in Britain came directly under the command of the

Royal Air Force, but it was agreed that the Polish units would not be sent outside British territory without the express consent of the Polish government (PSZ, II, Pt.i, 187–8). After the fall of France in June 1940 Polish forces regrouped on British soil. On 5 Aug. 1940 the Anglo-Polish Military Agreement was signed. According to Article I, 'The Polish Armed Forces (comprising land, sea, and air forces) shall be organised and employed, under British Command, as the Armed Forces of the Republic of Poland Allied with the United Kingdom' (*ibid.*, 297–304). Under this agreement the position of the Polish navy did not alter significantly from that under the agreement of 18 Nov. 1939. The Polish air force on the other hand was reorganized from personnel 'selected for service by a joint board composed of Polish and British representatives' (*ibid.*, 301). In effect the Polish air force became a branch of the Royal Air Force. The recruited pilots were given the rank of second lieutenant. There were over 3,000 of these men together with several thousand ground crew. In 1941 it was numerically the strongest Allied air force in Britain: see Sayre, *op. cit.*, 24.

After June 1940 the Polish army suffered a fall in numbers. Only 19,451 officers and men of the Polish forces in France reached Britain. Col. J. Lunkiewicz, 'Naczelne Władze Polskich Sił Zbrojnych na Obczyźnie w latach 1939–1945' (The Polish High Command in exile, 1939–1945), *Bellona*, no. 2 (Apr.–June 1957), 42–55. Polish military authorities were allowed to call up Polish citizens resident in Britain. The Polish army was to 'be so used as to form one theatre of operations under the command of the Polish Commander in that theatre'. However, these forces would be 'under British Command, in its character as the Allied High Command' (Art., 3, App. II of Military Agreement, 5 Aug. 1940. PSZ, II, Pt. i. 297–304).

Members of the Polish army were subject to Polish military law and were tried in Polish military courts. This provision was extended to the Polish navy and air force by the Anglo-Polish protocol concerning jurisdiction over the Polish armed forces of 22 Nov. 1940: *ibid.*

Salaries of the Polish armed forces were made equal to those of the officers and men of corresponding categories in the British armed forces. The cost of putting this provision of the Military Agreement into effect was to be 'refunded out of the credit granted by His Majesty's Government to the Polish Government to finance the cost of mounting the Polish Military effort' (*ibid.*). The amount of credit made available to the Polish authorities for this purpose was fixed at £3,500,000 a year (subject to various adjustments), under the Agreement for the provision of Funds for Polish Land Forces of 25 Feb. 1941. General Sikorski's preliminary budget for the Polish land forces, put before the Council of Ministers on 29 June 1941, estimated an expenditure of £3,801,860. A figure of £301,860 was added to the credit of £3,500,000 granted by the War Office to cover costs of 'official military activity' (PRM-K 104(16), 29 June 1941, PISM).

71. Minutes, PRM-K 103(29) 26 June 1940, PISM. These minutes are typed on notepaper headed 'Republique de Pologne. Presidence du Conseil. Angers'. The latter is crossed out and London typed in its place.

72. Minute by Strang, assistant secretary at the Foreign Office, 4 July 1940, PRO, FO 371, 24474/C/7639.

73. Minutes, PRM-K 103(30) 6 July, 1940, PISM.

74. Minutes, PRM-K 103(31) 8 July, 1940, PISM.

75. Minutes, PRM-K 103(32) 11 July, 1940, PISM.

76. *Ibid.*

77. Minute by Roberts, 17 July 1940, PRO, FO 371, 24474/C/7629/252/55.

78. Kennard to Halifax, 18 July 1940, PRO, FO 371, Enclosure C. C/7639/252.

79. Minutes, PRM-K 103(35) 19 July 1940, PISM.
80. Minute by Strang, 20 July 1940, PRO, FO 371, 24474/C/7639.
81. *Ibid.*
82. Letter, Savery to Brigadier Charles Bridge, 15 Sept. 1940, PRO, FO 371, 24474/C/10115.
83. See minute by Roberts, 30 July 1940 on a record of impressions gained by Major Perkins of M.I.5 who accompanied Sikorski on his visit: PRO, FO 371, 24474/C/7639.
84. Minutes, PRM-K 103(33) 12 July 1940, PISM.
85. Raczynski, *op. cit.*, 60.
86. Minutes, PRM-K 103(37) 6 Aug. 1940, PISM.
87. Minutes, PRM-K 103(38) 19 Aug. 1940, PISM.

3　Anglo-Polish relations and the pact with Russia, 1941

1. Letter, Churchill to Sikorski, 24 Jan. 1940, PRO, FO 371, 26735/C/732.
2. Letter, Sikorski to Churchill, 30 Jan. 1940, PRO, FO 371, 26732/C/1107.
3. Minute by Churchill, 15 Mar. 1941, PRO, FO 371, 26732/C/2980.
4. Eden to Halifax, 28 Mar. 1941, PRO, FO 371, 26735/C/3096.
5. J. Ciechanowski, *Defeat in Victory* (1948), 32.
6. E. Raczynski, *In Allied London* (1963), 6. The ambassador, who appears to have made his entry in his diary between 25 June and 18 July 1940 identifies Retinger, Litauer and Cazalet as Sikorski's collaborators. The closest of the three was Retinger, on whom an FO minute reads: 'On personal points it is quite clear that Retinger has, for good or for ill, enormous influence with the Prime Minister. The latter laughs at him, it is true, and calls him *'le cousin du diable'*, but he is clearly regarded as a sort of household pet and everything of importance is discussed with him. It is no good, therefore, trying to circumvent Retinger. . . . [He] plays role of *eminence grise* to G.S.' Minute by H.M. Jebb, 1 Jan. 1941, PRO, FO 371, 26722/C/188. See J. Pomian (ed.), *Joseph Retinger, Memoirs of an Eminence Grise* (1972).
7. Letter, Naval Intelligence Dept., Admiralty, to Major General Beaumont Nesbitt, 25 July 1940, PRO, FO 371, 24482/C/8027/27/7177/55.
8. Minute, PRM-K 104(1) 7 January 1941, PISM.
9. Minute, H.M. Jebb, PRO, FO 371, 26722/C/188. See DPSR, I, no. 84, 102–3 which should, however, be read together with the original. As printed it accords a certainty to Sikorski's views which is not borne out in the full record.
10. Minute, H.M. Jebb, PRO, FO 371, 26722/C/188.
11. Minutes, PRM-K 104(3a) 15 Feb. 1941, PISM.
12. Letter, Savery to Roberts, reporting Sikorski's speech of 15 Jan. 1941 when Bevin opened the Polish Employment Office at 18 Devonshire Street, London: PRO, FO 371, 26738/C/835. The same file contains press cuttings from the *Glasgow Herald* of 4 Feb. 1941 giving an account of a speech delivered by S. Litauer (see note 6 above) to a group of Glasgow editors. He described Polish war aims to them as 'the reconstruction of Poland as an independent State within boundaries which will ensure security'.
13. Transcript of speech with minute by Makins, 26 Feb. 1941, PRO, FO 371, 26738/C/2088.
14. Reply to Parliamentary Question (Mr Wedgwood) 19 Mar. 1941, PRO, FO 371, 26738/C/2774.

15. Enclosure in letter, Bruce Lockhart to Strang, 31 June 1941, PRO, FO 371, 26739/C/3226.
16. *Parliamentary Debates* 5 (Commons), CCCLXV (1940), 40.
17. DPSR, I, note no. 80, 574.
18. *Manchester Guardian*, 31 May 1941.
19. DPSR, I, No. 85, 1903–8.
20. *Ibid.* The Council of Ministers decided on Kazimierz Bartel for the post: PRM-K, 104 (12) 19 June 1941, PISM. Bartel had been prime minister five times between 1926 and 1930.
21. DSPR, I, No. 85, 103–8.
22. Minutes, PRM-K (12) 19 June 1941, PISM.
23. Minutes, PRM-K (12a) 22 June 1941, PISM.
24. For the text of Churchill's speech see his *The Second World War*, III (1960), 331–3.
25. Minutes, PRM-K 104(14) 25 June 1941, PISM.
26. See DPSR, I, note no. 78, 573–4. A valuable account of this enormous transfer of population is given in Anon., *The Dark Side of the Moon* (1946). See also J. Coutouvidis, 'T.S. Eliot's Preface to *The Dark Side of the Moon* and his model of society in the light of Polish experience', *Bull. Literature and History*, North Staffordshire Polytechnic (summer 1986). Zajdlerowa's account can be corroborated by the personal reminiscences of those who survived the Russian hardships. A typical experience was recounted to me by Mrs B. Wacewicz, now living in London. Her father, Major W. Bucior, served as *Starosta* in Trembowla in 1939. He met Sikorski on 17 Sept. 1939, en route for exile, but refused to leave his post. He was taken into captivity by the NKVD and was subsequently killed at Katyn. See A. Moszyński, *Lista Katynska (The Katyn List)* (1974), 31. Also confirmed by note from General Rudnicki, 23 Oct. 1946, RAF Bushy Park. His family was deported to Russia and eventually reached Tanganyika via the Middle East and later the U.K. See references in J. Coutouvidis, 'The Matsis Papers: a Greek settler in Tanganyika', *Immigrants and Minorities, 2*, no. 2 (July 1983), 171–84.
27. Churchill, *op. cit.*, 348–9.
28. Minutes, PRM-K 104(15) 28 June 1941, PISM.
29. Eden to Bagallay (acting-counsellor at the British Embassy to Moscow. He took charge of British interests in the Soviet Union in the interregnum between Seeds and Cripps) 24 June 1941, PRO, FO 371, 26775/C/7016.
30. Record of a conversation between Sikorski and Bevin, 3 July 1941, PRO, FO 371, 26755/C/7458. Sikorski's eighth point suggests that Poland's western frontier was to be shaped in the context of negotiations over her eastern frontier. Nevertheless, see S.M. Terry, *Poland's Place in Europe. General Sikorski and the Origin of the Oder-Neisse Line, 1939–1943* (Princeton, 1983).
31. Minute by Strang, 4 July 1941, PRO, FO 371, 26755/C/7458.
32. In his conversation with Eden, Sikorski spoke of 300,000 prisoners. To his ministers he mentioned 200,000 (Minutes PRM-K 104(14) 25 June, 1941, PISM). See also note 26 above.
33. Record of a conversation between Eden and Maisky, 4 July 1941, PRO, FO 371, 26755/C/7421.
34. Eden to Dormer, 4 July 1941, PRO, FO 371, 26755/C/7422.
35. Eden to Cripps, 4 July 1941, PRO, FO 371, 26755/C/7423.
36. Minutes, PRM-K 104(16) 5 July 1941, PISM.
37. Record of conversation between Sikorski and Maisky, 5 July 1941, PRO, FO 371, 26755/C/8593 on which Eden minuted, 'This seems as good as could be expected in the circumstances.' See also DPSR. I, no. 91, 117–19.
38. Zaleski to Eden, 7 July 1941, PRO, FO 371, 26755/C/7590 and DPSR, I, no. 92, 119–22.

39. Zaleski to Eden, 8 July 1941, PRO, FO 371, 26755, and DPSR, I, no. 93, 122–8.
40. Minute by Strang, 11 July 1941, PRO, FO 371, 26755/C/7591.
41. Record of conversation between Sikorski and Maisky, 11 July 1941, PRO, FO 371, 26755 and DPSR, I, no. 94, 128–32.
42. Eden to Cripps, 16 July 1941, PRO, FO 371, 26755/C/7804.
43. Minutes, PRM-K 104(17) 12 July 1941, PISM.
44. See DPSR. I, no. 96, 132–4.
45. Minute by Makins, 13 July 1941, PRO, FO 371, 26757/C/8596.
46. Minute by Strang, 13 July 1941, *ibid*. Churchill did send, as suggested, a very sympathetic letter to Sikorski.
47. Note attached to record of conversation, Dormer with Raczkiewicz, 21 July 1941, PRO, FO 371, 26756/C/8127.
48. Record of conversation, Dormer with Raczkiewicz, *ibid*.
49. Dormer to Eden, 25 July 1941, PRO, FO 371, 26756/C/8306.
50. *Ibid*.
51. Minute by Cadogan, 29 July 1941, *ibid*.
52. Minutes, PRM-K 104(18) 21 July 1941, PISM. On 18 July Eden sent Zaleski a note emphasizing Britain's resolve not to recognize territorial changes effected during the war. See DPSR, I, no. 102, 138–9.
53. Minutes, PRM-K 104(18) 21 July, PISM.
54. Reported by Ridsdale to Roberts, 22 July 1941, PRO, FO 371, 26756/C/8217.
55. Minute by Strang, 28 July 1941, PRO, FO 371, 26756/C/8479.
56. Minutes, PRM-K 104(19) 28 July 1941, PISM.
57. See DPSR, I, no. 106, 141–2 for text of treaty.
58. See DPSR, I, Note no. 106, 580.
59. Letter, Paderewski to Sikorski, 8 Oct. 1939, 3, PRM/7 PISM.
60. Churchill, *op. cit.*, 337.
61. E. Estorick, *Stafford Cripps: a biography* (1949), 248.
62. See Raczynski, *op. cit.*, 344–6 for his 'open letter' in reply to Lloyd George's article.
63. See PSZ, II, pt. i, 330.
64. D.N. Dilks (ed.), *The Diaries of Sir Alexander Cadogan, 1938–1945* (1971).
65. *Ibid*.
66. See DPSR, I, no. 225, 365.

4   The growing isolation of the London Poles, 1942–1944

1. See Herbert Feis, *Churchill Roosevelt Stalin. The War they Waged and the Peace they Sought* (1957), 10–13 and United States: Foreign Relations of the United States, Diplomatic Papers (FRUS) (Washington, 1959) I, 768–9.
2. See W.S. Churchill, *The Second World War*, III, *The Grand Alliance* (1950), 385–6, 392–5.
3. Feis, *op. cit.*, 24, note 24.
4. See Churchill, *op. cit.*, 409.
5. See DPSR, I, nos 123–4, 167–70.
6. Churchill, *op. cit.*, 416–18.
7. R.E. Sherwood, *The White House Papers of Harry L. Hopkins* (1948), I, 395–6.
8. Churchill, *op. cit.*, 414–15.
9. See S. Kot (ed.) *Conversations with the Kremlin and Dispatches from Russia* (1963), 42–4.
10. DPSR, I, no. 128, 174–5.

11. See *ibid.*, no. 112, 147–8 for the text of the agreement.
12. *Ibid.*, no. 159, 233–7.
13. J. Ciechanowski, *Defeat in Victory* (1948), 82. See also A. Sharp, 'The origins of the "Teheran formula" on Polish frontiers', *J. Contemporary History, 12*, II (April 1977), 381–93.
14. See J. Erickson, *The Road to Stalingrad. Stalin's War with Germany* (1975), 281–92.
15. Churchill, *op. cit.*, 469.
16. *Ibid.*, 471–2.
17. FRUS (1941), I, 195.
18. DPSR, I, no. 176, 269–71.
19. W.S. Churchill, *The Second World War*, IV, *The Hinge of Fate* (1950), 293.
20. See Erickson, *op. cit.*, 273–7.
21. DPSR, I, no. 206, 328.
22. *Ibid.*, no. 194, 310–11.
23. *Ibid.*, no. 229, 370–1.
24. FRUS (1942), III, 568–9.
25. DRSR, I, no. 180, 277.
26. *Ibid.*, no. 293, 301–10.
27. Figure based on statistics supplied to the War Office in London from C. in C. Persia/Iraq, 9 Sept. 1942. PRO, FO 371, 31087/C/8796.
28. N. Davies, *God's Playground, A History of Poland* (1981), II, 464.
29. Rowecki to London, no. 140, 1 July 1942, File 3.20.20. VI (4140/42) *Studium Polski Podziemnej* (The Archives Polish Underground Study Trust, London (APUST). The report 'Soviet Communists Action in Poland' is not reproduced in their collection *Armia Krajowa w Dokumentach* (*The AK in documents*) *1939–45* (1970–) but see vol. II, *1941–43* (1973), no. 314, 274, note 4. A translation of the report, with certain omissions, was forwarded to British authorities and is to be found in PRO, FO 371, 31098/C/11247.
30. See summary of reports in letter, Savery to Roberts, 3 Sept. 1942, PRO, FO 371, 26775/C/8644. The same file contains an interesting note from Raczynski to the effect that such actions had put paid to German plans for a German sector in Warsaw. Despite the risk to Polish lives the Polish government was nevertheless willing to cooperate with Soviet authorities in identifying the dispersed military targets. *Ibid.*, C/8916.
31. See summary of reports in letter, Savery to Roberts, 23 Feb. 1941, PRO, FO 371, 26723/C/1827 and C/278.
32. Minuted by C.W. Harrison, 27 Dec. 1942, PRO, FO 371, 31098/C/12980.
33. Sikorski to Grot-Rowecki, 28 Nov. 1942, I, no. 278, 457–8 DPSR and no. 357, 269–71 *Armja Kraiowa w Dokumentach*, II (1973).
34. Ciechanowski, *op. cit.*, 151–2.
35. DPSR, I, no. 285, 473–4.
36. Ciechanowski, *op. cit.*, 154–5.
37. DPSR, I, no. 292, 486.
38. DPSR, I, no. 295, 489–501.
39. DPSR, I, no. 296, 501.
40. Sherwood, *op. cit.*, 706–7.
41. Ciechanowski, *op. cit.*, 156.
42. DPSR, I, no. 305, 523–4. Of a number of studies concerning Katyn, the best is by J.K. Zawodny, *Death in the Forest, The Story of the Katyn Forest Massacre* (1971). One may perhaps add a point that emerged during discussion at the Symposium on General Sikorski, SSEES, London, 28 Sept. 1983: there appears to be a relationship between the question of the 'Red Legions' discussed on p. 44 above and the incidence of slaughter at Katyn; a lull occurred while Soviet

authorities reviewed their options over the fate of their Polish prisoners.

43. DPSR, I, no. 306, 524.
44. *Ibid.*, I, no. 307, 525.
45. *Ibid.*, I, no. 310, 530.
46. *Ibid.*, I, no. 312, 532.
47. Letter, Savery to Roberts, 30 July 1940, PRO, FO 371, 24474/C/8090. Also quoted in J. Coutouvidis, 'The formation of the Polish Government-in-Exile and its relations with Great Britain, 1939–1941' (Ph.D. thesis, University of Keele, 1975), 224. For an investigation into the causes of Sikorski's death, see D. Irving, *The Death of General Sikorski* (1967).
48. See PRO, FO 371, 31094/C/10225.
49. J. Pomian (ed.), *Joseph Retinger, Memoirs of an Eminence Grise* (1972), 144.
50. DPSR, I, no. 295, 489–501.
51. J.R.M. Butler (ed.), *The Grand Strategy* (1956), V, 321–2.
52. FRUS (1943), II, *The First Quebec Conference*, Documents and Supplementary Papers, 1030.
53. *Ibid.*
54. DPSR, II, note no. 38, 716–17.
55. *Ibid.*, note no. 39, 718.
56. *Ibid.*, no. 39, 54–6. See also J. Erickson, *The Road to Berlin. Stalin's War with Germany*, II (1983), 264.
57. See FRUS (1943), III, 508.
58. Earl of Avon, *The Eden Memoirs. The Reckoning* (1965), 403.
59. See memo., Eden to Hull, Quebec 23 Aug. 1943. FRUS (1943), III, 1113–16.
60. *Ibid.*
61. DPSR, II, no. 41, 61–4.
62. FRUS (1943), I, 622–3.
63. *Ibid.*, 624–8.
64. *Ibid.* See pp. 639, 667–8, 762–3.
65. Minute on memo., Raczynski to Eden, 'The problem of Central and South-Eastern Europe', 17 Dec. 1942, PRO, FO 371, 31091/C/12841/464/55.
66. *Ibid.*
67. Minute by Eden on telegram from Halifax to Eden, 9 Dec. 1942, no. 5994, PRO, FO 371, 31091.
68. As for note 64 above.
69. DPSR, II, no. 47, 74–80.
70. A. Polonsky (ed.), *The Great Powers and the Polish Question 1941–45. A Documentary Study in Cold War Origins* (1976), 158, note 1.
71. *Ibid.*, no. 75, 158.
72. Churchill, *op. cit.*, V, 319–20.
73. V. Mastny, *Russia's Road to the Cold War. Diplomacy, Warfare, and the Politics of Communism, 1941–45* (New York, 1979), 132.
74. DPSR, II, no. 68, 121.
75. *Ibid.*, no. 70, 123.
76. Polonsky, *op. cit.*, 32.
77. J. Reynolds, 'Lublin v. London – The party and the underground movement in Poland 1944–1945', *J. Contemporary History*, 16, IV (Oct. 1981), 617–48.
78. An excellent account of the causes of the rising is to be found in J. Ciechancowski, *The Warsaw Uprising of 1944* (1974).
79. Quoted in R.F. Leslie (ed.), *The History of Poland since 1863* (1980), 269.
80. Polonsky, *op. cit.*, 35.
81. *Ibid.*, no. 112, 220–1.
82. Erickson, *op. cit.*, 271.

83. Davies, *op. cit.*, 478.
84. R.F. Leslie, in his valuable review of Polonsky's *The Great Powers and the Polish Question* . . ., in *History, 62*, no. 204 (Feb. 1977).
85. DPSR, II, no. 214, 372–4.
86. *Ibid.*, no. 237, 405–13.
87. *Ibid.*
88. *Ibid.*
89. *Ibid.*
90. *Ibid.*
91. *Ibid.*
92. DPSR, II, no. 238, 415–16.
93. *Ibid.*, no. 239, 416–22.
94. *Ibid.*
95. DPSR, II, no. 257, 450–7.
96. *Ibid.*, no. 269, 469.
97. *Ibid.*, no. 272, 476–7.
98. D.N. Dilks (ed.), *The Diaries of Sir Alexander Cadogan, 1938–1945* (1971), 684.
99. DPSR, II, no. 281, 491.
100. Minuted in PRO, FO 371, 26775/C/9563.
101. See minutes on the comprehensive report produced by the Polish Ministry for Foreign Affairs in May 1941, 'L'Occupation Allemande et Sovietique de la Pologne', publication of which was suppressed, PRO, FO 371, 26724/C/4932.
102. A phrase used by Arthur Koestler in his book *The Yogi and the Commissar* to convey the other-worldliness of the Russia whose wastelands imprisoned millions. It became the title of a book as explained in Anon., *The Dark Side of the Moon* (1946), 13. See above, p.327, n.26.
103. W.S. Churchill, *War Speeches, 1939–45*, compiled by C. Eade (1942), III, 90.
104. Minutes of a conversation between Jebb and Kulski, 20 Nov. 1942, PRO, FO 371, 31088/C/11601.
105. *Ibid.*
106. Polonsky, *op. cit.*, 45.
107. *The Times*, 23 Feb. 1985.

5   From the KPP to Lublin

1. M. Malinowski, *Geneza PPR* (2nd edn, Warsaw, 1975), 362–3.
2. See A. Polonsky (ed.), *The Great Powers and the Polish Question 1941–1945* (1976), 13–48. Polonsky (p. 47) makes the point that: 'As Churchill repeatedly told Mikołajczyk, the Western Powers were not prepared to go to war with the Soviet Union over Poland. The essential fact was that control of Poland was seen as vital by the Soviet Union, as it was not by Great Britain or the United States.'
3. See A. Korboński, *Politics of Socialist Agriculture in Poland 1945–1960* (New York and London, 1965), 38–40.
4. See J.K. Zawodny, *Death in the Forest, The story of the Katyn Forest Massacre* (1971) and above pp. 80, 87.
5. For the dissolution of the KPP, see further: J. Kowalski, *Komunistyczna Partia Polski 1935–1938* (Warsaw, 1975), chs XI, XII; M. Malinowski, 'Przyczynek do sprawy rozwiązania KPP' Z pola walki (1968), no. 3 (43), 3–24; A. Litwin, 'Tragiczne dzieje KPP (1935–1938)', *Zeszyty Historyczne 36* (1976), 215–31.
6. *Narada informacyjna dziewięciu partii* (Warsaw, 1947), 22–3.

7. In a message from the KC PPR to the CBKP dated 12 Jan. 1944 Gomułka admitted that 'despite the fact that the political line expressed in its programme in no sense resembles that of a communist party, the PPR is considered to be one not only by conservative and reactionary elements, but also by the working class.' See W. Gomułka, *Artykuły i przemówienia*, I (Warsaw, 1962), 61.

8. 'In Warsaw there were slogans in every street, on every house: PPR – enemy, agent of Moscow . . . The PPR is an enemy . . . A large part of society believed in this and also that the KRN was inspired by Moscow, that everyone involved in it was rolling in money and the expression "Jewish work" became generally accepted.' Gomułka quoted in J. Borkowski, 'Pertrakcje przedwyborcze między PPR i PPS a PSL (1945–6)', *Kwartalnik Historyczny*, R. LXXI z. 2 (1964), 429–30.

9. J. Kowalski, *Trudne lata. Problemy rozwoju polskiego ruchu robotniczego 1929–1935* (Warsaw, 1966), 295.

10. See further W. Ważniewski, *Bolesław Bierut* (Warsaw, 1976); N. Bethell, *Gomułka: His Poland and His Communism* (1972); H. Rechowicz, *Aleksander Zawadzki. Życie i działalność* (Katowice, 1969); Z. Jakubowski, 'Franciszek Jóźwiak "Witold" (Zarys działalności politycznej i państwowej),' *Z pola walki* (1974), no. 2 (66), 225–68.

11. The German Communist Party received 17% of the votes in the November 1932 elections. The Communists received 13% of the votes in Czechoslovakia in November 1925, coming second.

12. Kowalski, *KPP* . . ., 69–70.

13. Kowalski, *Trudne* . . ., 61.

14. Kowalski, *KPP* . . ., 61.

15. J. Holzer, *Mozaika polityczna drugiej Rzeczypospolitej* (Warsaw, 1974), 231, 515. Resolutions were passed at both the IV (1936) and V (1937) Plenums of the KPP criticizing sectarian and ultra-Leftist elements in the party for failing correctly to understand the party's new line. See Kowalski, *KPP* . . ., 209, 339–40.

16. 'Przemówienie tow. Wiesława na plenarym posiedzeniu KC PPR w dniu 3 czerwca 1948 roku,' *Zeszyty Historyczne*, 34 (1975), 60.

17. Holzer, *Mozaika* . . ., 226–33, 512–33.

18. Gomułka wrote in 1948 that 'from 1925 to 1935 . . . the KPP either questioned the right of Poland to Upper Silesia and Pomorze, or employed the slogan of the right of these territories to secede from Poland, since they had been annexed by Polish imperialism. This was without doubt a misuse of the slogan of the right of national self-determination . . . the application of the right of self-determination in those areas would without doubt have implied the negation of Poland's independence. 'Wyjaśnienie sekretarza generalnego KC PPR Władysława Gomułki w związku z jego referatem i projektem rezolucji biura politycznego,' *Zeszyty Historyczne*, 34 (1975), 81–2.

19. A. Polonsky, *Politics in Independent Poland 1921–1939* (Oxford, 1972).

20. 'Wyjaśnienie sekretarza generalnego . . .', *op. cit.*, 81.

21. In 1935 membership of the major trade union federations in Poland was as follows: *Związek Stowarzyszeń Zawodowych w Polsce* (mainly PPS) – 283,000 members; *Związek Związków Zawodowych (Sanacja)* – 147,000 members; *Zjednoczenie Zawodowe Polskie* (NPR) – 129,000 members; *Chreścijańskie Zjednoczenie Zawodowe* (Catholic) had 78,000 members in 1933. The *Lewica Związkowa* (KPP) had 51,000 members in 1933. See Kowalski, *Trudne* . . ., 251–3 and *PPR Rezolucje, odezwy, instrukcje i okólniki komitetu centralnego, viii 1944–xii 1945* (Warsaw, 1959), 62.

22. See N. Davies, *White Eagle, Red Star. The Polish-Soviet War 1919–1920* (1972), especially 150–9.

23. Holzer, *Mozaika* . . ., 226.

24. For the connection between the stance of the KPP on the national question and

the extent of its membership amongst Polish Jews, see for instance
W. Bieńkowski, *Motory i hamulce socjalizmu* (Paris, 1969), 45–6.

25. See for instance A. Zawadzka-Wetz, *Refleksje pewnego życia* (Paris, 1967), 43–4 on Bierut's attitude.

26. In a telegram to Dimitrov (12 Jan. 1943), Finder estimated the proportion of KPP veterans in the PPR at one-third: 'Depesze KC PPR do Georgii Dymitrowa (1942–43)', *Z pola walki* (1961), no. 4 (16), 178. One historian commenting on this estimate has suggested that the non-KPP members of the PPR were drawn from former trade unionists, 'united front socialists' and other 'left-wing anti-fascist forces', as well as the peasant movement, but that 'the former KPP . . . formed the basic cadre in rebuilding the party . . .': J. Naumiuk, *PPR na Kielecczyźnie* (Warsaw, 1976), 75–6.

27. 'Depesze KC . . .', 178.

28. N. Kołomejczyk, *PPR 1944–1945* (Warsaw, 1965), 275.

29. PSZ, III (1950), 123.

30. Technically, the PPR was not a member party of the Communist International. However, the PPR maintained regular radio contact from 1941–4 (with an interruption from Nov. 1943 to Jan. 1944) with Georgi Dimitrov. Dimitrov was secretary-general of the Comintern until its dissolution in May 1943 and until 1944 headed a commission which continued to coordinate the Soviet Party's links with other Communist Parties. From spring 1944 the PPR also established direct communications with the Central Bureau of Polish Communists in the USSR, see A. Przygoński, *Z zagadnień strategii frontu narodowego PPR 1942–1945* (Warsaw, 1976), 217. Despite its formal autonomy and although the PPR continued to liaise closely with Dimitrov after May 1943, the dissolution of the Comintern may well have been an important factor prompting the greater freedom of manoeuvre with which the PPR leadership approached strategic questions from mid-1943: see J. Jagiełło, *o Polską drogę do socjalizmu* (Warsaw, 1984), 46.

31. PPR statements in Jan.–Feb. 1942 spoke of 'putting an end to the split in the Polish working-class', see W. Góra (ed.), *Kształtowanie się podstaw programowych PPR w latach 1942–1945* (Warsaw, 1958), 13–16.

32. *Ibid.*, 13.

33. Przygoński, *Z zagadnień . . .*, 103–15.

34. M. Spychalski, 'Informacja przedstawiciela KC PPR na zebraniu komunistów polskich w Moskwie 8 czerwca 1944 r.', *Z pola walki* (1961), no. 4 (16), 184.

35. T. Sierocki, 'PPR-owska koncepcja jedności ruchu robotniczego w latach 1942–48', *Z pola walki* (1976), no. 4 (76), 6.

36. F. Baranowski, 'Z dziejów nurty lewicowego powojennej PPS', *Z pola walki* (1974), no. 3 (63), 26–7.

37. M. Spychalski, *Wspomnienia o partyjnej robocie (1931–44), Archiwum ruchu robotniczego*, II (Warsaw, 1975), 296.

38. Przygóński, *Z zagadnień . . .*, 83.

39. Malinowski, *Geneza . . .*, 463. Przygóński, *Z zagadnień . . .*, 49–51 suggests that Malinowski exaggerates the problem.

40. Malinowski, *Geneza . . .*, 360.

41. *Ibid.*, 351–2, 361n.

42. *Ibid.*, 463; Przgóński, *Z zagadnień . . .*, 49.

43. See Góra, *Kształtowanie się . . .*, 27–31.

44. Malinowski, *Geneza . . .*, 465–6.

45. *Ibid.*, 465–6.

46. Góra, *Kształtowanie się . . .*, 79.

47. Malinowski, *Geneza . . .*, 357n, 361, 356.

48. See further: Spychalski, *Wspomnienia* . . ., 296–8, 314–19; Przygoński, *Z zagadnień* . . ., 84; M. Malinowski, *Marceli Nowotko* (Warsaw, 1976), 82–5; Bethell, *op. cit.*, 51–3; *Polski Słownik Biograficzny*, XXIII/2, 297; P.T., 'O tajemniczej śmierci M. Nowotki i B. Mołojcá', *Zeszyty Historyczne, 59* (1982), 210–20; W. Jabłonski, 'Wyjaśnienia i uzupełnienia do artykułu "O tajemniczej śmierci M. Nowotki i B. Mołojca"', *Zeszyty Historyczne, 62* (1982), 234–6.
49. Przygoński, *Z sagadnień* . . ., 110–11.
50. Z.S. Siemaszko, 'Grupa Szańca i NSZ', *Zeszyty Historyczne, 21* (1972), 12.
51. S. Korboński, *Polskie państwo podziemne* (Paris, 1975), 102.
52. Prygoński, *Z zagadnień* . . ., 97.
53. *Ibid.*, 96–103; Góra, *Kształtowanie się* . . ., 58–63, 66–81, 93–6.
54. W. Gomułka, 'Polemika z "Archiwum Ruchu Robotniczego"', *Zeszyty Historyczne, 39* (1977), 4. This article was first published in the Paris émigré journal *Zeszyty Historyczne*. It was subsequently published in Poland in *Archiwum ruchu robotniczego, IV* (1977).
55. 'Z archiwów polskich komunistów List KC PPR "do tow. D" z 7.03.1944r', *Zeszyty Historyczne, 26* (1973), 187.
56. I. Blum (ed.), *Organizacja i działania bojowe ludowego Wojska Polskiego 1943–45. Wybór źródeł, IV, Działalność aparatu polityczno-wychowawczego* (Warsaw, 1963), 57–61.
57. Przygoński, *Z zagadnień* . . ., 20.
58. Gomułka, 'Polemika . . .', 5–6.
59. For the KRN manifesto (15 Dec. 1943) see W. Góra (ed.), *W walce o sojusz robotniczo-chłopski. Wybór dokumentów i materiałów 1944–1949* (Warsaw, 1963), 7–9.
60. Gomułka, 'Polemika . . .', 5.
61. *Ibid.*, 6–8.
62. Gomułka, 'Polemika . . .', 5.
63. Spychalski, *Wspomnienia* . . ., 335.
64. B. Syzdek, *PPS w latach 1944–1948* (Warsaw, 1974), 49n; A. Reiss, *Z problemów odbudowy i rozwoju organizacyjnego PPS 1944–1946* (Warsaw, 1971), 26–8.
65. Gomułka, *Pismo KC PPR do CBKP w ZSRR z 12.1.44r, Artykuły* . . ., I, 61.
66. B. Drukier (D.K.), 'Na marginesie polemiki Gomułki', *Zeszyty Historyczne, 43* (1978), 215; Przygoński, *op. cit.*, 172n.
67. Przygoński, *Z zagadnień* . . ., 199, 201; Syzdek, *op. cit.*, 45–6.
68. Bierut knew both Szwalbe and Osóbka-Morawski well before the war. See Ważniewski, *op. cit.*, 39; H. Rechowicz, *Bolesław Bierut 1892–1956* 20, 24, 55.
69. Kowalski had been an activist on the radical wing of the 'Liberation' Peasant Party (*PSL Wyzwolenie*) in the early 1920s and was later one of the leaders of the pro-Communist Independent Peasant Party (*Niezależna Partia Chłopska*) and the Peasant self-help movement (*Samopomoc Chłopska*). He joined the KPP in the late 1920s and worked for the agricultural section of the Central Committee. He was in regular contact with the PPR from its formation in 1942. See further: *Polski Słownik Biograficzny* t. XIV/4 z. 63, 575–7; Z. Hemmerling, *Władysław Kowalski* (Warsaw, 1977).
70. Gomułka, 'Polemika . . .', 16; Drukier, 'Na marginesie . . .', 217.
71. 'Z archiwów . . .', 187.
72. Gomułka, 'Polemika . . .', 31.
73. F. Zbiniewicz, *Armia Polska w. ZSRR* (Warsaw, 1963), 13.
74. Thus the total number of ex-members of the KPP who had been drafted into the political apparatus of the Polish army by the first half of 1944 was just 350, see Zbiniewicz, *Armia Polska* . . ., 58.
75. For the texts of these 'theses', see Blum (ed.), *Organizacja* . . ., 98–100. (number one), 110–20 (number two). A slightly different version of number one is cited

in W. Sokorski, *Polacy pod Lenino* (Warsaw, 1971), 98–100. Number three is in Góra, *Kształtowanie się* . . ., 474–87.

76. Zbiniewicz *Armia Polska* . . ., 149–73.
77. *Ibid.*, 167–8.
78. Blum (ed.), *Organizacja* . . ., 98–100.
79. *Ibid.*, 110–20.
80. Przygoński, *Z zagadnień* . . ., 145–6.
81. *Ibid.*, 212.
82. Blum (ed.), *Organizacja* . . ., 110–20.
83. Przygoński, *Z zagadnień* . . ., 209–11.
84. *Ibid.*, 226.
85. Zbiniewicz, *Armia Polska* . . ., 186, 324.
86. Gomułka, *Pismo KC PPR do CBKP w ZSRR z 12.1.44, Artykuły* . . ., I, 61–76. Published in translation by A. Polonsky and B. Drukier (eds), *The Beginnings of Communist Rule in Poland, December 1943–June 1945* (1980), 193–202.
87. 'Z archiwów . . .', 189. Lengthy excerpts from this letter were published in Przygoński, *Z zagadnień* . . ., 227–33, 258–9. See also Polonsky and Drukier, *Beginnings* . . ., 203–7.
88. Polonsky and Drukier, *Beginnings* . . ., 212–13.
89. Przygoński, *Z zagadnień* . . ., 272.
90. *Ibid.*, 228, 255–8.
91. R. Halaba, *Stronnictwo Ludowe 1944–1946* (Warsaw, 1966), 18.
92. Gomułka, 'Polemika . . .', 34.
93. J. Pawłowicz, *Z dziejów konspiracyjnej KRN 1943–44* (Warsaw, 1961), p. 75; Przygoński, *Z zagadnień* . . ., 254–9.
94. In February the émigrés had advised the PPR 'to take steps to expand the KRN's political base. These should take the form of an appeal to members of the PPS, SL, ND and other military and civil bodies. The aim should be a broad national front'; Polonsky and Drukier, *Beginnings* . . ., 203.
95. Gomułka, 'Polemika . . .', 28.
96. Gomułka, *op. cit.*, 30–1.
97. *Nowe drogi* (1948), no. 11, 20.
98. Przygoński, *Z zagadnień* . . ., 261.
99. *Dyskusje w PPR w sprawie zjednoczenia sił demokratyznych (Notatki protokolarne z posiedzeń KC PPR maj–czerwiec 1944 r), Archiwum ruchu robotniczego*, II, *op. cit.*, 156–7. See also Polonsky and Drukier, *Beginnings* . . ., 214–15.
100. At the meeting Stalin agreed in principle to recognize the KRN as the representative of the Polish nation and to open diplomatic relations with its executive organ as and when this was formed. In reply to doubts expressed by the KRN delegates as to the possibility of winning over elements from the London camp while there was a chance of a resumption in relations between the U.S.S.R. and the Government-in-Exile, Stalin is reported to have said 'you may be sure that the London Government in its present composition will never be recognised by the U.S.S.R. As regards our recognition of the KRN, we will consider this further . . . but you must first of all establish an executive body.' J.S. Haneman, 'U progu Polski Ludowej', *Z pola walki* (1969) (46), 142–3.
101. *Dyskusje w PPR* . . ., 157–60. See also Polonsky and Drukier, *Beginnings* . . ., 216–20.
102. W. Wąsowicz and L. Socha, 'Z archiwum Bolesława Bieruta', *Krytyka, 8* (1981), 76.
103. Membership of the Central Committee was as follows: Gomułka (secretary), Bierut, Jóźwiak, Aleksander Kowalski, Ignacy Loga-Sowiński and Hilary Chełchowski.

104. *Dyskusje w PPR* . . ., 161–3. See also Polonsky and Drukier, *Beginnings* . . ., 223–6.
105. See M. Malinowski (ed.), *Publicystyka konspiracyjna PPR 1942–45 Wybór dokumentów*, III (Warsaw, 1967), 299–308.
106. *Nowe Drogi* (1948), no. 11, 20–3, 46, 95–7.
107. Przygoński, *Z zagadnień* . . ., 280, 283. The ZPP declaration was published in *Wolna Polska*, 1 July 1944.
108. Przygoński, *Z zagadnień* . . ., 290–3.
109. Extracts from accounts by Franciszek Jóźwiak (Franek, Witold) to the PZPR Central Committee (AZHP 8516, delivered 2 and 6 Sept. 1959), Polonsky and Drukier, *Beginnings* . . ., 452.
110. Przygoński, *Z zagadnień* . . ., 283.
111. In fact, conspiratorial security was so tight that Spychalski was not even officially told the identity of Gomułka and Bierut before his departure for the Soviet Union. Spychalski, *Wspomnienia* . . ., 355–6.
112. Haneman, *op. cit.*, 144.
113. K. Kersten, *Polski Komitet Wyzwolenia Narodowego* (Lublin, 1965), 37–9; Przygoński, *Z zagadnień* . . ., 283–7; T. Żeńczykowski, 'Geneza i kulisy PKWN', *Kultura*, no. 7–8 (1974), 138–69. The minutes of the Presidium of the head office of the ZPP for 15 and 18 July 1944 were published in *Protokoły prezydium zarządu głównego Związku Patriotów Polskich w ZSRR (czerwiec 1943–lipiec 1944r), Archiwum ruchu robotniczego*, II, 63–153. See also Polonsky and Drukier, *Beginnings* . . ., 21–2, 233–44.
114. *Manifesto PKWN* (Warsaw, 1974). A significantly different version of the text of the manifesto is given in T. Żeńczykowski, *Geneza* . . ., 164–9.
115. Przygoński, *Z zagadnień* . . ., 291.

6 'Lublin' and 'London', July to December 1944

1. *Protokół zebrania delegatów PPR z Lubelszczyzny, 5.8.1944, Pierwsze kroki PPR po wyzwoleniu, Archiwum ruchu robotniczego*, I (Warsaw, 1973), 355. A translation of the minutes of this meeting is in A. Polonsky and B. Drukier (eds), *The Beginnings of Communist Rule in Poland, December 1943–June 1945* (1980), 258–65.
2. Speech to XII Plenum KC PZPR, 9 July 68, W. Gomułka, *Z kart naszej historii* (4th edn, Warsaw, 1970), 455.
3. 'Z archiwów polskich komunistów: List KC PPR "do tow. D" z 7.03.1944r. 'List Biura Komunistów Polskich w ZSRR do KC PPR z dn. 18.VIII.44r', 191–4, *Zeszyty Historyczne*, 26 (1973). See also extracts published in A. Przygoński, *Z zagadnień strategii frontu narodowego PPR 1942–1945* (Warsaw, 1976), and translation in Polonsky and Drukier, *Beginnings* . . ., 230–2.
4. 'Z archiwów . . .', 191.
5. 'Okólnik komitetu obwodowego PPR w Lublinie o zadaniach partii w organizowaniu władzy ludowej (sierpień 1944r.)', *Z pola walki* (1959), no. 2 (6), 120.
6. K. Kersten, *Polski Komitet Wyzwolenia Narodowego, 22 VII–31 XII 1944* (Lublin, 1965), 49. Bierut appears to have consistently handled top level contacts between Lublin and Moscow in 1944–5. The first visit by Gomułka to Moscow of which there is evidence was made in June 1945.
7. J. Gołębiowski and W. Góra (eds), *Ruch Robotniczy w Polsce Ludowej* (Warsaw, 1975), 405. However, there is some doubt if Radkiewicz was a full member, Przygoński, *Z zagadnień* . . ., 316 and *Pierwsze kroki PPR po wyzwoleniu*,

Archiwum Ruchu Robotniczego, I (1973), 392 omit Radkiewicz's name. Gomułka states that the membership of the Politburo was decided at a meeting in Lublin attended by himself, Bierut, Zawadzki, Berman, Minc and Zambrowski. Gomułka nominated Jóźwiak, despite their political differences. However, Bierut opposed his nomination and Jóźwiak was not elected: W. Gomułka, 'Polemika. z "Archiwum Ruchu Robotniczego"', *Zeszyty Historyczne, 39* (1977), 35–6. Zambrowski and Spychalski became members in spring 1945.

8. N. Kołomejczyk, *PPR 1944–1945 (Studia nad Rezwojem Organizacyjnym Partii)* (Warsaw, 1965), 22–3.

9. *Ibid.,* p. 20. The national strength of the AL in mid-1944 is generally estimated by party historians as between 50,000 and 65,000. This figure includes not only partisans, but also non-combatant support. The combined strength of AL guerrilla units (July 1944) seems to have been between 6,000 and 8,000 troops: *20 lat LWP. II sesja naukowa poświęcona wojnie wyzwoleńczej narodu polskiego 1939–45* (Warsaw, 1967), 142.

10. Kołomejczyk, *PPR . . .,* 275.

11. *Ibid.,* 40.

12. *Ibid.,* 41–2. See also B. Hillebrandt and J. Jakubowski, *Warszawska organizacja PPR 1942–1948* (Warsaw, 1978), 216–17.

13. *Instrukcja organizacyjna KC PPR dla organizacji partyjnych na wyzwolonych terenach Polski (10.9.1944), PPR . . . viii 1944–xii 1945,* 27. The instruction was drafted by Gomułka and approved by the Politburo meeting on 15 Sept. The minutes of this meeting published in Polonsky and Drukier, *Beginnings . . .,* 280 record only that the matter was discussed.

14. Kołomejczyk, *PPR . . .,* 45, 275.

15. Kołomejczyk, *PPR . . .,* 40.

16. R. Buczek, *Stronnictwo Ludowe w latach 1939–45* (1975), 175.

17. *Protokół zebrania delegatów PPR z Lubelszczyzny 5.8.44, Pierwsze kroki . . .,* 356.

18. The strength of the *Bataliony Chłopskie* and associated units as of 30 June 1944 has been estimated as 173,000 troops. Buczek, *SL . . .,* 172.

19. Minutes of the PKWN (extracts), 4 Oct. 1944: Polonsky and Drukier, *Beginnings . . .,* 295. The incident appears to have assumed considerable significance in shaping the policy of 'Lublin' towards 'ROCh'. Stalin was highly critical of the decision to release the 'ROCh' delegates. Minutes of the PPR Central Committee (extracts), 9 Oct. 1944: *ibid.,* 300. Gomułka returned to the incident at a meeting of the leadership of the PPR and PPS in Sept. 1945 as evidence of the unwillingness of 'ROCh' to cooperate with the PKWN in 1944. R. Halaba, *Stronnictwo Ludowe 1944–1946* (Warsaw, 1966), 131.

20. *Ibid.,* 40–2.

21. *Ibid.,* 42, 51.

22. Kołomejczyk, *PPR . . .,* 34.

23. Halaba, *Stronnictwo . . .,* 61.

24. *Ibid.,* 60.

25. Kersten, *PKWN . . .,* 61; E. Olszewski, *Początki władzy ludowej na Rzeszowszczyźnie 1944–47* (Lublin, 1974), 98; *Resolution of the KRN Presidium, 11 Sept. 1944:* Polonsky and Drukier, *Beginnings . . .,* 279.

26. *Report on Kotek-Agroszewski (undated), ibid.,* 354. The candidates were S. Agroszewski, A. Witos, S. Janusz, J. Maślanka and J. Czechowski, see Halaba, *Stronnictwo . . .,* 47.

27. *Ibid.,* 48–9, 53; H. Słabek, *Polityka agrarna PPR* (1st edn, Warsaw, 1967), 212–15.

28. A. Reiss, *Z problemów odbudowy i rozwoju organizacyjnego PPS 1944–1946* (Warsaw, 1971), 51; T. Sierocki, *Warszawska organizacja PPS 1944–1948* (Warsaw, 1976), 62–4.

29. *Ibid.*, 63.
30. *Protokół zebrania delegatów PPR z Lubelszczyzny, 5.8.44, Pierwsze kroki* . . ., 358.
31. J. Naumiuk, *Polska Partia Robotnicza na Kielecczyźnie* (Warsaw, 1976), 202, 217. In Mielec (Rzeszów province) PPS activists formed the core of the PPR organization set up there in 1944. See the speech by W. Zawadzki to the party conference held in Lublin on 10–11 Oct., *Pierwsze kroki* . . ., 373.
32. J. Bardach, 'O dziejach powojennej PPS', *Kwartalnik Historyczny*, R. LXXIX z. 3 (1972), 686–7.
33. *Barykada Wolności* 9 Nov. 1944 – cited in B. Syzdek, *Polska Partia Socjalistyczna w latach 1944–1948* (Warsaw, 1974), 379n.
34. Bardach, 'O dziejach . . .', 687. See also Reiss, *Z problemów* . . ., 63, 69–70. The PPR was also concerned to put pressure on the leadership of the PPS to take a harder line against former WRN elements in the party, see Minutes of the Politburo of the PPR Central Committee, 3 Dec. 1944, Polonsky and Drukier, *Beginnings* . . ., 391.
35. Sierocki, *Warszawska* . . ., 64.
36. Letter from Julian Finkielsztajn to Comrade Pukhlov, 10 Oct. 1944, Polonsky and Drukier, *Beginnings* . . ., 304–5.
37. Sierocki, *Warszawska* . . ., 62.
38. F. Mantel, 'Szkice pamiętnikarskie', *Zeszyty Historyczne 7* (1965), 129.
39. *Ibid.*, 118.
40. Minutes of the Politbureau of the PPR Central Committee, 9 Nov., 14 Dec. 1944, Polonsky and Drukier, *Beginnings* . . ., 364, 395.
41. Minutes of the Politbureau of the PPR Central Committee, 14 Dec., 17 Dec. 1944, *ibid.*, 394, 397–8.
42. Minutes of the Politbureau of the PPR Central Committee, 14 Dec. 1944, *ibid.*, 395.
43. B. Hillebrandt and J. Jakubowski, *Warszawska Organizacja PPR 1942–1948* (Warsaw, 1978), 230–1.
44. *Sprawozdanie Warszawskiego Komitetu Wojewodzkiego PPR z działalności w okresie 15.11.44–1.1.45r, Pierwsze kroki* . . ., 387.
45. W. Gomułka, *Sytuacja obecna i zadania Partii Referat wygłoszony na naradzie PPR w Lublinie 10.10.1944r, Artykuły* . . ., I, *op. cit.*, 117. The PPS leadership had revived its youth section (OM TUR) a couple of days before, see Reiss, *Z problemów* . . ., 65.
46. Minutes of the Politbureau of the PPR Central Committee, 9 Nov. 1944, Polonsky and Drukier, *Beginnings* . . ., 364.
47. E. Puacz, 'Powstanie warszawskie w protokołach PKWN', *Zeszyty Historyczne, 10* (1966), 178.
48. E. Osóbka-Morawski, 'Pamiętniki ministra' *Polityka*, no. 42 (1973).
49. Reiss, *Z problemów* . . ., 51–2; Sierocki, *Warszawska* . . ., 65.
50. *Ibid.*, p. 66; Syzdek, *op. cit.*, 80 says the membership was about 5,000; Reiss, *Z problemów* . . ., 67n, 69 gives a figure of 7,663.
51. W. Jurgielewicz, *Organizacja LWP (22 vii 44 – 9 v 45)* (Warsaw, 1968), 381, gives the strength of the First Army as 107,810 on 1 Aug. 1944. M. Plikas (ed.), *Mała kronika LWP 1943–73* (Warsaw, 1975), 484, gives a figure of 100,777 (20.7.1944). F. Zbiniewicz, *Armia Polska w ZSRR* (Warsaw, 1963), 324 says 107,000.
52. Kersten, *PKWN* . . ., 96–7.
53. *Ibid.*, 104.
54. Kersten, *PKWN* . . ., 110.
55. Przygoński, *Z zagadnień* . . ., 319.
56. I. Blum (ed.), *Organizacja i działania bojowe ludowego Wojska Polskiego 1943–1945. Wybór źródeł*. IV (Warsaw, 1963), 234–8. Report dated 30 June 1944.

57. M. Turlejska (ed.), *Z walk przeciwko zbrojnemu podziemiu 1944–47* (Warsaw, 1966), 77. See also J. Czapla, 'KBW w latach 1947–65', *Wojskowy Przegląd Historyczny*, no. 3 (1965).
58. Kersten, *PKWN* . . ., 118.
59. H. Słabek, *Dzieje polskiej reformy rolnej 1944–48* (Warsaw, 1972), 80.
60. Minutes of the Politbureau of the PPR Central Committee, 17 Dec. 1944, Polonsky and Drukier, *Beginnings* . . ., 398.
61. Minutes of the PKWN (extracts), 4 Oct. 1944, Polonsky and Drukier, *Beginnings* . . ., 295.
62. Minutes of the PPR Central Committee (extracts), 9 Oct. 1944, Polonsky and Drukier, *Beginnings* . . ., 302.
63. Minutes of the Politbureau of the PPR Central Committee, 17 Dec. 1944, Polonsky and Drukier, *Beginnings* . . ., 398. Other sources give a figure of 12,934 for the strength of the MO in Dec. 1944, J. Czapla (ed.), *W walce o utrwalenie władzy ludowej w Polsce 1944–47* (Warsaw, 1967), 221.
64. Minutes of the PPR Central Committee (extracts), 9 Oct. 1944, Polonsky and Drukier, *Beginnings* . . ., 300.
65. W. Zawadzki told the 10–11 Oct. 1944 PPR conference that in the urban areas of Rzeszów province the bulk of party members were in the militia. In Jarosław district for instance, of 100 members, 45 were in the militia and 20 in the UB, *Pierwsze kroki* . . ., *op. cit.*, 373.
66. M. Turlejska (ed.), *W walce ze zbrojnym podziemiem 1945–47* (Warsaw, 1972), 12. According to one estimate an average of almost 35,000 Red Army or Polish army troops were deployed in Lublin Poland for each 1000 sq. km of territory, Olszewski, *Początki* . . ., 103.
67. Minutes of the PKWN (extracts), 4 Oct. 1944, Polonsky and Drukier, *Beginnings* . . ., 294.
68. The strength of the AK (including affiliated formations such as the Peasant Battalions) was probably about 40,000–60,000 in Lublin okręg; about 18,000–30,000 in Białystok okręg; about 19,000–24,000 in Rzeszów province; about 5,000 in the Sandomierz-Opatów bridgehead; and perhaps 20,000 in the liberated parts of Warsaw province, see PSZ, III, 123; I. Caban and Z. Mańkowski, *ZWZ i AK w okręgu Lubelskim 1939–1944*, I (Lublin, 1971), 81; H. Majecki, *Białostocczyzna w pierwszych latach władzy ludowej 1944–48* (2nd edn, Warsaw, 1977), 12; Olszewski, *Początki* . . ., 103; P. Matusek, *Ruch oporu na ziemie opatowsko-sandomierskiej 1939–45* (Warsaw, 1976), 230.
69. PSZ, 556.
70. *Armia Krajowa w Documentach 1939–1945 no. 709 Bor to Sosnkowski, 22 July 1944*, IV (1977).
71. J. Ciechanowski, *The Warsaw Rising of 1944* (1974), 166.
72. PSZ, III , 556.
73. T. Walichnowski, *U źródeł walk z podziemiem reakcyjnym w Polsce* (Warsaw, 1975), 119.
74. See I. Caban and E. Machocki, *Za władzę ludu* (Lublin, 1975), 53–5 for the position in Lublin province; Turlejska *W walce* . . ., 220–21 for the situation in Rzeszów province.
75. Ciechanowski, *Warsaw Rising*, 190–211.
76. *Ibid.*, 188.
77. Turlejska, *W. walce* . . ., 12–13.
78. Minutes of the PKWN (extracts), 3 Aug. 1944, Polonsky and Drukier, *Beginnings* . . ., 256.
79. Minutes of the PKWN (extracts), 2 Aug. 1944, *ibid.*
80. This account is based on Caban and Machocki, *op. cit.*, 36–9; PSZ, III, 626;

Kersten, *PKWN* . . ., 30–1, 47; S. Korboński, *Polskie państwo podziemne* (Paris, 1975), 165.

81. *Protokół zebrania delegatów PPR z Lubelszczyzny 5.8.1944, Pierwsze kroki* . . ., 357.
82. *nr. 1050 Cdr. Żoliborz to Cdr. Warsaw okręg, 12.9.1944, AK w Dokumentach* . . ., IV.
83. H. Majecki, *Białostocczyzna w pierwszych latach władzy ludowej 1944–48* (2nd edn, Warsaw, 1977), 44.
84. *nr. 1163 Bor to podokręg Rzeszów, 26.9.1944, AK w Dokumentach* . . ., IV.
85. *nr. 985 Bor to Nowogródek okręg, 2.9.1944, ibid.*
86. *nr. 1052 Mikołajczyk to Bor, 13.9.1944r, ibid.*
87. Turlejska, *W walce* . . ., 13.
88. *nrs 1065, 1089, 14, 16.9.1944, AK w Dokumentach* . . ., IV.
89. Minutes of the Politbureau of the PPR Central Committee, 17 Dec. 1944, Polonsky and Drukier, *Beginnings* . . ., 397.
90. *Rezolucja KC PPR o sytuacji politycznej i zadaniach partii 26.9.44, PPR* . . . *viii 1944–xii 1945*, 30–7.
91. *Protokół konferencji sekretarzy komitetów powiatowych i aktywu PPR terenów wyzwolonych 10–11.10.44, Pierwsze kroki* . . ., 364.
92. *Ibid.*, 373.
93. Minutes of the PKWN (extracts), 4 Oct. 1944, Polonsky and Drukier, *Beginnings* . . ., 294.
94. I. Blum, 'Sprawa 31pp', *Wojskowy Przegląd Historyczny*, no. 3 (1965), 45.
95. *Okólnik KC PPR o zadaniach komitetów folwarcznych w realizowaniu reformy rolnej 26.9.44, PPR* . . . *vii 1944–xii 1945, op. cit.*, 39–41.
96. *Instrukcja KC PPR o zadaniach organizacji partyjnych w przeprowadzeniu prac przygotowawczych dla podziału ziemi obszarniczej 28.9.1944, ibid.*, 42–5.
97. Minutes of the PKWN (extracts), 4 Oct. 1944, Polonsky and Drukier, *Beginnings* . . ., 295.
98. Minutes of the PPR Central Committee (extracts), 9 Oct. 1944, *ibid.*, 300.
99. PPR National Conference (Selected Minutes), 12–13 Nov. 1944, *ibid.*, 371.
100. Minutes of the Politbureau of the PPR Central Committee, 29 Oct. 1944, *ibid.*, 359.
101. Blum, 'Sprawa . . .', 45.
102. Z.S. Siemaszko, 'Sprawa Berlinga', *Zeszyty Historyczne*, 38 (1976), 224–9.
103. Polonsky and Drukier, *Beginnings* . . ., 292.
104. *Protokół z posiedzenia PKWN z dnia 27 września 1944 w Lublinie*, Puacz, *op. cit.*, 192.
105. *Sprawozdanie Bolesława Bieruta na posiedzeniu KC PPR 9 października 1944r z rozmów z Józefem Stalinem, Archiwum Ruchu Robotniczego*, I, 351.
106. Polonsky and Drukier, *Beginnings* . . ., 300.
107. Minutes of the PPR Central Committee (extracts), 9 Oct. 1944.
108. At the PPR conference held in Lublin on 10–11 Oct. the PPR district secretary for Biała Podlaska, expressed the incomprehension of the *aktyw* over the delay in the land reform: 'Since the Red Army and the Party are in such a strong position, why wasn't reform carried out at once? After all, that was our great mistake in 1920.' *Protokół konferencji sekretarzy komitetów powiatowych i aktywu PPR z terenów wyzwolonych, 10/11.10.1944, Pierwsze kroki* . . ., 369.
109. Hillebrandt and Jakubowski, *op. cit.*, 216–17.
110. *Protokół konferencji sekretarzy komitetów powiatowych i aktywu PPR z terenów wyzwolonych, 10–11.10.1944, Pierwsze kroki* . . ., 377. In a letter to the editors of *Archiwum ruchu robotniczego* (II, 370), Konopka denied that he had called for an intensification of repression against the AK.
111. Minutes of the PPR Central Committee (extracts), 9 Oct. 1944, Polonsky and Drukier, *Beginnings* . . ., 301.

112. J. Borkowski, 'Nie tylko pod Lenino', *Miesięcznik literacki* no. 4 (1972), 87–91.
113. Olszewski, *Początki* . . ., 67.
114. *Protokół z posiedzenia PKWN dnia 15 września 1944r*, Puacz, *op. cit.*, 183–4.
115. Blum (ed), *Organizacja* . . ., 358.
116. Minutes of the PKWN, 15 Sept. 1944, Polonsky and Drukier, *Beginnings* . . ., 291.
117. Majecki, *op. cit.*, 46.
118. Meeting of the Politbureau and Central Committee of the PPR, 22 Oct. 1944, Polonsky and Drukier, *Beginnings* . . ., 356.
119. Ciechanowski, *Warsaw Rising*, 273.
120. *20 lat* . . ., *op. cit.*, 332.
121. Blum, 'Sprawa . . .', Z. Załuski, *Czterdziesty czwarty. Wydarzenia, obserwacje refleksje* (4th edn, Warsaw, 1969), 409–23.
122. W. Pobóg-Malinowski, *Najnowsza historia polityczna Polski*, III (1960), 778–92; J.J. Terej, *Na rozstajach dróg. Ze studiów nad obliczem i modelem Armii Krajowej* (Wrocław, 1978), 272–85.
123. PSZ, 910–14.
124. On 8 Sept. the NSZ killed nearly 100 Soviet and AL partisans at Rząbiec, powiat Włoszczowa, Walichnowski, *op. cit.*, 133.
125. Załuski, *op. cit.*, 459–63; Majecki, *op. cit.*, 46.
126. *Protokół konferencji sekretarzy komitetów powiatowych i aktywu PPR z terenów wyzwolonych, 10–11.10.44, Pierwsze kroki* . . ., 380.
127. Minutes of the Politbureau of the PPR Central Committee, 3 Dec. 1944, Polonsky and Drukier, *Beginnings* . . ., 391.
128. Przygoński, *Z zagadnień* . . ., 327.
129. Minutes of the Politbureau of the PPR Central Committee, Polonsky and Drukier, *Beginnings* . . ., 394–5.
130. A. Polonsky, *The Great Powers and the Polish Question 1941–1945. A Documentary Study in Cold War Origins* (1976). 37.
131. APUST t.16 L.dz.K 595/45 Sobol (Jankowski) to president and prime minister, 28 Dec. 1944.
132. APUST L.dz.K 516 and 517/45 Walkowicz (A. Bién) to president and prime minister, 25 Jan. 1945.
133. Gomułka, *Artykuły* . . ., I, *op. cit.*, 144.
134. *Protokół konferencji sekretarzy komitetów powiatowych i aktywu PPR z terenów wyzwolonych, 10–11.10.1944, Pierwsze kroki* . . ., 381.
135. *Instrukcja KC PPR w sprawie zadań organizacji partyjnych w walce z wypaczeniami reformy rolnej 25.10.1944, PPR . . . vii 1944–xii 1945*, 82.
136. 'Z materiałow listopadowej konferencji PPR w Lublinie w 1944r', *Z pola walki* (1959) no. 2 (6), 139–43; Słabek, *Polityka agrarna* . . ., 230–3.
137. Minutes of the PPR Central Committee (extracts), 9 Oct. 1944, Polonsky and Drukier, *Beginnings* . . ., 300.
138. Minutes of the Politbureau of the PPR Central Committee, 9 Nov. 1944, *ibid.*, 364.
139. Minutes of the Politbureau of the PPR Central Committee, 17 Dec. 1944, *ibid.*, 397.
140. Słabek, *Dzieje* . . ., 92.
141. Kołomejczyk, *PPR* . . ., 275.
142. W. Gomułka, H. Minc and R. Zambrowski, *Przemówenia na rozszerzonym plenum KC PPR w lutym 1945r.* (Katowice, 1945), 26.
143. Minutes of the Politbureau of the PPR Central Committee, 14 Dec. 1944, Polonsky and Drukier, *Beginnings* . . ., 394.
144. Kołomejczyk, *PPR* . . ., 275.

145. Syzdek, *op. cit.*, 79–80.
146. Minutes of the Politbureau of the PPR Central Committee, 3 Dec. 1944; Minutes of the Politbureau of the PPR Central Committee, 17 Dec. 1944; Polonsky and Drukier, *Beginnings* . . ., 391, 398.
147. Sierocki, *PPR-owska* . . ., 10–11.
148. The PKWN manifesto declared that 'Property stolen by the Germans from citizens – peasants, shop-keepers, (small) craftsmen, (small and medium-scale) industrialists, institutions and the Church – will be returned to its rightful owners', *Manifest PKWN* (1974 version), *op. cit.*, 20. The words in parenthesis are not included in the version of the manifesto published by T. Żeńczykowski, 'Geneza i kulisy PKWN', *Kultura*, no. 7–8 (1974), 167.
149. H. Słabek, 'Ogólne aspekty polityki PPS w kształtowaniu nowych stosunków przemysłowych', *Z pola walki* (1978) no. 1 (81), 43. Minutes of the PKWN (extracts), 7 Oct. 1944, Polonsky and Drukier, *Beginnings* . . ., 296–7.
150. J. Kaliński and Z. Landau (eds), *Gospodarka Polski Ludowej 1944–1955* (Warsaw, 1974), 82.
151. See further J. Reynolds, 'Communists, Socialists and workers: Poland 1944–48', *Soviet Studies*, 30.4 (Oct. 1978), 519–20.
152. B. Rumiński, speaking to an industrial conference in Praga, 14 Oct. 1944, quoted in J. Gołebiowski, *Nacjonalizacja przemysłu w Polsce* (Warsaw, 1965), 112.
153. Minutes of the Politbureau of the PPR Central Committee, 29 Oct. 1944, Polonsky and Drukier, *Beginnings* . . ., 359.
154. Gomułka, *Referat wygłoszony na naradzie partyjnej w Lublinie, 13.11.1944, Artykuły* . . ., I, 125–7.
155. *Ibid.*, 128–30; Meeting of the Politbureau and Central Committee of the PPR, 22 Oct. 1944, Polonsky and Drukier, *Beginnings* . . ., 356.
156. Gomułka, *Referat wygłoszony na naradzie w Lublinie, 13.11.44 Artykuły* . . ., I, 133, 135–6; *Okólnik KC PPR 'W sprawie ochotniczego zaciągu do Wojska Polskiego', 22.11.44, PPR* . . . *vii 1944–xii 1945*, 83–5.
157. Kołomejczyk, *PPR* . . ., 22.
158. Gomułka, *Referat wygłoszony na I ogólnokrajowej naradzie PPR, 27.5.1945, Artykuły* . . ., I, 281.
159. For example, Gomułka said that the 'majority' of the AK were 'hostile', Minutes of the Politbureau of the PPR Central Committee, 29 Oct. 1944, Polonsky and Drukier, *Beginnings* . . ., 359.
160. Gomułka, *Sytuacja obecna i zadania Partii. Referat wygłoszony na naradzie PPR w Lublinie, 10.10.1944, Artykuły* . . ., I, 112–13.
161. *Projekt uchwały rozszerzonego plenum KC PPR o zadaniach partii na wsi, 7.2.1945, PPR* . . . *vii 1944–xii 1945*, 96.
162. *Uchwała plenum KC PPR w sprawach politycznych, 26.5.1945, ibid.*, 141.
163. Hillebrandt and Jakubowski, *op. cit.*, 219–20. See also Sierocki, *Warszawska* . . ., 230.
164. Gomułka, *Sytuacja obecna i zadania Partii. Referat wygłoszony na naradzie PPR w Lublinie, 10.10.44, Artykuły* . . ., I, 98.
165. Przygoński, *Z zagadnień* . . ., 344.
166. List Berlinga do Gomułki, 20.x.1956, in J. Nowak, 'Sprawa gen. Berlinga', *Zeszyty Historyczne*, 37 (1976), 39.
167. Turlejska, *W walce* . . ., 14.
168. Minutes of the Politbureau of the PPR Central Committee, 17 Dec. 1944, Polonsky and Drukier, *Beginnings* . . ., 399.
169. Polonsky and Drukier, *Beginnings* . . ., 399.
170. Gomułka, *Nadszedł moment utworzenia rządu tymczasowego. Wywiad dla 'Rzeczypospolitej' opublikowany 7.12.1944, Artykuły* . . ., I, 141–5.

7 The spring crisis and the 'May turn', January to June 1945

1. Several of the best-known anti-Communist partisan leaders active in 1945–7: 'Ogień' (J. Kuraś), 'Bury' (R. Rajs), 'Wołyniak (J. Zdziarski), A. Żubryd, 'Mścisław' (M. Wadolny), for instance, were in 1944–5 members of the army, militia or UB.
2. Extracts of the minutes of the Plenum of the PPR Central Committee, 20–21 May 1945, A. Polonsky and B. Drukier, *The Beginnings of Communist Rule in Poland December 1943–June 1945* (1980), 435, 440. The first large KBW operation against the underground did not take place until Feb. 1946.
3. Polonsky and Drukier, *Beginnings . . .*, 427.
4. PSZ, 926.
5. APUST File 52 L.dz.K. 2404/45 Korboński to London, 27 Apr. 1945. I. Caban and E. Machocki, *Za władzę ludu* (Lublin, 1975), 97.
6. *Polegli w walce o władzę ludową* (Warsaw, 1970) 32–65. In 1945 61% of assassinations took place in Białystok, Lublin and Rzeszów provinces. A further 14% took place in Warsaw province, partially liberated in 1944.
7. W. Pobóg-Malinowski, *Najnowsza historia polityczna Polski 1864–1945*, III (1960), 854–5; S. Korboński, *Polskie państwo podziemne* (Paris, 1975), 215.
8. J. Czapla, *W walce o utrwalenie, władzy ludowej w Polsce 1944–47* (Warsaw, 1967), 51–2; T. Walichnowski, *U źródeł walk z podziemiem reakcyjnym w Polsce* (Warsaw, 1975), 120.
9. PSZ, 925–7.
10. H. Majecki, *Białostocczyzna w pierwszych latach władzy ludowej 1944–48* (2nd edn, Warsaw, 1977), 113; Pobóg-Malinowski, *op. cit.*, 877–8, analyses the extent to which the order was ignored.
11. *Ibid.*, 878–82; Czapla, *W walce . . .*, 52–3.
12. APUST File 52 L.dz.K. 1802/45 Rzepecki to Anders, 5 Apr. 1945; Korboński, *Polskie . . .*, 220–2; Pobóg-Malinowski, *op. cit.*, 856–73 discusses in detail developments in London and within the underground leadership, Nov. 1944 to Mar. 1945.
13. Aleksander Zawadzki, for example, spoke of the danger of civil war at the May 1945 Plenum. Extracts of the minutes of the Plenum of the PPR Central Committee, 20–21 May 1945, Polonsky and Drukier, *Beginnings . . .*, 429.
14. APUST File 52, L.dz.K 2313/45 Korboński to London, 26 Apr. 1945.
15. R. Szpała, 'Z dziejów MO i SB w pierwszych latach władzy ludowej w pow. Bielsk Podlaski', *Wojskowy Przegląd Historyczny* (1977), no. 4, 187.
16. Majecki, *op. cit.*, 121; Turlejska (ed.), *Z walk przeciko zbrojnemu podziemiu 1944–47* (Warsaw, 1966), 238 *and passim*.
17. Extracts of the minutes of the Plenum of the PPR Central Committee, 20–21 May 1945, Polonsky and Drukier, *Beginnings . . .*, 440.
18. F. Ryszka (ed.), *Polska Ludowa 1944–50. Przemiany społeczne* (Wrocław, 1974), 279, 285, 341.
19. B. Hillebrandt and J. Jakubowski, *Warszawska organizacja PPR 1942–1948* (Warsaw, 1978), 376–8, 349.
20. J. Kaliński and Z. Landau (eds), *Gospodarka Polski Ludowej 1944–1955* (Warsaw, 1974), 146–53.
21. I. Kostrowicka, Z. Landau and J. Tomaszewski, *Historia gospodarcza Polski XIX i XX wieku* (Warsaw, 1975), 486.
22. J. Gołębiowski, *Nacjonalizacja przemysłu w Polsce* (Warsaw, 1965), 222.
23. Ryszka, *op. cit.*, 357–8, 367. It is estimated that real earnings in 1945 did not rise

above 40% of the 1938 level. See A. Jezierski, *Historia gospodarcza Polski Ludowej 1944–68* (Warsaw, 1971), 120.

24. *Ibid.*, 93–4.
25. Extracts of the minutes of the Plenum of the PPR Central Committee, 20–21 May, 1945, Polonsky and Drukier, *Beginnings* . . ., 438.
26. 'Sprawozdanie KW PPR w Łodzi za okres od 15.4. do 15.5 1945r., Sprawozdania komitetów wojewódzkich PPR z 1945r.', *Z pola walki* (1971), no. 4 (56), 287.
27. Sprawozdanie KW PPR Warsaw, 25 Apr. 1945, quoted in Hillebrandt and Jakubowski, *op. cit.*, 261.
28. Hillebrandt and Jakubowski, *op. cit.*, 412.
29. R. Zambrowski, *O masową milionową partię* (Warsaw, 1946), 12.
30. W. Gomułka, H. Minc and R. Zambrowski, *Przemówienia na rozszerzonym plenum KC PPR w lutym 1945r.* (Katowice, 1945), 17.
31. W. Gomułka, *Referat wygłoszony na I ogólnokrajowej naradzie PPR, 27.5.1945, Artykuły* . . ., I, 265.
32. Extracts of the minutes of the Plenum of the PPR Central Committee, 20–21 May 1945; Polonsky and Drukier, *Beginnings* . . ., 433.
33. T. Sierocki, *Warszawska organizacja PPS 1944–1948* (Warsaw, 1976), 171; J. Kantyka, *Polska Partia Socjalistyczna na Śląsku i Zagłębiu Dąbrowskim w latach 1944–48* (Katowice, 1975), 185; E. Wojnowski, *Warmia i Mazury w latach 1944–1947* (Olsztyn, 1970), 91; J. Naumiuk, *Początki władzy ludowej na Kielecczyźnie 1944–47* (Lublin, 1969), 130; J. Naumiuk, *Polska Partia Robotnicza na Kielecczyźnie* (Warsaw, 1976), 359.
34. Gomułka, *Referat wygłoszony na I ogólnokrajowej naradzie PPR, 27.5.1945., Artykuły* . . ., I, 267.
35. *Dekret Rady Ministrów, O utworzeniu rad zakładowych, 6.2.45, PPR* . . . *vii 1944–xii 1945, op. cit.*, 267–75.
36. Gomułka, Minc and Zambrowski, *op. cit.*, 21.
37. J. Gołębiowski, *Problemy nacjonalizacja przemysłu* in *Uprzemysłowienie ziem polskich w XIX i XX wieku* (Warsaw, 1970) quoting a KCZZ report for April.
38. *Uchwała plenum KC PPR w sprawach gospodarczych, 26.5.45, PPR* . . . *viii 1944–xii 1945, op. cit.*, 145–52.
39. W. Góra, *Polska Rzeczpospolita Ludowa 1944–1947* (Warsaw, 1974), 129; see also B. Syzdek, *Polska Partia Socjalistyczna w latach 1944–1948* (Warsaw, 1974), 261–2; Gomułka, *Referat wygłoszony na I ogólnokrajowej naradzie PPR, 27.5.1945, Artykuły* . . ., I, 268.
40. 'Sprawozdania KW PPR . . .', 287.
41. *Uchwała w sprawie płac zarobkowych KCZZ, 21/22.4.45, Sprawozdanie KCZZ (listopad 1944–listopad 1945)* (Warsaw, 1945), 110–12.
42. H. Jakubowska, Walka o jednolite związki zawodowe w pierwszych latach Polski Ludowej, *Studia i materiały z dziejów Polski Ludowej, 12* (1978), 148.
43. 'Sprawozdania KW PPR . . .', 287.
44. Jakubowska, *op. cit.*, 149–50.
45. Zambrowski, *O masową* . . ., 30–1.
46. Sprawozdanie KW PPR Warsaw, 20 June 1945, quoted in Hillebrandt and Jakubowski, *op. cit.*, 435.
47. On the activity of the WRN see: K. Pużak, 'Wspomnienia 1939–45', *Zeszyty historyczne, 41* (1977), 128–34; Z. Zaremba, *Wojna i konspiracja* (1957), 305–6; Syzdek, *op. cit.*, 83–4; A. Reiss, *Z problemów odbudowy i rozwoju organizacyj nego PPS 1944–1946* (Warsaw, 1971), 213–14; Kantyka, *PPS na Śląsku* . . ., 161–2.
48. Pużak, *op. cit.*, 130.
49. In Kraków (June 1945), the PPS had some 31,000 members in the province as a

whole to 21,000 for the PPR. In the city itself (May 1945) the PPS led the PPR by 4,000 to 2,000 (May 1945) and in Katowice province by 23,000 to 20,000 (June 1945). See Z. Kozik, *Partie i stronnictwa polityczne w Krakowskiem 1945–1947* (Kraków, 1975), 23; Reiss, *op. cit.*, 189; Kołomejczyk, *PPR* . . ., 277; R. Wapiński, *Pierwsze lata władzy ludowej na wybrzeżu gdańskim* (Gdańsk, 1970), 31; K. Ćwik, *Problemy współdziałania PPR i PPS w województwie krakowskim 1945–48* (Kraków, 1974), 51.

50. Minutes of a meeting of the secretariat of the PPR Central Committee (extracts), 24 Apr. 1945, Polonsky and Drukier, *Beginnings* . . ., 423.

51. *Okólnik KC PPR 'w sprawie uporządkowania przynależności partyjnej i oczyszczenia szeregów partii z elementów niepożądnych (7.4.45) PPR . . . vii. 1944–xii. 1945, op. cit.*, 124–31.

52. *Ibid.*, 125. In 1944 Gomułka had described Poznań province as 'a blank page for the Party', PPR national conference (selected minutes), 12–13 Nov. 1944, Polonsky and Drukier, *Beginnings* . . ., 386.

53. Kołomejczyk, *PPR* . . ., 98–9, 277.

54. Zambrowski, *O masową* . . ., 54.

55. Kołomejczyk, *PPR* . . ., 95.

56. Extracts of the minutes of the Plenum of the PPR Central Committee, 20–21 May 1945, Polonsky and Drukier, *Beginnings* . . ., 428.

57. *Uchwała Plenum KC w sprawach organizacyjnych (26.5.45), PPR . . . viii 1944–xii 1945, op. cit.*, 154.

58. Extracts of the minutes of the Plenum of the PPR Central Committee, 20–21 May 1945, Polonsky and Drukier, *Beginnings* . . ., 430–1, 433.

59. *Ibid.*, 431, 439–40.

60. Gomułka, *Referat wygłoszony na rozszerzonym plenum KC PPR 6.2.1945r., Artykuły* . . ., I, 215.

61. Hillebrandt and Jakubowski, *op. cit.*, 434.

62. Gomułka, *Referat wygłoszony na rozszerzonym plenum KC PPR 6.2.1945r., Artykuły* . . ., I, 215.

63. Reiss, *op. cit.*, 106.

64. T. Sierocki, 'PPR-owska koncepcja ruchu robotniczego w latach 1942–48', *Z pola walki* (1976), no. 4 (76), 12.

65. J. Bardach, 'O dziejach powojennej PPS', *Kwartalnik Historyczny* R. LXXIX, 3 (1972), 688.

66. Ćwik, *op. cit.*, 49.

67. Syzdek, *op. cit.*, 107–8, 453.

68. Reiss, *op. cit.*, 109.

69. Extracts of the minutes of the Plenum of the PPR Central Committee, 20–21 May 1945, Polonsky and Drukier, *Beginnings* . . ., 435.

70. Kozik, *op. cit.*, 32.

71. *Ibid.*, 41–50; Extracts of the minutes of the Plenum of the PPR Central Committee, 20–21 May 1945, Polonsky and Drukier, *Beginnings* . . ., 429.

72. Kantyka, *PPS na Śląsku* . . ., 157; Bardach, 'O dziejach . . .', 688.

73. Extracts of the minutes of the Plenum of the PPR Central Committee, 20–21 May 1945, Polonsky and Drukier, *Beginnings* . . ., 437.

74. R. Halaba, *Stronnictwo Ludowe 1944–1946* (Warsaw, 1966), 84.

75. R. Buczek, *Stronnictwo ludowe w latach 1939–45. Organizacja i polityka* (1975), 378.

76. A. Wojtas, *Kryzys programu i polityka 'Rocha'. Powstanie SL 'Wola ludu'* (place of publication not given, 1976), 165.

77. *Ibid.*, 166; Halaba *Stronnictwo* . . ., 81.

78. *Ibid.*, 102–3; S. Jarecka-Kimlowska, *Związek Młodzieży Wiejskiej 'Wici'. Walka o oblicze ideowe i nowy model organizacyjny 1944–48* (Warsaw, 1972), 92–4.

79. Extracts of the minutes of the Plenum of the PPR Central Committee, 20–21 May 1945, Polonsky and Drukier, *Beginnings* . . ., 431–2.

80. *Ibid.*, 427.

81. *Ibid.*, 430.

82. Polonsky and Drukier, *Beginnings* . . ., 434, 436.

83. *Ibid.*, 425.

84. *Ibid.*, 430.

85. Polonsky and Drukier, *Beginnings* . . ., 429.

86. *Ibid.*, 424, 429.

87. Sprawozdanie KW PPR w Białymstoku za lipiec 1945r., Sprawozdania KW PPR . . ., *op. cit.*, 293.

88. Extracts of the minutes of the Plenum of the PPR Central Committee, 20–21 May 1945, Polonsky and Drukier, *Beginnings* . . ., 437.

89. *Ibid.*, 432.

90. S. Przywuski, 'PPS w woj. Gdańskim 1945–48. Powstanie organizacja i formy działania', *Z pola walki* (1978) no. 1 (81).

91. Extracts of the minutes of the Plenum of the PPR Central Committee, 20–21 May 1945, Polonsky and Drukier, *Beginnings* . . ., 426–7, 434.

92. Kozik, *op. cit.*, 50.

93. Central Party Control Commission resolution of 28 Nov. 1945 concerning Zawadzki, Włodzimierz (Jasny) and Minutes of a hearing with Włodzimierz Zawadzki, 26 Nov. 1945, Polonsky and Drukier, *Beginnings* . . ., 450–1; 'Protokoły z pos. Sekretariatu KC w dniu 15.XI.45, Protokół KC (1945)', *Zeszyty Historyczne*, 24 (1973), 147.

94. See for instance: Puzak, *op. cit.*, 134 *et passim*; K. Bagiński, 'Proces szesnastu w Moskwie', *Zeszyty Historyczne*, 4 (1964); Z. Stypułkowski, *Invitation to Moscow* (1951); Korboński, *Polskie* . . ., 220–2; *Polish Plotters on Trial. The full report of the trial of Polish diversionists in Moscow, June 1945* (1945).

95. APUST File 52, L.dz.K. 3346/45, Korboński to London, received 11 June 1945.

96. S. Wójcik, 'Stanowisko W. Witosa w 1945r.', *Zeszyty Historyczne*, 34 (1975), 200.

97. Extracts of the minutes of the Plenum of the PPR Central Committee, 20–21 May 1945, Polonsky and Drukier, *Beginnings* . . ., 426.

98. Gomułka, *Referat wygłoszony na I ogólnokrajowej naradzie PPR, 27.5.1945r., Artykuły* . . ., I, 283.

99. Extracts of the minutes of the Plenum of the PPR Central Committee, 20–21 May 1945; Polonsky and Drukier, *Beginnings* . . ., 428.

100. APUST File 52 L.dz.K. 3439/45, Korboński to London, 12 June 1945.

101. Gomułka, *Referat wygłoszony na naradzie PPR w Lublinie 10.10.1944r., 'Artykuły* . . .', I, 115.

102. *Uchwała plenum KC PPR w sprawie politycznych, 26.5.45 PPR . . . viii 1944 – xii 1945, op. cit.*, 141.

103. Gomułka, *Referat wygłoszony na I ogólnokrajowej naradzie PPR, 27.5.1945r., Artykuły* . . ., I, 284.

104. Z. Załuski, *Czterdziesty czwarty. Wydarzenia, obserwacje, refleksje* (4th edn, Warsaw, 1969), 460.

105. Extracts of the minutes of the Plenum of the PPR Central Committee, 20–21 May 1945, Polonsky and Drukier, *Beginnings* . . ., 432.

106. Gomułka, *Referat wygłoszony na I ogólnokrajowej naradzie PPR 27.5.1945r., Artykuły* . . ., I, 281–2.

107. APUST File 52 L.dz.K. 3439/45, *op. cit.*

108. Walichnowski, *op. cit.*, 135.

109. *Ibid.*, 136–7.

110. 'Protokół posiedzenia Głównej Komisji Politycznej dla spraw Walki z

Bandyhtyzmem, 8.6.45', *Z pola walki* (1965), no. 3 (31), 196–200.

111. *Instrukcja KC PPR o zadaniach grup agit-prop. przy jednostkach WP prowadzących walkę z bandami reakcyjnymi,* June 1945, *PPR . . . viii 1944 – xii 1945, op. cit.,* 174–8.

112. *Protokół pos. GKP . . ., op. cit.,* 198–200.

113. Gomułka, *Referat wygłoszony na I ogólnokrajowej naradzie PPR, 27.5.1945r., Artykuły . . .,* I, 265.

114. Kaliński and Landau (eds), *op. cit.,* 84.

115. *Uchwała KCZZ w spr. aprowizacji, 21–22.4.45, Sprawozdanie KCZZ . . ., op. cit.,* 121–2.

116. The decree came into force on 20 May. Election arrangements were governed by an order of the Ministry of Labour, 7 May. Ryszka, *op. cit.,* 313n.

117. *Uchwała plenum KC PPR w spr. gospodarczych, 26.5.45, PPR . . . vii 1944 – xii 1945, op. cit.,* 147.

118. Ryszka, *op. cit.,* 313n; see also Gomułka, *Wywiad dla redakcji czasopisma 'Trybuna Związkowca', 1.6.45, Artykuły . . .,* I, 288–92.

119. Kaliński and Landau (eds), *op. cit.,* 83.

120. *Ibid.,* 83.

121. *Ibid.,* 83.

122. J.M. Montias, *Central Planning in Poland* (2nd edn, Westport, Conn., 1974), 52.

123. Ćwik, *op. cit.,* 108.

124. *Uchwała plenum KC PPR w sprawach gospodarczych, 26.5.45, PPR . . . vii 1944–xii 1945, op. cit.,* 147–8.

125. Kaliński and Landau (eds), *op. cit.,* 86–9; Ryszka, *op. cit.,* 315.

126. Extracts of the minutes of the Plenum of the PPR Central Committee, 20–21 May 1945, Polonsky and Drukier, *Beginnings . . .,* 424.

127. *Uchwała plenum KC PPR w sprawach gospodarczych, 26.5.45, PPR . . . vii 1944 – xii 1945, op. cit.,* 147–8.

128. S. Jarecka-Kimlowska, *Z problemów spółdzielczości wiejskiej w Polsce w latach 1944–57* (Warsaw, 1977), 27–9.

129. Gomułka, Minc and Zambrowski, *op. cit.,* 20.

130. Extracts of the minutes of the Plenum of the PPR Central Committee, 20–21 May 1945, Polonsky and Drukier, *Beginnings . . .,* 438.

131. *Ibid.,* 430, 432.

132. *Ibid.,* 441.

133. Minutes of a meeting of the secretariat of the PPR Central Committee (extracts), 23 June 1945, Polonsky and Drukier, *Beginnings . . .,* 449.

134. *Protokół z posiedzenia Sekretariatu KC odbytego w dniu 8.8.1945r., Protokoły KC* (1945), *op. cit.,* 132.

135. *Uchwała plenum KC PPR w spr. politycznych, 26.5.45, PPR . . . viii 1944 – xii 1945, op. cit.,* 142.

136. Gomułka, *Przemówienie wygłoszone na XXVI Kongresie PPS, 29.6.1945r., Artykuły . . .,* I, 303.

137. When addressing Socialist audiences, the Communists stressed the joint leadership of the government coalition by 'the working class' – i.e. by the PPR and PPS, see *ibid.,* 302–3. Internally, however, the PPR continued to call on its activists to work to achieve a leading role for the party. Party members were instructed to work to 'ensure the leading role of the Party in the work of the state apparatus and among the Polish nation by strengthening the authority, activity and initiative of the Party and not through patronage and administrative means'. *Uchwała plenum KC PPR w sprawach politycznych, 26.5.45, PPR . . . vii 1944–xii 1945, op. cit.,* 142. Gomułka, in his commentary on the resolutions on the May Plenum, said that 'the PPR . . . has the aspiration to

lead in the democratic national front and in the Polish nation.' He added that 'the tasks which the Plenum of the KC PPR has placed on all Party organizations can be carried out only by arduous, self-sacrificing, day-in-day-out work by all members of the Party. Our Party will then be able to take its rightful place and will become the leading party of the nation.' Gomułka, *O uchwałach plenum KC PPR, maj 1945, Artykuły . . .*, I, 254. In contrast, at the Feb. 1945 Plenum he had emphasized that the party's leading role was well-established and followed from its marxist character: 'the correctness of our Party's assessment of political events and its political far-sightedness, which follows from the marxist character of the Party, also contributed to the fact that the PPR was from the beginning the leading party of the democratic front.' Gomułka, *Referat wygłoszony na rozszerzonym plenum KC PPR, 6.2.45, ibid.*, 202.

138. Extracts of the minutes of the Plenum of the PPR Central Committee, 20–21 May 1945, Polonsky and Drukier, *Beginnings . . .*, 441.

139. H. Rybicki, *Powstanie i działalność władzy ludowej na zachodnich i północnych obszarach Polski 1945–49* (Poznań, 1976), 48. The port of Szczecin remained under Soviet administration until Sept. 1947.

140. W.T. Kowalski, *Walka dyplomatyczna o miejsce Polski w Europie 1939–45* (Warsaw, 1966), 753; H. Bartoszewicz, 'Polsko-radzieckie stosunki gospodarcze, *Z pola walki* (1977), no. 1 (77), 281.

141. Rybicki, *op. cit.*, 29.

142. 'Sprawozdanie KW PPR Pomorza zachodniego (Koszalin) za grudzień, 1945r. i pierwszą dekadę stycznia 1946r., Sprawozdania KW PPR . . ., *op. cit.*, 336.

143. Extracts of the minutes of the Plenum of the PPR Central Committee, 20–21 May 1945, Polonsky and Drukier, *Beginnings . . .*, 440.

144. Calculated on the basis of a sample of data from *Polegli w walce . . ., op. cit.* The proportion of Red Army personnel as a percentage of the total number of government supporters and officials killed was, according to this source, as follows: 1944 (July–Dec.) 18.8%; 1945 (Jan.–June) 10.7%; 1945 (July–Dec.) 14.1%; 1946 (Jan.–June) 9.3%; 1946 (July–Dec.) 3.8%.

145. E. Reale, *Raporty: Polska 1945–46* (Paris, 1968), 247–53.

146. PRO, FO 371, 56428/N/5411.

147. Communiqué issued at the end of the Yalta conference (extract), 11 Feb. 1945: A. Polonsky, *The Great Powers and the Polish Question 1941–45. A documentary study in Cold War origins* (1976), 249–50.

148. *Ibid.*, 242n.1, 245n.3.

149. *Ibid.*, 254n.2.

150. *Ibid.*, 41.

151. *Ibid.*, 263n.

152. *Ibid.*, 263.

153. Extracts of the minutes of the Plenum of the PPR Central Committee, 20–21 May 1945, Polonsky and Drukier, *Beginnings . . .*, 440.

154. *Ibid.*

155. Polonsky, Communiqué issued at the end of the Yalta conference (extract), 11 Feb. 1945: *The Great Powers*, 251.

156. Gomułka, *Przemówienie wygłoszone na drugim plenarnym posiedzeniu przedstawicieli rządu tymczasowego i konsultantów z kraju i zagranicy, 18.6.1945r., Artykuły . . .*, I, 295–6.

157. Extracts of the minutes of the Plenum of the PPR Central Committee, 20–21 May 1945, Polonsky and Drukier, *Beginnings . . .*, 426–7.

158. *Ibid.*, 433–44.

159. *Ibid.*, 439–40.

160. *Ibid.*, 440.

8 National unity? June 1945 to February 1946

1. Minutes of a meeting of the secretariat of the PPR Central Committee (extracts), 23 June 1945, A. Polonsky and B. Drukier, *The Beginnings of Communist Rule in Poland December 1943–June 1945* (1980), 448.
2. A. Jezierski, *Historia gospodarcza Polski Ludowej 1944–1968* (Warsaw, 1971), 109.
3. V. Mastny, *Russia's Road to the Cold War* (New York, 1979), 299–300.
4. Minutes of a meeting of the secretariat of the PPR Central Committee (extracts), 23 June 1945, Polonsky and Drukier, *Beginnings . . .*, 449.
5. At Potsdam Bevin had obtained from Bierut the statement that elections would be held not later than early 1946: R. Buczek, 'Udział delegacji polskiej w konferencji poczdamskiej w 1945 r.', *Zeszyty historyczne*, 34 (1975), 121. Gomułka told the Central Committee Plenum of 10 Feb. 1946 that 'we wish to hold the elections more or less in the first half of this year': 'Sytuacja polityczna a sprawa wyborów do Sejmu Ustawodawczego z referatu Sekretarza Generalnego KC PPR na plenum KC PPR dnia 10.2.1946r.', *Z pola walki* (1964), no. 2 (26), 7. Mikołajczyk told the British early in 1946 that he expected 'that the election will take place at the end of June or beginning of July and that it will not be possible for the Communist Party to postpone the elections beyond that time'; PRO, FO 371, 56432 (conversation 14 Jan. 1946).
6. J. Borkowski, 'Pertrakcje przedwyborcze między PPR i PPS a PSL (1945–6)', *Kwartalnik Historyczny*, R. LXXI z. 2 (1964), 424.
7. 'Sytuacja polityczna . . .', 9.
8. Averell Harriman to acting secretary of state Grew: telegram Moscow 28 June 1945: A. Polonsky, *The Great Powers and the Polish Question 1941–1945. A documentary study in Cold War origins* (1976), 277.
9. Borkowski, 'Pertrakcje . . .', 424.
10. Gomułka, *Referat wygłoszony na zebraniu aktywu organizacji warszawskiej PPR, 21.10.1945r. Artykuły . . .*, I, *op. cit.*, 392.
11. Gomułka told the February 1946 Plenum that the opponents of the bloc were 'very numerous': 'Above all the PSL leaders themselves with Mikołajczyk in the fore do not wish to form an electoral bloc. Within the leadership of that party there is virtually nobody who is a sincere advocate of the conception of the electoral bloc. . . . In the grassroots too there are strong anti-bloc currents.' He added that after the first round of talks with the PSL 'we came away with the general impression that an agreement is unlikely', 'Sytuacja polityczna . . .', 11–12.
12. *Ibid.*, 10–11.
13. *Ibid.*, 11.
14. *Ibid.*, 8.
15. *Ibid.*, 9.
16. *Ibid.*, 12–13.
17. Gomułka, *Referat wygłoszony na zebraniu aktywu organizacji warszawskiej PPR, 21.10.1945r. Artykuły . . .*, I, 393.
18. 'Sytuacja polityczna . . .', 13.
19. There is some controversy over Witos's stance in 1945. See J. Borkowski, 'Kształtowanie się antymikołajczykowskiej opozycji w kierownictwie PSL 1946–47', *Polska Ludowa* (1962/1), no. 1, 86–8; S. Wójcik, 'Stanowisko W. Witosa w 1945r.', *Zeszyty Historyczne*, 34 (1975).
20. *Polski Słownik Biograficzny*, XXI/1 z.88, 152–4.
21. S. Mikołajczyk, *The Pattern of Soviet Domination* (1948); N. Bethell, *Gomułka. His Poland and his Communism* (1972), 108, 122; A. Bromke, *Poland's Politics. Idealism vs. Realism* (Cambridge, Mass., 1967), 51.

22. Averell Harriman to acting secretary of state Grew: telegram Moscow, 28 June 1945: Polonsky, *The Great Powers* . . ., 276–7.
23. S. Mikołajczyk, 'Na drodze czynnej i konstruktywnej polityki', *Jutro Polski*, 27 May 1945.
24. Report of a speech by Mikołajczyk in Poznań, 7 Oct. 1945, *Chłopski Sztandar*, 21 Oct. 1945. Mikołajczyk said that there were 'trouble-makers who whisper about the possibility of a new war. . . . We do not want one, we must not wish for one and there will not be one.'
25. J. Borkowski, 'Działalność PSL w latach 1945–47', *Rocznik dziejów ruchu ludowego* (1960), no. 2, 89.
26. S. Mikołajczyk, *My a państwo*, 28 Oct. 1945.
27. 'Wielka mowa Stalina', *Gazeta Ludowa*, 11 Feb. 1946.
28. PRO, FO 371, 56434/N/2648.
29. *Ibid.*, 56432.
30. *Ibid.*, 56432.
31. In Feb. 1946 Mikołajczyk sent his envoy, W. Zaremba, to London, to sound out the Foreign Office view on the elections and the extent to which Great Britain was prepared to support the PSL's opposition to a single list. Warner, the British official with whom Zaremba spoke, affirmed British support for free elections, but was careful to avoid giving any undertakings as to the future (*ibid.*, 56434/N/2154). British policy was in fact under review at this time. Bevin had suggested that it might be 'relying too exclusively on Mikołajczyk' and that this was encouraging him 'to take up an unduly intransigent attitude' on the elections (*ibid.*, 56434/N/2624).
32. 'Sytuacja polityczna . . .', 6–7.
33. *Chłopski Sztandar*, 21 Oct. 1945.
34. Mikołajczyk indicated his party's position on agricultural contingents in his speech in Poznań, 7 Oct. 1945: 'the peasants must deliver quotas regardless of whether it hurts them or not. . . . I call on you to fulfil this duty. On the other hand, if someone criticises the organisation of quota-collection itself, that is not quite anti-state activity.' *Ibid.* According to a Communist source, 'Kiernik's position at a meeting in Grodzisk virtually amounted to this: give quotas, but as they give you industrial products for the same prices', Sprawozdanie KW PPR Warsaw, 1.8–15.9.45, Sprawozdania KW PPR . . ., *op. cit.*, 298.
35. In mid-1946 the first secretary of the British Embassy asked Mikołajczyk what assurances Britain might demand of the Polish government. Mikołajczyk 'smiled sadly and replied that no assurance given by Bierut had any value, unless we took measures to ensure its implementation.' PRO, FO 371, 56444/N/10142.
36. Interview with Franciszek Wilk (London, 2 Feb. 1977).
37. *Chłopski Sztandar*, 6 Jan. 1946.
38. A. Dobieszewski and Z. Hemmerling, *Ruch ludowy w Wielkopolsce 1945–1949* (Warsaw, 1971), 100–1.
39. PRO, FO 371, 56432: conversation 23 Jan. 1946.
40. Z. Kozik, *Partie i stronnictwa polityczne w Krakowskiem 1945–1947* (Kraków, 1975), 214.
41. PRO, FO 371, 56432: conversation 14 Jan. 1946.
42. Zambrowski defined the tactics of the PPR at a meeting and the party secretariat in Aug. 1945: 'In the first phase our tactics rested on playing on the case for unity and giving the support of the democratic camp to the existing Peasant Party on forcing Mikołajczyk to form one united party on the platform of the existing SL in which the SL would have the majority.' 'Protokół z posiedzenia Sekretariatu KC odbytego w dniu 8.8.1945r., Protokoły KC (1945)', *Zeszyty Historyczne*, 24 (1975), 132.

43. Borkowski, 'Działalność . . .', 79–80; J. Borkowski, 'O powstaniu PSL i ukształtowaniu się jego naczelnych władz, *Polska Ludowa* (1964), no. 3, 62.
44. R. Halaba, *Stronnictwo Ludowe 1944–1946 Niektóre problemy rozwoju organizacyjnego i działalności politycznej* (Warsaw, 1966), 117–18; J. Borkowski, 'Rola i działalność Mikołajczykowskiego PSL (1945–47), unpub. doctoral thesis (1958), ch. 2.
45. Borkowski, 'Działalność . . .', 80–1.
46. Borkowski, 'O powstaniu PSL . . .', 64–5.
47. R. Halaba, 'Z zagadnień współpracy politycznej PPR z radykalnym SL w okresie lipiec 1945 – styczeń 1946', *Rocznik dziejów ruchu ludowego* (1962), no. 4, 78n.
48. Borkowski, 'O powstaniu PSL . . .', 66.
49. Bańczyk told a party meeting on 15 Sept.: 'There is a fear that we would be outnumbered by the PSL in a merger; that we might go too far to the right . . . the SL can be neither Right nor Left, but Centrist, close to the left-wing, since that is the mood of today', *ibid.*, 68.
50. At a meeting of the Supreme Council of the SL on 11 Feb. 1946 sections of the leadership of the PPS were heavily criticized for an 'incorrect attitude to the SL' and for 'favouring the reaction': Halaba, *Stronnictwo* . . ., 190.
51. Borkowski, 'Działalność . . .', 81–2; 'O powstaniu PSL . . .', 69–70.
52. Borkowski, 'Diałalność . . .', 81.
53. *Ibid.*, 82.
54. 'Sprawozdanie KW PPR Warsaw, 1.8.1945, Sprawozdania KW PPR . . .', 305.
55. H. Słabek, 'Wpływy partii wśród chłopów ziem dawnych 1944–48', *Z pola walki* (1974), no. 2 (66), 51.
56. At a meeting held with the leaderships of the PPR and PPS at the request of the SL on 11 Feb. 1946 Korzycki argued that 'the low-point of the crisis in the SL was after September. . . . If both workers' parties assist, the SL will grow and strengthen. The PSL cannot be counted on for anything.' Halaba, *Stronnictwo* . . ., 172–3.
57. *Ibid.*, 130–1.
58. Halaba, Z zagadnień . . ., 79–80.
59. Resolution of the Central Executive Committee of the PPS, 28 Sept. 1945, cited in B. Syzdek, *Polska Partia Socjalistyczna w latach 1944–1948* (Warsaw, 1974), 326.
60. T. Sierocki, *Warszawska organizacja PPS 1944–1948* (Warsaw, 1976), 254.
61. H. Rechowicz, *Pierwsze Wybory 1947* (Katowice, 1963), 15.
62. Halaba, *Stronnictwo* . . ., 154.
63. K. Ćwik, *Problemy współdziałania PPR i PPS w województwie krakowskim, 1945–1948* (Kraków, 1974), 309, 320.
64. Kozik, *op. cit.*, 176–7; E. Olszewski, *Początki władzy ludowej na rzeszowszczyźnie 1944–1947* (Lublin, 1974), 172, 190–1. Z. Robel, a PSL sympathizer, was governor of Kraków province until Dec. 1945. R. Gesing, a member of the leadership of the PSL, was governor of Rzeszów province, 1946–7.
65. Thus, for instance, on 13 Nov. 1945 responsibility for the administration of the new western and northern territories was transferred from Kiernik's Ministry of Public Administration to a new Ministry for the Recovered Territories under Gomułka. Subsequently the PSL was largely excluded from local government in this area.
66. For example, the PSL twice almost defeated the PPR during discussions in committee of the KRN on the Nationalization Law in early 1946. The PSL attacked the principle of compensating former owners and won support from spokesmen of the SL, PPS and SD. Shortly afterwards the PSL backed an SL amendment to give coops control of the food industry. In each case the support

of the Socialists enabled the PPR to vote the PSL down. See H. Słabek, 'Ogólne aspekty polityki PPR i PPS w kształtowaniu nowych stosunków przemysłowych, *Z pola walki* (1978), no. 1 (81), 52–5.

67. N. Kołomejczyk, *PPR 1944–45 (Studia nad rozwojem organizacyjnym partii)* (Warsaw, 1965), 290.

68. *Ibid.*, 287, 290.

69. *Ibid.*, 118–23.

70. R. Zambrowski, *O masową milionową Partię. Sprawozdanie organizacyjne KC wygłoszone na I Zjeździe PPR* (Warsaw, 1946), 40.

71. 'Sprawozdanie KW PPR Warsaw, 1.8.–15.9.45, Sprawozdania KW PPR . . .', 306.

72. Halaba, *Stronnictwo* . . ., 174–6; 'Montaż Zjazdu Samopomocy', *Jutro Polski*, 14, 21, 28 Apr. 1946. Zambrowski had told the First Congress of the PPR: 'we must dam the further penetration of the PSL into the ZSCh': Zambrowski, *O masową* . . ., 41.

73. S. Jarecka-Kimlowska, *Związek Młodzieży Wiejskiej 'Wici'* (Warsaw, 1972), 109–10.

74. J. Jakubowski, 'Polityka PPR i PPS wobec ZNP 1944–48', *Z pola walki* (1973), no. 4 (64), 41.

75. *Okólnik KC PPR w spawie pracy partyjnej wśród nauczycieli PPR . . . viii 44 – xii 45*, *op. cit.*, 201–3.

76. Zambrowski, *O masową* . . ., 40–1.

77. 'Uchwała Rady Jedności z dn. 1 VII 1945r., in T. Żeńczykowski, *Dramatyczny rok 1945* (1981), 216–23.

78. S. Korboński, *Polskie państwo podziemne* (Paris, 1975), 229–30.

79. W. Pobóg-Malinowski, *Najnowsza historia polityczna Polski 1864–1945*, III (1960), 882–3n, 274.

80. *Ibid.*, 884.

81. J. Czapla, *W walce o utrwalenie władzy ludowej w Polsce 1944–47* (Warsaw, 1967), 53—9, 64.

82. W. Góra, *Polska Rzeczpospolita Ludowa 1944–1974* (Warsaw, 1974), 161.

83. T. Walichnowski, *U źródeł walk z podziemiem reakcyjnym w Polsce* (Warsaw, 1975), 332. This source suggests that the figures are probably underestimates.

84. On WiN see: Czapla, *W walce* . . ., 64–76; S. Kluz, *W potrzasku dziejowym WiN na szlaku AK: Rozważania i dokumentacja* (1978). On the nationalist underground see: Czapla, *W walce* . . ., 78–105; J. Pilaciński, *NSZ – kulisy walki podziemnej 1939–46* (1976); Z.S. Siemaszko, *Narodowe Siły Zbrojne* (1982). The activity of the KWP Lasy is described in M. Turlejska (ed.), *W walce ze zbrojnym podziemiem 1945–1947* (Warsaw, 1972), 315–65; Ogień is dealt with in M. Turlejska (ed.), *Z walk przeciwko zbrojnemu podziemiu 1944–1947* (Warsaw, 1966), 170–237; J. Koźliński, *Podziemie na Pomorze 1945–47* (Gdynia, 1959) and '"Były żołnierz AK", 5-ta Brygada Wileńska AK mjr. Łupaszki', *Zeszyty Historyczne*, 21 (1972), 136–44 contains material on Łupaszko.

85. On the Ukrainian nationalist underground see: A. Szcześniak and W. Szota, *Droga do nikąd. Działalność OUN i jej likwidacja w Polsce* (Warsaw, 1973); Y. Tys-Krokmaliuk, *UPA Warfare in Ukraine* (Society of Veterans of Ukrainian Insurgent Army, USA, 1972).

86. Czapla, *W walce* . . ., 326–7.

87. Z.S. Siemaszko, 'Grupa Szańca i NSZ', *Zeszyty Historyczne*, 21 (1972), 24; J. Kowal, letter to the editor, *Zeszyty Historyczne*, 22 (1972), 152–3.

88. H. Majecki, *Białostocczyzna w pierwszych latach władzy ludowej 1944–48* (2nd edn, Warsaw, 1977), 147–8.

89. 'Sprawozdanie KW PPR . . .', 305–6, 321, 324–5, 329, 338. 'Pierwsze lata władzy ludowej w dokumentach PPR (1945–46)', *Z pola walki* (1974), no. 2 (66), 320.

90. Kozik, *op. cit.*, 118; *Robotnik*, 15 Aug. 1945.
91. 'Protokół z posiedzenia Komitetu Centralnego z dnia 20.9.1945r., Protokoły KC (1945)', *op. cit.*, 137–8.
92. 'Sprawozdanie KW PPR w Rzeszowie za okres od 15.10. do 15.11.1945r., Sprawozdania KW PPR . . .', 328.
93. Kozik, *op. cit.*, 273–4.
94. PRO, FO 371 56432.
95. W. Gomułka, *Referat wygłoszony na zebraniu aktywu organizacji warszawskiej PPR 21.10.1945r. Artykuły . . .*, I, *op. cit.*, 376.
96. *Ibid.*, 380–1.
97. *Chłopski Sztandar*, 14 Oct. 1945.
98. This seems to have been the view of some sections of the National Party at first. See Kozik, *op. cit.*, 171–3.
99. S. Bańczyk, 'Domagamy się wyborów w dniu 28 lipca' (speech to X session of the KRN), *Gazeta Ludowa*, 28 Apr. 1946.
100. Turlejska, *W walce . . .*, 268–70; Walichnowski, *op. cit.*, 248–9.
101. J. Borkowski, 'Miejsce PSL w obozie reakcji (1945–47)', *Z pola walki* (1959), no. 2 (6), 70–2.
102. 'Archiwista', 'Zestawienie wydarzeń dotyczących kierowania konspiracji w kraju po powstaniu warszawskim', *Zeszyty Historyczne*, 26 (1973), 207.
103. 'Deklaracja programowa WiN z dn. 2.IX.1945r. O Wolność Obywatela i Niezawisłość Państwa (Wytyczne ideowe)', in T. Zeńczykowski, *Dramatyczny Rok 1945* (1981), 229–33.
104. I. Caban and Z. Machocki, *ZWZ i AK w okręgu lubelskim 1939–44*, 2 vols (Lublin, 1971), 48–9; Turlejska, *W walce . . .*, 262–3.
105. Following his arrest in Nov. 1945, Col. Jan Rzepecki, the first 'President' of WiN, publicly called for an end to underground armed activity. His successor, Franciszek Niepokółczycki, who led WiN until he in turn was arrested in late 1946 was a former follower of Piłsudski from the eastern *kresy* and a more conservative and military figure. See S. Lis-Kozłowski, 'Teodor', *Zeszyty Historyczne*, 38 (1976), 180–92; *Polski Słownik Biograficzny*, XXIII/1, z.96.
106. 'Sprawozdanie KW PPR Warsaw, 1.8.–15.9.45, Sprawozdania KW PPR . . .', 309.
107. 'Protokół z posiedzenia Sekretariatu Centralnego Komitetu odbytego w dniu 15.11.1945r., Protokoły KC (1945)', 147.
108. *Ibid.*
109. *Ibid.*, 149.
110. L. Kieszczyński, 'Moja działalność w Łodzkiej Dzielnicy PPR – Górna Prawa, styczeń-czerwiec 1945', *Z pola walki* (1974), no. 2 (66), 296–7.
111. 'Uchwała plenum KC PPR w sprawie Bloku Wyborczego Stronnictwo Demokratycznych, PPR . . . i.46 – i.47', 33–4. The minutes of the Plenum which were recently published in *Archivum ruchu robotniczego*, 9 (1984), 238–313, confirm this judgment.
112. Gołębiowski, *Pierwsze lata 1945–1947* (2nd edn, Katowice, 1974), 327.
113. H. Roos, *A History of Modern Poland* (1966), 238.
114. 'Uchwała plenum KC PPR w sprawie głosowania ludowego, 2.6.46, PPR . . . i.46 – i.47', 119.
115. APUST File 52 L.dz.K 3567/45.
116. Kozik, *op. cit.*, 85.
117. *Komunikat z plenarnej konferencji Episkopatu Polski, Jasna Góra 4.10.45, Listy pasterskie episkopatu Polski 1945–1974* (Paris, 1975), 23–4.
118. A. Polonsky, *Politics in Independent Poland 1921–1939. The Crisis of Constitutional Government* (1972), 438.

119. P. Lendvai, *Anti-Semitism in Eastern Europe* (1971), 213.
120. PISM Ambasada R P Vatykan A.44.2 (1947), 2.
121. *Kościół katolicki w Polsce wobec zagadnień chwili, 28.10.45, Listy pasterskie episkopatu . . ., op. cit.*, 14.
122. PISM Ambasada R P Paryz A.46.I (1945–6).
123. PRO, FO 371, 56443/N/9185.
124. W. Bujak, 'Historia krajowej działalności SP 1937–1950' (unpublished doctoral thesis, Jagiellonian University, Kraków, 1971), 208–9.
125. K. Popiel, *Od Brześcia do 'Polonii'* (1967), 89.
126. Bujak, *op. cit.*, 212.
127. *Ibid.*, 213.
128. *Ibid.*, 195.
129. *Głos ludu*, 5 July 1946.
130. Bujak, *op. cit.*, 200.
131. *Ibid.*, 198–9.
132. R. Zambrowski, 'Dziennik', *Krytyka, 6* (1980), 86.
133. For the text, see J. Wójcik, *Spór o postawę* (Warsaw, 1969), 51–2.
134. L. Blit, *The Eastern Pretender. The Story of Bolesław Piasecki* (1965); A. Bromke, *Poland's Politics: Idealism vs. Realism* (Cambridge, Mass, 1967), 81–5 and ch. 11.
135. J. Wojcik, *Spór o postawę* (Warsaw, 1969), 60.
136. Kozik, *op. cit.*, 237.
137. *Ibid.*, 86; Bromke, *op. cit.*, 71–4.
138. Kozik, *op. cit.*, 84, 86.

9 The democratic bloc and the referendum, February to September 1946

1. J. Borkowski, 'Pertrakcje przedwyborcze między PPR i PPS a PSL (1945–6), *Kwartalnik Historyczny* R. LXXI z. 2 (1964), 431.
2. Mikołajczyk told the U.S. ambassador at the end of Feb. that the PPR had decided to postpone the elections for 6 to 8 months. In Apr., the Polish foreign minister told the U.S. ambassador that Sept. would be the earliest practical date for the elections and the prime minister informed the KRN that the elections would be held in the autumn. In the first half of Oct. Mikołajczyk told the British ambassador that the election date would be fixed when the PPR and PPS finalized their agreement and said that 19 Jan. – the date eventually chosen – had been mentioned: PRO, FO 371, 56434/N/2654, 56437/N/4475, 56438/N/5700, 56447/N/13136.
3. The secretariat of the Central Committee of the PPR met on 22 Feb. to plan the campaign. See Borkowski, 'Pertrakcje . . .', 432.
4. *Gazeta Ludowa*, 2 Mar. 1946.
5. W. Gomułka, *Przemówienie wygłoszone w Warszawie na wspólnej konferencji aktywu PPR i PPS 27.2.1946r.*, *Artykuły . . .*, II, *op. cit.*, 31.
6. *Ibid.*, 44–7.
7. Borkowski, 'Pertrakcje . . .', 432, 434.
8. Gomułka, *Przemówienie na manifestacji pierwszomajowej w Katowicach, 1.5.1946 r.*, *Artykuły . . .*, II, *op. cit.*, 108.
9. Gomułka, *Przemówienie na akademii pierwszomajowej w Warszawie, 30.4.1946 r.*, *Artykuły . . .*, II, *op. cit.*, 91–3.
10. *Ibid.*, 93–4.
11. Gomułka, *Przemówienie wygłoszone w Warszawie na wspólnej konferencji aktywu PPR*

i PPS, 27.2.1946 r., Artykuły . . ., II, *op. cit.,* 48.

12. Gomułka, *Przemówienie na akademii pierwszomajowej w Warszawie, 30.4.1946 r., Artykuły* . . ., II, *op. cit.,* 94.

13. Przemówienie wygłoszone w Warszawie na wspólnej konferencji aktywu PPR i PPS, 27.2.1946 r., *Artykuły* . . ., II, *op. cit.,* 53.

14. *Ibid.,* 53.

15. Ł. Socha, 'Interpelacje posłów PSL', *Krytyka,* 6 (1980), 155–8.

16. For example, the murder of W. Kojder, a leading activist from Kraków province and member of the national executive of the PSL, in Sept. 1945, and of B. Ścibiorek, secretary-general of *Wici* in Dec. 1945.

17. F. Wilk, 'Słownik biograficzny ofiar terroru PSL', *Zeszyty Historyczne,* 6 (1964), 7–15.

18. Socha, 'Interpelacje . . .', 151–5 and 'Protokół przesłuchania świadka', *Krytyka,* 6 (1980), 159–64.

19. 'Dokument MBP z 1945 r.', *Krytyka,* 6 (1980), 147.

20. Gomułka, *Przemówienie wygłoszone w Warszawie na wspólnej konferencji aktywu PPR i PPS, 27.2.1946 r., Artykuły* . . ., II, *op. cit.,* 45–7.

21. H. Rechowicz, *Pierwsze wybory 1947* (Katowice, 1963), 49.

22. T. Potomski, *SP na Górnym Śląsku w latach 1937–50* (Katowice, 1969), 68; W. Bujak, 'Historia krajowej działalność Stronnictwa Pracy 1937–50' (unpublished doctoral thesis, Kraków, 1971), 246–50; K. Popiel, *Od Brześcia do 'Polonii'* (1967), 169.

23. K. Ćwik, *Problemy współdziałania PPR i PPS w województwie krakowskim, 1945–1948* (Kraków, 1974), 145. (Włoszczowa and Grojec).

24. PRO, FO 371, 56441/N/7860.

25. J. Czapla, 'KBW w latach 1944–65', *Wojskowy Przegląd Historyczny* (1965), no. 3, 84; M. Turlejska (ed.), *W walce ze zbrojnym podziemiem 1945–1947* (Warsaw, 1972), 21–4 gives slightly different figures.

26. *Ibid.,* 26–7.

27. J. Naumiuk, *Początki władzy ludowej na Kielecczyźnie 1944–1947* (Lublin, 1969), 197.

28. *PPR. Resolucje, odezwy, instrukcje i okólniki komitetu centralnego, viii 1944–xii 1945,* 391; *i 1946 – i 1947,* 212.

29. Thus Kowalik, writing about Lower Silesia, admits that: 'Party activists occupied the top positions in local government [and] in every kind of commission which had direct contact with settlers. Sometimes the allocation of houses, farms, cows or horses depended on the party membership of the settler.' A. Kowalik, *Z dziejów Polskiej Partii Robotniczej na Dolnym Śląsku w latach 1945–1947* (Wrocław, 1979), 38–9.

30. J. Borkowski, 'Działalność PSL w latach 1945–47', *Rocznik dziejów ruchu ludowego* (1960), no. 2, 82; A. Reiss, *Z problemów odbudowy i rozwoju organizacyjnego PPS* (Warsaw, 1971), 317.

31. R. Zambrowski, *O masową milionową Partię* (Warsaw, 1946), 59. An analysis of the composition of the *aktyw* is given in N. Kołomejczyk, *PPR 1944–1945* (Warsaw, 1965), 296.

32. *Okólnik KC PPR w sprawie II kursu agitatorów i organizatorów wyborczych, PPR . . . i 1946 – i 1947, op. cit.,* 45.

33. *Okólnik KC PPR w sprawie masowej pracy partyjnej na terenie wsi, PPR . . . i 1946 – i 1946, op. cit.,* 60–1.

34. *Okólnik KC PPR w sprawie obchodów Święta Ludowego, 15.5.1946, PPR . . . i 1946–i 1947, op. cit.,* 92–6; *Instrukcja KC PPR w sprawie obchodów Święta Ludowego,* 15 May 1946, *ibid.,* 98–100.

35. J. Naumiuk, *Polska Partia Robotnicza na Kielecczyźnie* (Warsaw, 1976), 260–1.

36. A. Dobieszewski and Z. Hemmerling, *Ruch ludowy w Wielkopolsce 1945–1949* (Warsaw, 1971), 133.

37. PRO, FO 371, 56435/N/2521, 56434/N/2476.
38. R. Halaba, *Stronnictwo Ludowe 1944–1946* (Warsaw, 1966), 193.
39. See p.218.
40. Gomułka, Przemówienie wygłoszone w Warszawie na wspólnej konferencji aktywu PPR i PPS, 27.2.1946 r., Artykuły . . ., II, *op. cit.*, 45.
41. 'Sprawozdanie KW PPR za okres 1 viii do 15 ix 1945, Sprawozdania KW PPR z 1945 r.', *Z pola walki* (1971), no. 4 (56), 304.
42. E. Wojnowski, *Warmia i Mazury w latach 1945–1947. Życie polityczne* (2nd edn, Olsztyn, 1970), 139.
43. *Gazeta Ludowa*, 4 Oct. 1946. In Gdańsk province more than half the militia were dismissed between Oct. 1945 and Apr. 1946, see R. Wapiński, *Pierwsze lata władzy ludowej na wybrzeżu gdańskim* (Gdańsk, 1970), 118.
44. Zambrowski, *O masową* . . ., 52.
45. B. Hillebrandt and J. Jakubowski, *Warszawska organizacja PPR 1942–1948* (Warsaw, 1978), 399.
46. W. Góra (ed.), *PPR w walce o niepodległość i władzę ludu* (Warsaw, 1963), 108.
47. *Okólnik KC PPR w związku z utworzeniem ORMO, 8.3.46, PPR . . . i 1946 – i 1947, op. cit.*, 47–9.
48. B. Syzdek, *Polska Partia Socjalistyczna w latach 1944–1948* (Warsaw, 1974), 256n.
49. E. Olszewski, *Polska Partia Robotnicza na Lubelszczyźnie 1942–1948* (Lublin, 1979), 281.
50. M. Plikas (ed.), *Mała Kronika LWP 1943–73* (Warsaw, 1975), 255.
51. Z. Kozik, *Partie i stronnictwa polityczne w Krakowskiem 1945–1947* (Kraków, 1975), 249.
52. Borkowski, 'Pertrakcje . . .', 432.
53. H. Majecki, *Białostocczyzna w pierwszych latach władzy ludowej 1944–48* (2nd edn, Warsaw, 1977), 138.
54. Zambrowski, *O masową* . . ., 49.
55. *Okólnik KC PPR w sprawie pracy administracyjno-samorządowej na terenie powiatów, April 1947, PPR Rezolucje, odezwy, instrukcje i i okólniki komitetu centralnego i 1947–xii 1948* (Warsaw, 1973), 72–3.
56. Okólnik KC PPR w sprawie pracy partii na odcinku administracyjno-samorządowym, March 1946, PPR . . . i 1946–i 1947, *op. cit.*, 52.
57. J. Borkowski, 'Kształtowanie się antymikołajczykowskiej opozycji w kierownictwie PSL, 1946–1947', *Polska Ludowa* (1962), no. 1, 96.
58. *Okólnik KC PPR w sprawie pracy administracyjno-samorządowej na terenie powiatów, April 1947, PPR . . . i 1947–xii 1948*, 72.
59. For example, Wycech appointed a PSL sympathizer to run Kraków education authority, a position which according to the Communists he used to limit their influence. See Kozik, *op. cit.*, 202.
60. PRO, FO 371, 56437/N/4396, N/1893.
61. *Ibid.*, 56433/N/1893.
62. *Ibid.*, 56434/N/2476.
63. Borkowski, 'Pertrakcje . . .', 432; *Gazeta Ludowa*, 3 Mar. 1946.
64. PRO, FO 371, 56441/N/7860.
65. *Ibid.*, 56447/N/12480, 56452/N/16279.
66. *Ibid.*, 56441/N/7860.
67. Borkowski, 'Kształtowanie się . . .' 98.
68. For example, Mikołajczyk informed the Americans in confidence that he regretted their agreement in April 1946 to provide a $50m credit for the purchase of U.S. war surplus and a £40m trade loan to buy locomotives and coal cars. He suggested that a loan to help Polish agriculture would have strengthened his position, but that the credits had been given in a form which

gave 'the impression that the present Polish government can obtain credit from the US and is not viewed with disfavour by the US Government'. On 11 May, after Bliss Lane had flown to Paris to persuade Byrnes to suspend the credits, the State Department announced they had been frozen. The British Foreign Office, which had been highly critical of the U.S. decision to grant the loans, was given to understand that 'whilst they [the State Department] did not directly speak of financial sanctions in the event of the Polish government resorting to terrorist methods against Mikołajczyk and the opposition, the threat was implicit and fully appreciated.' See PRO, FO 371, 56438/N/5700/56440/N/6828; A. Bliss Lane, *I saw Poland Betrayed. An American Ambassador Reports to the American People* (3rd edn, Boston, 1965), 193–7.

69. PRO, FO 371, 56439/N/6206.
70. *Ibid.*, 56440/N/7139.
71. *Ibid.*, 56445/N/10451.
72. *Gazeta Ludowa*, 10,11,12 Apr. 1946.
73. S. Mikołajczyk, *The Pattern of Soviet Domination* (1948), 173–9.
74. Rechowicz, *Pierwsze wybory* . . ., 49; J. Gołębiowski, *Pierwsze lata 1945–1947* (2nd edn, Katowice, 1974), 331.
75. Borkowski, 'Kształtowanie się . . .', 91–3; Dobieszewski and Hemmerling, *op. cit.*, 109–10.
76. *Ibid.*, 108–9; PRO, FO 371, 56432.
77. *Ibid.*, 56439/N/6245.
78. *Robotnik*, 19 Apr. 1946, Gołębiowski, *Pierwsze lata* . . ., 331; Naumiuk, *Początki* . . ., 181; Hillebrandt and Jakubowski, *op. cit.*, 369; PRO, FO 371, 56439/N/5886, N/6901, N/7266.
79. See further: J. Reynolds, 'Communists, Socialists and Workers: Poland 1944–48' *Soviet Studies*, 30.4 (Oct. 1978), 524.
80. Hillebrandt and Jakubowski, *op. cit.*, 369.
81. *Ibid.*, 429–30.
82. *Gazeta Ludowa*, 4 May 1946; PRO, FO 371, 56439/N/7266; Kozik, *op. cit.*, 203–4; Gołębiowski, *Pierwsze lata* . . ., 374; J. Kantyka, *PPS na Śląsku i w Zagłębiu Dąbrowskim w latach 1939–1948* (Katowice, 1975), 251–2; Naumiuk, *Początki* . . ., 202. A detailed account of events in Gliwice appeared in *Jutro Polski*, 8 Dec. 1946.
83. *Gazeta Ludowa*, 9 Mar. 1946; Kozik, *op. cit.*, 308–9; Ćwik, *op. cit.*, 137–9.
84. PRO, FO 371, 56939/N/6206.
85. Borkowski, 'Pertrakcje . . .' 434.
86. *Robotnik*, 2 Mar. 1946.
87. *Robotnik*, 26 Aug. 1946.
88. During the February talks, Cyrankiewicz described part of the constituency of the PSL as 'pathologically ill' and in need of 'educational measures': Borkowski, 'Pertrakcje . . .', 429n. In June 1946 he called for 'ruthless struggle until the fascist source of infection is entirely destroyed': *Robotnik*, 7 July 1946.
89. Borkowski, 'Pertrakcje . . .', 432.
90. Żuławski was a major figure in the leadership of the PPS between the wars and was chairman of the party's Supreme Council in 1939. After Yalta he favoured the cessation of underground activity by the PPS and its unification with the 'Lublin PPS'. Talks between Żuławski and the 'Lublin PPS' were held during mid-1945, but broke down in the autumn, whereupon Żuławski and his followers formed a separate 'Polish Social Democratic Party'. However, permission to legalize this organization was refused. In December Żuławski and his followers were admitted to the PPS on an individual basis and at the meeting of the Supreme Council on 31 Mar. – 1 Apr. 1946, Żuławski and five of

his group were coopted as members. See further: A. Reiss, *Z problemów odbudowy i rozwoju organizacyjnego PPS 1944–1946* (Warsaw, 1971), 216–74; L. Cohn, 'Zygmunt Żuławski', *Krytyka*, 6 (1980), 184–9.

91.   *Robotnik*, 2 Mar. 1946.
92.   J. Hochfeld, 'List do towarzyszy z Labour Party', *Przegląd Socjalistyczny*, 1 Apr. 1946.
93.   Szwalbe set out the evolutionary approach of the PPS thus: 'according to the PPS we are not constructing a socialist system now or in the present historical period. Nevertheless, we want to arrange matters in such a way that the foundations of the new Poland created now will not have to be demolished when circumstances and the will of the majority of the nation calls – as we believe it will – for a socialist economy.' *Robotnik*, 10 Aug. 1946.
94.   The PPS leadership encountered considerable opposition to the bloc with the communists at the provincial conference of the PPS in Kraków on 16–17 March. Żuławski, who had led the criticism, was elected to the provincial committee with two of his followers. See Kozik, *op. cit.*, 308–9. At a meeting of secretaries of local committees of the PPS in Upper Silesia in April, 19 out of 23 speakers considered that party members were opposed to the bloc. Kantyka, *PPS na Śląsku . . .*, 245. See also T. Sierocki, *Warszawska organizacja PPS 1944–1948* (Warsaw, 1976), 266.
95.   Reiss, *op. cit.*, 270–2; J. Bardach, 'O dziejach powojennej PPS', *Kwartalnik Historyczny*, R. LXXX z. 3 (1973), 688–92; PISM Kol.97/30 (Arciszewski papers) Rada Naczelna FPPS w dn. 31 III i 1 IV 1946 r.; PRO, FO 371, 564371, 56437/N/4832.
96.   Syzdek, *op. cit.*, 336.
97.   F. Baranowski, 'Z dziejów nurty lewicowego powojennej PPS', *Z pola walki* (1974), no. 3 (63), 36; T. Sierocki, 'Dyskusje nad programem PPS w latach 1945–47', *Z pola walki* (1971), no. 4 (56), 157.
98.   *Robotnik*, 24 May 1946.
99.   *Ibid.*
100. Mikołajczyk told the executive that the PPS had told him that 'they aimed at us being in the bloc'. Borkowski, 'Kształtowanie się . . .', 432.
101. Borkowski, 'Pertrakcje . . .', 432.
102. *Uchwała plenum KC PPR w sprawie głosowania ludowego, 2.6.46, PPR . . . i 1946 – i 1947, op. cit.*, 119.
103. *Robotnik*, 8 June 1946.
104. In 1948, in a speech denouncing the policy of the party in 1946–7 which he had been prominent in shaping, Cyrankiewicz said that the PPS 'right' had endeavoured to 'galvanise such a group as *Nowe Wyzwolenie . . .* in order to have its own pawns to play in the countryside'. See *Przegląd Socjalistyczny*, Oct.–Dec. 1948.
105. *Robotnik*, 13 June 1946.
106. *Robotnik*, 21 June 1946.
107. Western journalists had heard by Jan. 1946 that a referendum was under consideration, see PRO, FO 371, 56434/N/2028. Gomułka mentioned, the possibility of a referendum in his speech on 27 Feb. *Przemówienie wygłoszone w Warszawie na wspólnej konferencji aktywu PPR i PPS 27.2.1946 r., Artykuły . . ., II, op. cit.*, 51.
108. Modzelewski, the Polish foreign minister, told Bliss Lane in April that September would be the earliest practicable time to hold the election, PRO, FO 371, 56437/N/4475.
109. *Ibid.*, 56439/N/6206; Borkowski, 'Kształtowanie się . . .', 97 and 'Pertrakcje . . .', 425n.

110. PRO, FO 371, 56439/N/6206.
111. Borkowski, 'Kształtowanie się . . .', 97–9 and 'Pertrakcje . . .', 435n.
112. PRO, FO 371, 56440/N/7127.
113. Borkowski, 'Pertrakcje . . .', 435.
114. *Jutro Polski*, 28 July 1946.
115. PRO, FO 371, 56443/N/8598.
116. A. Kraszewski, 'To były tylko trzy lata . . .', *Z pola walki* (1974), no. 3 (67), 118; S. Wójcik, PSL w walce z komunistami 1945–47 (typescript, n.d.), 24.
117. *Ibid.*, 24–5; PRO, FO 371, 56443/N/8598.
118. *Ibid.*, 56443/N/8983.
119. I Blum 'Z dziejów GZP WP 1944–56' *Wojskowy Przegląd Historyczny* (1963), 3–4, 226. According to this source 25,700 militia, 28,070 ORMO, 11,315 UB, 8,370 KBW and 36,400 Polish army troops were deployed during the referendum.
120. *Nowe Wyzwolenie*, 13 July 1946; Ćwik, *op. cit.*, 162–4.
121. Naumiuk, *Początki* . . ., 223.
122. J. Zasada, *Referendum w województwie poznańskim 30.VI.1946* (Poznań, 1971), 90; Olszewski, *Początki* . . ., 242.
123. PRO, FO 371, 56445/N/10451, 56443/N/8998. According to the PSL's figures, there was a 90% vote against the Communist camp in working-class centres, see *Jutro Polski*, 15 Dec. 1946.
124. Hillebrandt and Jakubowski, *op. cit.*, 373–4.
125. *Okólnik KC PPR w sprawie referendum – głosowania ludowego, May 1946 PPR . . . i 1946–i 1947, op. cit.*, 87.
126. Wójcik, 'PSL w walce . . .', 22.
127. Zasada, *op. cit.*, 58, Olszewski, *Początki* . . ., 230.
128. Ćwik, *op. cit.*, 150–1.
129. In Warsaw 44.4% of chairmen of local electoral commissions during the referendum belonged to the PPS, see Hillebrandt and Jakubowski, *op. cit.*, 375. In Katowice province 31.2% of the chairmen belonged to the PPS, see Kantyka, *PPS na Śląsku* . . ., 254.
130. Naumiuk, *Początki* . . ., 206–7. In Kielce province 35.6% of commission chairmen were PPS members, compared with 41.1% belonging to the PPR.
131. Olszewski, *Początki* . . ., 242; Ćwik, *op. cit.*, 149–50, 157–8, 162. The petition drawn up by the Left wing of the PPS in Aug. 1946 attributed the referendum result in Kraków to the 'complete paralysis of the united front', see Bardach, 'O dziejach . . .', 693.
132. Gomułka, *Przemówienie w Warszawie na zebraniu aktywu PPR i PPS, 6.7.46, Artykuły* . . ., II, *op. cit.*, 158–76.
133. PRO, FO 371, 56442/N/7641.
134. *Ibid.*, 56443/N/8804.
135. Mikołajczyk thought that 'he would lose all influence with the rank-and-file of his party' if he joined the bloc: *ibid.*, 56447/N/12480.
136. Borkowski, 'Pertrakcje . . .', 437–8n.
137. PRO, FO 371, 56444/N/10042.
138. *Ibid.*, 56444/N/9822.
139. *Ibid.*, 56443/N/8804.
140. PRO, FO 371, 56450/N/14980.
141. *Ibid.*, 56446/N/12336.
142. D. Yergin, *Shattered Peace. The Origins of the Cold War and the National Security State* (1978), 230.
143. *Gazeta Ludowa*, 31 July 1946, 7 Aug. 1946.
144. PPR reports for Aug. 1946 noted that the PSL 'has recently changed course and is tending to set up illegal circles', Hillebrandt and Jakubowski, *op. cit.*, 429. In

Olsztyn province a commissioner with 17 instructors was sent from party HQ to reorganize the local PSL. There followed a gradual disappearance 'of the normal organizational network . . . and its replacement by a network of secret delegates. . . . The most committed individuals [were] withdrawn from active work and formed into the so-called second team. . . . There was even talk of the existence of two provincial leaderships: the official and unofficial.' Wojnowski, *op. cit.*, 159–60. In Poznań province, in accordance with central instructions, 'the whole election campaign was run on conspiratorial lines', see Dobieszewski and Hemmerling, *op. cit.*, 145.

145. On 4 July 1946 a mob attacked a tenement in Kielce inhabited by Jews. In the ensuing violence 34 Jews were murdered and 6 militia men killed. In the days following, a further 31 Jews were murdered in the surrounding district. The trial of the alleged instigators of the pogrom was held within a week and 9 of the 12 defendants, who included militia men, were sentenced to death. Both the local UB and Militia commanders were briefly arrested in the aftermath of the incident. The party's version of events, repeated at the trial, was that the pogrom was organized by NSZ and Anders supporters. However, the PSL maintained that the pogrom had been inspired by the Communists to divert attention from the referendum fiasco (see Mikołajczyk, *op. cit.*, 186–8). An evaluation of the evidence by the British Embassy doubted this interpretation and attributed the pogrom to a Right-wing provocation against a background of small-town provincial anti-semitism, the incompetence of the security forces and the indifference of the local church authorities (PRO, FO 371, 56444/N/9871). See further M. Chęciński, *Poland: Communism, Nationalism Anti-Semitism* (New York, 1982), 21–34; K. Kersten, 'Kielce – 4 lipca 1946 roku', *Tygodnik Solidarność*, 4 Dec. 1981.

146. Borkowski, 'Pertrakcje . . .' 437.

147. *Robotnik*, 11 Aug. 1946.

148. *Gazeta Ludowa*, 13 July 1946.

149. *Robotnik*, 26 Aug. 1946.

150. Borkowski, 'Pertrakcje . . .', 436n.

151. *Jutro Polski*, 15 Dec. 1946.

152. Borkowski, 'Pertrakcje . . .', 437.

153. Borkowski, 'Miejsce PSL w obozie reakcji (1945–47)', *Z pola walki* (1959), no. 2 (6), 77.

154. *Gazeta Ludowa*, 26 July 1946. In June–July about 7 members of the PSL were murdered; in the period Aug.–Oct. 1946 at least 30 were killed, see F. Wilk, 'Słownik biograficzny ofiar terroru PSL', *Zeszyty Historyczne*, 6 (1964).

155. Mikołajczyk later acknowledged the role of the PPS in restraining the PPR. He told the PSL Supreme Council in Oct. that after the referendum 'it was decided to take the nation by the throat and pay it back for voting as it did. This did not come about. Here we must give credit to the Polish Socialist Party, which did not wish to take upon itself the responsibility for what would follow.' *Jutro Polski*, 15 Dec. 1946.

156. *Jutro Polski*, 15 Dec. 1946.

157. *Robotnik*, 29 July 1946, 2 Aug. 1946, 5 Aug. 1946, 6 Aug. 1946.

158. *Robotnik*, 29 July 1946.

159. *Robotnik*, 2 Aug. 1946.

160. Mikołajczyk, *The Pattern . . .*, 188.

161. Gomułka, *Nasze stanowisko. Artykuł opublikowany w 'Głosie Ludu', 18.8.46, Artykuły . . .*, II, *op. cit.*, 194–5; *Jutro Polski*, 8 Sept. 1946.

162. Bardach, 'O dziejach . . .', 696.

163. *Robotnik*, 6 Aug. 1946.

164. *Robotnik*, 7 Aug. 1946 (emphasis as in the original). Cyrankiewicz was later to repudiate what he described as 'certain tendencies to pseudonational demogoguery' in the leadership of the PPS in the period 1946–47, *Robotnik*, 18 Mar. 1948.
165. PRO, FO 371, 56445/N/10598.
166. Borkowski, 'Pertrakcje . . .', 437.
167. Bardach, 'O dziejach . . .', 696.
168. See: Bardach, 'O dziejach . . .'; F. Baranowski, 'W związku z artykułem Juliusza Bardacha "O dziejach powojennej PPS",' *Kwartalnik Historyczny*, R LXXX, z.3 (1973), 668–71; J. Bardach, 'O wewnętrznym zróżnicowaniu w PPS w latach 1944–1946', *ibid.*; Baranowski, 'Z dziejów . . .'. A commentary by E. Osóbka-Morawski, *Uwagi do artykułu F. Baranowskiego pt. 'Z dziejów nurtu lewicowego powojennej PPS'* has been placed in the party's Central Archive (CA KC PZPR sygn. 4063), but has not been published, see *Z pola walki* (1978), no. 3 (83) 342.
169. For example, in the Rzeszów provincial organization, see Olszewski, *Początki . . .*, 251.
170. *Robotnik*, 2 Aug. 1946; Bardach, 'O dziejach . . .', 696n.
171. Bardach, 'O dziejach . . .', 693–4.
172. B. Drobner, 'Nasze polityczne oblicze', *Naprzód*, 16 Aug. 1946; H. Wachowicz, 'List do przyjaciela z PPR', *Kurier Popularny*, 11, 12, 13 Aug. 1946.
173. *Głos ludu*, 18 Aug. 1946.
174. Borkowski, 'Pertrakcje . . .', 237.
175. PRO, FO 371, 56446, letter D. Healey to M. Phillips, 12 Sept. 1946.
176. Bardach, 'O dziejach . . .', 696. According to one source, the Leftist plotters planned either to intimidate the Supreme Council of the PPS, using an armed gang from Skowroński's organization in Kielce, or to split the party and form a second organization which would claim to be the PPS, see J. Holzer ('W.Pański'), *Agonia PPS, Socjaliści Polscy w sojuszu z PPR 1944–1948* (Warsaw, 1981), 15.
177. PRO, FO 371, 56446 letter D. Healey to M. Phillips, 12 Sept. 1946.
178. *Ibid.*, 56446/N/11074; L.M. Oak, *Free and Unfettered* (Newtown, Montgomery, 1947), 22–3.
179. Bardach, 'O dziejach . . .', 696.
180. *Robotnik*, 22 Aug. 1946.
181. PRO, FO 371, 56446/N/10853.
182. Borkowski, 'Pertrakcje . . .', 437; PRO, FO 371, 56446/N/11074. Under this formula the PPR with the SL and SD would have had less than half the seats in the bloc; 45% (not 50% as envisaged in the Feb. offer) and the PSL with the SP would have had more than one-third (35% as against 30% offered in Feb.), i.e. enough seats to block constitutional changes.
183. Syzdek, *op. cit.*, 355, 358.
184. Borkowski, 'Pertrakcje . . .', 437.
185. *Jutro Polski*, 15 Dec. 1946.
186. *Gazeta Ludowa*, 1 Sept. 1946.
187. 'Stenogram obrad Niezależnej Młodzieży Socjalistycznej w dniu 18 IX 1946 r.', *Krytyka*, no. 4 (1980), 59.
188. PRO, FO 371, 56447/N/12741.
189. Borkowski, 'Pertrakcje . . .', 438; 'Stenogram obrad NMS . . .', 59.
190. Borkowski, 'Pertrakcje . . .', 437n.
191. 'Stenogram obrad NMS . . .', 59.
192. *Ibid.*
193. *Ibid.*; *Robotnik*, 8 Sept. 1946.

194. Ćwik, *op. cit.*, 171; 'Stenogram obrad NMS . . .', 59.
195. *Robotnik*, 27 Sept. 1946. The decision seems to have been taken sometime before 17 Sept., when Szwalbe told a meeting of the provincial secretaries of the PPS that the PSL would not enter the bloc and that the PPS leadership had agreed 'to fight the PSL, but to fight in a reasonable way'. W. Stefaniuk, *Łódzka organizacja PPS 1945–1948* (Lodz, 1980), 121. Hochfeld implied the same at the ZNMS meeting on 18 Sept.: 'Stenogram obrad NMS . . .', 59.
196. PRO, FO 371, 56446/N/11370; Mikołajczyk, *The Pattern* . . ., 190–1; 'R', 'The Fate of Polish Socialism', *Foreign Affairs, 28*, no. 1 (Oct. 1949), 131.
197. Mikołajczyk, *The Pattern* . . ., 190–1.
198. Z. Brzezinski, *The Soviet Bloc* (4th edn, Harvard, 1971), 44.
199. PRO, FO 371, 56446/N/12336.
200. 'R', 'The Fate . . .', 131.
201. *Gazeta Ludowa*, 11 Sept. 1946.
202. S. Trepczyński and N.N. Rodionow (eds), *Polska Ludowa – Związek Radziecki 1944–1974. Zbiór dokumentów i materiałow* (Warsaw, 1974), 133.
203. *Robotnik*, 13 Sept. 1946.
204. 'Stenogram obrad NMS . . .', 57–8.
205. *Ibid.*, 57.
206. 'Stenogram obrad NMS . . .', 59–60.
207. *Ibid.*, 60.
208. See ch. 8, pp. 223–8.
209. *Komunikat z plenarnej konferencji Episkopatu Polski, Jasna Góra, 24.5.46, Listy pasterskie episkopatu . . .*, 38–9.
210. PRO, FO 371, 56443/N/9185.
211. *Ibid.*
212. Kozik, *op. cit.*, 234–5.
213. W. Bujak, 'Historia krajowej działalności Stronnictwa Pracy 1937–50' (unpublished doctoral thesis, Kraków, 1971), 271, 275.
214. *Ibid.*, 266–8, 234–5.
215. PRO, FO 371, 56436/N/3492.
216. Bujak, *op. cit.*, 290.
217. *Ibid.*, 277.
218. *Ibid.*, 281.
219. Gawrych was particularly vulnerable to Communist pressure. Before the war he had been active in the Silesian Christian Democratic movement and had run its anti-Communist intelligence section during the 1921 uprising. In the 1930s as a member of the Silesian *Sejm* he had joined the Right-wing National Party.
220. Bujak, *op. cit.*, 283. Felczak was absent ill and died a few days later. His replacement on the executive, another *Zryw* supporter, gave the group a majority of one.
221. Bujak, *op. cit.*, 295.
222. The membership of the SP at its peak in mid-1946 was probably about 100,000. In Silesia it has been variously estimated at 16,–60,000 members, see Gołębiowski, *Pierwsze lata . . .*, 333; Bujak, *op. cit.*, 250; T. Potomski, *SP na Gornym Śląsku w latach 1937–50* (Katowice, 1969), 68. In Kraków it had some 9,000 members, see Kozik, *op. cit.*, 230 and in Poznań about 10,000, see Bujak, *op. cit.*, 238. It was also fairly strong in Lodz city, Częstochowa and Bydgoszcz.
223. See above, p.235.
224. CAHSD/KW SP, Memoriał i uchwały KW SP 1946–47, letter from KW ZG SP to Prezydium KRN, 15 July 1946.
225. Popiel, *op. cit.*, 202–3.
226. PRO, FO 371, 56440/N/10034.

227. *Komunikat z plenarnej konferencji Episkopatu Polski, 8–10.9.46, Listy pasterskie episkopatu . . . op. cit.,* 45–6. This was confirmed in the Episcopate's statement of 22.10.46, see Popiel, *op. cit.,* 284.

228. The membership of the SP declined from about 27,000 at the end of 1947 to less than 18,000 in 1950 when the party was dissolved. Widy-Wirski had joined the communists in 1949; Stefan Brzeziński and others continued activity in the SD.

229. Popiel, *op. cit.,* 230–1, 272, 281.

230. Bujak, *op. cit.,* 290.

231. *Orędzie Episkopatu Polski w sprawie wyborów do Sejmu, 10.9.46, Listy pasterskie episkopatu . . ., op. cit.,* 40–4.

232. *Robotnik,* 15 Sept. 1946.

233. *Robotnik,* 7 July 1946, 14 July 1946.

10 'A mighty lightning offensive', September 1946 to spring 1947

1. *Gazeta Ludowa,* 10 Sept. 1946.

2. *Uchwała plenum KC PPR 'O najważniejszych momentach sytuacji politycznej Polski', 18.9.46, PPR . . . i 1946–i 1947, op. cit.,* 147.

3. *Ibid.,* 146.

4. *Ibid.,* 145.

5. *Ibid.,* 148.

6. *Ibid.,* 148.

7. *Ibid.,* 145.

8. H. Rechowicz, *Pierwsze wybory 1947* (Katowice, 1963), 56; cf. *Gazeta Ludowa,* 17,18 Oct. 1946.

9. For instance, the September Plenum political resolution made no mention of winning over 'democratic' elements from the PSL.

10. *Jutro Polski,* 29 Sept. 1946.

11. *PPR . . . i 1946–i 1947, op. cit.,* 212, *PPR . . . i 1947–xii 1948, op. cit.,* 287. The Sept. 1946 figure is given in J. Gołębiowski and W. Góra (eds), *Ruch robotniczy w Polsce Ludowej* (Warsaw, 1975), 36.

12. The percentage of peasants in the membership of the PPR declined from 28.1% at the beginning to 23.2% at the end of 1946; in the same period workers increased from 61.0% to 64.7%, *PPR . . . i 1946–i 1947, op. cit.,* 213.

13. On this point, see L. Kołakowski, *The Intelligentsia in Poland: Genesis of a Revolution,* ed. A. Bromberg (New York, 1983), 58.

14. F. Ryszka (ed.), *Polska Ludowa 1944–50. Przemiany społeczne* (Wrocław, 1974), 262.

15. PRO, FO 371, 56452/N/15949.

16. *Ibid.,* 56449/N/14649.

17. The Training Department of the Central Committee of the PPR was not established until Mar. 1947, see S. Kuśmierski, *Propaganda polityczna PPR w latach 1944–1948* (Warsaw, 1976), 96. See also *Wytyczne Sekretariatu KC PPR w sprawie szkolenia kadr i politycznego wychowania członków partii, February 1947, PPR . . . i 1947–xii 1948, op. cit.,* 33–7.

18. J. Szczeblewski, 'Problemy rozwoju organizacyjnego PZPR w okresie scalenia organizacji partyjnych po zjednoczeniu PPR i PPS (xii 1948–xi 1949)', *Z pola walki* (1967), no. 1 (37), 32–3; *Uchwała Sekretariatu KC PPR oceniająca przebieg obchodów Święta Ludowego, May 1948, PPR . . . i 1947–xii 1948, op. cit.,* 236.

19. The numerical strength of Communist parties in various East European states in relation to total population in 1946 was as follows:

	Poland	Czecho	Bulgaria	Hungary	Germany (Soviet)
Population (m)	23.90	12.08	6.97	9.20	20.51
				(1948)	
CP membership (m)	0.42	1.08	0.50	0.65	1.30
	(Sept. 46)	(Mar. 46)	(Mar. 46)	(Sept. 46)	(Apr. 46)

Z.K. Brzezinski, *The Soviet Bloc, Unity and Conflict* (rev. edn, Cambridge, Mass., 1971), 86; N. Kołomejczyk, *Rewolucje ludowe w Europie 1939–1948* (Warsaw, 1973), 352.

20. *Instrukcja KC PPR w sprawie pracy partyjnej trójki wyborczej w obwodzie głosowania, November 1946, PPR . . . i 1946–i 1947, op. cit.*, 167–70.

21. In 376 out of 527 polling districts in Kraków province, 345 out of 470 in Lublin province, 351 out of 386 in Rzeszów province: K. Ćwik, *Problemy współdziałania PPR i PPS w województwie krakowskim, 1945–1948* (Kraków, 1974), 190; H. Majecki, *Białostocczyzna w pierwszych latach władzy ludowej 1944–48* (2nd edn, Warsaw, 1977), 165; E. Olszewski, *Polska Partia Robotnicza na Lubelszc Zyźnie 1942–1948* (Lublin, 1979), 306, 308; E. Olszewski, *Początki władzy ludowej na rzeszowszczyźnie 1944–1947* (Lublin, 1974), 271.

22. Ćwik, *op. cit.*, 198.

23. *Ibid.*, 198; Olszewski, *PPR . . .*, 306.

24. *Instrukcja KC PPR dotycząca działalności agitacyjnej w obwodzie wyborczym, 1.12.46., PPR . . . i 1946–i 1947, op. cit.*, 173; *Uchwała Sekretariatu KC PPR o konieczności rozbudowy form organizacyjnych w miejskich i wiejskich organizacjach partyjnych, January 1947, PPR . . . i 1947–xii 1948, op. cit.*, 22.

25. Ćwik, *op. cit.*, 192; B. Hillebrandt and J. Jakubowski, *Warszawska organizacja PPR 1942–1948* (Warsaw, 1978), 380; Rechowicz, *Pierwsze . . .*, 93.

26. S. Kuśmierski, *op. cit.*, 247.

27. *Okólnik KC PPR w sprawie działalności ORMO, October 1946, PPR . . . i 1946–i 1947, op. cit.*, 149–51.

28. M. Plikas (ed.), *Mała kronika LWP 1943–73* (Warsaw, 1975), 255.

29. At the beginning of 1947, 56% of ORMO were members of the PPR: B. Syzdek, *Polska Partia Socjalistyczna w latach 1944–1948* (Warsaw, 1974), 371.

30. Kuśmierski, *op. cit.*, 249.

31. S. Wójcik, 'PSL w walce z komunistami 1945–47' (typescript in possession of author), 22, 29.

32. *Ibid.*, 33.

33. *Ibid.*, 29, 34.

34. *Ibid.*, 33.

35. Cf. B. Pasierb, *Ruch ludowy na Dolnym Śląsku w latach 1945–49* (place of publication not given, 1972), 150, Olszewski, *Początki . . .*, 287; J. Naumiuk, *Początki władzy ludowej na Kielecczyźnie 1944–1947* (Lublin, 1969), 259; R. Wapiński, *Pierwsze lata władzy ludowej na wybrzeżu gdańskim* (Gdańsk, 1970), 161; A. Dobieszewski and Z. Hemmerling, *Ruch ludowy w Wielkopolsce 1945–1949* (Warsaw, 1971), 147.

36. Wójcik, *PSL w walce*, 30.

37. K. Bagiński, 'Cenzura w Polsce', *Zeszyty Historyczne, 8* (1965), 146.

38. S. Mikołajczyk, *The Pattern of Soviet Domination* (1948), 199.

39. Bagiński, 'Cenzura . . .', 146.

40. *Ibid.*, 146–7.

41. *Ibid.*, 147–8.

42. Naumiuk, *Początki . . .*, 257.

43. E. Wojnowski, *Warmia i Mazury w latach 1945–1947. Życie polityczne* (2nd edn, Olsztyn, 1970), 161.

44. Z. Kozik, *Partie Stronnictwa polityczne w Krakowskiem 1945–1947* (Kraków, 1975), 217.

45. The PSL was banned in 29 districts by the time of the election, S. Korboński, *Polskie państwo podziemne* (Paris, 1975), 245.

46. Plikas, *op. cit.*, 253–5 gives slightly different figures for the numbers of KBW troops involved from L. Grot, 'Działalność ochronno-propagandowa wojska polskiego w czasie referendum (30.6.1946r) i wyborów do Sejmu RP (19.1.1947r)', *Wojskowy Przegląd Historyczny* (1974), no. 2, 199, quoted here.

47. *Ibid.*, 200.

48. *Ibid.*, 193.

49. Olszewski, *Początki* . . ., 280.

50. The strength of the Polish army was 165,000 in Apr. 1947, speech by K. Dąbrowski, *Sprawozdanie stenograficzne Sejmu Ustawodawczego*, I, 15 Apr. 1947.

51. PRO, FO 371, 56452/N/16280.

52. Mikołajczyk, *The Pattern* . . ., 201–24.

53. *Uchwała plenum KC PPR 'O najważniejszych momentach sytuacji politycznej Polski', 18.9.1946, PPR* . . . *i 1946–i 1947, op. cit.*, 147.

54. Ćwik, *op. cit.*, 178.

55. T. Sierocki, 'PPR-owska koncepcja jedności ruchu robotniczego w latach 1942–1948', *Z pola walki* (1976), no. 4 (76), 18.

56. *Ibid.*, 17.

57. *Ibid.*, 18.

58. T. Sierocki, *Warszawska organizacja PPS 1944–1948* (Warsaw, 1976), 270.

59. *Uchwała plenum KC PPR 'O najważniejszch momentach sytuacji politycznej Polski', 18.9.1946, PPR* . . . *i 1946–i 1947, op. cit.*, 147.

60. Syzdek, *op. cit.*, 365.

61. Sierocki, 'PPR-owska . . .', 19.

62. *Uchwała plenum KC PPR 'O najważniejszych momentach sytuacji politycznej Polski', 18.9.1946, PPR* . . . *i 1946–i 1947, op. cit.*, 143, 146.

63. W. Gomułka, *Przemówienie wygłoszone na adademii w Warszawie w 7 rocznicę śmierci M. Buczka, 10.9.1946, Artykuły* . . ., II, 223.

64. K. Janowski, Kształtowanie się jedności ruchu robotniczego na Dolnym Śląsku (1945–1948)', *Z pola walki* (1971), no. 3 (55), 63.

65. W. Stefaniuk, *Łódzka organizacja PPS 1945–1948* (Lodz, 1980), 120; cf. Syzdek, *op. cit.*, 359.

66. The talks seem to have been initiated at about the time of the September Plenum, 'Stenogram obrad Niezależnej Młodzieży Socjalistycznej w dniu 18 IX 1946 r.', *Krytyka*, no. 4 (1980), 59. Szwalbe told the Lodz PPS *aktyw* on 13 Oct. that the pact was being prepared, see Stefaniuk, *op. cit.*, 122. The PPS central executive agreed to negotiations on 25 Oct.: Syzdek, *op. cit.*, 368. According to some versions, the terms of the pact were outlined by Stalin during a visit by the PPR and PPS leaders to Moscow on 3 Nov.: L.M. Oak, *Free and Unfettered* (Newtown, Montgomery, 1947), 23 and 'R', 'The Fate of Polish Socialism', *Foreign Affairs, 28*, no. 1 (Oct. 1949), 132.

67. W. Stawiński, speaking to the PPS branch in Widzew, Lodz, 8 Nov. 1946, quoted in Stefaniuk, *op. cit.*, 124.

68. *Umowa o jedności działania i współpracy między PPR i PPS, 28.11.1946, PPR* . . . *i 1946–i 1947, op. cit.*, 204–7. In the discussion of the pact in the Supreme Council of the PPS on 4 Dec. Osóbka emphasized that the PPS would do all it could to win over the democratic and progressive forces in the PSL, see Syzdek, *op. cit.*, 370.

69. *Ibid.*, 369.

70. It seems that the replacement of Osóbka by Cyrankiewicz as prime minister was agreed by the PPS and PPR leaderships at this time. Hochfield implied this in an article published in *Robotnik*, 7 Feb. 1947.

71. Sierocki, *Warszawska* . . ., 275; cf. Syzdek, *op. cit.*, 369; Sierocki, 'PPR-owska . . .', *op. cit.*, 20.
72. Syzdek, *op. cit.*, 369; Kozik, *op. cit.*, 335–6.
73. Syzdek, *op. cit.*, 375.
74. *Ibid.*, 365–6.
75. *Ibid.*, 370.
76. Ćwik, *op. cit.*, 180, Kozik, *op. cit.*, 335, Olszewski, *Początki* . . ., 253.
77. Kantyka, *PPS na Śląsku i w Zagłębiu Dąbrowskim w latach 1939–1948* (Katowice, 1975), 268–73.
78. Ćwik, *op. cit.*, 179–80.
79. Sierocki, *Warszawska* . . ., 277.
80. Kozik, *op. cit.*, 338.
81. Stefaniuk, *op. cit.*, 132.
82. *Robotnik*, 23 Oct. 1946.
83. *Robotnik*, 15 Dec. 1946.
84. *Robotnik*, 23 Oct. 1946.
85. *Robotnik*, 27 Aug. 1946.
86. Stefaniuk, *op. cit.*, 133–4; Syzdek, *op. cit.*, 375.
87. *Robotnik*, 7 Dec. 1946.
88. *Robotnik*, 23 Dec. 1946.
89. Stefaniuk, *op. cit.*, 138.
90. K. Robakowski, *Rola i działalność PPS w Wielkopolsce i na Ziemi Lubuskiej w latach 1945–48* (Poznań, 1973), 126.
91. *Ibid.*, 126; Naumiuk, *Polska Partia Robotnicza na Kielecczyźnie* (Warsaw, 1976), 429–31.
92. Syzdek, *op. cit.*, 375. This figure presumably includes alternative members.
93. Rechowicz, *Pierwsze wybory* . . ., 142–45; Stefaniuk, *op. cit.*, 134–5. These figures are incomplete; an unknown number of PPS and PPR members are classified as 'trade union' nominees.
94. K.B. Janowski, *Polska Partia Socjalistyczna na Dolnym Śląsku w latach 1945–1948* (Wrocław, 1978), 123.
95. Naumiuk, *Początki* . . ., 245.
96. Ćwik, *op. cit.*, 198–9.
97. Olszewski, *PPR* . . ., 306.
98. Wojnowski, *op. cit.*, 182.
99. 20% had taken part in the referendum, see Syzdek, *op. cit.*, 344, 375.
100. For example, 80% in Białystok and Kielce, 70% in Gdańsk, 61% in Lublin provinces; Majecki, *op. cit.*, 171, Naumiuk, *Początki* . . ., 278, Wapiński, *op. cit.*, 135, Olszewski, *PPR* . . ., 309.
101. Syzdek, *op. cit.*, 375.
102. Zambrowski, writing in 1971 after his expulsion from the PZPR, distinguished between the 'full independence' of the PPS and the 'considerable (*znaczna*) independence' of the SL and SD; R. Zambrowski, 'Dziennik', *Krytyka*, 6 (1980), 70.
103. R. Halaba, *Stronnictwo Ludowe 1944–1946* (Warsaw, 1966), 195–8.
104. *Pierwsze lata władzy ludowej w dokumentach PPR . . . op. cit.*, 322.
105. N. Kołomejczyk and B. Syzdek *Polska w latach 1944–1949* (Warsaw, 1968), 162.
106. N. Kołomejczyk, 'Niektóre problemy rozwoju partii politycznych na Ziemiach Zachodnich w latach 1945–46', *Z pola walki* (1964), no. 2 (26), 175.
107. J. Gołębiowski, *Pierwsze lata 1945–1947* (2nd edn, Katowice, 1974), 346.
108. *Ibid.*, 346; Rechowicz *Pierwsze wybory* . . ., 142–5.
109. Kozik, *op. cit.*, 360–1.
110. Cf. Rechowicz, *Pierwsze wybory* . . ., 142–5; Naumiuk, *Początki* . . ., 278; Kozik,

op. cit., 362; Majecki, op. cit., 171; Wapiński, 135–6.

111. Kozik, op. cit., 416–7.
112. Cf. Uchwała Sekretariatu KC PPR oceniająca przebieg obchodów Święta Ludowego, May 1948, PPR . . . i 1947 – xii 1948, op. cit., 234–7.
113. Dobieszewski and Hemmerling, op. cit., 164.
114. N. Kołomejczyk, 'Polska na drodze ku demokracji socjalistycznej', Studia i materiały z dziejów Polski Ludowej, 12 (1978), 64. The SD had 2,740 members in Kraków province at the end of Jan. 1947; about 1,000 in Rzeszów province at the end of 1946; less than 800 in Lublin province and about 300 in Olsztyn province in the second half of 1946: Kozik, op. cit., 369; Olszewski, Początki . . ., 254; Olszewski, PPR . . ., 322; Wojnowski, op. cit., 185.
115. P. Winczorek, Miejsce i rola SD w strukturze politycznej (Warsaw, 1975), 107.
116. Stronnictwo Demokratyczne w latach 1937–1965 (Warsaw, 1967), 57, 63, 64; Kozik, op. cit., 167–9.
117. Cf. Majecki, op. cit., 164; Wapiński, op. cit., 135–6; Wojnowski, op. cit., 182, 185; Olszewski, Początki . . ., 272; Olszewski, PPR . . ., 306; Rechowicz, Pierwsze wybory . . ., 142–5.
118. Kozik, op. cit., 371.
119. Rechowicz, Pierwsze wybory . . ., 142–5; Janowski, PPS . . ., 123; Stefaniuk, op. cit., 134–5.
120. Gomułka, Przemówienie na uroczystym posiedzeniu łodzkiej organizacji PPR z okazji przyjęcia 50-tysięcznego członka partii, 1.1.47, Artykuły . . ., II, 334–5.
121. Sprawozdanie KW PPR za IX–X 1946, cited in Pasierb, Ruch . . ., 148–9.
122. CAHSD ZG SP, Akcja wyborcza 1946–7.
123. Majecki, op. cit., 162; Olszewski, Początki . . ., 260–1; Kozik, op. cit., 363–5; Wojnowski, op. cit., 185; Dobieszewski and Hemmerling, op. cit., 143, 169; Rechowicz, Pierwsze wybory . . ., 86; Wapiński, op. cit., 131.
124. Okólnik Sekretariatu KC PPR w sprawie Święta Ludowego, May 1947, PPR . . . i 1947–xii 1948, op. cit., 81.
125. Głos ludu, 15 Nov. 1946.
126. Rzeczpospolita, 23 Nov. 1946.
127. J. Wójcik, Spór o postawę (Warsaw, 1969), 59.
128. S. Kisielewski, 'Wspomnienia polityczne', Krytyka, 4 (1980), 143–5.
129. Ibid., 144.
130. Ibid., 145.
131. Bujak, op. cit., 332–4.
132. Brzeziński described the SP as having been founded 'on the organizational framework of the National Workers' Party', not mentioning the Christian Democratic tradition, Sprawozdanie stenograficzne Sejmu Vstawodawczego, I (Warsaw, 1947), 8 Feb. 1947, col. 50.
133. Bujak, op. cit., 320–3.
134. Ibid., 362.
135. Jutro Polski, 15 Dec. 1946.
136. PRO, FO 371, 56447/N/13136.
137. Jutro Polski, 15 Dec. 1946.
138. Jutro Polski, 1 Dec. 1946.
139. Jutro Polski, 8 Dec. 1946.
140. Jutro Polski, 1 Jan. 1946.
141. PRO, FO 371, 56452/N/16279.
142. Jutro Polski, 8 Dec. 1946.
143. A translation of the text is in Mikołajczyk, The Pattern . . ., 339–41.
144. PRO, FO 371, 56447/N/12480.
145. PRO, FO 371, 56452/N/16280.

146.   *Ibid.*, N/16289.
147.   A. Bliss Lane, *I Saw Poland Betrayed* (3rd edn, Boston, 1965), 231–7.
148.   *Jutro Polski*, 15 Dec. 1946.
149.   PRO, FO 371, 56451/N/15238, N/15295.
150.   *Jutro Polski*, 26 Jan. 1947.
151.   Naumiuk, *Początki* . . ., 259–60, 263.
152.   Olszewski, *PPR* . . ., 298.
153.   Olszewski, *Początki* . . ., 284.
154.   Wapiński, *op. cit.*, 131.
155.   Hillebrandt and Jakubowski, *op. cit.*, 429; Olszewski, *Początki* . . ., 257; Olszewski, *PPR* . . ., 278; Naumiuk, *Początki* . . ., 260. Wójcik confirms that the PSL's electoral organization operated in secret, '*PSL w walce* . . .', 28.
156.   *Ibid.*, 32.
157.   PRO, FO 371, 56447/N/12483.
158.   Kisielewski, *op. cit.*, 145.
159.   Popiel, *op. cit.*, 274–5.
160.   PISM Ambasada RP Paryż A46:1.
161.   *Ibid.*, Ambasada RP Watykan A44 48:2 (1947) 2.
162.   Olszewski, *Początki* . . ., 282; Naumiuk, *Początki* . . ., 263–4, 269.
163.   *Jutro Polski*, 8 Dec. 1946.
164.   L. Smosarski, 'Reakcyjne podziemie zbrijne w latach 1945–1948', *Z dziejów Polski Ludowej* (Warsaw, 1966), 385. Using Ministry of the Interior data, F. Kubica has calculated that some 60,000 people belonged to armed groups in 1946 (compared with 80,000 in 1945 and 46,000 in 1947), J. Czapla, *W walce o utrwalenie władzy ludowej w Polsce 1944–47* (Warsaw, 1967), 193–4. Walichnowski points out that this must be an underestimate of the numbers involved in the underground (which extended beyond the military organizations) as a whole: T. Walichnowski, *U źródeł walk z podziemiem reakcyjnym w Polsce* (Warsaw, 1975), 332. Some 55,000 people gave themselves up in the amnesty in spring 1947.
165.   For examples, guerrillas attacked St Michael's prison in Kraków on 18 Aug. releasing more than 200 prisoners, PRO, FO 371, 56446/N/10746; on 24 Sept. about 20 KBW troops and militia were killed in an ambush by guerrillas commanded by Hieronim Dekutowski ('Zapora'): I. Caban and E. Machocki, *Za władzę ludu* (Lublin, 1975), 375; WiN units commanded by 'Jastrząb' carried out a series of daring raids on towns in Lublin province between late Oct. and the end of Dec. *ibid.*, 380, Walichnowski, *op. cit.*, 228.
166.   Naumiuk, *PPR* . . ., 424–5.
167.   Olszewski, *PPR* . . ., 164.
168.   B. Dymek, *Pierwsze lata władzy ludowej na Mazowszu, Kurpiach i Podlasiu 1944–1948* (Warsaw, 1978), 158.
169.   The underground carried out 40 attacks on members of electoral commissions on 71 polling stations during the election campaign, see Walichnowski, *op. cit.*, 243.
170.   *Ibid.*, 222.
171.   Smosarski, *op. cit.*, 388.
172.   Walichnowski, *op. cit.*, 223.
173.   M. Turlejska (ed.), *W walce ze zbrojnym podziemiem 1945–1947* (Warsaw, 1972), 30.
174.   Caban and Machocki, *op. cit.*, 122.
175.   Czapla, *W walce* . . ., 71; Wojnowski, *op. cit.*, 139; Majecki, *op. cit.*, 168.
176.   J. Pilacinski, *Narodowe Siły Zbrojne. Kulisy walki podziemnej* (1976), 219.
177.   See pp.219–20.
178.   Pilaciński, *op. cit.*, 219.
179.   PISM PRM E/20.

180. For underground activity after 1947, see Walichnowski, *op. cit.*, ch. 9; Caban and Machocki, *op. cit.*; S. Wałach, *Świadectwo tamtym dniom* (Kraków, 1974) and *Był w Polsce czas* . . . (Kraków, 3rd edn, 1978); S. Kluz, *W potrzasku dziejowym: WiN na szlaku AK. Rozważania i dokumentacja* (1978). Majecki, *op. cit.*, ch. 7.
181. Hillebrandt and Jakubowski, *op. cit.*, 381.
182. Olszewski, *PPR* . . ., 310.
183. Rechowicz, *Pierwsze wybory* . . ., 136.
184. Pasierb, *Ruch* . . ., 152.
185. Rechowicz, *Pierwsze wybory* . . ., 136.
186. Olszewski, *Początki* . . ., 281.
187. Olszewski, *PPR* . . ., 310.
188. CAHSD Akty SP: ZG SP Akcja wyborcza 1946–7. The SP was officially credited with 3.1% of the votes in this constituency.
189. *Ibid.*
190. *Uchwała Sekretariatu KC PPR o konieczności rozbudowy form organizacyjnych w miejskich i wiejskich organizacjach partyjnych, January, 1947, PPR . . . i 1947–xii 1948, op. cit.*, 22.
191. Naumiuk, *Początki* . . ., 268.
192. Olszewski, *PPR* . . ., 312.
193. Olszewski, *Początki*, 286.
194. Wójcik, *PSL w walce* . . ., 34.
195. Ćwik, *op. cit.*, 200.
196. Olszewski, *Początki* . . ., 286–7; Pasierb, *Ruch* . . ., 152; Janowski, *PPS* . . ., 125.
197. Naumiuk, *Początki* . . ., 268–9.
198. Ćwik, *op. cit.*, 202.
199. Wójcik, *PSL w walce* . . ., 35.
200. Writing in 1971, Zambrowski recalled the 1946 referendum and the 1947 elections as 'bitter experiences' for the PPR leadership; Zambrowski, 'Dziennik', 92–3.
201. PRO, FO 371, 66092/N/2923.
202. *Ibid.*, 66091/N/1500.
203. Sprawozdanie stenograficzne . . ., 4 Feb. 1947, col. 37; 8 Feb. 1947, col. 60.
204. PRO, FO 371, 66093.
205. *Chłopski Sztandar*, 9 Feb. 1947.
206. A. Jezierski, *Historia gospodarcza Polski Ludowej 1944–1968* (Warsaw, 1971), 98; J. Kaliński, *Bitwa o handel 1947–1948* (Warsaw, 1970), 61–8.
207. PRO, FO 371, 66093/N/6707.
208. J. Fajkowski, 'Z działalności ruchu ludowego na Mazurach i Warmii w latach 1945–1949', *Rocznik dziejów ludowego*, 8 (1966), 266.
209. See, e.g., Dobieszewski and Hemmerling, *op. cit.*, 171–2.
210. Naumiuk, *PPR* . . ., 349, 439.
211. Fajkowski, 'Z działalności . . .', 261, 267.
212. Dobieszewski and Hemmerling, *op. cit.*, 106–7, 194.
213. *Ibid.*, 183.
214. *Ibid.*, 189; *Uchwała Sekretariatu KC PPR oceniająca przebieg obchodów Święta Ludowego, May 1948, PPR . . . i 1947–xii 1948*, 236–7.
215. J. Fajkowski (ed.), *Krótki zarys historii ruchu ludowego* (Warsaw, 1969), 253.
216. *Okólnik KC PPR w sprawie pracy administracyjno-samorządowej na terenie powiatów, April 1947, PPR . . . i 1947–xii 1948*, 73.
217. *Okólnik Sekretariatu KC PPR w sprawie reorganizacji gminnych rad narodowych, November 1947, PPR . . . i 1949–xii 1948*, 162–6.
218. Ryszka, *op. cit.*, 262–6.
219. Szczeblewski, 'Problemy rozwoju . . .', 29–30. Gomułka told the June 1948

Plenum that the party had still to overcome the problem of organizing itself in the countryside. He admitted that 'our Party does not sit in the countryside, or sits weakly . . .', *Przemówienie tow. Wiesława* . . ., *op. cit.*, 69.

220. Fajkowski, *Krótki zarys* . . ., 253.
221. R. Zambrowski, 'Na nowym etapie', *Nowe drogi* (1947), no. 2, 13.
222. J. Hochfeld, 'Problematyka nowego okresu', *Przegląd Socjalistyczny* (1947), no. 3 (17), 4–9.
223. S. Szwalbe, 'Na nowym etapie', *Przegląd Socjalistyczny* (1947), no. 3 (17), 3.
224. *Ibid.*, 3.
225. *Robotnik*, 11 Feb. 1947.
226. Szwalbe, 'Na nowym etapie', 3–4.
227. Gomułka, *Przemówienie wygłoszone na akademii pierwszomajowej w Warszawie, 30.4.1947, Artykuły* . . ., II, 412.
228. Gomułka, *Z przemówienia na plenum Komitetu Centralnego PPR, 13.4.1947 r, Artykuły* . . ., II, 391.
229. *Ibid.*, 388.
230. R. Werfel, 'Istota naszego państwa i problem biurokratyzmu', *Nowe drogi* (1947), no. 3, 118.
231. *Ibid.*, 114.
232. *Ibid.*, 118.
233. *Ibid.*, 122.
234. *Ibid.*, 125.
235. *Ibid.*, 125.
236. *Ibid.*, 130.
237. Kantyka, *Na drodze* . . ., 293; *Instrukcja KC PPR w sprawie wymiany tymczasowych legitymacji członkowskich na stale, 27.5.1947, PPR . . . i 1947–xii 1948*, 83–5.
238. Kantyka, *Na drodze* . . ., 293.
239. Gomułka, *Z przemówienia na plenum Komitetu Centralnego PPR, 13.4.47, Artykuły* . . ., II, 395.
240. J. Drewnowski, 'Proces Centralnego Urzędu Planowania w 1948 roku', *Zeszyty Historyczne, 28* (1974), 39–60.
241. This account is largely based on J. Holzer, *Agonia PPS Sojaliscei Polscy w sojuszu z PPR 1944–1948* (Warsaw, 1981) 18–22.
242. R. Zambrowski, 'Na nowym etapie', 14.
243. Gomułka, *Z przemówienia na plenum Komitetu Centralnego PPR, 13.4.1947, Artykuły* . . ., II, 388.
244. Gołębiowski, *Pierwsze lata* . . ., 348.
245. *Okólnik Sekretariatu KC PPR o udziale partii w działalności RTPD, 22.10.1947, PPR . . . i 1947–xii 1948*, 142.
246. *Listy pasterskie episkopatu* . . ., 52–5.
247. Berman told the Aug.–Sept. 1948 Plenum that there had been mention 'of certain hesitations, of a lack of understanding of the new situation a year ago at the September session of the Information Bureau when we were unable at first to grasp the point of an open, public co-ordination of revolutionary forces on an international scale', *Nowe drogi* (1948), no. 11, 113. In 1956 he told the Oct. Plenum that 'we had a different view on the Information Bureau than the Soviet comrades and we defended our position. I recall that I was sharply criticised by Zhdanov', *Nowe drogi* (1956), no. 10, 90.
248. *Narada informacyjna dziewięciu partii* (Warsaw, 1947), 58.
249. *Ibid.*, 64.
250. Gomułka, *Przemówienie na manifestacji we Wrocławiu, 25.11.1947, Artykuły* . . ., II, 486–9.
251. Gomułka, *Przemówienie wygłoszone na akademii pierwszomajowej w Warszawie,*

   30.4.1947, Artykuły . . ., II, 411–12.
252. Gomułka, *Jedność 'mechaniczna' czy ideologiczna? Artykuły* . . ., II, 431–41.
253. Gomułka, *Z przemówienia na plenum Komitetu Centralnego PPR, 13.4.1947 Artykuły*
   . . ., II, 395. Gomułka argued that the party should learn 'Polish Marxism'.
254. J. Holzer ('W. Pański'), *Agonia PPS*, 21.
255. *Przemówienia tow. Wiesława* . . ., 54–71.

Bibliography

Unpublished Documentary Sources

APUST – Archive of the Polish Underground Study Trust, London
  Z kraju do Centrali 1944–5:
    file 16 (Z kraju od Delegata lub via Delegat, I–XII 1944)
    file 52 (Z kraju i do kraju, II–VII 1945)
    file 53 (Z kraju, XI 1944 – VII 1945)
CAHSD – Centralne Archiwum Historyczny Stronnictwa Democratycznego, Warsaw
  Akty Stronnictwa Pracy:
    Programy SP
    KW SP Memoriał i uchwały KW
    SP 1946–47
    ZG SP Akcja wyborcza 1946–7
LPA – Labour Party Archives, London
  International Department:
    Box 4 Poland (PPS) 1946
    Box 9 Poland (PPS) 1947
    File: International Socialist Conference 1946–7
PISM – Archive of the Polish Institute and Sikorski Museum, London
  Dziennik Czynności Naczelnego Wódza
  Protokóły Posiedzeń Rady Ministrów (PRM – K, 102)
  Prezydium Rady Ministrow (PRM/1–20)
  Akta Rady Narodowej RP (A.5/1a)
  Min. Spraw Zagranicznych (A.11. 49/WB/1, 2) (A.12.49/WB/3)
  Arciszewski papers (Kol.97)
  Ambasada RP Watykana (A.44)
  Ambasada RP Paryż (A.46)
PRO – Public Records Office, London
  Chamberlain's Cabinet, CAB 23: Minutes and Conclusions
  War Cabinet, CAB 65: Minutes and Conclusions
  Foreign Office – Poland (FO 371/55): General Correspondence

Interviews

Aleksander Bobkowski (Geneva, 2, 5, 7 August 1967)
Adam Ciołkosz (London, 8, 17, 24 November 1976)
Bolesław Drukier (London, 7, 10 December 1976)
General Marian Kukiel (London, 15 October 1972)
Feliks Mantel (Paris, 21 March 1977)
Count Edward Raczyński (London, 18 January 1972)
Franciszek Wilk (London, 2 February 1977)

Published Documentary Sources

Archiwum ruchu robotniczego, vols I, II, IV (Warsaw, 1973–7)
Armia Krajowa w Dokumentach 1939–1945, vols I–V (1970–81)
Bierut, Bolesław, *O partii* (Warsaw, 1952)
Blum, Ignacy (ed.), *Organizacja i działania bojowe ludowego Wojska Polskiego 1943–1945, Wybór źródeł*, vol. IV, *Działalność aparatu polityczno-wychowawczego* (Warsaw, 1963)
Buczek, Roman, 'Dokumenty. PRL w 1946r.', *Zeszyty Historyczne*, 31 (1975), 158–70
Cyrankiewicz, Józef, 'Wchodzimy w nowy okres pewni i świadomi swojej drogi. Przemówienie sekretarza generalnego CKW PPS na zebraniu sprawozdawczym komitetów obywatelskich bloku demokratycznego 25 stycznia 1947r.', *Z pola walki* (1964), no. 4 (28), 90–4
'Depesze KC PPR do Georgii Dymitrowa (1942–43)', *Z pola walki* (1961), no. 4 (16), 174–80
Documents on Polish-Soviet Relations, 1939–1945, vols I–II (1961–7)
'Dokument Ministerstwa Bezpieczeństwa Publicznego z 1945r.', *Krytyka*, 6 (1980), 147
Drzewiecki, Wacław, 'Stanisław Mikołajczyk o sytuacji w kraju. Rozmowa przeprowadzona w dniu 17 listopada 1947', *Zeszyty Historyczne*, 44 (1978), 7–13
Dyskusje w PPR w sprawie zjednoczenia sił demokratycznych (Notatki protokolarne z posiedzeń KC PPR maj-czerwiec 1944r.) Archiwum ruchu robotniczego, vol. II (1975), 154–63.
Gomułka, Władysław, *Artykuły i przemówienia*, vols I–II (Warsaw, 1962–4)
Gomułka, Władysław, *O naszej partii* (2nd edn, Warsaw, 1969)
Gomułka, Władysław, *Z kart naszej historii* (4th edn, Warsaw, 1970)
Gomułka, Władysław, Minc, Hilary and Zambrowski, Roman, *Przemówienia na rozszerzonym plenum KC PPR w lutym 1945r.* (Katowice, 1945)
Góra, Władysław (ed.), 'Działalność grup operacyjnych w zakresie tworzenia administracji polskiej i uruchamiania przemysłu na terenach wyzwolonych', *Z pola walki* (1964), no. 2 (26), 197–213
Góra, Władysław, *Kształtowanie się podstaw programowych PPR w latach 1942–45. Wybór materiałów i dokumentów* (Warsaw, 1958)
Góra, Władysław, 'Sprawozdania resortów (ministerstw) z pierwszych lat Polski Ludowej', *Materiały i studia z najnowszej historii Polski*, 3 (1967), 227–54
Góra, Władysław, *W walce o sojusz robotniczo-chłopski. Wybór dokumentów i materiałow 1944–1949* (Warsaw, 1963)
Malinowski, Marian (ed.), *Publicystyka konspiracyjna PPR 1942–1945. Wybór artykułów*, vols I–III (Warsaw, 1961–7)
Manifest PKWN (Warsaw, 1974)
Lato, Stanisław and Stankiewicz, Witold (eds), *Programy Stronnictw Ludowych. Zbiór dokumentów* (Warsaw, 1969)
Listy pasterskie episkopatu Polski 1945–1974 (Paris, 1975)
Listy pasterskie prymasa Polski 1946–1974 (Paris, 1975)
Narada informacyjna dziewięciu partii (Warsaw, 1947)
'Okólnik komitetu obwodowego PPR w Lublinie o zadaniach partii w organizowaniu władzy ludowej (sierpień 1944r)', *Z pola walki* (1959), no. 2 (6), 119–24
Osóbka-Morawski, Edward, 'Pamiętniki ministra', *Polityka* (1973), no. 42
'Pierwsze dni władzy ludowej w świetle sprawozdań działaczy Polskiej Partii Robotniczej', *Z pola walki* (1961), no. 4 (16), 200–13
Pierwsze kroki PPR po wyzwoleniu, Archiwum ruchu robotniczego, vol. I (1973), 354–89
'Pierwsze lata władzy ludowej w dokumentach PPR (1945–1946)', *Z pola walki* (1974), no. 2 (66), 299–323
Polish Plotters on Trial. The full report of the trial of Polish Diversionists in Moscow, June 1945 (1945)
Polonsky, Antony, *The Great Powers and the Polish Question 1941–1945. A documentary*

study in Cold War origins (1976)

Polonsky, Antony and Drukier, Bolesław, *The Beginnings of Communist Rule in Poland December 1943–June 1945* (1980)

Polskie Siły Zbrojne w Drugiej Wojnie Światowej, vols I–III (1950–9)

PPR. Rezolucje, odezwy, instrukcje i okólniki komitetu centralnego, vii 1944–xii 1948, vols I–III (Warsaw, 1959–73)

'Protokół posiedzenia Głównej Komisji Politycznej dla spraw Walki z Bandytyzmem odbytego dnia 8 czerwca 1945r.', *Z pola walki* (1965), no. 3 (31), 196–200

'Protokoły KC (1945)', *Zeszyty Historyczne*, 24 (1975), 132–59

'Przemówienie tow. Wiesława na plenarnym posiedzenie KC PPR w dniu 3 czerwca 1948 roku', *Zeszyty Historyczne*, 34 (1975), 54–71

Puacz, Edward, 'Powstanie warszawskie w protokołach PKWN', *Zeszyty Historyczne*, 10 (1966), 175–92

Reale, Eugenio, *Raporty: Polska 1945–46* (Paris, 1968)

Rocznik Statystyczny 1947, 1948, 1949 (Warsaw, 1948–50)

Sprawozdanie KCZZ (listopad 1944–listopad 1945) (Warsaw, 1945)

'Sprawozdania komitetów wojewódzkich Polskiej Partii Robotniczej z 1945r.', *Z pola walki* (1971), no. 4 (56), 279–351.

Sprawozdanie stenograficzne Sejmu Ustawodawczego, vol. I (Warsaw, 1947)

Spychalski, Marian, 'Informacja przedstawiciela KC PPR na zebraniu komunistów polskich w Moskwie 8 czerwca 1944r.', *Z pola walki* (1961), no. 4 (16), 181–99

'Stenogram obrad Niezależnej Młodzieży Socjalistycznej w dniu 18 IX 1946r.', *Krytyka*, 4 (1980), 47–63.

'Sytuacja polityczna a sprawa wyborów do Sejmu Ustawodawczego z referatu Sekretarza Generaslnego KC PPR na plenum KC PPR dnia 10 lutego 1946r.', *Z pola walki* (1964), no. 2 (26), 5–13

Trepczyński, S. and Rodionow, N.N. (eds), *Polska Ludowa – Związek Radziecki 1944–1974. Zbiór dokumentów i materiałów* (Warsaw, 1974)

'Uchwały Rady Jedności Narodowej w sprawie Jałty', ed. Tadeusz Żeńczykowski, *Zeszyty Historyczne*, 33 (1975), 55–90.

U.S. Department of State, Foreign Relations of the United States, Diplomatic Papers (Washington, D.C., 1955–1963), vols for 1943–1945 indexed Poland

Wąsowicz, Wera and Socha, Łukasz, 'Z Archiwum Bolesława Bieruta', *Krytyka*, 8 (1981), 74–123

'Wyjaśnienie sekretarza generalnego KC PPR Władysława Gomułki w związku z jego referatem i projektem rezolucji biura politycznego', *Zeszyty Historyczne*, 34 (1975), 71–85

'Z archiwów polskich komunistów: List KC PPR "do tow. D" z 7.03.1944r. List Biura komunistów polskich w ZSRR do KC PPR z dn. 18.VII.44r., A. Lampe Zagadnienie', *Zeszyty Historyczne*, 26 (1973), 186–202

'Z materiałów listopadowej konferencji PPR w Lublinie w 1944r.', *Z pola walki* (1959), no. 2 (6), 128–43

Zambrowski, Roman, *O masową milionową Partię. Sprawozdanie organizacyjne KC wygłoszone na I Zjeździe PPR* (Warsaw, 1946)

Zawadzki, Aleksander, 'Bilans pierwszego roku władzy ludowej na Śląsku. Przemówienie wygłoszone na posiedzeniu Wojewódzkiej Rady Narodowej w Katowicach, 29 stycznia 1946r.', *Z pola walki* (1964), no. 2 (26), 14–38

Memoirs

Bagiński, Kazimierz, 'Proces szesnastu w Moskwie', *Zeszyty Historyczne*, 4 (1964), 74–123

Bliss Lane, Arthur, *I Saw Poland Betrayed. An American Ambassador Reports to the American People* (3rd edn, Boston, 1965)

Borkowicz, Leonard (ed.), *Komuniści. Wspomnienia o KPP* (Warsaw, 1969)

'"Były żołnierz AK", 5–ta Brygada Wileńska AK mjr Łupaszki', *Zeszyty Historyczne, 21* (1972), 136–44

Chajn, Leon, *Kiedy Lublin był Warszawą (viii–xii 1944r.)* (Warsaw, 1964)

Gomułka, Władysław, 'Polemika z "Archiwum Ruchu Robotniczego"', *Zeszyty Historyczne, 39* (1977), 3–36

Góra, Władysław *et al.* (eds), *Takie były początki* (Warsaw, 1965)

Haneman, Jan Stefan, 'U progu Polski Ludowej', *Z pola walki* (1969), no. 2 (46), 136–58

Harriman, W. Averell and Abel, Elie, *Special Envoy to Churchill and Stalin 1941–1946* (1976)

Kieszczyński, Lucjan, 'Moja działalność w Łódzkiej Dzielnicy PPR – Górna Prawa, styczeń – czerwiec 1945r.', *Z pola walki* (1974), no. 2 (66), 269–97

Kisielwski, Stefan, 'Wspomnienia polityczne', *Krytyka, 4* (1980), 138–56

Korboński, Stefan, *Warsaw in Chains* (1959)

Kraszewski, Antoni, 'To były tylko trzy lata . . .', *Z pola walki* (1974), no. 3 (67), 107–25

Mantel, Feliks, 'Szkice pamiętnikarskie', *Zeszyty Historyczne, 7* (1965), 90–132

Mikołajczyk, Stanisław, *The Pattern of Soviet Domination* (1948)

Orłowska, Edwarda, 'Wspomnienia z woj. Białostockiego z roku 1944', *Z pola walki* (1959), no. 2 (6), 144–9

Popiel, Karol, *Od Brześcia do 'Polonii'* (1967)

Ptasiński, Jan, *Walki ciąg dalszy 1945–1946* (Warsaw, 1979)

Pużak, Kazimierz, 'Wspomnienia 1939–45', *Zeszyty Historyczne, 41* (1977), 3–196

Sokorski, Włodzimierz, *Polacy pod Lenino* (Warsaw, 1971)

Spychalski, Marian, 'Warszawska społeczna – Fragmenty ze wspomnień', *Z pola walki* (1977), no. 1 (77), 203–40

——, Wspomnienia o partyjnej robocie (1931–44), *Archiwum ruchu robotniczego*, vol. II (1975), 266–356

——, 'Ze wspomnień', *Z pola walki* (1976), no. 4 (76), 139–64

Steinsbergowa, Aniela, *Widziane z Ławy obrończej* (Paris, 1977)

Stypulkowski, Zbigniew, *Invitation to Moscow* (1951)

Światło, Józef, *Za kulisami bezpieki i partii* (New York, 1955)

Wójcik, Stanisław, 'Stanowisko W. Witosa w 1945r.', *Zeszyty Historyczne, 34* (1975), 197–202

Zambrowski, Roman, 'Dziennik', *Krytyka, 6* (1980), 20–118

Zaremba, Zygmunt, *Wojna i konspiracja* (1957)

Zawadzka-Wetz, Alicja, *Refleksje pewnego życia* (Paris, 1967)

Books and Special Studies

Andrzejewski, Jerzy, *Popiół i Diament* (Warsaw, 1948)

'Archiwista', 'Zestawienie wydarzeń dotyczących kierowania konspiracji w kraju po powstaniu warszawskim', *Zeszyty Historyczne, 26* (1973), 207–16

Bagiński, Kazimierz, 'Cenzura w Polsce', *Zeszyty Historyczne, 8* (1965), 129–52

Baranowski, Feliks, 'W związku z artykułem Juliusza Bardacha "O dziejach powojennej PPS", *Kwartalnik Historyczny*, R.LXXX z.3 (1973), 668–71

——, 'Z dziejów nurty lewicowego powojennej PPS', *Z pola walki* (1974), no. 3 (63), 25–47

Bardach, Juliusz, 'O dziejach powojennej PPS', *Kwartalnik Historyczny*, R.LXXIX z.3 (1972), 685–99

Bardach, Juliusz, 'O wewnętrznym zróżnicowaniu w PPS w latach 1944–46', *Kwartalnik Historyczny*, R.LXXX z.3 (1973), 672–4

Bartoszewicz, Henryk, 'Polsko-radzieckie stosunki gospodarcze', *Z pola walki* (1977), no. 1 (77), 278–82

Barwicz, Romuald, 'Ube a sowiecka służba bezpieczeństwa', *Kultura*, no. 6 (273) (1970), 77–100

Bethell, Nicholas, *Gomułka. His Poland and His Communism* (1972)

Bieńkowski, Władysław, *Motory i hamulce socjalizmu* (Paris, 1969)

Blit, Lucjan, *The Eastern Pretender. Boleslaw Piasecki: His Life and Times* (1965)

Blum, Ignacy, 'Sprawa 31pp. Tło, przebieg i charakter masowej dezercji żołnierzy 31pp w 1944r.', *Wojskowy Przegląd Historyczny* (1965), no. 3, 40–73

——, *Z dziejów aparatu politycznego Wojska Polskiego Szkice i dokumenty* (Warsaw, 1957)

——, 'Z dziejów Głównego Zarządu Politycznego WP 1944–56', *Wojskowy Przegląd Historyczny* (1963), no. 3–4

——, *Z dziejów WP w latach 1945–48* (Warsaw, 1960)

Błagowieszczański, Igor, *Dzieje I Armii Polskiej w ZSRR, maj–lipiec 1944r.* (Warsaw, 1972)

Borkowski, Jan, 'Działalność PSL w latach 1945–47', *Rocznik dziejów ruchu ludowego* (1960), no. 2, 72–105

——, 'Kształtowanie się antymikołajczykowskiej opozycji w kierownictwie PSL, 1946–47', *Polska Ludowa (1962), no. 1, 85–99*

——, 'Miejsce PSL w obozie reakcji (1945–47)', *Z pola walki* (1959), no. 2 (6), 56–79

——, 'Nie tylko pod Lenino', *Miesięcznik literacki* (1972), no. 4, 87–91

——, 'O powstaniu PSL i kształtowaniu się jego naczelnych władz', *Polska Ludowa* (1964), no. 3, 59–73

——, 'Pertrakcje przedwyborcze między PPR i PPS a PSL (1945–6)', *Kwartalnik Historyczny*, R.LXXI z.2 (1964)

——, 'Rola i działalność Mikołajczykowskiego PSL 1945–47' (unpublished doctoral thesis, Warsaw, 1958)

Bromberg, Abraham, *Poland: Genesis of a Revolution* (New York, 1983)

Bromke, Adam, *Poland's Politics: Idealism vs. Realism* (Cambridge, Mass., 1967)

Brzezinski, Zbigniew K., *The Soviet Bloc. Unity and Conflict* (rev. edn, Cambridge, Mass., 1971)

Buczek, Roman, *Stronnictwo ludowe w latach 1939–45. Organizacja i polityka* (1975)

——, 'Udział delegacji polskiej w konferencji poczdamskiej w 1945r.', *Zeszyty Historyczne* (34) (1975), 85–133

Bujak, Waldemar, 'Historia krajowej działalności Stronnictwa Pracy 1937–50' (unpublished doctoral thesis, Kraków, 1971)

Caban, Ireneusz and Machocki, Edward, *Za władzę ludu* (Lublin, 1975)

Caban, Ireneusz and Mańkowski, Z., *ZWZ i AK w okręgu lubelskim 1939–44*, 2 vols (Lublin, 1971)

Chabros, Tadeusz, *Kronika wydarzeń w Lublinie 22 VII 1944–1 II 1945* (Lublin, 1974)

Chęcinski, Michał, *Poland: Communism, Nationalism Anti-Semitism* (New York, 1982)

Ciechanowski, Jan M., *The Warsaw Uprising of 1944* (1974)

Cohn, Ludwik, 'Zygmunt Żuławski', *Krytyka*, 6 (1980), 184–9

Coutouvidis, John, 'Lewis Namier and the Polish Government-in-Exile, 1939–40', *Slavonic and East European Rev.*, 62, no. 3 (July 1984), 421–8

——, 'Government-in-Exile: the transfer of Polish authority abroad in September 1939', *Rev. Int. Studies*, 10, no. 4 (Oct. 1984), 285–96

Czapla, Jan, 'KBW w latach 1944–65', *Wojskowy Przegląd Historyczny* (1965), no. 3

——, *W walce o utrwalenie władzy ludowej w Polsce 1944–47* (Warsaw, 1967)

Ćwik, Kazimierz, *Problemy współdziałania PPR i PPS w województwie krakowskim, 1945–1948* (Kraków, 1974)

Davies, Norman, *White Eagle, Red Star. The Polish-Soviet War 1919–20* (1972)
——, *God's Playground. A History of Poland*, 2 vols (1981)
Dobieszewski, Adolf and Hemmerling, Zygmunt, *Ruch ludowy w Wielkopolsce 1945–1949* (Warsaw, 1971)
Drukier, Bolesław, *Początki Polski Ludowej. Szkice i przyczynki* (Warsaw, 1966)
Drukier, Bolesław ('D.K.'), 'Na marginesie polemiki Gomułki', *Zeszyty Historyczne*, 43 (1978), 214–25
Duraczyński, Eugeniusz, *Wojna i okupacja, wrzesień 1939–kwiecień 1943* (Warsaw, 1974)
20 lat WP. II sesja naukowa poswięcona wojnie wyzwoleńczej narodu polskiego 1939–45 (Warsaw, 1967)
Dymek, Benon, *Pierwsze lata władzy ludowej na Mazowszu, Kurpiach i Podlasiu 1944–48* (Warsaw, 1978)
Dziewanowski, M.K., *The Communist Party of Poland. An Outline of History* (2nd edn, Cambridge, Mass. and London, 1976)
Erickson, John, *Stalin's War with Germany*, vols I–II, (1975–83)
Fajkowski, Jozef, *Krotki zarys historii ruchu ludowego* (Warsaw, 1969)
——, 'Z działalności ruchu ludowego na Mazurach i Warmii 1945–1949', *Rocznik dziejów ruchu ludowego*, 8 (1966), 229–75
Garas, J.B., *Oddziały GL i AL 1942–45* (Warsaw, 1963)
Gepna, Jolanta, 'Powstania i organizacja Centralnego Urzędu Planowania', *Dzieje Najnowsze*, R.V. (1973), no. 4, 261–72
Gerhard, Jan, *Łuny w Bieszczadach*, 2 vols (3rd. edn, Warsaw, 1962)
Gołębiowski, Janusz, *Nacjonalizacja przemysłu w Polsce* (Warsaw, 1965)
——, *Pierwsze lata 1945–1947* (2nd edn, Katowice, 1974)
——, *Walka PPR o nacjonalizację przemysłu* (Warsaw, 1961)
Gołębiowski, Janusz W. and Góra, Władysław (eds), *Ruch robotniczy w Polsce Ludowej* (Warsaw, 1975)
Góra, Władysław, *Polska Rzeczpospolita Ludowa 1944–1974* (Warsaw, 1974)
—— (ed.), *PPR w walce o niepodległość i władzę ludu* (Warsaw, 1963)
Góra, Władysław and Halaba, Ryszard, 'Z problemów I Zjazdu PPR', *Z pola walki* (1962), no. 2 (18), 3–25
Grot, Leszek, 'Działalność ochronno-propagandowa WP w czasie referendum (30.6.46) i wyborów do Sejmu RP (19.1.47)', *Wojskowy Przegląd Historyczny* (1974), no. 2, 173–200
Halaba, Ryszard, *Stronnictwo Ludowe 1944–1946. Niektóre problemy rozwoju organizacyjnego i działalności politycznej* (Warsaw, 1966)
——, 'Z zagadnień współpracy politycznej PPR z radykalnym SL w okresie lipiec 1945–styczeń 1946r.', *Rocznik dziejów ruchu ludowego* (1962), no. 4, 64–92
Halaba, Ryszard and Kołomejczyk, Norbert, *Z dziejów PPR w woj. bydgoskim 1945–47* (Bydgoszcz, 1962)
Hemmerling, Zygmunt, *Władysław Kowalski* (Warsaw, 1977)
Hillebrandt, Bogdan and Jakubowski, Józef, *Warszawska organizacja PPR 1942–1948* (Warsaw, 1978)
Holzer, Jerzy, *Mozaika polityczna drugiej Rzeczypospolitej* (Warsaw, 1974)
——, *PPS. Szkice dziejów* (Warsaw, 1977)
—— ('Wacław Pański'), *Agonia PPS. Socjaliści Polscy w sojuszu z PPR 1944–1948* (Warsaw, 1981)
Jabłoński, W. 'Wyjaśnienia i uzupełnienia do artykuły "O tajemniczej śmierci M. Nowotki i B. Mołojca"', *Zeszyty Historyczne*, 62 (1982), 234–6
Jagiełło, Jerzy, *O Polską drogę do socjalizmu* (Warsaw, 1984)
Jakubowski, Halina, 'Walka o jednolite związki zawodowe w pierwszych latach Polski Ludowej', *Studia i materiały z dziejów Polski Ludowej*, vol. 12 (1978), 117–66
Jakubowski, Józef, 'Franciszek Jóźwiak "Witold" (Zarys działalności politycznej i

państowowej)', *Z pola walki* (1974), no. 2 (66), 225–68

Jakubowski, Jósef, 'Polityka PPR i PPS wobec ZNP 1944–48', *Z pola walki* (1973), no. 4

——, 'Struktura organizacyjna PPR (1944–1948)', *Materiały i studia z najnowszej historii Polski*, 3 (1967), 145–64

Janczewski, George H., 'The origin of the Lublin Government', *Slavonic Studies*, 50, no. 120 (1972), 410–33

Janowski, Karol B., 'Kształtowanie się jedności ruchu robotniczego na Dolnym Śląsku (1945–1948)', *Z pola walki* (1971), no. 3 (55), 59–81

——, *Polska Partia Socjalistyczna na Dolnym Śląsku w latach 1945–1948* (Wrocław, 1978)

Jarecka-Kimlowska, Stanisława, *Związek Młodzieży Wiejskiej 'Wici'. Walka o oblicze ideowe i nowy model organizacyjny 1944–48* (Warsaw, 1972)

——, *Z problemów spółdzielczości wiejskiej w Polsce w latach 1944–1957* (Warsaw, 1977)

Jezierski, Andrzej, *Historia gospodarcza Polski Ludowej 1944–1968* (Warsaw, 1971)

Jurgielewicz, Wacław, *Organizacja LWP (22 vii 44–9 v 45)* (Warsaw, 1968)

Kaliński, Janusz, *Bitwa o handel 1947–1948* (Warsaw, 1970)

——, 'Wpływ sytuacji rynkowej na warunki bytowe ludności lipiec 1946–grudzień 1948r.', *Kwartalnik Historyczny*, R.LXXVI z.2 (1969), 319–35

Kaliński, Janusz and Landau, Zbigniew (eds), *Gospodarka Polski Ludowej 1944–1955* (Warsaw, 1974)

Kantyka, Jan, *Na drodze do jedności. Z problemów współdziałania PPR i PPS w województwie śląsko-dąbrowskim* (Katowice, 1973)

——, *Polska Partia Socjalistyczna na Śląsku i w Zagłębiu Dąbrowskim w latach 1939–1948* (Katowice, 1975)

Kersten, Krystyna, 'Kielce – 4 lipca 1946 roku', *Tygodnik Solidarność*, 4 Dec. 1981

——, *Polski Komitet Wyzwolenia Narodowego, 22 VII–31 XII 1944* (Lublin, 1965)

——, 'Przemiany struktury narodowościowej Polski po II wojnie światowej, geneza i wyniki', *Kwartalnik Historyczny*, R.LXXVI z.2 (1969), 337–66

Kluz, Stanisław, *W potrzasku dziejowym: WiN na szlaku AK. Rozaważania i dokumentacja* (1978)

Kołomejczyk, Norbert, 'Niektóre problemy rozwoju partii politycznych na Ziemiach Zachodnich w latach 1945–46', *Z pola walki* (1964), no. 2 (26), 155–75

——, 'Polska na drodze ku demokracji socjalistycznej, *Studia i materiały z dziejów Polski Ludowej*, 12 (1978), 5–71

——, *PPR 1944–1945 (Studia nad rozwojem organizacyjnym partii)* (Warsaw, 1965)

——, *Rewolucje ludowe w Europie 1939–1948* (Warsaw, 1973)

Kołomejczyk, Norbert and Syzdek, Bronisław, *Polska w latach 1944–1949. Zarys historii politycznej* (Warsaw, 1968)

Korboński, Andrzej, *Politics of Socialist Agriculture in Poland, 1945–1960* (New York and London, 1965)

Korboński, Stefan, *Polskie państwo podziemne* (Paris, 1975)

Kostrowicka, I., Landau, Zbigniew and Tomaszewski, J., *Historia gospodarcza Polski XIX i XX wieku* (Warsaw, 1975)

Kowalik, Anastazja, *Z dziejów Polskiej Partii Robotniczej na Dolnym Śląsku w latach 1945–1948* (Wrocław, 1979)

Kowalski, Józef, *Trudne lata. Problemy rozwoju polskiego ruchu robotniczego 1929–1935* (Warsaw, 1966)

——, *Komunistyczna Partia Polski 1935–1938. Studium historyczne* (Warsaw, 1975)

Kowalski, Włodzimierz T., *Walka dyplomatyczna o miejsce Polski w Europie* (Warsaw, 1966)

——, *Polityka zagraniczna RP 1944–47* (Warsaw, 1971)

Kowalski, Zbigniew, *Polska Partia Robotnicza na Śląsku Opolskim. Studium rozwoju organizacyjnego* (Wrocław, 1973)

Kozik, Zenobiusz, *Partie i stronnictwa polityczne w Krakowskiem 1945–1947* (Kraków, 1975)
Koźliński, Jerzy, *Podziemie na Pomorzu w latach 1945–47* (Gdynia, 1959)
Kuśmierski, Stanisław, *Propaganda polityczna PPR w latach 1944–1948* (Warsaw, 1976)
Lane, David and Kolankiewicz, George, *Social Groups in Polish Society* (1973)
Lendvai, Paul, *Anti-Semitism in Eastern Europe* (1971)
Leslie, R.F. *et al.*, *The History of Poland Since 1863* (1980)
Lis-Kozłowski, S., 'Teodor', *Zeszyty Historyczne*, 38 (1976), 180–92
Litwin, Aleksander, 'Tragiczne dzieje KPP (1935–1938)', *Zeszyty Historyczne*, 36 (1976), 215–31
Machejek, Władysław, *Rano przeszedł huragan* (Warsaw, 1960)
Majchrowski, J.M., *Stronnictwo Pracy. Działalność polityczna i koncepcje programowe 1937–45* (Warsaw–Kraków, 1979)
Majecki, Henryk, *Białostocczyzna w pierwszych latach władzy ludowej 1944–48* (2nd edn, Warsaw, 1977)
Malara, Jean and Ray, Lucienne, *La Pologne d'une occupation à l'autre 1944–52* (Paris, 1952)
Malinowski, Marian, *Geneza PPR* (2nd edn, Warsaw, 1975)
——, *Marceli Nowotko* (Warsaw, 1976)
——, 'Przyczynek do sprawy rozwiązania KPP', *Z pola walki* (1968), no. 3 (43), 3–24
——, 'Wywiad PPR i GL z pomocą dla frontu wschodniego', *Z pola walki* (1977), no. 3 (79), 241–8
Mastny, Vojtech, *Russia's Road to the Cold War. Diplomacy, Warfare and the Politics of Communism 1941–1945* (New York, 1979)
Matusek, P., *Ruch oporu na ziemie opatowsko-sandomierskiej 1939–45* (Warsaw, 1976)
McCauley, Martin (ed.), *Communist Power in Europe 1944–1949* (1977)
Miś, Władysław, *Od wojny do pokoju. Gospodarka Polski w latach 1944–46* (Warsaw, 1978)
Montias, John M., *Central Planning in Poland* (2nd edn, Westport, Conn., 1974)
Naumiuk, Jan, *Początki władzy ludowej na Kielecczyźnie 1944–1947* (Lublin, 1969)
——, *Polska Partia Robotnicza na Kielecczyźnie* (Warsaw, 1976)
Nowak, Jan, 'Jeszcze w sprawie Berlinga', *Zeszyty Historyczne*, 41 (1977), 210–15
——, 'Sprawa gen. Berlinga', *Zeszyty Historyczne*, 37 (1976), 39–60
Oak, Liston M., *Free and Unfettered* (Newtown, Montgomery, 1947)
Olszewski, Edward, *Początki władzy ludowej na rzeszowszczyźnie 1944–1947* (Lublin, 1974)
——, *Polska Partia Robotnicza na Lubelszczyźnie 1942–1948* (Lublin, 1979)
Pasierb, Bronisław, *Rok pierwszy. Z problemów życia politycznego Dolnego Śląska w latach 1945–1946* (Wrocław, 1972)
——, *Ruch ludowy na Dolnym Śląsku w latach 1945–49* (place of publication not given, 1972)
——, *Życie polityczne Dolnego Śląska 1945–50* (Wrocław, 1979)
Patrykiejew, Włodzimierz, *Powstanie i umacnianie władzy ludowej na terenie powiatu zamojskiego 1944–1947* (Lublin, 1974)
Pawłowicz, Jerzy, *Strategia frontu narodwego PPR III 1943–VII 1944* (Warsaw, 1965)
Pilacinski, Jerzy, *Narodowe Siły Zbrojne. Kulisy walki podziemnej* (1976)
Plikas, M. (ed.), *Mała kronika LWP 1943–73* (Warsaw, 1975)
Pobóg-Malinowski, Władysław, *Najnowsza historia polityczna Polski 1864–1945*, vol. III (1960)
Polegli w walce o władzę ludowa. Materiały i zestawienia statystyczne (Warsaw, 1970)
Polonsky, Antony, *Politics in Independent Poland 1921–1939. The Crisis of Constitutional Government* (1972)
Polska w latach 1944–1949
Polski Słownik Biograficzny

Potomski, Tadeusz, *SP na Gornym Śląsku w latach 1937–50* (Katowice, 1969)

Przygoński, Antoni, *Z zagadnień strategii frontu narodowego PPR 1942–1945* (Warsaw, 1976)

Przywuski, Stanisław, 'PPS w województwie Gdańskim 1945–48. Powstanie, organizacja i formy działania', *Z pola walki* (1978), no. 1 (81), 155–77

'P.T.', 'O tajemniczej śmierci M. Nowotki i B. Mołojca', *Zeszyty Historyczne, 59* (1982), 210–20

'R', 'The Fate of Polish Socialism', *Foreign Affairs, 28*, no. 1 (Oct. 1949), 125–42

Raina, Peter K., *Władysław Gomułka. Życiorys polityczny* (1969)

Rechowicz, H., *Pierwsze Wybory 1947* (Katowice, 1963)

Reiss, A., *Z problemów odbudowy i rozwoju organizacyjnego PPS 1944–1946* (Warsaw, 1971)

Reynolds, Jaime, 'Communists, Socialists and Workers: Poland 1944–48', *Soviet Studies, 30/4* (Oct. 1978), 516–39

——, 'Lublin vs. London: The Party and the Underground Movement in Poland 1944–45', *J. Contemporary History, 16* (1981), 617–48

Robakowski, Kazimierz, *Rola i działalność PPS w Wielkopolsce i na Ziemi Lubuskiej w latach 1945–48* (Poznań, 1973)

Roos, Hans, *A History of Modern Poland from the Foundation of the State in the First World War to the Present Day* (1966)

Rutkowski, Stanisław, 'PPR w siłach zbrojnych w latach 1944–48', *Wojskowy Przegląd Historyczny* (1977), no. 4, 37–49

Rybicki, Hieronim, *Powstanie i działalność władzy ludowej na zachodnich i północnych obszarach Polski 1945–1949* (Poznań, 1976)

Ryszka, Franciszek (ed.), *Polska Ludowa 1944–50. Przemiany społeczne* (Wrocław, 1974)

Siemaszko, Z.S., 'Grupa Szańca i NSZ', *Zeszyty Historyczne, 21* (1972), 3–26

——, *Narodowe Siły Zbrojne* (1982)

——, 'Sprawa Berlinga', *Zeszyty Historyczne, 38* (1976), 224–9

Sierocki, Tadeusz, 'Dyskusje nad programem PPS w latach 1945–47', *Z pola walki* (1971), no. 4 (56), 137–74

——, 'Kronika ważniejszych wydarzeń w PPS (1944–1948)', *Polska Ludowa* (1966), no. 5, 203–34; (1967), no. 6, 149–82

——, 'PPR-owska koncepcja jedności ruchu robotniczego w latach 1942–48', *Z pola walki* (1976), no. 4 (76), 3–28

——, 'Struktura organizacyjna PPS (1944–1948)', *Materiały i studia z najnowszej historii Polski, 3* (1967), 165–91

——, *Warszawska organizacja PPS 1944–1948* (Warsaw, 1976)

Słabek, Henryk, *Dzieje polskiej reformy rolnej 1944–48* (Warsaw, 1972)

——, 'Ogólne aspekty polityki PPR i PPS w kształtowaniu nowych stosunków przemysłowych', *Z pola walki* (1978), no. 1 (81), 35–70

——, *Polityka agrarna PPR (Geneza i realizacja)* (1st edn, Warsaw, 1967)

——, 'Wpływy partii wśród chłopów ziem dawnych 1944–48', *Z pola walki* (1974), no. 2 (66), 39–55

Smosarski, Ludomir, 'Reakcyjne podziemie zbrojne w latach 1945–1947', *Z dziejów Polski ludowej* (Warsaw, 1966), 351–89

Socha, Łukasz, 'Interpelacje posłów PSL; Protokół przesłuchania świadka', *Krytyka, 6* (1980), 148–64

Stefaniuk, Władysław, *Łódzka organizacja PPS 1945–1948* (Lodz, 1980)

Stronnictwo Demokratyczne w latach 1937–1965 (Warsaw, 1967)

Syzdek, Bronisław, *Polska Partia Socjalistyczna w latach 1944–1948* (Warsaw, 1974)

Szczeblewski, Jan, 'Problemy rozwoju organizacyjnego PZPR w okresie scalenia organizacji partyjnych po zjednoczeniu PPR i PPS (grudzień 1948–listopad 1949)', *Z pola walki* (1967), no. 1 (37), 25–40

Szczeblewski, Jan, 'Przygotowania organizacyjne do zjednoczenia PPR i PPS, *Z pola walki* (1966), no. 4 (36), 93–104

Szcześniak, A. and Szota, W., *Droga do nikąd. Działalność OUN i jej likwidacja w Polsce* (Warsaw, 1973)

Szpała, R., 'Z dziejów MO i SB w pierwszych latach władzy ludowej w pow. Bielsk Podlaski', *Wojskowy Przegląd Historyczny* (1977), no. 4

Terej, Jerzy Janusz, *Idee, mity, realia. Szkice do dziejów Narodowej Demokracji* (Warsaw, 1971)

——, *Na rozstajach dróg. Ze studiów nad obliczem i modelem Armii Krajowej* (Wrocław, 1978)

——, *Rzeczywistość i polityka. Ze studiów nad dziejami najnowszymi Narodowej Demokracji* (Warsaw, 1971)

Terry, Sarah Meiklejohn, *Poland's Place in Europe* (Princeton, 1983)

Turlejska, Maria (ed.), *W walce ze zbrojnym podziemiem 1945–1947* (Warsaw, 1972)

—— (ed.), *Z walk przeciwko zbrojnemu podziemiu 1944–47* (Warsaw, 1966)

——, *Zapis pierwszej dekady 1945–54*, (Warsaw, 1972)

Tys-Krokhmaliuk, Yuriy, *UPA Warfare in Ukraine* (Society of Veterans of Ukrainian Insurgent Army, USA, 1972)

Uprzemysłowienie ziem polskich w XIX i XX wieku (Warsaw, 1970)

Wałach, Stanisław, *Był w Polsce czas . . .* (3rd edn, Kraków, 1978)

——, *Świadectwo tamtym dniom* (Kraków, 1974)

Walichnowski, Tadeusz, *U źródeł walk z podziemiem reakcyjnym w Polsce* (Warsaw, 1975)

Wapiński, Roman, *Pierwsze lata władzy ludowej na wybrzeżu gdańskim* (Gdańsk, 1970)

Ważniewski, Władysław, *Bolesław Bierut* (Warsaw, 1976)

Werth, Aleksander, *Russia: The Postwar Years* (1971)

Wilk, Franciszek, 'Słownik biograficzny ofiar terroru PSL', *Zeszyty Historyczne*, 6 (1964), 7–15

Winczorek, Piotr, *Miejsce i rola Stronnictwa Demokratycznego w strukturze politycznej* (Warsaw, 1975)

Wojnowski, Edmund, *Warmia i Mazury w latach 1945–1947. Życie polityczne* (2nd edn, Olsztyn, 1970)

Wojtas, Andrzej, *Kryzys programu i polityki 'Rocha'. Powstanie SL 'Wola ludu', 1943–1944* (place of publication not given, 1976)

Wójcik, Józef, *Spór o postawę* (Warsaw, 1969)

Wójcik, Stanisław, 'Na 30-lecie wyborów w Polsce', *Zeszyty Historyczne*, 43 (1978), 16–43

——, 'PSL w walce z komunistami 1945–47' (typescript in possession of author)

Yergin, Daniel, *Shattered Peace. The Origins of the Cold War and the National Security State* (1978)

Załuski, Zbigniew, *Czterdziesty czwarty. Wydarzenia, obserwacje, refleksje* (4th edn, Warsaw, 1969)

Zasada, Jerzy, *Referendum w województwie poznańskim, 30 VI 1946* (Poznań, 1971)

Zawodny, J.K., *Death in the Forest. The Story of the Katyn Forest Massacre* (1971)

Zbiniewicz, Frederyk, *Armia Polska w ZSRR. Studia nad problematyką pracy politycznej* (Warsaw, 1963)

Żeńczykowski, Tadeusz, 'Geneza i kulisy PKWN', *Kultura* (1974), no. 7–8, 138–69

——, *Dramatyczny Rok 1945* (1981)

Żochowski, Stanisław *NSZ. O Narodowych Siłach Zbrojnych* (1983)

Newspapers and Periodicals

Chłopi i Państwo, PSL-Lewica
Chłopski Sztandar, PSL weekly
Dziennik Ludowy, SL
Dziś i Jutro Catholic (Piasecki)
Gazeta Ludowa, PSL daily
Głos Ludu, PPR daily
Jutro Polski (London), PSL
Kurier Popularny, PPS Lodz
Lewy Tor, PPS Left
Naprzód, PPS Kraków
Nowe drogi, PPR theoretical organ
Nowe Wyzwolenie, PSL 'Nowe Wyzwolenie'
Piast, PSL Kraków
Przegląd Socjalistyczny, PPS theoretical organ
Robotnik, PPS daily
Robotnik (London), PPS in exile
Rzeczpospolita, PKWN and semi-official
Trybuna Wolności, PPR
Tygodnik Powszechny, Catholic
Wolna Polska (Moscow), ZPP
Wola ludu, SL 'Wola ludu'
Zielony Sztandar, SL

Index

Note: Illustration references are indicated by italic numerals